LA TERRA CONOSCIVTA FIN QVI

HAMMOND

ATLAS OF

WORLD
RELIGIONS

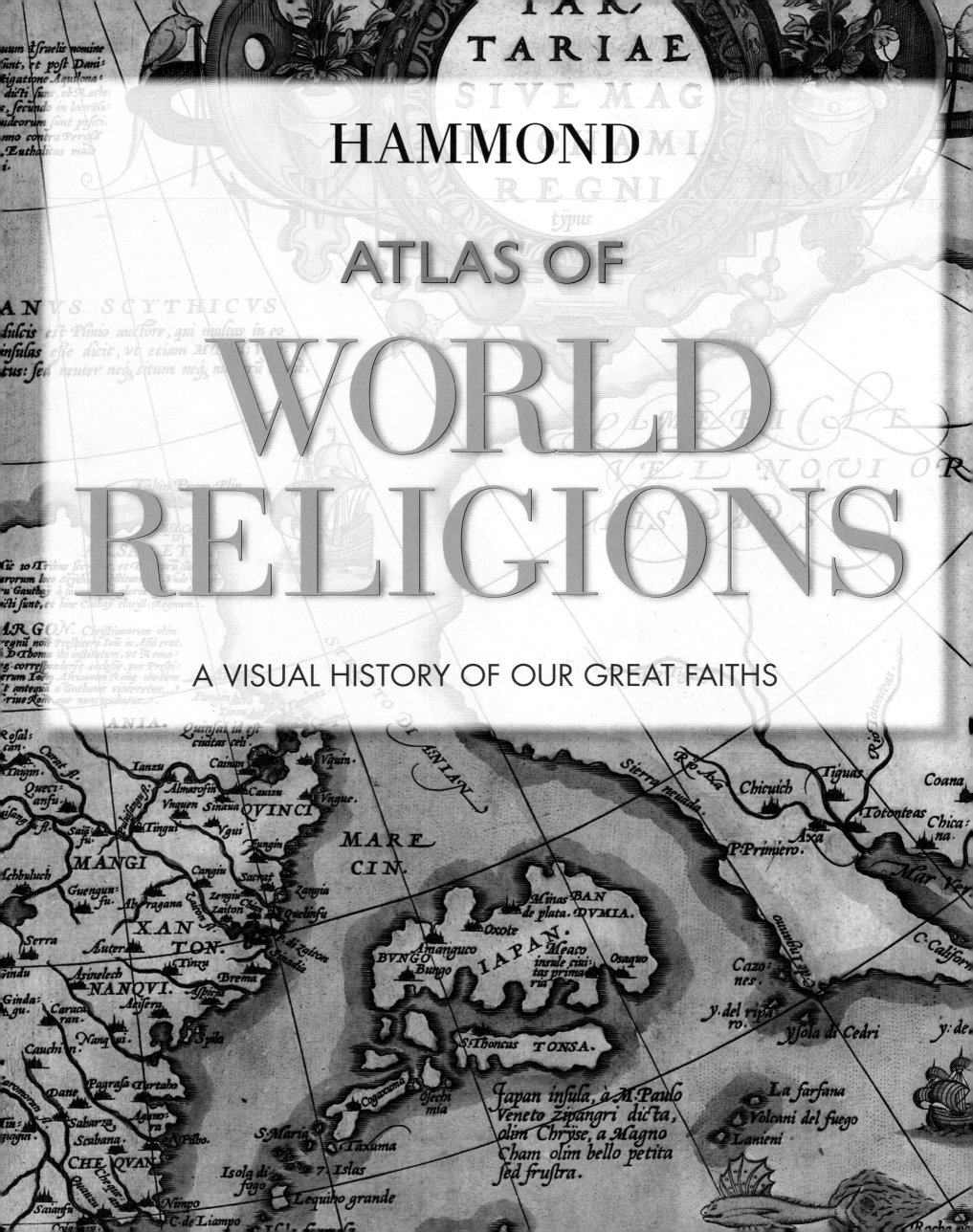

HAMMOND

ATLAS OF

WORLD RELIGIONS

A VISUAL HISTORY OF OUR GREAT FAITHS

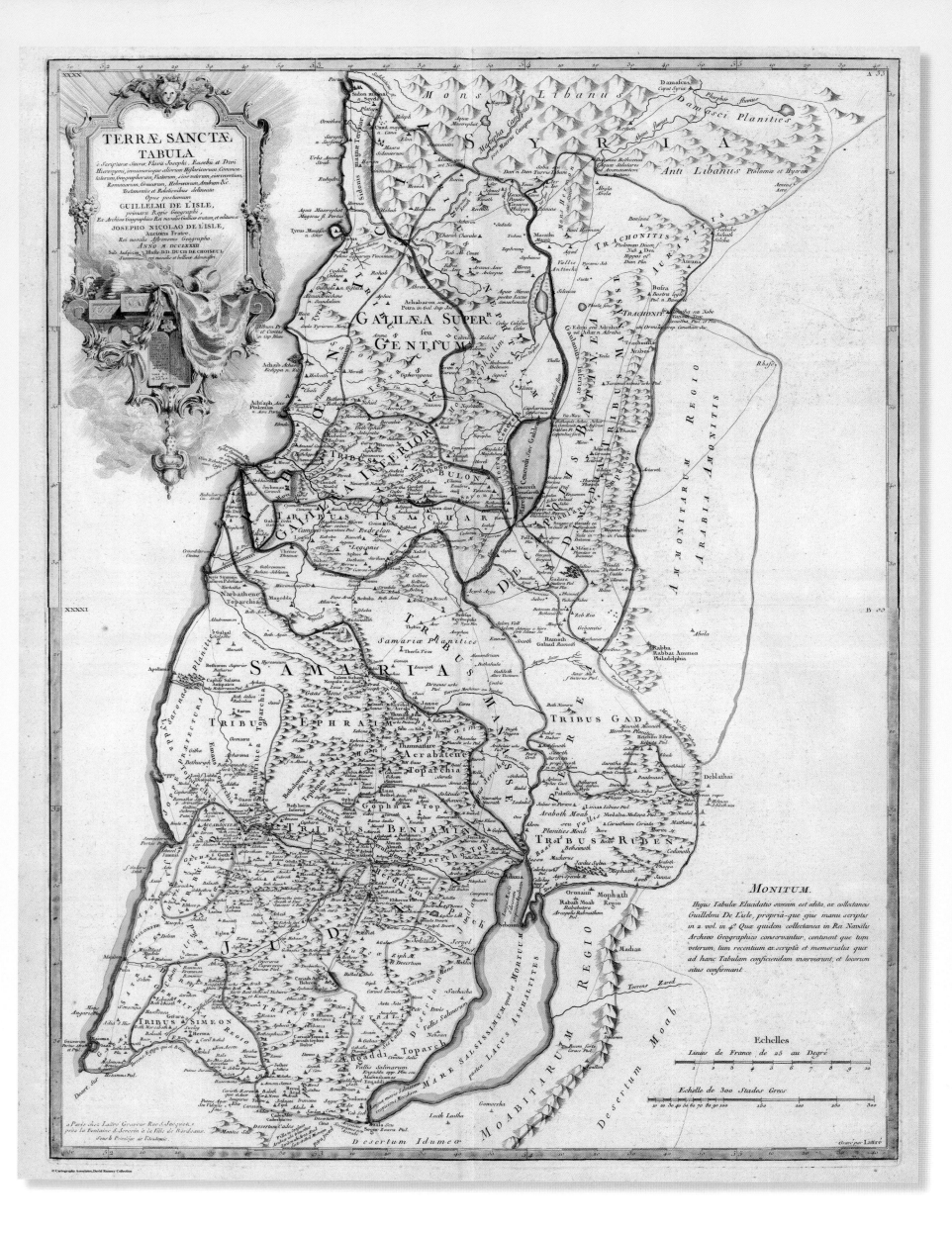

TERRÆ SANCTÆ TABULA

è Scripturæ Sacræ, Flavii Josephi, Eusebii et Divi
Hieronymi, innumerorumque aliorum Historicorum Commen-
tatorum, Geographorum, Viatorum, cive veterum, sive recentiorum,
Romanorum, Græcorum, Hebræorum, Arabum &c.
Testimoniis et Relationibus delineata

Opus posthumum
GUILLELMI DE L'ISLE,
primarii Regis Geographi,
Ex Archivis Geographicis Rei navalis Gallicæ erutum et editum a
JOSEPHO NICOLAO DE L'ISLE,
Auctoris Fratre,
Rei navalis Astronomo Geographo.
ANNO M.DCCLXXXII.
Sub Auspiciis Illustr. D.D. DUCIS DE CHOISEUL

MONITUM.

Hujus Tabulæ Elucidatio seorsim est edita, ex collectanea
Guillelmi De L'Isle, propriâque ejus manu scriptis
in 2. vol. in 4º Quæ quidem collectanea in Rei Navalis
Archivo Geographico conservantur, continent que tum
veterum, tum recentium ex scriptis et memorialia quæ
ad hanc Tabulam conficiendam inservierunt, et locorum
situs confirmant

Echelles
Lieues de France de 25 au Degré

Echelle de 300 Stades Grecs

à Paris chez Lattré Graveur Rue S. Jacques,
près la Fontaine S. Severin à la Ville de Bordeaux.
Avec le Privilege de l'Académie.

Gravé par Lattré.

CONTENTS

Detail from a 1562 Spanish-Dutch map of the Americas. Reflecting the spirit of the times, which had developed a new appreciation for Greek and Roman mythology, the cartographers chose a figure resembling a classical water god to display the Portuguese coat of arms.

Published in the United States and U.S. Territories, Canada, the United Kingdom, South Africa, Australia, and New Zealand by HAMMOND WORLD ATLAS CORPORATION, part of the Langenscheidt Publishing Group, 36-36 33rd Street, Long Island City, NY 11106

HAMMOND

Executive Director Publishing Karen Prince

Produced for HAMMOND WORLD ATLAS CORPORATION by

HYLAS PUBLISHING
129 MAIN STREET
IRVINGTON, NY 10533
WWW.HYLASPUBLISHING.COM

HYLAS PUBLISHING
Publisher Sean Moore
Editorial Director Aaron R. Murray
Art Director Brian MacMullen

Contributing Authors Stuart A.P. Murray; Robert Huber; Elizabeth Mechem; Sarah Novak; David West Reynolds, PhD; Tricia Wright; Thomas Cussans

Project Editor Jo Rose
Copyeditor Glenn Novak
Contributing Editors Suzanne Lander, Elizabeth Mechem, Lisa Purcell
Designers Neil Dvorak, Gus Yoo, Lisa Purcell, Holly Lee
Production Eunoh Lee
Picture Researcher Ben DeWalt
Editorial Assistants Rachael Greene, Gabrielle Kappes, Casey Tolfree, Will Vunderink, Emma Frankel
Indexer Jessie Shiers

Cartography Neil Dvorak

Cover Design Gus Yoo and Brian MacMullen

Printed and bound in Italy

ISBN-13: 978-084-370995-7

Half title: map of the world by a Ming dynasty cartographer, c. 1800. **Title page:** map of northern Asia by Belgian cartographer Abraham Ortelius (1527–98). **vii:** Arab geographer Muhammad al-Idrisi's map of the known world, showing Europe, Asia, and northern Africa in 1154. **End papers:** map of the world in 1565, drawn by Italian cartographer Paulo Forlani.

Front cover: Center: statue of the Buddha. Left, top to bottom: the Lotus Temple in Delhi, India; statues of gods at a Hindu temple; a Torah scroll. Right, top to bottom: mosque in Alexandria, Egypt; mosaic depicting Jesus Christ; Torii gates at the Fushimi Inari Shrine in Kyoto, Japan. Background: a 1587 European-made map of the world. **Back cover:** Left: the Golden Temple in Amritsar, India. Right: Spas-na-krovi Cathedral in St. Petersburg, Russia. Background: cartographer Christiaan van Adrichem's (1533–85) map of Jerusalem.

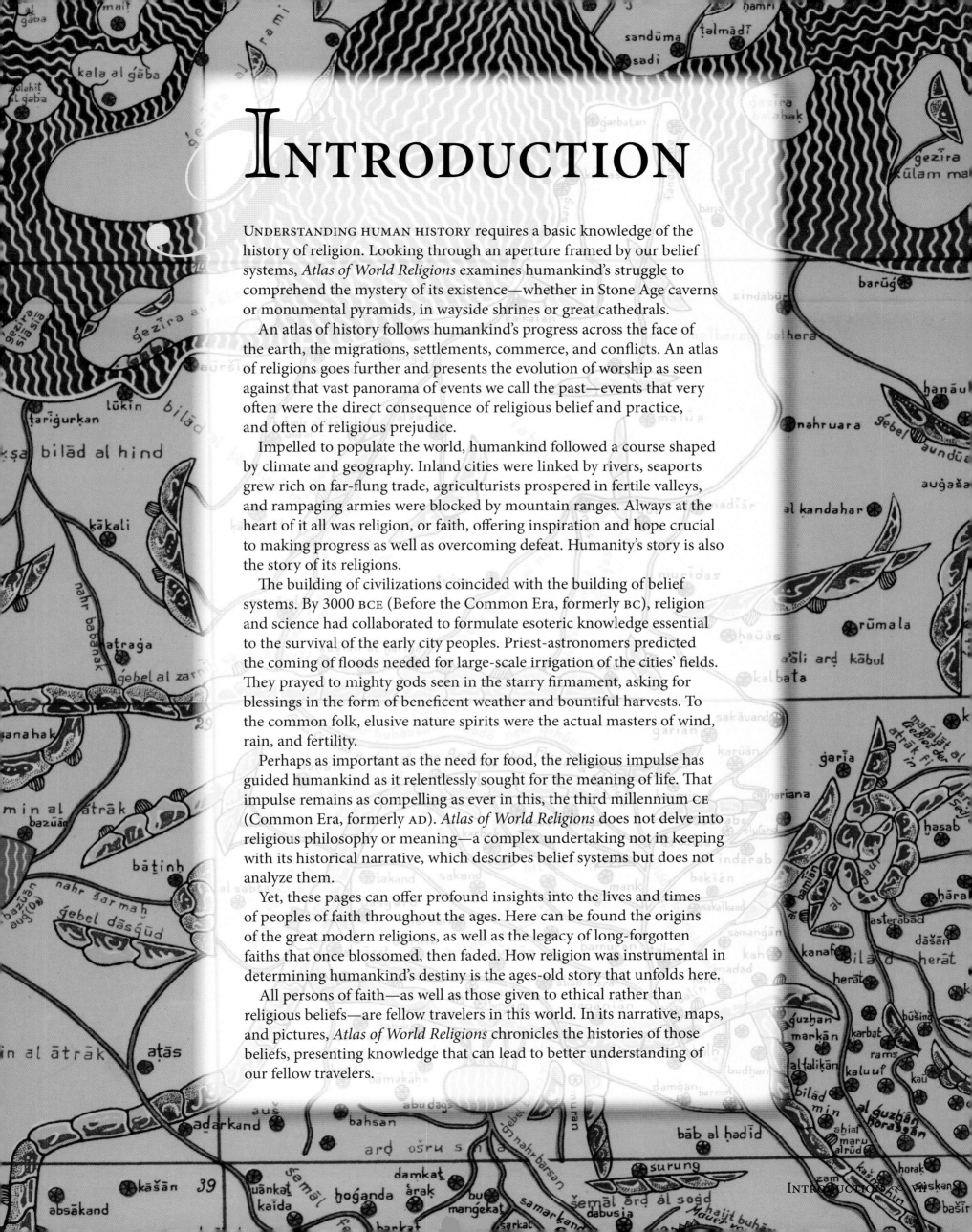

INTRODUCTION

UNDERSTANDING HUMAN HISTORY requires a basic knowledge of the history of religion. Looking through an aperture framed by our belief systems, *Atlas of World Religions* examines humankind's struggle to comprehend the mystery of its existence—whether in Stone Age caverns or monumental pyramids, in wayside shrines or great cathedrals.

An atlas of history follows humankind's progress across the face of the earth, the migrations, settlements, commerce, and conflicts. An atlas of religions goes further and presents the evolution of worship as seen against that vast panorama of events we call the past—events that very often were the direct consequence of religious belief and practice, and often of religious prejudice.

Impelled to populate the world, humankind followed a course shaped by climate and geography. Inland cities were linked by rivers, seaports grew rich on far-flung trade, agriculturists prospered in fertile valleys, and rampaging armies were blocked by mountain ranges. Always at the heart of it all was religion, or faith, offering inspiration and hope crucial to making progress as well as overcoming defeat. Humanity's story is also the story of its religions.

The building of civilizations coincided with the building of belief systems. By 3000 BCE (Before the Common Era, formerly BC), religion and science had collaborated to formulate esoteric knowledge essential to the survival of the early city peoples. Priest-astronomers predicted the coming of floods needed for large-scale irrigation of the cities' fields. They prayed to mighty gods seen in the starry firmament, asking for blessings in the form of beneficent weather and bountiful harvests. To the common folk, elusive nature spirits were the actual masters of wind, rain, and fertility.

Perhaps as important as the need for food, the religious impulse has guided humankind as it relentlessly sought for the meaning of life. That impulse remains as compelling as ever in this, the third millennium CE (Common Era, formerly AD). *Atlas of World Religions* does not delve into religious philosophy or meaning—a complex undertaking not in keeping with its historical narrative, which describes belief systems but does not analyze them.

Yet, these pages can offer profound insights into the lives and times of peoples of faith throughout the ages. Here can be found the origins of the great modern religions, as well as the legacy of long-forgotten faiths that once blossomed, then faded. How religion was instrumental in determining humankind's destiny is the ages-old story that unfolds here.

All persons of faith—as well as those given to ethical rather than religious beliefs—are fellow travelers in this world. In its narrative, maps, and pictures, *Atlas of World Religions* chronicles the histories of those beliefs, presenting knowledge that can lead to better understanding of our fellow travelers.

PART ONE

THE RELIGIONS OF THE ANCIENT WORLD

IN ANCIENT TIMES, AS CIVILIZATIONS DEVELOPED along the Tigris and Euphrates rivers and in the Valley of the Nile, human settlement also took root in Europe and East Asia. Whether in prosperous West Asian cities surrounded by fertile agricultural lands, or in the scattered clearings of endless European forests, humanity built homelands that were the foundation for all that was to come.

In the Indus Valley of northwest India and the Yellow River valley of eastern China, two great civilizations arose simultaneously. Each developed religious traditions that are still practiced today. In India, Hinduism sprang from an amalgam of two main cultures: the settled farmers of the Indus Valley and the nomadic Aryans from central Asia. In China, shamanistic traditions served the powerful early dynasties, until the time of the great reformer and teacher Confucius. Buddhism, which arose in India around 500 BCE, would eventually link these two ancient civilizations.

Thousands of years ago intrepid adventurers sailed across vast stretches of sea to colonize Australia and Oceania. Other peoples migrated from Siberia to Arctic North America, eventually reaching the tip of South America. And in the Mediterranean, the rich Minoan civilization of Crete gave way to the Greek Mycenaean era that Homer celebrated in his epic poems of gods and heroes.

No matter how sophisticated or simple were these civilizations, they all were anchored by religious practices and looked to ageless myths for answers—myths that shared many fundamental aspects. From the beginning, human beings all over the earth defined themselves by their faith.

Much as later seafarers did, early humans probably used features of the night sky to navigate in their travels, and many societies mapped their myths onto the heavens, identifying constellations with gods, heroes, and sacred stories.

Early Humans and Religion

THE PREHISTORIC AGES OF THE WORLD have, by definition, no written record to reveal how early humans thought or what they believed. The origins of mankind are shrouded by the mists of time, but could reach back one million years. Scientists, historians, clergy, and philosophers can only make educated guesses about the spirituality of those countless generations that lived and died before the advent of writing—and history—around 3500 BCE.

Archaeological evidence from the Paleolithic period (the Old Stone Age, 500,000–8000 BCE) indicates that important human customs were guided by religious impulses. Modern religions are said to have roots in Paleolithic spirituality, which is witnessed by sacred places, sculptures, paintings, stone engravings, and burial sites. That early humans recognized powers higher than themselves and acknowledged life after death is especially evident in their funereal practices.

Proof of ancient religious customs is found in burial pits, where human skeletons were laid in fetal positions, bound hand and foot alongside the bones of oxen or skulls of bears that seem intentionally placed there. The possible meanings of wall paintings discovered in the recesses of pitch-black caves have filled the writings of researchers and theorists for centuries. Most conclusions about the faith of prehistoric man remain, however, only conjecture.

Did early man have the intellectual capacity to construct a religious system? In answer, the power of that intellect is seen in the achievements of those first humans, who fabricated shelters, fashioned tools, made clothing, invented the bow, hunted and fought giant creatures. The intellect that enabled the human species not only to survive but to prosper against great odds proved just as potent in the creation, practice, and perpetuation of religion.

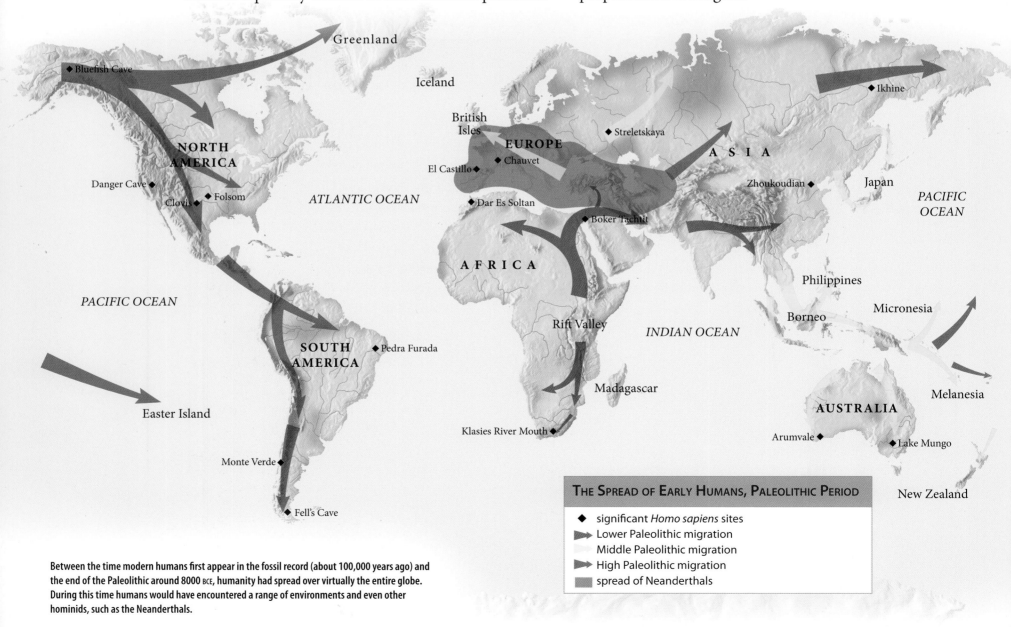

THE SPREAD OF EARLY HUMANS, PALEOLITHIC PERIOD

◆ significant *Homo sapiens* sites
➤ Lower Paleolithic migration
   Middle Paleolithic migration
➤ High Paleolithic migration
   spread of Neanderthals

Between the time modern humans first appear in the fossil record (about 100,000 years ago) and the end of the Paleolithic around 8000 BCE, humanity had spread over virtually the entire globe. During this time humans would have encountered a range of environments and even other hominids, such as the Neanderthals.

"See!" said the uncle, pointing with his spear to a star as his nephew listened. "That one is Mami-ngata, 'Our Father.' You see him, and he sees you."
—FROM THE MYTHS OF SOUTHEAST AUSTRALIA'S KULIN TRIBE

The Great Rift Valley, which runs for 4,000 miles (6,500 km) from Jordan to Mozambique, has yielded some of archaeology's most valuable fossils of early human ancestors, including the famous *Australopithecus* called Lucy.

ANCIENT EVIDENCE OF FAITH

Stone Age burial customs indicate humans believed in preparing the dead for another world that was to come. In the Middle Paleolithic period, flint axes and stone scraping tools accompany burials in southern France, apparently in the belief that such things would be needed after death. Bodies have been found placed in red ocher, along with shells, bones, and ivory. Researchers wonder whether the ocher and shells had significant symbolic or religious meaning.

The special treatment of human skulls, found around the world, also suggests there was some notion of another realm of unseen powers. Discovered in Bavaria were more than thirty skulls, all facing west. The heads had been severed, cut off with flint knives, ceremonially dried, and preserved. Decapitated bodies were laid in Chinese caves 500,000 years ago, also with the heads preserved. Skulls made into drinking cups have been found in

ICE AGE ART

Paleolithic cave art and decorated rock shelters, animals carved from bone, and female figures in stone have been found around the world. Apparently linked to rituals for communicating with otherworldly spirits, this artwork suggests early man shared a religio-magical outlook on life that went beyond basic methods of survival.

The limestone caves of southern Europe contained carved ivory statues, clay models, and amber pendants. Still-colorful ancient paintings of deer, oxen, bison, and horses survive on cave walls that had not been seen by humans since the paintings were made 15,000 to 20,000 years ago. Australian rock paintings and engravings possibly dating as far back as 45,000 BCE employ crescents, spirals, dots, and sometimes hand stencils—but their meanings and purposes can only be guessed at. Rock paintings have been termed "picture magic."

This ancient art amazes modern researchers but leaves them with more questions than answers. One interpretation seems certain:

early man possessed systems of faith, practiced religious rituals, and believed in another world beyond the physical dimension.

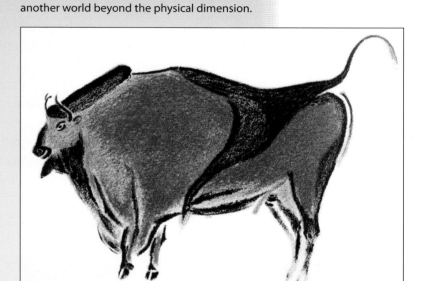

Bison figure prominently in much European cave art, perhaps because they were a significant food source.

French caves, and in a small chamber in an Italian cavern a skull was found inside a circle of stones. The brain appears to have been removed, perhaps for ceremonial purposes.

Other evidence of ancient religious beliefs is seen in cave paintings, engravings, and sculptures dating to the High Paleolithic period, between 40,000 and 12,000 BCE. These are particularly found in deep limestone caverns in France and Spain. Some subjects appear to be female humans, while others are of animals stuck with spears

and marked with red ocher, as if wounded. Female paintings and statues could be linked to fertility and goddess rituals, while other figures appear to be nature spirits, with attributes of both animals and humans.

THE ICE WITHDRAWS

Humankind is believed to have originated as erect hominids in East Africa more than four million years ago. Modern humans—the species *Homo sapiens*—appeared by 100,000 BCE and migrated northward to Europe and eastward into South Asia and China. The bitter cold climates of the "ice age," or glacial period, began to moderate by about 70,000 BCE. As glaciers melted and withdrew, and the resulting rising seas had not yet covered ancient land bridges, human migration pushed north and east and on into North and South America.

By 50,000 years ago humans had reached Australia, and by 30,000 years ago many of the islands of the southwestern Pacific were inhabited by people capable of building vessels and navigating long ocean voyages. Evidence from Chile to Oregon indicates likely habitation by humans by 12,000 BCE and possibly much earlier. Skillfully made blades and spearheads found in Clovis, New Mexico, are estimated to date to 9,500 BCE, and 9,000-year-old basketry has been discovered in Danger Cave, Utah.

Nestled against a section of the Great Rift Valley escarpment, Lake Manyara in Tanzania is still as scenic today as it must have been at the dawn of humanity. The Great Rift Valley has yielded some of the earliest hominid fossils ever discovered.

The Neolithic Period

THE NEOLITHIC PERIOD BEGINS around 8000 BCE with the era in which stone tools and weapons were formed by polishing and grinding. Previously, most tools and blades were made by the cruder method of chipping or flaking stone.

In the Neolithic period the earth's climate, geography, and living organisms became comparable to what now exists. Most of the great mammals, such as the mammoth, woolly rhinoceros, and giant deer, had become extinct. The glaciers were retreating, and the northerly climates moderating, so new human migrations drifted into uninhabited regions. Instead of remaining only hunter-gatherers, much of mankind began cultivating the land, domesticating herds and flocks, and settling into permanent communities.

New methods for harvesting, grinding, and storing grain were developed, and pottery appeared. Boats were being built, and mining extracted materials for tools, weapons, artwork, and adornments. Religious concepts, as reflected in burial practices, became more subtle and complex.

Burial in the Neolithic period sometimes included ritually burning the body, and there is indication of sacrifice. Some apparently important personages are found buried with other human remains that seem to belong to subordinate individuals. This suggests ritual killing of servants or close associates to accompany the deceased in the afterlife. Such sites become increasingly frequent late in the Neolithic period in archaeological finds from Mesopotamia and China. These burials may indicate offerings to the dead or to invisible powers beyond the physical world.

Neolithic civilizations appeared from southeastern and northwestern Europe to northern Africa and the Nile Valley, Southwest Asia, East Asia, and the Americas. The world's first great farming civilization appeared in what would become known as the Fertile Crescent, which reached from Mesopotamia to the Mediterranean.

For the most part, Neolithic peoples survived by hunting and gathering, with agricultural development restricted to the Fertile Crescent and valleys along the Indus, Yellow, and Yangtze rivers. Distinctive art styles, hinting at religious motives, can be identified at several hunter-gatherer archaeological sites.

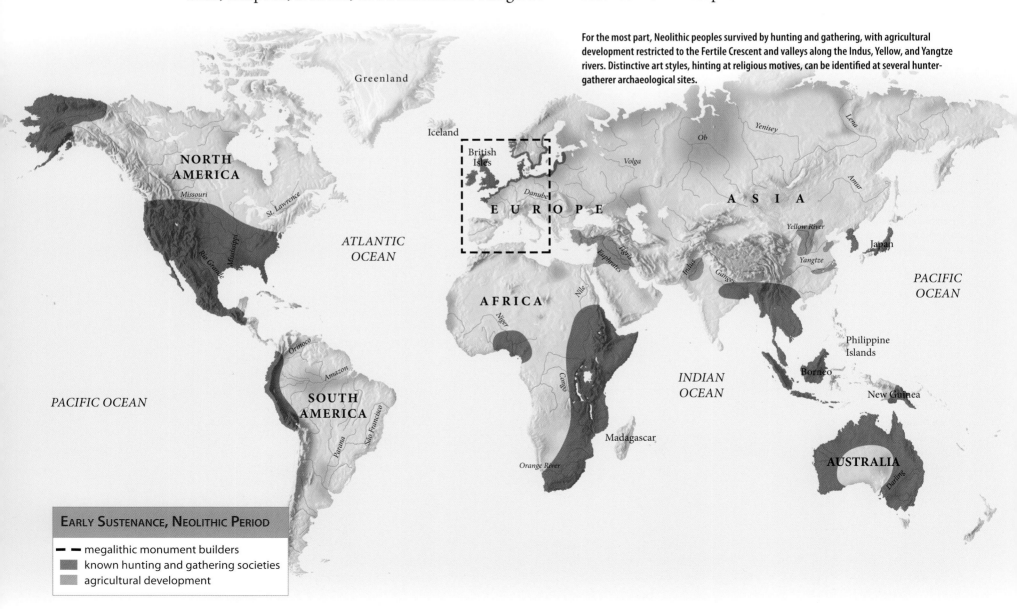

EARLY SUSTENANCE, NEOLITHIC PERIOD

- – – megalithic monument builders
- known hunting and gathering societies
- agricultural development

The heavens declare the glory of God;
And the firmament showeth his handiwork.
—PSALM 19

CANNIBALISM AND RITUAL SACRIFICE

In the first millennia of the Neolithic period evidence of cannibalism becomes more widespread. This practice appears to have been ritualistic. Cannibalism as manifested in modern "uncivilized" societies is generally intended to transfer certain of the victim's powers to the one who consumes the victim. Neolithic cannibalism rituals could also have been part of a sacrifice to appease mighty forces—whether the natural elements or higher powers.

In Neolithic agricultural communities the ritual of sacrificial death—animal or human—appears closely tied to prospects for a successful harvest. Rites that seem designed to promote fertility or agricultural abundance at harvest time often included human sacrifice. The remains of women and children have been found in what appear to be ceremonial pits.

Polytheism developed to account for the various forces of nature, which were in turn dominated or guided by supreme divine entities—sometimes male, at other times female. Female fertility images—"Great Mother" or "Earth Mother" images—were widespread well before the Neolithic period. Another notion taking shape was of "Father Sky" and "Mother Earth" and their unity as a couple, the parents of all existence.

A group of menhirs at Callanish, on Scotland's Isle of Lewis, some of which stand more than sixteen feet (4.8 m) high.

STANDING STONES

The Neolithic period is notable for the placement of huge stones, megaliths, on sites in northwestern Europe. These sites, often including burials, are considered sacred places. These megalithic sites may have been the focus of ancestor worship and seem to be monuments intended to endure for many centuries. Tall standing stones, or menhirs, are also found in some Neolithic constructions.

The Neolithic tomb of Newgrange, Ireland, incorporated a precisely calibrated double entrance; the sun's rays enter the tomb through the upper "roof box" on the winter solstice, illuminating exactly the passage and the inner burial chamber. This may have been intended to ritualistically represent the masculine sky (the sun beam) entering the feminine earth (the womblike tomb).

ANIMALISM AND THE HUNT

Painted images of animals and of creatures that display both human and animal features are increasingly prolific in the Neolithic period. Close ties between animals and humans are suggested by such images, which are consistent with the concept of "animalism." This is a belief that requires the hunter to ask forgiveness of the hunted—often by ritual dancing, imitating the animal, and carrying out rites to guarantee the rejuvenation and abundance of the game. Animalism is considered the forerunner of "totemism," which itself expresses a complex and intertwined relationship among humans, animals, and natural objects and forces.

There is also evidence that hunting ceremonies—perhaps actually practice sessions—involved the use of an animal hide to replicate the quarry. In Neolithic Siberia, for example, a bearskin was draped over a clay form, and hunters (dancers) fired arrows and stabbed with spears in imitation of the hunt. Such ceremonies continued into more recent times in Eurasia and North America, where hunters still depended on killing bears for food. The depiction of spears and arrows on images of game animals could suggest a belief in magic power to aid in the hunt.

In this same era, hoofed animals, especially sheep, oxen, and bulls, became leading candidates for ritual sacrifice. Horses, on the other hand, were being domesticated for beasts of burden rather than food, although they appear as special sacrifices near the end of the Neolithic period. The nomads of Central Asia led the way in breeding larger and stronger horses that one day would be used for war.

A typical Folsom point, with a leaflike shape and a long groove running nearly the entire length of the blade.

Shaman: The One Who Knows

WRITING HAD NOT YET BEEN INVENTED by the close of the Neolithic period sometime after 5000 BCE, but religious practices were becoming ever more complex. For millennia, certain communal leaders had been regarded as having special powers of healing and the ability to communicate with the ancestors. These were sorcerers, or "shamans," a term from Asia, meaning "he who knows."

Early in the twentieth century three young brothers exploring caves in southern France squeezed their way through a small hole, looking for cave paintings. They found themselves in a chamber, where their lights revealed a recess, much like a window, and in it was a carved and painted figure with a human face and limbs and several animal features.

This image combined a man's beard with the eyes of an owl, horns of a stag, claws of a lion, and tail of a horse. Over the decades, this often-visited cave became famous, named "Les Trois Frères," after the three brothers. Its mysterious image also won fame as "The Sorcerer," and is considered to represent a god or a priest. Some say it symbolizes a shaman who has the ability to change form and cast spells to guarantee a successful hunt. The sorcerer/shaman appears to be performing a sacred dance, the type of religio-magical ceremony practiced by shamans throughout the ages.

Shamanism was an important feature of Neolithic life, for the shaman was the intermediary between ordinary human beings and spirit-world deities that governed nature and animals. Shamans were leaders in the nomadic hunter-gatherer stage of human development and could be either male or female.

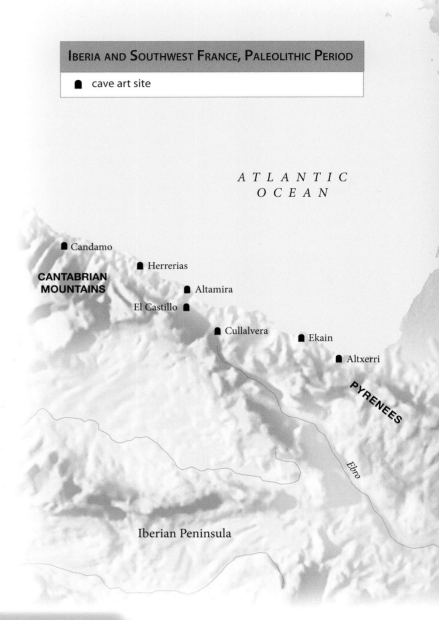

IBERIA AND SOUTHWEST FRANCE, PALEOLITHIC PERIOD

■ cave art site

ATLANTIC OCEAN

Candamo

CANTABRIAN MOUNTAINS

Herrerias

Altamira

El Castillo

Cullalvera

Ekain

Altxerri

PYRENEES

Ebro

Iberian Peninsula

A SACRED DUTY

In a cave in the Pyrenees Mountains of southern France, small models of male and female bison stand near a mounded clay platform that shows the marks of dancing feet. This scene suggests rituals may have been performed in Neolithic times to promote propagation of the bison, or perhaps to show respect and ask the animal to allow itself to be caught and killed.

As with the creator of "The Sorcerer" of Les Trois Frères, these dancers under flickering tallow torches could have been shamans fulfilling a sacred duty to their people—and to the spirits of the animals that sustained them.

A reproduction of ocher-stained artwork in Altamira Cave. Animals occur frequently, perhaps for shamanistic purposes.

A CHOSEN ONE

The shaman or sorcerer was recognized as the individual most able to communicate with the spirit world. The wisest shamans had the ability to interpret relationships between the living and their ancestors. They could heal sickness and could "divine," or foretell, the future.

The shaman was believed to have the guidance of certain disembodied entities, dwellers of the spirit world, sometimes identified as animals. The shaman was a "chosen one," selected by such spirits to communicate with them.

To achieve status as a shaman, the candidate had to endure difficult trials, even torture or severe illness, until he or she surrendered and fully accepted this demanding role in life. The shaman is said to fall into a state of ecstasy at will to communicate with the spirits, often to speak for them to the people. As evidenced

When addressing animals in a spiritual way with his songs, or using the drum, the conjurer [says], "You and I wear the same covering and have the same mind and spiritual strength," [meaning] their equality was spiritual and embraced or eclipsed the physical.

—FROM "HUNTING IS A HOLY OCCUPATION," ABOUT THE
NASKAPI PEOPLE OF THE LABRADOR PENINSULA

The preponderance of cave art sites in southeastern Europe suggests an artistic culture responding to a religious sensibility. The high occurrence of animals indicates their central importance to this ancient society.

Angles-sur-l'Anglin

Montgaudier
Roc-de-Sers

Lascaux

Le Gabillou
Laugerie Basse
Dordogne
Les Combarelles
Font-de-Gaume

Ebbou

Pech-Merle

La Baume-Latrone

Montespan
Le Mas d'Azil
Gargas
Le Tue d'Audoubert
Niaux
Les Trois
Frères

Mediterranean Sea

Loire

Rhône

The Venus of Willendorf, named after the Austrian village where it was found, measures a little more than four inches (10 cm) tall and dates to around 20,000 BCE. The limestone carving was stained with ocher.

by modern practice, the shamanic trance state is said to be a spiritual journey, often followed by an awakening and revelation.

Certain instruments and objects are used in the shaman's practice, including drums, rattles, special headgear, and a wooden staff. Charms and fetishes are employed to cast spells or divine the future.

OBJECTS OF SPELLS AND WORSHIP

Shamanism is predicated on the belief that the visible world is one with the invisible and pervaded by forces and spirits that affect all living beings. The shaman's knowledge includes manipulation and creation of charms, amulets, and fetishes that, when used properly, impart authority and power.

Fetishes are believed to have supernatural or magical power, usually to protect the bearer from harm or illness. These objects are cherished and concealed until used in rituals by shamans. Fetishes can be parts of animals that are to be hunted, or a lock of hair of an individual who is to be the object of a magic spell.

Among the most common Paleolithic artifacts of worship after 30,000 BCE are small female statues known collectively as "Venuses." These figures, which often have accentuated breasts and buttocks, have been found from Siberia to Anatolia and Spain. The ancient concept of woman as the producer of life, with inherent life-giving powers, is thought to have come before the notion of man as the "begetter" of life in cooperation with woman.

Nine female figures dance around a small male figure in a cave painting in the Spanish Pyrenees. In many ancient scenes, the male—perhaps a shaman—is represented by such a figure, possibly symbolizing a creative force that enters the world in order to procreate with woman and thus sustain humanity.

Paleolithic sculptures and paintings and engravings of fertility scenes were likely created to promote the renewal of life from generation to generation.

MESOPOTAMIA
The Fertile Crescent

THE SEMIARID REGION "BETWEEN THE RIVERS," as Mesopotamia is translated, was made productive and bountiful by 3500 BCE, largely through complex irrigation systems. The waters of the rivers Tigris and Euphrates, flowing southeastward from the Anatolian mountains, were diverted into canals, ditches, aqueducts, and pools to nourish the fields. Mesopotamian agriculture flourished, populations increased, and cities were founded.

The peoples of ancient Mesopotamia did not take their wealth and abundance for granted. They attributed their success in planting and harvesting to the gods, and their religious practice established an elaborate pantheon of deities whose blessings, or wrath, determined the destiny and fortunes of the people and their civilizations. Sacred blessings meant rainfall, freedom from locusts, and prosperity. Wrath of the gods meant drought, plagues, and famine.

The heart of the Mesopotamian city was the temple, dwelling place of the deity who was supreme lord of the realm. In the temple were the priests, many of them originally scribes who developed writing in part to keep track of the harvests and taxes. In the early temples were storage rooms for grains and crops, and there, too, were kept the first libraries, intended to maintain official documents recording agriculture, administration, and trade.

The king-priest stood at the head of an earthly hierarchy that reached into the heavenly order of invisible deities. The king carried the mantles of protector in time of war as well as that of the nation's father, the high magnificence who led his people in religious practices to please the gods and assure the harvest for another year. The king, priests, and leading scribes understood the phases of the moon, predicted the changing of the seasons by observing and studying the stars, and could anticipate the time of floods.

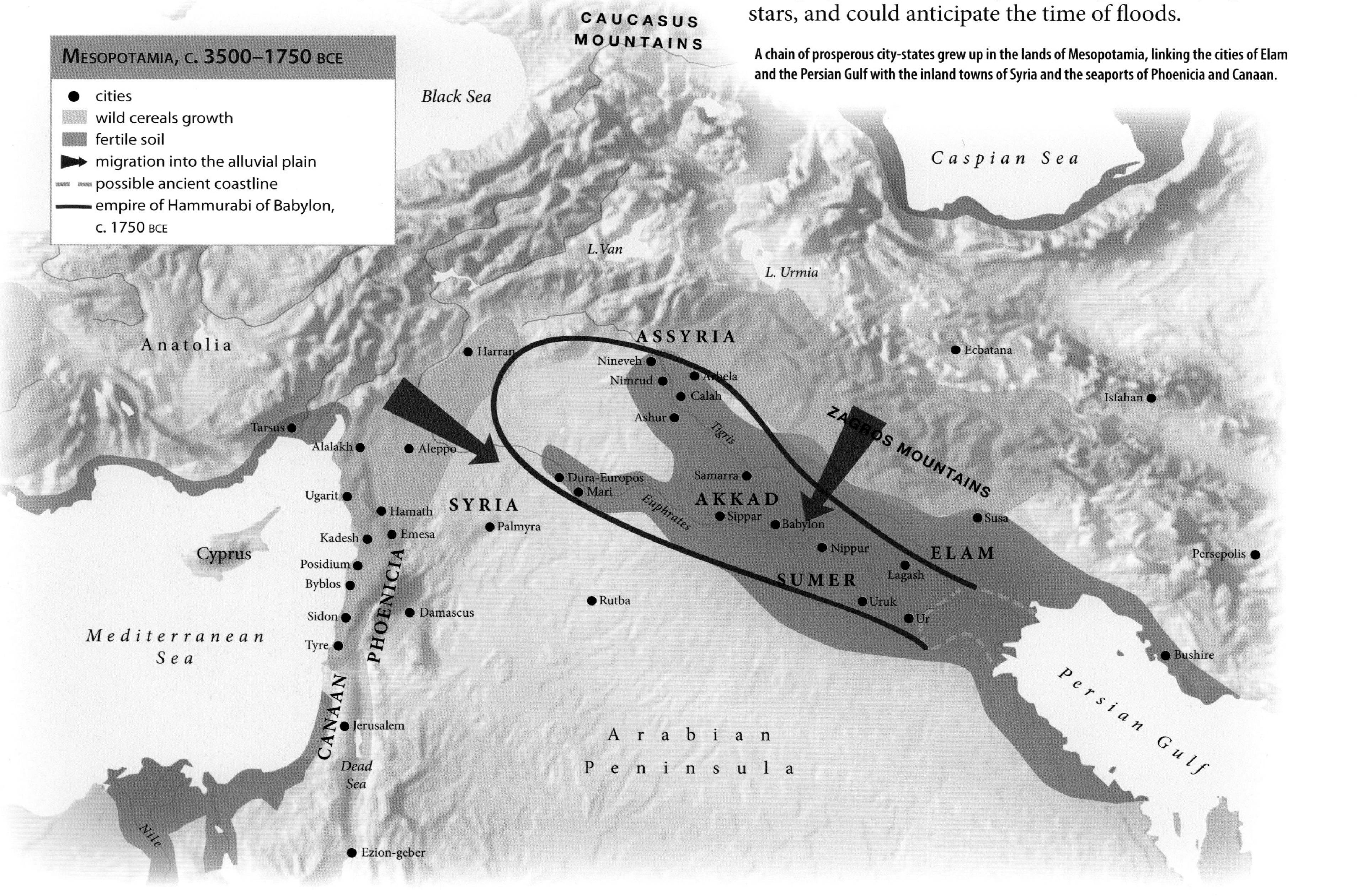

A chain of prosperous city-states grew up in the lands of Mesopotamia, linking the cities of Elam and the Persian Gulf with the inland towns of Syria and the seaports of Phoenicia and Canaan.

MESOPOTAMIA, C. 3500–1750 BCE

- ● cities
- wild cereals growth
- fertile soil
- ➤ migration into the alluvial plain
- – – possible ancient coastline
- ▬ empire of Hammurabi of Babylon, c. 1750 BCE

I am the salvation-bearing shepherd, whose staff is straight. . . . on my breast I cherish the inhabitants of the land of Sumer and Akkad. . . . in my deep wisdom have I enclosed them. . . .

—HAMMURABI, KING OF BABYLON (1792–1750 BCE)

The earliest collections of tablets were mainly economic records used by administrators and political leaders to keep track of business transactions, taxes, and other financial matters of the government.

With the development of the written word there arose a need for documents concerning storage and organization. These documents led to the first libraries, usually established in temples, where scribes worked, recording and copying. Eventually, literary works appeared and also were copied. Libraries contained epics, myths, and scientific, historical, and philosophical tracts. No longer would religious teachings be handed down only orally to future generations.

The earliest known form of writing, cuneiform, used pictograms—symbols—which were cut into clay tablets with a reed stylus.

King Sargon I (2334–2279 BCE), shown in this relief, brought Akkadia to its zenith, extending the empire from the Persian Gulf to the Mediterranean.

CRADLE OF CIVILIZATION

Agriculture was the driving force behind the first organized state religions of Mesopotamia. The cities of Uruk, Babylon, Nineveh, and Ashur grew and prospered, and Mesopotamia—the lands of the Tigris and Euphrates—would one day become known as the "Cradle of Civilization."

Although cities also began to rise in Egypt, the Indus Valley, and China in the fourth millennium BCE, it was Mesopotamia that led humanity into the urban world of temples, royalty, governments, great armies, commerce, alliances, and conquest.

Civilization developed in the agriculturally rich "Fertile Crescent" that arched from Mesopotamia westward to the Jordan River, down the Mediterranean coast, and into the Nile Valley. The achievements of the Sumerians, Assyrians, Babylonians, Hittites, West Semitic peoples, and Hurrians paralleled the rise and fall of their economic progress. Always, gratitude—or blame—was directed toward their gods, the king, and the priesthood.

Sumerians, whose written language dates to the fourth millennium BCE and is the oldest in the region, worshipped the mother goddess Nammu, who with the sky god Anu gave birth to great gods of the earth, to the animals, and to humankind. The principal god of Babylon was Marduk, once a god of agriculture who was elevated to be the highest in the empire's pantheon.

In the reign of Hammurabi in Babylon, 1792–1750 BCE, the peoples of Mesopotamia would be guided by his written code of laws. The prologue to the Code of Hammurabi enumerates the essential characteristics required of a just ruler.

THE FIRST WRITING

The Fertile Crescent was the birthplace of writing, which appeared sometime before 3000 BCE. At first writing was done on various materials, including bones, skins, clay, and papyrus. Early Mesopotamian documents were clay tablets inscribed with cuneiform writing, done with a stylus, or small stick, which made wedge-shaped cuts (*cunea*, in Latin) on tablets of damp clay.

THE GODS CALLED HIM BY NAME

The Code of Hammurabi sets out detailed penalties for crimes, regulations for commerce, and rules for husbands and wives, but the code first of all asserts the king's own obligations and duties to his people, beginning in the first lines of the prologue:

"When Anu the Sublime, King of the Anunaki, and Bel, the lord of heaven and earth, who decreed the fate of the land, assigned to Marduk, the overruling son of Ea, God of righteousness, dominion over earthly man, . . . they called Babylon by his illustrious name, made it great on earth, and founded an everlasting kingdom in it, whose foundations are laid so solidly as those of heaven and earth; then Anu and Bel called by name me, Hammurabi, the exalted prince, who feared God, to bring about the rule of righteousness . . . so that I should . . . enlighten the land, to further the well-being of mankind."

The cuneiform writing on this stele, or stone column, is part of the second-millennium BCE Code of Hammurabi, the 282 official laws established by King Hammurabi to govern Babylon's vast empire.

MESOPOTAMIA
The Mesopotamian Cosmogony

Just as the first organized civilizations and cities developed in Mesopotamia, so did the first organized religions. The king represented the gods on earth, but his city was owned by the gods, who were to be served by the inhabitants. The lord of the wind and air, Enlil, who was also counselor to the gods, lived in the temple of the city of Nippur. Enlil was the son of the god An and the goddess Ki—whose combined names make up the Sumerian word for universe, *an-ki*.

The king's gods were also the gods of the state and the empire. The religion of the imperial court was usually accepted by those peoples who were brought into the empire, whether by conquest or by treaty. With the advent of ships and sea travel, fast-growing commerce also spread religious doctrine and traditions from people to people. By the second millennium BCE, many civilizations shared similar myths and narratives—legends and creation stories that became cornerstones for the leading religions of the period.

The Mesopotamian cosmogony—theories or stories having to do with the creation of the world—is laid out in the second-millennium BCE Babylonian epic poem *Enuma Elish*, meaning "when on high." In this epic, which begins with the universe in a state of chaos, the warrior deity Marduk, son of Ea, becomes the champion of a younger generation of gods. Marduk's battle with merciless elder gods results in the forming of heaven and earth from the essence of his vanquished enemies. Marduk was the supreme deity of the Babylonian empire.

Such creation myths, including the Sumerian *Epic of Gilgamesh*, with its "great flood" narrative, were carried on through the generations to appear and reappear in the cosmogony, traditions, and beliefs of faiths such as Christianity, Judaism, and Islam.

Trade routes connected the ancient cities of the Fertile Crescent, allowing goods to travel from the Persian Gulf into Egypt, the Mediterranean, and beyond. Abraham, the biblical patriarch, would certainly have followed some of these routes as he made his way from Ur to Harran, Jerusalem, and finally Egypt.

ANCIENT MESOPOTAMIA, 3300–1750 BCE

- ● cities
- — trade routes
- --- possible routes for Abraham's journey
- --- possible ancient coastline
- ▒ fertile soil

[T]hey went forth from Ur of the Chaldeans to go to the land of Canaan. . . . Now the Lord said to Abram, "Go from your country and your kindred and your father's house to the land that I will show you. And I will make of you a great nation, and I will bless you, and make your name great, so that you will be a blessing."
—BOOK OF GENESIS

The war side of the so-called Standard of Ur, discovered in that city's royal cemetery and dated to approximately 2500 BCE. The exemplary craftsmanship, with fine inlay of lapis lazuli, shell, stone, and mother-of-pearl, suggests the power of the early Ur dynasties.

OUT OF MESOPOTAMIA CAME ABRAHAM

The Jewish patriarch Abraham—first known as Abram—is said in the Book of Genesis to have come from Ur, city of the Chaldeans, in Mesopotamia, seeking the land of Canaan. Historians believe this could have been around 2000 BCE. Instead of reaching Canaan, Abraham and his family settled in Haran, northern Mesopotamia. Later, at the Lord's directive, Abraham departed Haran and wandered in the wilderness. Because he faithfully obeyed the voice of God, Abraham was promised that his descendants would be given the land of Canaan.

Abraham is considered the patriarch of the Israelites, Ishmaelites, and Edomite peoples. Israelites are the ancestors of the Jews, Ishmaelites are the ancestors of Arab peoples, and Edomites were a Semitic-speaking people whose lands ranged from the Sinai Peninsula to the southerly tip of the Dead Sea.

The name Abraham has been translated as "father of many nations," and because of his place as patriarch—or "exalted father" in another translation—Judaism, Christianity, and Islam are referred to as the "Abrahamic" religions.

A Sumerian goddess appears on this stele, recovered from the ancient city of Girsu (modern Telloh, in Iraq) and dated to approximately 2120 BCE.

THE EPIC OF GILGAMESH

The mythic exploits of an Uruk king, Gilgamesh, were handed down in legend and song for thousands of years. The *Epic of Gilgamesh* is considered to have originated with the Sumerians, known for long narrative poems on the nature of the world. The epic tells the story of Gilgamesh, a harsh but intrepid king, one part human and two parts god, as he fights monsters and seeks for the tree of life.

The epic includes a narrative of a catastrophic flood that destroyed the city of Shurippak, on the bank of the Euphrates. Only Utnapashtim, warned by the god Ea, survives the flood, after building a great vessel to carry "the seed of all living things," Utnapashtim's kinfolk, and chosen craftsmen, as well as animals, wild and domesticated.

Gods of Shurippak are enumerated in the epic:

There were Anu, their father,
Valiant Enlil, their counselor,

Ninurta, their herald.
Ennuge, their irrigator,
Ninigiku-Ea was also present with them.

Utnapashtim's vessel survives the flood, and he himself is transformed from human to deity.

PALACES AND ZIGGURATS

Archaeological sites throughout Mesopotamia reveal major temple and palace complexes from as early as the fourth millennium BCE. Since much of the region is arid and has little available stone, most structures were made from mud brick, although palaces and temples had magnificently decorated cut-stone walls. Assyrian palaces such as those at Nimrud and Nineveh are famed for stone slabs adorned with pictorial and written carvings narrating accounts of the king's achievements.

Royal palaces were residences as well as centers for worship, with courtyards for ceremonies and shrines to the deities. In the city of Ur, the priestesses of the moon god, Nanna, lived in a complex of courtyards, sanctuaries, great halls, and burial sites.

Massive stepped structures, known as ziggurats, have been discovered throughout Mesopotamia and the Fertile Crescent. Ziggurat means "rising high up." They are believed to have been temples, erected generation after generation, one building placed upon the one beneath. These moundlike structures, with enormous main staircases, towered over the mostly mud-brick houses of the city.

The massive ziggurat of Ur, appearing today with some modern restorations, has stood since about 2100 BCE, when the king Ur-Nammu built it as a place of worship for the god of the moon. Three staircases ascend the front of the ziggurat and were perhaps restricted to priests.

MESOPOTAMIA
Land of Faith and Science

THE ROLLING AGRICULTURAL LANDS of Mesopotamia were rich and prosperous but difficult to defend from powerful invaders such as the Hittites of Anatolia, who sacked Babylon in 1600 BCE. Nor could city states resist their empire-building neighbors such as the Akkadians in 2330 BCE, and the Assyrians in 1350 BCE.

Conquerors brought their own gods, but these alien deities were often interchangeable with local gods, many known by both names. Enki, the Sumerian lord of the earth and god of wisdom and fresh water, was also the Akkadian god Ea. Sumer's Asarluhhi, king of the gods, was Babylon's Marduk. The Sumer goddess of love and war, Ianna, also queen of heaven and earth, was Ishtar to the Akkadians.

The status of gods rose and ebbed according to the fortunes of the peoples who worshipped them. Just as Marduk was raised to be the king of the gods when Babylon flourished, so did Ashur become supreme when the Assyrians dominated Mesopotamia. Myths and legends were carried down through the generations, as with the Sumerian *Epic of Gilgamesh,* still important a thousand years later to the Assyrians of the seventh century BCE.

Myths could be changed by successive conquerors. Marduk's symbolic conquest of Tiamet, dragon goddess of creative chaos—narrated in the *Enuma Elish*—was recast by the Assyrians as the victory of their chief god, Ashur. The triumphs of armies became also the triumphs of state religions, but many traditions—including religious festivals—were shared in common.

Throughout the Bronze Age (c. 3000–1000 BCE) and into the Iron Age, Mesopotamian religion was polytheistic (except for the monotheistic Jews), with hundreds of deities, and so widespread that it influenced the beliefs of the peoples of Persia, Mycenae, and Greece.

A succession of empires, each with its own culture but often blending or adopting elements of rival belief structures, dominated Mesopotamia through the Bronze Age and early Iron Age.

EMPIRES OF MESOPOTAMIA, SECOND MILLENNIUM BCE

- • cities
- – – possible ancient coastline
- —— maximum extent of Hittite Empire
- —— maximum extent of Assyria
- —— maximum extent of Babylonia
- Israel
- Judah

In that day the Lord with his hard and great and strong sword will punish Leviathan, the fleeing serpent, Leviathan, the twisting serpent, and he will slay the dragon that is in the sea.
—Book of Isaiah

Wars and Conquest

Warfare was a recurring aspect of life in the Fertile Crescent, and kingdoms fell and rose, some great, some lesser-known. The might of Egypt pressed northward and was contested in some of the greatest battles of the ancient world, such as at Kadesh, on the Orontes River, a standoff between the Egyptians and Hittites in 1288 BCE.

Babylon's dominance rose and then receded in the second millennium BCE and rose again by the reign of Nebuchadnezzar II in the sixth century BCE. The peoples of Canaan, the Philistines, and the kingdoms of Judah and Israel were often in the middle of these struggles. They, in turn, engaged in their own bitter conflicts, made alliances, and carried out rebellions against the professional armies of Assyria, Babylon, and Egypt.

Nebuchadnezzar defeated Egyptian forces again and again, and he put down local uprisings in Syria, Palestine, and Phoenicia. In 587 BCE his forces—termed Chaldeans by this time—captured Jerusalem, ending the Kingdom of Judah. Many Jews were forced to depart for his capital city, Babylon.

Fifty years later an invasion by Cyrus the Great of Persia overwhelmed Babylon, and descendants of those Jewish captives were permitted to return to Jerusalem, ending the period known as the "Babylonian captivity."

A Shared Religious Tradition

The priests of Mesopotamia envisioned the world as a disk surrounded by vast space, beyond which was the realm of heaven, all of it embraced by waters. Mesopotamian gods were powerful but often bore the same characteristics and flaws as human beings. They fought among themselves in the heavens and in the underworld.

While pondering on the ways of the gods, priest-magicians in Mesopotamian temples developed a profound understanding of astronomy. The movements of heavenly bodies were understood in terms of the godly pantheon. In Babylonian mythology the zodiac is the result of Marduk's defeat of Tiamet, described as a dragon. The constellation Draco can symbolize Tiamet, also the god of chaos and termed a "leviathan"—or enormous—sea serpent. A similar struggle between God and a sea serpent is described by Isaiah, the eighth-century BCE Jewish prophet. The Book of Isaiah contains prophecies, myths, and teachings also found in the faiths of Babylon, Assyria, Canaan, and Egypt, to name but a few.

A fresco shows Marduk, on the right, slaying the monstrous figure of Tiamat, in the center.

The Priest-Scientists

Marduk's triumph over the serpent god of chaos created the order of the stars and heavenly bodies, an order that marks the passage of time—the days, seasons, and years. Temples became astronomical observatories, and the science of astronomy combined with newly evolved mathematics to calculate celestial movements, eclipses, and solstices, and also led to measuring time and space.

Mesopotamian religion and science combined to discover means to calculate the travel of the sun, establish a calendar with a seven-day week (days with 24 hours), and divide the circle into 360 degrees. The wheel was invented, and the war chariot naturally followed.

Commerce and conquest helped broadcast the seeds of religion and science, including medicine, and established the Fertile Crescent, from Babylon on the Euphrates to Thebes on the Nile, as a birthplace of scholarship and wisdom. Cities such as Babylon were famed for their centers of learning—learning that was disseminated far and wide—and flourished long after Mesopotamia had diminished in power and influence.

A seated statue of Gudea, a prince of Lagash in the mid-twenty-first century BCE. The statue is dedicated to the god Ningishzida; the prince oversaw intensive restoration and building of temples.

The ruins of ancient Babylon, neatly excavated, fascinate modern tourists even as the city once enchanted the Mesopotamian world.

Worship in the Valley of the Nile

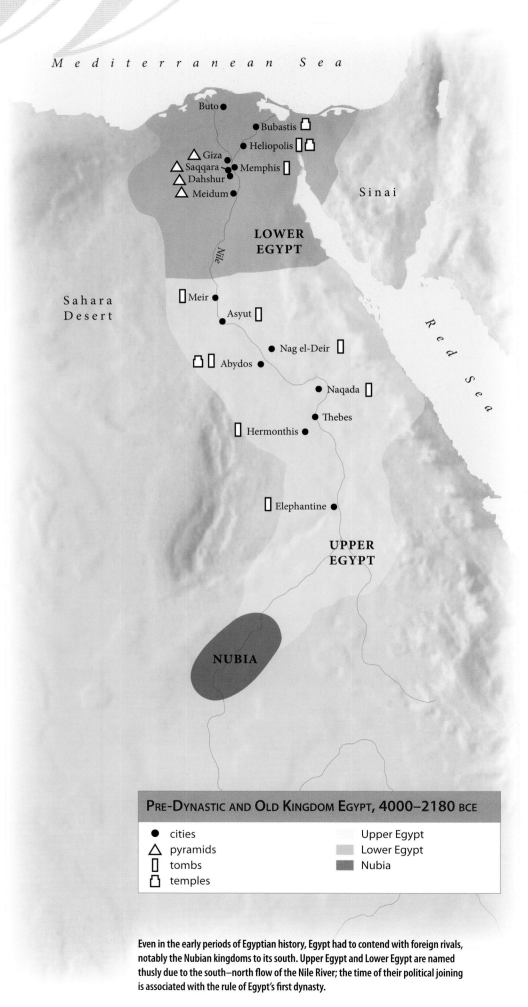

Mediterranean Sea

Buto

Bubastis

Heliopolis

Giza

Saqqara   Memphis

Dahshur

Meidum

LOWER EGYPT

Nile

Sinai

Sahara Desert

Meir

Asyut

Nag el-Deir

Abydos

Naqada

Thebes

Hermonthis

Red Sea

Elephantine

UPPER EGYPT

NUBIA

Pre-Dynastic and Old Kingdom Egypt, 4000–2180 bce

- ● cities
- △ pyramids
- ▯ tombs
- ⌂ temples

- Upper Egypt
- Lower Egypt
- Nubia

Even in the early periods of Egyptian history, Egypt had to contend with foreign rivals, notably the Nubian kingdoms to its south. Upper Egypt and Lower Egypt are named thusly due to the south–north flow of the Nile River; the time of their political joining is associated with the rule of Egypt's first dynasty.

As in Mesopotamia, agriculture stimulated the development of ancient Egypt, which grew up along the Nile River before 5000 BCE. Also like Mesopotamia, Egypt was semiarid and its crops required systematic control of the river waters. The lower Nile's annual floods covered vast lands that had to be evacuated and allowed to dry out before planting.

Predicting floods was one of the most important functions of Egyptian astronomy, and priests mastered the ability to announce the time of the river's rising, which happened at the summer solstice, when the star Sirius appeared before the sun rose above the horizon.

Egypt is said to have acquired wheat and barley from Mesopotamia and wild cereals from the Sahara, once a fertile, well-watered region. Saharan rock art dating to 6000 BCE depicts game animals that went extinct when the area became arid.

Villages and fortified towns grew up along the Nile, where by 4000 BCE there existed an Upper Kingdom and Lower Kingdom. The warrior-king Menes united these kingdoms by the third millennium BCE, an era when hieroglyphics—Greek for "sacred carvings"—came into use. Egyptian hieroglyphics, or picture-writing, were inscribed on temples and buildings, telling of gods and their legends, of wars and conquests, and describing the reigns of divine sovereigns—pharaohs—whose role was to link humanity with the gods.

The pharaoh was originally designated as the only priest who could perform the daily temple ritual and thus was known as "Lord of the Ritual."

The ancient Egyptian era that lasted until approximately 2180 BCE is known as the Old Kingdom. It was also called the "Pyramid Age," for the great monuments built during this time.

Among the world's most fabulous structures, the three enormous pyramids at Giza were built for Old Kingdom pharaohs between 2550 and 2490 BCE. The center pyramid, Khafre's, is actually smaller than the Great Pyramid, beyond, but appears taller because it was placed on higher ground.

The Narmer Palette may represent a pharaoh, Narmer, unifying Upper and Lower Egypt. The palette dates to the thirty-first century BCE, and its antiquity and possible meaning have led some to wonder if Narmer and Menes are the same person. The palette also shows some of Egypt's earliest hieroglyphs.

THE LAND OF PYRAMIDS

Among the more than one hundred identified pyramids of ancient Egypt, none are grander than those at Giza, believed to have been erected in the middle of the third millennium BCE.

Many pyramid structures exist within a fifty-mile stretch of the Nile. Giza's are the largest, with the Great Pyramid of the pharaoh Khufu one of the most enormous buildings humanity has ever erected. The Great Pyramid, diminished slightly by time, originally rose to 481 feet (147 m). There is endless speculation about the purpose of pyramids, large and small, and their various builders apparently had different purposes. The most common interpretation is that most pyramids were intended as tombs to pharaohs, designed to establish a closer union between the world of the living and the deceased ruler in the afterlife.

Some pyramid complexes contain tombs of pharaohs and high priests. Others, such as the Great Pyramid, contain chambers and shafts that suggest tombs and rites, but no burials have been found there.

THE EGYPTIAN CREATION MYTH

The *Book of Overthrowing Apophis* is from a later period in Egyptian history, but it preserves documents related to early religious beliefs. In this work, the divine act of creation involves the defeat of Apophis, also known as Apep, chief god of the powers of darkness and adversary of the sun god, Re.

Apep is portrayed as a huge serpent in the watery abyss of original chaos, as described in the opening of the story of creation:

> The Lord of All, after having come into being, says: I am he who came into being as Khepotri [the Becoming One]. When I came into being, the beings came into being, all the beings came into being after I became. . . . I thought in my heart, I planned in myself. . . . I ejected Shu [the air], before I spat out Tefnut [the moist], before any other who was in me had become. . . . Shu and Tefnut jubilated in the Watery Abyss in which they were [and] produced Geb and Nut; Geb and Nut produced out of a single body Osiris, Horus the Eyeless One, Seth, Isis, and Nephthys, one after the other among them. Their children are numerous in this land. . . .

In the end I will destroy everything that I have created, the earth will become again part of the Primeval Ocean, like the Abyss of waters in their original state. Then I will . . . have changed myself back into the Old Serpent who knew no man and saw no god.
—ATUM-RE, THE FIRST AND CHIEF GOD OF EARLY EGYPT, FROM THE BOOK OF THE DEAD, CHAPTER 175

An obelisk graces the ruins of Karnak. Their slender shape is reminiscent of a ray of light, and Egyptian obelisks are thought to represent the sun god, Re.

WRITING AND PAPYRUS

One of the world's earliest known forms of writing, with examples dating as far back as 3400 BCE, Egyptian hieroglyphs make extensive use of animal and natural forms.

In ancient Egypt, papyrus—the forerunner of paper—became widely used for writing. The papyrus reed grew along the backwaters of the Nile, where it was harvested to be made into flat sheets. Easy to store and handle as official documents and literature, papyrus became more widely used than the earlier medium, clay tablets.

Egypt long maintained its prestige in the civilized world in part because it was the only practical source of precious papyrus, a valuable trade commodity. The secrets of producing papyrus in sheets were jealously guarded.

One disadvantage to papyrus, however, was that it was susceptible to deterioration. Clay tablets, on the other hand, were extremely durable in the dry climates of Egypt and Mesopotamia. Relatively few papyrus scrolls have survived the centuries, while archaeologists have discovered more than 400,000 clay tablets buried in once-lost cities covered by shifting desert sands.

Part One: The Religions of the Ancient World ❧ 15

Egypt's Enduring Deities

EGYPT WAS POWERFUL AND PROSPEROUS century after century and remained largely undisturbed by outside threats. By the period known as the Middle Kingdom (2040 to 1786 BCE) Egypt's immediate sphere of influence extended into Canaan and southward to Nubia. For millennia Egyptian culture strongly influenced peoples from Mesopotamia to southern Europe.

Around 1800 BCE Egypt suffered invasion and eventual conquest by the Hyksos—termed the "Shepherd Kings"—who brought horses from southwest Asia and used bronze weapons that were superior to Egyptian arms. After a century the Egyptians rose up and defeated the Hyskos and by 1469 BCE had extended their empire to Libya and distant Anatolia.

From generation to generation Egyptians carried forward previous religious ideas, added new ones, and integrated them in their spiritual lives. Myths and rituals could be revised but were usually kept alive with due respect and veneration. Egyptian religion was intimately entwined with daily culture and offered society its guiding ethics. Over the earthly realm stood the pharaoh, whose sacred duty was to establish and maintain order, or *ma'at,* which encompasses truth and justice both on earth and in the afterlife.

Egypt is famed for its ancient temples, such as the spectacular complex at Thebes, a capital city during the Middle Kingdom period. The Karnak temples of Thebes stand on the east bank of the Nile, across the river from many tombs and palaces, including those of pharaohs Tutankhamen, Amenhotep III, and Rameses III.

Egyptian temples were dedicated to one god or another, and there were numerous major and minor deities—often interchangeable with one another and with different names and powers, depending on the practices and beliefs of the region.

Karnak, an enormous temple complex in the ancient city of Thebes, exudes an aura of power even in its current ruinous state. Primarily active in the Middle and New Kingdoms, the largest precinct of Karnak was dedicated to Amun-Ra (or Re), with smaller areas dedicated to local Theban gods.

TOMBS OF PHARAOHS, TEMPLES TO GODS

Each Egyptian temple had its prominent deities, some represented as humans, some as animals. Bull gods were widespread, as were rams and falcons. The moon god Thoth and Osiris, ruler of the dead, had human forms; other gods were hybrids of animals and humans, such as the jackal-headed Anubis, pictured in funerary paintings as weighing—judging—the hearts of the dead.

Egyptian temples and tombs were built with an astronomical orientation, depending on the religious importance of certain heavenly bodies to the priests. Relying on basic observations of the polestar and the constellations Orion and the Great Bear, temple builders calculated positions of rooms and windows so that light would enter specific openings at precise times of the year. In this way, the temple became a celestial calendar, capable of accurately anticipating the progress of the sun, stars, and planets for integration into religious ceremonies.

Ancient tombs of royalty and of the lesser nobility are found up and down the Nile Valley, some cut into rock and others in flat-roofed mastabas—rectangular structures of stone or mud brick. The earliest known temples, from the Old Kingdom, are designed with roofs of stone slabs held up by stone columns. Sometimes called mortuary temples, these were intended both as tombs and as enduring memorials to those interred there.

The psychopomp (guide of the dead) Anubis, in his usual jackal (or dog)-headed form. He is associated with the mummification process and occasionally appears fully canine.

By the Middle Kingdom, Egypt had extended trade routes into the surrounding deserts and had begun to build some of the most impressive temples of its history. Dating to this period are the early temples of Karnak; in the New Kingdom the area would be much enhanced by the glorious tombs in the Valley of the Kings across the river.

MIDDLE KINGDOM EGYPT, C. 2040–1786 BCE

- ● cities
- △ pyramids
- ⌂ tombs
- ⌂ temples
- ▢ oases
- — trade routes
- Egyptian control

GODS IN THE SKIES

The gods in the changing and complex Egyptian pantheon often were identified with heavenly bodies, beginning with the sun-god, Re. The gods had different forms and represented various earthly powers and natural forces.

Dominant cults came and went over the centuries. Now Horus, the sky god with the falcon's head, was raised to the highest standing; then it was his adversary, Seth (Set). The pharaoh was the incarnation on earth of Horus, who was the chief god of Lower Egypt, while Seth was chief god of Upper Egypt.

Seth's nature changed according to the current dominant cult, and at times he stood on the prow of the sun god's vessel. According to changing myths, Seth was both partner and rival of Horus and the murderer of Osiris—whose brother or son Seth was at one time or another.

The stars of the northern night sky were deities known as the Imperishable Ones, because they were always visible no matter the season. The planets were gods who journeyed in ships across the heavens and were named the "stars that know no rest." Mars was identified with Horus, as "Horus of the Horizon," or "Horus the Red." Saturn was the "Bull of the Sky," Venus was the "God of the Morning," and Mercury was Sebegu, a deity associated with Seth.

The star Sirius was personified by the goddess Sopdet, whose husband, Sah, was the constellation Orion.

THE MYSTERIOUS SPHINX

Egyptologists debate the origins of the pyramids, temples, and monuments, particularly of the Sphinx, which sits on the Giza plateau.

With a human head and the body of a lion, the Sphinx is said to have been erected in the middle of the third millennium BCE. Some, however, contend that that was when the Sphinx was first discovered, buried in the desert sands. A thousand years later, Pharaoh Thutmose IV excavated the half-buried Sphinx and raised an engraved stele, or stone, between its forelimbs.

The words on the stele recounted a dream Thutmose once had as a prince, while slumbering beside the Sphinx, "in the shadow of this mighty god." The Sphinx told Thutmose he would become pharaoh if he cleared away the "sand of the desert whereon I am laid." Thutmose did so and restored the Sphinx, whose soft limestone composition had already suffered considerably from the elements.

Sphinx is Greek for a mythic creature, half human, half animal, but the original Egyptian name is unknown. The Sphinx has been eroded by wind and weather over the more than 4,500 years of its known existence. Part of the face is conspicuously missing. Although the Sphinx has been prayed to for centuries by Egyptian peasants hoping for a bountiful harvest, its true meaning remains a mystery.

Measuring 241 feet long, 20 feet wide, and 65 feet high (73 by 6 by 20 m), the Great Sphinx dominates the region to the east of Khafre's pyramid. Next to the Sphinx is an ancient temple and a causeway running to the pyramid, fueling suspicions that they form an integral whole.

Ancient Gods, New Beliefs

NEW KINGDOM EGYPT, C. 1500 BCE

- ● cities
- △ pyramids
- ⬚ tombs
- ⬚ temples
- ▨ Egypt under Thutmose III

Anatolia

● Carchemish

● Ugarit

Cyprus

SYRIA

● Byblos

PALESTINE

● Tyre

CANAAN

● Jerusalem

Mediterranean Sea

Buto ●   ● Piramesse

   ● Bubastis ⬚

   ● Memphis ⬚⬚

   ● Ankyronpolis

Sinai

⬚ Beni Hasan ●

   ● Hermopolis Magna ⬚

   ● Akhetaten ⬚

*Sahara
Desert*

△⬚ Abydos ●

   ● Deir el-Ballas

   ● Thebes ⬚⬚

Red Sea

   ● Kom Ombo ⬚

Elephantine ●

NUBIA

The New Kingdom of Egypt stretched far into Nubia in the south and as far north as Anatolia. Egyptian influence spread farther still, and the glory of New Kingdom pharaohs is reflected in the enormous structures they built and ornate styles they favored.

PROSPERITY BROUGHT A NEW WAVE of monument building in Egypt with the advent of the era known as the New Kingdom, around 1500 BCE. The state god was Amun, whose center of worship was at Thebes, where many magnificent edifices and temples were erected.

Internal conflict rent Egyptian society apart around 1350 BCE, when the pharaoh Akhenaten sought to promote the worship of the sun disk, Aten, as the only god. Open hostility developed between the pharaoh and the powerful priestly class. The death of Akhenaten around 1334 BCE brought an end to Egypt's brush with monotheism, and the priests joined the next pharaoh, Tutankhamen, in returning to the older forms of worship.

The outer reaches of the Egyptian empire had become vulnerable in this time of strife, and Syria and Palestine were lost to invasion and rebellion. Much of the following centuries were filled with conflicts that allowed Phoenicians to establish colonies on the Egyptian coast. In the seventh century BCE an Ethiopian army conquered Egypt, and wars continued over the next two centuries. There were notable Egyptian victories, including two over Babylon, but then came conquest by the Persians in 525 BCE.

Throughout these times, many Greek mercenaries fought for Egypt, settling in their own permanent colonies while mingling their cultures and religions with those of the locals. Much of the philosophy and religion of the rising Greek culture harked back to Egypt and its ancient traditions and faiths.

Also influenced by—and influencing—Egyptian culture and religion were the many Jews who had migrated to Egypt and settled there. Around 1250 BCE they were led by their prophet Moses in the "Exodus" out of Egypt, seeking Canaan, the land promised by Yahweh to Abraham.

A relief from the royal tomb at Amarna shows Akhenaten, the largest figure, and his smaller queen, Nefertiti, worshipping Aten as a sun-disk. The curiously elongated body parts of the royal family are part of a distinctive art style, one restricted to Akhenaten's reign.

Protective spells, scenes from the Book of the Dead, and depictions of the deceased worshipping various gods often decorated coffins. Such imagery guided the spirit on its dangerous journey through the underworld.

BELIEF IN A LIFE AFTER DEATH

The faiths of Egyptians, Jews, and Greeks intermingled with those of Anatolians, Mesopotamians, and other peoples of the Fertile Crescent to produce the seeds of the monotheistic Abrahamic religions. The Greeks adopted much of the polytheistic practices and beliefs that had made Egypt such a rich and diverse society, known for allowing others to practice their own religions as they saw fit.

An important aspect of Egyptian religious customs not adopted by the Greeks was the ritual of mummifying the dead. The essence of Egyptian faith was belief in an afterlife, for which the body of the deceased was prepared for preservation lasting as long as possible. These burial practices varied from century to century and depended on the wealth and status of the deceased. The general protocol was to remove and preserve the internal organs and brain, and then the body was wrapped in linen and coated with plaster or resin.

Amulets, personal tokens, jewelry, and food for the departing journey were placed beside the body, which often was enclosed by an elaborately decorated case in the shape of the person who occupied it. Mummifying, and the accompanying funeral rituals, were intended to bless and protect the deceased in the life after death.

Thou sole god, there is no other like thee!
Thou didst create the earth according to thy will, being alone:
Everything on earth which walks with feet,
And that are on high, flying with their wings.
Thou dost set each man in his place and supply his needs.
—FROM THE HYMN TO ATEN

This afterlife was the continuation of the earthly life, and the realms of the living and dead were two halves of the same unity. The belief in an afterlife may have imparted a unique sense of optimism to Egyptian worship.

AKHENATEN'S MONOTHEISM

The cult of Aten, a name for the god of the sun, developed in Egypt by the middle of the second millennium BCE. The cult glorified the physical orb of the sun, known as *aten*, without referring to its mythological characteristics. This belief likely was derived from earlier worship of the sun god, Re.

Previous deities symbolized by the sun, including Re, Horus, and Amun, were now superseded by the symbol of the sun disk, with its rays streaming toward the earth. At the end of each ray is a hand offering the hieroglyphic symbol for life.

Only a small circle of believers, mainly an educated elite, adhered to the cult of Aten, but they were led by the pharaoh, Akhenaten. Their rituals included the "Hymn to Aten," the sun who gives life to all nature and creates and sustains all peoples of the world.

Thou dost appear beautiful on the horizon of
    heaven,
O living Aten, thou who wast the first to live.
When Thou hast risen on the eastern
    horizon,
Thou hast filled every land with thy beauty.

EGYPTIAN COFFIN TEXTS

The interiors of coffins from the Middle Kingdom were usually inscribed with religious expressions that became known as "coffin texts." The following text praises the creator, who brought forth Hahu, the wind:

I was the Primeval Waters, he who had
    no companion when my name came
    into existence.
The most ancient form in which I came
    into existence was as a drowned one.
I was he who came into existence as a
    circle, he who was the dweller in his
    egg.
I was the one who began, the dweller in
    the Primeval Waters.
First Hahu emerged for me, and then I
    began to move.
I created my limbs in my glory.
I was the maker of myself, in that I
    formed myself according to my desire
    and in accord with my heart.

A map of ancient Egypt, produced in England in 1831 and developed largely from classical authors such as Strabo, Ptolemy, and Pliny the Elder.

CANAAN AND PHOENICIA

Crossroads of Empire

THE REGION BORDERED by the Mediterranean coast to the west and Anatolia to the north served as a crossroads between the empires of Egypt and Mesopotamia. Known by the last centuries of the second millennium BCE as Canaan and Phoenicia, it included Syria, the Levant, and the Hebrew kingdoms of Judah and Israel. Much of the region is also called ancient Palestine.

Inhabited by Semitic peoples who mainly spoke Aramaic, these lands contained some of the world's oldest cities—by the ninth millennium BCE Jericho had been established in the Jordan Valley. For the most part, the land was desert, its inhabitants occupied with small-scale farming and herding. Unlike Egypt and Mesopotamia, Canaan-Phoenicia did not have extensive irrigation systems for agriculture. Instead, rainwater was crucial to the crops.

Canaanite-Phoenician religious practice is divided into two main eras. Canaanite religious beliefs were dominant until 1200 BCE, but by the first millennium BCE the peoples of Syria, the Levant, and the coastal cities were becoming known as Phoenicians. Rising in influence and wealth as their trading vessels ranged far and wide, Phoenicians planted colonies around the Mediterranean and beyond. Their belief system, formerly identified as Canaanite, became termed Phoenician.

Canaanite-Phoenician religion had a pantheon of local deities and intermixed the various concepts and beliefs of neighbors and conquerors. Canaanite-Phoenician cities and villages each had their own pantheons, with one local deity usually recognized as supreme, as El. Most ancient Semitic faiths used the term "El" to signify their chief god. In Hebrew, *El* means "power," and in Aramaic it means "first."

Most Canaanite-Phoenician gods symbolized forces of nature, and El symbolized water, the natural element most needed by this arid land. El was depicted as a wise father-figure.

The Promised Land of the Bible—Canaan—had been settled for centuries by the time the Israelites arrived. Many stories of the area's other inhabitants, the Canaanites, and even some of their religious practices can be found in the Bible.

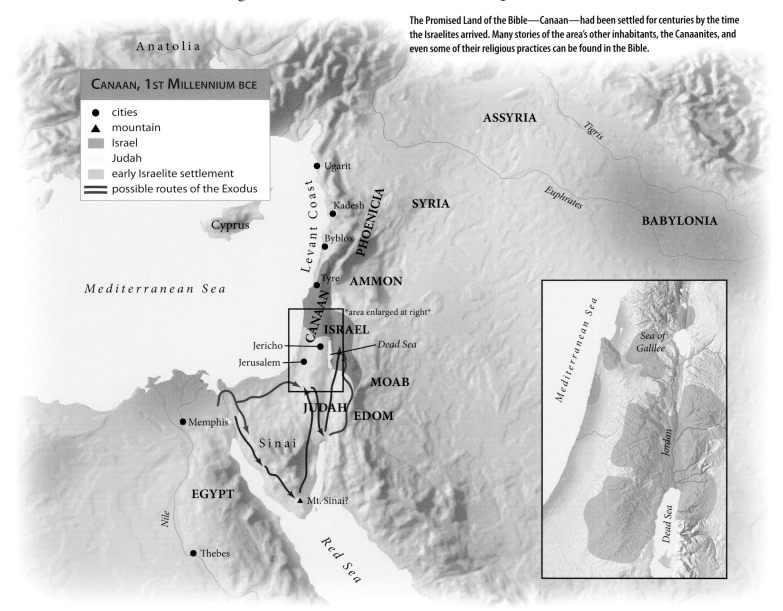

Lo, also it is the time of His rain.
Baal sets the season,
and gives forth His voice from the clouds.
He flashes lightning to the earth.
—FROM THE BAAL CYCLE, *AN EPIC POEM FROM UGARIT,*
CELEBRATING THE EXPLOITS OF THE GOD BAAL

For centuries the route that the Israelites took from Egypt to Canaan has fascinated scholars. Many are particularly interested in locating Mount Sinai (which may be the Mount Horeb mentioned elsewhere in the Bible), where Moses is said to have received God's commandments. On this 1843 English map, Mount Sinai is identified as modern-day Jebel Músa (Gebel Musa) on the Sinai Peninsula.

BAAL AS DEMON

The cult of bull worship was pervasive in West Asia, and Baal was often represented by a bull. Over the centuries monotheism took root among the Hebrews, and the name "Baal" came to mean evil, or a demon.

To first-millennium BCE Hebrew prophets, the worship of more than one god, Yahweh, was akin to worshipping Baal. The sixth-century BCE prophet Jeremiah called on his people to stop worshipping the nature gods, a practice he declared an "abomination": "Then shall the cities of Judah and inhabitants of Jerusalem go and cry to the gods to whom they offer incense: but they shall not save them at all in the time of their trouble. For according to the number of your cities are your gods, O Judah; and according to the number of the streets of Jerusalem you have set up altars to the abomination, altars to burn incense to the Ba'al."

With his divinity signified by his distinctive headgear, this bronze statue of Baal stands in a pose typical of Southwest Asian storm gods, with one foot forward and one arm raised, perhaps about to unleash lightning.

AT WORSHIP

The Canaanite-Phoenician faithful worshipped both in temples and at shrines in the balmy open air of the Mediterranean. Small groups used sacred groves on hillsides for intimate religious observances, while important temples had courtyards to accommodate large public worship.

Sanctuaries often were marked by a tree or by an uncut stone, without statues or temple altars. Scholars believe the powers being venerated at such places were considered to be natural forces rather than a personified entity.

Animal sacrifice was practiced in the Canaanite period, the ritual led by the priesthood or the king. Hymns from the region have been discovered in Egyptian library archives, and later Jewish literature used Canaan-Phoenician religion and traditions as an important source.

THE LAND OF BAAL AND WARFARE

Subordinate to El was the powerful god Baal, or Ba'al, the god of rain, also known as the "Rider of the Clouds." The deity Mot, who represented aridity and death, was Baal's main adversary.

Baal is a Semitic term meaning "lord" or "master" and referred to any honored deity. Baal Haddad was the name for a lord of rain, thunder, fertility, and agriculture. *Baal* was also an honorific for important men, with *baalat* meaning "lady," and also used for goddesses.

Archaeological excavations of temples from the city of Ugarit reveal places of worship dedicated to Baal and to his father, the god Dagan, of whom little is known. Phoenician scholars made Ugarit a center of their literary world and are credited with developing the first cuneiform writing. Ugarit's excavations yielded large libraries of clay tablets, some

describing the worship of many gods, including local gods and gods revered in other lands.

The Phoenicians originally called themselves by a name that translates as "Canaanite." Among the peoples of Canaan-Phoenicia were Arabian Semites, believed to have lived in the region since the fourth millennium BCE. The first Phoenicians are thought to have appeared around 3000 BCE, originally from the Persian Gulf. The Hebrews appeared around 1200 BCE, and soon afterward seaborne Greek invaders arrived. Known as the Sea Peoples, the Greeks destroyed a number of ancient cities, including Ugarit.

Local feuds kept the various kingdoms embroiled in conflict, and the period between 1200 and 800 BCE was known as the time of the "Warring States." Assyrian invasions came and went, resulting in conquest and revolt, including a sharp defeat of the invaders at Jerusalem in 701. The rise of Babylon and incursions by Egyptian forces brought further invasion and occupation, with Jerusalem falling to Babylon's Nebuchadnezzar II in 587 BCE.

Like most of their neighbors, the Phoenicians were polytheists. Here, a fragment of carved stone from Ugarit mentions several of these ancient deities.

Phoenicia's Empire of Commerce

In ancient Hebrew, *cana'ani* (Canaanite) means "merchant," an appropriate name for the Phoenicians, who actually referred to themselves as Canaanites and were famed merchant-traders. Phoenicia included the seaports of Byblos, Tyre, Beirut, and Sidon.

The Phoenicians rose to wealth and power because of their vast trading empire, and they seldom made war to achieve their ends. The peoples of many ancient towns were influenced by the Phoenicians, whose alphabet and system of writing were exported, as were their religious customs. Phoenicia was at its zenith by the ninth century BCE, her colonies widely sowing the seeds of West Asian culture and religion.

Intrepid Phoenician seafarers sailed westward through straits known to the Greeks as the Pillars of Herakles. Termed the Strait of Gibraltar in modern times, its original Greek name is also still used, with Herakles changed to the Latin, Hercules. This name is believed to refer to Melqart, the Phoenician "God of the City," for whom a temple was built just west of the strait. This temple was famous for its two majestic bronze pillars—the pillars of Melqart (Herakles). Melqart was the guardian god of the Phoenician city of Tyre.

For centuries, Phoenician seafarers passed through these straits and into the Atlantic Ocean. Many settled along the coast of western Europe, and some perhaps went as far as North America.

Of all the worldly accomplishments of the ambitious Phoenicians, one of the greatest was Carthage, the city founded around 800 BCE on the North African coast. Carthage became the hub of the Punic Empire, which would be challenged by Rome late in the first millennium BCE.

Only thirteen miles across, the Strait of Gibraltar is where the Mediterranean Sea meets the Atlantic Ocean. For many years it marked the western edge of Phoenicia's vast trading dominion and was the site of the pillars of Melqart.

WORSHIP ON HIGH PLACES

The concepts of immortality or life after death—essential to Egyptian and Mesopotamian religions—were not important aspects of Canaanite-Phoenician faith. Life was a gift of the gods and could be taken away at their whim. Humanity existed to serve the deities, who were many and localized, so they lacked large followings.

Wherever they settled, Phoenicians created outdoor sites for worship called "bamah," meaning "high place." Here they often erected two pillars, one of stone for a male god and one of wood for a goddess. Bamahs were also placed in front of temple buildings. It was believed that a temple structure was necessary to house the god Baal, who needed it to perpetuate his power.

Phoenician temples were rectangular, usually with a room for the altar or a space for a statue that faced the entrance.

SACRIFICE TO THE GODS

Unlike the civilizations of Egypt and Mesopotamia, where most people lived in cities dominated by a few major deities, Phoenicia's population was too small, too diverse, and too widely scattered to worship one supreme god.

Egyptian and Mesopotamian peoples were at first organized by large-scale, systematic irrigation and agriculture that defined their duties and roles in society. The main basis of many Canaanite-Phoenician communities was their strong West Semitic, Amorite tribal alliances. Local Amorite gods bore names such as Ammu, Abbu, and Ahku, which indicated they belonged to specific tribes.

Unlike royalty in Egypt and Mesopotamia, Phoenician kings did not expect their peoples to worship them. Scholars speculate that Phoenician rulers had such small states that they could not in good conscience elevate themselves to be divine. The king did, however, have ultimate responsibility for the fate of his people, and that obligation may have called for human sacrifice to win over the gods.

The Phoenician scholar Sanchuniathon wrote about one such ruler: "And when great dangers from war beset the land, he adorned the altar, and invested his son with the emblems of royalty and sacrificed him."

There is evidence that animal sacrifice was

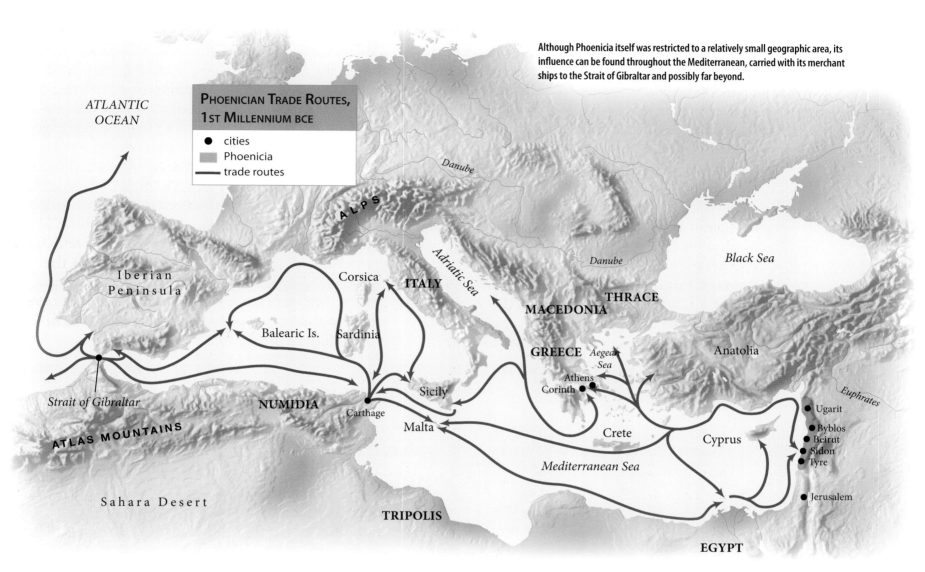

Although Phoenicia itself was restricted to a relatively small geographic area, its influence can be found throughout the Mediterranean, carried with its merchant ships to the Strait of Gibraltar and possibly far beyond.

PHOENICIAN TRADE ROUTES, 1ST MILLENNIUM BCE

● cities
▨ Phoenicia
— trade routes

ATLANTIC OCEAN

Danube

ALPS

Black Sea

Danube

Corsica

ITALY

Adriatic Sea

THRACE

MACEDONIA

Iberian Peninsula

Balearic Is.

Sardinia

GREECE

Aegean Sea

Anatolia

Athens

Corinth

Euphrates

Strait of Gibraltar

NUMIDIA

Carthage

Sicily

Malta

Crete

Cyprus

Ugarit
Byblos
Beirut
Sidon
Tyre

ATLAS MOUNTAINS

Mediterranean Sea

Jerusalem

Sahara Desert

TRIPOLIS

EGYPT

---

a custom of Phoenician religions as well as of the Hebrews. Whether the Phoenicians carried out human sacrifice, however, remains controversial among scholars.

HEBREW GODS

The King James Bible phrase "O heavenly beings," neglects the more accurate translation of the ancient Hebrew, "O sons of gods;" although Judaism is monotheistic, Canaan was a land of many deities.

Ascribe to the Lord, O sons of gods,
   ascribe to the Lord glory and strength.
Ascribe to the Lord the glory of his name;
   worship the Lord in holy array.

The Lord sits enthroned over the flood;
   the Lord sits enthroned as king for ever.
May the Lord give strength to his people!
   May the Lord bless his people with peace!

–Psalm 29

Eventually, long-standing West Asian religious practices such as ancestor worship (and likely human sacrifice) were rejected by the Hebrew prophets, who scorned the Canaanite-Phoenician worship of nature gods, especially those referred to as Baal. Yahweh, god of Moses and of the Hebrews, allowed no other gods before him. In the seventh century BCE King Josiah of Judah called for the exclusive worship of Yahweh and outlawed the priests of other religions, many of whom were put to death.

PHOENICIANS AND HEBREWS

Many religious concepts were held in common throughout West Asia, which included Canaan-Phoenicia, the Hebrew lands, and Anatolia.

The Hebrews were closely linked to neighboring Canaan-Phoenicia, sharing similar languages, political interests, and traditions of worship. In the tenth century BCE, the Hebrew king Solomon contributed to the growing power of the Phoenicians when he allied with Hiram of Tyre. After the death of Solomon,

his kingdom split into two—Israel in the north and Judah, with Jerusalem, in the south.

Most original Phoenician writings—scholarly and religious—have been lost because they were recorded on parchment, which could not withstand the rigors of time. Yet a number have survived as hymns and verse adapted by the Hebrews and found in the Bible's Old Testament. Archaeological excavations from the ancient Phoenician city of Ugarit uncovered literary works that indicate Phoenician hymns were used by the Hebrews. King David's Psalm 29, for example, appears almost identical with an Ugarit hymn, sung before sea journeys, to the storm god Baal.

In the Bible, distraught Israelites begin to worship a golden calf while Moses is away. The choice of a calf may not have been arbitrary: zoomorphic (animal-shaped) gods are found throughout the ancient world, and in Southwest Asia cattle in particular seem to have carried heavy symbolism.

The Golden Age of Judaism

THE PEOPLE OF ISRAEL enjoyed a golden age in the tenth century BCE—or at least, most of it. At the start of the century the charismatic King David ruled and greatly extended his lands by conquest. Then, from roughly 965 to about 926 BCE, David's son Solomon ruled Israel, earning praise for his wisdom and massive building projects. But in the last quarter of the century, the kingdom split in two, never to regain its former glory.

The Israelites had come to Canaan some two centuries earlier, at which time they conquered the local peoples and settled in twelve tribal areas with separate leaders, called judges. According to the Hebrew scriptures, the tribes were descended from the twelve sons of Abraham's grandson Jacob (renamed Israel). After migrating to Egypt during a famine, Jacob's family had settled there, and their descendants were eventually enslaved. The scriptures tell how the prophet Moses freed them and led them to the land of Canaan, which had been promised them. The people made a covenant with their God, Yahweh, to keep his commandments in turn for his protection.

In about 1025 BCE the tribes united into a kingdom. Their second king was David, formerly a shepherd and a singer of psalms. David not only expanded his kingdom, but instituted an age of learning. But when he announced his intention to build a temple in the newly won city of Jerusalem, the prophet Nathan told him that God had reserved that privilege for Solomon. However, he assured David that his kingdom would last forever.

Solomon did build the temple and added to the kingdom's wealth and wisdom, but upon his death the kingdom was split in two. The north broke away and established a separate kingdom, known as Israel. The south continued to be ruled by David's descendants, but was called Judah.

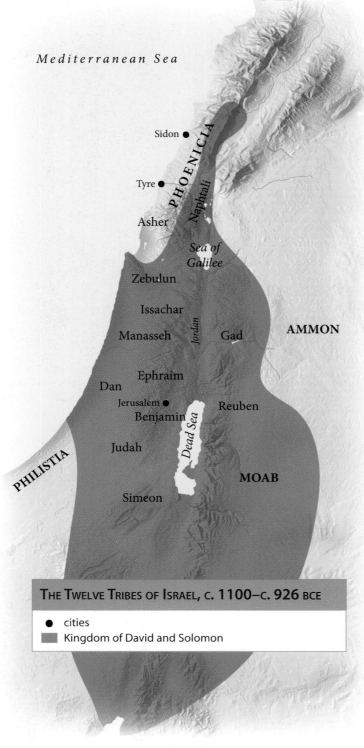

THE TWELVE TRIBES OF ISRAEL, C. 1100–C. 926 BCE

● cities
■ Kingdom of David and Solomon

The Bible speaks of a deliberate and planned division of territory among the tribes of Israel following their entry into Canaan. For perhaps two centuries the Israelites lived on their allotted land, before joining into a single, unified kingdom.

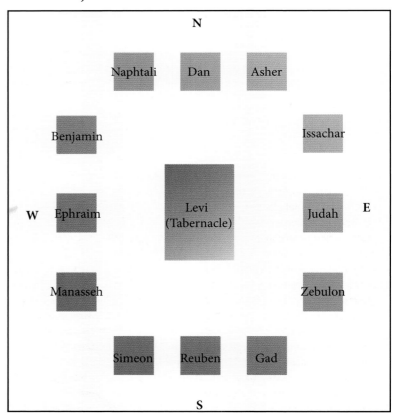

According to the Bible, the tribes of Israel traveled through the desert in a very organized fashion, surrounding the tabernacle with three tribes on each of the four sides and the thirteenth tribe, Levi, accompanying the tabernacle in the center.

One of the most popular stories of David in Jewish, Christian, and even secular traditions focuses on his boyhood defeat of the gigantic Philistine champion, Goliath. The victory routs the Philistine army, which the Bible says had encroached upon Israelite territory in Judah.

FALL AND EXILE

For the next two centuries the two kingdoms were ruled by kings who, like the people, were said to be sometimes faithful to their covenant with God and sometimes not. Prophets, who claimed to speak for God, kept warning the people to change their ways or face destruction. Most refused to listen. In 722 BCE the Assyrians conquered Israel and scattered the people. They also attacked Judah in 701 but failed to enter Jerusalem.

Other prophets warned the people of Judah (the Jews) to mend their ways, but again, according to the Hebrew scriptures, few listened. Judah was invaded by the newly powerful Babylonians. By 587 BCE the Babylonians had destroyed Jerusalem and the temple and then carried most of the Jews back with them to Babylon, where they remained in exile. When the Persian conqueror Cyrus the Great overthrew the Babylonians in 539 BCE, he freed the Jews. Some remained in Babylon under the Persians, but many returned home.

LOOKING TO THE FUTURE

Back in Jerusalem the Jews rebuilt their city and temple as best they could. Although their exile had ended, they were still under foreign rule, this time by the Persians, and the line of David seemed to have come to an end. From then on, the Jewish people, prompted by the prophets, would look for a messiah, a special figure anointed by God, who would deliver them from their enemies, reestablish the kingdom of Israel, and reign over an era of world peace. They believed that this messiah would be a descendant of King David.

Because of thy temple at Jerusalem
kings bear gifts to thee.
—PSALM 68

King Solomon's judgment concerning the disputed motherhood of an infant epitomizes his reputation as a wise and just ruler; when he commands that each claimant be given half the child, one woman refuses, as the solution would kill the infant. Famously, Solomon then declares that she must be the true mother and awards the child to her.

THE JERUSALEM TEMPLE

When Solomon's temple was dedicated in about 953 BCE, it was long overdue. Since the days of Moses, the chief place of worship for the Israelites had been a portable tabernacle. This building had been constructed in the Sinai wilderness just after Moses presented the people with the Ten Commandments. The stone tablets of the law were kept in a specially constructed chest known as the Ark of the Covenant, and the ark in turn was housed in the tabernacle, which could be dismantled for traveling during the Israelites' forty years of wandering in the wilderness. The new temple changed that. It was a permanent stone structure situated prominently on a hilltop (Mount Zion) in the heart of Jerusalem. It was reportedly so beautiful that people traveled from far-off lands to see it.

The structure itself was rectangular with a pillared portico facing east, a nave, and an inner sanctuary—the holy of holies in which the Ark of the Covenant was kept. There was a gold incense altar in the nave and a large bronze altar in the surrounding courtyard for offering animal sacrifices. Worship services included processions, chanting, and the singing of psalms, some of them composed specifically for certain celebrations.

The temple was the only legitimate place for the Israelites to worship, and the men were required to make three annual pilgrimages to celebrate major feasts there. Worship at other temples or at shrines in the high places (on hilltops) was considered idolatry, though in later times prayer services could be offered in local synagogues. Priests and temple workers were all from the tribe of Levi (one of Jacob's twelve sons), and the high priest was traditionally a descendant of Moses's brother, Aaron.

An artist's depiction of the massive Temple of Solomon.

Stones of Magic, Stones of Faith

AS EXTENSIVE AGRICULTURE DEVELOPED in the Fertile Crescent, giving rise to cities and large populations, the scattered peoples of western Europe continued mainly as hunter-gatherers and fishermen until farming methods appeared by 5000 BCE. Knowledge of agricultural techniques and tools spread north and west from Anatolia, promoting animal husbandry—mainly pigs and cattle—and the planting of crops such as wheat and barley.

Agricultural progress moved through the Balkans and followed the valleys of great rivers, such as the Danube, Elbe, and Rhine. Other developmental corridors led up the Italian peninsula and penetrated the Rhône Valley, while the southern and eastern coasts of the Iberian Peninsula also came under cultivation. Trade in western European metal goods as well as in the raw materials required to make them (tin and copper), followed similar routes, bringing about considerable cultural exchange by the second millennium BCE.

The earliest archaeological evidence of religion in prehistoric Europe consists of the hundreds of megalithic structures of various designs. "Megalith" means large stone, while "megalithic" refers to structures made with large stones. Although their original functions are unknown, many such structures are considered to be tombs, while others apparently served as astronomical calendars. Ancient lore, known from the end of the first millennium CE, suggests that some standing stones and stone circles (henges) were believed to possess certain supernatural powers. Springs and wells—described by locals throughout the historic period as holy or sacred—are often found near megalithic constructions.

According to a twelfth-century legend, water that was splashed over Stonehenge, the great circle of southern England, cured wounds. Some medieval scholars believed a magic power found at these structures aided ancient priests in their work of casting spells, prophesying, and communing with natural and divine forces.

Despite the intense labor required to build such monumental structures, some 25,000 or more megaliths survive in Europe, suggesting they were of crucial importance to the cultures that built them.

MEGALITHIC EUROPE, 3RD–2ND MILLENNIUM BCE

- Neolithic tombs
- region of megalithic structures

● stone circles

STONE CIRCLES IN NORTHWEST EUROPE

The stones are great
And magic power they have.
Men that are sick, Fare to that stone
And they wash that stone
And with that water bathe away their sickness.
—FROM BRUT, A TWELFTH-CENTURY ENGLISH EPIC
POEM NARRATING THE MYTHICAL FOUNDING OF BRITAIN

At the time of construction, around 3000 BCE, the Belas Knap long barrow tomb measured some 200 feet (61 m) in length. One of a number of similar tombs in Gloucestershire, England, Belas Knap was used to house human remains over a long period.

EUROPE'S MEGALITHIC STRUCTURES

Although their true ages are often undetermined, some megalithic works are the oldest major constructions in Europe, with some thought to be as old as third-millennium BCE Egyptian pyramids.

Many megalithic works are found along the coasts of western Europe. They range from the Strait of Gibraltar in the south to the most northern Scottish islands and across the North Sea to Scandinavia. Megalithic sites are especially numerous in southwestern Spain, western France, and on the shores of the Baltic Sea. They are prominent in Great Britain and Ireland and can be found on the Mediterranean islands of Corsica and Sardinia, across the Strait of Gibraltar in North Africa, and far to the east in Anatolia.

There is still only speculation as to the actual purpose of megalithic works and the beliefs of those who built and used them. Often, chambers that appear to be recesses for tombs are skillfully aligned with the sun, whose rays penetrate these depths at the solstices. Many standing stones appear to be aligned with each other and also with sites and land features at a distance. The most common megalithic structure in Europe is the dolmen, formed by massive upright stones topped with flat capstones.

The ancient communities of the great plain that reaches from the Rhine River eastward to the Vistula River had many stone-built tombs, termed barrows. Also known as gallery graves, and one of the most common megalithic types, barrows had individual chambers arranged under long mounds. In Germany they are called *Steinkisten*, in Ireland, court tombs, and in Britain, long barrows.

Throughout north-central Europe by the second millennium, there were many large communal cemeteries containing urns filled with cremated human remains. Burials of apparently wealthy individuals contained pottery, copper figures, and bronze artifacts, including valuables from as far away as the Mediterranean lands.

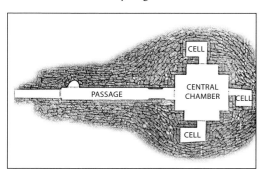

On the winter solstice, the sun's last rays illuminate the passage and the central chamber of Maes Howe, the largest of Orkney's passage tombs. The precision engineering indicates the extent of Neolithic abilities and perhaps some of its designers' religious beliefs.

SKARA BRAE

Most dolmens and other, tomblike megaliths are believed to have originally been covered with mounded earth. Stone dwellings were also sometimes earth-covered. One of the oldest known such dwelling places was at Orkney, on the northern tip of Scotland, where a cluster of stone-built houses and buildings was occupied by 3100 BCE.

Called Skara Brae, the community was likely occupied with fishing and collecting shellfish, as were most coastal villages in the north. The walls are of laid-up stone banked against earthen mounds. With no trees growing on the island, the inhabitants framed roofs using driftwood and whalebone, covering them over with turf and thatch.

There is no evidence of religious practices in this little community huddled against the northern seas, but nearby archaeological sites bear witness to the faith of their builders. These sites include Maes Howe, with its chambered sandstone cairn (pile of stones) and a tomb that is illuminated at winter solstice. Nearby, too, are stone rings and standing stones, among other works that likely testify to the religious beliefs of the ancient folk of the north.

The main entrance to the Neolithic village of Skara Brae, on the Orkney Islands, Scotland. Both furniture and walls were constructed of local stone, perhaps because the only available wood would have drifted in from the nearby sea.

Norse and Germanic Polytheism

As the tribes of northern Europe grew in numbers and strength during the second millennium BCE, competition for control of territory and domination of natural resources brought on warfare. Fortified settlements arose to protect farming and fishing populations, and social culture, including religious practice, became more formalized.

Manifestations of early northern Germanic and Norse polytheism can be seen by 1600 BCE in Scandinavian stone carvings that apparently picture gods and spirits. Norse culture and religion were entwined with those of other northern Germanic peoples from the European mainland and the British Isles.

Norse mythology was handed down orally through the first millennium BCE. By the time it was recorded—beginning around 1000 CE—the Norse creation myth described a world composed of fire and ice that collided to create the giant, Ymir, and the cow Audhumla. From Ymir's body sprang a race of giants, or Jotun, and from the licking of Audhumla on a salt stone was created Buir, grandfather of the three great gods, Odin, Vili, and Ve. Eventually, the gods slew Ymir, whose body became the soil, blood became the waters, bones the stones, brains the clouds, and skull the heavens. Sparks from Audhumla became the stars.

The gods, led by Odin—chief of the Norse pantheon—created two human beings, Ask and Embla, out of two trees, ash and elm. The humans were favored by the gods, who built a protective wall around their realm, known as Middle Earth. Eventually, humanity and the gods will be overwhelmed by chaos. In a final cataclysm known as Ragnarök, all the world—including chaos—will be swept away, and a pure new world will arise. This myth is found in the eddic (mythological) poem *Völuspá*, or *Sibyl's Prophecy*, as told by a *völva*, or seeress, also known as a sibyl.

In the Baltic Sea region, amber deposits inspired Scandinavian and Germanic trading. Bronze Age trade routes brought German, Norse, Celtic, and other peoples into contact.

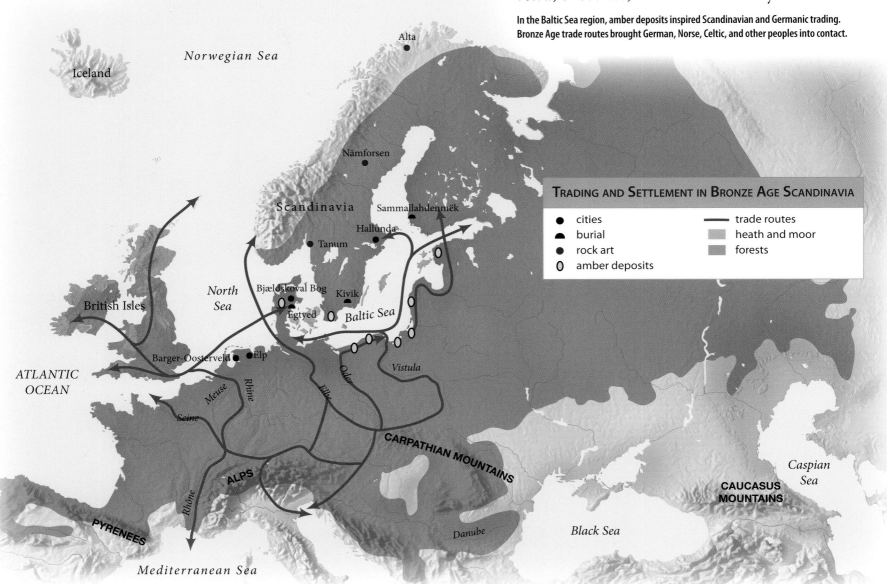

TRADING AND SETTLEMENT IN BRONZE AGE SCANDINAVIA

- ● cities
- ◖ burial
- ● rock art
- ○ amber deposits
- — trade routes
- heath and moor
- forests

The three central figures on this Viking Age rune stone are often interpreted as three of the primary Norse gods, Odin with his spear, Thor with his hammer, and Frey with vegetation.

The Cosmic Tree

Norse religious symbolism centers on the tree of the world, Yggdrasil, a huge ash that comprises nine worlds. A serpent, or dragon, chews at the roots of this cosmic tree. At Yggdrasil's base three *norns*, or fates—representing the past, present, and future—spin out the world's destiny. Yggdrasil means the "steed of Ygg," Ygg being another name for Odin.

According to the Scandinavian eddic poem *Hávamál*, or *Sayings of the High One*, Odin

> . . . hung
> on the windswept tree
> for nine full nights

until his ordeal gained him occult wisdom that would give him power in the nine worlds, and he learned the meaning of secret runes and of nine magic songs.

Much of the speculation concerning the early religious beliefs of the northern Germanic peoples is based on the works of Roman writers, including Julius Caesar, conquering general of the first century BCE, and the historian Tacitus of the first century CE. Although their interpretations are flawed, colored by a Roman perspective, both evoked broad outlines of early Germanic and Norse polytheism.

In some cases Romans identified Germanic gods with more familiar deities, describing a leading pagan god as similar to their own Mercury, and a goddess as akin to Isis, the Egyptian divinity often described as the mother of leading gods.

Both Norse and German peoples may have venerated trees, particularly the ash and possibly the oak. Tacitus wrote that the Germanic peoples believed temple structures to be unsuitable places for their gods to dwell. Instead, various groves and woods were considered sacred places for individual gods. Tacitus described divination as a powerful influence, often done by a priest throwing twigs cut from a fruit tree. He then, "with eyes lifted up to heaven takes up every piece thrice, and having done thus forms a judgment" interpreting the future or the prospects for some course of action.

Human Sacrifice

Evidence exists of human sacrifice in southern Scandinavia and north Germanic lands as well as in the British Isles. Norse legends tell of kings being sacrificed to appease the gods in time of famine, and of a king sacrificing nine sons in an effort to prolong his own life. Tacitus describes a Germanic goddess, whom he names Nerthus, as an "earth goddess"

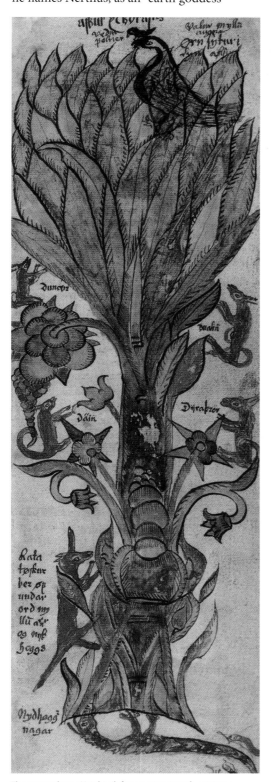

The great ash tree Yggdrasil, from a seventeenth-century CE Icelandic manuscript.

to whom slaves in her service were ritually drowned.

Discovered in the peat bogs of Denmark's Jutland peninsula were the perfectly preserved bodies of men who had been strangled—perhaps in some ritual sacrifice. Although the reason for their deaths and interment are unknown, their strangulation suggests a possible connection to the god Odin, who is often associated with ritual hanging.

Rock Art

By the advent of the Scandinavian Bronze Age, around 1800 BCE, the Norse were highly skilled woodworkers and boatmen. They may have used bronze tools to etch stone carvings, or petroglyphs, into flat rocks. These images show long vessels powered by many oars, as well as hunters, and farmers at their work, one using an ox and plow. Other glyphs show what appear to be women grieving and a funeral boat, while others seem to illustrate religious rituals.

The "King's Grave" tomb at Kivik, Sweden, has stone engravings of folk dressed in robes, as if at a funeral or some ceremony. Images suggesting the sun and fertility rituals are also depicted in north European rock art.

Rock carvings from Tanum, Sweden, show actual and perhaps ritual life in Bronze Age Scandinavia. Here, figures brandish axes while boats can be seen above them; unfortunately, their meanings remain unclear.

I remember yet the giants of yore,
Who gave me bread in the days gone by;
Nine worlds I knew, the nine in the tree
With its mighty roots beneath the mould.
—From the Norse epic Völuspá,
or Sibyl's Prophecy

WESTERN EUROPE
The Ancient Celts

Mountain chains were a barrier between much of Europe and the Mediterranean lands in ancient times, and forests covered most of the continent. By the middle of the first millennium BCE the peoples of the central and western forests became known to the Greeks, who called them *Keltoi*. Romans later named them Gauls.

In the previous millennium Celtic tribes had migrated outward from the deep woods of the upper Danube, gradually moving northwest into Britain and Ireland and southwest into the Iberian Peninsula. Celts, called Galatians, also lived in central Anatolia, where they may have originated.

The many Celtic tribes spoke different dialects and never created a unified empire or society. They may have adopted elements of local culture, appropriating sacred sites or even certain religious practices of the peoples they invaded. The Norse and Germans inter-mingled with the Celts and shared several mythological beliefs, including an apparent reverence for the sun and thunder as divine powers. The ancient Celts had no written language, and what is recorded about them derives from the later works of Greeks and Romans.

The ancient Celts were polytheists, considering all of nature to be sacred and imbued with divinity. They worshipped many gods and goddesses—as many as four hundred Celtic deities have been named (usually in Latin), but most were local gods. The two names most encountered are Belenus and Grannus, whom the Romans identified with Apollo. The god Cernunnos had the horns of a stag and may have been a god of animals or comparable to the Greek Pan. Sucellus carried a hammer and was a god of agriculture, forests, and strong drink. The chief Celtic god was Lug Lámfota, Lug of the Long Hand, who appears in Swedish rock carvings. Lugh, as the name is also spelled, was a god of the sun, light, and the harvest.

It is unclear where the Celtic people came from originally, but they quickly spread across Europe, supplanting or mingling with peoples already there.

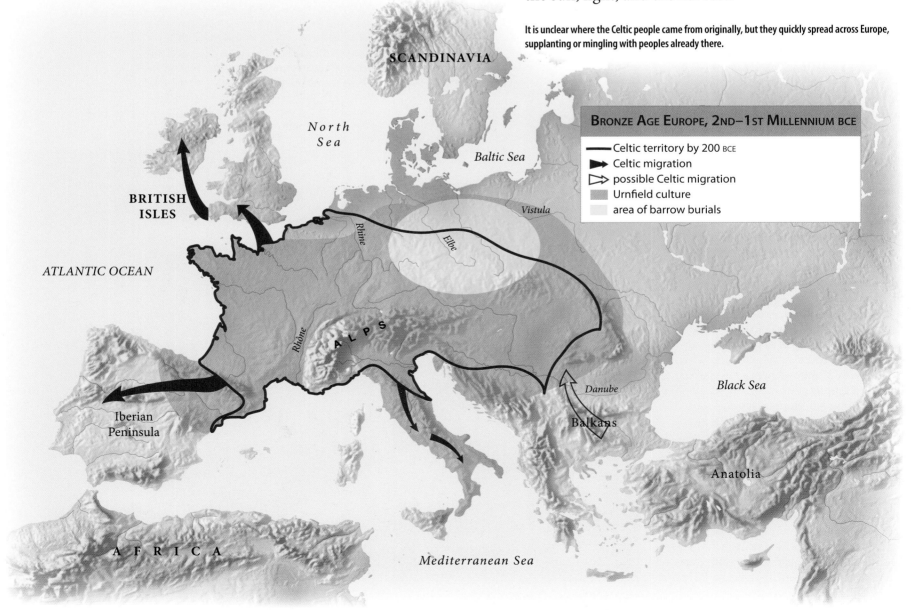

BRONZE AGE EUROPE, 2ND–1ST MILLENNIUM BCE

— Celtic territory by 200 BCE
▶ Celtic migration
▷ possible Celtic migration
▨ Urnfield culture
▨ area of barrow burials

Who spreads light in the gathering on the hills?
Who can tell the ages of the moon?
Who can tell the place where the sun rests?
—From an invocation by the mythic druid
Amergin, leader of the first Celtic invaders to
Ireland; excerpted from The Song of Amergin

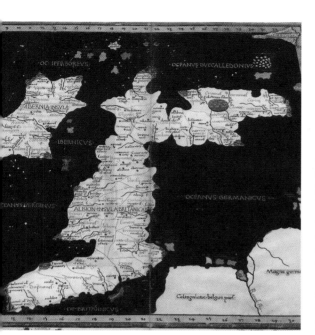

In the first or second century CE, the Greek scholar Ptolemy created a world map (later reproduced) that included the earliest references to tribes on the British Isles.

Sacred Groves and Graves

Other ancient Celtic deities included a god of healing, a goddess of plenty, and the most famous goddess, Epona, depicted mounted on a mare. Epona was revered as the goddess of mares and foals and protector of mounted warriors and travelers on horseback. Epona is also considered a fertility goddess.

The ancient Celts did not construct temple buildings, for their holy places were outdoors, often along rivers or beside springs, and in sacred groves, especially among oaks. Burial fields were also considered sacred places by the Celts, and researchers define phases of ancient Celtic culture according to types of graves and burial customs.

One of the major periods is the Tumulus culture of central Europe, 1600–1200 BCE, distinguished by burials in long mounds, or tumuli. The Urnfield culture followed, lasting until the eighth century BCE and extending from the Baltic to the eastern Mediterranean. This phase is unique for its cemetery fields of buried urns containing cremated remains.

The Celts were ruled by a noble class and led in battle by warriors who won reputations as fierce fighters. Celtic priests were chosen from warrior families and were required to undergo many years of education and training. Known as druids, this priestly class had great authority and could overrule chiefs and kings, even to the point of stopping conflicts and ordering reconciliation. Druids were sages and skilled healers and believed in an immortal soul and reincarnation.

The etymology of the term *druid* includes Latin and Greek meanings ("son of the oak") as well as Proto-Celtic ("steadfast and wise seer"), Old Irish and modern Irish ("magician"), and modern Gaelic ("enchanter").

Druids: Students and Teachers

According to Julius Caesar, who encountered druids in Gaul and Britain at the close of the first millennium BCE, they knew "much about the stars and celestial motions, and about the size of the earth and universe, and about the essential nature of things, and about the powers and authority of the immortal gods; and these things they teach to their pupils."

Classical writers came to compare the druids with the Chaldean astronomers of Babylon and the sixth-century BCE Pythagoreans, who were known as "those that study all." Much of what the druids taught and practiced may have been derived from much older cultures, especially in Britain, Ireland, and western France, where druids had their strongest influence. There is some speculation they may have practiced religious rites at older sacred sites, such as Stonehenge.

Where and how druids trained has been a question since at least the time of Julius Caesar, who believed the best druid teachers could be found in Britain; it does seem certain, given their purely oral traditions, that druidical teaching relied heavily on memorization, as Caesar also reports. Receiving an education from the druids was key to the training of minstrels and bards.

This unidentified Celtic deity wears a torque around his neck, indicating nobility and power. The boar, carved into his torso, was a potent symbol in Celtic societies and is one of the most frequently encountered animals in Celtic art and literature.

The Urnfield Culture

"Grave gifts" often accompanied the remains found in Celtic Urnfield cemeteries and ranged in value according to the status of the individual. Gifts included jewelry, weapons, ceramic bowls and cups, and sometimes burned animal bones that suggest a sacrifice, an offering, or perhaps food for the soul's coming journey.

The remains of apparently wealthy persons have been found interred in wooden structures with stone floors. Other rich burials contain additional human remains, often women and children, who may have been sacrificed to accompany the deceased in the next world.

A panel from the ornate Gundestrup Cauldron (first or second century BCE), often interpreted as a depiction of the god Cernunnos, surrounded by the animals of the forest.

Early Greece and Crete

UNTIL ABOUT 2000 BCE the geographic regions that were to become Greece were populated by simple farmers and fisherman who lacked the sophistication of their neighbors to the east. These early peoples used simple stone tools to work the land, and some ventured out to sea to trade with nearby neighbors. They spoke a language that had no resemblance to the later Greek dialects but that made frequent use of the sounds *nth* and *ss*, as in the names Corinth and Knossos.

In about 2000 BCE a wave of Indo-Europeans swept down from the north and occupied much of the Greek peninsula. They brought with them their own language (an early form of Greek) and their principal sky god, Zeus, who personified light, weather, and fertility. The culture on the Greek mainland began to change, but the island of Crete to the south was not invaded. It developed its own rich culture.

Although Homer, in his *Iliad* (probably composed in the eighth or seventh century BCE), refers to the Greeks collectively as "Achaeans," just who the Achaeans were or where they came from is not clear. In any case, by the seventh century BCE, three distinct groups would be discernible in Greece: Ionians, Aeolians, and Dorians, each with its own dialect of the Greek language. According to later legends these peoples were descendants of the warlike king Hellen and his three sons, Xathus (father of Ion), Aeolus, and Dorus—all of whom are described in literature as "delighting in horses." King Hellen himself gave his name to the country, which is *Hellas* in Greek. The people were called *Hellenes*, and the adjective *Hellenic* refers to all things Greek. The English word "Greece" comes from the Latin *Graecus,* the Romans' name for the Hellenes.

Minoan Crete was a place of grandeur, situated between the sea traders of Phoenicia, the islands of Greece, and the glory of Egypt. Kings outfitted their palaces richly, free to capitalize on natural resources and trade while developing a unique—and, to scholars, still mysterious—culture.

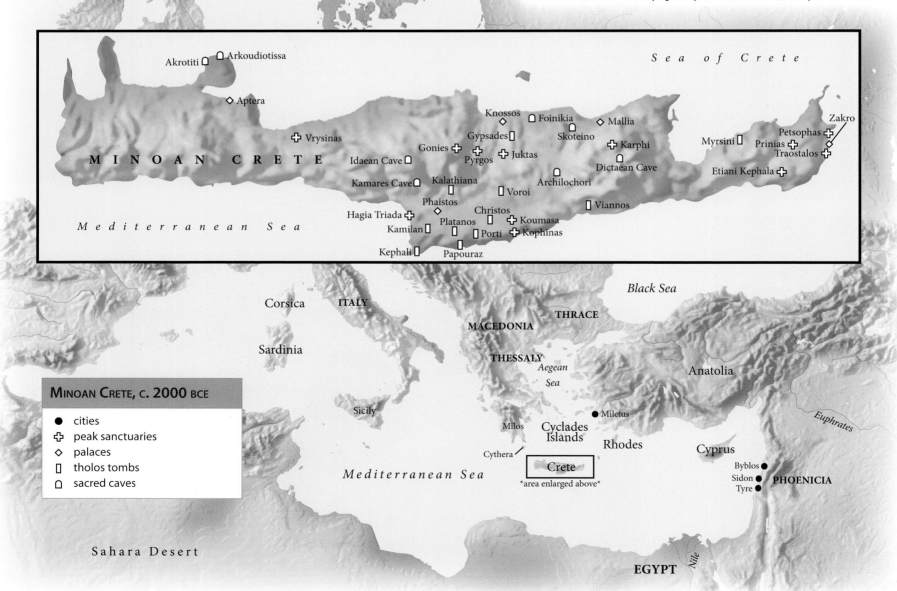

MINOAN CRETE, C. 2000 BCE

- ● cities
- ✚ peak sanctuaries
- ◇ palaces
- ▯ tholos tombs
- ⌂ sacred caves

There is a land called Crete . . . ringed by the wine-dark sea with rolling whitecaps—handsome country, fertile, thronged with people well past counting—boasting ninety cities. . . . Central to all their cities is the magnificent Cnossos, the site where Minos ruled and each ninth year conferred with almighty Zeus himself.
—HOMER, THE ODYSSEY (TRANSLATED BY ROBERT FAGLES)

MINOAN CIVILIZATION

Life in Crete centered on a number of king's palaces, each consisting of a large hall surrounded by a maze of small rooms. The earliest Cretan community was Knossos, dating back to 6100 BCE. Minos, an early king of Knossos, lent his name to the Cretan culture, which is known as the Minoan civilization.

By 2000 BCE Crete was a thriving Bronze Age community that was sending ships to trade in Syria and the Cyclades Islands and trading with the Greek mainland through agents on Melos. After an earthquake struck the island in about 1700 BCE, some palaces were rebuilt on a grander scale and the Cretans began keeping written records using a now indecipherable script called Linear A. Earlier records had been in pictographs.

Over the next two centuries Crete was the center of the Aegean world, with outposts in Cythera and Rhodes and in Miletus on the coast of Asia Minor. Cretans also traded with Egypt, Sicily, Italy, and directly with the Greek mainland. The island continued to grow rich in both wealth and art. It was, in effect, the first great civilization of Europe. Although minimally influenced by Southwest Asian cultures, Crete had its own personality. Much Minoan art depicts the beauties of nature and such joyful pastimes as dancing and the sport of bull leaping.

Crete's days of glory ended in about 1450 BCE, when invaders from the Greek mainland took over the major Cretan strongholds. The invaders also brought with them a new form of writing—Linear B, the earliest surviving texts in Greek. Most of the palaces of Crete were destroyed at that time, either by the invaders or by shock waves initiated by the explosion of a volcano on the island of Thera to the north of Knossos.

MINOAN RELIGION

Little is known about Minoan religion, but it was dominated by a female deity who was associated with bulls, snakes, and fertility. The Cretan goddess was also depicted as a bird and sometimes bore a shield. She may survive to some degree as the goddess Athena, who lived on the Acropolis at Athens with a sacred bird, a snake, and a shield. There were no large temples on Crete, but shrines were included inside the palaces. Cretan leaders were buried in tombs and offered libations, suggesting that they were worshipped as deities.

Discovered in the ruins of the Minoan place of Phaistos, the so-called Phaistos Disk dates to the second millennium BCE. Its purpose and inscription remain mysteries.

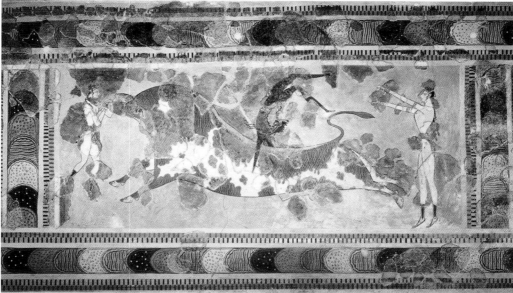

This fresco of what must have been the very dangerous sport of bull-leaping decorated the palace of Knossos. Bulls generally figure heavily in Minoan art and religion.

The extraordinary palace at Knossos dominated Crete, and hence the Minoan civilization, for centuries. In Greek mythology it is the home of King Minos.

KING MINOS AND THE MINOTAUR

Minos was a common name for kings in Crete, but the original King Minos entered Greek mythology as the son of Zeus (disguised as a bull) and Europa, wife of a king of Knossos. When Minos became king, he refused to sacrifice a white bull to Poseidon, and so Poseidon made Minos's wife fall in love with the bull and bear an offspring that was half human and half bull—the monstrous Minotaur, who demanded regular human sacrifices. Eventually, the Athenian hero Theseus traveled to Crete, where Minos's daughter Ariadne fell in love with him and gave him a ball of string to mark his path as he tracked down the Minotaur, who was confined in a vast labyrinth (possibly inspired by the mazelike palace at Knossos). Theseus killed the Minotaur and took Ariadne away with him, only to desert her later on the island of Naxos.

The bull-headed Minotaur of Greek mythology may suggest the importance of bulls to the Minoan civilization.

Mycenaean Culture

AFTER INVADING CRETE, Greeks from the mainland replaced the Minoans as the leading naval power in the Aegean. They engaged in trade with nations far and wide and had settlements in Crete, Cyprus, and Cilicia (the south coast of modern-day Turkey). Greeks also established trading stations in Syria and Palestine and traded with Egypt, Italy, Sicily, and Troy in Asia Minor.

Over the years the Greeks had been building up their own civilization, which was more militaristic than that of the Minoans. There was no single political unit, but only small kingdoms. Rulers and lesser lords lived in palaces, while peasants and craftsmen lived in nearby villages. Court records were kept on clay tablets in Linear B writing (with symbols representing syllables).

The typical Greek palace was a fortified stone structure that featured a large room (megaron) with a central hearth and a pillared portico at the front—a design that would later resurface in classic Greek temples. Leaders were buried in tombs with entrance corridors leading to burial chambers that were topped by huge domes of squared masonry. The bodies were laid in shafts that also contained treasures.

In 1876 the German archaeologist Heinrich Schliemann discovered the ruins of one such palace at Mycenae in the northeastern Peloponnesus and gave the name Mycenaean to the entire culture. In actuality, though, Mycenaean culture spread across Greece as far as Thessaly, where there was a palace associated with the mythic hero Achilles. Schliemann dubbed his first Mycenaean find the House of Atreus, associating it with the father of the heroes Agamemnon and Menelaus, who figure prominently in the Trojan War in Greek mythology. The tomb, which had a forty-foot dome, was built around 1330 BCE. Treasures buried with the king included gold face masks, inlaid daggers and other weapons, and ornate jewelry.

Although most Mycenaean settlements were clustered around the Aegean Sea, trade routes throughout the Mediterranean brought the Mycenaeans into contact with numerous cultures.

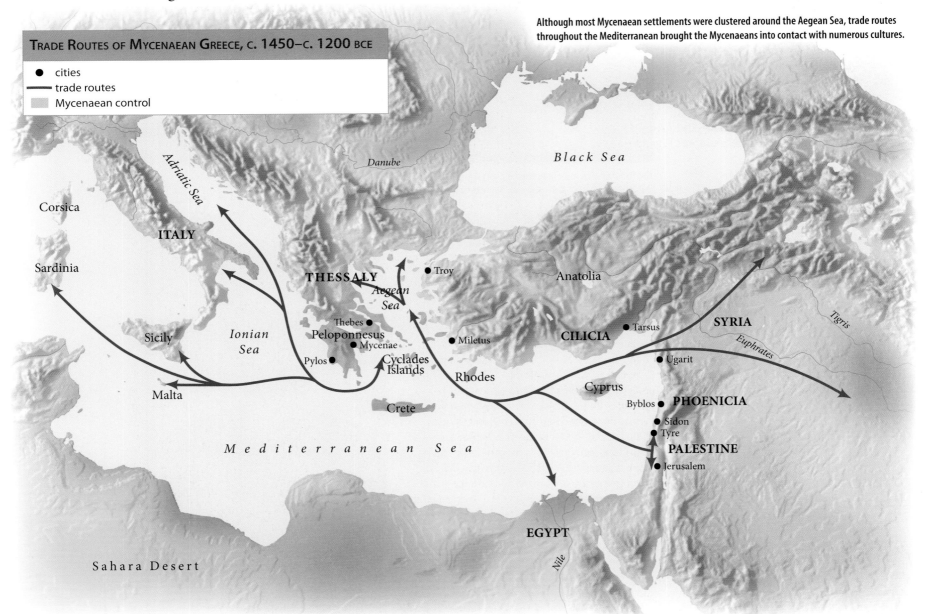

TRADE ROUTES OF MYCENAEAN GREECE, C. 1450–C. 1200 BCE

- ● cities
- — trade routes
- ▨ Mycenaean control

Among the objects discovered in the noble graves at Mycenae was this bronze dagger, elaborately decorated with a hunting scene.

Nine days the arrows of god swept through the army.
On the tenth Achilles called all ranks to muster—
The impulse seized him, sent by white-armed Hera
Grieving to see Achaean fighters drop and die.
—HOMER, THE ILIAD (TRANSLATED BY ROBERT FAGLES)

DISAPPEARANCE OF THE MYCENAEAN CULTURE

Soon after 1200 BCE the Mycenaean palaces were destroyed, writing disappeared, and bronze was no longer manufactured. Little is known of what occurred on the Greek mainland over the next 400 years. When writing reemerged in the eighth century, it used a form of the Phoenician alphabet—an early version of the Greek alphabet in use today.

Nothing certain is known of the causes of that dark period in Greek history, but theories abound. According to one prominent theory, Mycenaean warriors supplemented the riches they accumulated in trading by raiding foreign lands, including Egypt, Cyprus, and Troy. When a resulting war with Troy took the Mycenaeans away to fight in Asia Minor, foreign invaders moved in, and when the Mycenaeans returned home from war, the invaders defeated them. These foreigners, generally referred to as Dorians, pushed some Mycenaeans across the Aegean to the coast of Asia Minor. Soon almost all the shores of the Aegean were occupied by peoples who spoke some dialect of Greek.

Whatever the causes of the collapse, soon after 1150 BCE Mycenaean culture was no more. In the coming centuries

A gold funerary mask discovered in a royal grave at Mycenae. Dating to about 1550 BCE, it was once believed to belong to the legendary king Agamemnon and still bears the name Mask of Agamemnon.

the palaces fell into further ruin, but their ghostly presence must have fed the imaginations of the people who lived after the days of glory. Consequently, legendary tales of mighty heroes of the past emerged and were passed along by word of mouth, culminating in the great epics of the blind poet Homer.

Excavated tombs at Mycenae. Visible on the right-hand side is the circular shaft of Grave Circle A, in which Mycenaean kings or nobles were buried with rich trappings.

HOMER AND THE TROJAN WAR

Although history tells us nothing of the final days of the Mycenaean people, stories of that era are preserved in the epic poems of Homer, who lived some four centuries later. In his *Iliad*, Homer tells of a war with Troy that lasted ten years, culminating in the fall of Troy and the return home of the Mycenaean heroes.

Homer's epics were culminations of a long history of oral poetry handed down from generation to generation and mixed in time and place of composition. They used epithets and poetic formulas and phrases, selecting the ones that best fit the regular meter of the poetry. The time of composition is uncertain, but *The Iliad* was possibly written down in 725–675 BCE, when alphabetical writing came into use in Greece. It is possible that Homer himself wrote down the poems.

In *The Iliad* the Greek deities interact directly with humans, often influencing their actions. While Zeus is preoccupied with making love (often with human women), the goddess Aphrodite instigates a love affair between the mortals Helen, wife of King Menelaus of Lacedaemon (Sparta), and Paris, a prince of Troy. Paris abducts Helen and brings her to Troy, and war follows.

In the course of telling his story of the war, Homer also describes various religious rituals, including cremation, which allowed a hero's remains to be transported back home for ceremonial entombment and hero worship. Homer's religious views, however, are more likely to reflect those of his own time than those of the Mycenaeans.

The Fall of Troy, by eighteenth-century painter Johann Georg Trautmann. According to Homer, Mycenaean warriors took the city through the trickery of the Trojan horse.

Greek Gods and Goddesses

When the Indo-Europeans swept down into Greece in about 2000 BCE, they added the worship of Zeus to local religious observances. Over the centuries, as the Mycenaeans traveled abroad they adopted still other deities from the lands they visited, greatly expanding the pantheon with gods from Crete and from Asia Minor, and even farther east. Myths were intermingled, resulting in new beliefs that sometimes contradicted the original ones.

In about 750 BCE the Greek poet Hesiod wrote his *Theogony*, a kind of succinct verse genealogy for Greek gods and goddesses. According to Hesiod, in the beginning, Chaos came into being and then Eros, the god of sexual love. Out of Chaos came Gaea (Earth), who bore Uranus (Heaven) and mated with him to bring forth twelve Titans. The youngest of the Titans was Cronus, who castrated his father, Uranus, and took his place as head of all the gods. From Uranus's genitals sprang Aphrodite, the goddess of love. Cronus and his sister Rhea produced six more gods. The youngest of these, Zeus, then overthrew his father and became head of the gods. Some aspects of these stories seem to trace back to thirteenth-century BCE Hittite mythology and the eleventh-century BCE Babylonian creation epic *Enuma Elis*.

The twelve main deities live on Mount Olympus, often quarreling with one another to the advantage or disadvantage of humanity. In addition to them, Hesiod names about three hundred more deities. Some are merely personified abstractions, such as Sleep and Victory. Others have specific jobs, such as Atlas, who holds up the heavens. Still others are fully fleshed out, with their own stories and strong personalities, and they move about like human beings.

POSEIDON
God of the sea and of earthquakes, Poseidon was also associated with horses. He probably began as an earth fertility spirit, whose nature changed when the Greeks settled by the sea.

ZEUS
Father of all the gods, Zeus governed the skies and the weather, wielding thunderbolts as his weapons. He was also an amorous god, coupling with both goddesses and humans and siring multitudes of other gods and heroes. Myths of his childhood are associated with Crete.

HERA
Both the sister and wife of Zeus, Hera was the goddess of marriage and women. She probably developed from the Minoan earth goddess.

HESTIA
Goddess of the hearth, Hestia was often worshipped in private homes. She comes out of Mycenaean culture, where hearths were first used.

APOLLO
Sun god and guardian of young men, Apollo was also the god of prophecy, healing, music, and archery, and protector of the herds. He probably originated in Asia Minor and, before that, northern Asia.

ARTEMIS
Virgin goddess of wild animals and hunting, Artemis was also associated with childbirth and the moon. Her origins were Southwest Asia, where she was probably more sexual, as seen in the many-breasted images of Artemis at Ephesus.

MOUNT OLYMPUS

HERMES
Inventor of the lyre, Hermes was messenger to Zeus, guide to travelers in this world, and the escort of the dead. He was also patron of merchants, secrets, cunning, tricks, and even thieves. He may have been Minoan in origin and was associated with Arcadia in the central Peloponnesus, where he may have been worshipped before the Greeks arrived.

ATHENA
Goddess of wisdom, the arts, and war, Athena was later regarded as protector of cities. She developed from the Minoan snake goddess but in Greek mythology is said to have sprung from the head of her father, Zeus.

APHRODITE
Goddess of love and beauty. She appeared late in Greece, probably brought from Phoenicia via Cyprus as a version of the Semitic fertility goddess Astarte.

HEPHAESTUS
God of fire, Hephaestus was a master craftsman. Although he was lame and unattractive (alone among the gods) he was married to the beautiful Aphrodite. When Prometheus stole fire from heaven, Hephaestus helped Zeus take revenge. He originated in Asia Minor, and the center of his cult was Lemnos, a volcanic island in the Aegean.

PLUTUS
God of wealth—originally agricultural wealth, but later wealth of all kinds. His mother was Demeter, goddess of crops and the fertile earth.

ARES
God of war, Ares was Thracian in origin and appears less important than his Roman counterpart, Mars, would be.

Thus there is no way of deceiving or evading the mind of Zeus, since not even Iapetos' son, sly Prometheus, escaped the weight of his wrath, and for all his cleverness a strong fetter holds him in check.

—HESIOD'S THEOGONY (TRANSLATED BY M. L. WEST)

GREEK GODS

Although the Greeks acknowledged hundreds of deities, twelve gods and goddesses reigned supreme from their home on Mount Olympus in Thessaly (northeastern Greece)

In addition, Dionysus, the god of wine, came from the north and was Asian in origin. He often displaced Hestia in the Olympic pantheon. Hades, the god of the underworld, remained in his domain and never ascended Mount Olympus.

RELIGIOUS RITES

Ancient Greek religion had no body of doctrine, and its priests were not set apart from the lay members of society. Most priests and priestesses saw to the administration of temples and other sacred sites, where they also officiated at rituals and sometimes offered advice.

The first Greek temples were built in the eighth century BCE. Temple services included hymns, prayers, processions, and animal sacrifices, which were offered to obtain protection or some favor of a deity. The Greeks normally sacrificed animals instead of practicing human sacrifice. However, Bronze-Age Greeks may have practiced human sacrifice, for Homer and others tell how Agamemnon set out to sacrifice his daughter Iphigenia to Artemis, who substituted a deer at the last minute. (In a similar story in the Hebrew book of Genesis, God commands Abraham to sacrifice his son Isaac but substitutes a ram at the last minute.)

A fifth century BCE depiction of the hero Heracles with the goddess Athena on a *kylix*, or drinking cup.

In addition to the temples there were cult centers to which both rulers and common people went to consult oracles. The most famous was at Delphi, where Apollo was believed to possess the priestess, or Pythia, and speak through her. In exchange for a sacrifice and prayers, priests would write down the oracle's answers to questions or solutions to problems. However, these responses, in verse, were often hard to interpret.

Although the Olympian gods and others reigned over all of Greece, the people also worshipped local heroes, such as the Trojan War hero Achilles in Thessaly. Typically, the people offered prayers and sacrifices at the tomb of the hero in the belief that he could help or harm them. If a hero died away from home, his remains (sometimes cremated) were brought back and placed in a tomb.

PROMETHEUS, CHAMPION OF MEN

Though not one of the Olympians, the rebellious demigod Prometheus was dear to the people. The son of the Titan Iapetus, he created the first man from clay and had the goddess Athena give him life. Prometheus was also a trickster who repeatedly rebelled against Zeus. At one point, when Zeus refused to give men fire, Prometheus stole fire from heaven and gave it to them. Zeus punished Prometheus by chaining him to a rock in the Caucasus, where every day an eagle ate his liver, which grew back at night. Zeus also punished the men for accepting the fire by sending down a curse in the form of Pandora, a woman with a covered box (actually a stoppered jar). Even though Pandora was forbidden to open the box, she did, and all the evils of the world spilled out.

Prometheus, chained and tormented by the eagle.

The Temple of Apollo at Delphi dates to the fourth century BCE, but the site was sacred for centuries before that. Most famously, the site housed the Oracle, a female priestess, who by the eighth century BCE was reputedly foretelling future events.

Greek City-States Emerge

THE DARK AGE THAT FOLLOWED the dissolution of the Mycenaean civilization ended in the eighth century BCE when the new Greek alphabet was put into use and trade between the Greeks and the rest of the Mediterranean world began to expand. Over the next three centuries, the so-called Archaic period in Greek history, various new forms of government appeared, ending with a rudimentary form of democracy.

As Greek marketplaces grew, communities began to gather into large defensive units resulting in political systems based on a single city—*polis* in Greek (from which comes our word "politics"). Early city-states were ruled by hereditary kings, but soon these kings were overthrown and rule was taken over by oligarchies, or small groups of wealthy citizens. Leaders of these oligarchies came to power in various ways. Some were chosen by lot, some were elected, and still others rotated in office. Sometimes the leaders ruled in conjunction with a council or assembly.

Generally, leaders of the city-states were wealthy and could be unfair to the nonruling classes. Consequently, many were overthrown by populist leaders called tyrants, who promised to take care of the people. Some of these tyrants honored their pledges to protect the people, but others did not.

By the sixth century several powerful city-states had emerged, including Athens, Sparta, Corinth, and Thebes. Athens and Corinth, with their large and strategically located seaports, became major maritime and mercantile powers as well.

Powerful city-states crowded together on the Greek homeland, establishing colonies across seas and struggling for dominance at home.

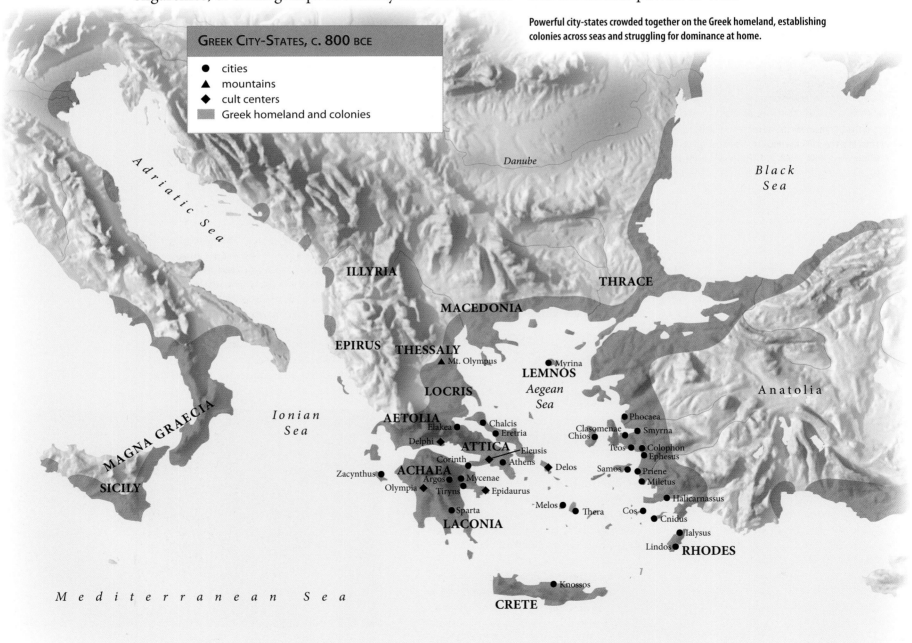

GREEK CITY-STATES, C. 800 BCE

- ● cities
- ▲ mountains
- ◆ cult centers
- ▬ Greek homeland and colonies

Adriatic Sea
Danube
Black Sea
ILLYRIA
THRACE
MACEDONIA
EPIRUS
THESSALY
▲ Mt. Olympus
LOCRIS
● Myrina
LEMNOS
Aegean Sea
Anatolia
Ionian Sea
AETOLIA
Flakea ●
● Chalcis
● Eretria
Delphi ◆
ATTICA
Eleusis ◆
● Phocaea
Clasomenae ●
● Smyrna
Chios ●
Corinth ●
Athens ●
Teos ●
Colophon ●
● Ephesus
MAGNA GRAECIA
Zacynthus ●
ACHAEA
Argos ●
● Mycenae
● Delos
Samos ●
Priene ●
● Miletus
Olympia ◆
Tiryns ●
◆ Epidaurus
SICILY
● Sparta
● Melos
Thera ●
Cos ●
Halicarnassus ●
LACONIA
Cnidus ●
Ialysus ●
Lindos ●
RHODES
Mediterranean Sea
● Knossos
CRETE

Some wicked men are rich, some good are poor;
We will not change our virtue for their store:
Virtue's a thing that none can take away,
But money changes owners all the day.
—VERSE BY SOLON (TRANSLATED BY JOHN DRYDEN)

According to Ovid, Orpheus met his death at the hands of vicious maenads, who tore him to pieces after the musician tragically lost his love, Eurydice, to Hades. Here, nineteenth-century painter Gustave Moreau shows an unnamed maiden tenderly cradling Orpheus's head on his lyre.

THE RISE OF ATHENS

In 621 BCE a lawgiver named Draco wrote a comprehensive code of laws for Athens. Although it was intended to improve things in the city-state, the code was unduly harsh, dictating death for most offenses. (Today harsh measures are still said to be draconian.)

A period of acute economic distress followed, and in about 594 Solon, a poet and wise statesman, was given full authority to institute reforms for Athens. Solon instituted a semi-constitutional system of aristocratic government and replaced Draco's law code with a more humane one. However, some Athenians opposed Solon's reforms, and from 527 to 510 the tyrant Pisistratus and his sons ruled Athens.

Meanwhile, Sparta in the southern Peloponnesus continued under the rule of landed kings, who vigorously trained their men for war, and in 650 BCE Sparta established a permanent militarist regime under a dual monarchy. In 510 the Spartans went to Athens, overthrew the tyrants there, and tried to install their own tyrant, but the Athenians resisted. In 508 the Athenian leader Cleisthenes instituted reforms that turned Athens into a kind of democracy—with power being held by an assembly of all the male citizens. This was the start of the classical period of Greek civilization.

MYSTERY CULTS

Throughout the Archaic era the Olympian gods and goddesses continued to be worshipped, but in the late fifth century BCE certain mystery cults emerged, possibly because orthodox Greek religion offered no hope of an afterlife. One such cult in Epidaurus centered on the physician Asclepius, who was so good at healing that it was said he could raise the dead. People flocked to Epidaurus seeking cures from diseases.

Another cult, at Eleusis (near Athens) centered on Demeter, goddess of crops, whose daughter Persephone was abducted by Hades and spent four months each year in the underworld but returned to earth each spring so that her mother would be joyful enough to ensure the harvest. Dionysus, god of wine, offered women in his cult freedom from tension as they engaged in ecstatic rites, even tearing apart living animals.

Finally, a mystery cult revolved around the musician Orpheus, who when his wife, Eurydice, died, descended into the underworld and with his music charmed the deities into restoring Eurydice to him. Unfortunately, Orpheus broke his agreement not to look at Eurydice on the way back home, and he lost her again. Nevertheless, his cult promised life after death for followers who performed certain rites and abstained from eating meat. Orpheus himself supposedly wrote texts to guide his followers.

Dionysus was god not only of the physical intoxication produced by alcohol, but also of the madness, frenzy, and divine inspiration that drinking could provoke. Myths about him are often quite brutal, with his mythical followers, such as the male satyrs or female maenads, becoming insane and violent in his worship.

OLYMPIC GAMES

Sports were always a major activity among the Greeks. In *The Iliad*, Homer describes elaborate athletic competitions that were held during the funeral celebrations for Achilles' friend Patroclus. Young aristocrats were trained in various sports as well as in military matters, music, and poetry.

Beginning in 776 BCE a group of men from various city-states initiated a summer religious festival that featured athletic competitions in honor of Zeus. The games, which were held at Olympia on the Peloponnesus, fostered peace among the city-states, and participants were assured safe conduct to and from the games even in times of war. The games continued to be held every four years until 394 CE. They were revived in 1896 to foster international peace and continue to this day.

The ruins of Olympia, for centuries the site of the Olympic Games.

Greek Colonization and the People of Italy

WHILE THE CITY-STATES WERE THRIVING on mainland Greece under kings, oligarchs, and tyrants, Greeks spread across the Mediterranean and even beyond. Greek settlements that had been established earlier in Asia Minor grew rapidly, and new settlements were added by the various city-states. Some of the colonies were established as simple trading posts but then grew larger. Others were founded because the people needed more land. A sense of adventure led to the founding of still other colonies.

Colonization began in the eighth century BCE along the coast of Asia Minor. Unable to gain more than a foothold there, due to resistance from people of the interior, Greeks at Miletus ultimately established colonies along the shores of the Black Sea. Other city-states established colonies in Sicily, Italy, and even Spain.

By the sixth century BCE there were Greek colonies in northern Africa between Egypt and Carthage.

Generally, the Greeks sailed to new lands in long boats powered by fifty oars, seized and fortified land, and established replicas of their native city-states. They absorbed little of the cultures upon which they intruded but often influenced the local peoples. This included the colonies in southern Italy, known as Magna Graecia.

In addition to the Greeks who settled in Magna Graecia, the Italian peninsula was occupied by a variety of different peoples. Sometime before 1000 BCE Indo-Europeans had migrated to Italy from the north, and not too long after that, most of the people in Italy were speaking some sort of Indo-European language—including Latin along the lower Tiber River and to the southeast in the region of Latium.

By 500 BCE, three groups of people lived in Italy: the Greeks, whose colonies by now spread throughout the Mediterranean; the Italic-speaking tribes of south and central Italy; and the Etruscans.

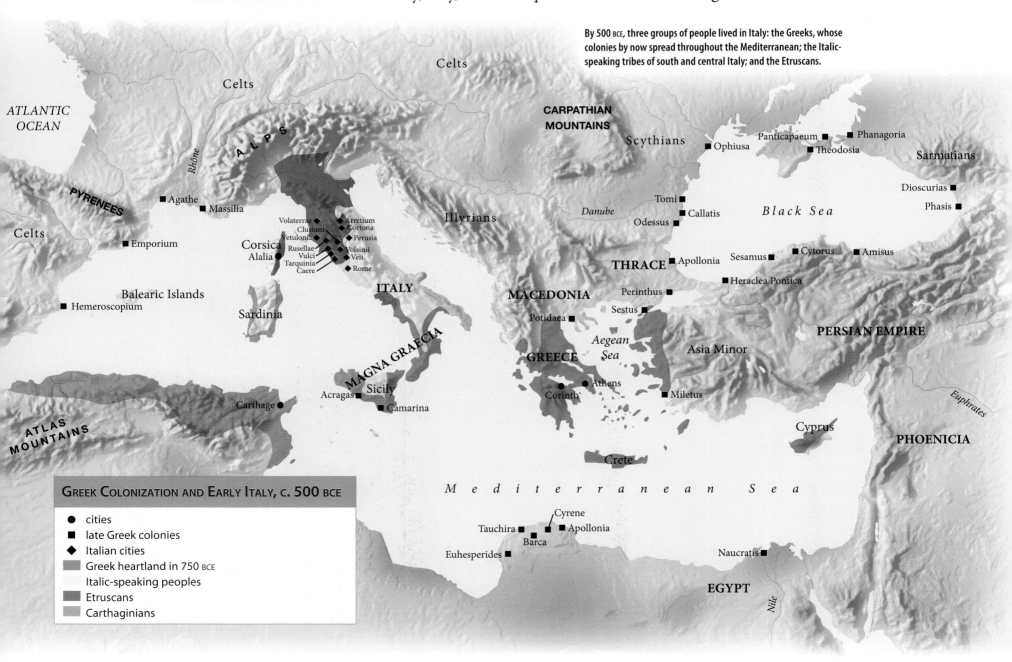

GREEK COLONIZATION AND EARLY ITALY, C. 500 BCE

- ● cities
- ■ late Greek colonies
- ◆ Italian cities
- Greek heartland in 750 BCE
- Italic-speaking peoples
- Etruscans
- Carthaginians

Romulus made a beginning with the foundation of the city. He had sent for men from Etruria to direct every action within the founding with certain sacred offerings and rules and to teach how it was prescribed in the Sacred Law.
—PLUTARCH'S PARALLEL LIVES, "THE LIFE OF ROMULUS"

THE FOUNDING OF ROME

According to legend, the city-state of Rome was founded in 753 BCE by the brothers Romulus and Remus, who had been nursed as infants by a she wolf. (According to another legend the boys were descended from Aeneas, the Trojan hero who came to Italy after his city had been destroyed in the Trojan War.) After Remus's death Romulus became the first king of Rome (which inherited his name). The seventh and last king of Rome was the tyrannical Tarquinius Superbus (Tarquin the Proud). The Romans deposed him and established a republic in 509 BCE.

ETRUSCANS LEAVE THEIR MARK

Tarquinius's family was said to have descended from the Etruscans, who had appeared in Italy in the eighth century, though historians disagree about their origins. The Etruscans settled along the coast of what is now Tuscany and prospered through trade, agriculture, crafts, and the mining of copper, lead, and iron. Following the example of the Greeks and Phoenicians with whom they traded, they built twelve to fourteen city-states in Italy. These were ruled by kings, but a sacred alliance united the city-states economically and politically. Although the Etruscans left no written literature, many inscriptions survive in their tongue (using the Greek alphabet), showing that Etruscan is not an Indo-European language.

Although the Etruscans were often highly influenced by the cultures they encountered in trading throughout the Mediterranean, they also retained inherited native beliefs. Their religion was dominated by the idea of fate, and they continually sought to know the will of the gods, resorting to reading the entrails of animals or the flights of birds, and finding signs in lightning and thunder. The demigod Tages and the nymph Vegoe handed down precepts about rituals, destiny, human conduct, and life beyond the grave. Many of the gods and goddesses of the Etruscans seem to be versions of the Greek and Roman deities worshiped in Italy. Apulu, for instance, seems to be an Etruscan version of Apollo.

Often the Etruscans fought with Phoenicians and Greeks for control of trade in the western Mediterranean. About 535 BCE they allied with the Carthaginians and defeated the Greeks in a naval battle. The Latins threw off Etruscan rule late in the sixth century, and in 509 BCE the Etruscans were driven out of Rome. From then on their influence waned.

The Pyrgi Tablets record the dedication of a temple to the goddess Ashtaret, known as Astarte in Mesopotamia. The text repeats in the Etruscan language and in Phoenician, reinforcing the existence of cultural ties in the ancient Mediterranean world.

ETRUSCAN BURIAL CUSTOMS

Etruscans put great energy into their burial rites. Generally, each city-state had a large necropolis nearby. The dead were buried in large tombs that were dug into the rock beneath the ground and made to resemble actual Etruscan homes. In some tombs, beds and chairs were carved out of the rock. The walls of the tombs were decorated with colorful paintings depicting funerary banquets, games, and dancing. Others show outdoor activities that may reflect a bright view of the afterlife. (Tombs of the fourth century would take on a more somber tone.) Still other wall paintings show episodes from mythology. One grave at Tarquinia shows the Trojan horse of Greek mythology, indicating how easily the Etruscans melded their religion with foreign myths. The bodies were placed in these tombs and surrounded with household goods, armor, weapons, and anything else they may have needed in the life to come. Life after death would be comfortable.

One common type of Etruscan tomb appears in the form of a mound. Constructed of earth and stone, these mounds often resemble Etruscan houses, suggesting a belief in a realistic afterlife.

Etruscans were masters of necropolis building, with different styles in different locales. At Sutri, tombs cut directly into rock are still visible.

Part One: The Religions of the Ancient World ✧ 41

PERSIA
Ancient Persia

THE PERSIAN PLATEAU SPREADS more than one thousand miles across Southwest Asia, from the Caspian Sea in the northwest toward the Arabian Sea in the south. A region of tall mountain ranges and deep basins, the plateau encompasses much of modern Iran and portions of Afghanistan and Pakistan. In the fourth and third millennia BCE, pastoral and nomadic peoples lived in this mountainous land, which had few important towns.

While great cities and organized agriculture flourished in Mesopotamia and the Fertile Crescent to the west, most of the Persian uplands remained sparsely settled. In the southwest lowlands, however, the Elamite civilization grew in the shadow of the Zagros Mountains. By the third millennium BCE, Elam was expanding as a regional power on Babylon's doorstep, with influence far across the Persian highlands to the north and east.

Elam, with the city of Susa as its capital, was closely involved with the Mesopotamian states, including Sumer, Assyria, and Babylonia—trading with them and often making war. The polytheism of Mesopotamia influenced the Elamites, who stood between the civilized city-states and the scattered pastoralists of the plateau. By the first century BCE, the most powerful peoples of

The frieze of archers from the palace at Susa (in modern Khuzistan Province, Iran) dates to c. 510 BCE but may continue a style developed by Elamites, who themselves took it from Babylon centuries earlier.

the plateau were the Medes and Parthians. Among these semi-migratory peoples there developed a deep religious tradition centered on nature worship, especially of fire and water.

The personification of these elements laid the foundations for organized worship that gave rise to Apas, goddess of water, and Atar, the god of fire. Prayers and libations were offered daily to these deities by elders of each household. Other nature gods and goddesses were also worshipped, including a lord of the sky, an earth goddess, and a bull who was protector of domestic animals. The sun and moon also were objects of worship in the lands that would become known as Persia.

THE BATTLE OF THE STALLIONS

The Aryan god Tishtrya, known as the "God of the Dog Star," was said to protect the clouds that bring rain. Each year, in the form of a white stallion, Tishtrya goes down to the great sea, Vourukasha, source of all rivers, and battles with a black stallion—Apaosha, the "Demon of Death." After his victory, Tishtrya dashes into the sea, and the resulting tumult throws water into the air to be gathered up into the clouds by Vata, the rain bringer. Thus was precious rain again showered over the lands of the Aryans.

Zoroastrians continued an ancient festival, carried into modern times, to celebrate the spring. Among the main features of the festival are traditional horse races that hark back to the mythic battle of the stallions.

THE ROYAL SAGES

The ancient Aryans had a complex language system as well as sophisticated religious customs and myths. Their ancestors were said to have been taught by "royal sages," with the greatest being Yima, the leading ruler and teacher from a mythic golden age.

The supreme deity, Mazda, warned Yima that the sinful world would be destroyed by snow and ice, and commanded him to build an underground sanctuary. There Yima was

to bring a chosen people, along with seed for trees, fruits, and flowers, as well as pairs of useful animals. Thus were the Aryans to be restored after the crisis.

Another royal sage was Kava-Ushan, a king whose prayers overcame the forces of evil and who was surrounded by a sacred halo. A third royal sage was Thrae-taona, a great physician and healer.

A winged disk, reminiscent of Egyptian designs, represented the god Ahura Mazda in early Persian art. This depiction appears in the ruins of Persepolis, an ancient Persian capital city.

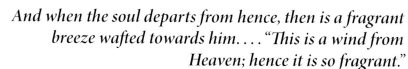

And when the soul departs from hence, then is a fragrant breeze wafted towards him. . . . "This is a wind from Heaven; hence it is so fragrant."

—AS A SAVED SOUL PREPARES TO ENTER HEAVEN, THE
SPIRIT OF WISDOM REPLIES TO HIS QUESTIONS; FROM AN
ANCIENT ZOROASTRIAN TEXT, MENOK I KHRAT

LANDS OF ELAM AND ARYANS

The Persian plateau was known to the classical Mediterranean world as Aranya, "Land of the Aryans," or Eran in Middle Persian, which eventually became Iran in modern Persian. The ancient inhabitants are sometimes referred to as "Indo-Iranians," considered to be the ancestors of various peoples from Iran to the Indian subcontinent.

An early Aryan legend describes this people coming from the north, from a motherland that was overwhelmed by ice and snow that destroyed their civilization. They migrated southward, into the mountains and tablelands, making homes in the fertile valleys and moving down through ancient Bactria and what is now Afghanistan.

By the third millennium BCE Elam was thriving but also was often at war or in thrall to its Mesopotamian neighbors. Elamite power

steadily grew until, at the end of the second millennium BCE, an Elamite king captured Babylon itself and carried off the stela that bore the Code of Hammurabi. In the end, however, the Babylonians conquered Elam, which became a weak federation of countries until the seventh century BCE, when the Assyrians finally destroyed Susa and punished Elam by sowing its fields with salt to ruin them.

In these ancient times the Aryan peoples practiced what became known as Paoiryotkaesha (the Ancient Faith), also termed Mazdayasna—the Faith that worships Mazda, the Great Lord of All. Ahura Mazda is the traditional name for the "Supreme Lord," or the "Lord of Life" and the "One Life from Whom All Proceed."

Ahura Mazda was the supreme deity, but a broad pantheon of gods and goddesses continued to be revered—including a god of war and a goddess who brings rain. Early in the

first millennium BCE there appeared a prophet known as Zoroaster (first called Zarathustra), who taught the people to worship only Ahura Mazda. The teachings of Zoroaster had won a great following by the sixth century BCE, but they also brought about a deep cultural schism with regard to traditional Aryan religious beliefs and practices.

The sack of Susa, perpetrated by Ashurbanipal of Assyria in 639 BCE, was particularly brutal. As recorded on this stele (commissioned by the victor), Ashurbanipal destroyed Elamite palaces, tombs, and temples, and even salted the fields.

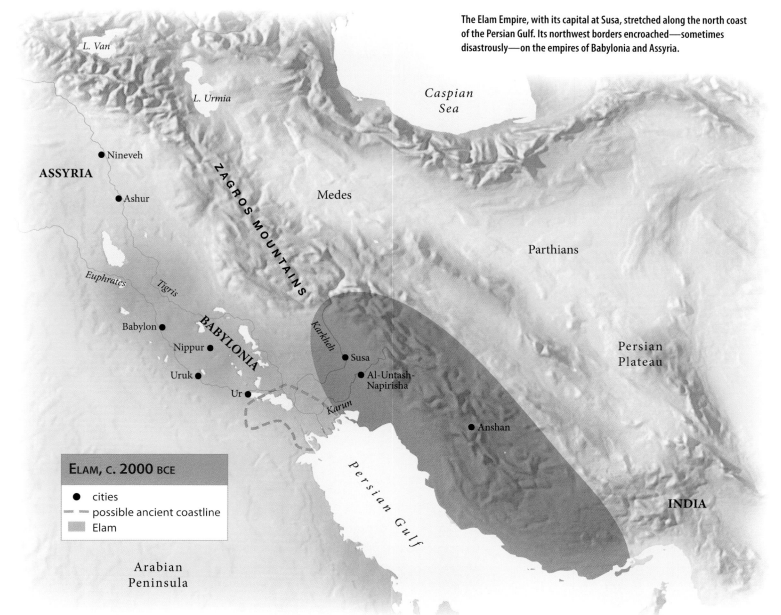

The Elam Empire, with its capital at Susa, stretched along the north coast of the Persian Gulf. Its northwest borders encroached—sometimes disastrously—on the empires of Babylonia and Assyria.

L. Van

L. Urmia

Caspian Sea

• Nineveh

ASSYRIA

• Ashur

Medes

ZAGROS MOUNTAINS

Parthians

Euphrates

Tigris

Babylon •

BABYLONIA

Nippur •

Karkheh

• Susa

Persian Plateau

Uruk •

• Al-Untash-Napirisha

Ur •

Karun

• Anshan

ELAM, C. 2000 BCE

• cities
- - - possible ancient coastline
  Elam

Persian Gulf

INDIA

Arabian Peninsula

Persia

Emperor Cyrus and Zoroastrianism

THE FADED GLORY OF ELAM was succeeded in the sixth century BCE by the rising Persian Empire, which united the peoples of the Persian plateau. Emperor Cyrus the Great defeated all competitors, including the ruler of Babylon, and named his dynasty (and empire) Achaemenid after his ancestor Achaemenes, a warrior chief who trained the first great Persian army. With the capture of Babylon in 539 BCE, Cyrus permitted the Jews to return to Jerusalem, where they rebuilt their temple.

Cyrus extended his empire to the northeast, dying on campaign in 530 BCE. In his lifetime, Cyrus was an adherent of Zoroastrianism, which became the Persian Empire's established religion. The resulting religious turmoil brought about persecution of nonbelievers, but eventually there was a consolidation of ancient religious traditions with official Zoroastrianism.

The date of Zoroaster's birth, somewhere on the Persian plateau, is debated, but evidence points to sometime near the beginning of the first millennium BCE. It is said that he was called to his holy task as teacher around his thirtieth year, and that after years of wandering in the wilderness communing with his god, he received heavenly visions and was taught by angels, from whom he ultimately received perfect knowledge.

Although he is considered a prophet, Zoroaster never claimed this title, instead calling himself an "invoker." He is described as a priest, or at least someone with priestly training. Zoroaster's soul attained great elevation, yet he is not considered a divine being, but as one gifted by divine inspiration.

Zoroaster taught that the individual has the free will to choose between the forces of good (*ahuras*) or evil (*daevas*), and the soul will face the consequences of that choice in the afterlife. His monotheism evolved from the original ancient faiths that imbued the cultures of the Persian plateau.

The vast expanse of the Persian Empire enabled Zoroastrianism—the chosen religion of Persia's great early emperors—to spread far beyond its origins on the Persian plateau.

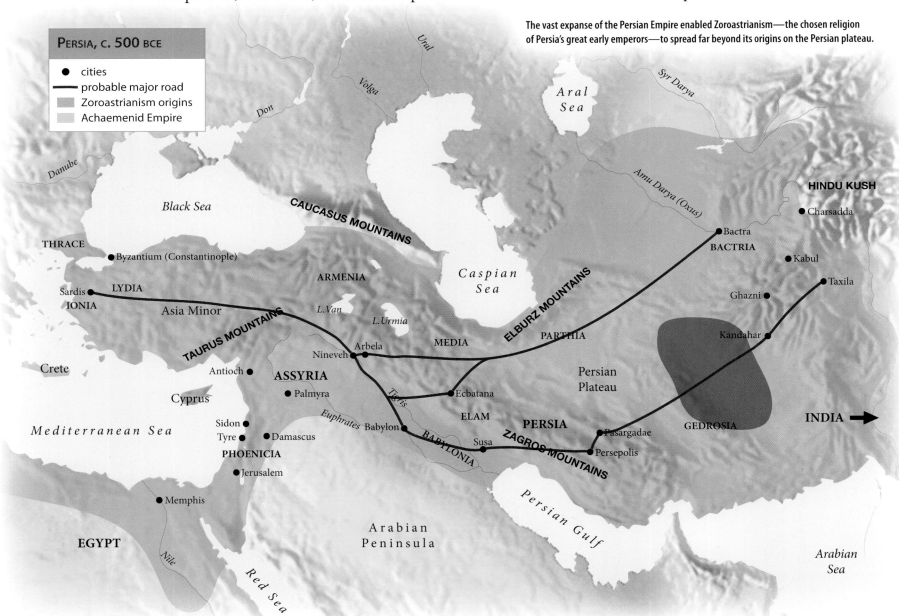

PERSIA, c. 500 BCE

- cities
- probable major road
- Zoroastrianism origins
- Achaemenid Empire

Small gold plaques showing various figures, many of whom appear in Median clothing. Approximately fifty of these were discovered in what was probably a temple near the Oxus River, and some speculate that the plaques served as votive offerings to the gods.

You, Wise One, Who have fashioned the world, the waters, and the plants by Your most progressive mentality, grant me, in accordance with good mind's doctrine, immortality, wholeness, steadfast strength, and endurance.
—GATHA SONG 16

O men and women, it is true that wrong is attractive and appears to have advantages. But it alienates one away from one's self. It ends in woefulness and bad reputation. It destroys happiness for the wrongful. It defiles truths. With these, you shall be destroying your mental life.

But the reward of this Fellowship shall be yours as long as you remain united in weal and woe with all your heart in wedlock. Thus the mentality of the wrongful disappears. However, if you abandon the Fellowship, then the last word you shall utter is "woe."

ZARATHUSTRA'S GATHAS

The primary sacred text of Zoroastrian literature is the Avesta, which contains the hymns known as the Gathas, many of which are said to have been composed by Zoroaster himself. Even older Indo-Iranian wisdom—including an oral tradition of heroic poetry—was incorporated into the Gathas, which were organized over several centuries and written in a version of the Avestan language akin to Sanskrit from the second millennium BCE. (The Old Iranian Avestan language is known primarily from the Avesta texts.)

The Gatha hymns are incorporated into the Yasna, the primary collection of Zoroastrian literature for worship. "Yasna" means oblation, or worship, and is the name for the recitation of these verses during worship.

Gatha Song 1, titled "Humbly I Pray," begins with a supplication to Ahura Mazda, the supreme deity:

Mazda, Wise God, with a bow and uplifted arms, I pray. First, I ask for support through progressive mentality. Then I pray that I may perform all my actions, based as they are on the wisdom of good mind, precisely according to the laws of righteousness so that I please You and the soul of the Living World.

For all the sublime wisdom and religiosity of Zarathustra's Gathas, they also served to impart practical advice, such as Song 17, addressing young married couples:

[Zarathustra says] These words I speak to the charming brides, and to you, bridegrooms. Do bear them in mind. Comprehend them with your consciences. Master the life which belongs to good mind. May you each win the other through righteousness. It will, indeed, be a good acquisition for each of you.

AN ANCIENT LAW

The original Indo-Iranian faith taught that the universe was governed by a natural law that maintained the course of existence—including the regular movement of the sun and the progression of day following night. This fundamental law, which ordered everything, was known as *asha* in the Avestan language. Ethical purity of the individual was essential to this natural order, and any departure from ethical living disturbed it. Lying and distortion of the truth were contrary to asha, for one's given word was sacred—a solemn oath known as Varuna, or bond, which must never be violated.

The pledge was said to have a latent power that was itself a divine force. The accusation by a wise elder that one had broken an oath could bring tests by ordeal, involving immersion in water or running a gauntlet of fire. The truthful individual was expected to come through safely.

A page from the Avesta, the sacred text of Zoroastrianism.

A replica of a bas-relief statue, thought to represent Cyrus the Great, from the emperor's palace at Pasargade. The wings might suggest divine endorsement of Cyrus's kingship.

INDIA

Ancient India, New Discoveries

THE SUBCONTINENT OF INDIA is the birthplace of two major world religions, Hinduism and Buddhism. Its long recorded history and its rich culture have made India the subject of much scholarship. But recent archaeological discoveries have opened up new questions about the origins of civilization in India and shed new light on its religious traditions.

Excavations begun in the late nineteenth century uncovered a previously unknown civilization that flourished in the Indus Valley during the Bronze Age. From about 3500 to 1700 BCE, the Indus Valley was home to an urbanized and sophisticated civilization, often called the Harappan civilization for one of its largest cities, Harappa (its ruins lie in the Punjab and Sindh regions of Pakistan). The Harappan civilization flourished at roughly the same time as the Egyptian and Sumerian civilizations. Carved by waters from the Himalayan, Hindu Kush, and Sulaiman mountain

ranges, the Indus Valley was a fertile agricultural region and was ideally situated, with river access to the Arabian Sea to allow for trade into the Persian Gulf. Harappan artifacts have been unearthed as far north as the Sumerian city of Nineveh, in present-day Iraq.

At least three major cities made up the Indus Valley civilization. Harappa, one of the largest of these cities, lay in the foothills of the mountains, on a tributary of the Indus. Downstream were the cities Mohenjo-Daro and Chanhu-Daro. Excavations of these settlements have revealed large public buildings, granaries, citadels, streets laid out on a grid pattern, and evidence of advanced agricultural practices. Artifacts dating back as far as the fourth millennium include agricultural implements, female figurines, and fertility symbols. A picture has emerged of an advanced civilization, and this picture has changed the way we think about the birth of Indian culture.

Although concentrated in the lower Indus Valley, Harappan artifacts have been found as far away as Mesopotamia, indicating cultural contact and the existence of trade routes.

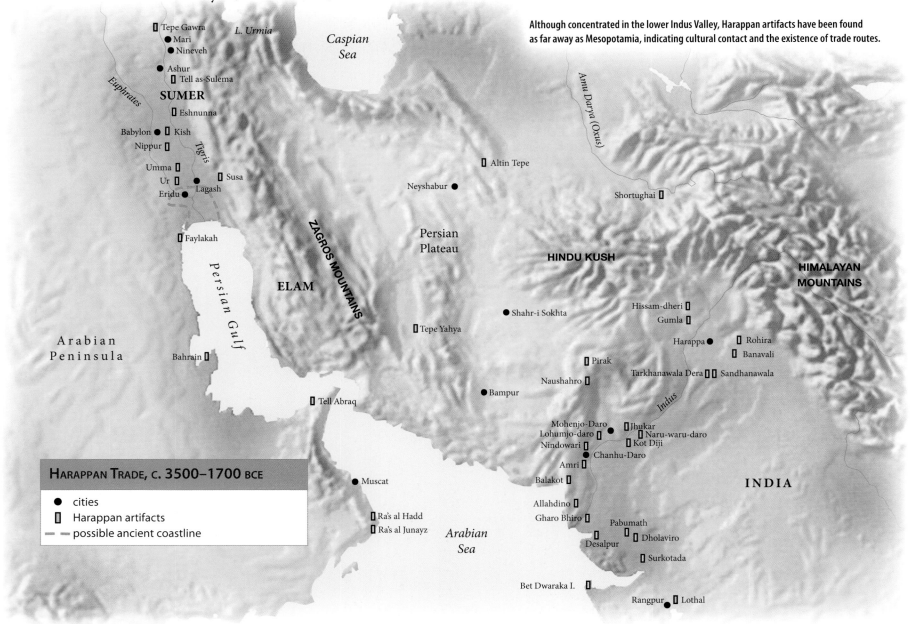

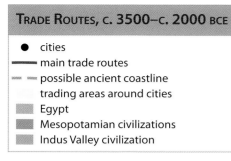

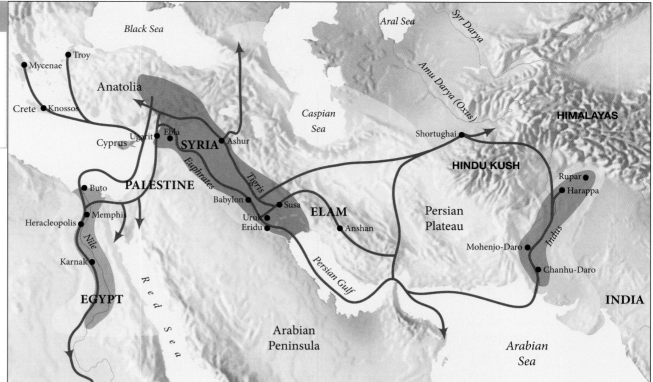

TRADE ROUTES, C. 3500–C. 2000 BCE

- • cities
- —— main trade routes
- – – possible ancient coastline
- trading areas around cities
- Egypt
- Mesopotamian civilizations
- Indus Valley civilization

Black Sea
Aral Sea
Syr Darya
Mycenae
Troy
Anatolia
Caspian Sea
Amu Darya (Oxus)
HIMALAYAS
Crete Knossos
Ugarit Ebla
Cyprus
SYRIA Ashur
Shortughai
Rupar
Harappa
HINDU KUSH
Euphrates
Tigris
Buto
PALESTINE
Babylon
Susa
Persian Plateau
Heracleopolis
Memphis
Uruk
Eridu
ELAM
Anshan
Mohenjo-Daro
Indus
Nile
Persian Gulf
Chanhu-Daro
Karnak
EGYPT
Red Sea
Arabian Peninsula
Arabian Sea
INDIA

THE ARYANS: NEW BELIEFS, NEW RITUALS

The decline of the Indus Valley civilization is nearly as mysterious as its beliefs. Climate change, coupled with natural disasters, may have been a major culprit; this once-fertile region is now an arid landscape. Ancient cities that once were river towns or ports are now ruins on a barren steppe.

By 1500 BCE, just a few centuries after the collapse of Harappa, a new people had established dominance in the region. Called Aryans, these nomads from Central Asia gradually migrated into northern India. Some evidence of violence and flight has been found in Harappan settlements, so there was probably a period of conflict in the overlap of the Aryans and the Indus Valley civilization. The pottery, beads, and burial mounds dating from this transition period show rapid change. Urns were shaped and inscribed differently, and beads were made from new materials. Crops seem to have changed from primarily wheat to mostly rice, probably another indicator of climate change.

The Aryans brought with them an orally transmitted religion based on sacred teachings known as the Vedas. The long-held belief that Hindu religion derived primarily from the Vedas is now being challenged. With the new discoveries in the Indus Valley, scholars now look to pre-Vedic civilization for important clues to the complex and varied beliefs of Hinduism.

Excavations at Harappa, in present-day Pakistan, reveal a well-planned city, with carefully delineated workers' areas, a large citadel, and massive granaries occupying more than 9,000 square feet (836 sq m).

MYSTERIES IN SOAPSTONE, CLAY, AND BRONZE

The religious beliefs and rituals of the Indus Valley civilization remain largely a mystery. Archaeological digs have unearthed numerous steatite (soapstone) seals, as well as clay and bronze figurines. These artifacts tell us much: female figurines bedecked with jewelry seem to prefigure Hindu deities like Lakshmi, a mother goddess or fertility symbol. Other figures, including humans sitting in a yogic position, could indicate that the meditative and transcendental traditions in contemporary South Asian religions have their roots here in the Indus Valley. One commonly recurring image in Harappan art is a horned male figure, while images of potency—bulls, elephants, and tigers—figure prominently.

Yet there is still a missing key: the written Harappan language. Intricate script on the soapstone seals has yet to be deciphered. Pottery and urns were also inscribed. It is believed that the seals may have been used to identify goods that

were meant for export. While we can guess at the purpose of the seals, without the key of language, the precise meaning of the Indus Valley symbols and pictures remains unclear. Excavations are still being carried out, and archaeologists are even analyzing the "handwriting" of the Harappan inscriptions. Are these pictograms? An alphabet? An early record of Sanskrit, or one of the Dravidian languages now spoken in southern India? The mystery has yet to be solved.

Harappan seals, carved in steatite, depict animals and mysterious symbols, whose meanings remain obscure.

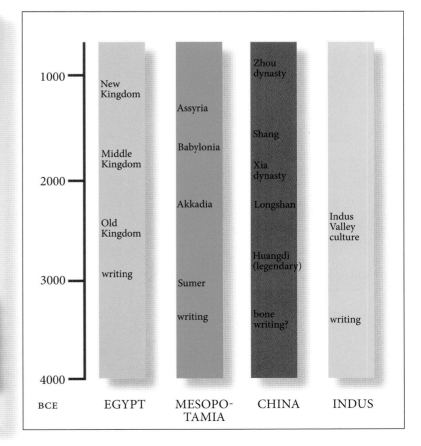

BCE	EGYPT	MESOPO-TAMIA	CHINA	INDUS
1000	New Kingdom	Assyria	Zhou dynasty	
	Middle Kingdom	Babylonia	Shang	
2000		Akkadia	Xia dynasty	
	Old Kingdom		Longshan	Indus Valley culture
3000	writing	Sumer	Huangdi (legendary)	
		writing	bone writing?	writing
4000				

The Birth of Hinduism

NORTHERN INDIA WAS A LOCUS of great and lasting changes during the first millennium BCE. Chief among these changes was the introduction of the Vedas, the sacred works brought into the subcontinent by the nomadic Aryan peoples around 1500 BCE.

The Vedas, initially an oral tradition passed from one generation of the priestly class to the next, were considered to be received sacred wisdom, the divine truth transmitted directly from God to the sages. Indeed, the very word *veda* means "knowledge" in Sanskrit, the dominant language of the Aryans and the primary classical language of India. Vedic deities, rituals, and beliefs remain an integral part of today's Hindu religion and can be found embedded in Buddhist and Jain beliefs as well.

Hinduism itself is not a unified set of beliefs; rather it is a collection of traditions, most of them arising from the Vedic beliefs, but some incorporating beliefs and customs from indigenous or outside traditions. The name "Hindu" is merely the Persian translation of the Sanskrit word *Sindhi*, the name for the Indus River. So in many ways, Hinduism refers more to geography than to one canon of beliefs. Its spread and variety are the result of migration, and societal and political developments.

The deities of the nomadic Aryans differed from those of the agrarian Indus Valley civilization. Instead of ritual bathing in a river (a key Hindu practice that seems to have pre-Vedic origins), Vedic worship was centered on fire and ritual sacrifice. The upper castes presented burnt offerings of food or animals to the gods, hoping to receive divine favors. Scholars disagree about whether human sacrifice was a part of Vedic worship. The Vedas were integral to these solemn rituals, laying out specific incantations, prayers, hymns, and directions to be followed during the sacrifice.

Sophisticated agricultural practices, far-reaching trade, and an ordered society were hallmarks of the ancient Indus Valley civilization, which thrived for at least a millennium. The nomadic Aryan peoples migrated here from Central Asia around 1500 BCE, forever changing the region's culture and religion.

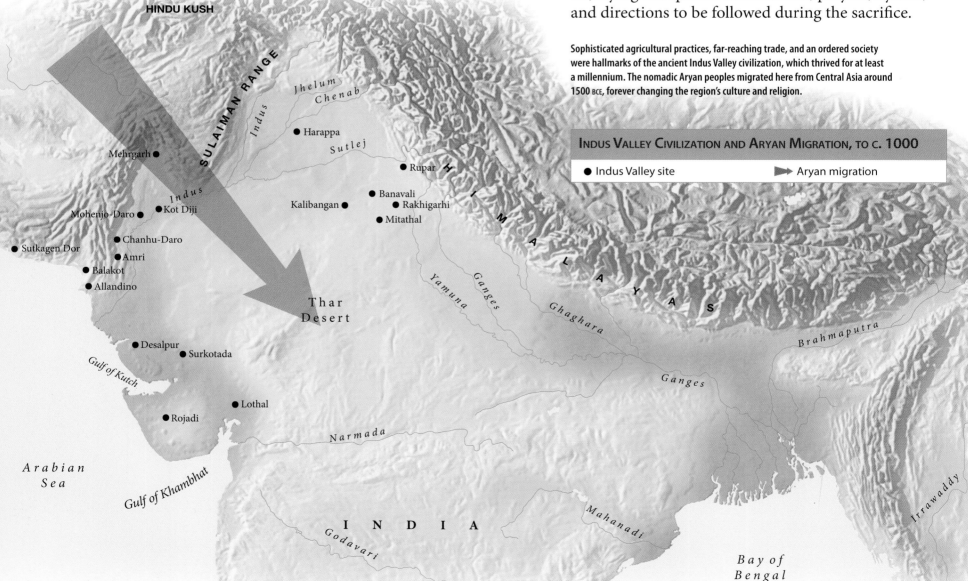

HINDU KUSH

SULAIMAN RANGE

Jhelum
Chenab
Indus
Sutlej

Harappa
Mehrgarh
Rupar
Banavali
Rakhigarhi
Kalibangan
Mitathal
Mohenjo-Daro
Kot Diji
Chanhu-Daro
Sutkagen Dor
Amri
Balakot
Allandino

Thar
Desert

Yamuna
Ganges
Ghaghara
HIMALAYAS
Brahmaputra

Desalpur
Surkotada

Ganges

Lothal
Rojadi

Narmada

Gulf of Kutch

Arabian
Sea

Gulf of Khambhat

INDIA
Godavari

Mahanadi

Bay of
Bengal

Irrawaddy

INDUS VALLEY CIVILIZATION AND ARYAN MIGRATION, TO C. 1000

● Indus Valley site   ➤ Aryan migration

A fragment of the Rig Veda, from an early nineteenth-century manuscript. This sacred text derives from ancient orally transmitted teachings. The earliest written versions appeared in the first millennium BCE.

THE FOUR VEDAS

The Vedas are collected into four separate bodies of work. The Rig Veda, considered the oldest of these, dates to at least the second millennium BCE. Beginning as an oral tradition, the Vedas were written down gradually, probably during the period between 600 and 300 BCE. Their long history makes them among the most ancient of religious texts still in use today. The four Vedas are

- Rig Veda, made up of 1,028 hymns of praise. Many of the later Vedas borrow from or elaborate on these original verses.
- Yajur Veda, primarily a set of directions for priests performing ritual sacrifice. This text is written mostly in short paragraphs of prose rather than verse.
- Sama Veda, like the Rig Veda, a series of hymns and chants, focused on the soma rites. Soma was a mind-altering beverage made from an herb and used in Vedic rituals.
- Atharva Veda, the newest (c. 900 BCE) of the four Vedas and concerned more with nonsacrificial rituals, such as weddings and burials, and with practical wisdom, such as attaining longevity.

Each of the Vedas is separated into four sections. The first is a set of mantras, written in verse, called the Samhitas. This section is followed by the Brahmanas, which are essentially commentary on the verses themselves. Following the Brahmanas are the Aranykas, sometimes called "forest books"; this section of the Veda is intended for those living an ascetic life outside the community.

The Upanishads are the final, somewhat free-form portion of the Vedas. Many take the form of a conversation or dialogue, delving into metaphysical, spiritual, and philosophical questions. The Upanishads are not only the end portion of the Vedas, but are considered a stand-alone body of learning. The root of the word translates as "to sit down near," as a student would sit near a teacher to gain wisdom and knowledge. The Upanishads were collected and written down over time; together their teachings are known as the Vedanta, or the culmination of the Vedas.

THE VEDIC PANTHEON

Aryan gods were seen as manifestations of natural forces and elements. The Vedas name thirty-three gods in all, each representing either the earth, the atmosphere, or the sky. These three elements are each ruled over by a dominant god.

The god of fire, Agni, is the first deity praised in the opening stanzas of the Rig Veda, fire being the element most central to Vedic practices. Fire is seen as a consuming force of nature, shared in by humans, who both consume and are consumed. An offering to the god of fire is intended to appease his unremitting appetite.

Indra, the lord of the heavens, is the Vedic god of the sky, thunder, and war. He is even more revered than Agni and is often referred to as the king of the gods. Legends tell of how Indra freed the waters for use by humans and animals by slaying the dragon Vritra, who had locked up the waters.

Varuna rivals Indra for power in the heavens. He is all-watching, all-seeing, said to employ the stars as his spies. He metes out justice where he sees fit. He is a god of water, and in the middle Vedic period he is associated with the ocean, coinciding with the Aryans' arrival at the coast. The Vedic gods are all male and are seen as bestowing gifts. When there is misfortune, this is because of demons that the gods have not yet conquered.

Indra, the Vedic lord of the heavens, is shown with his wife, Sachi, in this seventeenth-century Rajasthani painting. They are riding Airavata, the white elephant who is said to have made the clouds.

A bronze statue of Indra, one of the Vedic deities who remained an important figure in the Hindu pantheon.

INDIA
Changing Society, Emerging Religions

VEDIC TRADITIONS AND BELIEFS swept through northern India during the first millennium BCE. Archaeological findings of Painted Gray Ware, the pottery used by this culture, show a rapid movement from the Indus Valley eastward toward the Ganges. With this movement came increased contact with indigenous cultures, religious beliefs, deities, and rituals. The Vedic tradition began to adapt and evolve, as the society moved from nomadic to agrarian to urban. The discovery of iron-forging techniques led to new prosperity.

During this prosperous period in the Indus and Ganges valleys, kingdoms and empires began to take shape, and society became more stratified. While there had long been a priestly class in the Vedic tradition, the new hierarchy enumerated four estates, or *varnas*. The

priests, scholars, and nobles were the Brahmins; next in the hierarchy were the warrior class, the Kshatriyas, which included knights and kings. Farmers, merchants, and artisans made up the Vaishya group, while servants and peasants made up the Sudra class. This rigidly defined vertical organization of society may have opened the way for new religious traditions.

The most sacred rite of sacrifice was open only to the top three tiers of the social order established in the Indus and Ganges valleys; the servant class was essentially disenfranchised in both the material and spiritual realms. It has been suggested that the renunciatory and ascetic religious movements that sprang up around 500 BCE are the result of this disenfranchisement of a large portion of the population, who may have willingly embraced beliefs that made a virtue out of poverty.

The large number of religiously significant archaeological sites in northern India identify the region as one of the world's foremost incubators of influential religions.

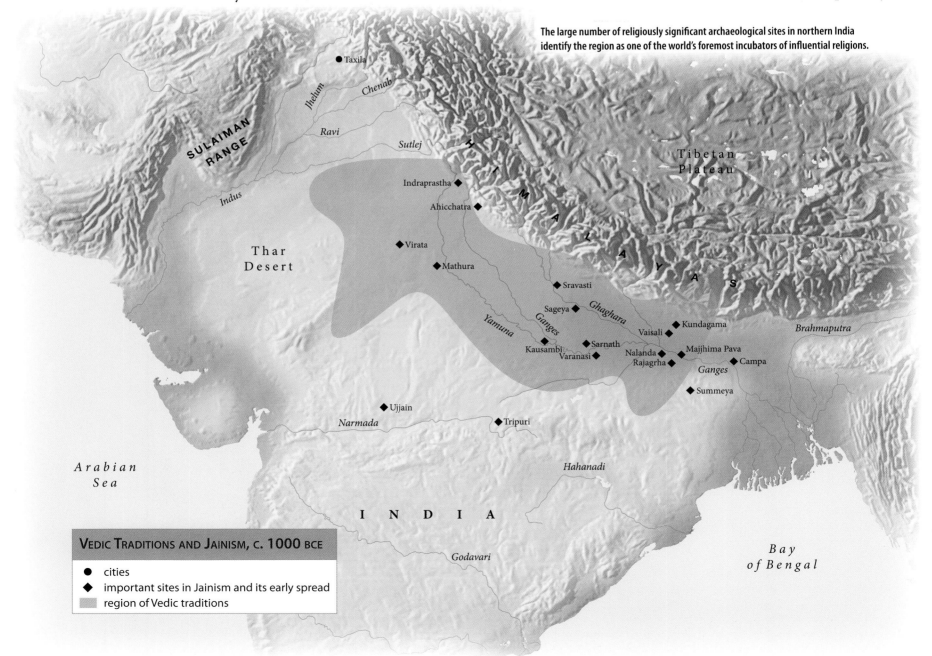

VEDIC TRADITIONS AND JAINISM, C. 1000 BCE

- ● cities
- ◆ important sites in Jainism and its early spread
- region of Vedic traditions

One of the most important sacrifices in Vedic tradition was that of a white stallion. Associated with royal assumption of power, the Asvamedha ritual, as it was called, appears briefly in the Rig Veda, and related rituals may have been practiced as late as the eleventh century CE. Similar practices appear elsewhere in Indo-European civilizations.

Mahavira, the twenty-fourth tirthankara, and one of the great holy figures of Jainism.

The Ascetics

Buddhism, Jainism, and the Ajivika religion originated in India during the years surrounding 500 BCE. These ascetic traditions renounced the worldly and corporeal in favor of the spiritual. They called for fasting, denial of physical comforts, and mendicancy. Some scholars believe that the ascetic movement merely picked up a submerged thread of belief that dated back to pre-Aryan civilization in northern India.

While there are important differences in theology among these three traditions, they share a common and essential belief in karma, which is literally defined as "actions" or "deeds." One's actions through the course of a lifetime are believed to affect the outcome of the next life. The concept of reincarnation is closely linked to karma, with the belief that one will be continually reborn until attaining enlightenment (Buddhism) or *moksha* (Jainism), thereby liberating the soul from the cycle of rebirth. Buddhism and Jainism both forbid the harming or destruction of any sentient being. It follows that these beliefs would reject the sacrifice essential to Vedic practices.

The ascetics, marginalized from the dominant society, soon came to be organized by visionary leaders into a number of sects, Buddhism and Jainism among them. While the founders of these traditions came from noble birth, Buddhism and Jainism initially gained a following among the Sudra class. In short measure, though, the ascetic beliefs gained ground in all levels of society, especially as they were carried abroad by trade, warfare, and migration. While Jainism and Buddhism are still practiced today, the Ajivika tradition, a renunciatory movement, declined around the fourteenth century CE.

Mahavira: Jainism Takes Root

According to Jain belief, time is separated into two half-cycles, each of which lasts some millions of years. In each of these half-cycles, twenty-four teachers, called *tirthankaras,* will appear in succession. A tirthankara is seen as one who will ford the river of rebirth, leading followers to moksha, or liberation. Born around 599 BCE in the Ganges Valley, Mahavira is the twenty-fourth tirthankara of the current age. While he is often called the founder of Jainism, a more correct view is that Mahavira was a key teacher of an ancient tradition.

Mahavira was born Prince Vardhamana, a member of the warrior Kshatriya class and son of King Siddhartha and Queen Trishala. Legend says that the god Indra placed him into the womb of his birth mother, rescuing him from a Brahmin mother's womb; in Jain belief, a tirthankara must be born into the warrior class. At the age of thirty, Vardhamana renounced the world and became an ascetic, spending twelve years in intense meditation and fasting. He acquired the name Mahavira, which literally means "great hero," and acknowledgment of the difficulty and austerity of the spiritual path he followed. Mahavira gathered twelve disciples, who created the Jain scriptures from his teachings. By the time of his death in 527 BCE, Mahavira had gained a large following. During the ensuing centuries, Jainism grew and spread south and westward through the Indian subcontinent.

Elaborate carvings decorate the fifteenth-century CE Jain temple at Ranakpur. Image worship, which encouraged such intricate carvings, had developed within a few centuries after Mahavira's death.

INDIA
The Life of the Buddha

THE ASCETIC MOVEMENT IN INDIA gave rise to a new tradition that would eventually spread throughout Asia, changing the face of the world's religions. The new tradition was Buddhism, and its founder was Siddhartha Gautama, who came to be known as the Buddha, or Shakyamuni Buddha. *Buddha* literally means "the enlightened one"; in Buddhist belief, Gautama Buddha is not a deity, but one who has come to see the truth. He is regarded as the twenty-fourth Buddha, the latest in a succession of Buddhas.

Born around 563 BCE in Lumbini, near the present Indian-Nepalese border, Gautama was a member of a royal family in the city of Kapilavastu. Protected by his family's wealth and status, he married, and fathered a son. Legend says that Gautama's father carefully arranged for his son to never see evidence of human misery. At age twenty-nine, however, Gautama left the palace enclosure and witnessed human suffering and misery for the first time. He saw in succession an aged man, a sick man, a corpse in a funeral procession, and finally a wandering ascetic holy man. These experiences in the life of the Buddha are known as the Four Signs.

Shortly after witnessing these signs, Gautama left home and began a long period of renunciation, fasting, and meditation, including several years sitting under a great tree known as the Bodhi tree in Bodh Gaya, in present-day Bihar. Legend says that here he was visited by a series of worldly temptations delivered by a malevolent deity, Mara. Resisting these, Buddha finally achieved enlightenment. He gathered five disciples in a deer park in Sarnath and gave his first sermon.

For the rest of his life, Buddha traveled throughout the plain of the Ganges, teaching and gaining followers. Gautama Buddha died at the age of eighty at Kushinagar in present-day Uttar Pradesh. His body was cremated, and his ashes were taken by his disciples to form the first Buddhist temples, or stupas.

Siddhartha Gautama, as well as the Buddhist religion he founded, probably traveled on well-established trade routes near the great Ganges River.

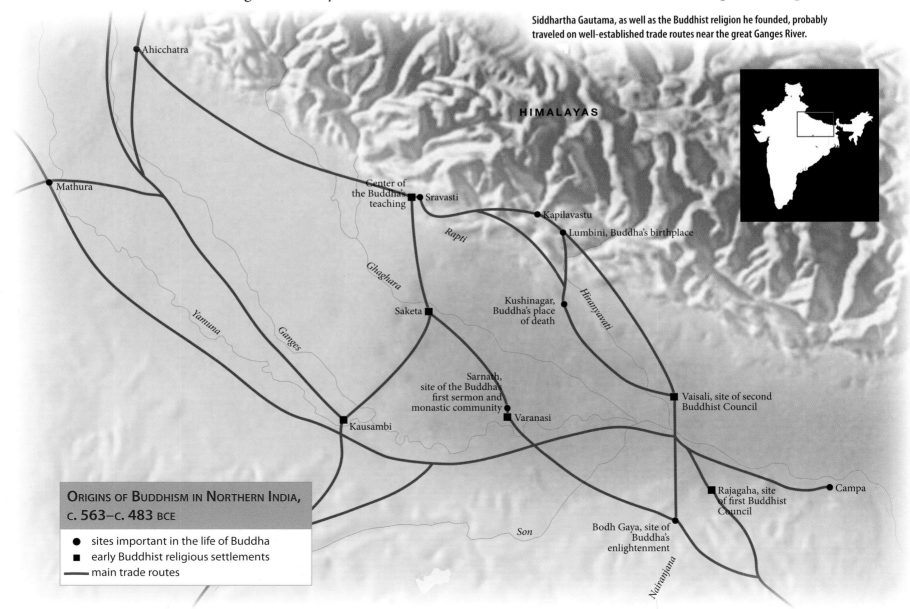

ORIGINS OF BUDDHISM IN NORTHERN INDIA,
C. 563–C. 483 BCE

- ● sites important in the life of Buddha
- ■ early Buddhist religious settlements
- — main trade routes

THE FOUR NOBLE TRUTHS

The core belief of Buddhism, the Four Noble Truths, arose from the Four Signs. What Buddha witnessed of the human condition, and his subsequent reflection on the causes of this condition, led him to classify the truth in four parts. In this case, the word "noble" means enlightened or pure.

1. *Dukkha*: Suffering is inevitable. Suffering refers here to the inevitable aging, disease, and death of the physical body. But it also includes nonphysical suffering: mental, emotional, or spiritual pain. Suffering is rooted in the notion of impermanence. Happiness, satisfaction, health, and indeed life itself are impermanent states of being.

2. *Samudaya*: The origin of suffering is attachment. In various Buddhist traditions, attachment is also known as clinging, craving, or desire. The vain attempt to hold that which is transitory leads to suffering, as we are destined to lose what we strive to hold. Foremost among these objects of attachment is the notion of the "self," which is seen as being as transitory as a moment in time.

3. *Nirodha*: The cessation of suffering is possible. Once the transitory nature of all things is understood, it is possible to live free of suffering. This does not mean that one is free from adversity; rather, that the suffering in the face of adversity can be eliminated by recognizing and practicing nonattachment.

4. *Magga*: The middle path will end suffering. By following these precepts, a person can attain a state of nonattachment. The Eightfold Path is the delineation of the Fourth Noble Truth.

THE EIGHTFOLD PATH

During Buddha's period of renunciation, it is said that he subsisted on one grain of rice a day. When his body was nearly withered, he recognized that extreme self-denial, like extreme self-indulgence, does not lead to enlightenment. He came to believe in a middle path of moderation, laid out in the principles of the Eightfold Path. By following this path, Buddhists believe one can be freed of delusions and eventually attain nirvana.

The numerical sequence doesn't mean that these principles are to be mastered or practiced in any particular order; rather, they are seen as interdependent aspects of one's ideal state. The first two steps confer wisdom, the next three delineate ethical conduct, and the final three address mental discipline. Meditation is the central practice of Buddhism and considered essential to achieving these steps. The steps of the Eightfold Path are:

1. Right Understanding
2. Right Intention
3. Right Speech
4. Right Action
5. Right Livelihood
6. Right Effort
7. Right Mindfulness
8. Right Concentration

One of the most popular early symbols of Buddha were his footprints. Called Buddhapada, the symbol represented Buddha's transcendence and his earthly existence. This example dates to the first century BCE and hails from Gandhara.

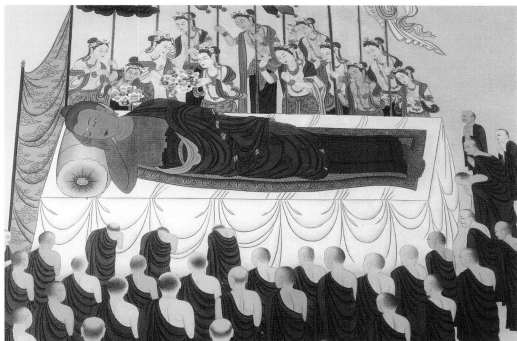

Monks gather at the Parinirvana, or death of Siddhartha Gautama, the Buddha, in 483 BCE.

A rock carving from the Gandhara region of India, dating to the first or second century CE, shows the Buddha departing his sheltered palace life.

China's Ancient Roots

STONE TOOLS FOUND in northeastern China, at Xiaochangliang, date back 1.36 million years. Peking Man, a *Homo erectus* mummy found at Zhoukoudian near Beijing, dates back some 400,000 years. But these clues merely tell us that hominids lived on these lands many millennia ago. What of the culture that eventually became modern China?

Many Neolithic cultures flourished in ancient China and have left behind a wealth of artifacts that point to widely varied beliefs and practices. The two cultures that have been most widely studied are the Yangshao and the Longshan. The Yangshao (5000–1500 BCE) inhabited north and northwest China, and the Longshan (2500–1700 BCE) was centered mostly in the east, around the Yellow River. Sophisticated pottery, jade, masks, burial grounds, sacrificial sites, and evidence of silk production are all signs that archaeologists can use to piece together a picture of advanced agricultural cultures with highly stratified societies.

Rock carvings are another clue to beliefs and practices of ancient peoples. Symbols frequently depict herding, hunting, and religious rituals involving the sun, the moon, and animals. One of the most recent discoveries in China is a series of rock carvings, or petroglyphs, in Damaidi, in present-day Ningxia Province. These appear to date to the ninth millennium BCE. What makes these carvings different from the pictographs found elsewhere, though, is a series of symbols that appear to be precursors of modern Chinese characters.

These findings underscore the belief that Chinese culture is among the world's oldest. As such, its traditional religions are part of a long continuum of varied beliefs. Daoism, Confucianism, and the Chinese branches of Buddhism all have roots in the country's ancient spiritual beliefs. It has long been the case in China that different doctrines and practices can harmoniously coexist. Contemporary Chinese often select various elements of different native religions to call their own. This plurality of worship, ritual, and creed reflects the sweeping landscape of China's geography and history.

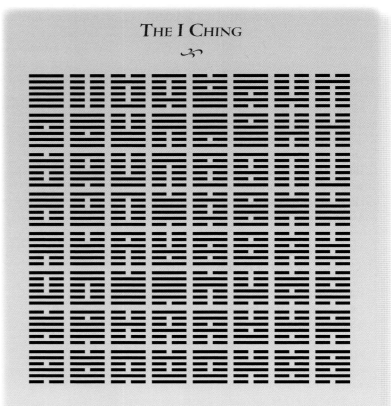

THE I CHING

Opposites attract. Or do they? In the ancient Chinese system of beliefs, the balance between opposites was the primary source of understanding the universe. Pairs of opposites in nature are seen as dynamic forces that interact to create harmony, or lack of harmony. Dark and light, female and male, earth and sky, north and south—in Chinese philosophy, these opposites are expressed as yin and yang. The yin-yang symbol is familiar to westerners and is the symbol for Daoism, the belief system that most closely follows these precepts.

Yin and yang are also the primary components of the I Ching (Yi Jing), an ancient Chinese philosophy and system of divination. In the I Ching, yin, the female, negative energy, is represented as a broken line, and yang, the male, positive energy, is represented as a solid line. Legend says that eight trigrams—stacked combinations of broken and solid lines—were revealed to the mythical god-emperor Fuxi. The eight trigrams were later combined, one on top of the other, and appeared as sixty-four hexagrams. Used as a divination tool, the arrangement of the hexagrams points to the outcome of a question. Yarrow stalks or coins are the traditional tools for Yi Jing divination.

While captured by the last ruler of the Shang dynasty (1600–1046 BCE), King Wen, first of the Zhou dynasty, made an arrangement and began an explanation of the I Ching hexagrams. This version is known as the King Wen sequence. In the sixth century BCE, Confucius made an exhaustive study of the hexagrams. This work, known as the *Book of Changes*, or *I Ching (Yi Jing)*, became one of the Five Classics of Chinese culture.

With its invention credited to the first of China's legendary emperors, Huangdi, tea has remained central to Chinese history and culture and is still grown in massive quantities today.

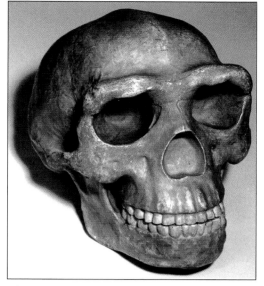

Peking Man, discovered at Zhoukoudian, near Beijing, in 1923, is a fossilized *Homo erectus* skeleton, dating from 550,000 to 230,000 years ago. *Homo erectus* became extinct about 200,000 years ago, and *Homo sapiens* became dominant.

THREE SOVEREIGNS AND FIVE EMPERORS

Before China's dynastic period was the era known as the time of the Three Sovereigns and Five Emperors. These legendary rulers are said to have controlled the region around the Yellow River before the Xia dynasty came to power around 2100 BCE.

The Three Sovereigns, sometimes called the Three August Ones, are mythological figures said to represent the heavens, the earth, and humanity. Legend says that heaven and earth, in the forms of the god Fuxi the goddess Nüwa, were husband and wife, or perhaps brother and sister, who created humankind in the form of the god Shennong. These three sovereigns, and the forces they represent, are part of China's indigenous creation myth. They lie at the heart of the religious and philosophical belief systems that are the bedrock of Chinese culture.

Written Chinese history begins with the reign of the Yellow Emperor, Huangdi, the first of the Five Emperors. History and mythology are closely entwined in the stories of these legendary rulers of the area around the Yellow River. Huangdi in particular is the subject of much lore. He is credited with having invented tea, silk, and writing, and he is sometimes regarded as the ancestor of all Han Chinese. Legend ascribes a nearly hundred-year reign to the Yellow Emperor, from 2697 to 2598 BCE. It is said that he communicated with the gods through shamanism and divination. Huangdi's reign set the precedent for the Mandate of Heaven, the belief that a ruler is divinely chosen. Ensuing Chinese dynasties used the Mandate of Heaven to reinforce the legitimacy of their rule.

This distinctively boat-shaped pot, painted with a fishnet pattern in the Yangshao style, was discovered in Shaanxi Province.

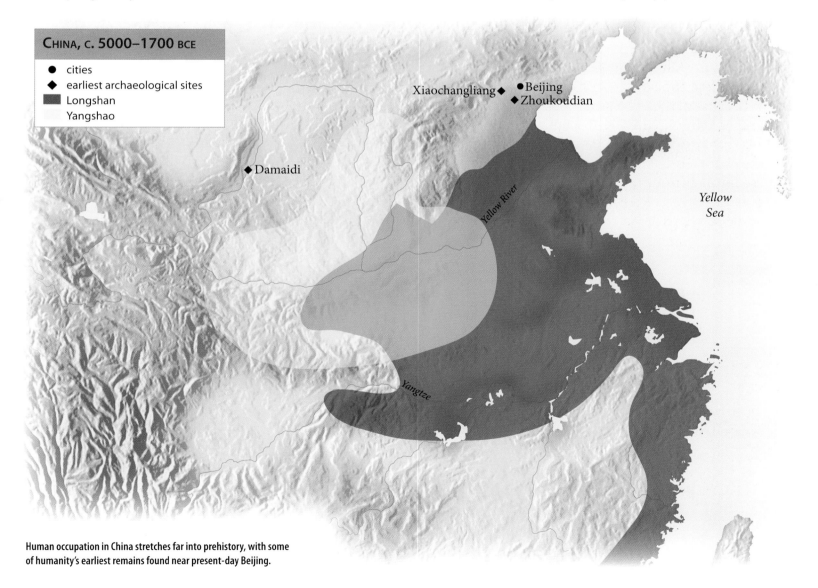

CHINA, C. 5000–1700 BCE
- ● cities
- ◆ earliest archaeological sites
- ■ Longshan
- Yangshao

Xiaochangliang ◆ ● Beijing
◆ Zhoukoudian

◆ Damaidi

Yellow River

Yellow Sea

Yangtze

Human occupation in China stretches far into prehistory, with some of humanity's earliest remains found near present-day Beijing.

China's Earliest Dynasties

CHINA'S DYNASTIC PERIOD BEGINS with the Xia dynasty (2100–1600 BCE). There is some dispute among historians about whether the Xia dynasty really existed, and until recently little archaeological evidence was found. The Xia dynasty ended badly, with a notoriously corrupt leader, Jie, who was plagued by natural disasters, poor military choices, and indulgent practices—all seen as lack of favor from, or obedience to the gods. Legend says that during Jie's reign it snowed in the summer, ruining crops and throwing society into confusion. This strange weather pattern may have been the result of volcanic winter brought on by the seventeenth-century eruption of the Thera volcano in the Aegean. Unlucky, unpopular, and dissolute, Jie was eventually overthrown by Tang, leader of the westerly Shang dynasty.

The Shang dynasty flourished for six hundred years (1600–1046 BCE) and was marked by prosperity, if not peace. The ambitious Shang kings, particularly those of the later Shang period, built an impressive army and set about annexing neighboring lands to the east and south. The society that grew up about this military system was highly stratified, with slaves and prisoners often treated as sacrificial victims. The last Shang king, Shang Zhou, was corrupt and ineffectual. His people rebelled and joined the Zhou, ushering in the next great Chinese dynasty.

The Shang kings amassed great wealth and spent it improving conditions for the aristocratic class. The arts and sciences were well supported, and the Shang developed advanced calendars based on astronomy and mathematics. This period is often credited with producing the earliest writing in China, though ancient rock carvings have since been found that seem to contradict this.

Much of what we know of the Shang dynasty comes from inscriptions carved into tortoise shells and ox bones, known as oracle bones. Over 150,000 of these artifacts have been excavated from Yin, the ancient capital city of the Shang dynasty, in modern Henan Province. These inscriptions tell us much about the religious beliefs of the Shang peoples.

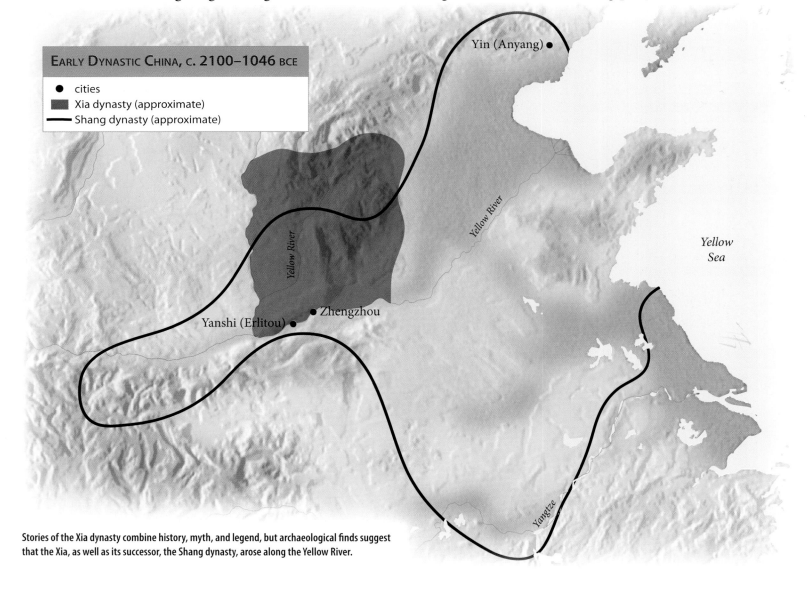

EARLY DYNASTIC CHINA, C. 2100–1046 BCE

● cities
▨ Xia dynasty (approximate)
━ Shang dynasty (approximate)

Yin (Anyang) ●

Yellow River

Yellow Sea

Zhengzhou ●
Yanshi (Erlitou) ●

Yangtze

Stories of the Xia dynasty combine history, myth, and legend, but archaeological finds suggest that the Xia, as well as its successor, the Shang dynasty, arose along the Yellow River.

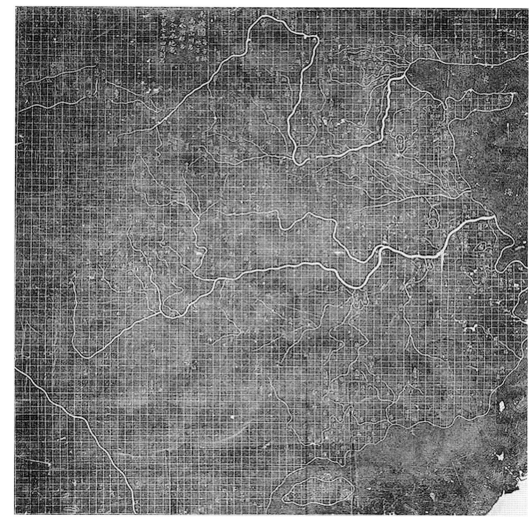

A rubbing taken from an inscribed stone in Xi'an. The stone shows one of the oldest maps in the world, noting provinces paying tribute to the legendary emperor Yu of the first dynasty. It is approximately 4,000 years old.

*In the next ten days
there will be no disaster.*
—ORACLE BONE INSCRIPTION,
CHING-HUA

Knives and coins from the Shang dynasty (on the left) and the Zhou dynasty (on the right).

ONE GOD, MANY ANCESTORS

Worship in the Shang dynasty was focused on two primary sources of otherworldly power. The first of these was Di, or Shangdi, an omnipotent deity, sometimes called the Lord on High.

Di ruled over a pantheon of lesser gods, most of them related to elements in nature. There were gods of rain, wind, sun, and gods of fertility and harvest. There were malevolent gods who caused mayhem and destruction. But Di was the supreme deity over all.

The Shang also practiced an elaborate form of ancestor worship. The ancestors of the aristocratic class in particular were believed to reside in a high court with other gods and spirits. They were seen as somewhat temperamental ghosts who must constantly be appeased through rituals and sacrifices. Offerings were made on a ten-day cycle. Shang-era people believed in an afterlife, a kind of heaven where they would be reunited with their ancestors. This veneration of past relatives is the basis for the Confucian ideal of filial piety, one of the foundations of Chinese society.

THE ORACLE BONES

One of China's most important archaeological finds, the oracle bones were discovered in 1899 by a university chancellor, Wang Xirong. Marketed as "dragon bones," the ancient shells and bones were said to be a cure for malaria. The scholar became fascinated by the arcane inscriptions covering the bones. He discovered that these were tools of divination and records of historical events dating back several millennia. The characters, known as "oracle bone script," are relatively close matches for many modern Chinese characters and appear to use similar structures of grammar and vocabulary.

Foretelling the future, or divining, was practiced in many ancient cultures, using a variety of methods. In the case of the Shang oracle bones, a tortoise shell or ox scapula (shoulder blade), or even the bones or skulls of humans, were carved with several pits or gouges. The diviner, or even the king himself, would ask a question that could be answered in the positive or negative.

The bone was heated over fire until a crack developed; the shape of the crack was the answer to the diviner's question. The diviner would then carve into the bone the date of the divining session, the question asked, the answer given, and even sometimes the outcome, perhaps to prove the accuracy of the method. For example, if an oracle bone foretold an auspicious hunting expedition, and the king indeed came back with a good kill, then this result was added to the records on the bone.

Oracle questions were often about military issues, but nearly as many were about domestic affairs: agriculture, childbirth, travel, weather, and hunting expeditions—a favorite pastime of the ruling class. Before a ritual or sacrifice, the oracle was consulted to determine the proper procedure. Often a question would be directed toward an ancestor, asking for advice or approval on important decisions. If an ancestor were angered, it could mean ruin for a king or even a dynasty.

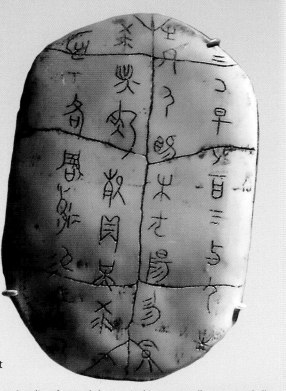

A replica of an oracle bone—in this case actually a tortoise shell.

EAST ASIA

Confucius: The Great Teacher

CONFUCIUS IS MANY THINGS to many people. Some see him as a demigod, akin to the great mythological sages who are said to have ruled ancient China. To others he is a social and political reformer who organized Chinese society into a form we still recognize today. For some, Confucius is the model of a great teacher and master. And still more regard him as China's most venerable philosopher and writer, a man of surpassing wisdom and eloquence.

In his *Analects*, Confucius called himself a "transmitter and not a maker, believing in and loving the ancients." He saw himself as a conduit, one man who gathered and synthesized the wisdom of China's ages and presented it in a structured format for application to practical life. Indeed, when speaking of Chinese culture, it is nearly impossible to separate philosophy, art, religion, and social structure. These elements are all threads of the same fabric of beliefs; Confucius is credited with weaving them together. Most scholars agree that through all the social and political upheavals in China's history, this fabric still holds strong. Confucian beliefs are also essential to the cultures of Korea, Japan, and Vietnam.

Some, particularly in the West, have questioned whether Confucianism—and its cousin tradition, Daoism—is a religion or a philosophy. The answer may be that they are both. Eastern traditions favor a more integrated approach to subjects that are often separated from one another in Western culture. Concepts of the divine are so deeply embedded in ancient Chinese thought that they are manifest in all the teachings of Confucius. The reason to act ethically and righteously stems from the ineffable laws of the universe, the *Dao*, the way.

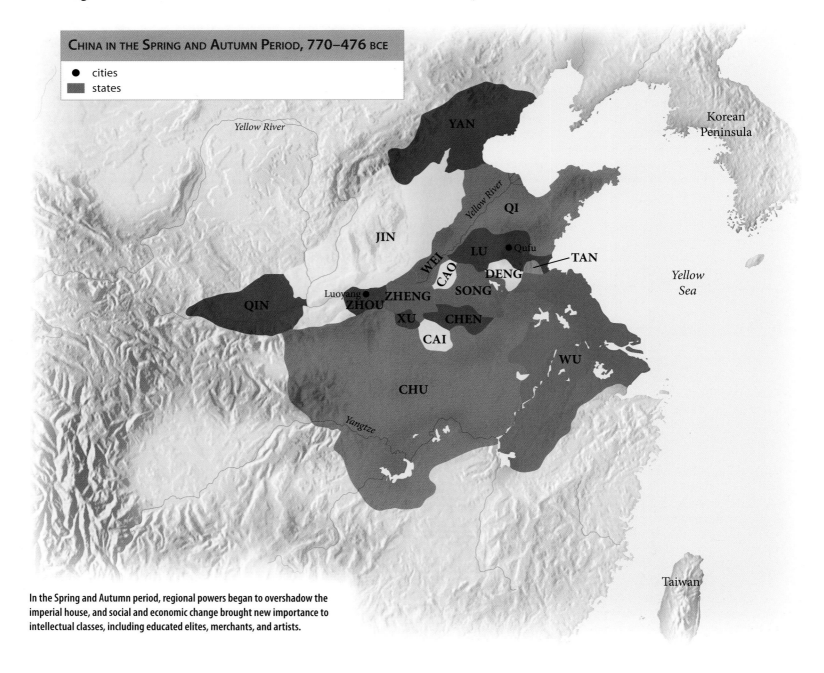

CHINA IN THE SPRING AND AUTUMN PERIOD, 770–476 BCE

● cities
▮ states

Yellow River

Korean Peninsula

YAN

Yellow River

QI

JIN

LU ● Qufu

WEI

CAO

DENG

TAN

Yellow Sea

Luoyang ● ZHENG SONG

QIN ZHOU

XU CHEN

CAI

WU

CHU

Yangtze

Taiwan

In the Spring and Autumn period, regional powers began to overshadow the imperial house, and social and economic change brought new importance to intellectual classes, including educated elites, merchants, and artists.

*What you do not wish for yourself,
do not do to others.*
—ANALECTS OF CONFUCIUS

The entrance to Confucius's grave site and the sacred forest beyond. The Chinese characters read Zhi Sheng Lin, the name of the cemetery.

THE LIFE OF CONFUCIUS

Much of what we know about the life and the teachings of Confucius comes to us from his *Analects* (*Lunyu*), or teachings, which were posthumously written by his disciples and then modified in the ensuing centuries. The Confucius pictured in the *Analects* is a careful, courtly man, eminently concerned with filial piety, honor, and integrity. He considered these traits, along with study and self-reflection, the true hallmarks of nobility, rather than rank or power. The cardinal virtue in Confucius's world-view was *ren*: benevolence, or simply humanity.

Born in 551 BCE in the state of Lu, in what is now the city of Qufu, Shandong Province, Confucius belonged to the social class called *shi*—educated but often poor members of the lower aristocracy. The name "Confucius" is a Latinized version of Kong Fuzi, or K'ung Fu-tzu, which means "great master Kong"—Kong being Confucius's surname. He lived during the Spring and Autumn period (770–476 BCE) of the Eastern Zhou dynasty.

Confucius was three years old when his father died. Growing up in well-educated poverty, he worked menial jobs, married at age nineteen, and when his mother died secluded himself for three years of study and reflection. He began to study the ancients and soon gathered disciples as he shared his teachings. Confucius finally achieved a post in government, as minister of crime, and used the position to enact political reforms. He traveled for over a decade in neighboring states but returned eventually to his home state of Lu, where he is buried.

Confucius died in 479 BCE. He summed up his own life thus: "At fifteen, I had my mind bent on learning. At thirty, I stood firm. At forty, I had no doubts. At fifty, I knew the decrees of Heaven. At sixty, my ear was an obedient organ for the reception of truth. At seventy, I could follow what my heart desired, without transgressing what was right."

Today, Confucius is often portrayed as an elderly, bearded gentleman, with his hands crossed in front of his chest.

The grave of Confucius stands in the middle of a large cemetery of Kong family members in the town of Qufu, in Shandong Province (ancient Lu). Nearby are the Kong family mansion and the largest Confucian temple in the world.

THE FIVE CLASSICS

Confucius is traditionally credited with compiling the body of learning known as the Five Classics. Most modern scholars question the extent of Confucius's work on these five books, but the texts have come to represent the essential canon of Confucian belief. A sixth book, the *Classic of Music*, may have once been included in this collection. Confucius had an almost spiritual reverence for music, and it is said that he sometimes played a qin—a kind of zither—to accompany his oral teachings. The Five Classics are

• *The Classic of Changes* (also called the *Yi Jing*, or *I Ching*). A book of divination that expresses the essential Chinese belief in the eternal nature of change, represented by the opposing forces of nature, which are in constant flux.
• *The Classic of Poetry* (*Shi Jing*). This collection of songs, odes, and hymns draws from Chinese folk tradition, religious liturgy, and ceremonial ritual.
• *The Classic of Rites* (*Li Ji*). The meaning and mores of court ritual, ceremony, and rites of sacrifice are laid out in forty-nine chapters. What remains of the *Classic of Music* is included in this book.

• *The Classic of History* (*Shu Jing*). Ancient Chinese history from the time of the mythological rulers through the Xia, Shang, and Zhou dynasties. Portions of this book are said to be the earliest examples of Chinese prose.
• *The Spring and Autumn Annals* (*Chun Qiu*). The official records of the state of Lu, from 722 to 481 BCE, and the first such history using the format of the annal, or yearly listing of events.

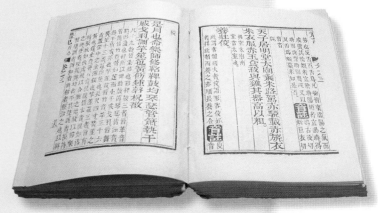

A page from *The Classic of Rites*.

EAST ASIA
Gods and Spirits: Ancient Japan and Korea

MODERN JAPAN AND KOREA have distinctly different cultures and ethnicities. While they have some religious traditions in common—Buddhism in particular—the Japanese and Korean views toward religion and its everyday practice are very different from one another. Even so, there is evidence that these two countries were once connected by a land bridge, allowing free movement between them.

It is thought that the archipelago of Japan, which today consists of four major and many hundreds of smaller islands, was connected to the continent of Asia during the last ice age. Hunter-gatherers entered Japan through two points. The first was from the north, from modern-day Russia, through Sakhalin Island, and onto what is now the island of Hokkaido. The second route was likely through the Korean peninsula, onto the northern tip of modern-day Kyushu. As climate warmed and sea levels rose, the islands of Japan

became separated from one another and from the mainland. The indigenous Jomon culture flourished here for some 10,000 years, until the Yayoi people arrived around 300 BCE. The Yayoi, of Mongolian or northern Chinese ethnicity, brought iron tools, rice cultivation, and Daoist religion from the mainland. They merged with the Jomon people to create the distinct ethnicity, culture, and religion of Japan.

The ethnic ancestors of modern Koreans probably arrived on the Korean peninsula from northeastern China. Ethnic migrations in mainland China may have bypassed the Korean peninsula, allowing a distinct culture to develop. Pottery found from the Bronze Age (c. 3000 BCE), called the Jeulmun period, resembles Jomon pottery found in Japan, sharing similar shapes, manufacture, and comb-pattern markings. Such findings underscore the belief in the shared ancestry of ancient Korea and Japan.

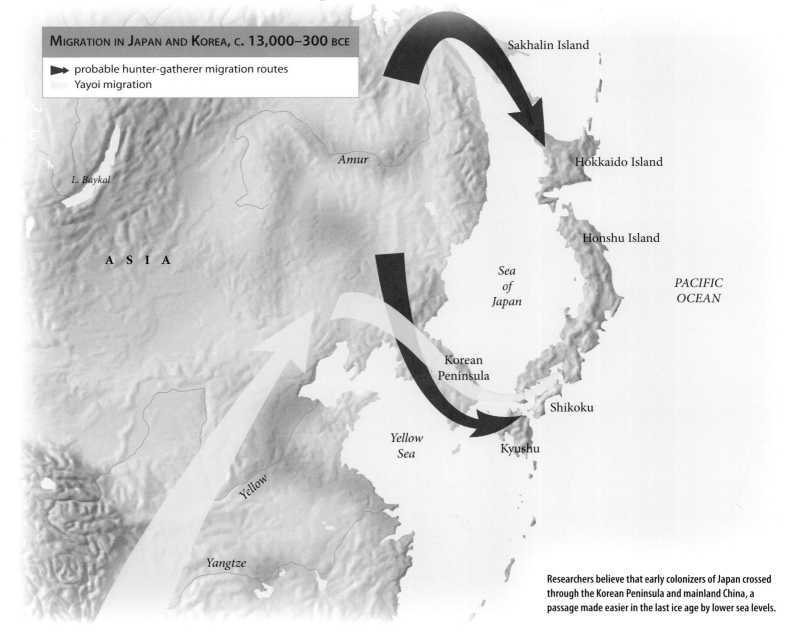

MIGRATION IN JAPAN AND KOREA, C. 13,000–300 BCE

▶ probable hunter-gatherer migration routes
Yayoi migration

Sakhalin Island

Amur

L. Baykal

Hokkaido Island

Honshu Island

ASIA

Sea
of
Japan

PACIFIC
OCEAN

Korean
Peninsula

Shikoku

Yellow
Sea

Kyushu

Yellow

Yangtze

Researchers believe that early colonizers of Japan crossed through the Korean Peninsula and mainland China, a passage made easier in the last ice age by lower sea levels.

A nineteenth-century depiction of Izanami and Izanagi stirring the primordial ocean with a spear in order to create land.

Best known for its sixth-century CE "floating" shrine, Itsukushima Island has been a sacred Shinto site for thousands of years and, in keeping with Shinto's emphasis on natural forms of divinity, is today considered one of Japan's most scenic places.

THE KAMI, JAPAN'S NATIVE SPIRITS

Shinto, the native religion of Japan, has roots in the ancient Jomon culture. The name *Shinto* derives from the Chinese *shin dao,* meaning "the way of the gods." But before the religion had a name, or any elements of Chinese Daoism, it had rituals, beliefs, legends, and above all, an elaborate creation story.

Traditional Japanese beliefs begin with the *kami,* sacred spirits of nature. The sun, moon, trees, rocks, ocean, mountains, and rivers were all believed to be inhabited by kami. Kami were present in the heavens and on earth, but they originated in the heavens. In Japanese mythology, there were seven generations of gods, culminating with Izanagi and Izanami, male and female—perhaps brother and sister—who created the islands of Japan using a jeweled spear. They begot several children as well, but Izanami died giving birth to the fire-god, Kagutsuchi. After this, Izanami ceased to be a goddess of creation and became a goddess of death.

The mythological Japanese underworld, Yomi, claimed Izanami after her death. Her husband determined to seek her out there, but he was too late; Izanami had eaten of the food of the dead. After a narrow escape from Yomi, Izanagi performed a cleansing ritual and gave birth from his left eye to a daughter, Amaterasu, the sun goddess, and from his right eye a son, Tsukuyomi, the moon god. He also begot a jealous sibling, Susano'o, the

god of storms, out of his nose. Of the three, Amaterasu, whose name means "that which illuminates the heavens," is the most powerful and important Shinto deity.

The ancient Japanese culture employed shamans in the performance of sacred worship rites. These men, and perhaps women, were intermediaries between the gods and the people, though this distinction is less valid in a religion that sees humans as also imbued with kami, or divine spirit. Formal ritual is an important part of contemporary Japanese religion; its roots lie in its most ancient spiritual beliefs.

GOJOSEON: KOREA'S FIRST KINGDOM

Korea's long history of human habitation is crystallized in mythology with an ancient kingdom known as Gojoseon. This kingdom, translated as "old Joseon," was the realm of a legendary god-king, Dangun Wanggeom (also called Tan'gun). Dangun is said to have founded his kingdom in 2333 BCE on the border between Manchuria and modern-day North Korea.

Legend says that Dangun was the grandson of heaven, descended from the lord of the

heavens, Hwanin. Hwanin had a son, Hwanung, who wished to live on the earth. Finally the father was persuaded, and allowed his son to descend to Mount Baekdu, on the Taebaek mountain range, accompanied by 3,000 helpers. Dangun was born from the union of Hwanung and Ungnyeo, a bear who had been transformed into a woman. In Korean mythology, these are the progenitors of the Korean people. This mythology has retained popularity as a means of expressing the particular quality of Korean culture and as a way to distinguish its origins from those of its powerful neighbor, China.

It is worth noting that the symbol of the bear is also important in the Jomon culture of ancient Japan. Indeed, the bear is central to the symbolism and mythology of the Ainu ethic group of Japan, who are believed to be directly descended from the Jomon.

A Jomon vessel dating to the fourth millennium BCE shows comb-pattern markings and decoration made with a slim cord or rope.

In Korean mythology, Mount Baekdu, located on the border of North Korea and China, is the legendary place of origin of the Korean people. Rising more than 9,000 feet (2,744 m) high, it is the highest mountain on the Korean peninsula.

AMERINDIAN
Migration from Asia

It seems likely that the first humans came to the Americas from Siberia. Some 20,000 or more years ago, when ice age glaciers impounded huge quantities of the world's water, sea levels fell to some 300 feet lower than they are today, exposing a land bridge at what is now the Bering Strait, between Siberia and Alaska. Humans crossed over into North America and gradually migrated south. They spread out across North America and continued south, reaching the tip of South America by 9000 BCE.

The last group of immigrants crossed the Beringia land bridge in about 8000 BCE, at which time the last ice age ended and the melting glaciers released the pent-up waters, which covered the land bridge. Many of this last group of immigrants remained in the Arctic regions and became the ancestors of the Aleuts and Inuits.

Although none of the religious ideas of the early Arctic tribes survive, numerous myths of the later Inuits may carry on the traditions of their ancient forebears. According to one Inuit creation myth, Raven, a man with a raven's beak, created the world. When he was still a boy, Raven was playing with a bladder that had been kept over his father's bed. When the bladder broke, daylight escaped, but his father took the bladder away and kept it safe, preserving some darkness, lest it always be day. In this way night and day began. Later Raven used his spear to draw the land up out of the water.

By 10,000 BCE humans had reached the Americas, most probably from Siberia when sea levels were lower and ocean crossings simpler. By 500 BCE humans had settled widely over North America, and several distinct culture groups had emerged.

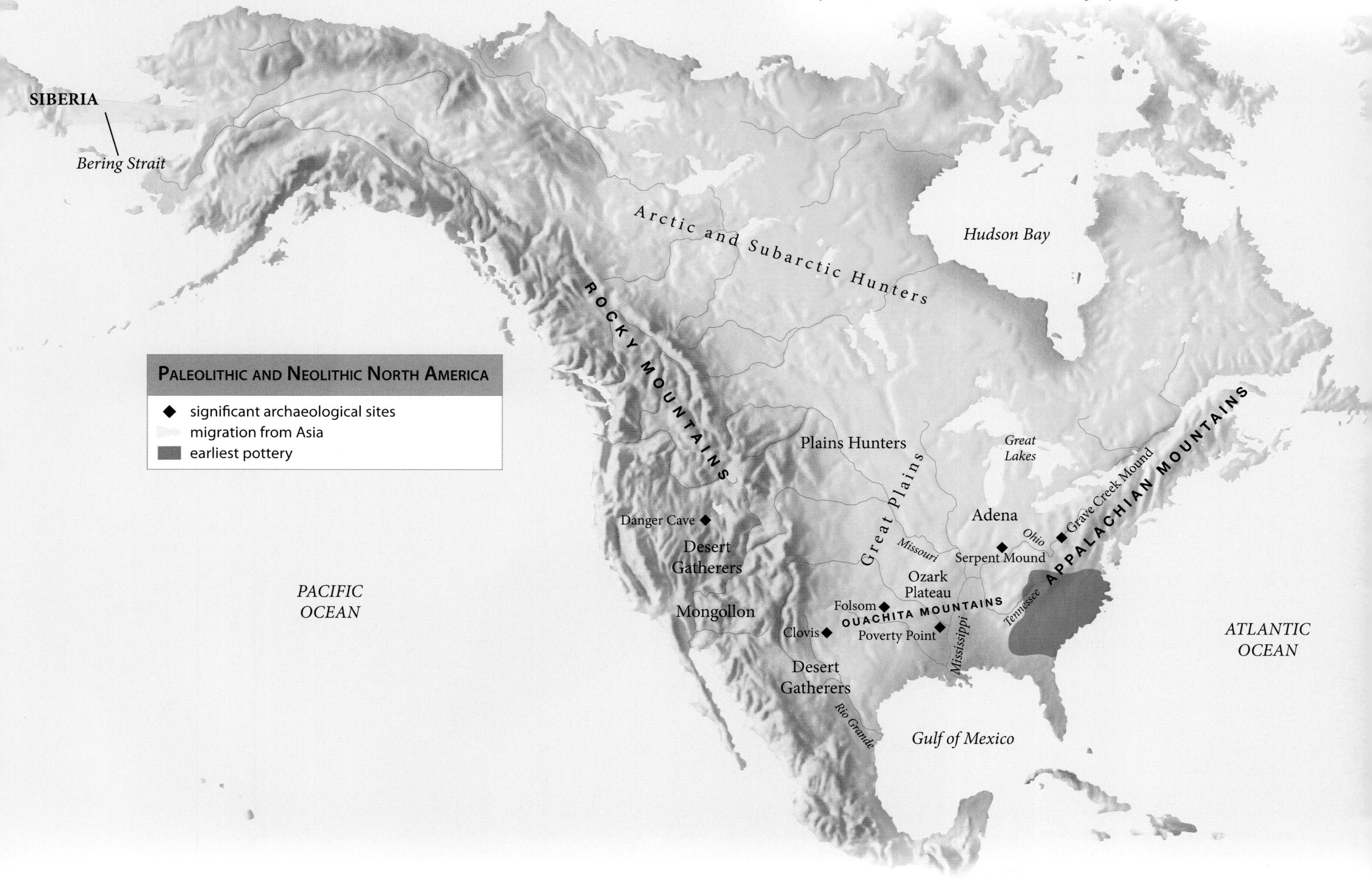

SIBERIA

Bering Strait

Arctic and Subarctic Hunters

Hudson Bay

ROCKY MOUNTAINS

PALEOLITHIC AND NEOLITHIC NORTH AMERICA

◆ significant archaeological sites
migration from Asia
earliest pottery

Plains Hunters

Great Lakes

Great Plains

APPALACHIAN MOUNTAINS

Grave Creek Mound

Adena

Ohio

Danger Cave ◆

Missouri

Serpent Mound ◆

Desert Gatherers

Ozark Plateau

PACIFIC OCEAN

Mongollon

Folsom ◆

OUACHITA MOUNTAINS

Tennessee

ATLANTIC OCEAN

Clovis ◆

Poverty Point ◆

Mississippi

Desert Gatherers

Rio Grande

Gulf of Mexico

*Look at me, friend!
I come to ask for your dress
Since there is nothing you cannot be used for.
I come to beg for this,
Long-life maker.*
—KWAKIUTL PRAYER TO A CEDAR TREE

EARLY NORTH AMERICANS

Most of the early inhabitants of North America were hunters and gatherers, or fishermen along the coasts. They generally kept on the move, possibly pursuing game or milder climates or fleeing enemies. Generally they traveled in small numbers, but sometimes, as in the Great Plains, they grouped together to pursue large herds of buffalo or other prey. Some settled down. In about 4500 BCE the first pottery appeared in Georgia and the first copper implements were made in the Great Lakes region. Sometimes while the men were out hunting, women did small-plot farming.

In about 1000 BCE a people now known as the Mogollon settled in the highlands of Arizona and New Mexico. They grew corn and other crops. At first they lived in shallow pit houses but later in multiroom complexes. They would eventually develop fine pottery, starting with plain earthenware but evolving into colorful vessels adorned with figures of animals and people, which may or may not have had religious significance. Their culture would peak in the second century CE.

MOUND BUILDERS

Between 500 BCE and 100 CE people in east-central North America apparently gathered together around ceremonial earth mounds for some sort of rituals, but the nature of their religious beliefs remains unknown. Although the mounds would come to be named for the later Hopewell Indians, the earliest were built by the Adena, a woodland people of the Ohio River Valley, in about 500 BCE.

The Adena built their mounds as part of a burial ritual, piling earth atop a burned

Danger Cave—actually a series of caves in the Utah desert near Wendover, Nevada—shows evidence of human occupation from 11,000 BCE.

mortuary building. The buildings themselves were likely intended to keep and maintain the dead until their final burial was performed. Before the construction of the mounds, utilitarian and grave goods would be placed on the floor of the structure along with the dead. Then the body, goods, and building were all burned to honor the dead, and a mound was constructed over everything. Often a new mortuary structure would be placed atop a new mound. After a series of such repetitions, a prominent earthwork would remain. Grave Creek Mound, which is 62 feet high and 240 feet in diameter, is the largest conical type burial mound in the United States. It is located in Moundsville, West Virginia.

Grave Creek Mound took one hundred years and more than 60,000 tons of earth to build. It is unknown why this mound should be so much larger than other Adena mounds.

POVERTY POINT MOUNDS

Mounds serving a purpose different from those of the Adena were constructed between 1650 and 700 BCE in the Mississippi River floodplain in northeastern Louisiana. The central construction consisted of six rows of five-foot-high concentric ridges, forming a partial octagon with five aisles. The outermost ridges (three-quarters of a mile in diameter) probably served as foundations for dwellings. A large bird-shaped mound at the back of the configuration may have been used for religious ceremonies. The site is known as Poverty Point, after a nineteenth-century plantation that had to cope with poor soil.

The building of the Poverty Point site was an amazing undertaking. Laborers carried earth to the site in baskets that weighed fifty pounds when full and worked with simple hand tools. The construction also required widespread trading. Stone implements found there were made with raw materials from the Ouachita and Ozark mountains and from the Ohio and Tennessee river valleys. Soapstone for vessels came from the Appalachian foothills. The inhabitants of Poverty Point were obviously among the most advanced of all the early peoples in North America up to the year 500 BCE.

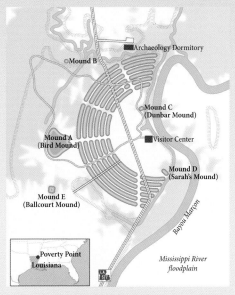

A schematic drawing of Poverty Point.

Mesoamerica and South America

WHEREAS LIFE IN NORTH AMERICA stayed relatively simple through 500 BCE, at least two highly sophisticated cultures emerged—one in Mesoamerica (from Mexico to Panama) and another in the South American Andes. But first there were small advances.

Pottery appeared in Ecuador and Colombia as early as 4000 BCE, and by 1000 BCE it had even reached the Amazon. Often the pottery included figurines of nude females, which may have been associated with a fertility cult. At Monte Albán, near Oaxaca, Mexico, sculptures of dead men were found with unreadable hieroglyphs added near the heads of the figures— possibly the names of the individuals represented. Accompanying slabs bear calendrical notations. And so the Monte Albánites seem to be the first peoples in the Americas to develop writing or refer to the calendar in written form.

Pyramid structures have been found at some sites, including two at Río Seco in the Andes. Between 1500 and 1200 BCE, a twenty-six-foot-high pyramidlike mound was erected at Ocós, on the Pacific coast of Mesoamerica. The mound probably once supported some kind of building, suggesting a highly stratified society in which the leader of the people resided in a high palace. Later Mesoamericans would build pyramids as the final resting places of great leaders. A large tiered pyramid, which seems to have been used for religious purposes, was built between 800 and 600 BCE at Cuicuilco on the Mexican plateau. Finally, in Guatemala soon after 600 BCE, the Mayans began building small ceremonial centers with modest-size pyramid platforms—hints at the splendors to come.

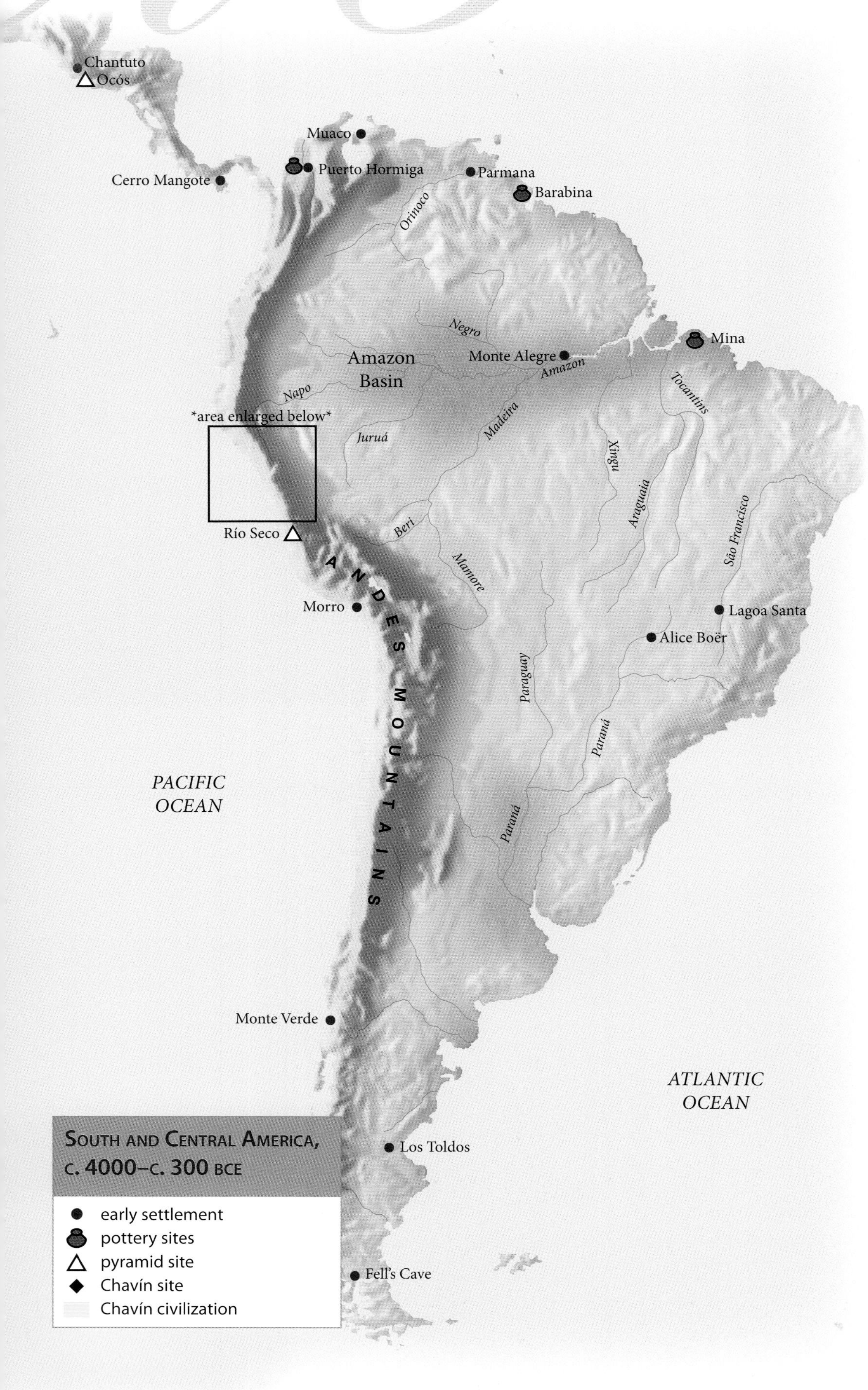

Map labels (main map)

Chantuto
Ocós
Muaco
Cerro Mangote
Puerto Hormiga
Parmana
Barabina
Orinoco
Mina
Negro
Amazon Basin
Monte Alegre
Amazon
Napo
Tocantins
area enlarged below
Juruá
Madeira
Xingu
Beri
Araguaia
São Francisco
Río Seco
Mamoré
Morro
ANDES MOUNTAINS
Lagoa Santa
Paraguay
Alice Boër
Paraná
Paraná
PACIFIC OCEAN
Paraná
Monte Verde
ATLANTIC OCEAN

Legend

SOUTH AND CENTRAL AMERICA, C. 4000–C. 300 BCE

- ● early settlement
- ⬗ pottery sites
- △ pyramid site
- ◆ Chavín site
- ▢ Chavín civilization

Los Toldos
Fell's Cave

By about 1000 BCE, civilizations in South and Central America were designing complex artwork and monumental structures. Unlike the great early civilizations in Asia, these grew not near fertile river valleys but in the more surprising environments of dense jungle and high mountains.

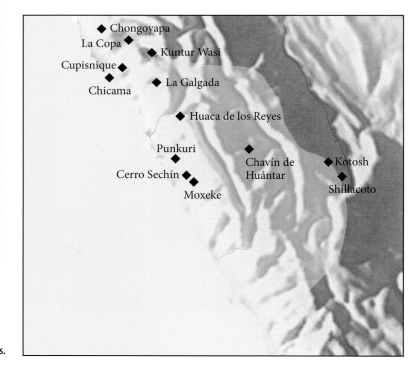

Chongoyapa
La Copa
Kuntur Wasi
Cupisnique
La Galgada
Chicama
Huaca de los Reyes
Punkuri
Chavín de Huántar
Kotosh
Cerro Sechín
Moxeke
Shillacoto

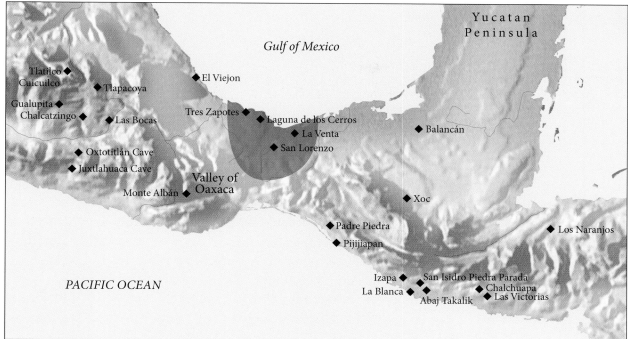

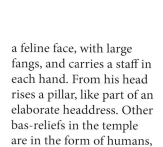

Gulf of Mexico

Tlatilco
Cuicuilco
Tlapacoya
El Viejon
Gualupita
Chalcatzingo
Las Bocas
Tres Zapotes
Laguna de los Cerros
La Venta
San Lorenzo
Balancán
Oxtotitlán Cave
Juxtlahuaca Cave
Valley of Oaxaca
Monte Albán
Xoc
Padre Piedra
Los Naranjos
Pijijiapan
PACIFIC OCEAN
Izapa
San Isidro Piedra Parada
La Blanca
Chalchuapa
Abaj Takalik
Las Victorias

a feline face, with large fangs, and carries a staff in each hand. From his head rises a pillar, like part of an elaborate headdress. Other bas-reliefs in the temple are in the form of humans, jaguars, eagles, snakes, and crocodiles. They may have been intended as attendants to the gods rather than objects of worship.

Chavín is noted for its fine artwork, as found in painted textiles, pottery, and especially stone carvings. It would have a strong artistic influence on the people of what is now northern and central Peru until about 200 BCE.

The helmets worn by the colossal stone Olmec heads lead some to suspect that the figures represent ballplayers in a game known from Olmec figurines.

THE OLMEC

The earliest of the two great primitive American cultures, the Olmecs, first appeared in about 1150 BCE at San Lorenzo, Mexico. There a large ceremonial structure stood at the end of a long rectangular court that was defined by two long parallel mounds and some 200 small mounds supporting houses of pole and thatch. Throughout the complex stood massive basalt sculptures—many in the form of colossal human heads. Some of these heads weighed as much as forty tons and stood up to nine feet high.

San Lorenzo was destroyed (perhaps by invaders) around 900 BCE, but the culture continued to thrive elsewhere, notably at La Venta on an island in the Tonalá River. The site includes large structures and tombs. Kings or priests there wore concave mirrors around their necks to impress the populace with their supernatural powers. (The mirrors could project pictures onto flat surfaces and even start fires.) Basalt monuments, including colossal heads, were also found at La Venta. The Olmec influence spread far and wide throughout Mesoamerica until about 300 BCE.

THE CHAVÍN

In the Peruvian Andes yet another remarkable culture appeared about two centuries after the start of the Olmec civilization. The Chavín emerged in about 900 BCE and quickly grew. Although there were numerous Chavín temples, the chief temple seems to have been the one at Chavín de Huántar, which is situated at an elevation of 10,530 feet on a tributary of the Marañón River. It was also the only Chavín site with a town attached.

The temple at Chavín is a gigantic structure of rectangular stone blocks with interior galleries at different levels and shafts to provide ventilation. In a U-shaped section of the temple stands a fifteen-foot-high white granite figure in the shape of a human with snakes for hair and fangs in the upper jaw. This is sometimes known as the smiling god, to distinguish him from the so-called standing god that was once kept in another part of this temple and that is also duplicated in many of the other Chavín temples.

The standing god is a bas-relief sculpture on a large stone. The semihuman figure has

Sculptures like these, called "tenon-heads," decorated the exterior walls of Chavín. They combine human and feline elements.

OLMEC RELIGION

The Olmec pantheon consisted of deities that were hybrids between a jaguar and a human infant. There is actually a whole spectrum of such figures in Olmec art, ranging from almost entirely feline to mostly human. They were generally shown crying or snarling with open mouth. Nothing is known of the nature of these gods, as the Olmecs left no written records. The figures may not actually represent gods at all, or they may present aspects of a single deity. Some scholars hold that the Olmecs practiced shamanism.

A 3,000-year-old jade Olmec ax, carved in the shape of a human-jaguar. The skill of the carving and the choice of subject suggest the ax was a ritual object.

Australia

About 50,000 years ago humans first settled in Australia, which because of lower sea levels was then joined as a single landmass with New Guinea and Tasmania. Sometime during the next 10,000 years New Guinea and Tasmania were settled. Then, in about 28,000 BCE, a new wave of immigrants arrived in the Solomon Islands. These early settlers must have been hardy, for they sailed from Asia across vast spans of sea to reach their new homes. However, the trip was probably not as arduous as it would be today, as lower sea levels may have created a kind of land bridge in certain areas, limiting the amount of sailing the pioneers had to do. Even so, they were not soon emulated, for no new peoples came to Australia or Oceania for the next 25,000 years.

When sea levels rose to their present level—probably between 6000 and 5000 BCE—the coasts of Australia were submerged, making the small continent even smaller and cutting it off from New Guinea and Tasmania. By this time Aborigines were scattered through much of the land, and they continued to live as they had in the past and as they would for thousands of years to come.

The Aborigines never took up agriculture, and there were no animals in Australia suitable for herding. Consequently, they lived by hunting and gathering. For this they formed tribes made up of several small groups. The tribes generally lived in a spot associated with the leader's totemic ancestor.

Some 50,000 years ago the islands of New Guinea, Australia, and Tasmania were part of the same landmass. Settlement patterns tended to follow rivers and shorelines, and as a result several of the earliest archaeological sites are now underwater.

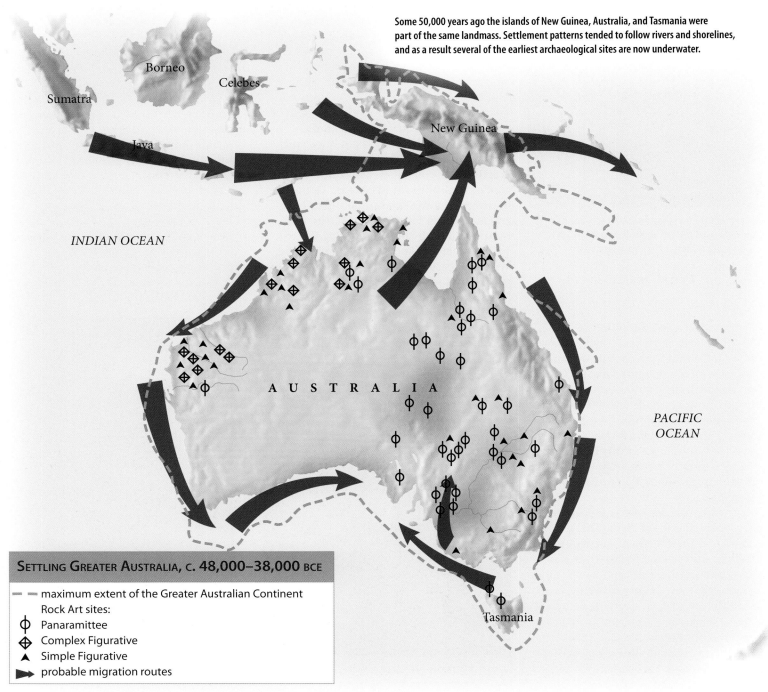

SETTLING GREATER AUSTRALIA, C. 48,000–38,000 BCE

- – – maximum extent of the Greater Australian Continent
  Rock Art sites:
- ⏀ Panaramittee
- ⏀ Complex Figurative
- ▲ Simple Figurative
- ➤ probable migration routes

When the emu egg was hurled up to the sky it struck a great pile of wood that had been gathered by a cloud man named Ngoudenout. It hit the wood with such force that the pile instantly burst into flame, and flooded the earth with the soft, warm light of dawn.

—FROM AN ANCIENT ABORIGINE DREAMING

One of the earliest art forms at Kakadu (in Australia's Northern Territory) are large, naturalistic figures, often of kangaroos and sometimes completed with red ocher, as here.

SPIRITUAL ANCESTORS

The Aborigines believe, as they have for millennia, that each individual is the incarnation of one of the *wandjinas*, the ancestral spirits (human or animal) who had made the earth habitable and supplied it with animals, plants, and natural phenomena. A man is expected to continue the good work of his totemic ancestor. For example, a man with a kangaroo ancestor is obligated to act out rituals to insure a sufficient supply of kangaroo meat for his tribe. He also has to tell stories to keep the memory of his ancestor fresh. The actual ancestor, who was born out of eternity, is currently resting until it is time for him to be reborn again. By enacting rituals and telling stories, known as the Dreaming, the Aborigines assure themselves of maintaining a continuity of life.

ROCK ART

The Aborigines keep in touch with their ancestors through art as well as ritual and storytelling. Cave art of incredible antiquity is found in many parts of the continent, some of it going back at least 43,000 years. The earliest paintings, in a style known as Panaramittee, are characterized by small circles, crescents, radiating lines, footprints, or animal tracks.

According to legend they were painted by birds who pecked the rock until their beaks bled and then used the blood as paint and their tails as brushes.

A second style of paintings, termed the Simple Figurative, is characterized by silhouettes of humans or animals. A final category, the Complex Figurative, which is found only in the north and west, consists of four substyles. In the Dynamic substyle, stick human figures wear ornaments and carry spears and boomerangs; some have animal heads or are shown with now-extinct animals, such as the Tasmanian wolf. In the Estuarine substyle, crocodiles predominate; and in the X-ray substyle, people or animals are depicted with their internal organs showing. Finally, some paintings simply show ceremonial feathered fans.

A unique group of paintings, found only near Kimberley in Western Australia, represent wandjinas, the ancestral spirits of the Dreamings, which are depicted with large white faces and no mouths. Aborigines believe that the wandjinas created their own images in these paintings and continue their existence through them. To this day the oldest living member of the local Aborigine tribe is responsible for maintaining the figures.

Australian Aborigines still paint in caves first decorated about 20,000 years ago in Australia's Kakadu National Park. Often figures are repainted or painted over, leaving a legacy of multiple styles and stories.

DREAMTIME AND ITS STORIES

Aborigines are committed to storytelling, and in sessions they refer to as Dreamtime they pass tales down from generation to generation. By keeping these stories alive they remain in touch with their ancestral spirits, who came from the time before time began. Each tale, or Dreaming, is instructive or mythic and often involves animals, as many of the ancestral spirits were animals. In one Dreaming some animals discover that the drought they are suffering occurred because a giant frog had swallowed all the water in the land. The animals group together and keep trying to make the frog laugh. When an eel finally succeeds in doing so, the frog laughs so hard that all the water he had swallowed rushes out of his mouth like rolling thunder. The drought is over. By retelling this tale the Aborigines may hope for continued good weather.

Oceania

ALTHOUGH AUSTRALIA HAD BEEN SETTLED at a very early date, the numerous islands to the north and east of it, known collectively as Oceania, remained uninhabited for thousands of years afterward. Oceania is actually made up of three major island groups. Micronesia consists of islands north of the equator, ranging from the Marianas and Palau in the west to the Marshall Islands in the east. Melanesia is made up of the islands of the southwestern Pacific from New Guinea to Fiji. Polynesia includes the islands found within the vast triangle drawn from Hawaii in the north to New Zealand in the southwest and Easter Island in the far southeast.

New Guinea, Tasmania, and the Solomon Islands were settled by 28,000 BCE, but little is known of these early settlers. Then, in about 4000 BCE, domestic Asian plants and animals mysteriously appeared in New Guinea and fields were drained, allowing agriculture to be added to the hunting-and-gathering lifestyle of the islanders. No further colonization of Oceania was forthcoming over the next two millennia.

A new wave of settlers came to Oceania in about 2000 BCE and settled in the islands of western Melanesia. Beginning in about 1400 BCE the colonists included a group of merchants probably from Indonesia, who became known for their pottery, which was in a style known as Lapita. Over the centuries, these Lapita merchants continued to move eastward, reaching Fiji by 1300 BCE. Three or four centuries later they went from Fiji to Tonga and Samoa at the western edge of Polynesia. In Samoa (and to a lesser degree Tonga) the people slowly came to adopt a more Indonesian way of life. When these people eventually spread to the more distant islands of Polynesia, beginning in about 150 BCE, they took this culture with them.

Nearly 230 miles separate the western edge of the Solomon Islands and the Santa Cruz Islands, the first great leap eastward made by the Lapita more than 3,000 years ago. Even greater distances awaited these early explorers, who must have developed sophisticated sailing techniques despite their Neolithic technology.

LAPITA SETTLEMENT IN OCEANIA, C. 2000–C. 900 BCE

— maximum spread of Lapita culture
Lapita migration
non-Lapita pottery discoveries

As welcoming as islands of the South Pacific are, it must have been a daunting journey for the Lapita to travel to them. Researchers speculate that cloud banks, birds, and ocean currents may have given them the clues they needed to reach land, but the specifics of their amazing travels remain mysterious.

EARLY SETTLERS

Oceania was settled by a succession of migrations from Southeast Asia, with each group of immigrants bringing in different aspects of the culture that was to take root in Oceania. And so various groups introduced agriculture, tools, pottery, and artifacts made from shells, bone, and coral. In Micronesia, immigrants who may have been from the Philippines introduced houses with stone pillars, stepped tombs, and even stone money.

Religion varied from island to island, but most of the people worshipped gods who gave them land and taught them crafts, and revered tribal ancestors and the spirits of the recent dead. Tribespeople kept in touch with their deities through dreams, prophets, and mediums and participated in ritualistic song and dance. To prepare them for manhood, boys went through complex rituals that included bloodletting. Myths were used to teach. For example, stories about Aluluei, a god of seafaring, were used to train navigators.

LAPITA PEOPLE

The immigrants who made the most lasting contributions to Oceania's culture were the so-called Lapita people, named after the style of pottery they brought with them. (Lapita is the name of a site in New Caledonia where much of this pottery was found.) The Lapita people probably came from Indonesia and settled first in the Solomon Islands in about 1400 BCE. They lived on small islands or on the coasts of larger islands, building houses on stilts at the water's edge. They fished, raised pigs, chickens, and dogs, and grew fruit and nut trees. They also made exquisite pottery.

The Lapita people traveled far over the centuries, and whenever they moved on to a new island they brought along animals, plants, tools, and other goods, thereby enriching the life in the many islands they colonized. They also brought along their distinctive pottery, spreading it far and wide.

Lapita pottery came in many forms, including dishes, jars, and bowls. Decoration was pressed into the pottery with toothed stamps. The simplest designs were geometrical. Others incorporated stylized faces. Lapita pottery flourished only until about 140 BCE but still managed to influence the art of Polynesia, whose more distant islands were still being settled.

An intricate pottery pattern (from the Solomon Islands, c. 1000 BCE) characteristic of the Lapita style. The "Lapita face" motif, visible on the right despite the piece's fragmentary state, recurs on Lapita pottery, but its meaning is not fully understood.

OCEANIA'S CANOES

For these island people, who did a lot of fishing and traveled from island to island, boats were of primary importance. Generally, they used some version of the outrigger canoe, which could negotiate shallow waters as well as deep and then be hauled ashore with little trouble. The hulls of these canoes were either carved out of large logs or assembled from planks when large trees were unavailable. Often these canoes were equipped with sails, and on some a second canoe was used in place of the outrigger float, creating a double canoe. In Micronesia the boats were often highly decorated and were so important to the islanders that sometimes shrines were built in the shape of boats. For longer trips the islanders packed families, animals, plants, and supplies into very large double canoes. These canoes were up to 150 feet long and included small huts with thatched roofs. Still, the prospect of sailing one through the vast waters of the Pacific must have been daunting.

Canoes of Oceania had to navigate shallow waters—filled with attractive but dangerous rocks and corals—as well as the open sea, where waves regularly climb to over ten feet (3 m) high. Clearly, canoe design must have been quite advanced.

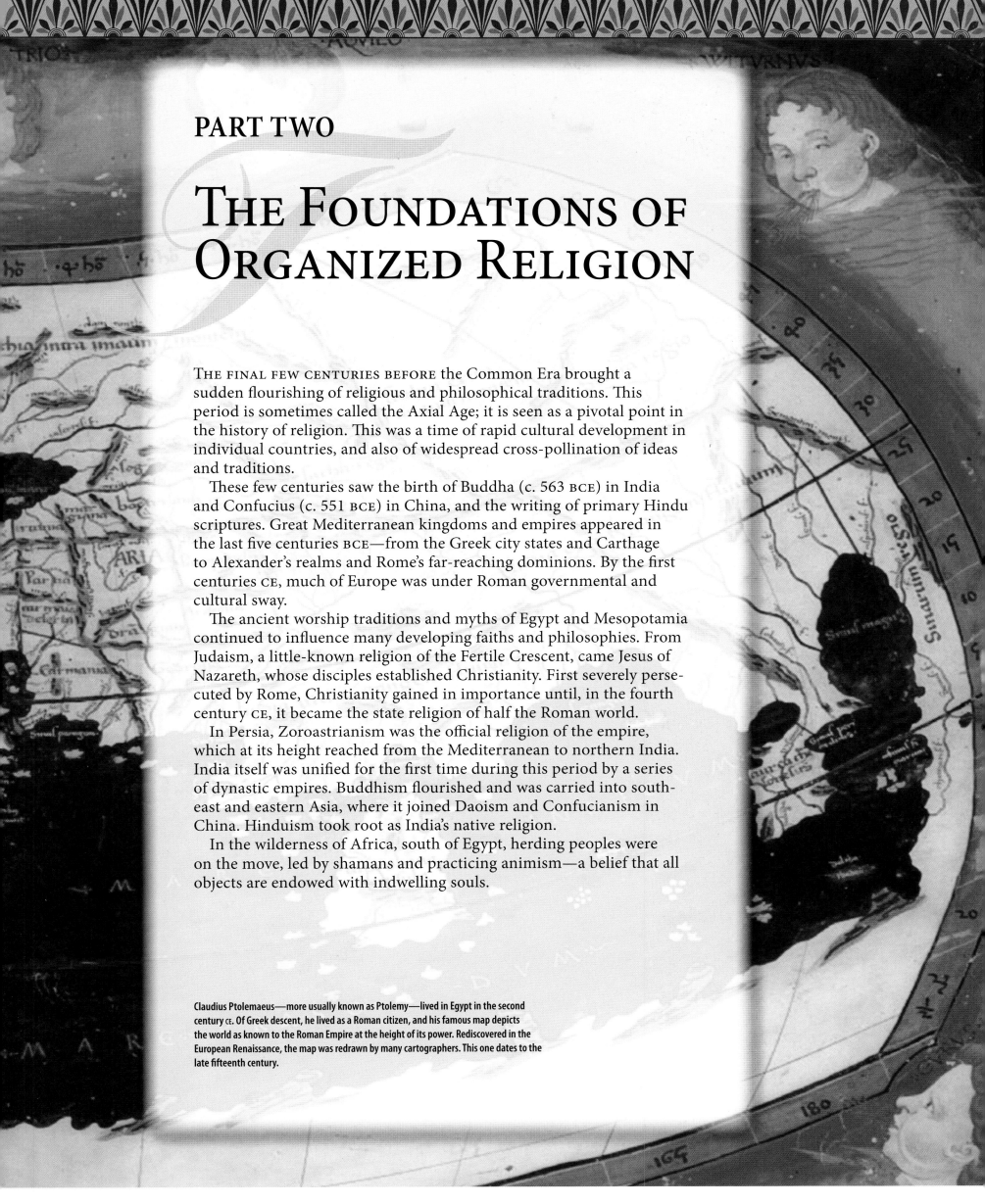

PART TWO

THE FOUNDATIONS OF ORGANIZED RELIGION

THE FINAL FEW CENTURIES BEFORE the Common Era brought a sudden flourishing of religious and philosophical traditions. This period is sometimes called the Axial Age; it is seen as a pivotal point in the history of religion. This was a time of rapid cultural development in individual countries, and also of widespread cross-pollination of ideas and traditions.

These few centuries saw the birth of Buddha (c. 563 BCE) in India and Confucius (c. 551 BCE) in China, and the writing of primary Hindu scriptures. Great Mediterranean kingdoms and empires appeared in the last five centuries BCE—from the Greek city states and Carthage to Alexander's realms and Rome's far-reaching dominions. By the first centuries CE, much of Europe was under Roman governmental and cultural sway.

The ancient worship traditions and myths of Egypt and Mesopotamia continued to influence many developing faiths and philosophies. From Judaism, a little-known religion of the Fertile Crescent, came Jesus of Nazareth, whose disciples established Christianity. First severely perse-cuted by Rome, Christianity gained in importance until, in the fourth century CE, it became the state religion of half the Roman world.

In Persia, Zoroastrianism was the official religion of the empire, which at its height reached from the Mediterranean to northern India. India itself was unified for the first time during this period by a series of dynastic empires. Buddhism flourished and was carried into south-east and eastern Asia, where it joined Daoism and Confucianism in China. Hinduism took root as India's native religion.

In the wilderness of Africa, south of Egypt, herding peoples were on the move, led by shamans and practicing animism—a belief that all objects are endowed with indwelling souls.

Claudius Ptolemaeus—more usually known as Ptolemy—lived in Egypt in the second century CE. Of Greek descent, he lived as a Roman citizen, and his famous map depicts the world as known to the Roman Empire at the height of its power. Rediscovered in the European Renaissance, the map was redrawn by many cartographers. This one dates to the late fifteenth century.

Classical Greek Civilization

IN THE DAYS OF THE PROTO-DEMOCRATIC city-state of Athens (Attica), philosophy and the arts flourished, stimulated by a new intellectual freedom, though devotion to the old gods diminished. However, even though Athens was luxuriating in the golden age of Greek culture, the city-state was also plagued by wars.

Early in the fifth century BCE the Athenians warded off invasions by the Persians, winning decisive victories at Marathon (490 BCE) and Salamis (480). In the years that followed Athens joined with other states of the eastern Aegean to form a loose maritime confederation. The city-state quickly grew wealthy, increasingly dominating the league and siphoning off its riches, thereby alienating the Spartans.

Taking advantage of Athens' new prosperity, the great statesman Pericles, who controlled Athens at the time, promoted learning and the arts, making the city-state a leading center of philosophy, literature, and art. Pericles also promoted building and was responsible for the construction of the Parthenon. But, perhaps inevitably, Sparta went to war with Athens. The so-called Peloponnesian War lasted from 431 to 404 BCE.

Greece never recovered from this war, and in the third century BCE Philip II of Macedon swept down from the north and forcibly united Greece with his

The Parthenon, dedicated to Athena Parthenos (Athena the Virgin), has stood in Athens since its completion in 432 BCE. One of the most recognizable buildings of ancient Greece, it is considered a pinnacle of classical Greek architecture.

own lands by 337 BCE. Philip's son, Alexander the Great, went on to conquer the Persian Empire and extend his own power to cover vast spaces, bringing Greek culture and religion to the East during what is known as the Hellenistic age. In 196 BCE Rome defeated the Macedonians and declared Greece to be free, but the Romans kept the Greeks under their thumb, and in 27 BCE Augustus Caesar officially turned Greece into the Roman province of Achaea.

RATIONAL VERSUS MYTHICAL

In the golden age of Athens there were no religious constraints on thinking, and as the city-state prospered, learning increased. Bands of traveling teachers, called Sophists, taught those eager to learn. Soon magic was dismissed and science was based on rational analyses of empirical observations. Even history was based on careful analyses of observed facts for the first time, making Herodotus the Father of History for his studied account of the Persian wars.

It was also a golden age of philosophy. Socrates turned rational theory away from the external world, urging Athenians to turn from material power to moral principles—a viable alternative to cultic worship. Plato thought people could be guided in their moral choices by seeking the transcendental idea of the good, while Aristotle advocated practical philosophy to help people make right choices.

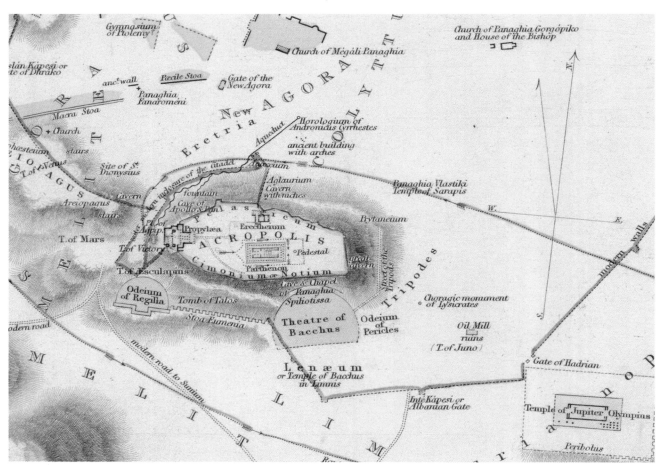

A nineteenth-century map of ancient Athens. Clearly visible below the Parthenon is the large Theater of Bacchus (Dionysus), underscoring the literally close relationship between theater and religion.

The intersection between theater and ritual is suggested by this Greek theater mask of Dionysus, which dates to the second or first century BCE.

DRAMA AND RELIGION

Early in the fifth century BCE, a new art form, drama, developed in Athens out of the mystery cult of the wine god Dionysus. It had begun as rituals involving choral singing and dancing in animal costumes, but then actors stepped away from the chorus and enacted tragic stories that had nothing to do with Dionysus. The tragedies were performed at religious festivals. Later, comic plays were added. Interestingly, these great plays reflect the changing attitudes of the Greeks toward their gods.

In the earliest surviving tragedies, the playwright Aeschylus sought to justify the gods for the seeming harm done to humans. In the *Oresteia*, Aeschylus traces a chain of revenge killings—seemingly prompted by the gods—that involved three generations. In the end the deities Apollo and Athena participate in the trial of the hero Orestes, and Athena sets things right.

Sophocles and Euripides were concerned less with the gods and more with the internal struggles of their heroes. However, Sophocles' *Antigone* shows how a king precipitates disaster by placing his own man-made regulations above divine law. The comedy writers were downright irreverent to the gods, and Aristophanes' comedy *Plutus* (about the god of wealth), openly parodies Greek myths. After the Macedonians conquered Greece, the only new plays were secular comedies.

DETERIORATION OF CLASSICAL RELIGION

In explaining humanity's relationship to the cosmos, philosophers began to openly undermine the myths that were the basis for Greek religion. The Sophists explained away the myths. Plato wanted to exclude Homer's stories of the gods and goddesses from the educational curriculum. By the end of the fourth century BCE, the old religion was critically weakened and only the mystery cults had large followings.

In the third century BCE the situation accelerated. The Stoic Cleanthes spoke of the supreme divinity "Zeus who interpenetrates all," but this entity was more a philosophical concept than a deity who could be worshipped. Epicurus believed that the gods existed but did not interact with humans in any way.

The collapse of religion in Greece corresponded to a weakening of political institutions, so that Greek religion became more individual practice than state religion. People turned for comfort to philosophy or to the mystery cults, and sometimes to astrology. During the Hellenistic period they found new gods from the East to worship.

Major centers of intellectual thought flourished in Greek cities like Athens, Corinth, and Sparta. Combining philosophy and elements of both native and foreign religions, traditions that began here in the second half of the first millennium BCE still have currency in Western thought.

GREECE, C. 400 BCE

● cities
▲ mountains

As many as 14,000 people could sit in the theater of Epidaurus, the best preserved of the ancient Greek theaters. Like other theaters, this one was located near a temple (in this case dedicated to Asclepius, the god of healing).

The Republic of Rome

AFTER THE ESTABLISHMENT of the republic in 509 BCE, Rome was governed by elected consuls and a senate of magistrates and priests. In addition to proposing legislation to be ratified by a popular assembly, these men also sent out armies to protect Rome. These military campaigns enriched the city but escalated into empire building.

By 264 BCE Rome controlled the entire Italian peninsula and wielded great power. However, in order to gain control of the Mediterranean, Rome went to war with the Punic Empire of the Carthaginians, which had evolved from the Phoenician settlement of Carthage in northern Africa. The Carthaginians controlled trade routes from Spain to the Asian coast, and Rome managed to eject them from Sicily, Sardinia, and Corsica. Then, when the Carthaginians attempted to establish an empire in Spain, the Romans threatened to squash them. However, the

Carthaginian general Hannibal attacked first, moving his army and elephants up from Spain and down across the Alps. Rome drove the Carthaginians out of Italy and attacked and destroyed Carthage, which they later rebuilt as a Roman colony. In the second century BCE Rome took over Spain, northern Africa, and Macedonia/Greece—eagerly bringing home Greek art and adopting Greek culture and religion. Finally, they expanded deep into western Asia.

In Italy itself a period of turbulence began in 233 BCE as slave revolts and civil wars erupted and ambitious Roman generals attempted to dominate politics. One such general, Julius Caesar, conquered Gaul in 59–49 BCE, then marched on Rome and took over the government. He was assassinated in 44 BCE for refusing to honor the republican system. After more civil wars Gaius Octavius became the first emperor of Rome in 27 BCE. He ruled as Augustus Caesar.

After Carthage had been defeated in 146 BCE, Rome no longer faced a single mighty rival and grew to cover territories from the Atlantic Ocean to the Caspian Sea, from northern France to northern Africa.

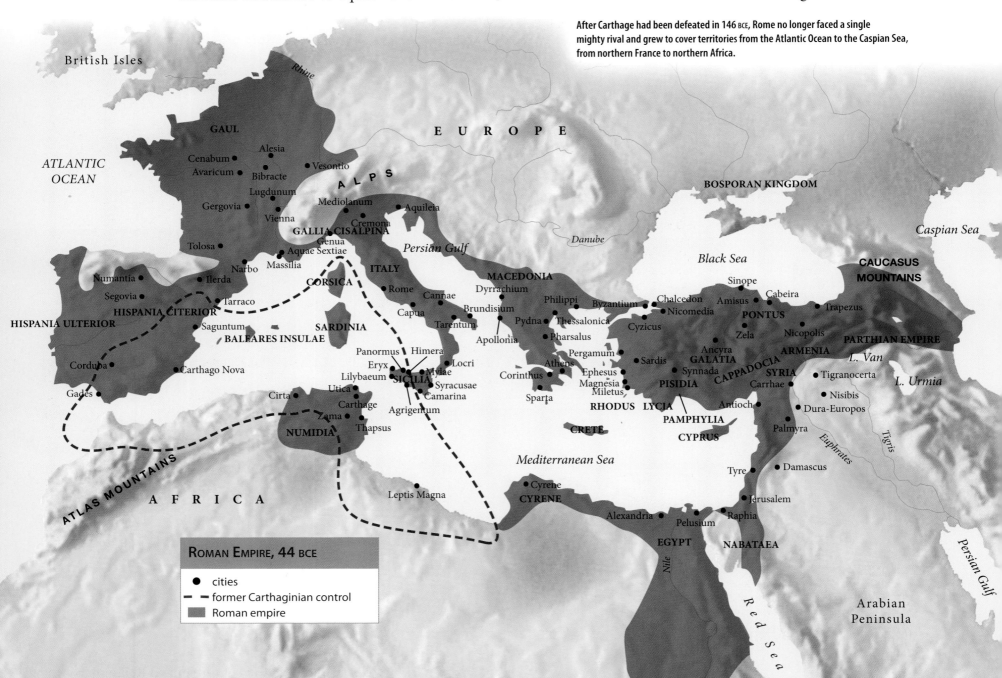

ROMAN EMPIRE, 44 BCE

● cities
╌ ╌ former Carthaginian control
▬ Roman empire

*Captured Greece led her conqueror captive,
and brought the arts to the rural Latins.*
—FROM HORACE'S EPODES

GODS AND GODDESSES

At a glance it almost seems that Rome had no religion of its own, as over the centuries it absorbed so many beliefs from others— beginning with the Etruscans, Greeks, and Carthaginians who lived or traded in Italy. However, the earliest Latins seem to have engaged in a kind of nature worship, which gradually evolved with their culture.

The early deities were evoked in prayer but seem to have been little more than embodiments of abstract concepts, such as Ceres, goddess of agriculture; Fides, goddess of good faith; and Janus, the god of comings and goings whose two faces adorned many entranceways. In time the number of deities increased, and they took on personalities.

In the beginning the chief deities were Diana, goddess of the moon and hunt, and Jupiter, another name for the Indo-European Zeus. Jupiter was a weather god and ultimately the chief deity. Diana was for a time seen as representing night to Jupiter's day. She was the goddess of women and fertility in early times, but later merely the goddess of the hunt and of travelers.

Other major gods included Mars and Venus, he the father of Romulus and she the mother of Aeneas—both mortals associated in myth with the founding of Rome. Mars began as a god of agriculture but was known mainly as a god of war. Venus was a goddess of love. Finally, Vesta, the goddess of the hearth, was first worshipped in private homes but later in a temple that kept an eternal flame tended by unmarried women—the vestal virgins.

Wolves recur throughout Roman religion, notably in Rome's foundation myth (when a she-wolf suckled Romulus and Remus), and possibly in the etymology of the festival of Lupercalia, from Latin *lupus* (wolf).

THE LITURGICAL CALENDAR

From early times Romans celebrated religious festivals according to a set calendar. The earliest surviving calendar, from the first century bce, outlines a solar year that is closely linked to the agricultural cycle. Each day is assigned its religious, legal, and political nature, and important festivals are described. During the Lupercalia, a purification festival in February, naked priests ran through the city, striking bystanders with strips from the hide of a sacrificed goat. In March, priests dressed as soldiers danced through the streets honoring Mars, the god of war. Spring and summer festivals focused on the harvest and storage of food. In December, Saturn, a god of sowing, was honored in the seven-day festival of Saturnalia, in which masters served servants, gifts were exchanged, and revelry ran rampant.

DIVINATION

Because predicting the outcome of their actions was important to the Romans, one of their earliest borrowings from the Greeks was the prophetess Sibyl, whose cult originated in a Greek community in southern Italy in the eighth century BCE. Sibyl is said to have sold her prophetic writings, known as the Sibylline Books, to the Etruscan Roman king Tarquinius, who deposited them on Capitoline Hill in Rome. Through the centuries that followed, Romans often consulted the Sibylline Books in times of trouble.

Priests watched for disruptions in nature— such as storms, abnormal births, or wild animals roaming the streets. They interpreted these disruptions as signs of a breach between the gods and the people and recommended remedies to placate the gods. Priests also

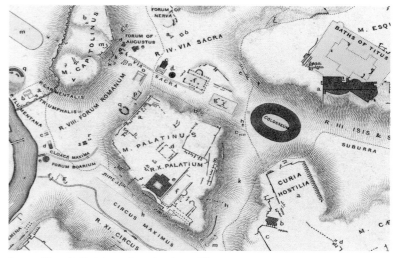

A map of Rome in the late empire and early republic.

consulted the *auspices*, signs sent by Jupiter about upcoming events, such as battles. The auspices, observed from such things as the flight of birds, were generally vague.

The main forum of Rome, centrally located near the Palatine and Capitoline hills, served as meeting place, open market, and political center, as well as primary religious site.

ROME

The Augustine Age

ALREADY HIGHLY REGARDED as the adopted son of Julius Caesar, Augustus had dazzled the people with his defeat of Mark Antony and Cleopatra in 30 BCE, which brought him Egypt as a personal domain and led to his being made ruler of the entire Roman Empire. Apt as he was at making war, however, Augustus quickly stopped the unbridled expansion of the past. He even set limits to the growth of the empire during his reign, halting it at the Rhine and Danube to the north and the Euphrates to the east. The Rhine-Danube frontier proved hard to hold, though, as the northern tribes continually tried to press southward. Still, Rome managed to hold the line for several centuries. Augustus had, in effect, established a long-lasting peace, known as the Pax Romana.

Augustus reshaped Rome's government into a system capable of controlling a vast empire, which the former republican system had been ill equipped to do. He restored the prestige of the Senate, though not its power, and he reorganized the army and took full responsibility for the defense of all parts of the empire. He also appointed himself pontifex maximus, chief high priest, and from that time on the Roman emperor would be the focus of all religious ritual. In 19 BCE Rome gave Augustus the right to rule by decree, making him absolute ruler.

The emperor was central to the empire, and his images appeared everywhere in the form of statues and coins. Rome quickly adopted the Hellenistic practice of emperor worship. Julius Caesar had already been deified, and all emperors from Augustus on would be worshipped as gods as well.

In the long peace known as the Pax Romana (Roman Peace), cultural traditions were, for the most part, free to blend and spread without interference from political authorities. Mystery cults, usually focusing on one mythological figure, became particularly popular in this period.

EMPIRE OF AUGUSTUS, 14 CE

- ● cities
- ● origins of mystery religions
- ■ empire of Augustus, 14 CE

A statue of Caesar Augustus, dressed not as an emperor but in his robes as pontifex maximus (high priest).

THE WANE OF TRADITIONAL RELIGION

During the period of Rome's expansion into distant lands, many new gods and goddesses and new rites and rituals had been absorbed into the Roman religion. Greece supplied most of them, and a majority of the Roman deities were basically the old Greek gods and goddesses with Latin names. Even the mythology had been adapted to Roman use.

By the time Augustus came to power, however, the people were beginning to find the old religion overly ritualized and fossilized. Consequently, Augustus, in initiating emperor worship, also urged a revival of traditional religion and personally participated as chief priest. As time went on, however, the people were ever more drawn to exotic new religions from the distant parts of the empire, and mystery cults grew in popularity.

OVID'S METAMORPHOSES

The Greeks had Hesiod to write about their gods. The Romans had Ovid, a poet who wrote numerous works about love and other topics but also recast, in a much lighter tone, tales of the gods and heroes of Greek and Roman mythology. In 8 ce Ovid completed his *Metamorphoses*. This poem in fifteen books retells important myths, concluding each with a transformation of someone or something into a bird, tree, rock, star, or the like. The book progresses through history, beginning with the first great transformation (chaos into order) and ending with the deification of Julius Caesar and a tribute to Augustus. Some 250 myths fall in between. For example, when pursed by Apollo, the nymph Daphne turns into a laurel tree. Acteon, a young hunter who accidentally sees the goddess Diana naked, is turned into a stag and attacked by his own dogs. Romulus, founder and first king of Rome, is transformed into Quirinus, the god of peaceful and prosperous communities. The fact that so many of Ovid's stories come from Greek mythology demonstrates the extent to which the Romans had adopted Greek culture and religion.

Here Jove with Hermes came; but in disguise
Of mortal men conceal'd their deities.
One laid aside his thunder, one his rod;
And many toilsome steps together trod.
—FROM OVID'S METAMORPHOSES

Construction on Rome's Pantheon—*pantheon* is from the Greek for "shrine of all the gods"—was begun in 27 BCE. The Pantheon was rebuilt by Emperor Hadrian in the second century. In 609 CE, it was dedicated as the Church of the Santa Maria Rotonda.

SECRECY AND SACRIFICE

The major mystery cults were those of Cybele, Isis, and Sabazius (akin to Dionysus), all of which developed in Greece; Osiris from Egypt; and Mithraism from far distant Persia. All these cults had a system of authority based on the initiation of members. All offered some sort of secret knowledge, generally involving reversals of traditional ideas of reality, morality, life, and death.

One of the most popular of the mystery cults was Mithraism. Mithras was a god of light and truth, and a warrior in the battle against evil, whose worship was open only to men. At the heart of Mithraism was the tauroctony, in which Mithras slew a sacred bull and released its blood to renew and nurture life. Symbols associated with this primordial event related to the holy mysteries of sacrifice, life through death, and the triumph of good over evil through Mithras's struggle in a dark cave. Compassion, composure, and restraint were demanded by Mithras's creed, fostering a moral discipline that suited the natures of many career military men.

A second-century CE Roman statue of Mithras killing a bull, the most sacred animal in Mithraic tradition. The snake, dog, and scorpion—which attacks the bull's genitals—are also symbolically potent.

ROME
Christianity's Beginnings

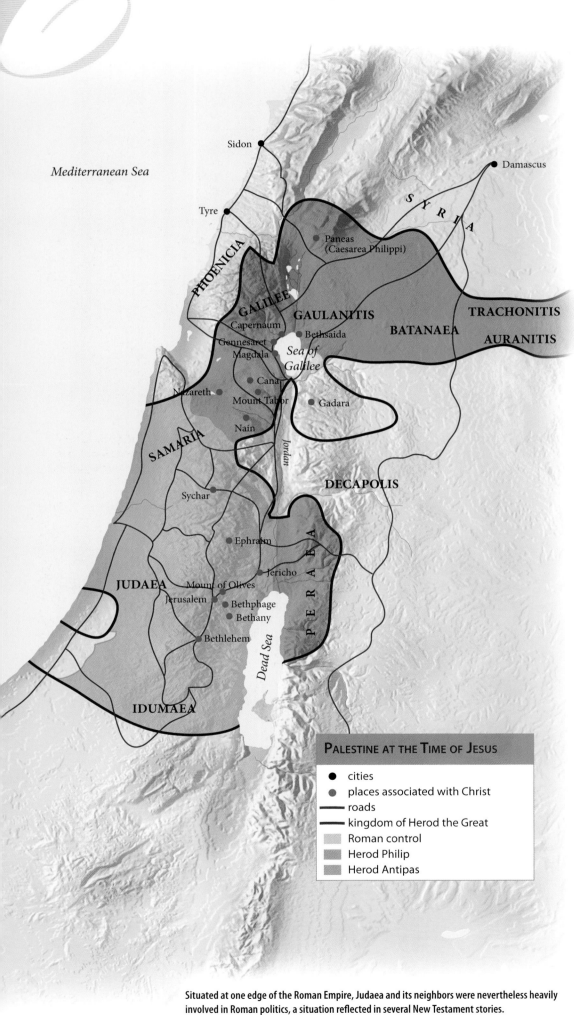

Mediterranean Sea

Sidon

Damascus

S Y R I A

Tyre

PHOENICIA

Paneas
(Caesarea Philippi)

GALILEE

GAULANITIS

Capernaum

TRACHONITIS

Bethsaida

BATANAEA

AURANITIS

Gennesaret
Magdala

Sea of
Galilee

Cana

Nazareth

Mount Tabor

Gadara

Nain

Jordan

SAMARIA

DECAPOLIS

Sychar

Ephraim

PERAEA

Jericho

JUDAEA

Mount of Olives

Jerusalem

Bethphage

Bethany

Bethlehem

Dead Sea

IDUMAEA

PALESTINE AT THE TIME OF JESUS

- ● cities
- ● places associated with Christ
- —— roads
- —— kingdom of Herod the Great
- Roman control
- Herod Philip
- Herod Antipas

Situated at one edge of the Roman Empire, Judaea and its neighbors were nevertheless heavily involved in Roman politics, a situation reflected in several New Testament stories.

In a backwoods area of Palestine, a far corner of the Roman Empire, a Jewish carpenter, Jesus of Nazareth, stepped into history and came to be heralded by his followers as the "Savior of the World"—a title already appropriated by Augustus Caesar, but used of Jesus in a different sense. Jesus's followers saw him as the Messiah, or Christ (*Christos* in Greek), whom the Jews awaited, and as one who would forgive their sins and grant them eternal life after death. Soon after Jesus died, a new religion known as Christianity spread his teachings throughout the Mediterranean world. In time Christianity would reach across the entire Western world and into the East and would profoundly affect the course of world history.

Jesus was born in about 7 BCE in Bethlehem, a small town near Jerusalem, the Jewish religious center. Christian scriptures tell stories of Jesus's birth in what would have been a familiar classical heroic style. In one account, local Jewish shepherds and wise men from the East (possibly Zoroastrians) honor the infant, thus emphasizing the Christian belief in Jesus as king of all the world. In another story, when Herod the Great, king of Judaea under Roman supervision, hears that a new "king" had been born in Bethlehem, he jealously has the town's infant boys slaughtered, but Jesus is taken to safety in Egypt until Herod's death. And so Jesus's infancy parallels that of the Hebrew prophet Moses, who had similarly been saved from slaughter at childbirth in Egypt.

In Western Christian traditions, the number of magi, or wise men, who come to recognize the infant Christ as king of the Jews is set at three, possibly because the Gospels describe the magi bringing three gifts: gold, frankincense, and myrrh.

A depiction of Jesus preaching to local fishermen, his first followers, on the shores of the Sea of Galilee.

For God so loved the world that he gave his only Son, that whoever believes in him should not perish but have eternal life.
—GOSPEL OF JOHN

DEATH AND RESURRECTION

As Jesus was celebrating the Jewish feast of Passover, he offered his disciples bread and wine, saying they were his body and blood, which he told them would be offered as a sacrifice for the forgiveness of humanity's sins. After supper Jesus was arrested, charged with calling himself king of the Jews, found guilty, and put to death by crucifixion. Christians later saw his death as a onetime sacrifice that resulted in God's forgiving all the sins of the world. However, the Gospels do not end with the crucifixion, but relate that on the third day after his death Jesus rose from the dead and told his followers that all that had happened to him had been prophesied in the Hebrew scriptures. He promised to return at some unspecified time and to send a spirit to guide them in the meantime. He was then lifted into the sky and left this earth—which his followers saw as his return to God.

A twelfth-century armilla, or shoulder amulet, showing the resurrection of Jesus Christ. Flanked by angels, a haloed Jesus steps out of his sarcophagus, overlooking two sleeping guards.

THE MINISTRY OF JESUS

Virtually all we know of the life of Jesus comes from the four books of Christian scripture known as the Gospels. These were written some time after Jesus's death as theological reflections on his life and teachings. According to the Gospels, Jesus grew up in Nazareth, a town in rural Galilee, under the care of his mother, Mary, and her husband, Joseph. In about 27 CE Jesus left home and traveled south along the Jordan River. There John, a desert preacher, was calling for repentance and offering the people the cleansing ritual of baptism. While John was baptizing Jesus he pointed him out as the expected Messiah. Jesus then returned to Galilee to begin a three-year ministry.

Jesus chose twelve disciples (sometimes called apostles) to travel with him and help him. Then, according to the Gospels, he went from town to town preaching, miraculously healing the ill and disabled and proclaiming the Kingdom of God, a time when God would rule over all and good would prevail.

When Jesus preached he often used parables, stories that made a moral point. His main topic was love, and he held that the greatest Jewish law was to love both God and neighbor. The Gospels relate that Jesus opposed some of the regulations of the Jewish religious leaders. Some of these leaders considered him a threat to their authority and tried to silence him.

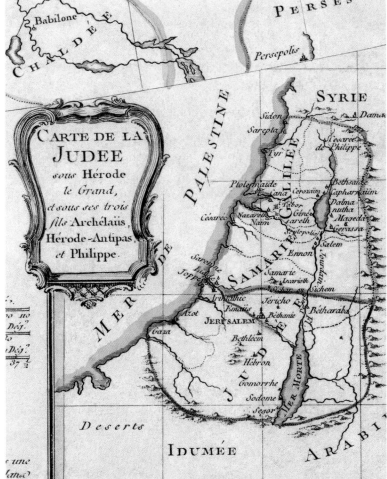

A late eighteenth-century French map of Judaea under Herod the Great and his three sons.

THE BEATITUDES

In his teaching Jesus stressed love, and blessed people who lived simply and lovingly. He began his so-called Sermon on the Mount with eight such blessings, or beatitudes:

Blessed are the poor in spirit, for theirs is the kingdom of heaven.
Blessed are those who mourn, for they shall be comforted.
Blessed are the meek, for they shall inherit the earth.
Blessed are those who hunger and thirst for righteousness, for they shall be satisfied. Blessed are the merciful, for they shall obtain mercy.
Blessed are the pure in heart, for they shall see God.
Blessed are the peacemakers, for they shall be called sons of God.
Blessed are those who are persecuted for righteousness' sake, for theirs is the kingdom of heaven.
Blessed are you when men revile you and persecute you and utter all kinds of evil against you falsely on my account. Rejoice and be glad, for your reward is great in heaven, for so men persecuted the prophets who were before you.

The Christian Church

WITHIN DAYS AFTER Jesus had left them, his disciples began to preach to the Jews who had come to Jerusalem from far and wide to celebrate Pentecost, a harvest feast. According to the Acts of the Apostles, a book written later in the first century, Peter, Jesus's chief disciple, managed to convert 3,000 people in one day. With their numbers increased, the followers of Jesus continued to spread the so-called gospel ("good news") about Jesus—that he was the Messiah promised by the Hebrew scriptures and had risen from the dead. The belief in Jesus's resurrection was from the start the primary article of Christian faith.

The early followers of Jesus, who came to be known as Christians, gathered in close-knit groups and continued to attend synagogue services, as practicing Jews. However, they also gathered privately to talk about Jesus and reenact his "Last Supper," including the consumption of his body and blood. Unfortunately these reenactments would later be misreported as cannibalism, and Roman officials put some Christians to death on that charge. As the Christians continued to grow in numbers and preach publicly, they came into conflict with the Jews who did not accept Jesus, and some of these Jews persecuted them. One of the persecutors, Paul of Tarsus, eventually came to believe in Jesus and became an apostle, or missionary, himself.

Paul worked arduously to spread faith in Jesus, making three long missionary journeys. At each place he stopped, Paul preached first to the local Jews, then to the Gentiles (non-Jews). Many came to believe in Jesus, and Paul established churches to which he began writing letters after moving on. These letters later became part of the Christian scriptures, or New Testament, and were the first books of the New Testament to be written.

Paul's extensive journeys throughout the eastern Mediterranean are the first major examples of a missionary trend that continued in Christian tradition through modern times.

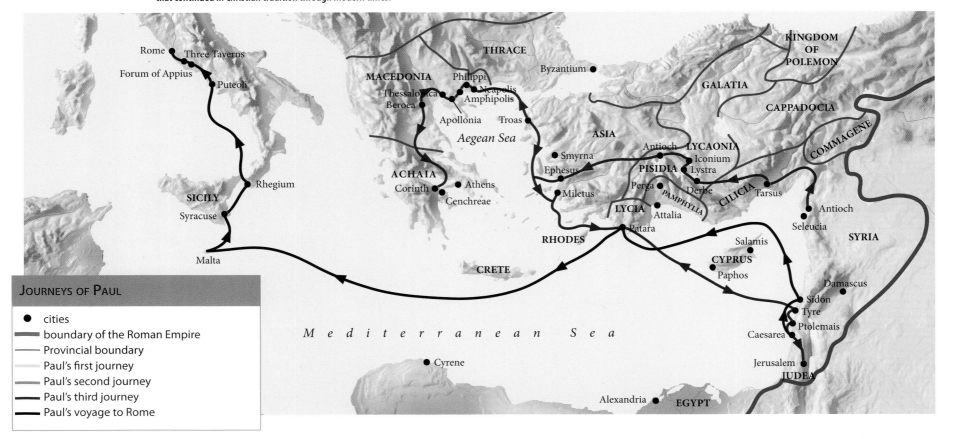

JOURNEYS OF PAUL

- ● cities
- ── boundary of the Roman Empire
- ── Provincial boundary
- ── Paul's first journey
- ── Paul's second journey
- ── Paul's third journey
- ── Paul's voyage to Rome

Conversion has played a significant role in the history of Christianity since the earliest days. Perhaps the most famous convert to Christianity is Paul (Saul) of Tarsus. Paul became a missionary, and is depicted here preaching in Athens.

Caesar gave orders that they should now demolish the entire city [Jerusalem] and temple, but should leave as many of the towers standing as were of the greatest eminency.
—JOSEPHUS'S WARS OF THE JEWS

synagogue, the men making the complaint were arrested, and war broke out between the Jews and the Romans. Nero sent troops to Palestine, led by his best general, Vespasian, and they defeated the Jewish troops in Galilee. Ultimately, Vespasian's son Titus became emperor and inherited the dispute. Titus's army wiped out the Jewish forces and leveled the city of Jerusalem, destroying the temple, in 70 CE. Titus returned to Rome and paraded through the streets brandishing the sacred menorah he had taken from the Jewish temple. To this day the temple has not been rebuilt.

Detail of a relief from the Arch of Titus in Rome, 81 CE. The relief shows Roman soldiers carrying the menorah that they had removed from the Temple of Jerusalem in 70 CE.

PERSECUTIONS

Friction between Christians and Jews intensified. After years of proclaiming the Christian faith, Paul was arrested in Jerusalem for illegally bringing Gentiles into restricted areas of the Jewish temple. He insisted on being tried in Rome, as was his right as a Roman citizen, believing he would be treated more fairly there. He sailed to Rome, where, while awaiting trial, he was kept under loose house arrest. From prison Paul continued writing letters to distant Christian communities.

Roman authorities at first considered Christianity to be a Jewish sect (and so exempt from worshipping Roman deities), but they soon began to see it as separate, and when Christians refused to acknowledge the emperor as god, they were sometimes put to death. When a fire broke out in 64 CE and destroyed much of the city of Rome, Emperor Nero quickly blamed the city's Christians and instigated a fierce persecution in which Christians were brutally murdered—even torn apart by

dogs or turned into living torches. Paul was probably put to death by beheading during this persecution. In addition, Peter, who was serving as head of the church in Rome, was crucified upside down. And so the two foremost leaders of the early church were dead.

THE DESTRUCTION OF JERUSALEM

The Pax Romana was deeply shaken in Judaea in the 60s CE because of the perceived cruel disregard of the Roman governors. When Jewish leaders complained that Greeks had offered pagan sacrifices at the door of their

The third-century Christian scholar Origen reported that Peter had requested that his cross be inverted. Debates have raged about the specifics of his death ever since.

WRITING THE GOSPELS

Because early Christians expected Jesus to return imminently, they wrote nothing down, relying on word of mouth to pass along his sayings and actions. But after many of the people who had known Jesus personally died, Christians feared that the traditions about Jesus might be lost. Consequently, probably between 60 and 85 CE three men wrote books about Jesus, called Gospels. Although the authors are unknown, second-century sources identified them as Matthew, Mark, and Luke.

Each Gospel was directed at a specific group of readers. Mark wrote to Christians facing persecution, and so he emphasized Jesus's suffering. Matthew, addressing Jews who had become Christians, alluded to Jewish customs and scriptures and emphasized the Christian church. Luke directed his Gospel to Gentile Christians unfamiliar with Judaism, and painted Jesus as a savior who came for men and women of all backgrounds.

At the turn of the first century someone named John wrote a fourth Gospel. Unlike the earlier three it is less an account of Jesus's

thoughts and deeds than a theological discourse attempting to show that Jesus was truly God. Although the Gospels differ, they do not contradict one another. Rather they offer the same subject from different perspectives.

The beginning Gospel of John in the Codex Alexandrinus, one of the earliest copies of the Greek Bible. Now incomplete, the manuscript dates to the fifth century CE.

ROME
The Early Church

After the destruction of Jerusalem and its temple in 70 CE, Jewish worship shifted to the synagogues, and for a time Christians worshipped with them. Friction between Christian and non-Christian Jews increased, however, and the Christians were eventually expelled from the synagogues and became a distinct sect. Because of vigorous missionary efforts, Christianity spread quickly and widely, and each city or town had its own church, or congregation. By the second century, large churches or groups of churches were overseen by men called bishops (or sometimes presbyters). Because a new bishop could be anointed (installed) only by an already anointed bishop, and because the first bishops were Jesus's apostles, "episcopal," or bishop-based authority was seen as being passed down directly through an unbroken chain from the twelve disciples specifically chosen by Jesus.

Though sporadic, Roman persecution of the Christians continued and claimed the lives of many prominent Christians, including Ignatius, bishop of Antioch, who welcomed martyrdom as a way of reaching God. Many Christians agreed with Ignatius, and martyrs were greatly revered. In 311 some Christians in Africa refused to recognize their new bishop because he had been anointed by a bishop who had not resisted the Roman authorities during a persecution ordered by Diocletian. The result was the Donatist schism, a split in the African church named for one of the bishops involved. It persisted for centuries.

Roman distrust of Christianity continued until Constantine became emperor of the western half of Rome, which had split in two. According to tradition, before the decisive battle at the Milvian Bridge near Rome, Constantine had a vision of a cross and came to believe it was through that cross that he won the battle and became emperor of the West. In 313 he and Licinius, emperor of the East, jointly promulgated the Edict of Milan, which offered religious freedom to all.

In the late third century, the emperor Diocletian fundamentally reorganized the administration of the Roman Empire. His reforms were the starting point for the ultimate split of the Roman Empire in half, a political restructuring that would have enormous effects on Christianity, Judaism, and Islam.

DIVIDED ROME, FOURTH CENTURY

- ● cities
- western Roman Empire
- eastern Roman Empire

A mosaic of Jesus Christ as the Good Shepherd—a common form of early Christian iconography, before the crucifix became current in the mid-first millennium—decorates the fifth-century tomb in Ravenna, Italy, traditionally associated with Galla Placidia (effectively the Roman Empire's last ruler).

Let me be fodder for wild beasts—that is how I can get to God. I am God's wheat and I am being ground by the teeth of the wild beasts to make a pure loaf for Christ.
—LETTER TO THE ROMANS BY IGNATIUS, BISHOP OF ANTIOCH AND MARTYR

JEWISH WARS AND WRITINGS

The revolt of the 60s had been a disaster for the Jews, and some of them, organized as a political party called the Zealots, still greatly resented being ruled by the Romans. In 115 the Zealots found a new leader, Bar Kokhba ("Son of a Star"), who was believed by some to be the Messiah—the "star" that that would "come out of Israel," according to an ancient Jewish prophecy of a messianic king in the line of King David. The Zealots captured the Roman-held city of Jerusalem and its environs and declared their holdings an independent nation. Roman troops laid siege to the Jewish strongholds, which fell one by one. Then, in 135, they stormed the last Jewish fortress and killed Bar Kokhba. In all, some half million Jews were killed in the revolt. It was the last serious attempt to establish an independent Jewish state until modern times.

Meanwhile, great progress was being made in preserving Jewish thought. In the second century the canon of Jewish scripture was officially set, and future additions, subtractions, or revisions were forbidden. Early in the third century learned rabbis undertook the gargantuan task of writing down, and so preserving, all the oral traditions that had accumulated over the centuries. The resulting volume, the Mishnah, provided a supplement to the Jewish scriptures. Later, debates on the Mishnah were recorded in the Gemara and added to the Mishnah to form a gigantic compilation known as the Talmud.

DIVERSE SECTS

As Christianity spread to the outskirts of the Roman Empire, the customs and beliefs of some regional groups began to have an impact. The Ebionites, a second-century group of Jewish Christians in the Trans-Jordan, held that Jesus was only one in a long line of prophets and not born the son of God but adopted. They continued to follow many of the older Jewish rituals and led ascetic lives.

In the third century, Montanus, an ex-priest of the mystery cult of Cybele in

Phrygia, Asia Minor, converted to Christianity and proclaimed himself the channel for the outpouring of the "Spirit of truth" promised by Jesus in John's Gospel. Montanus and two women, Priscilla and Maximilla, prophesied that the end of the world was near. So the Montanists gave up their homes and possessions and lived ascetically, preparing for Jesus's return. The cult spread into Syria, northern Africa, and the West.

Mani, a third-century Christian from Babylon, claimed to be the last and greatest of a line of prophets who included Zoroaster, the Buddha, and Jesus. He advocated a form of gnosticism, stressing dualism and direct communication with God.

Saint Helena was Constantine's mother and a devout Christian. Here, a nineteenth-century painting depicts her return from the Holy Land bearing Christ's true cross, which she reportedly discovered—a legendary theme that spread throughout the Christian world in the second half of the first millennium.

GNOSTICISM

Christians were slow to formulate an official core of beliefs, but conservative bishops, whose theology was rooted in monotheism and anchored in the Hebrew scriptures, were seriously challenged and spurred to do so by Gnosticism. Emerging late in the first century, Gnosticism was not a religion, but a movement that encompassed a wide variety of sects centered on the idea of *gnosis* ("knowledge" in Greek).

Valentinus, the second-century leader of a sect in Rome, taught that there were two worlds and two gods. Our everyday world was created by the inferior god of the Hebrew scriptures and embodies darkness and evil. The other world is one of light and knowledge ruled by a Supreme Being. The Gnostic elect had access to the mysteries of this world, which brought salvation and could teach and enlighten a receptive few others. However, most people were incapable of enlightenment and could not be saved. Because everything in the material world is evil, including the human body, the Gnostics denied that Jesus was human.

Christian authorities fought hard against the Gnostics and by the third century managed, for the most part, to silence them, burning most of their writings. However, some manuscripts were hidden away and came to light again in the twentieth century.

In the Gospels, Judas Iscariot, a disciple of Christ, identifies Jesus to Roman guards by giving him a kiss. His betrayal, attributed variously in the Gospels to avarice or Satanic possession, was viewed very differently by Gnostic sects, which saw Judas as instrumental in Christ's plan to save humanity.

ROME

Last Years of the Roman Empire

AFTER GRANTING RELIGIOUS FREEDOM to the entire empire, Constantine and Licinius separately ruled their western and eastern sectors, but Licinius began persecuting the Christians again, even though Constantine backed them. The emperors went to war, and Licinius was defeated and executed in 324. Constantine became sole ruler of the Roman Empire and built a new capital, Constantinople, on the site of the ancient Greek city of Byzantium.

At the time Christians were fairly numerous, making up as much as 10 percent of the empire's population, and they came from all levels of society. Constantine seems to have viewed Christianity as a potential unifying force, and he promoted the religion vigorously. He built magnificent churches, brought church leaders into the inner circles of the empire, and used his power to influence theological debates.

In 337 Constantine himself was baptized a Christian on the feast of Pentecost, the same feast on which the first Christians had begun spreading the word of Jesus. Constantine died the same day.

Christianity thrived in the centuries to come, but the Roman Empire did not. In 410 Visigoths sacked Rome, and the empire never recovered. However, in northern Africa, Augustine, the Christian bishop of Hippo Regius, soon wrote a theological masterpiece, *The City of God,* justifying Christianity and refuting critics who claimed that Rome fell because the people had abandoned the old gods. Meanwhile, in Bethlehem, Jerome, another great Christian scholar, had recently completed his Latin translation of the Bible, which would stand as the main version of the Christian scriptures for centuries to come. The Roman Empire was in its death throes, but Christianity was not.

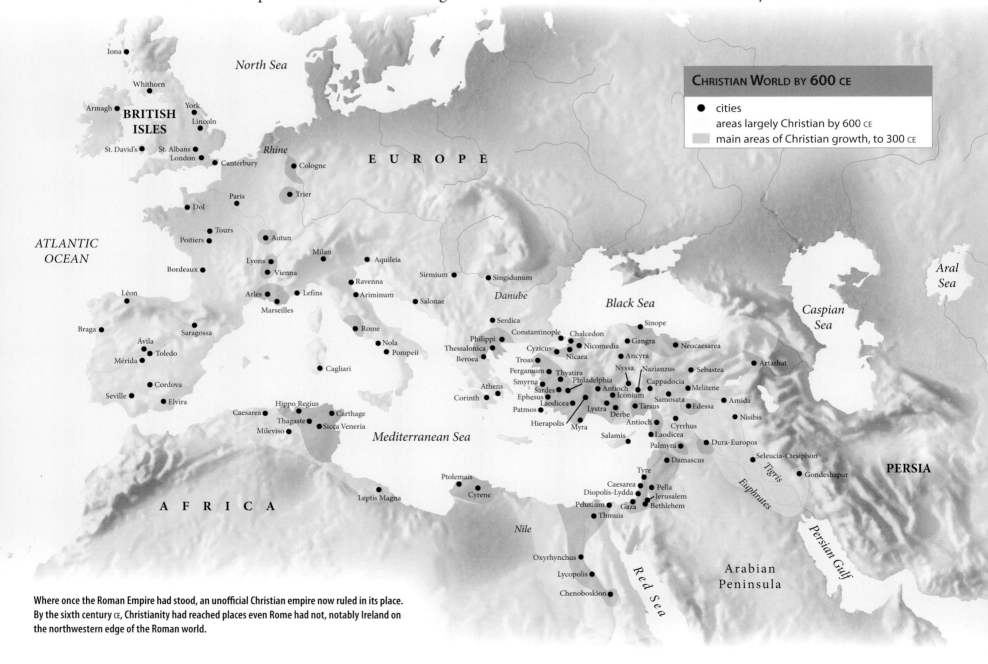

Where once the Roman Empire had stood, an unofficial Christian empire now ruled in its place. By the sixth century CE, Christianity had reached places even Rome had not, notably Ireland on the northwestern edge of the Roman world.

> *On every Lord's Day—his special day—come together and break bread and give thanks, first confessing your sins so that your sacrifice may be pure.*
> —THE DIDACHE, A SECOND-CENTURY CHRISTIAN MANUAL

CHRISTIAN WORSHIP AND SCRIPTURE

In the second and third centuries, Christians generally worshipped in a large room of a house or in an unused temple. As they had from the start, the services centered on the celebration of the Lord's Supper. The congregation also said prayers, sang hymns, and read from the Hebrew scriptures and from what they referred to as the memoirs of the apostles. These must have been the Gospels and letters written by Paul and other prominent church leaders.

It was not until the fourth century that these "memoirs" were gathered together and considered a part of Christian scripture. Looking at what was being read during worship services, church leaders compiled lists of the writings they considered scripture. By the end of the fourth century a collection of twenty-seven "books" was agreed upon and called the New Testament. This was appended to the Hebrew scriptures, or Old Testament; Christians believed that the prophecies of the Old Testament were fulfilled in Jesus. The New Testament contains twenty-one letters, the four Gospels, the Acts of the Apostles (a chronicle of the early church), and the Revelation to John, a book of consolation written during the time of the Diocletian persecution, envisioning a time to come when evil would be punished and good prevail.

THE BEGINNINGS OF MONASTICISM

Beginning in the third century, Christians wishing to escape the distractions of the world began to move into the deserts, where they lived simple, ascetic lives devoted to prayer. The first of these hermits may have been Anthony of Egypt, who for twenty years lived in an abandoned fortress near the Red Sea. Others imitated Anthony, and one of them, Pachomius, established the first community of Christian hermits and wrote regulations to govern their daily routines, including shared meals, work, prayer, and discipline. This was the first monastic rule. Similar communities were soon established throughout Egypt, the Sinai, and caves in the volcanic hills of Cappadocia in Asia Minor. From these early communities the great monastic orders of the Middle Ages would emerge.

The unforgiving but naturally pocketed landscape of Cappadocia attracted both Christians fleeing persecution and early monastic communities.

DEVELOPMENT OF THE CHRISTIAN CREED

Once the church authorities set out to establish a core of essential beliefs, they did not have an easy time of it. Theological disagreements raged on for years and were often antagonistic and personal. Many involved the nature of Jesus. Was he man or God or both? A number of church councils were held at which theologians tried to hammer out a basic creed that could be used as the basis for acceptance into the church at baptism.

Constantine himself finally became involved in 325 and ordered church leaders to convene a council at Nicaea (a town near Constantinople) to settle these bitter disputes over dogma. The result was the Nicene Creed, which holds that Jesus was both fully God and fully man and that he is one with God the Father and the Holy Spirit, constituting the Holy Trinity. Although the Nicene Creed went through minor revisions at later councils, in its final form it was accepted by all Christians for centuries. However, the debate on the exact nature of the Trinity continued and was one of the chief issues of contention that led to the eventual split between the eastern and western churches in the eleventh century.

Since its creation in 383, Saint Jerome's Vulgate and certain derivatives have served as the standard Bible of the Roman Catholic Church. At the time, Latin was the common ("vulgar") language, prompting Pope Damascus to commission a translation from the Greek.

A mosque from 1453 to 1935, Hagia Sophia is today a museum, but when first constructed in 532 to 537, it was the largest cathedral in the world and remained the focal point for eastern Christendom for centuries.

European Religion and the Roman Empire

THE GEOGRAPHY OF WESTERN RELIGION TODAY is largely a legacy of the ancient Roman Empire. Jesus's followers in Palestine lived under the Pax Romana, which fostered the excellent communications by which Christianity was spread via missionaries as well as correspondence such as the letters of the apostle Paul. The well-governed, well-connected empire provided the early church fathers with a tremendous foundation upon which Christianity would become the religion of all Europe.

The empire's solid integration was no accident. More than any empire that had come before it, Rome expanded with a systematic approach that progressively blended conquered territories with the heartland, until the inhabitants generally thought of themselves not as defeated peoples but as part of greater Rome. Rome's codified system of laws was applied to annexed territories, and conquest was followed not only by the construction of extensive beneficial infrastructure, but also by cultural integration.

Important local gods, such as Sulis at the Bath thermal springs in England, were identified with Roman deities (in this case, Minerva) and shown appropriate respect with fine temples and elaborate ritual, acknowledgments that greatly reduced popular resentment of the new rulers. Local people were furthermore gradually afforded opportunities to become fully naturalized Roman citizens and thus had a vested interest in learning the universal language of Latin and participating in the success of the Roman state.

Colonial governments initially staffed by occupying Roman forces gradually incorporated meritorious locals, who then served as role models to the rest of the populace. The integration that Rome offered was not merely superficial: by the later empire, the Roman Senate was filled with members from throughout the far-flung provinces. The empire's effective unity gave church missionaries an incomparable advantage. When the Roman state officially adopted Christianity, it was not long before all Europe became "Christendom."

If not always encouraged, foreign gods were usually tolerated by the Roman Empire. Often, Romans would identify them with Roman gods, allowing regional syncretism. Religious conflicts rarely erupted, and usually involved gods not associated with a parallel Roman one.

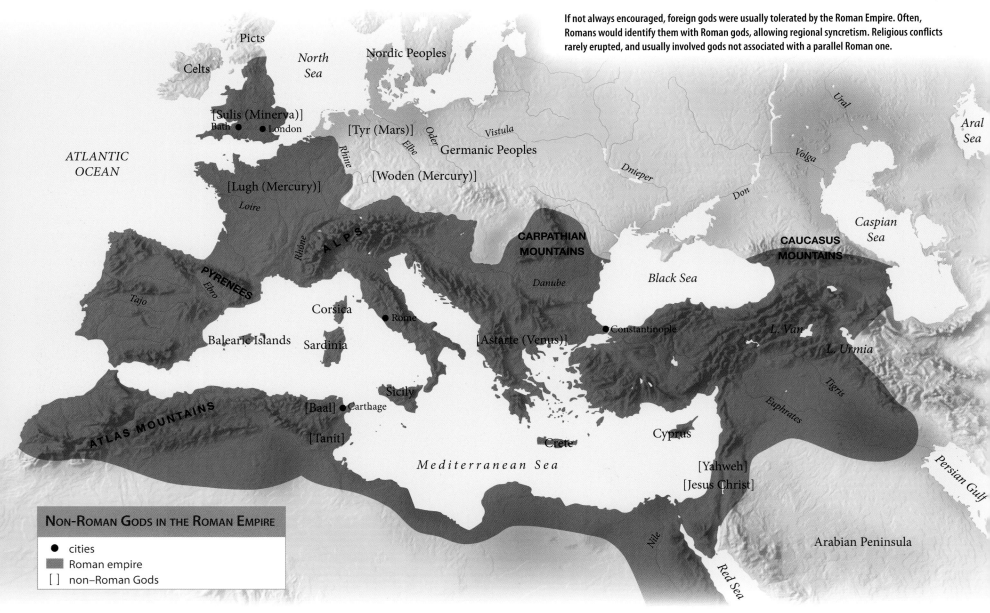

NON-ROMAN GODS IN THE ROMAN EMPIRE

● cities
▪ Roman empire
[ ] non–Roman Gods

The head of Sulis-Minerva from Bath, England, is all that remains of a Roman bronze statue that once graced the sacred, reputedly therapeutic, natural springs.

CLASSICAL POLYTHEIST TOLERANCE

Classical polytheism saw the world as ruled by divine forces of many different magnitudes and natures. When the Romans encountered other religions and new divinities, as they frequently did during their expansion into Europe, it was generally presumed that behind local deity names probably lay at least some of their familiar gods. When discussing foreign religions, Classical authors constantly align local gods with Olympian counterparts. Reverence could be shown, and prayer petitions made, in countless different modes and rites. Classical polytheism accommodated innumerable local traditional ritual practices, and there was always room for a few more.

To this point of view, novel gods and religions represented no threat and might offer valuable new elements. The Sibylline Books prompted Rome to introduce the Epidauran worship of the medical healing god Asclepius after a plague in 293 BCE. Worship of the great agrarian mother-goddess Cybele was brought in from Anatolia in 205–204 BCE.

The Classical polytheist tradition led contrasting faiths to seek common ground and build shared understanding, rather than to resent each other's differences. As embodied in Roman imperial policy, this outlook was highly tolerant, and peoples added to the empire through annexation or conquest normally had little to fear for gods deeply beloved by their culture.

The concept of crusading, or fighting against a different religion because of matters of theological disagreement, would have struck the Romans as baffling and illogical. If someone else believed, or conducted their worship rituals, in a fashion offensive to divine powers, then surely the offended god or goddess would take care of exacting any required retribution. Indeed, mortals warring on the deity's behalf might therefore seem not devout, but presumptuous.

RARE ROMAN INTOLERANCE

Rome's tolerance on matters of religion could be overstepped, on rare occasions, by violating basic Roman values or threatening the welfare of the community. The Phoenician cults of Baal and Tanit, which Rome encountered in its North African rival Carthage, involved human sacrifice, and archaeological excavation of tophet shrine ruins in Carthage has uncovered deposits of the tiny bones that remain from the ritual incineration of some 20,000 children. This practice horrified the normally tolerant Romans and incited strong sentiment against Carthage. The wildly orgiastic bacchanalia—festivals celebrating Bacchus, the Greco-Roman god of wine—were suppressed as subversive in Rome in 186 BCE, a fate also suffered by some Celtic druids in European provinces during the first century CE. Jews' refusal to show even token reverence to the gods of the Roman state might seem a serious affront, but an early treaty provided a special legal exception that excused the Jews from obligation, and their periodic conflicts with Rome were political rather than religious.

A Phoenician custom, tophets were burial sites for sacrificed children. This one, at Carthage, roused the anger of the usually amenable Romans, for whom human sacrifice was an unacceptable form of worship.

PRIESTS WITHOUT DOGMA

The nonauthoritarian, nondogmatic nature of Classical polytheism contributed to the tolerance fostered by the Roman state religion. The religious beliefs underlying Classical polytheism were sustained through oral traditions and the folktales of myth. Great writers' accounts of particular myths might win lasting fame, but were not regarded as theologically definitive.

Priesthoods of Classical polytheism throughout Roman Europe were often held on a rotating basis by whoever had been elected to a particular political office. Some priesthoods were annually elected; others were appointed by the state for varying durations; still others were hereditary positions occupied by members of privileged families. Priests typically supervised religious rituals such as seasonal processions, the making of sacrifices, or the taking of auspices. Ritual traditions were passed down with their associated priesthoods. These posts required responsible service, but not the priest's spiritual leadership of a congregation. The fact that there was no elaborate orthodoxy meant that Roman priesthoods did not require lifetime dedication and were thus open to anyone of suitable social status. Any prominent citizen in a Roman city would hold a variety of priesthoods in his career, and there was no class of official priests who operated separately from government and society.

Classical polytheism thus belonged to all, rather than to any master authority with an interest in suppressing alternative viewpoints. It would generally take blatant disrespect toward the public gods to make a community feel insulted and bring on the accusation of impiety. As far as the finer points of theology were concerned, philosophers and average citizens alike were free to hold whatever views they might choose.

It was within this environment that the apostles first carried Christian worship from Judaea to the shores of Europe.

Rome was suspicious of bacchanalias in the second century BCE, a sentiment that became magnified in the early centuries CE, when Christians associated the festivities with the Devil.

Mystery Religions in the Roman Empire

FROM THE LOFTY PERCH of his massive temple atop the Capitoline Hill at the center of Rome, Jupiter watched over the welfare of the Roman state and served as the ultimate authority for its laws. With his constant philandering and his shrewdly political double-dealing, Jupiter was never represented as a model of decent behavior. He was in charge only because he was the strongest, and the favor of such a divinity was purchased via rituals and sacrificial offerings.

While Rome was a primitive city-state fighting for its existence, the formal public religion served its needs and focused the reverence of the people toward respect for the state. But as Rome prospered and grew in the final centuries BCE, its culture developed in sophistication, and like the Hellenistic Greeks before them, growing numbers of Romans sought comfort for their inner spiritual concerns—most particularly, their fears about what lay beyond death.

Faiths called "mystery religions" grew to serve these private emotional needs, complementing the public state religion. The mystery faiths offered a savior figure, whose grace could ensure one's happiness in an after-life. Salvation could not be bought by mere money; a savior asked for moral purity. At the heart of these religions lay the mystery of the salvation they offered their initiates.

In the first centuries CE, three leading mystery religions competed within the arena of the Roman Empire: Isis worship from Egypt, Mithraism from Persia, and Christianity from Palestine. From their Eastern origins, each spread far and wide along the trade routes of the unified lands under the Pax Romana. To the one tradition that emerged from the three would fall the legacy of the Roman Empire, which thus shaped the map of European religion for the next two thousand years.

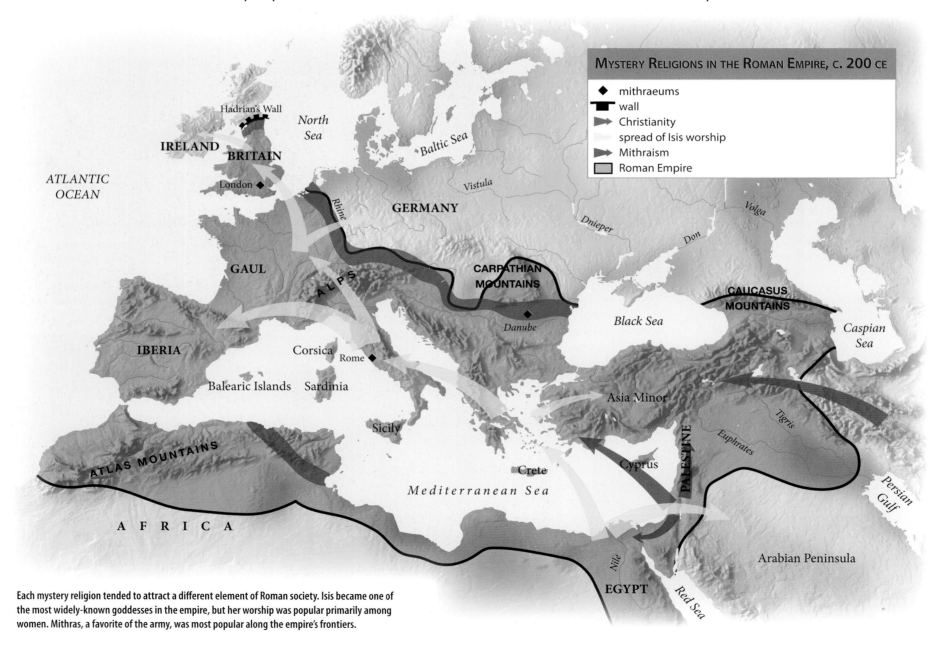

MYSTERY RELIGIONS IN THE ROMAN EMPIRE, C. 200 CE

- ◆ mithraeums
- ▬ wall
- ➤ Christianity
- spread of Isis worship
- ➤ Mithraism
- ▢ Roman Empire

Each mystery religion tended to attract a different element of Roman society. Isis became one of the most widely-known goddesses in the empire, but her worship was popular primarily among women. Mithras, a favorite of the army, was most popular along the empire's frontiers.

Roman soldiers carried Mithraism to the dangerous frontiers of the Roman Empire. Here, the remains of a mithraeum in Britain near Hadrian's Wall, which once marked the edge of Roman civilization.

MITHRAS, PERSIAN GOD OF LIGHT AND TRUTH

The god Mithras emerged from Persian Zoroastrianism in the first century BCE as the focus of his own distinctly Roman mystery tradition. His combat for the salvation of humankind struck a harmonic chord with the dedicated soldiers who built and protected the empire, and Roman legionaries eventually carried the worship of Mithras with them wherever they marched, from Dura Europos in Mesopotamia to Hadrian's Wall in Britain, and across the European frontier.

Followers of Mithras met in small congregations, and their places of worship, called Mithraea, were often built partly underground, to recall the holy cave where Mithras had fought his greatest battle against evil. Roman Mithraea are often of the finest quality. Mithras was also widely worshipped by well-to-do merchants who had earned their prosperity through hard work. Mithras's personal struggle offered such followers a sympathetic individual savior who had endured hardship and suffering to serve the good of mankind, and who extended his grace to those who would take up the task themselves. The adherence of Mithras's followers to their moral code was so well known that the early Christian father Tertullian admonished fellow Christians not to be outdone by the Mithraists.

EARLY CHRISTIANITY AND SYNCRETISM

His followers practiced baptism, shared a sacred supper, worshipped on Sunday instead of the Jewish sabbath Saturday. On December 25 they joyously celebrated the birth of their savior—none other than Mithras. Meanwhile, the priests who used purifying holy water, and candles in the sanctuary, did so in service of the Egyptian goddess Isis. Today all these practices are associated with Christian worship. By the fourth century, many of the popular features of its rival religions had been incorporated into Christianity, helping the faith to grow and appeal to new converts through the age-old process of syncretism.

For millennia, syncretistic borrowings among denominations had been commonplace. Church fathers concerned about doctrinal purity established the concept of orthodoxy, to halt such outside influences. Yet while competing Christian denominations fought bitterly over the purity of their theology, the use of outside worship practices was not so tightly policed. Christianity's adoption of familiar and comforting practices, as well as popular symbols, imagery, and prayers from outside faiths, helped ease the transition for non-Christians when all other religions were outlawed and Christianity became an obligation rather than a choice throughout Roman Europe. Even the physical assets of other mystery religions sometimes survived into Christianity: Mithraea can be found serving as the crypts under many of the oldest Christian churches.

Softly glowing candles are a familiar sight in Christian churches and rituals all over the globe, but their use may originate with other early religions, notably the cult of the Egyptian-Roman goddess Isis.

ISIS, THE EGYPTIAN GODDESS

The worship of Egyptian gods spread into the eastern Mediterranean with the development of close trade connections in the Classical Greek world. The composite Egyptian-Greek god Serapis originally symbolized the Egyptian pantheon. The goddess Isis eventually outshone all other Egyptian deities, however, for it was through her divine love that

A third to seventh century BCE example of an Egyptian sistrum, a ritual instrument used primarily by priestesses in honor of one or more of the myriad Egyptian goddesses.

her husband Osiris was resurrected. In this sacred rebirth was the promise of immortality for the soul. The mysteries of Isis were taught throughout the Roman world and involved elaborate and impressive rites. Rituals featured distinctive traditional Egyptian rattles called sistra and the use of water from the Nile. In time Isis was identified with myriad other female deities, and sung as "Thou of Countless Names." She came to represent virtually every good quality. Isis was deeply loved by people of all walks of life and is frequently pictured on the tombstones of Roman women.

A Roman sistrum, similar in form and function to the more ancient Egyptian sistra, but usually dedicated to Isis alone.

Christianity and Religious Persecution

CHRISTIANITY PRESENTED a special problem for the policy of religious tolerance in the Roman Empire. In Classical polytheism, the Olympian gods protected the welfare of the Roman people in return for appropriate worship. Christians, in denying the existence of the whole Olympian pantheon, seemed dangerously impious and disloyal. And their evangelistic fervor set them apart from the similarly monotheistic Jews; Christians passionately sought new converts and thus eroded public support for the religion that unified the empire.

Nero's famous persecution of Christians in 64 CE was an anomaly. Christians enjoyed relative safety throughout most of the first century, and persecution that did occur tended to be local and sporadic. While refusal to acknowledge the state gods was criminal by Roman law, the general policy toward Christianity in practice was on the order of "don't ask, don't tell."

The second-century emperor Trajan ordered that

accused Christians be given every chance to clear themselves: a simple recantation or a token pinch of incense would give them their freedom. However, many early Christians welcomed death by martyrdom as a guaranteed route to heavenly bliss, much as Muslim extremists do today. This attitude made Christians exasperatingly intractable to Roman efforts at accommodation.

Political instability in the third century produced alternating circumstances for early Christians, as some emperors, such as Philip, tolerated the growing movement, while others, such as Decius, tried to forcibly reassert the state religion to unify the citizenry against the rising threat of barbarian incursions. It was only after Constantine's conversion to the new faith and the toleration ordered by his Edict of Milan in 313 CE that Christianity finally reached complete acceptance by Rome.

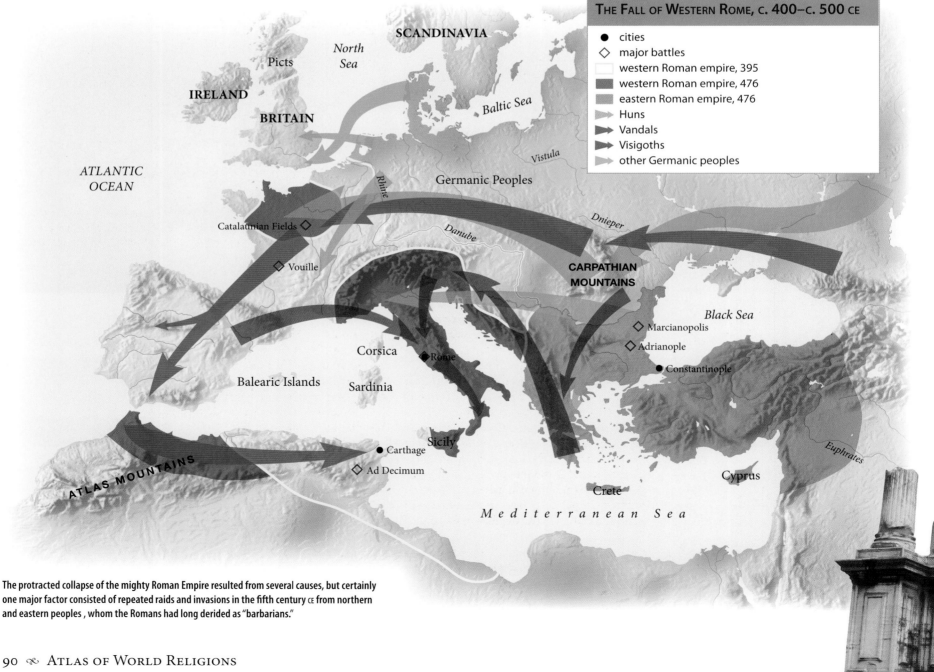

THE FALL OF WESTERN ROME, C. 400–C. 500 CE

- ● cities
- ◇ major battles
- ☐ western Roman empire, 395
- western Roman empire, 476
- eastern Roman empire, 476
- → Huns
- → Vandals
- → Visigoths
- → other Germanic peoples

The protracted collapse of the mighty Roman Empire resulted from several causes, but certainly one major factor consisted of repeated raids and invasions in the fifth century CE from northern and eastern peoples, whom the Romans had long derided as "barbarians."

Anyone who denies that he is a Christian, and gives proof—that is, by making supplication to our gods— shall obtain pardon by his repentance, even if he was under suspicion in the past.
—The emperor Trajan, in Letters of the Younger Pliny

Imperial Christianity

Constantine's conversion was a landmark development for Christianity, but he kept his options open. For another eleven years he continued to offer worship to "the unconquered Sun" as well as Jesus Christ. It was only after the Council of Nicaea in 325 CE that Christianity emerged supreme.

The Roman emperor Theodosius completed the triumph of Christianity in 391, outlawing Classical polytheism and closing the great temples, many of which were destroyed. After burning continuously for the thousand years of Rome's rise, the eternal flame in the Roman Forum was snuffed out.

On Theodosius's death four years later, the empire split permanently into eastern and western halves, never to reunite. This Roman political division left a direct religious legacy in the schism between the Roman Catholic and the (Eastern) Orthodox Church, a major breach that remains in Christianity to this day.

Constantine had moved to centralize Christianity under his absolute control, and set himself up as the dictatorial head of the church, a position inherited by emperors after him. As the new imperial religion, Christianity increasingly controlled religious thought with an iron hand. Alternative views were labeled "heresy," and heretics were often punished

Europe outside Christendom

Beyond the borders of the fallen Roman Empire lived rugged Germanic and Scandinavian peoples who continued to practice their indigenous religion. These northern tribes had never been Romanized into Classical polytheists, and since they lived outside the empire's authority, no one compelled them to convert to official Christianity before the empire ceased to exist. Living wild and free from any dominating authority, these warrior tribes would give rise to the Vikings, whose religion we call Norse, and whose raids on Christian Europe led eventually to their settlement of conquered territories—where even the Norsemen adopted Christianity.

The pocket of northern Europe that lay outside the Roman Empire is far more than a historical footnote. It is only because this region was independent of the Roman religions that the Norse legacy of the fearsome warrior gods Thor, Woden, Freya, and Tyr left its imprint on European civilization. Because the Roman Empire's northward expansion halted in Germany, the Norse divinities survive into the very heart of modern daily life: the English-speaking world acknowledges the old Viking gods every week on Tyr's day, Woden's day, Thor's day, and Freya's day.

with death. Tolerance itself was now considered heresy. Christianity had spread easily throughout the Roman Empire because of religious tolerance. It was a sad irony that once in power, the church would champion religious restriction unprecedented in Europe.

Over the succeeding centuries the legacy of imperial Christianity would carve a record of bitter and bloody persecution, a phenomenon that figured into many of Europe's wars and that perhaps reached its culmination in the Spanish Inquisition. The faith's history in this regard forms a tragic contrast with its gentle founder's exhortations to "judge not, lest ye be judged," and to "love thy neighbor as thyself."

The Barbarian Invasions

Beyond the northern and eastern fringes of the Roman Empire lived tribes that the Romans knew as "barbarians," such as the Goths and the Vandals. By the third century CE, these migratory peoples, originally Scandinavian, were mostly living in the Balkans, preying upon the neighboring Roman territories. Shortly after the Visigoths converted to Arian Christianity, they destroyed a Roman consular army and killed the emperor Valens himself in the decisive battle of Adrianople (in modern Turkey) in 378 CE. From this watershed point the barbarians pressed deeper and deeper into the rich provinces of the empire, leaving a trail of devastation behind them.

The Western, European half of the Roman Empire did not long survive its forced conversion to Christianity. Nineteen years after

The ruins of the Temple of Vesta in Rome, where Vestal Virgins once tended the sacred flame of the empire. Tradition associated the flame with the empire's well-being, perhaps with some justification. Soon after the flame was extinguished the Roman Empire began to dissolve.

A nineteenth-century painting of Gaesaric's sack of Rome shows Pope Leo I convincing the Vandals not to burn the city or commit murder—a plea which worked, according to tradition.

Theodosius had banned Classical polytheism, the chieftain Alaric led his Visigoths to sack and burn Rome in 410. Vandal barbarians under Gaeseric looted and raped their way through the city in 455 CE, their wanton smashing of all good things memorialized in the modern word "vandalism." The sack of imperial Rome was a catastrophe that struck to the foundations of Western civilization. The Western empire never recovered, its strength bleeding away until its final collapse in 476.

The barbarian tribes continued their destructive migrations until the European empire was strewn with wreckage, whereupon they finally settled down in the ruins—the Visigoths in today's France and Spain. Most of the barbarian tribes had converted to Christianity shortly before they began their apocalyptic invasions. And so, ex-Roman and barbarian alike, it was a Christian Europe that hunkered down for the long centuries of ignorance and brutality that came to be called the Dark Ages.

EUROPE
Wisdom and Warriors

By 500 CE the Celtic world was restricted to the British Isles and pockets in France and Spain; the Roman Empire had absorbed the rest of their once-vast European territories. In those unconquered regions, the Celts continued to develop regional cultures, adopting Christianity in spurts but still retaining indigenous beliefs and social customs. Ironically, it is in those areas that became Christian earliest, Ireland and Wales, where we know the most about their pagan beliefs, for Christianity brought the written word—and some early scholars were less Christian than others.

As Icelanders and Anglo-Saxons would later, early Celtic Christians wrote about their own insular mythologies, as well as Christian theology. Occasionally one culture would impress another enough to earn mythological associations; thus King Arthur developed in Wales out of the fifth-century Saxon invasion of Britain, and in Ireland Scandinavia would become Lochlainn, a place resembling the Celtic Otherworld of gods, monsters, and heroes.

Most Celtic and Anglo-Saxon literature was written during or just after the Viking Age, which is sometimes said to have lasted from sunrise on June 8, 793, until sunset on September 25, 1066: from the first recorded Viking raid, on Lindisfarne Abbey in northeastern England, to the Battle of Stamford Bridge, again in northern England, when Harald Hardrada (Hard-rule) of Norway died. During this period, Vikings sailed to Russia and to North America, and even joined the court of the Byzantine emperor, but their literature would flower later, primarily in Iceland in the mid-thirteenth century. Even at that late period, elements of a pre-Christian society persisted. Like their Celtic and Germanic neighbors, the Vikings operated in tribes and small kingdoms, worshipped a plethora of gods, sang about warrior heroes, respected poets for their specialized knowledge, and watched the natural world for signs of divine displeasure.

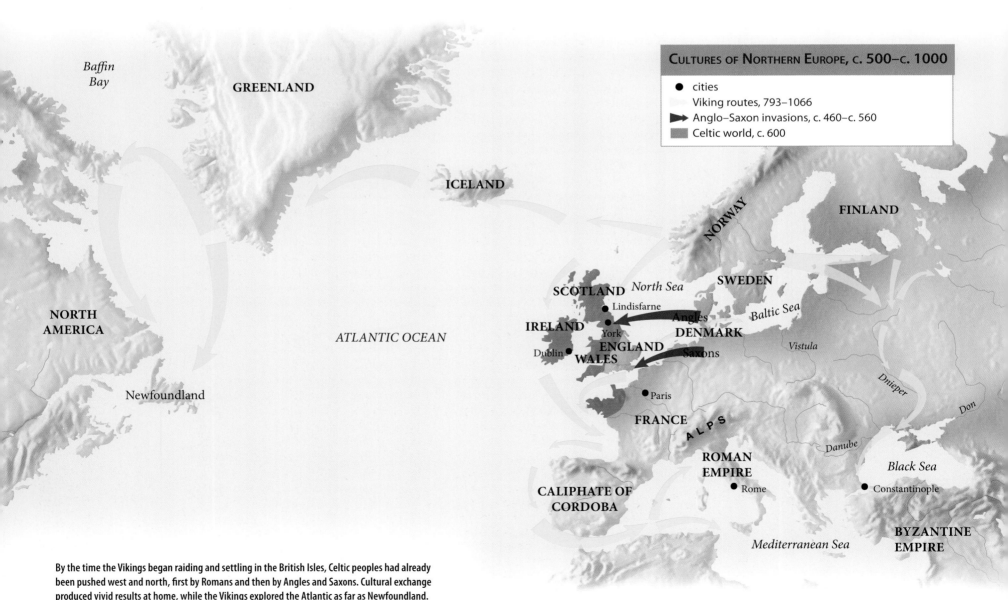

CULTURES OF NORTHERN EUROPE, c. 500–c. 1000

- • cities
- Viking routes, 793–1066
- ➤ Anglo–Saxon invasions, c. 460–c. 560
- Celtic world, c. 600

By the time the Vikings began raiding and settling in the British Isles, Celtic peoples had already been pushed west and north, first by Romans and then by Angles and Saxons. Cultural exchange produced vivid results at home, while the Vikings explored the Atlantic as far as Newfoundland.

"The man who would have done the deed is Cú Chulainn," said Fergus. "It is he who would have cut down the tree with one blow from its root, and he who would have killed the four men as quickly as they were killed, and he who would have come to the border accompanied (only) by his charioteer."
—TÁIN BÓ CÚAILNGE (TRANSLATION BY CECILE O'RAHILLY)

THE AGE OF THE POET

Among other similarities, all three cultures shared a reverence for poets and poetry, tending to view their bards as divinely inspired. Esoteric knowledge was imagined to be the result of drinking the brew of the gods—a myth particularly developed in Iceland. According to the myth, the mead of poetry is brewed from the blood of the wisest man and the spit of the gods, and is distributed by the god of poetry, Odin, to his favorites. The myth is recounted in one of the primary texts of Norse mythology, the Prose Edda, written in the mid-thirteenth century as a primer on traditional poetry, which often incorporated mythological motifs. At the time, Icelandic poets were renowned throughout Europe.

One of the favorite subjects for a northern European poet was the hero, usually a semidivine man who achieved great deeds or protected his society from harm, whether supernatural or not. Three of the greatest heroes, all of whose stories were written down between the eighth and twelfth centuries, were Cú Chulainn of Ireland, Sigurd of Nordic myth (Siegfried in German), and Beowulf of Anglo-Saxon fame. All of these typify the hero of northern European mythology: a great warrior who fights monsters, often displaying more than a hint of the monstrous himself.

KING ARTHUR

King Arthur, a semi-mythological, semi-legendary British hero, first appears in eighth-century Welsh literature. The historical King Arthur may have been a Welsh or Roman-British war chief who led the resistance against the Saxon invasions of the fifth century, but he quickly earned a place in Welsh—and subsequently Cornish, British, Scottish, and even French—mythology and legend. Elements of his story, popularized by the fifteenth-century *Le Morte d'Arthur*, seem strikingly Christian, notably his expected resurrection and his involvement with the Holy Grail. The Grail, though a later Christian addition, has struck some as reminiscent of Welsh and Irish cauldrons of life and plenty.

A fourteenth century tapestry depicts King Arthur as a contemporary Christian king, with bishops for companions.

WAR AND RELIGION

The Romans who experienced the battle rage of continental Celts and Germans often expressed shock, likening their cries and ferocity to those of ravening beasts. Later, Christians would say similar things about marauding Vikings, whom they saw as the devil's hordes. The evidence in both cases is one-sided, since there are no written accounts from the other side. But undeniably the mythologies of northern Europe emphasize a warrior elite, a religion of war expressed in gods like Tyr, god of justice and single combat; Thor, thunder god and giant-killer, always up for a good fight; and the Irish goddess Morrigan, who visits battlefields as a raven to feast on the fallen dead. This warrior culture is also evident in the ship-burials of the Anglo-Saxons, in which kings and nobles were placed with all their trappings of war in their greatest war machines—the ships themselves.

Accounts of warriors acting like animals may not, in fact, be hyperbole. The best evidence for cultlike warrior groups comes from Scandinavia, where the behavior of elite warriors, called berserkir (bear- or bare-shirts, whence English "berserk") or ulfhednar (wolf-shirts) is well attested. These men may have been dedicated to Odin; certainly their battlefield abandon and reports of invincibility and superhuman abilities suggest some divine associations.

Ravens and scenes of wolves devouring men decorate this lavish purse lid, discovered among other noble belongings at the Sutton Hoo ship burial in southeastern England.

A Viking-age rune stone illustrates one of the most famous scenes of Sigurd's career, the slaying of the dragon Fafnir by hiding in a pit and stabbing him from below. Although worn, the figure of Sigurd thrusting a sword through the dragon can be seen at the top.

The Decline of Egypt's Gods

AFTER OVERTHROWING the Ptolemaic dynasty in 30 BCE, Rome ruled over Egypt—Aegyptus, the Latin name for the province—but relatively few Roman citizens settled there. Greeks remained the ruling or elite class, with the official language, culture, and society remaining Hellenistic.

At first Rome showed respect for the ancient Egyptian religion, as well as for other prominent faiths, such as Judaism. When Rome suppressed the Jewish revolt of 70 CE and destroyed the Jerusalem temple, so many Jews fled to Egypt that Alexandria became the world center of Judaism. Intermittent strife between Greeks and Jews caused riots and resulted in punishment for Jewish residents, but Aegyptus was generally peaceful and prosperous through the second century CE.

Early Christianity, too, made inroads in Egypt, as well as in the former Carthaginian cities of North Africa and Phoenicia. Alexandria also became a leading center for Christians, many of whom may have been practicing Gnosticism. There is little surviving evidence of the nature of Christianity in those first centuries CE, and some scholars speculate that in later years the heretical nature of early Christianity caused embarrassment to the established church, so any records of Gnosticism were eliminated.

With the rise of Christianity to the status of official Roman religion in the fourth century CE, the worship of ancient Egyptian gods faded away. Politically powerful Christians began in their turn to persecute "pagan" faiths, and the old Egyptian religious customs had to be practiced in secret.

Traditional religious leaders lost authority, and the old customs lost their appeal to native Egyptians, who made up the bulk of the lower social classes. Meanwhile, Christianity found wide acceptance with its teachings that uplifted the poverty-stricken and theoretically made all worshippers equal in the eyes of the church.

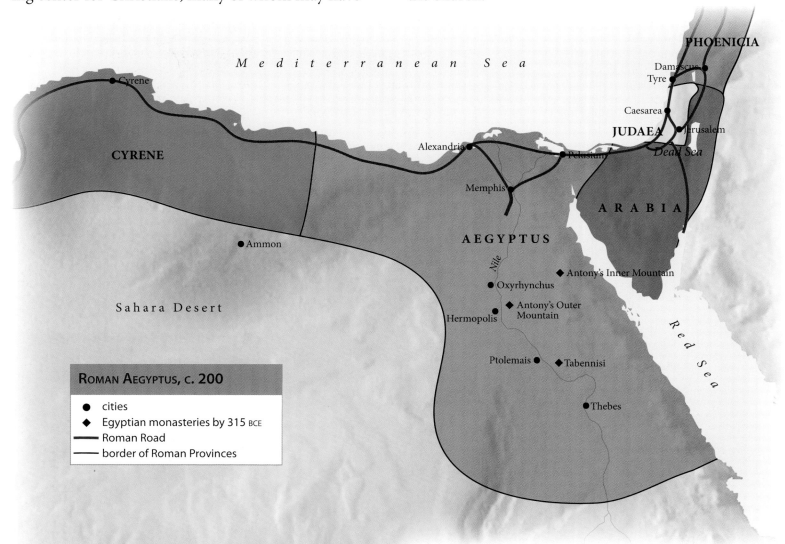

ROMAN AEGYPTUS, C. 200

- ● cities
- ◆ Egyptian monasteries by 315 BCE
- ── Roman Road
- ── border of Roman Provinces

Although no longer a mighty empire, Egypt (now the Roman province Aegyptus) nevertheless retained hallmarks of its former glory. Several of its gods entered the nebulous Roman pantheon, while its reputation as a place of mysterious knowledge spread and its champion city, Alexandria, became a crowning jewel of the empire.

That which is Below corresponds to that which is Above, and that which is Above corresponds to that which is Below, to accomplish the miracle of the One Thing.

—Hermes Trismegistus, in The Emerald Tablet; from Secret of the Emerald Tablet by Gottlieb Latz (translation by Dennis W. Hauck)

The Vanishing Gods of the Pyramids

Although some formal temple worship—of the much-loved Isis, for example—continued in Egypt into the fifth century CE, the decrease in priests and priestesses caused a corresponding decline in religious learning. With Greek as the most important language, even the ability to read hieroglyphics virtually disappeared. So, too, did the temples themselves—some converted into churches, others were abandoned. In Alexandria, the magnificent old-religion temple of Serapis remained a focus of traditional Egyptian worship.

In the fourth century CE, bitter conflicts developed among Egyptian Christians, and Alexandria became the scene of Christianity's first major schism. The party known as Arians, which considered Jesus not fully divine, was accused of heresy by the establishment in Rome. Arians refused to submit to the established Christian church, and the resulting dispute became more than simply philosophical debate. The two sides took up arms and fought in Alexandria's streets. Rome's archbishop in the city was deposed and reinstalled a number of times, and during the clashes the Serapis temple was attacked and destroyed.

As Egypt became a melting pot, and at times a boiling cauldron, of Christian denominations—Arianism, Manichaeanism, Gnosticism, and the first monastic movement, among others—the ancient religion of the Pyramid Age almost vanished. The Egyptian language was rescued, however, with the appearance of the newly developed Coptic language, which combined ancient Egyptian with the Greek alphabet. Many Egyptian Christians adopted Coptic, which became the method of proselytizing in Egypt. Yet the faith of the pharaohs was further diminished.

Still, the fount of Egyptian religious and philosophical tradition would continue to provide timeless wisdom. Among the most enduring philosophical concepts to have come out of Egypt is Hermeticism, with its mythic figure Hermes Trismegistus, the author of its teachings, which have parallels in Gnosticism and early Christianity. Widely known and studied in later centuries, Hermes is considered a combination (syncretism) of the Greek deity Hermes (Mercury to the Romans) and the Egyptian god Thoth—both gods of writing and of spiritual magic, and guides of souls to the afterlife.

The restored mosaic dome of an Arian baptistery in Ravenna, Italy. Dating to the late fifth or early sixth century, the scene shows the baptism of Jesus Christ. The baptistery was converted to an oratory in 565, after Arianism had lost its authority, but the dome was left intact.

Hermes Trismegistus

History does not indicate that an actual Egyptian priest existed with the Hellenic name Hermes Trismegistus, but a body of spiritual and philosophical writings is attributed to that name. Plato said Egyptian temples had secret halls containing religious texts from 9,000 years previous, and an early Christian author stated that writings (mainly in Greek) of Hermes laid out the traditional training of Egyptian priests.

Some religious scholars and philosophers speculated that the author had to be a contemporary of Moses. Others believed the works were written in the first centuries ce rather than by some ancient Egyptian priest.

The writings of Hermes Trismegistus became the basis for philosophical and religious beliefs collectively known as Hermeticism. The best-known surviving texts attributed to Hermes Trismegistus include *The Corpus Hermeticum* (sixteen Greek books) and *The Emerald Tablet* (a short discussion of spiritual wisdom). Legend has it that Alexander the Great himself discovered *The Emerald Tablet* at Hebron in Judaea, inside the very tomb of Hermes.

Hermeticism teaches of the oneness and goodness of God, of reincarnation of the divine aspect of humanity, and describes various levels of existence—particularly of a macrocosm and microcosm, which are cosmically interrelated. In this regard *The Emerald Tablet* contains a phrase that became famous among spiritual seekers and philosophical thinkers: "As above, so below."

By the 1400s, after centuries of obscurity, and rejection by religious authorities, these Hermetic teachings from Egypt would become a potent influence in the world's religious and philosophical discourses.

Above: A seventeenth-century depiction of Hermes Trismegistus.

Left: Paired Coptic (on top) and Arabic inscriptions can be found throughout Egypt. Combining elements of both Greek and Egyptian, Coptic was a language of choice for many early Christians in the region.

Religion, Philosophy, Wisdom

THROUGHOUT THE SECOND HALF of the first millennium BCE, wide-ranging commerce and frequent military conquests brought the peoples of West Asia and the Mediterranean together, by choice or compulsion. Cultures and languages intermingled and influenced one another, especially in the intercourse of religious customs and secular philosophical concepts.

From Greek city-states to Persia's agricultural regions and the empire of Carthage, much was shared of the ancient myths and deities. Respect for foreign gods and belief systems was part of the fabric of civilized life, and a traveler would be likely to pray to the local deities while remembering the gods of home.

The name of the Canaanite-Phoenician god Baal, for example, was familiar to all Mediterranean peoples. To the Carthaginians, he was chief god of their ancestors; to the Romans, he was Saturn; to the Greeks, he was Cronus. Baal in his various aspects was widely regarded as a fertility god alongside Ashtart, the corresponding female figure—Ishtar in Mesopotamia, Astarte in Egypt and Judaea, and Aphrodite in the Greek lands.

Knowledge, too, was shared and disseminated. The Mesopotamian religions, and particularly the priest-scientists of Assyria and Babylonia, gave the world the twelve-constellation zodiac, a product of their studies of the stars and the movements of heavenly bodies. Studying the firmament and understanding its changing aspects from season to season and year to year led to new scientific developments, including navigation by sighting on the positions of stars. The priest-scientists of Mesopotamia imparted such learning, which became widely known as "Chaldean wisdom," after a name for southern Babylonia. Chaldean was a term for individuals who were knowledgeable in Babylonian literature and science, especially astronomy and astrology.

ALEXANDRIA: THE CENTER OF LEARNING AND RELIGION

Most faiths professed a belief in the power of the stars and planets to influence world conditions in general and an individual's fortunes in particular. With the assignment of deities to the planets and constellations—the sun and moon being most prominent—these powers were personified and could be worshipped and petitioned in temples and through oracles dedicated to the respective gods.

Just as the cities of Mesopotamia were revered for their learned priests and scribes and for the growing store of wisdom in their libraries and educational institutions, Egypt held a lofty place in the religious culture of the age. Although her days as a great power had passed, Egypt was a spiritual beacon because of her long-standing religious traditions and places of worship, which influenced the beliefs of most Mediterranean and West Asian peoples.

Egypt had been ruled by Persians for generations until regaining independence briefly at the close of the fifth century BCE. The Persians returned, later to be ousted by Alexander of Macedon's invasion in 332 BCE. Received by the Egyptians as a deliverer from Persia, Alexander gave proof of the importance of the Egyptian gods when he worshipped them at Memphis. Next, he undertook a pilgrimage through the desert to the oracle of Amun, one of Egypt's most important deities. Alexander is said to have followed birds who led him to the remote oasis. There, a kinship between Amun and Zeus was proclaimed, and the priests declared Alexander a deity, descended from Amun.

Alexander soon left Egypt to invade the Persian Empire, with his destiny assured by the oracle's prediction that he would be a great conqueror. Before his departure, he founded a new city, Alexandria, at the mouth of the Nile.

Alexander's triumphs over the next ten years spread Hellenic culture widely, and it took root in the cities he captured or founded, from the Mediterranean to the Himalayas. More than any other of these cities, Alexandria blossomed and prospered, eventually laying claim to the mantle of Hellenic culture and to its educational tradition, rich in reading and writing and libraries. Although many cities were named after him, Alexander's imperial jewel was Egypt's Alexandria, where he was laid to rest after his death at the age of thirty-two.

A mosaic zodiac from Beit Alpha synagogue in Israel. Dating to the fifth or sixth centuries CE, the zodiac combines Mesopotamian astrology and Hebrew descriptions.

A LIBRARY FOR THE MUSES

Alexandria's most renowned cultural treasure was its Great Library, or Royal Library, established by the third century BCE under the Ptolemaic dynasty that assumed kingship of Egypt upon Alexander's death.

By the second century BCE no library could match that of Alexandria in Egypt for size and importance. The Alexandrian Library was essentially a temple, dedicated to the nine muses, the goddesses of the arts—among them poetry, music, singing, and oratory. A building so dedicated was more than just a place to keep records and books. It was termed a museum, a place of the muses, a temple that housed the wisdom of the ages.

The Alexandrian Library became a world center for scholarship, literature, and books. Termed the Great Library to distinguish it from others in the city, it acquired the largest holdings of the day, including many works of philosophers, priests, and literati from Hellenic lands. The highest estimates claim 400,000 scrolls (often complete books) were stored at the Great Library. Some scrolls were acquired by purchase—in many cases Alexandria bought whole private libraries—but for the most part they were added one at a time by scribes laboriously copying original documents, often from clay tablets.

Over the centuries the Great Library suffered from fires and conquest, but the city remained famous as the world's leading repository of learning and wisdom. Alexandria retained her status even during Rome's ascendancy, from the second century BCE to the first centuries CE.

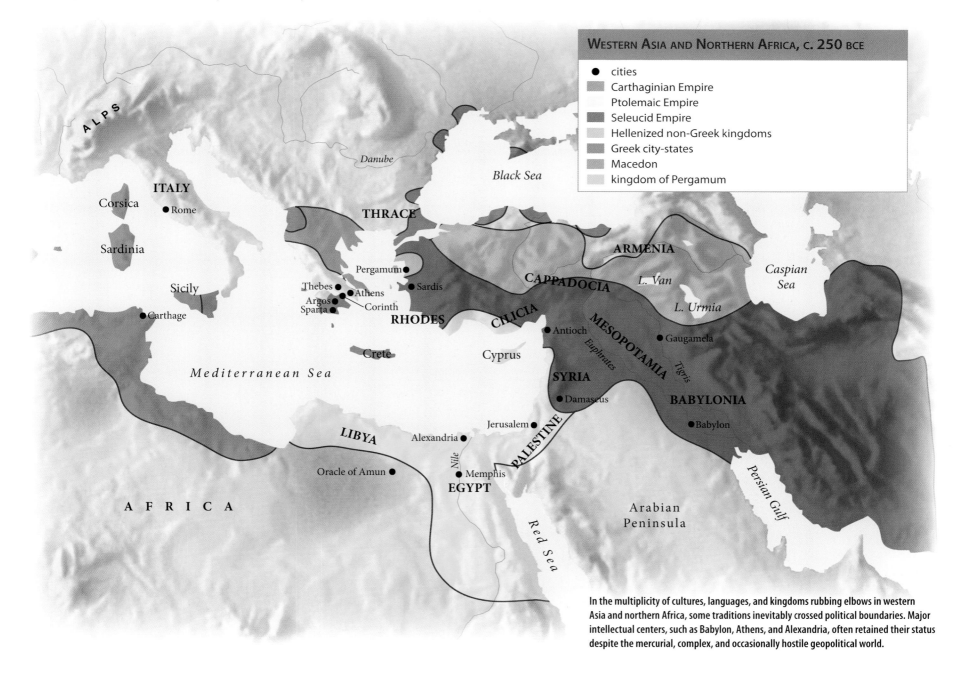

> *Thus the soul, since it is immortal and has been born many times and has seen all things both here and in the other world, has learned everything that is.*
> —PLATO, FROM A DIALOGUE ON THE IMMORTALITY OF THE SOUL

One of the Seven Wonders of the Ancient World, the lighthouse on Pharos Island guided ships into Alexandria's harbor for nearly 1,800 years. As a marvel of engineering, it illuminated Alexandria's standing as an intellectual capital of the world.

An Alexandrian mathematician, cartographer, and astronomer, Claudius Ptolemaeus (more usually known as Ptolemy) developed a cosmology that was to endure in the West until the sixteenth century, combining Greek, Mesopotamian, and Egyptian systems of knowledge.

WESTERN ASIA AND NORTHERN AFRICA, C. 250 BCE

- cities
- Carthaginian Empire
- Ptolemaic Empire
- Seleucid Empire
- Hellenized non-Greek kingdoms
- Greek city-states
- Macedon
- kingdom of Pergamum

In the multiplicity of cultures, languages, and kingdoms rubbing elbows in western Asia and northern Africa, some traditions inevitably crossed political boundaries. Major intellectual centers, such as Babylon, Athens, and Alexandria, often retained their status despite the mercurial, complex, and occasionally hostile geopolitical world.

Part Two: The Foundations of Organized Religion ❧ 97

An Empire of Hellenic Culture

ALEXANDER THE GREAT's decade-long conquest of the Achaemenid Empire, which had ruled Persia and much of Mesopotamia, opened floodgates of cultural exchange between the Mediterranean lands and the East. The vast empire Alexander created—reaching to the borders of India—was characterized by local rulers, often subordinate commanders, establishing cities and states populated by Greek colonists and native peoples.

Greek language and culture penetrated an immense region, spreading Hellenistic philosophy, government, and religion. Greek temples became the centers of cities as far east as the upper Indus River. The larger towns usually had a citadel (acropolis), gymnasiums, and libraries (public and private). Libraries often had temples attached for the patrons to exercise their faith as well as their minds.

Simultaneously, seeds of religion, science, and culture drifted westward from the conquered lands and found fertile ground throughout the Mediterranean.

Mithraism, an offshoot of Zoroastrianism, acquired adherents from Mesopotamia to Carthage and beyond. Mesopotamian astrology became important to many Greek philosophers, especially the mystics, who were fascinated by eastern religious thought and wisdom. Even the most forward-thinking intellects of Greece, and later Rome, were attracted by astrology's purported powers of divination.

The Greek myths and pantheon remained revered by Hellenistic philosophers, some of whom also became followers of cults honoring Egyptian deities. Osiris, the Egyptian god of nature and of the dead, and his wife, Isis—perhaps the best-loved Egyptian deity—became the objects of a new Greek cult that appealed to the philosopher Plato, who also studied and incorporated the teachings of Zoroaster into his works.

Although Alexander's empire did not last long as a political entity after his death at Babylon in 323 BCE, the peoples he brought together were changed forever.

In a long line of ancient Mediterranean-based empires, that of Alexander the Great stands out. Not only was it one of the largest, stretching more than 3,000 miles (4,800 km) east to west, but Alexander himself conquered much of the territory personally. The emperor became a legend in his own time, but his empire disintegrated rapidly after his death.

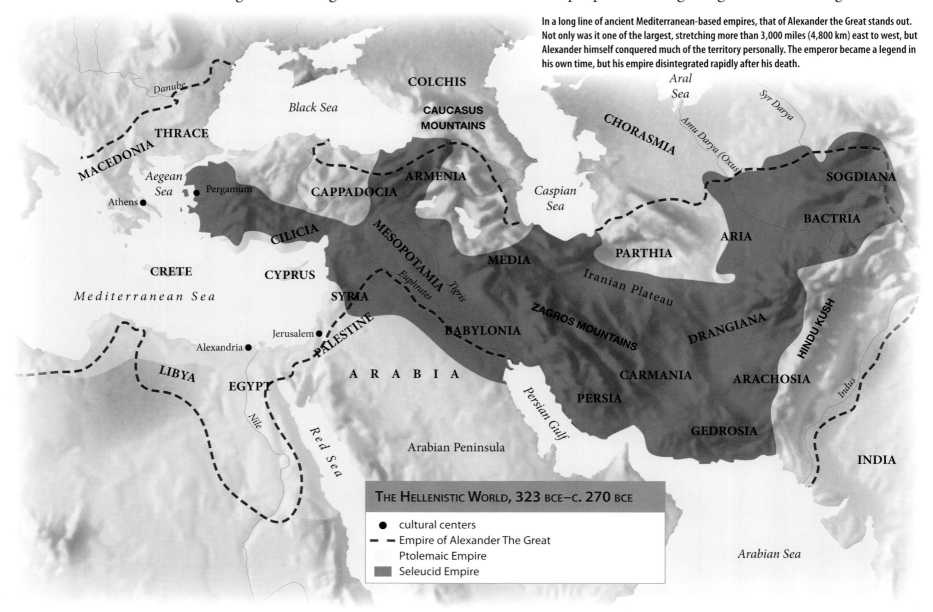

THE HELLENISTIC WORLD, 323 BCE–c. 270 BCE

- ● cultural centers
- - - Empire of Alexander The Great
-   Ptolemaic Empire
-   Seleucid Empire

The library of Celsus in Ephesus was built in the second century CE and could house up to 12,000 scrolls. It is one of the best remaining examples of Roman library architecture.

And Judas, and his brethren, and all ... Israel decreed, that the day of the dedication of the altar should be kept in its season from year to year for eight days ... with joy and gladness.
— 1 MACCABEES

A Hellenic bust of Isis, dating to the second century CE and bearing little resemblance to the Egyptian goddess of the Old, Middle, or New Kingdoms.

SELEUCIDS COMPEL HELLENIZATION

As the hub of Hellenistic civilization moved away from Athens, the leading focal points of culture and religion developed at Alexandria in Egypt and at Pergamum in western Anatolia. Both became great centers of learning, and a fierce rivalry between them lasted for generations, each striving to be more important and more beautiful than the other. Pergamum was western Anatolia's greatest Hellenistic city and, with its magnificent theater and library, a worthy competitor to Alexandria.

The rivalry was so stiff that Alexandria forbade the export of papyrus to Pergamum in order to make it more difficult for that city's scribes to copy books. Papyrus grew exclusively along the Nile and was used to produce the world's most important writing surface. In response, Pergamum developed its own writing material made from the skins of calf, sheep, or goat. Harking back to its origins, it is known as pergamenum in Latin, pergament in Germanic languages, and parchment in English.

As Roman legions replaced Greek phalanxes around the Mediterranean, new powers developed on the Persian plateau. Independent-minded Hellenistic cities and states fought the Seleucid dynasty that came to rule most of Persia, Syria, and Babylonia from 312 to 60 BCE. The Seleucids, descended from one of Alexander's generals, intensified the process of Hellenizing their empire. In many cases subjects were compelled by force to accept Greek religion, government, and philosophy, and many cities were given Greek names. Religions that resisted such change were persecuted.

Although Zoroastrianism had been allowed to flourish under the religiously tolerant Achaemenid dynasty, little is known of its standing in the Seleucid Empire. The Jews of Judaea, however, famously revolted against religious oppression. In the second century BCE they refused imperial edicts to worship Greek gods and abandon their own faith. Led by the four Maccabee brothers, they won independence that would endure for more than a century.

In joyous triumph, the Jews ritually cleansed and rededicated the Jerusalem temple, installing a Maccabee as high priest. The Hanukkah festival annually celebrates this Jewish victory and the temple's rededication.

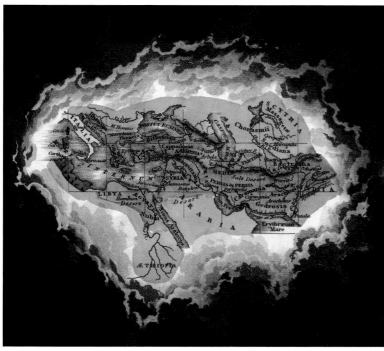

A nineteenth-century map uses clouds to emphasize the "known world" of ancient Persia and Alexander's Macedonian empire, shown in pink.

LIBRARIES, BOOKS, AND IDEAS

In the later centuries of the first millennium BCE, libraries were at the heart of the world's great cultures, whether Egyptian, Greek, Roman, Babylonian, or Persian. Books and libraries reached virtually every corner of the civilized world, contributing to a dynamic exchange of ideas that inspired religious thinkers and rational philosophers alike. Libraries preserved an ever-increasing body of literature—mostly written on papyrus scrolls—being produced as never before by rulers, priests, generals, scientists, philosophers, and poets.

Publishing meant laboriously copying documents that had been purchased or borrowed or traded for copies of other documents. Books were in demand everywhere, and armies of scribes were kept busy turning them out. In the last centuries BCE, libraries grew in importance, both as places to read and as repositories of a people's beliefs and their relationships with the deities.

As documents, sacred teachings could be preserved, copied, stored, read, and shared in libraries, while oral tradition could not. Oral teachings, once the prerogative of priests and scholars, were transformed into books and documents that could be handed down to be studied by future generations.

Books recorded knowledge, customs, and religious beliefs, and religious writings of every kind were sought out and translated. By the end of the first century BCE in much of the Mediterranean world and West Asia, the written word, libraries, and their role in disseminating religious thought had laid the groundwork for the appearance and rapid rise of Christianity.

The Rise of Judaism

JUDAISM WAS ONE OF the earliest monotheistic faiths, along with Egypt's fourteenth-century BCE cult of the pharaoh Akhenaten and first-millennium BCE Zoroastrianism. Scholars debate just when the Hebrews ceased being henotheistic—that is, crediting the existence of other people's gods while believing that one's own god was superior—and became truly monotheistic.

The traditional Jewish view holds that the patriarch Abraham practiced monotheism, while others maintain that Jewish monotheism took root during the Babylonian exile of the sixth century BCE. The destruction of the temple at Jerusalem in this time and the seventy-year "Babylonian Captivity" caused exiled Jewish scholars to worry that their religious heritage—a mainly oral tradition—might be lost, so they compiled and edited the Torah, a volume that contains the first five books of the Hebrew Bible. By the first century CE, leading Jewish scholars were recording their oral discourses and many of the teachings that had been handed down. This led to the publishing of a compilation known as the Talmud, completed in the first centuries CE. A supplement to the scriptures, the Talmud explains the 613 laws enumerated in the Torah.

The publishing of the Hebrew Bible earned Jews the name "People of the Book," for Judaism was structured by the written word. Its cornerstone was the Tanakh—the Hebrew Bible—and scholarly commentaries on it.

Jewish communities developed throughout the Fertile Crescent, from Mesopotamia to Egypt, by the close of the first century BCE, and Alexandria was a major center of Judaism, with more than a million Jewish residents. Ptolemaic rulers brought thousands of Jewish soldiers and their families to Egypt, settling them throughout the kingdom. The Delta district along Alexandria's waterfront was mainly Jewish, with a large number of families tracing their ancestry in Egypt back many centuries, well before the Persian occupations.

THE PENTATEUCH

The Torah, meaning "doctrine" or "teaching," is considered the inspired word of Yahweh, the Hebrew God, as it was imparted to Moses when he led the Israelites from Egypt to seek the Promised Land. At Mount Sinai Moses received the famous Ten Commandments, which are also revered by Christians, and an additional 603 commandments. These commandments, or laws, became the fundamental guidelines of Jewish life, addressing issues that range from everyday habits to profound ethical and religious matters.

The first five books of the Hebrew Bible are Genesis, Exodus, Leviticus, Numbers, and Deuteronomy. Their Hebrew titles can be translated, respectively, as: "In the beginning," "Names," "And he called," "In the desert," and "Discourses." Genesis is the creation legend; Exodus is the story of Moses and the flight from Egypt; Leviticus contains religious instruction; Numbers narrates the Israelite approach to the Promised Land, and Deuteronomy consists mainly of addresses by Moses to the Israelites, calling upon them to obey God as they prepare to enter Canaan, the Promised Land.

The importance of an enduring set of laws such as the Torah—and the writings that interpret them—was emphasized by the Jewish dispersion, or Diaspora, that resulted from the eventual destruction of the two Jewish kingdoms established in the land of Canaan. The northern kingdom of Israel was conquered by the Assyrians in the eighth century BCE, and Judah, with Jerusalem, fell to the Babylonians in the sixth century BCE.

The Diaspora scattered the Jews far and wide, but with the writing down and publishing of the Torah and Talmud, the faithful could practice their religion, no matter where they lived, and be in accord with Jews everywhere in the world. Other religions had no such written codification of their canon, which had to be interpreted by individual priests and scribes and was based mainly on oral tradition.

A Greek inscription from a synagogue in Hamat Tiberias, Israel, constructed by 286 BCE. The inscription underscores the strong Hellenic influence in Jewish life by the end of the first millennium BCE.

Torah scrolls, when intended for ritual purposes, are still handwritten today, following a tradition dating to at least the time of the Diaspora. The Torah contains the Pentateuch, or the first five books of the Hebrew Bible.

The Lord is my strength and my song,
and he has become my salvation;
this is my God and I will praise him,
my father's God, and I will exalt him.
—FROM THE BOOK OF EXODUS: MOSES IS
CELEBRATING THE ESCAPE OF THE ISRAELITES

JEWS IN THE HELLENIC WORLD

In Hellenized Egypt the Jews were the second-largest minority after the Greeks, who made up the ruling class and would continue as the elite even throughout the following Roman era. As with most peoples of the age, the Jews of Egypt were absorbed in a generation or two by the pervasive culture and political power of Greece. Since Hellenized Jews spoke only Greek, the Hebrew Bible was translated at Alexandria in the third century BCE.

These scriptures were named the Septuagint because they were said to have been translated by seventy divinely inspired scholars. Other historians contend the Hebrew scriptures were actually translated over three centuries. Whatever the actual time required, the Greek translations attest to the cultural Hellenization of most Jews by the end of the first millennium BCE.

The importance of Jews, politically and culturally, to Alexandria and Egypt paral-

A fifteenth-century depiction of the Maccabean Revolt, which established an independent Jewish kingdom in Israel in about 164 BCE. The kingdom lasted a century, eventually falling to Roman control.

lels the dynamic rise of Judaism throughout West Asia and the Mediterranean during this period. Even after Rome's conquest in 30 BCE of Cleopatra, ending the Ptolemaic dynasty, Jewish social status and political influence remained considerable in Egypt. The main synagogue in Alexandria, designed in the style of a Greek basilica, was long one of the Roman Empire's most magnificent buildings. Resistance to Roman rule in the Jewish homeland during the second century BCE brought on brutal Roman suppression, which caused a further dispersion of Jews.

By the last decades BCE, Jewish communities were thriving from southern Gaul to northern Germany, in the former Carthaginian colonies of northeast Africa, in central Italy, along the Aegean shores of Greece and Asia Minor, and in the cities of Mesopotamia. Uniting this people was their faith, set down in writing and published, so that all Jews could study the scriptures and worship in common, wherever they resided, within or without the Roman Empire.

By the first century CE, many more Jews lived outside of Judaea than inside. Since traditional Jewish belief holds that the physical territory of ancient Canaan is holy and given by God to the Jews, this geographical dispersion did not occur without deep cultural concern.

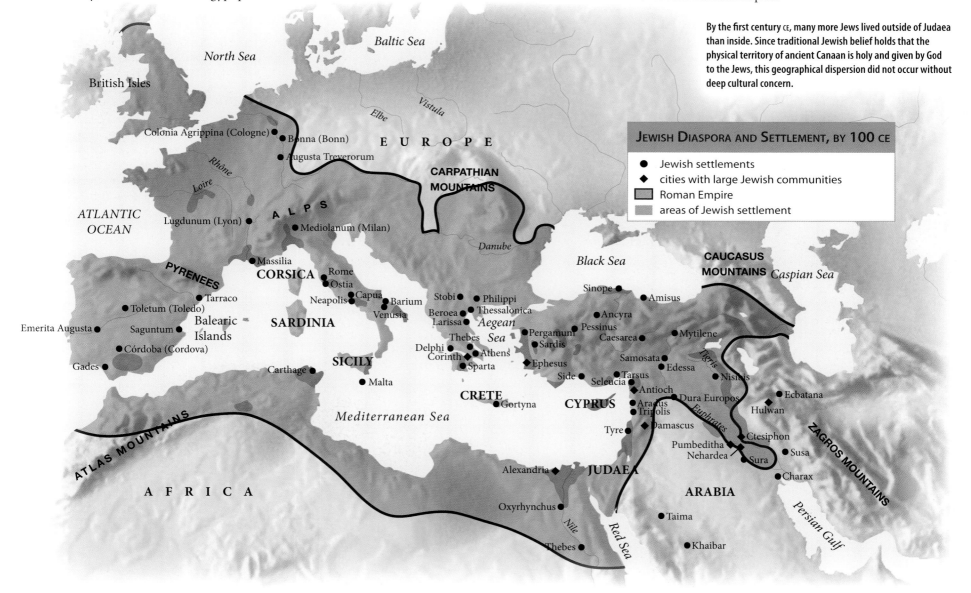

JEWISH DIASPORA AND SETTLEMENT, BY 100 CE

- ● Jewish settlements
- ◆ cities with large Jewish communities
- ▨ Roman Empire
- ▨ areas of Jewish settlement

Baltic Sea
North Sea
British Isles
ATLANTIC OCEAN
EUROPE
Colonia Agrippina (Cologne)
Bonna (Bonn)
Augusta Treverorum
Elbe
Vistula
Rhône
Loire
Lugdunum (Lyon)
Mediolanum (Milan)
ALPS
CARPATHIAN MOUNTAINS
Danube
Massilia
PYRENEES
CORSICA
Rome
Ostia
Capua
Neapolis
Barium
Venusia
Tarraco
Toletum (Toledo)
Saguntum
Emerita Augusta
Córdoba (Cordova)
Gades
Balearic Islands
SARDINIA
SICILY
Carthage
Malta
Black Sea
Stobi
Philippi
Thessalonica
Beroea
Larissa
Aegean Sea
Thebes
Delphi
Corinth
Athens
Sparta
Sinope
Amisus
Ancyra
Pessinus
Caesarea
Pergamum
Sardis
Ephesus
Side
Mytilene
Samosata
Edessa
Tarsus
Seleucia
Antioch
Aradus
Tripolis
Damascus
Tyre
Dura Europos
Nisibis
Ecbatana
Hulwan
Tigris
Euphrates
Ctesiphon
Pumbeditha
Nehardea
Sura
Susa
Charax
ZAGROS MOUNTAINS
CAUCASUS MOUNTAINS
Caspian Sea
CRETE
Gortyna
CYPRUS
Mediterranean Sea
ATLAS MOUNTAINS
AFRICA
Alexandria
JUDAEA
Oxyrhynchus
Nile
Red Sea
Thebes
ARABIA
Taima
Khaibar
Persian Gulf

Zoroastrianism and Manichaeanism

FROM ALEXANDER'S FORMER EMPIRE on the Persian plateau, kingdoms and states both large and small rose and fell, many to be absorbed by the Parthians after 250 BCE. These hard-riding Scythian people from the north built an empire that endured almost five centuries. The Parthians held back Roman eastward expansion and came to control—and grow rich from—the Silk Road trade routes, which opened around the first century BCE, linking the Mediterranean to India and China.

Around 224 CE a Persian uprising overthrew the Parthians and established a new Persian empire. The defeated Parthians resisted with occasional revolts, but many eventually fled eastward to India. The new Persian dynasty, the Sassanids, claimed to be of a priestly caste, rightful heirs to the Achaemenids and protectors of Zoroastrianism, which again became the state religion. Ancient traditions from Achaemenid times were commingled with teachings of Zoroaster to fashion official religious doctrine.

The Sassanid, or Sassanian Empire aggressively advanced Zurvanism, a divergent form of Zoroastrianism. The chief deity, Zurvan, was considered the primordial creator, not Ahura Mazda, who was relegated to the status of a subordinate god. Ahura Mazda was considered a twin deity, along with Angra Mainyu, better known as Ahriman. These twins were equal but opposite divinities—Ahura Mazda benevolent and Ahriman malevolent. Zurvan, their father, had brought them into being with the task of creating heaven and hell and "everything in between."

Zurvanism took several different forms. One version professed that human destiny was determined by the stars and planets—a doctrine thought to have been influenced by Chaldean astrology as well as by Aristotelian theories of chance and fortune. Some translations of Zurvan use the term "Fate."

The Persian empires were squarely between East and West Asia, and although Zoroastrianism and related native faiths remained supreme, both Eastern and Western religions traveled regularly across the Persian plateau, along the enormously lucrative Silk Road.

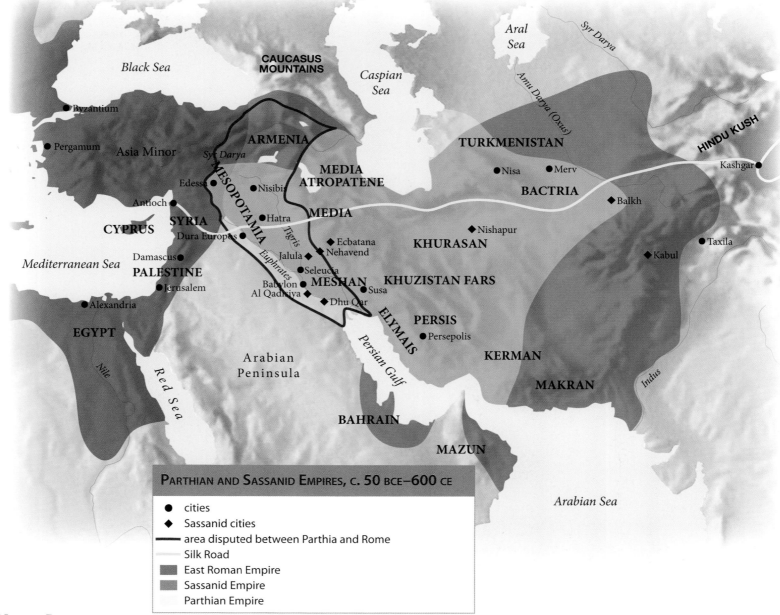

PARTHIAN AND SASSANID EMPIRES, C. 50 BCE–600 CE

- ● cities
- ◆ Sassanid cities
- —— area disputed between Parthia and Rome
- —— Silk Road
- ▓ East Roman Empire
- ▓ Sassanid Empire
- ▓ Parthian Empire

The ruins of Taq Kisra, a Parthian and Sassanid palace in Ctesphion, include a wonder of Persian architecture: the great arch soars 110 feet (34 m) high and remains one of the largest single-span arches in the world.

THE DISCIPLES OF MANI

The Sassanid Empire expanded in every direction, eventually reaching the Mediterranean, and became a worthy competitor for Rome and Byzantium. Sassanid forms of Zoroastrianism spread northward to the Caucasus and eastward along the Silk Road to China, where temples were built and survived for centuries. Soon after a military conquest, the Sassanids would build their temples on captured territory to establish the dominance of the dynasty's faith.

Followers of other faiths were often repressed, particularly those Christians who had ties to Rome—the Sassanid archenemy. Christians who were loyal to the breakaway Babylonian patriarchate were accepted by the Sassanids, and many lived in the empire's western regions, particularly in Mesopotamia.

Manichaeanism, a fast-growing Gnostic religion that arose in Babylonia in the third century CE, was also suppressed by the Sassanids. The founding prophet, Mani (c. 210–276 CE), who had Parthian heritage as well as a Judeo-Christian family background, wrote several sacred texts in Aramaic. These subsequently were translated into many languages, spreading the religion from the Persian empire into Europe, Egypt, and East Asia.

At first the Sassanid king Shapur I (c. 215–272 CE) supported and promoted Manichaeanism, which became one of the world's most popular religions. When widespread influence of Manichaeanism threatened the authority of politically powerful religions,

however, it brought on harsh persecution, especially from Zoroastrians and Christians. Mani, whose followers considered him the new Jesus, is believed to have been executed as a heretic by the Sassanid government. And soon after Christianity became the religion of Roman emperors in the fourth century CE, the Romans outlawed Manichaeanism and had many of its followers put to death.

Mani described himself as a "disciple of Jesus Christ," as well as a "comforter" and as one who "intercedes on behalf" of seekers after truth. He journeyed throughout the Persian empire teaching that there were two natures—one the realm of light, which was peaceful, and the other the realm of darkness, which was in constant conflict. The human being was the focus of the cosmic struggle between this dualism.

Manichaeanism influenced, and was influenced by, other contemporary faiths, including Zoroastrianism, Judaism, Christianity, and Buddhism. The religion's teachings were perpetuated for centuries by future generations of Gnostics, especially in South and East Asia and in Europe. The Coptic Christians of Egypt preserved some of Mani's best-known writings.

A tenth-century depiction of Manichaeans from Kocho, a city along the northern leg of the Silk Road; Manichaeanism flourished in central Asia for centuries after the Western kingdoms exiled it.

A Sassanian relief from c. 230 CE shows Ahura Mazda, on the right, handing a ring symbolizing kingship to Ardashir I, the founder of the Sassanid Empire. Ardashir's horse tramples the Parthian king Artaban V, while Ahura Mazda's tramples Ahriman.

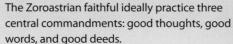

ZOROASTRIAN WORSHIP

The Zoroastrian faithful ideally practice three central commandments: good thoughts, good words, and good deeds.

The religion worships nature, especially the deified sun, moon, and stars. A Zoroastrian must protect the earth and show reverence to Ahura Mazda, venerating his creations and the supernatural forces that guard them. Fire pervades all creation and is always central in Zoroastrian ceremonies. Believers face a fire during prayers, or else turn to the sun or moon (heavenly fires).

Fire is not a symbol, but rather a sacred entity that aids humanity in return for nourishment and veneration. Worshipping fire is the same as invoking truth in the mind and heart of the Zoroastrian believer.

Fire remains centrally important to the Zoroastrian faith.

Empire Comes to India

ALEXANDER THE GREAT BROUGHT more than Hellenic culture and influence when he invaded northern India in 327 BCE. He brought along with him the very idea of empire, changing India forever. Indeed, a unified India, emerging as one nation covering the entire subcontinent, was a by-product of Alexander's invasion. Religious and cultural changes were part of these sweeping reforms.

When Alexander arrived, the region just south of the Himalayan foothills had already been divided into a number of small states, or polities. Chandragupta Maurya, leader of one of these small states, managed to drive out Alexander and to adopt his strategies of empire at the same time—annexing armies in order to build an ever larger force. Chandragupta went on to annex the Nanda Empire in Maghada, one of the larger Indian polities. Before his death in 298 BCE, Chandragupta had extended his rule to cover much

of the continent; India's first empire, known as the Mauryan Empire, was born. Two generations later, Emperor Ashoka (268–232 BCE) inherited his grandfather's empire and pushed even farther south, until his reign extended to the present-day region of Mysore. Evidence of Ashoka's influence can be found as far south as Sri Lanka.

Early in Ashoka's reign, after the exceptionally violent conquest of Kalinga, in east-central India, the emperor converted to Buddhism. He is said to have been shocked and grieved by the carnage of the battles, taking personal responsibility for the massive loss of life. His conversion was complete, and his imperial vision now took the form of uniting the continent in one religion as well as in one great political state. Ashoka's reign was pivotal in Indian history. It stood for great military and political might and at the same time was responsible for the spread of the pacifist teachings of Buddhism.

Although the famous Silk Road, north of Tibet, did not reach into India, many trade routes found their way to the subcontinent. However, due perhaps in part to its sheltering mountain ranges and oceans, India exported more religious traditions than it imported.

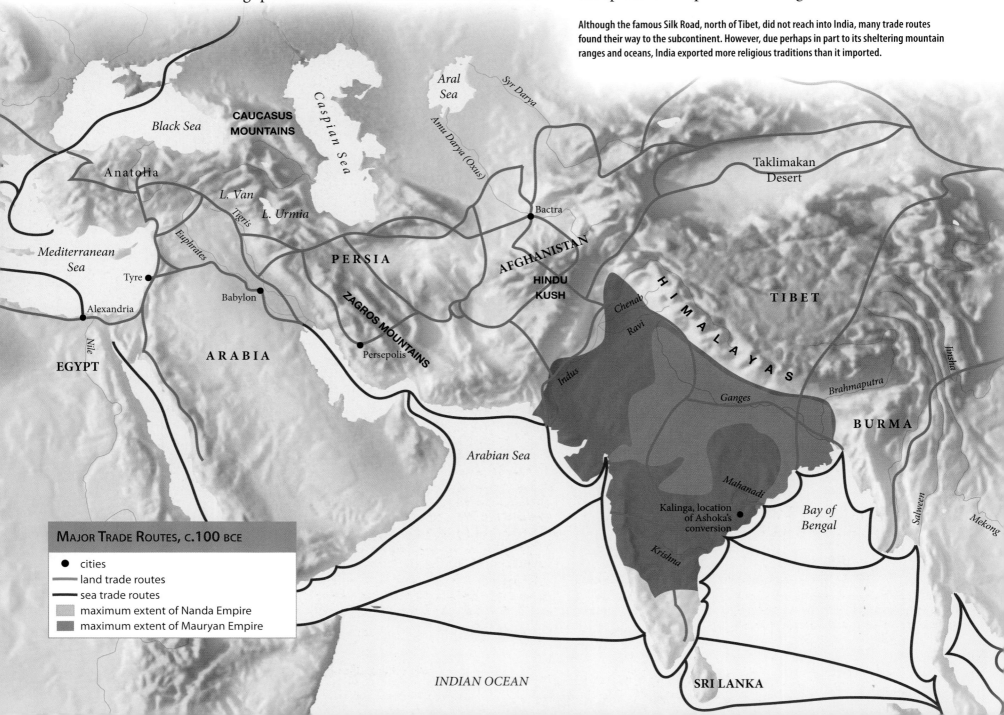

MAJOR TRADE ROUTES, C.100 BCE

- ● cities
- land trade routes
- sea trade routes
- maximum extent of Nanda Empire
- maximum extent of Mauryan Empire

Map labels: Aral Sea, Syr Darya, Black Sea, CAUCASUS MOUNTAINS, Caspian Sea, Amu Darya (Oxus), Taklimakan Desert, Anatolia, L. Van, Tigris, L. Urmia, Bactra, Mediterranean Sea, Euphrates, PERSIA, AFGHANISTAN, HIMALAYAS, TIBET, Tyre, Babylon, ZAGROS MOUNTAINS, HINDU KUSH, Chenab, Ravi, Jinsha, Alexandria, Persepolis, Nile, ARABIA, Indus, Ganges, Brahmaputra, BURMA, EGYPT, Arabian Sea, Mahanadi, Bay of Bengal, Salween, Mekong, Kalinga, location of Ashoka's conversion, Krishna, INDIAN OCEAN, SRI LANKA

Traditionally the site where Siddhartha Gautama became the Buddha, Mahabodhi Temple in the state of Bihar, eastern India, developed from a shrine built by Emperor Ashoka in the third century BCE. Today's temple complex dates to the fifth or sixth century CE and contains a bodhi tree. Legend says that this was grown from a cutting (provided by Ashoka) of the original bodhi tree, beneath which Buddha attained enlightenment.

THE FIRST BUDDHIST MISSIONS

Emperor Ashoka wasn't content to keep his new religion to himself and began proselytizing with as much fervor as he had shown as a conqueror. In his own country he built and expanded universities and stupas—temples housing the remains of the Buddha. Farther afield, he dispatched missionaries who traveled west through West Asia to the Mediterranean and into North Africa, east to Burma, south into Sri Lanka, and north into Central Asia.

The ease with which Ashoka's missionaries were able to travel to such distant lands is a testament to the interdependence of religion, trade, politics, and warfare. While it may seem that these entities make strange bedfellows, the first Buddhist missionaries were able to travel on established trade routes, both by land and by sea. The resources for such extensive travel came in this case from a robust economy and a powerful leader. The fact that such violent invasions and conquests led to the dissemination of a message of peace and tolerance is one of the great ironies of history.

Ashoka's missionaries certainly encountered many other religious traditions during their journeys. Scholars are still examining the impact Buddhism may have had during this crucial period in the history of so many world religions.

ASHOKA'S EDICTS: THE DHARMA CARVED IN STONE

One of Ashoka's greatest legacies is a series of stone pillars and rock carvings proclaiming the glory of the dharma, or truth, presenting essential teachings of Buddhism, and calling for religious tolerance. These carvings are known as the edicts of Ashoka, and together constitute some of the oldest surviving scripts in India.

Some of the edicts were carved into stone walls and rock faces; others were carved onto massive pillars, forty to fifty feet high and topped with an ornate capital. The script used on most of these is Brahmi, the root script of India, using the language of the region where it was placed: Maghadi in the northeast of India, and a form of Sanskrit in the west. One bilingual pillar in present-day Afghanistan, then under Indo-Hellenic influence, is written in both Aramaic and Greek. Pillars were appropriately placed at important sites in the life of the Buddha, such as Lumbini, Buddha's birthplace.

Dhamma [dharma] is good, but what constitutes Dhamma? [It includes] little evil, much good, kindness, generosity, truthfulness, and purity.
—PILLAR EDICT (TRANSLATED BY S. DHAMMIKA)

Ashoka's edicts clearly spelled out his remorse for the brutality of his wars. "Whatever efforts I am making is to repay the debt I owe to all beings to assure their happiness in this life, and attain heaven in the next," is the inscription on one of the rock edicts. This apology was accompanied by specific instructions to implement a system of social welfare, justice, tolerance, moderation, and piety. It is unclear whether his edicts had a great deal of impact on the daily lives of his subjects; the Indian subcontinent contained a wide variety of ethnicities, languages, and cultural traditions, even as it does now. But old traditions were reshaped, and new traditions born in the wake of Ashoka's reforms.

Nearly 2,000 miles (3,200 km) separate Ashoka's southernmost edicts in Sri Lanka, and the northernmost, near the intersection of the Himalayas and the Hindu Kush. The number of and distance between the edicts testify to Ashoka's zeal about his Buddhist religion.

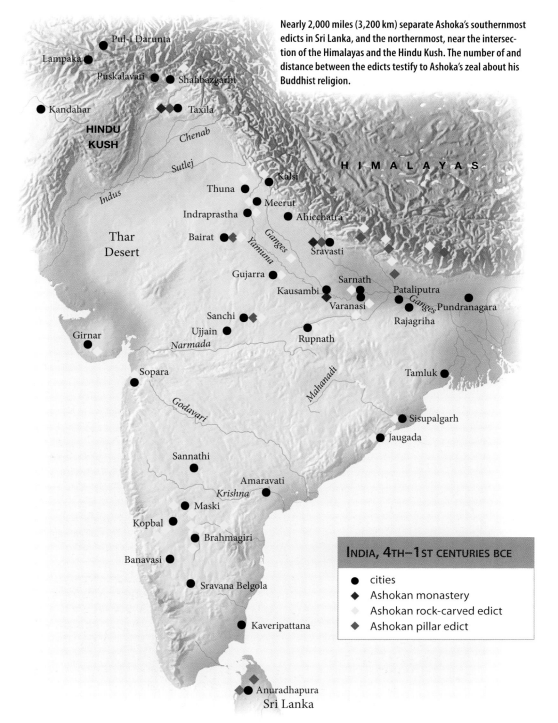

INDIA, 4TH–1ST CENTURIES BCE

- ● cities
- ◆ Ashokan monastery
- ◇ Ashokan rock-carved edict
- ◆ Ashokan pillar edict

Early Buddhism in India

THE CENTURIES FOLLOWING the death of the Buddha saw his teachings gathered, inscribed, and spread through all of India, and through all of Asia shortly thereafter. But the tradition was originally an oral one, and the guardians of Buddha's teachings did not always agree either on words or interpretations. So began a series of councils, then subdivisions into individual schools, and an eventual schism into the two main branches of Buddhism that still are practiced today.

The Buddhist monastic tradition had begun to take shape during Buddha's lifetime. The teacher and his disciples traveled widely, giving discourses as they

Although the Buddha did not venture out of a small region in northern India, within a few centuries of his death Buddhism had traveled throughout India and Sri Lanka and soon would spread far beyond.

went. During the rainy season, they retired for several months of meditation and contemplation. This practice furthered the division of Buddhist adherents into monks (*bikkhu*) and laity. The monastic centers established by Buddha grew in importance after his death, and new ones were founded throughout northern India. After his death, Buddha's remains were divided; the temples built to house his relics were called stupas, borrowing the ancient Indian name for royal burial mounds.

Even during Buddha's lifetime, women were ordained as nuns, or *bikkhuni,* with certain restrictions. The first woman to be ordained was Buddha's maternal aunt, Prajapati, who had raised him. Women have played an important role in most branches of Buddhism ever since.

Buddhism expanded rapidly in the last few centuries before the Common Era. Ashoka's missions were an important part of this expansion and popularization. Finally, though, it was the written canon, beginning in the first century BCE, that firmly established Buddhist traditions in South Asia and eventually in East Asia as well.

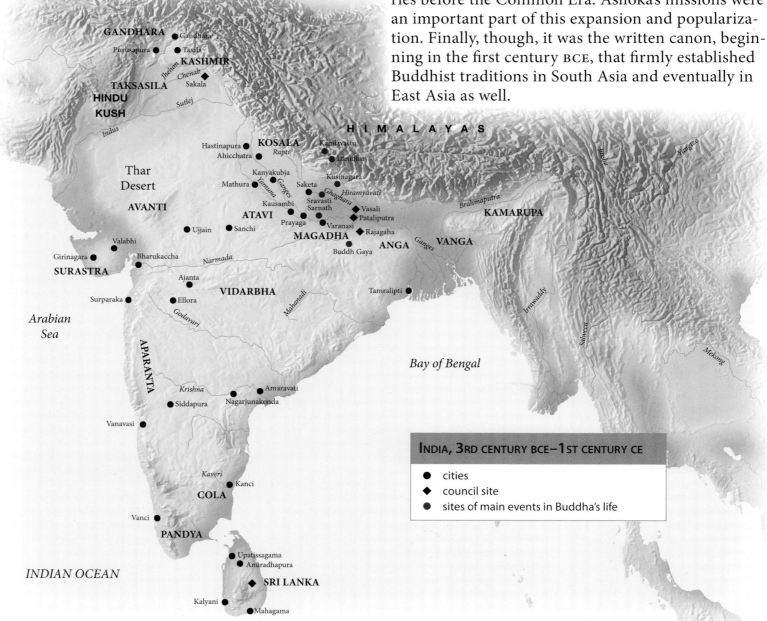

INDIA, 3RD CENTURY BCE–1ST CENTURY CE

- ● cities
- ◆ council site
- ● sites of main events in Buddha's life

A modern painting depicting Ananda, Buddha's cousin and disciple, reciting Buddha's teachings at the First Council.

EARLY BUDDHIST COUNCILS

Most schools of Buddhism fix the year of Buddha's death at around 483 BCE. Shortly after his death, or *parinirvana*, Buddha's closest disciples came together in the city of Rajagaha, at present-day Rajgir, in the Maghada kingdom; this gathering is known as the First Buddhist Council. The community, or *sangha*, was intent on capturing the words of their teacher before his sermons faded from memory. Beginning with Ananda, Buddha's cousin and close companion, the disciples recited Buddha's words from memory.

Roughly a century later, around 383 BCE, the Second Buddhist Council was convened in Vasali, or Vaishali, with the purpose of cleaning house. Elders had drawn up a list of ten points of practice that young monks had been disregarding, most notably, that they had begun to accept money. Around 700 monks gathered for this council. After the gathering, the first splintering of the sangha began, with different schools from different regions breaking off to form their own sects.

The Third Buddhist Council was held around 250 BCE in Pataliputra (modern-day Patna), the ancient capital of Bihar. The council was held under the sponsorship of the emperor Ashoka, again with the intent to purify the practices of monks. More schisms erupted from this council, however; the eventual division of Buddhism into the Theravada and Mahayana schools had its origins in this gathering. The fruit of the council, however, was the development of a Buddhist canon, called the Pali Tipitaka, still an oral tradition at the time of Ashoka.

TWO BRANCHES, TWO COUNCILS

The Fourth Buddhist Council, held after the schism between the Theravada and Mahayana schools, is not one single occurrence. Each branch of Buddhism recognizes its own Fourth Council.

For the Theravada school, the Fourth Council came at a time of crisis in Sri Lanka, an important center for Buddhism in the first century BCE. Many monks had died from starvation during a period of prolonged drought. The Pali Tipitaka was finally written down, c. 83 BCE, probably as a response to this loss of life. It was feared that the orally transmitted teachings of Buddha might be lost or forgotten by the surviving monks. The original Pali Tipitaka scriptures were written on palm leaves. *Tipitaka* in Pali means "three-part basket"; the name refers to the three parts of the canon: the Vinaya, or rules of conduct; the sutta, or discourse of the Buddha; and the Abhidamma, a philosophical analysis of the nature of reality.

Another Fourth Buddhist Council was held in Kashmir, under the Kushan emperor Kanishka, around 100 BCE. This council, not recognized by the Theravada school, was attended by about 500 monks and is seen as the inception of the Mahayana school of Buddhism. Some scholars believe that this northern school was influenced by the philosophical traditions of the Greeks; Indo-Hellenistic rule dominated northern India at this time. The Mahayana school rejected the Tipitaka, in favor of the study of the sutras, or transcriptions of Buddha's discourses, and chose Sanskrit as its liturgical language. The Theravada school continued to use Pali, which accounts for the various spellings of many Buddhist terms. As Mahayana Buddhism arrived in the West earlier than Theravada did, most westerners are more familiar with Sanskrit spellings.

The Mahayana branch of Buddhism favored the bodhisattva way, with the goal of enlightenment as a step to alleviating the suffering of all beings. *Mahayana* literally means "great vehicle." This school originally referred to the Theravada school as *Hinayana*, or "lesser vehicle," believing its practice to focus solely on self-attainment. The use of "Hinayana" is offensive to many Buddhists.

THE BUDDHA IMAGE

The first images of the Buddha appeared in northern India in the first or second century CE. Many show the influence of Hellenistic sculpture, with voluminous drapery and an idealized face that recalls heroic Greek statuary. These images are known as Greco-Buddhist, and the most noteworthy ones are found near Gandhara, present-day Kandahar, in Afghanistan. As Buddhism spread throughout Asia, however, representations of the Buddha took on characteristics of each region's indigenous art and sculpture. Most Buddha images show him in meditation and include scenes or symbols from his life or past lives.

The detailed draping of Buddha's garment in this 1st to 2nd century CE Gandhara statue clearly recalls Hellenistic statuary.

The Changing Hindu World

Buddhism swept through India in the last centuries before the Common Era, carried on the wave of empire. Beginning with the Mauryan emperors, including Ashoka (268–232 BCE), Buddhism enjoyed royal patronage and grew in influence. But what of the indigenous religion of India, the traditions that fostered the Buddha's own beliefs? Not surprisingly, these began to change and evolve as well—changes born in part from necessity, and in part as a natural progression of ideas. The views of the Mauryan emperor Ashoka regarding the sacred ritual of Vedic sacrifice were quite clear: carved onto a rock wall, one of his edicts proclaims, "Here in my domain no living beings are to be slaughtered or offered in sacrifice."

The Mauryan Empire didn't last more than a few centuries, and a series of invasions and coups made northern India a battleground for political domination and religious patronage. King Pushyamitra Sunga, who overthrew the Mauryans in 185 BCE, tried to do away with Buddhism. He destroyed temples, monasteries, and stupas. But soon another set of kings who favored Buddhism came to power, like Kanishka, the Kushan ruler who dominated India in the first century BCE. Finally, under the rule of the Gupta emperors (320–550 CE), India enjoyed a balance between its religious traditions. The Gupta emperors didn't favor one religion over another, preserving Buddhist holy sites, Jain monasteries in the south, and giving ample patronage to the arts and literature. Under this period of stability and prosperity, the Hindu faith evolved and flourished, giving rise to the classical period of Hinduism.

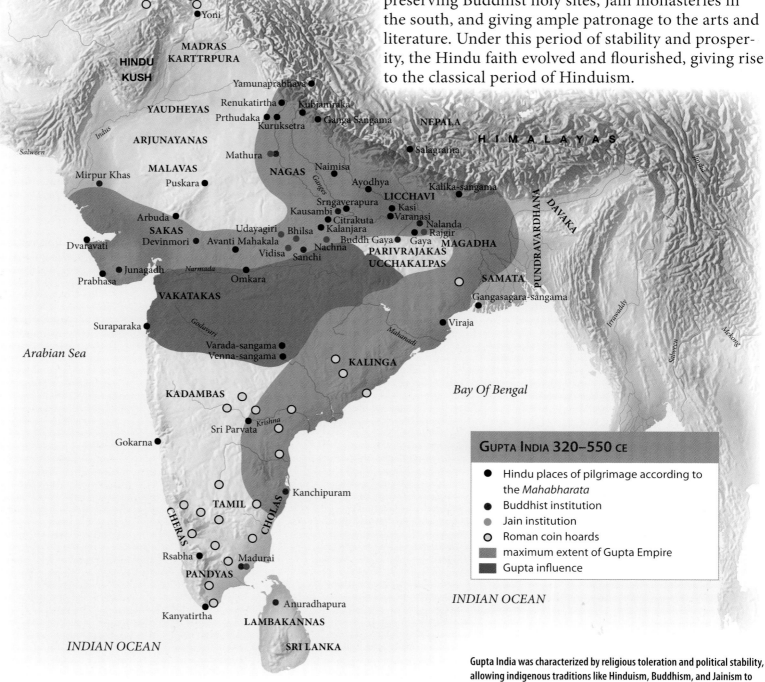

Gupta India was characterized by religious toleration and political stability, allowing indigenous traditions like Hinduism, Buddhism, and Jainism to flourish amid prosperous trading relationships with distant empires.

Brahma is often depicted with four heads and four arms. The number recurs throughout Hinduism, as in the four Vedas, varnas (or social classes), and ashramas (or correct life stages), and represents cosmic wholeness, as does Brahma himself.

THE HINDU TRIMURTI: OLD GODS, NEW ROLES

As Vedic sacrifice fell from favor, the gods who presided over these earlier rituals—Agni, god of fire, for example—began to decline in importance while other gods took their place.

Vishnu and Shiva rose to become the two most revered gods in the rich Hindu pantheon, with Brahma, the creator and seed of all life, as the third member of what came to be called the Hindu trinity, or *trimurti*.

Brahma, Vishnu, and Shiva are creator, preserver, and destroyer, respectively. These three gods are not seen as separate entities, but

as manifestations of a supreme sacred being, known as Brahman, or simply God. When considered in this light, root Hindu worship appears essentially monotheistic, but cults and sects focused on the worship of a particular god make Hinduism seem to be anything but. The cults of Shiva and Vishnu, whose followers are known as Shaivas and Vaishnavas respectively, flourished under Gupta rule of India.

SHIVA AND VISHNU

Both Shiva and Vishnu existed to some degree in pre-Vedic times. Shiva, in particular, can be traced back to the Indus Valley civilization. Images from this ancient culture show a Shiva-like fertility god. He appears as a minor deity in the Vedas. Known as the destroyer, Shiva is also present at creation. He is associated with male energy and is often represented as a phallus, or lingam, joined with a female symbol, a yoni. Shiva is usually represented in art with a third eye, matted hair, and a double-sided drum, a symbol of the duality of destruction and creation. He rides a white bull, Nandi, or a tiger-skin—both symbols of fertility.

Vishnu, like Shiva, appears as a minor god in the Vedas. During the post-Vedic period, though, he took on new importance. He is known as the preserver or the pervader, immanent in all aspects of existence. His followers call him Ishvara and consider him a supreme being. Many Hindu gods appear in a variety of forms, but Vishnu is especially known for his manifestations, or incarnations, known as his ten *avatars*. It is believed that Vishnu has appeared in nine of these earthly forms so far. Krishna and Rama are his most revered avatars; like Vishnu, they are represented in art with blue skin, believed to be the color of infinity. In the Hindu pantheon, Buddha is considered to be Vishnu's ninth avatar. The tenth—yet to appear—is Kalki, a horseman who will appear at the end of the world's present cycle.

By the first century CE, Nandi was recognized as the bull who carries the god Shiva. Statues of him in animal, human, and mixed form appear in or near temples to Shiva, and some scholars believe that before the first century, the bull form represented Shiva himself.

THE TAMIL WORLD

The southern tip of India escaped much of the political tumult of northern India's first empires. The region was ruled by three stable dynasties: the Cheras, Pandyans, and Cholas. Language marks the separation of this region from the rest of India. The indigenous Dravidian language in this region is Tamil, while north and central Indian languages are mostly Indo-European.

Tamil has a rich literary and cultural tradition. Its golden age, known as the Sangam age, was roughly between 200 BCE and 200 CE. Sea trade was vigorous between the Tamil region and points west, east, and south; caches of Roman coins have been found in Tamil areas. The region exported pearls, textiles, and ivory, but its most important export may have been Buddhism. Jainism and Buddhism both arrived in southern India at roughly the same time

(c. 250 BCE), and Jainism took root here as the major religion. It was from the busy ports of southern India and Sri Lanka, though, that Buddhism was carried to the rest of Southeast Asia at the beginning of the Common Era.

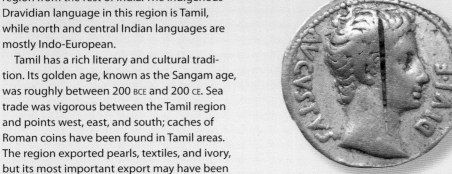

A Roman coin, showing Emperor Augustus, from a hoard discovered in Pudukottai, Tamil Nadu State, in southern India.

Hindu Epics in the Classical Age

EVERY GREAT CULTURE has its classical age, when the arts and literature flourish and peace and prosperity are the rule. For India this period was the time of the great empires—first the Mauryan Empire (323–185 BCE), and later the Gupta Empire (320–550 CE).

During India's classical age, which lasted roughly until the Islamic period in the eleventh century, literature in particular came to the fore. The legends, stories, histories, and teachings that made up a long oral tradition were gathered and written down for the first time. The Puranas, which outlined the beliefs of various aspects of Hinduism, and various sects emerged from this period. More important, though, the two great Sanskrit epics, the *Ramayana* and the *Mahabharata*, date from and define India's classical age.

These two great poetic works brought together many threads of Indian thought, history, and religious teachings. So in one sense they helped to define a culture that was already present. But they have an even more important place in history, as they laid the groundwork for the future of the Hindu religion and for Indian literature as well. This was no small feat for a religious tradition that has such diversity of origins and beliefs and such a wealth of legends, sects, and deities.

Both the *Ramayana* and the *Mahabharata* are considered to be mytho-historical—that is, they describe historic events but infuse the history with mythological, mystical, and religious elements. The *Mahabharata*, for example, tells the story of real wars, battles, and events—already ancient history when the epic was written during the last centuries before the Common Era. But gods and goddesses take major roles in the action, and the epic heroes are often indistinguishable from deities.

Although the *Ramayana* is mythical in outlook, the route of the hero-god can be constructed on a map because the text describes the myth in terms of known geographical locations. The location of some sites, however, like the fortress Lanka, can only be guessed at.

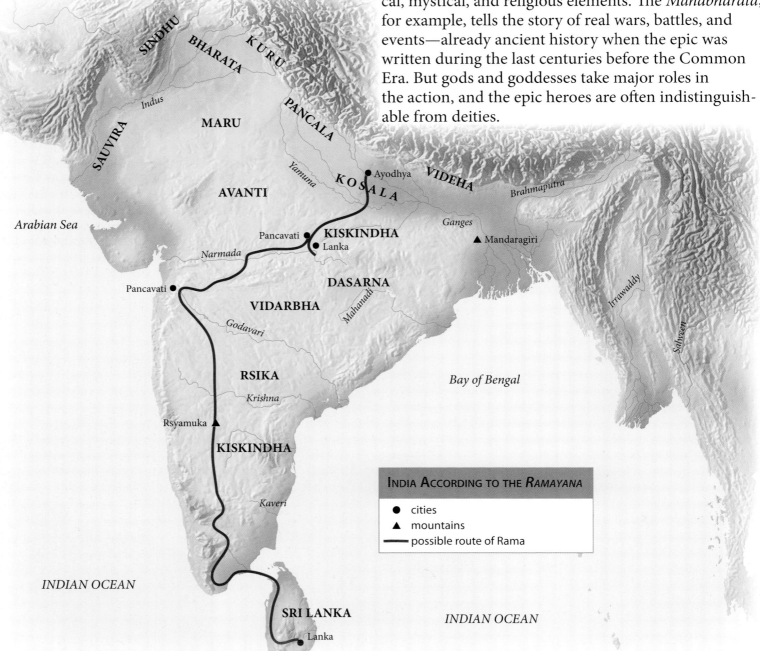

INDIA ACCORDING TO THE *RAMAYANA*

● cities
▲ mountains
— possible route of Rama

There are two forces: fate and human effort.
All men depend on and are bound by these;
there is nothing else.
—MAHABHARATA, *BOOK OF THE SLEEPING WARRIORS*

Sanskrit text from the *Ramayana*, one of the great Hindu epics; the *Ramayana* is made up of 24,000 couplets.

A modern statue of Hanuman, a monkey-headed god who features prominently in the *Ramayana*.

THE *RAMAYANA*

The *Ramayana* was written sometime between 200 BCE and 200 CE by the poet Valmiki. It tells the story of the great hero Rama, who is one of Vishnu's incarnations, or avatars. Prince Rama was born to deliver the gods from the demon Ravana. If he needed more incentive than freeing the gods, it soon came: the demon abducted Rama's faithful wife, Sita, and held her captive in his fortress in the city of Lanka. To rescue her, Rama enlisted the help of the monkey-headed god, Hanuman, general of an army of such *vanaras*, or monkey-men. Rama's half brother, Lakshma, also figures prominently in the epic. These characters, their actions, and the allegorical truths and lessons they represent are essential components of Indian culture and Hindu beliefs.

THE *MAHABHARATA*

The *Mahabharata*, India's greatest epic poem, is also one of the world's most important works of literature. It is certainly one of the longest, with a total of over 74,000 verses. Long an orally transmitted work, the *Mahabharata* was probably committed to writing during the Gupta period (320–550 CE). Legend holds that the epic was written by the poet and Brahmin Vyasa, a semi-mythological figure himself.

Written in classical Sanskrit, the epic tells the story of the struggles of the Bharata dynasty. The centerpiece is a war between two branches of the dynasty, the Kauranas and the Pandavas, the latter represented by five brothers. The most widely read section of the book, often read as a stand-alone work, is the *Bhagavad Gita*.

Bhagavad Gita is translated as "Song of the Divine One." The text, in eighteen chapters, is a dialogue between Arjuna, one of the five Pandava brothers, and his charioteer Krishna. Krishna, though, is no mere charioteer—he is an incarnation of the god Vishnu. He advises Arjuna on the battlefield, where the warrior is conflicted when he sees that his enemies in battle are also his relatives. What is his duty to his family, and what is his duty to God? Krishna's discourse with Arjuna touches on a wide spectrum of ethical and spiritual questions. The *Bhagavad Gita* is widely regarded as the most concise and poetic presentation of the core precepts of Hinduism.

THE VISUAL ARTS IN GUPTA INDIA

Religious tolerance was one of the hallmarks of the Gupta dynasty. While the great Hindu epics emerged from this period, a rich tradition of Buddhist visual art took hold as well. A supreme example of this art is the series of paintings and sculptures in the Ajanta Caves in southwestern India, in the present-day state of Maharashtra. These twenty-nine caves were mostly man-made and were part of a Buddhist monastic complex, which also includes ornate stupas, residence halls, and pillars. The paintings themselves focus on the Jataka tales, which in Theravada Buddhism refers to the stories of the Buddha's previous lives. They are considered unique among early South Indian art for their sophisticated technique and painstaking execution.

A painting from the Ajanta Caves in southwestern India, a World Heritage site since 1983.

The Eastward Journey of Buddhism

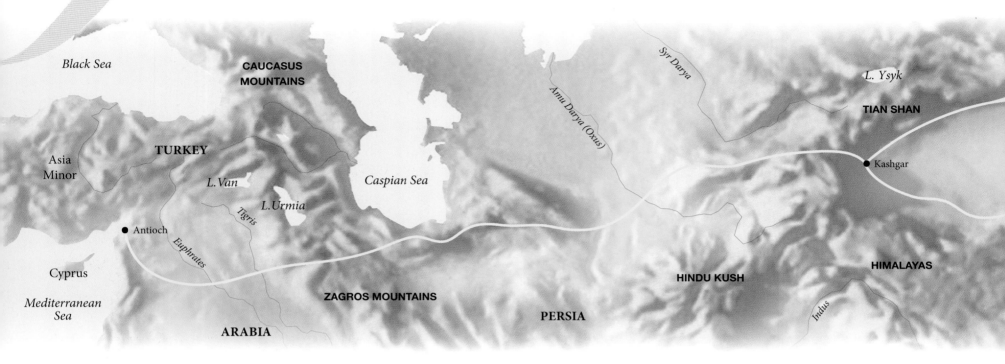

The major branches of Buddhism were disseminated eastward along different routes, traveling primarily along preexisting trade routes. Foremost of these was the overland Silk Road, which stretched some 4,000 miles (6,400 km) across most of Asia.

THE ARRIVAL OF BUDDHISM was the most significant religious development in East and Southeast Asia during the millennium that spans the dawn of the Common Era. Along with Hinduism, Buddhism is one of the few religions to have spread so widely through largely peaceful means, unattached to warfare, invasion, forcible conversion, or colonization.

By 500 CE, roughly a millennium after the birth of the Buddha (c. 563 BCE), the tradition that he founded in India had spread as far east as the Pacific Ocean. Each of the cultures that received Buddhist teachings absorbed some elements of the *dharma*, or doctrine. These principles of Buddhism were often commingled with the extant religious traditions, so that during this period Buddhism not only gained in geographic spread, but in variety of worship and practice as well.

Buddhism traveled east from India over two principal routes, generally carrying the two main branches of the religion to different regions. The Theravada school, one of the original eighteen schools of Buddhism that flourished under Indian emperor Ashoka (268–232 BCE), was carried east from the island of Sri Lanka, an early Buddhist center established by Ashoka's son, Mahinda. This branch of Buddhism is still the

dominant religion in most of Southeast Asia. Mahayana Buddhism, the other main branch of the religion, took a different route east, largely carried on the Silk Road through Central Asia into China,

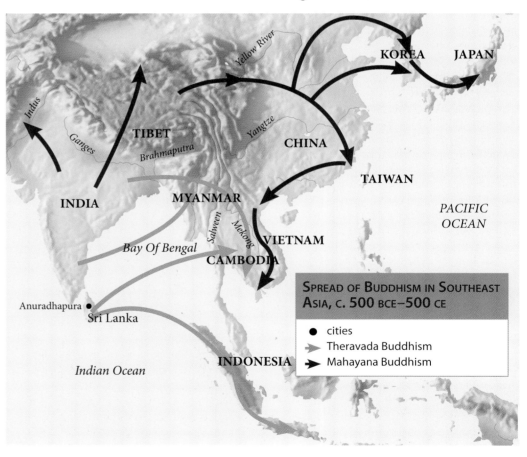

SPREAD OF BUDDHISM IN SOUTHEAST ASIA, C. 500 BCE–500 CE

- cities
→ Theravada Buddhism
→ Mahayana Buddhism

Vietnam, and Korea. Eventually, Mahayana Buddhism reached Japan, though not until it had been well established in mainland East Asia. Another important branch of Buddhism was later established in Tibet, in the seventh century CE.

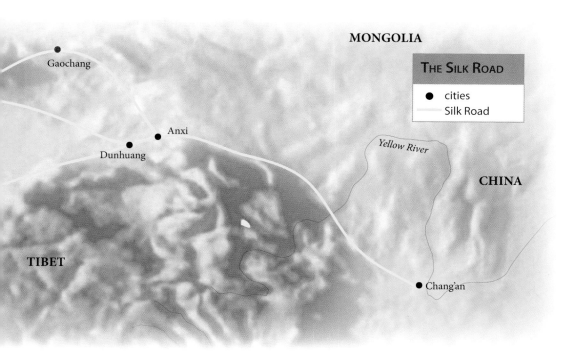

First built in 652 CE in Chang'an (modern Xi'an), the Big Wild Goose Pagado was rebuilt in 704 and indicates the importance of Buddhism by this time in this eastern city along the Silk Road.

THE NORTHERN ROUTE

Silk production in China, according to legend, began in 3000 BCE with the mythical Yellow Emperor, whose wife was said to have initiated the craft. While other products from China were exported in trade, it was silk that was the

THE ANCIENT SPLENDOR OF ANURADHAPURA

In Sri Lanka's north-central region, the city of Anuradhapura once rose high above the dense jungle. One of the ancient world's largest and most splendid cities, Anuradhapura covered over 250 square miles. Archaeological finds have been supported by descriptions of the city found in the early Sri Lankan Pali text the *Mahavamsa*.

During the fourth century BCE, when Buddhism arrived on the island, a succession of kings built enormous temples and stupas, which housed relics of the Buddha. Many are still standing today. The largest of these is the Jetavanaramaya stupa, the tallest brick structure ever built and the highest structure in the ancient world after the pyramids of Giza. Other magnificent buildings here include the Maha Vihara, a Theravadin temple, and the Abhayagiri Vihara, a Mahayana temple. Several important large monasteries surrounding the city have recently been excavated.

Anuradhapura was said to be the home of the legendary king Ravana, according to the Hindu text the *Ramayana*.

most prized. Hence the name the "Silk Road," which describes the ancient trade routes that have long connected China to points east (Korea and Japan), west (India, western Asia, and Europe), and southwest (the east coast of Africa). Along these routes China imported several important products, including jade and gold. Buddhism, especially Mahayana Buddhism, which was centered in northern India, traveled along these roads as well.

Monks, merchants, and pilgrims traveled the dusty and sometimes treacherous route from India to China. Along the way, Buddhist centers were established in Central Asia, often coexisting with the many other cultural and religious traditions that were found along these roads, primarily Turkish and Persian. The earliest documented pilgrim to come from China to India seeking Buddhist teachings was Fa Xian (338–422 CE), who traveled as far west as Lumbini, Buddha's birthplace in northern India, before returning to China by way of Southeast Asia.

EAST BY SOUTHEAST

Sri Lanka was one of the earliest Buddhist centers outside mainland India. The Theravada school was the dominant form here for centuries, beginning with the arrival of some 250 monks brought by Mahinda around 250 BCE. Already a major trade hub, with marine routes linking the island to Southeast Asia, Sri Lanka became a starting point for Buddhist missionaries. At the same time, both merchants and missionaries were carrying Buddhism eastward from mainland India as well. Indian culture and religion had already influenced many Southeast Asian countries, so Buddhism essentially became another layer of

Indian religion. Buddhism in Southeast Asia remains a syncretic religion, fusing elements of Hinduism, Buddhism, and indigenous spirit worship and shamanism.

Myanmar (Burma) was an early adopter of Buddhism, beginning in the time of Emperor Ashoka. The Mon ethnic group was dominant here in the early centuries of the Common Era; at its height in the twelfth century, the Mon kingdom incorporated much of present–day Thailand and Laos. It is believed that Theravada Buddhism spread from the southern region of Myanmar to Thailand and Cambodia, both countries where Theravada Buddhism is still widely practiced.

Buddhism in Indonesia took a different route, arriving later (in the seventh century), thriving through the Middle Ages, and then falling off with the arrival of Islam in the fifteenth century. Compared with other Southeast Asian countries, Vietnam had stronger trade and cultural links with China than with India, and Mahayana Buddhism became the dominant religion there.

Jetavanaramaya stupa in Sri Lanka rises more than 400 feet (122 m) high.

EAST ASIA
Laozi: Legendary Daoist Master

CHINA IS SOMETIMES CALLED the "Land of the Three Ways," a reference to the three religious traditions that coexist in this vast country: Daoism, Confucianism, and Buddhism. All three traditions incorporate many elements of ancient Chinese beliefs. And all three can trace their formal origins to the same short period of time, roughly the fifth century BCE. In the case of Confucianism and Buddhism, these years followed the lives of their founders, who were contemporaries—Confucius (551–479 BCE) in China and Buddha (563–483 BCE) in India. Daoism (or Taoism) is traditionally associated with the legendary sage Laozi (Lao Tzu), who is said to have lived at around the same time.

Daoism is named for the Chinese word *Dao* (*Tao*), usually translated as "the way," "the path," or "the order of the universe." The Dao, sometimes likened to the Greek Logos, is seen as ineffable, existing beyond description, naming, or rational comprehension. The seminal text of Daoism ascribed to Laozi, the *Dao De Jing* (*Tao Te Ching*), begins: "The Dao that can be spoken of is not the constant Dao. The name that can be named is not the constant name."

Many believe that Daoism is the purest form of ancient Chinese belief. Others view Laozi and Confucius as representing two opposing schools of thought. In the *Zhuangzi*, a later Daoist text, a character named Lao Dan—thought to be another name for Laozi—often proposes simple, pointed challenges to Confucius's teachings. Daoism represents an alternative to the Confucian emphasis on structured learning, formal knowledge, rectitude, and absolute respect for authority. Rather, Daoism embraces the paradox, relativity, and process of eternal change that it sees in the cycles of nature.

As in other East Asian traditions, mountains are viewed as sacred places in Daoism and are often visited on pilgrimages. The five sacred mountains of Daoism are Tai Shan, Heng Shan Bei, Hua Shan, Heng Shan Nan, and Song Shan; they represent the four cardinal directions and the center.

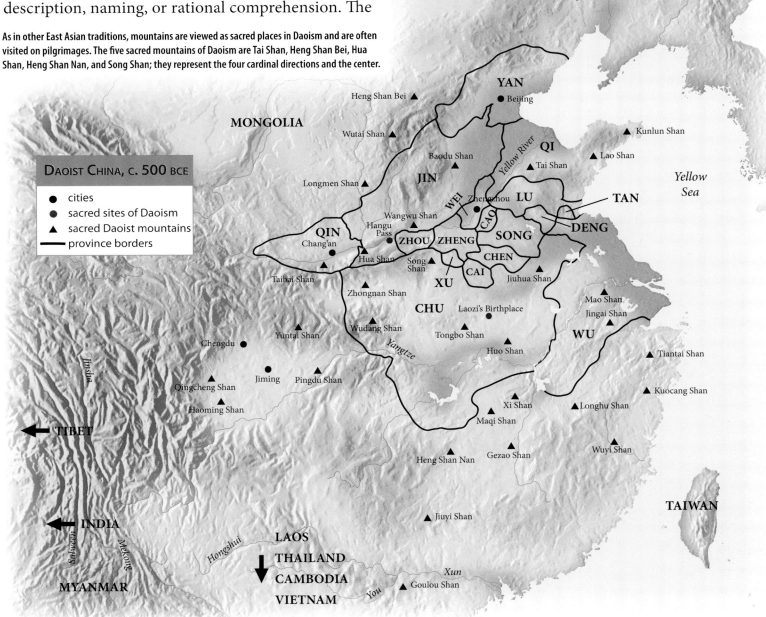

DAOIST CHINA, C. 500 BCE
- ● cities
- ● sacred sites of Daoism
- ▲ sacred Daoist mountains
- ━ province borders

Human beings follow the earth.
Earth follows heaven.
Heaven follows the Dao.
The Dao follows nature.
—*THE DAO DE JING*

LAOZI'S LIFE AND LEGEND

Laozi the man is an enigma. Scholars disagree about whether he lived at all, or is the stuff of legend. The scant knowledge we have comes from *The Records of the Grand Historian* (c. 109–91 BCE), by Sima Qian. Religious adherents of Daoism revere Laozi in his later incarnation as a deity, in keeping with the Daoist belief in immortality. Hence, his life story and the legends attached to his character have become part of canonical belief.

Laozi is said to have lived sometime between the sixth and fourth centuries BCE. One theory holds that Laozi is an amalgam of several sages and philosophers who lived during the time of Confucius. Others place him as a direct predecessor or successor to Confucius. Laozi's story was retold numerous times during the several centuries following his death, each account according him higher mystical and religious stature. Traditional accounts place Laozi's birthplace in the state of Chu, in present-day Luyi County, Henan Province. Laozi is said to have been born after eighty-one years of gestation, so he emerged with white hair and the long ears associated with wisdom and age. This physical description helps explain the honorific name: *Laozi* literally means "old master" or, alternatively, "old child."

According to legend, Laozi was employed in the imperial library of the court of Zhou, where he had access to the documents and wisdom of the Yellow Emperor. At the age of 160, Laozi traveled to the far western borders of China. When he reached the Hangu Pass, he was stopped by the guard, Yin Xi, and asked to impart his wisdom. The result was the orally delivered *Dao De Jing*, which is considered the essential scripture of Daoism.

Although a meeting like this one—in which Confucius presents the infant Buddha to Laozi—almost certainly never happened, the three traditions these figures represent certainly did blend throughout Chinese history.

A painting depicts the mysterious Laozi, the philosopher and central figure of Daoist tradition.

THE YIN YANG

The yin yang symbol, which is closely associated with Daoism, predates any formal religious tradition. This familiar black-and-white symbol expresses the constant flux in nature between opposing forces—a universal and ceaseless dynamic. Daoism sees human activity and natural cycles alike as subject to this immutable principle. The symbol is rooted in the ancient Chinese creation story, which sees humanity as born of the union between the gods of heaven (male) and earth (female). The same concepts are embedded in the *I Ching* (*Yi Jing*), or *Book of Changes*.

In the yin yang symbol, black represents yin and white represents yang. Yin is female, dark, receptive, and soft and is of the earth and the night. Yang is male, light, creative, and hard and is of the heavens and the day. The curved line separating them represents flux, or change—always maintaining a precise equilibrium. The dot of both black and white embedded in the other expresses the notions of interrelatedness and potential for change: because each contains a seed of the other, yin may become yang, and vice versa.

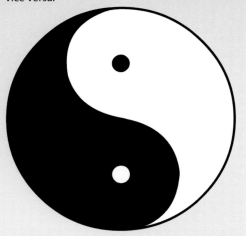

The yin yang symbol represents the unity of opposing forces in the universe.

Classical Daoist Scriptures

THE ESSENTIAL SCRIPTURES of Daoism were composed during a period of political and social upheaval in China. The two principal texts, the *Dao De Jing* (or *Tao Te Ching*) and the *Zhuangzi* (*Chuang Tzu*) form the basis of what is known as philosophical Daoism, which later developed into religious Daoism. Both books are concerned not only with philosophical and mystical questions, but also with a form of governance based on the principles of the Dao, or the way.

Several centuries separate these two books—the *Dao De Jing* (c. 500 BCE) is traditionally dated to the Spring and Autumn period of the Eastern Zhou dynasty, a time when a long and dissolute reign was coming to a close. The *Zhuangzi* (c. 300 BCE) was a product of the turbulent years known as the Warring States period (475–221 BCE), which was marked by bloody civil

wars. The two books show markedly different attitudes toward the individual's involvement in society, and the role of the sage or philosopher.

While polities battled for supremacy, Chinese philosophy was enjoying its golden age. The Warring States period was also a time of rich intellectual inquiry, a period known as the Hundred Schools of Thought. The Daoists Zhuangzi, author of the eponymous text, and Liezi belong to this period, as does the philosopher Mozi and the important Confucian theorist Mencius. The political philosophy of Legalism was born during these years. Scholars have linked this era's political strife to the flowering of philosophy and religion, suggesting that the deepest inquiry into human nature and divinity may grow out of the suffering caused by civil strife and war.

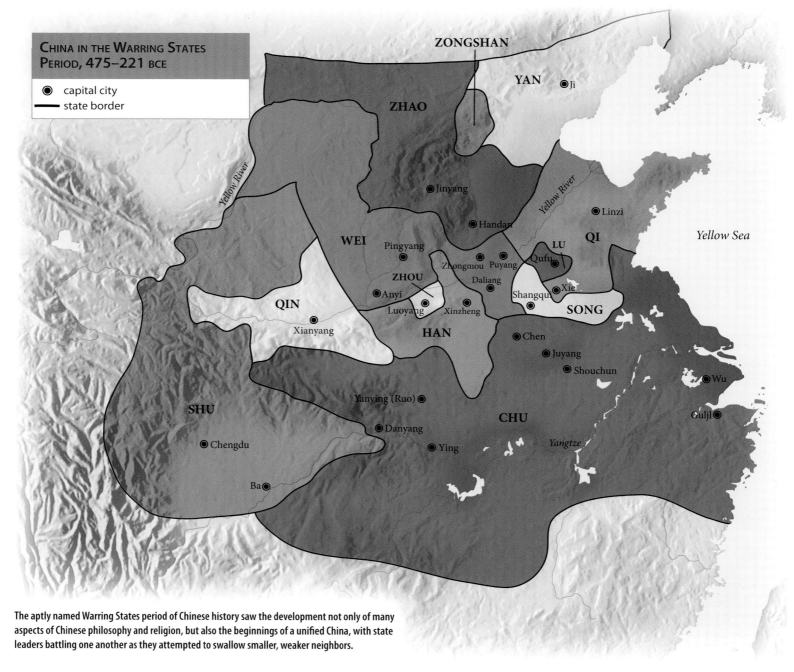

CHINA IN THE WARRING STATES PERIOD, 475–221 BCE

● capital city
— state border

The aptly named Warring States period of Chinese history saw the development not only of many aspects of Chinese philosophy and religion, but also the beginnings of a unified China, with state leaders battling one another as they attempted to swallow smaller, weaker neighbors.

While Daoism emphasized simple—though profound—philosophy, the environment in which it developed was becoming increasingly complex. The glass used in this fourth or third century BCE vase suggests foreign influence, indicating growing cultural and political interactions.

*Understanding that rests in what
it does not understand is the finest.*
—THE ZHUANGZI

THE DAO DE JING

Whether or not Laozi really lived, and whether or not he was the author of the book that bears his name, the *Dao De Jing* stands as one of the world's most important religious texts. Historians generally agree that the *Dao De Jing* had more than one author and that it was compiled over the course of several centuries. The wisdom and words contained in the book, however, likely have a much older origin, predating written history.

The name of the book is a clue to its contents: *Jing* here means "book," or "classic"; *Dao* translates as "the way," and *De* is understood as "virtue," "power," or "property." So the title roughly translates as "The Book of the Way and the Power." There are two parts to the *Dao De Jing*, which is composed in eighty-one chapters. The first half (chapters 1–37) concerns the Dao, the source of all in the universe, and the constant that exists beneath all outward change: "The way is unimpeded harmony." Several themes recur throughout the text: what it means to be a sage; the cyclical nature of the universe, or eternal return; and the power of the soft and yielding over the hard and fixed.

The second half of the *Dao De Jing* (chapters 38–81) concerns the De, with many ideas on the practices of ideal governance, underlined by Daoist belief: "Use straightforwardness for civil governance, use surprise for military oper-

WU WEI

The concept of *wu wei* is a central tenet of Daoism. Literally translated, wu wei means "inaction," "without action," or "without effort." Sometimes wu wei is explained as "the action of nonaction," or in familiar contemporary terms as "going with the flow." In the *Dao De Jing*, wu wei is likened to water traveling always along the path of least resistance, seeking the easiest path downstream, skirting obstacles, and proceeding with no effort. Soft water can wear down hard rock: "Nothing in the world is softer than water, yet nothing is better at overcoming the hard and strong. This is because nothing can alter it." Acting with such noneffort is the way to be in harmony with the Dao.

Perhaps it is no wonder that Daoism, flourishing near the world's third-longest river, the Yangzte, incorporated the imagery of water into its belief system.

ations; use noninvolvement to take the world." Deceptively simple, these verses were consulted and studied by Chinese rulers for centuries after the *Dao De Jing* was composed.

THE ZHUANGZI

The second of the two essential Daoist scriptures is the *Zhuangzi*. Its eponymous author was Zhuang Zhou (Chuang Tzu); *zi* is an honorific, meaning "master." The first seven, or "inner," chapters are ascribed to Zhuangzi himself, while the remaining are considered to have been written by his disciples or students. Composed against the backdrop of the pro-

tracted Warring States period, the *Zhuangzi* is less concerned with the ideal governance of a country by sages and wise counselors, and more concerned with personal understanding. By liberating the mind and the self from social constraints, and practicing a detached view of the world, the sage could see the relative nature of the universe. Breaking down distinctions between "being" and "nonbeing," *Zhuangzi* proposes that all hierarchies, all right and wrong, good and bad are human constructs, and merely a delusion. A section of the Zhuangzi is called "Discussion on making all things equal." The philosopher counsels, "Right is not right. So is not so. If right were really right it would differ so clearly from not right that there would be no need for argument. Forget the years; forget distinctions. Leap into the boundless and make it your home."

Told mostly in parables and allegories, many with a paradox at their core, the *Zhuangzi* is both playful and profound. Many sections poke fun at Confucius, who is characterized as being "after the sham illusion of fame and reputation and [not knowing] that the Perfect Man looks on these as so many handcuffs and fetters!" Often Laozi enters the picture, as Lao Dan, and helps the fun along. It is worth noting that both Laozi and Zhuang Zhou are from the same southern Chinese region of Chu, while Confucius is from the northeastern state of Lu.

A twentieth-century depiction of Laozi.

THE BUTTERFLY DREAM

One of the best-known stories in the *Zhuangzi* is known as "The Butterfly Dream." It is used to illustrate the relative nature of reality, proposing that consciousness itself may be a delusion. Zhuang Zhou places himself in the story:

Once Zhuang Zhou dreamt he was a butterfly, a butterfly flitting and fluttering around, happy with himself and doing as he pleased. He didn't know he was Zhuang Zhou. Suddenly he woke up and there he was, solid and unmistakable Zhuang Zhou. But he didn't know if he was Zhuang Zhou who had dreamt he was a butterfly, or a butterfly dreaming he was Zhuang Zhou. Between Zhuang Zhou and a butterfly there must be some distinction! This is called the Transformation of Things.

A butterfly—here a symbol in a paradoxical story that questions our view of reality.

The Rise and Fall of Confucianism

The bloody Warring States period in China was brought to a decisive end in 221 BCE with the establishment of China's first empire. The Qin (Chin) dynasty, presided over by the ruthless Qin Shi Huangdi, ushered in China's imperial period. The rule of the Qin was brief, ending in 206 BCE, but it served to unify China and set a precedent for two millennia of imperial rule. In the brief years of his reign, Qin Shi Huangdi left a staggering legacy: he initiated work on the Great Wall of China, he standardized Chinese writing, roads, and coinage, and when he died, he was buried in a vast mausoleum guarded by an army of terracotta warriors.

China's first emperor, who favored the philosophy of Legalism, was intent on suppressing Confucian teachings. He is responsible for acts known as the "burning of the books and burying of the scholars." On the orders of Qin Shi Huangdi, hundreds of Confucian scholars were buried alive, and most of the extant Confucian texts were burned.

The Qin dynasty was succeeded by the more stable Han dynasty (206 BCE–220 CE). During these centuries Confucianism was revived, becoming recognized as the official state religion, with formalized rites and rituals. Rather than imposing a rule of law, as did the punitive Qin dynasty, the Han dynasty sought to rule according to Confucius's idea of harmony, with exemplary rulers governing a people whose civil actions stem from an internalized sense of duty.

Today the world's most famous symbol of China, the Great Wall was built to protect China from northern peoples, and its construction helped establish the idea of an empire in China, rather than a series of contentious states.

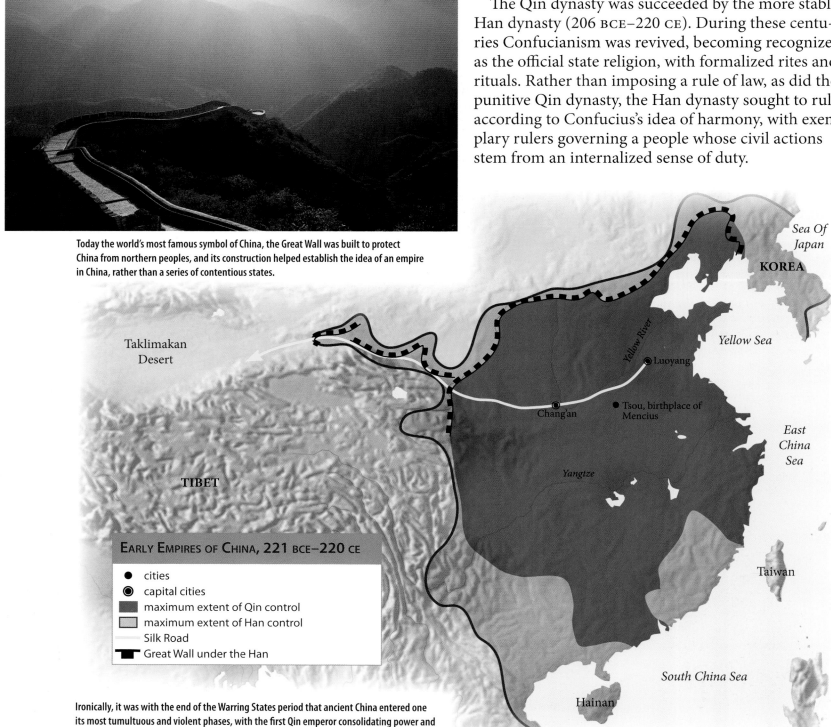

EARLY EMPIRES OF CHINA, 221 BCE–220 CE

- ● cities
- ◉ capital cities
- ■ maximum extent of Qin control
- □ maximum extent of Han control
- — Silk Road
- ▬ Great Wall under the Han

Ironically, it was with the end of the Warring States period that ancient China entered one its most tumultuous and violent phases, with the first Qin emperor consolidating power and restricting religious practice. The Han dynasty's subsequent assumption of power ensured the existence of a Chinese empire for close to 2,000 years.

HAN: THE FIRST CONFUCIAN STATE

The first Chinese state to incorporate Confucian teachings was the Han dynasty. Lasting for over four centuries, the Han was marked by prosperity and expansion. Separated into two periods, the Western, or Former, Han ruled until 9 CE from their capital in Chang'an. Then power shifted to another branch of the family, the Eastern, or Later, Han dynasty, whose capital was Luoyang, in present-day Henan Province. The Silk Road was firmly established, allowing for trade not only of goods but of ideas; Buddhism entered China along this route. During the Han period the arts and sciences flourished, particularly under Emperor Wu (141–87 BCE); and Sima Qian (145–90 BCE) wrote his invaluable *Records of the Grand Historian*. Han expansionism is largely responsible for the widespread Confucian influence in such countries as Korea, Japan, and Vietnam.

Confucian ideas took hold gradually with Han rulers, adopted initially to maintain the position of the growing aristocracy. According to Confucius, social harmony stems from a proper balance within the five relationships: between ruler and subject, father and son, elder brother and younger brother, husband and wife, and friend and friend. The first four are hierarchical relationships, in which it is the duty of the superior to assume responsibility for the inferior, and the duty of the inferior to act with obedience and respect. Filial piety is interwoven throughout; respect for one's superiors and elders even extends as far as the emperor, who must pay proper homage to his ancestors and the gods, or be in danger of forfeiting the Mandate of Heaven, the Chinese equivalent of divine right to rule.

The Later Han dynasty was a marvel of technological sophistication and trade with cultures as far west as Rome. Yet an agrarian

A bronze vase, elaborately decorated with geometric designs and depictions of tigers, from the Han dynasty.

THE TERRACOTTA ARMY

The massive terracotta army faces east, the direction of the emperor's enemies, emphasizing the implicit belief in their efficacy as guards. Accompanying the soldiers—who were given individualized faces—are many other artifacts of war, some symbolic and some, like weapons, actual.

A grand army of warriors guards the tomb of China's first emperor, the tyrannical Qin Shi Huangdi. They stand arrayed for combat, impassive, alert, heavily armored—and entirely made of clay. Known as the Terracotta Army, some 8,000 life-size figures were buried with Qin Shi Huangdi in his city-size mausoleum. Discovered in 1974 by local farmers in Xian, Shaanxi Province, the figures date from 210 BCE; they have been called the eighth wonder of the ancient world. Historians speculate that the emperor may have become mentally unstable from ingesting mercury in his quest for immortality. Indeed, rivers of mercury were believed to have flowed through the tomb, in which hundreds of concubines and countless craftsmen were buried alive with their dead ruler. The statues were originally painted bright colors. Recent scholarship suggests that the bright purple paint on some of the figures was the work of Daoist alchemists, who were experimenting with methods for creating artificial jade.

crisis and a severe famine eventually led to a revolt known as the Yellow Turban Rebellion (184–205 CE), centered in Confucius's home state of Lu, in present-day Shandong Province. The Yellow Turbans were an early sect of religious Daoism, followers of the "Way of Supreme Peace." The rebellion was crushed, but it toppled the Han dynasty and with it the supremacy of Confucianism. Buddhism and religious Daoism grew up from the uncertainty that followed the demise of the Han.

MENCIUS, THE SECOND SAGE

Mencius is the Latinized name of the scholar Mengzi (or Meng Tzu), who is popularly called the "second sage" of Confucianism. Mencius (c. 371–289 BCE) lived during the Warring States period. His eponymous writings further elaborated Confucian ideas.

Mencius is best known for his belief that humankind is essentially good, that "all men have a mind that cannot bear to see the sufferings of others." Mencius gives the following example: "If men suddenly see a child about to fall into a well, they will without exception experience a feeling of alarm and distress." From this feeling arise what Mencius termed the "four principles"—benevolence (*ren*), righteousness (*li*), propriety (*yi*), and knowledge (*zhi*). Since these qualities, sometimes called the "four beginnings," are as innate as the four limbs, they are a kind of human birthright. Mencius stands in direct opposition to his contemporary Xun Zi, whose belief in the essential evil in human nature gave rise to the harsh policies of Legalism.

Mencius, on the right, and Confucius. Two of China's most famous philosophers, they developed between them the major traditions of Confucianism.

Buddhism Takes Root in China

THE FIRST BUDDHIST TEXTS to reach China were of two kinds. One was Chinese writings taken directly from the oral teachings of traveling missionaries. The other came in the form of Chinese transcriptions of the sutras from Sanskrit. Buddhist scriptures, mostly of the Mahayana school, arrived in China close to the beginning of the Common Era, carried along the Silk Road.

One of the earliest Chinese Buddhist centers was Luoyang, said to be the eastern terminus of the Silk Road. Legend says that the Han emperor Ming, whose capital was in Luoyang, dreamed of a sixteen-foot-high "golden man." When he was told that such a god was worshipped in India, Ming dispatched envoys. His delegation returned around 68 BCE with two monks, a sutra in forty-two parts, and a large statue of the Buddha, carried on a white horse. White Horse Temple was built at Luoyang soon after this, and a temple still stands on the site today.

After the fall of the Han dynasty in 220 CE, China one again became fractured. The period that followed, known as the Three Kingdoms, was one of disunity, with regional empires each claiming succession from the Han. It was a religiously driven rebellion, the Daoist Yellow Turbans, that toppled the Confucian Han, and now religion in China became more of an open book. Buddhism first reached China during the Han dynasty, but it took root during the period of disunity, and thrived during the later Tang dynasty.

EARLY CHINESE BUDDHIST SCHOOLS

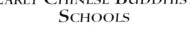

The relations between the Confucian establishment and the new religion from India were strained at best. Confucian teaching was hostile toward many Buddhist practices, particularly its monastic tradition. Monks, who sequestered themselves from society, who didn't marry and continue family lines, were seen as betraying the core value of filial piety. Buddhism and Daoism, on the other hand, found a natural affinity. Daoist emphasis on the open-endedness of many philosophical questions meshed well with Buddhism. Chinese Buddhist traditions are often overlain with Daoist precepts. In particular, the concept of emptiness seen in both Laozi's and Zhuangzi's teachings is a core concept of the Chan school of Buddhism.

After the fall of the Han, several Chinese Buddhist schools emerged. Most adopted a specific sutra as their central focus of worship. Two of the earliest and most influential were the Pure Land (*Jing Tu* or *Ching Tu*) and the Chan schools. The Pure Land school, still very active worldwide, venerates Amitabha Buddha, or the Buddha of infinite light. Amitabha was said to have dwelt in a land of pure bliss, called Sukhavati, which devotees could enter by accumulating enough merits during this lifetime. One would then dwell eternally in this realm, free from rebirth. Chanting Amitabha's name as a mantra is a central form of Pure Land devotion.

The other primary form of early Chinese Buddhism was the Chan school, the name being derived from the Sanskrit *dhyana*, which means meditation, concentration, or awareness. A back-to-basics form of Buddhism, Chan strove to imitate the Buddha's own path to enlightenment through sitting meditation and mindfulness of the present moment. Chan later became *Son* in Korea, and *Zen* when it reached Japan.

Originally constructed in 68 CE at Luoyang, White Horse Temple remains a sacred Buddhist site today.

BODHIDHARMA

A legendary Buddhist monk named Bodhidharma was said to have traveled east from India in either the fifth or sixth century BCE. Bodhidharma is credited with introducing Chan Buddhism to China. While visiting Emperor Wu of Liang, the monk was said to have had this exchange:

The emperor asked, "What is the meaning of Buddhism?"

"Nothing holy. Vast emptiness," answered Bodhidharma.

"Who is standing before me now?" asked the emperor.

"I don't know," came the answer.

Bodhidharma was thereafter banished from the court of Liang. He settled at Shaolin monastery in present-day Henan Province, where he is said to have meditated for nine years facing a wall, "listening to the ants scream." Bodhidharma is often shown in Buddhist art as a wild-eyed, bearded character with distinctly Western features. Some scholars also credit Bodhidharma with introducing a form of movement that flourished at Shaolin, becoming the basis for the martial art kung fu.

In modern Japan, Bodhidharma appears as wobbly Daruma (his Japanese name) doll. Traditionally, Daruma dolls fulfill wishes and symbolize the same characteristics of optimism and spiritual balance present in much-earlier Chinese legends about Bodhidharma.

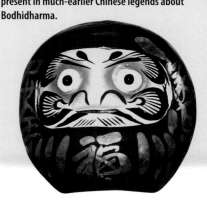

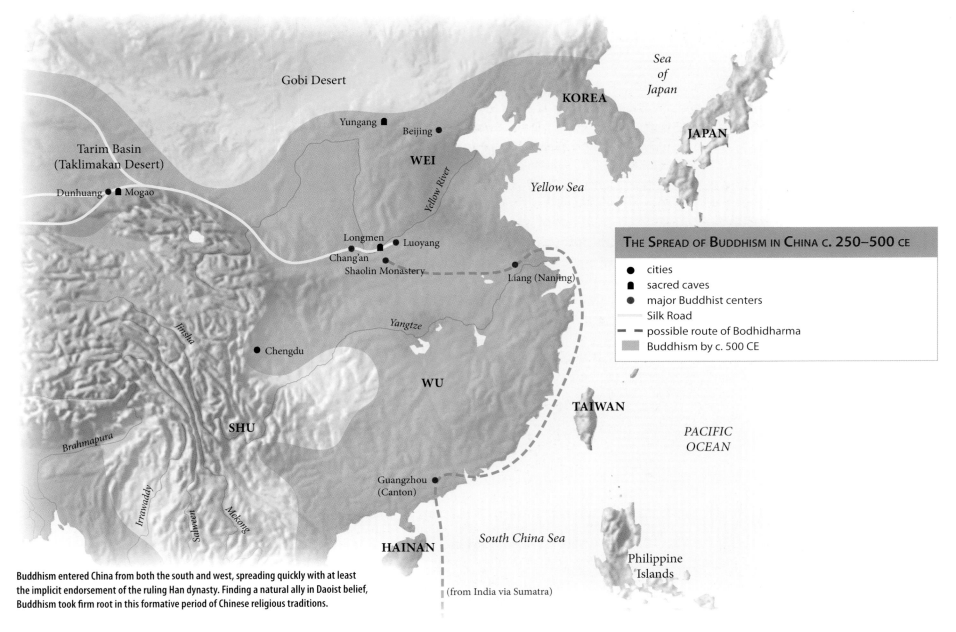

Gobi Desert

KOREA

Sea
of
Japan

JAPAN

Yungang · Beijing

WEI

Tarim Basin
(Taklimakan Desert)

Yellow Sea

Yellow River

Dunhuang · Mogao

Longmen · Luoyang
Chang'an
Shaolin Monastery

Liang (Nanjing)

THE SPREAD OF BUDDHISM IN CHINA C. 250–500 CE

- · cities
- ▪ sacred caves
- ● major Buddhist centers
- — Silk Road
- – – possible route of Bodhidharma
- ░ Buddhism by c. 500 CE

Yangtze

Jinsha

· Chengdu

WU

TAIWAN

PACIFIC
OCEAN

SHU

Brahmapura

Irrawaddy

Salween

Mekong

Guangzhou
(Canton)

HAINAN

South China Sea

Philippine
Islands

(from India via Sumatra)

Buddhism entered China from both the south and west, spreading quickly with at least
the implicit endorsement of the ruling Han dynasty. Finding a natural ally in Daoist belief,
Buddhism took firm root in this formative period of Chinese religious traditions.

This limestone relief, dating to c. 570, is one of the earliest known depictions
of Sukhavati (the Pure Land) in China. Once, the relief was vividly painted, highlighting
Amitabha's reception of newly reborn souls to his sacred land.

THE CAVES OF THE THOUSAND BUDDHAS

The Tarim Basin, in present day Xinjiang, China,
was a treacherous pass from west to east. Here
the northern and southern branches of the Silk
Road diverged, skirting the vast Taklimakan
Desert. To the east, one of the oases,
Dunhuang, is the site of the remarkable Mogao
Caves, known as the Caves of the Thousand
Buddhas. The caves form a complex of 492
temples, decorated with murals, sculpture, and
paintings. The Buddhist art here spans a period
of 1,000 years. In the early twentieth century, a
cache of ancient manuscripts was discovered
here as well, some dating from the fifth century
CE. Buddhist, Daoist, Confucian, and Nestorian
Christian documents were among those found.

The caves take their name from a legend:
a fourth-century traveling monk had a vision
here of a thousand golden Buddhas and initiated the practice of painting murals on the
cave walls. The Mogao Caves take their place
alongside the Longmen Grottoes and the
Yungang Grottoes as the three most important
examples of ancient Chinese Buddhist art.

The Caves of the Thousand Buddhas have drawn visitors
since the fourth century, first as a Buddhist pilgrimage site,
then as an archaeological treasure trove, and, since 1987,
as a World Heritage site.

AFRICA
Witch Doctors and Sacred Ancestors

EGYPT RESTED ATOP the continent of Africa like a glorious crown, having developed one of the world's earliest great civilizations. Later, Phoenicians and Greeks had visited, traded with, and even settled in Egypt and other parts of northern Africa, bringing their own religions; but the Greeks considered the people living south of Egypt to be the farthermost of mankind and called them Ethiopians ("burnt faces").

In fact, these "Ethiopians" were probably Nubians, occupying the northeastern parts of the Sudan region. Egypt and Nubia vied for power over each other through the millennia, and in the second millennium BCE Egypt divided Nubia's territories in half, naming the southern portion Kush. Then, much later (591 BCE), when Egypt invaded Kush and captured its capital, Napata; the Kushite king moved farther south and established a new capital at Meroë.

By the first century CE, Meroë had become one of a number of major iron-smelting centers. Meanwhile, a few proto-urban communities had appeared in the Niger River valley, and a trading post in northwestern Africa had grown into the Kingdom of Ghana, which was to prosper through much of the first millennium. Finally, traders from southern Arabia crossed the Red Sea and established a large trading center to the southeast of Meroë. Over the previous centuries the people there had traded with Phoenicians, Jews, and Greeks, but at this point the region grew into the Kingdom of Aksum, which gradually came to be known as Ethiopia (corresponding in location to modern-day Ethiopia). It soon controlled all the trade between the Nile Valley and points south.

Farther south, the numerous tribes remained isolated. Only merchants from Aksum or a few eastern ports seemed to penetrate even partway into the continent, and none ventured far from the coastlands.

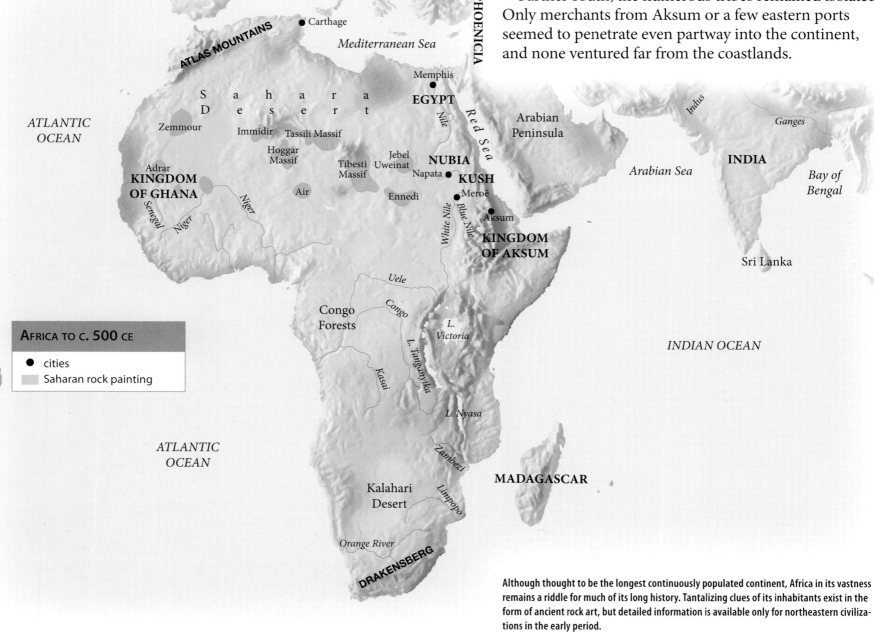

AFRICA TO C. 500 CE
- ● cities
- Saharan rock painting

Although thought to be the longest continuously populated continent, Africa in its vastness remains a riddle for much of its long history. Tantalizing clues of its inhabitants exist in the form of ancient rock art, but detailed information is available only for northeastern civilizations in the early period.

And behold, an Ethiopian, a eunuch, a minister of the Candace, queen of the Ethiopians, in charge of all her treasure, had come to Jerusalem to worship and was returning; seated in his chariot, he was reading the prophet Isaiah.

—ACTS OF THE APOSTLES

AFRICAN RELIGION

The Sahara Desert, which cuts across Africa from the Atlantic Ocean to the Red Sea, served to divide the Mediterranean cultures from those in the more southern regions. Because nothing was written down in sub-Saharan Africa, and regional cultures developed at different rates, little is known about the religions practiced before the arrival of Europeans in the late eighteenth century. What we do know comes from the oral traditions of the peoples who often moved from place to place, borrowing from one another's cultures.

Most sub-Saharan Africans seem to have believed in a single creator god (variously named) to whom they prayed for protection or prosperity. Often, in African mythology, the first man the god creates is a trickster, who steals from him to benefit other human beings. Many Africans also appealed to sacred ancestors to fulfill their needs. Others performed dances and other rituals to bring or stop rain. Misfortunes were blamed on witchcraft, and witch doctors were sometimes used to fend off its effects. Fetishes gave the bearer power to cause or ward off harm. Good behavior was also essential. Nzambi, one of the many creator gods, withdrew from earth because of the crimes of the people.

Nubian pyramids at Gebel Barkal, built by Meroë royalty, illustrate both strong Egyptian influence and native design. While the choice of a pyramid for a tomb clearly reflects Egyptian sensibility, Nubian pyramids are much narrower, with a steeper incline.

SAHARAN ROCK PAINTING

Although it is one of the world's fiercest deserts, the Sahara has enjoyed periods of heavy rainfall in the distant past. The last such period was the sixth millennium BCE, when humans fished in the Sahara's lakes, raised livestock, and hunted elephants, rhinoceros, and giraffes. But by the third millennium, desert conditions had returned and the people moved south. Fortunately, however, the aridity of the desert preserved many fossils, as well as the cave art of those long-ago peoples.

Some of the cave paintings go back to 6000 BCE and reflect the hunting lifestyle of the people. Some of the many animals portrayed are now extinct, such as the giant buffalo. Although the paintings seem to include some of the patterns found in Egyptian art, the overall character of the Saharan cave art is too unlike Egyptian art to be derived from it. In any case the paintings preserve glimpses of a lifestyle long lost.

Today an infamously inhospitable stretch of arid, sun-baked desert, the Sahara historically experienced periods of humidity, allowing humans and animals to live there with relative ease.

CHRISTIANITY COMES TO ETHIOPIA

According to the Acts of the Apostles in the Christian Bible, Philip, an early Christian leader, baptized an Ethiopian eunuch who was traveling home from Jerusalem. This Ethiopian was a high official in the court of the Candace of Ethiopia—probably Meroë, whose queens were called Candace. According to tradition, this official returned home and established Christianity there, making Ethiopia the first Christian country in Africa.

It is more likely, however, that Christianity came to Ethiopia in the fourth century. When two Christians from Tyre, Frumentius and Edisius, were returning from India on a merchant ship, they were captured and brought to the Ethiopian court, where they preached Christianity. Other missionaries arrived in the fifth century and helped spread Christianity, and by the early sixth century the Kingdom of Aksum had become an important Christian community. Christianity thrived in Ethiopia until the coming of Islam in the seventh century.

Philip, named by Christians "the Evangelist," and the Ethiopian eunuch travel by litter, a scene described in Acts of the Apostles.

THE AMERICAS
North America

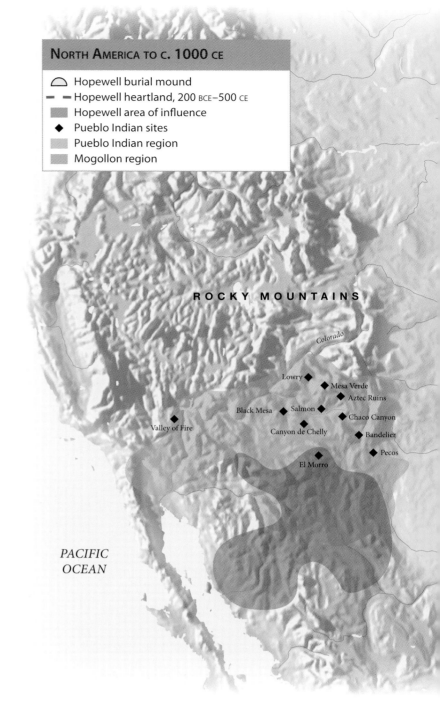

NORTH AMERICA TO C. 1000 CE

⌒ Hopewell burial mound
– – Hopewell heartland, 200 BCE–500 CE
▢ Hopewell area of influence
◆ Pueblo Indian sites
▢ Pueblo Indian region
▢ Mogollon region

ROCKY MOUNTAINS

Colorado

Lowry ◆   ◆ Mesa Verde
        ◆ Aztec Ruins
Black Mesa ◆   Salmon ◆   ◆ Chaco Canyon
Valley of Fire ◆   ◆ Bandelier
        Canyon de Chelly   ◆ Pecos
        El Morro ◆

PACIFIC OCEAN

THE INDIANS OF NORTH AMERICA continued to develop, sometimes building on the cultures that had preceded them. The Adena, for example, had built elaborate burial mounds through most of the first millennium BCE, but in about 200 BCE they were eclipsed by the Hopewell culture, which continued building mounds until about 500 CE. The Hopewell (named for a later owner of one of the mound sites) were hunters and gatherers, but they also fished and farmed, cultivating corn and other crops. They built thousands of villages across the Midwest and traded goods obtained from places as far apart as the Great Lakes and the Gulf of Mexico. They buried their leaders in the elaborate mounds they built, filling them with treasures obtained in their trading. Although their mound-building suggests that they believed in life after death, nothing more is known of the Hopewell religion.

The Hopewell were succeeded, in turn, by other mound builders, the Mississippians, who improved farming techniques and built large cities in the Mississippi Valley. Their largest city, Cahokia, had a population of some 20,000. The Mississippians had a highly stratified society, including leaders, artisans, and priests. Their religious symbols and motifs of rank appear in their art. One such symbol is a flying human figure with winglike tattoos around the eyes.

Meanwhile, in the Pacific Northwest, life was focused on the sea. The people lived in large plank houses with gabled roofs and fished the game-filled waters. They also excelled at woodworking, building seagoing canoes, carving their family emblems into totem poles, and creating elaborate wooden masks. A few wealthy families controlled each village, and a favorite event was the potlatch, a feast that lasted for days, during which the host demonstrated his wealth by lavishing his guests with food and gifts.

At the center of the city of Cahokia in the present-day Mississippi Valley rose the enormous Monks Mound, the largest earthworks construction in North America. Its base covers 14 acres (6 ha), and its highest terrace is 100 feet (30.5 m) high.

An image of a deer etched into a rock wall in the Valley of Fire, Arizona. Many ancient Pueblo Indian (Anasazi) petroglyphs have been found, but for the most part their meanings remain elusive.

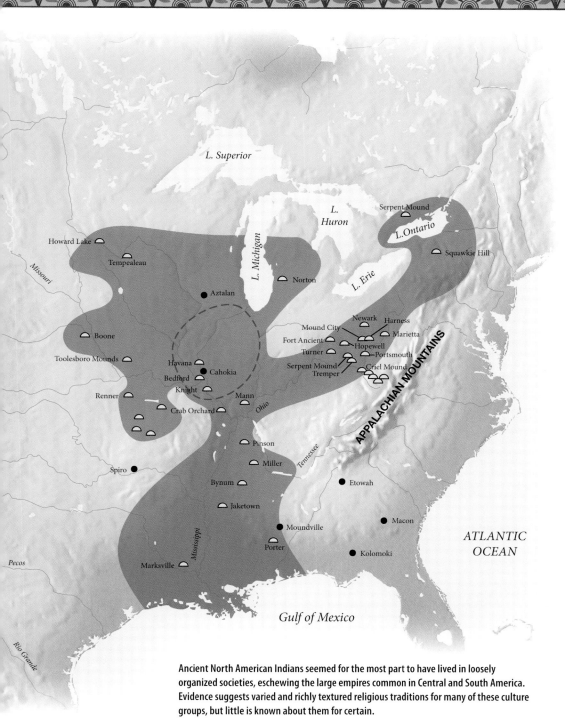

L. Superior

L. Huron

Serpent Mound

L. Ontario

Squawkie Hill

Howard Lake

Tempealeau

L. Michigan

L. Erie

Norton

Missouri

Aztalan

Boone

Mound City   Newark   Harness

Fort Ancient   Marietta

Toolesboro Mounds   Havana   Turner   Hopewell   Portsmouth

Bedford   Cahokia   Serpent Mound   Criel Mound

Knight   Tremper

Renner   Mann

Crab Orchard   Ohio

Pinson

Miller

Spiro   Bynum   Tennessee

Jaketown   Etowah

Mississippi   Moundville   Macon

Porter

Pecos   Marksville   Kolomoki

Rio Grande

APPALACHIAN MOUNTAINS

ATLANTIC OCEAN

Gulf of Mexico

Ancient North American Indians seemed for the most part to have lived in loosely organized societies, eschewing the large empires common in Central and South America. Evidence suggests varied and richly textured religious traditions for many of these culture groups, but little is known about them for certain.

May I always walk with beauty all around me.
—REFRAIN OF A NAVAJO PRAYER

PUEBLO INDIAN RELIGION

The Pueblo Indians found significance in all their surroundings and even designed their housing complexes to evoke their religious beliefs. This is particularly obvious in the designs of their kivas, or ceremonial rooms. Each of these large rooms was built around a sunken pit with a hole at the bottom, which recalled the myth of the people's origins. According to the myth, the first humans climbed into the sunlight through a hole in the ground, led by the Great Spirit. Then, guided by the Great Spirit, these first humans wandered for years seeking food and fleeing from danger. When they finally arrived at their present home, the Great Spirit taught them to plant and harvest corn and to build their great housing complexes. Then, after appointing twin warrior gods to guard them, the Great Spirit returned to his own domain beyond the clouds. The myth, then, basically speaks of emerging from dark to sunlight, from ignorance to wisdom.

Cliff-cut dwellings at Cliff Palace, Mesa Verde, Colorado. Visible in the foreground are several large, circular, subterranean kivas. Cliff Palace includes twenty-three kivas in all.

EMERGENCE OF THE PUEBLO CULTURE

Among the most distinctive peoples to emerge in the first centuries of the Common Era were the so-called Pueblo Indians—known to the Navajos as the Anasazi, or "enemy ancestors." They first appeared in the Southwest in about 200 BCE, as simple farmers. At first they lived in pit houses, later in long row houses, often two rooms wide. They grew corn and other crops, perhaps even cotton. Over the centuries they spread out, and their housing grew more complex. From 1050–1300 CE, they constructed dozens of stone and adobe apartment complexes, some of which were built into high cliffs.

At Mesa Verde (in what is now Colorado) a number of such complexes were built into shallow caves or under rock overhangs along the canyon walls. The individual dwellings were fashioned from blocks of hard sandstone, which were held together and plastered over with adobe mortar. Cliff Palace, which is one of the Mesa Verde complexes, is built in an alcove of a sandstone cliff. It is 89 feet wide, 59 feet deep, and 288 feet long (27 by 59 by 88

m) and contains about 150 rooms, including twenty-three round sunken rooms, or kivas, used for ceremonial purposes.

Another impressive Pueblo community was constructed in Chaco Canyon in the ninth century. This community, in flat, open country (now part of New Mexico), was made up of several hundred interlinked rooms surrounded by a single wall. Eventually it became the center of a network of settlements that extended 100 miles (160 km) to the north, south, and west. Its population ultimately reached about 4,000.

LATER PEOPLES

In about 1000 CE bands of Athabascans moved into the Southwest from the far north, bearing bows and arrows. They lived in structures made by piling logs against three poles that were joined at the top and covering the outside with mud. These newcomers were formidable hunters and raiders, and over the next few centuries they repeatedly raided the local farming communities and finally drove out the Pueblo Indians. They were the ancestors of the Navajos.

Mesoamerica

BETWEEN 200 BCE AND 900 CE two great cultures flourished in Mesoamerica. One was Teotihuacán, which played a role similar to that of the earlier Olmec, which probably influenced its people. The other was the mighty Maya culture.

Teotihuacán was probably the largest city in the pre-Columbian Americas, reaching a population of up to 150,000. Situated near the site of the future Mexico City, it was built up gradually between the first and sixth centuries CE. At the northern and southern ends of Teotihuacán's main avenue stood pyramids of the sun and moon. A temple to the creation god Quetzalcoatl (the Feathered Serpent) dominated the center of the city. Lining the stairs of this temple were alternating sculptures of Quetzalcoatl and the Fire Serpent (bearer of the sun on its daily journey across the sky). Little is known of the people of Teotihuacán, but they strongly influenced much of first-millennium

Mesoamerica and even the later Toltec and Aztec cultures. Teotihuacán faded into obscurity after 600 CE.

The Maya, who had emerged in Guatemala in about 600 BCE, reached maturity by 200 CE and flourished until roughly 900 CE. Influenced by the Olmec, the Maya built lavish ceremonial centers to their gods, developed astronomy to the point of forecasting eclipses, discovered the concept of zero in mathematics, and vastly improved earlier calendar systems. They also developed a sophisticated writing system containing hundreds of symbols. The Maya wrote their own history, giving the lineages of rulers and describing their often bloody battles. They even wrote books on bark, though all but three of these have been lost. Maya art is fairly naturalistic and was used along with written inscriptions for narrative purposes—or sometimes to depict a kind of ball game, a version of which is still played in Mexico today.

Having forged a mighty civilization in the dense jungles of the Yucatan Peninsula, the Maya Empire still haunts the imagination, with massive pyramids and elaborate carvings hinting at the depth of the people's ritual life. How their civilization thrived in such apparently inhospitable surroundings still puzzles scholars. The tropical rain forest made travel, construction, and agriculture quite difficult.

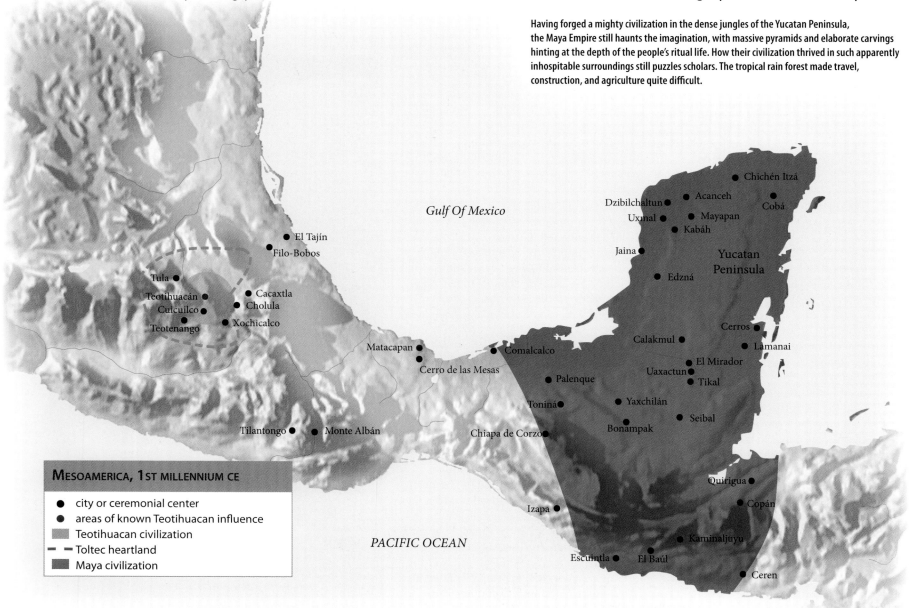

MESOAMERICA, 1ST MILLENNIUM CE

- ● city or ceremonial center
- ● areas of known Teotihuacan influence
- Teotihuacan civilization
- – – Toltec heartland
- Maya civilization

*The skulls piled up and
the blood pooled.*
—MAYA INSCRIPTION

MAYA CEREMONIAL CENTERS

Scattered throughout the Maya empire at its peak were about fifty major ceremonial centers of great majesty. At these centers pyramid temples and palaces surrounded a large plaza. A tomb was often hidden in the base of a temple pyramid, and a local leader was buried there—possibly with the idea that his spirit had become one with the god from whom he was descended. Altars and inscribed stone slabs, or steles, were often positioned in front of the temples.

Tikal was the largest of the ceremonial centers, with roughly 3,000 structures (large and small) in an area of six square miles (15.5 sq km). Its six pyramid temples were adorned with wooden lintels engraved with scenes of Maya lords enthroned in splendor. Palenque, possibly the most beautiful of the centers, had palaces with mansard-type roofs and stucco reliefs of rulers and gods. The central palace was a lavish structure with many galleries and interior courts.

The Maya believed in a full pantheon led by Itzamná, a creation god later envisioned as Kukulcán, or the Feathered Serpent (Quetzalcoatl in other cultures). Itzamná and other gods created a succession of worlds, each unsatisfactory, before settling on the present world. Different gods and goddesses were assigned to the sun and moon, corn, and the like. The underworld was a dark realm ruled over by sinister lords with jaguar emblems.

Priests led worship services involving incense, prayers, dances, bloodletting, and animal (and later human) sacrifice. Sorcerers and medicine men were considered prophets as well as dispensers of medicine and healers of disease. They used potions, chants, prayers, and bleeding to practice their craft.

The tops of three Tikal pyramids emerge from the thick forest canopy, which effectively hid the ruins of the largest Maya city for centuries.

LATER MESOAMERICAN CULTURES

For reasons that have never been discovered, Maya civilization declined in the ninth century, never to recover. With the Maya gone, the various states fought one another for supremacy in Mesoamerica, and there was a consequent emphasis on the military.

According to later Aztec myths, over the next few centuries a people known as the Toltec ruled central Mexico from their capital in Toulon—possibly the modern city of Tula, which is just north of Mexico City. Excavations at Tula reveal impressive sculptured columns and exquisite figurative pottery, whose creators could have been the Toltec. However, the Toltec may be a mere fiction used by the Aztec to symbolize the great builders who had preceded them. The Aztecs themselves would come into power in 1428 and remain the dominant force in Mexico until the coming of the Spanish, led by Hernán Cortés, in 1519.

The face of Quetzalcoatl, the "feathered serpent," as he appears on the temple at Teotihuacán. A number of stone heads depicting the deity project from the walls of the temple.

A MAYA MYTH

In addition to recording history, the inscriptions left by the Maya also relate myths that informed the people's religion. In one such myth, twins, summoned to play a ball game against the lords of the underworld, are defeated and sacrificed. The compassionate daughter of an underworld lord finds the head of one of the twins hanging from a tree, and the head spits into her hands, impregnating her. Banished to the world above, she gives birth to twin sons. Years later the twins go to the underworld, defeat the lords, and resurrect the body of their father, who is the god of corn. Then the triumphant twins bring food back to their people and rise up to become the sun and the moon.

The fantastic ruins of Teotihuacán, viewed from the top of the Pyramid of the Moon. The Avenue of the Dead runs through the middle of the great city; to the left can be seen the Pyramid of the Sun.

THE AMERICAS
South America

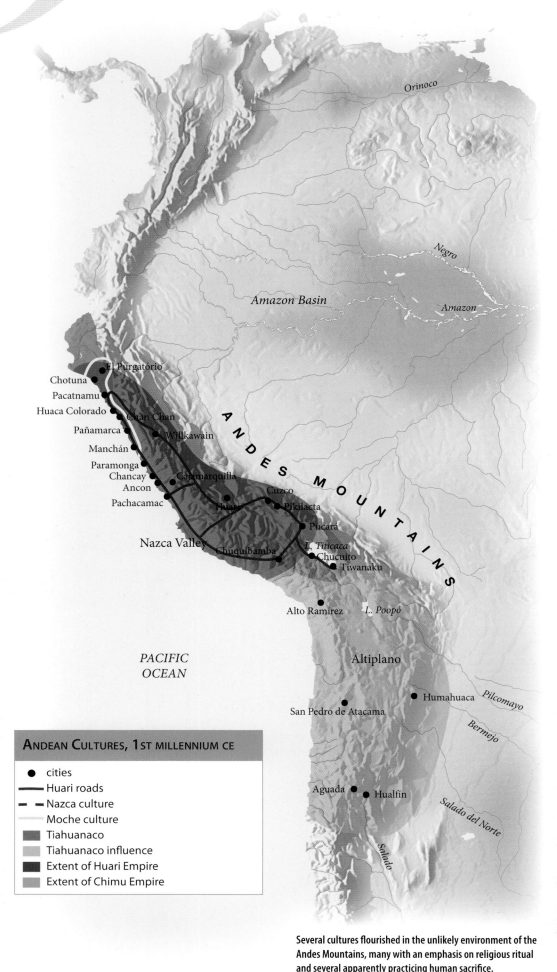

LITTLE IS KNOWN OF THE EARLY CULTURES of South America, but in the Andes, urban civilization was well under way by the start of the first millennium CE. A number of peoples there went on to build elaborate temples in which to worship their gods, or create other projects of vast proportions.

In about 200 BCE, a small-scale civilization began to emerge in the Nazca Valley near the southern coast of what is now Peru. For the most part, the people led a quiet life, producing elaborate textiles and ceramic art ornamented with stylized figures of people, animals, and plants. The Nazca culture flourished until about 600 CE and might have gone unnoticed except for the gigantic geometric forms and animal shapes that the people etched into the nearby desert floor.

From the first to the eighth century CE a more powerful culture occupied a strip along the northern coast of Peru. These people, known as the Moche, managed to bring water into the dry region from distant rivers by digging elaborate irrigation channels. But they were also brilliant artisans and great builders. At their chief worship center they constructed two massive pyramid temples. Because one is larger than the other, they were dubbed the Pyramids of the Sun and Moon in later times. Excavated tombs in the area have revealed richly jeweled bodies of warrior priests. Further hints of the Moches' lifestyle come from their pottery, which depicts daily life and even shows Moche warriors sacrificing prisoners of war and drinking their blood.

Another culture that excelled in irrigation started up in the south central Andean highlands and grew into an empire based in the city of Tiwanaku.

ANDEAN CULTURES, 1ST MILLENNIUM CE

- ● cities
- —— Huari roads
- – – Nazca culture
- Moche culture
- Tiahuanaco
- Tiahuanaco influence
- Extent of Huari Empire
- Extent of Chimu Empire

Several cultures flourished in the unlikely environment of the Andes Mountains, many with an emphasis on religious ritual and several apparently practicing human sacrifice.

Suggestive of bloody rituals, the grim Moche "Decapitator" god is variously depicted in animal and human (or mixed) forms and is often holding a sacred tumi knife and a human head.

TIWANAKU

The city of Tiwanaku (or Tiahuanaco) was situated on the Altiplano, in what is now western Bolivia, near the southeast end of Lake Titicaca at an altitude of 12,000 feet (3,600 m). Construction probably began in about 200 CE. When the city was completed centuries later it consisted of many stone buildings and a massive pyramid. A large rectangular enclosure constructed of stone columns and blocks was faced with the monolithic Gateway of the Sun. The figures of the condor, sun god, and winged creatures that were carved into the stone gateway would be copied widely.

The irrigation method used by the people of Tiwanaku consisted of raising planting surfaces and separating them with small ditches. The water in the ditches absorbed the heat of the daytime sun and retained some of it through the nights, which tended to be frosty in the Altiplano. The warm water, then, kept the plants from freezing. Algae that formed in the ditches was used as fertilizer, further advancing productivity. This method, which enabled the farmers to prosper, was later used throughout the Andes. Prosperity led to power, and Tiwanaku extended its influence through warfare.

LATER ANDEAN CULTURES

The empire based on the city of Huari (or Wari) shared many of the characteristics of Tiwanaku, but it was more militant and grew through conquest. The Huari were also great road builders, which enabled them to further extend their reach. By 650 they controlled all of northern Peru. The city of Huari had monumental sculptures and seventy to eighty walled rectangular compounds that housed 20,000 to 30,000 people. Both the Huari and Tiwanaku cultures declined in about 1000 CE.

In the years that followed, the Chimú, a new empire originating on the northern coast of Peru, would extend political control southward while building new cities and developing trade. But the Inca, after founding Cuzco, would go on to eventually conquer both the Chimú and more than half of western South America. The Inca were solidly in power when the Spanish conquistador Francisco Pizarro invaded Peru in 1532.

NAZCA LINES

It must have taken hundreds of years to complete the designs that are etched into the desert floor of the Nazca Valley. And the figures are so gigantic that they can only be seen from the air. They extend over some 190 square miles (500 sq km) and include geometric patterns and stylized images of plants and animals, including a monkey, a killer whale, and a spider. A gigantic pelican alone is 935 feet (285 m) long.

No one today knows why these images were cut into the desert floor. Theories about astronomical or agricultural uses have all been disproved. And assertions that they were not man-made but the work of extraterrestrials have been discredited. A more serious recent theory is that the designs had some religious significance for the people, which was why they worked so long and hard to create them. And even if the people themselves could not see the designs—designs that could well have been religious symbols—the gods could have seen them from their place in the heavens.

An enormous bird, set amid other Nazca lines, decorates the Peruvian desert.

The monolithic Gateway of the Sun stands once again in Tiwanaku, after having crashed and broken in half centuries ago. The central figure holds a pair of staffs. Surrounding him are forty-eight winged creatures, sixteen of whom bear condor heads.

POLYNESIA
Taboos, *Mana*, and the Birdman Cult

With Australia, Micronesia, and Melanesia already settled, only the islands of Polynesia remained open. Polynesia is the easternmost of the three groups of islands to the north and east of Australia that are known collectively as Oceania. (Micronesia and Melanesia are the others.) Prominent among the settlers of Melanesia had been immigrants from Indonesia who created the distinctive style of pottery known as Lapita. The Lapita people had settled in Tonga and Samoa, the westernmost islands of Polynesia, in about 1000–900 BCE, but had gone no farther. Eventually, they grew restless again and sent settlers to the far distant islands of Polynesia. Wherever they went they took along their religion, which was based on ancestor worship and ruled by taboos.

In about 150 BCE the Lapita set out from Tonga and Samoa and established communities in the Marquesas and Society Islands (including Tahiti). In about 400 CE they moved on to the northern and eastern extremities of Polynesia, navigating vast stretches of open sea in canoes with only the stars to guide them. They colonized Hawaii far to the north and Easter Island in the distant east. Finally, in about 750 CE, others set out again and traveled south, reaching New Zealand. In time, the new settlers there developed their own culture, which came

The Hawaiian coast, as appealing today as it was centuries ago when Polynesian seafarers made their way across thousands of miles of empty ocean to find these stunning island homes.

to be known as Maori. Even today, New Zealand's Maoris regard the islands to the north as their homeland and refer to them as the birthplace of the gods, under the name Hawaiki (possibly a variant of *Savai'i*, Samoa). Although Hawaii later adopted that name, the Hawaiian Islands were not originally considered the ancestral home of the Polynesians. Their real ancestors were the seafaring Lapita people who had spread their culture throughout Polynesia, but whose primary home base was Samoa.

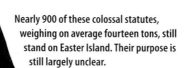

Nearly 900 of these colossal statutes, weighing on average fourteen tons, still stand on Easter Island. Their purpose is still largely unclear.

A weathered depiction, carved into reddish volcanic rock, of Makemake on Easter Island.

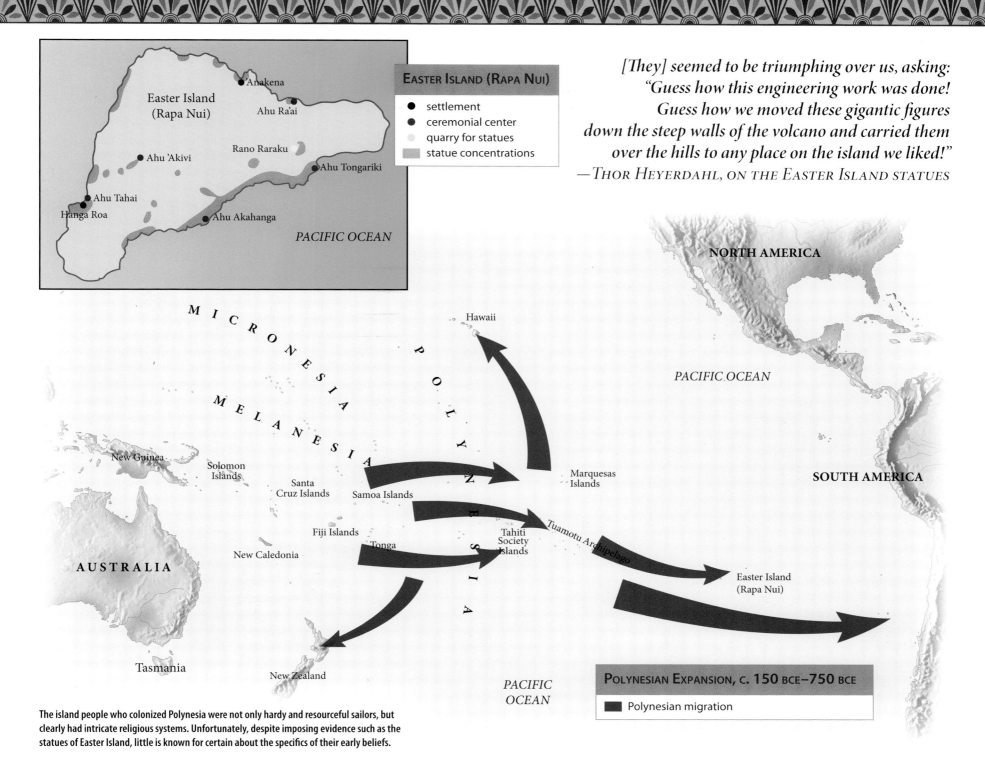

EASTER ISLAND (RAPA NUI)

- ● settlement
- ● ceremonial center
- ○ quarry for statues
- ▨ statue concentrations

Easter Island (Rapa Nui)

'Anakena
Ahu Ra'ai
Ahu 'Akivi
Rano Raraku
Ahu Tongariki
Ahu Tahai
Hanga Roa
Ahu Akahanga

PACIFIC OCEAN

[They] seemed to be triumphing over us, asking: "Guess how this engineering work was done! Guess how we moved these gigantic figures down the steep walls of the volcano and carried them over the hills to any place on the island we liked!"
—THOR HEYERDAHL, ON THE EASTER ISLAND STATUES

NORTH AMERICA

PACIFIC OCEAN

SOUTH AMERICA

MICRONESIA
MELANESIA
POLYNESIA

Hawaii

New Guinea
Solomon Islands
Santa Cruz Islands
Samoa Islands
Fiji Islands
Tonga
New Caledonia
Marquesas Islands
Tahiti Society Islands
Tuamotu Archipelago
Easter Island (Rapa Nui)

AUSTRALIA

Tasmania
New Zealand

PACIFIC OCEAN

POLYNESIAN EXPANSION, C. 150 BCE–750 BCE
■ Polynesian migration

The island people who colonized Polynesia were not only hardy and resourceful sailors, but clearly had intricate religious systems. Unfortunately, despite imposing evidence such as the statues of Easter Island, little is known for certain about the specifics of their early beliefs.

EASTER ISLAND

All we know for certain about Hawaii before the Europeans arrived in the eighteenth century is that it followed the Polynesian culture. However, we do know a bit more about Easter Island. Sitting alone, isolated in the vastness of the South Pacific Ocean, the tiny island (about three times the area of Manhattan island) is some 1,200 miles (1,900 km) from its nearest neighbor, Pitcairn Island. Still, colonists managed to find it and make it home, naming it Rapa Nui. Although Easter Island has no rivers, craters held freshwater, and a forest provided wood. The people managed to live well for a long while, planting crops, building houses, and fishing.

After a while, skilled craftsmen began building the gigantic sculptures for which Easter Island is now famous. These statues of gods and sacred chiefs were carved at a quarry of volcanic rock on the south coast. Once completed, they were moved (no one knows how) to one of the island's three hundred or so shrines. Each of these shrines consisted of a stone platform with a ramp

and a level court. The largest platforms were up to 200 feet long and 23-feet high (60 by 7 m) and held as many as fifteen statues.

There were once about a thousand statues on Easter Island, ranging in height from six to more than 30 feet (2 to 9 m). The statues' heads and torsos are rigid, the arms slender, and the hands elongated. The faces have large chins, long noses, and deep eye sockets through which the statue's *mana* (power and authority) was believed to emanate. Some of the statues have coral eyes with stone pupils.

Ultimately, Easter Island's resources became too sparse to support the population, and a powerful warrior class overthrew the hereditary chiefs. Claiming that the island's mana had dissipated, the warriors started a new religion, the Birdman cult, in which the warrior who found the first bird egg of the season became ruler for the next year. A new creator god, Makemake, replaced the old one, Tangaroa, and personal achievement was valued over heredity. The emblem of Birdman (a crouching human with a bird head) became the symbol for the new rulers. No more giant statues were created.

POLYNESIAN TABOOS

The Polynesians had an array of gods and myths, and they believed that all power and authority—mana—came from kinship with both these gods and with famous ancestors. Anyone who was wise, strong, or skillful had mana, and tribal chiefs embodied the mana of their people and land. To preserve the potency and holiness of mana, priests formulated taboos, or restrictions, to keep mana from being lost through contact with common things. Therefore, sacred shrines and the person and home of the tribe's chief were taboo. There were also taboos governing farming, fishing, and building, since these activities required the help and protection of the gods. Breaching a taboo could endanger the social order, and the gods themselves punished anyone who violated a taboo, directly inflicting sickness or defeat or withdrawing their protection. Taboos could be removed only through special rituals that involved incantations and purification.

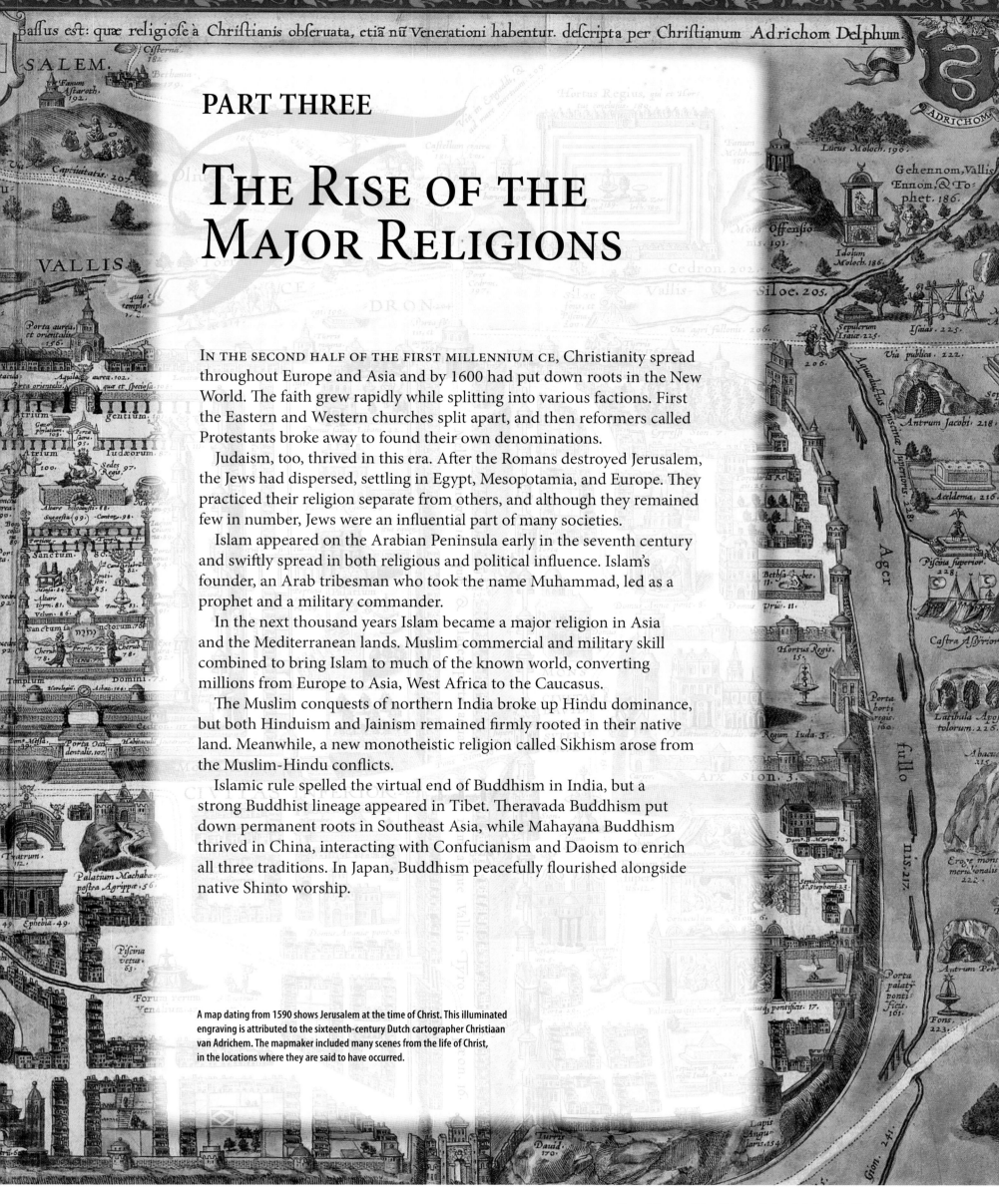

PART THREE

THE RISE OF THE MAJOR RELIGIONS

IN THE SECOND HALF OF THE FIRST MILLENNIUM CE, Christianity spread throughout Europe and Asia and by 1600 had put down roots in the New World. The faith grew rapidly while splitting into various factions. First the Eastern and Western churches split apart, and then reformers called Protestants broke away to found their own denominations.

Judaism, too, thrived in this era. After the Romans destroyed Jerusalem, the Jews had dispersed, settling in Egypt, Mesopotamia, and Europe. They practiced their religion separate from others, and although they remained few in number, Jews were an influential part of many societies.

Islam appeared on the Arabian Peninsula early in the seventh century and swiftly spread in both religious and political influence. Islam's founder, an Arab tribesman who took the name Muhammad, led as a prophet and a military commander.

In the next thousand years Islam became a major religion in Asia and the Mediterranean lands. Muslim commercial and military skill combined to bring Islam to much of the known world, converting millions from Europe to Asia, West Africa to the Caucasus.

The Muslim conquests of northern India broke up Hindu dominance, but both Hinduism and Jainism remained firmly rooted in their native land. Meanwhile, a new monotheistic religion called Sikhism arose from the Muslim-Hindu conflicts.

Islamic rule spelled the virtual end of Buddhism in India, but a strong Buddhist lineage appeared in Tibet. Theravada Buddhism put down permanent roots in Southeast Asia, while Mahayana Buddhism thrived in China, interacting with Confucianism and Daoism to enrich all three traditions. In Japan, Buddhism peacefully flourished alongside native Shinto worship.

A map dating from 1590 shows Jerusalem at the time of Christ. This illuminated engraving is attributed to the sixteenth-century Dutch cartographer Christiaan van Adrichem. The mapmaker included many scenes from the life of Christ, in the locations where they are said to have occurred.

The Temple Kingdoms of India

BY 500 CE THE GUPTA DYNASTY controlled a huge swath of northern India, from Sind and the Punjab in the west to Bengal in the east. At the same time much of the south of the subcontinent, nominally independent, consisted of little more than Gupta tributary states. Yet Gupta rule was threatened by imminent destruction, with warlike nomads from Central Asia massing on its northern frontier.

Against this unpromising background, a golden age of north Indian civilization took shape. It would last for at least 700 years. But like other civilizations of its time, Gupta India fell victim to barbarian invasions. By 511, following a crushing victory at Airikana by the Hephthalites (called "White Huns"—different from the Huns who invaded Rome), the Gupta Empire had been effectively obliterated.

Though Hun rule would prove short-lived, it was not until the mid-seventh century that, however uncertainly, native Indian centralized control arose again, that of the Pushyabhuti king, Harsha, who ruled, or claimed to rule, north India from Gujarat

to Bengal. Almost immediately, his kingdom came into conflict with a southern Indian dynasty, the Chalukyas. The conflict between them would set the pattern for much of the next 600 years as a series of smaller kingdoms and dynasties, principally in southern and central India, vied for supremacy. From about 750 to 950, these were the Palas in the northeast, the Gurjara-Pratiharas in the northwest, and, greatest of them all, the Rashtrakutas in the south.

Despite the political instability of this long period, the southern dynasties gradually came to displace the previous hegemony of northern India, especially with the rise of the Cholas from the middle of the tenth century. At much the same time, the increasingly vulnerable north was repeatedly ravaged by invasions from Turkic peoples from Central Asia, including after 1009 armies of the Muslim Mahmud of Ghazni, which looted temples and sacked towns across the entire region.

No fewer than six major kingdoms ruled enormous stretches of India between the seventh and twelfth centuries. Despite—or perhaps because of—this political turbulence, Hinduism flourished in this period; Adi Shankara, an eighth-century monk, founded four major monasteries as widely dispersed as Hinduism itself.

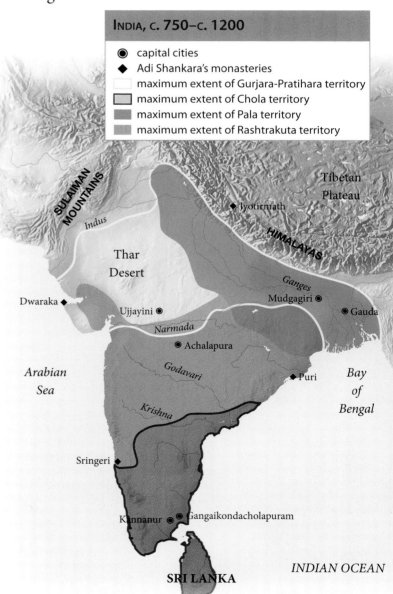

INDIA, C. 750–C. 1200

- ◉ capital cities
- ◆ Adi Shankara's monasteries
- ☐ maximum extent of Gurjara-Pratihara territory
- ☐ maximum extent of Chola territory
- ☐ maximum extent of Pala territory
- ☐ maximum extent of Rashtrakuta territory

INDIA, C. 640–C. 750

- ◉ capital cities
- ☐ territory claimed by Harsha of the Pushyabhutis
- ☐ maximum extent of the Chalukya territory
- ☐ former Gupta control

THE HINDU CONSOLIDATION

Paradoxically, whatever its political turmoil, this was an age that witnessed a supreme flowering of Indian culture and, inseparable from it, Hinduism. This was partly the result of growing trade links, especially with Southeast Asia, and more particularly because of the adoption of Hinduism by royal courts from the seventh century onward. Ruling families contributed lavishly to the building of a series of extraordinary, sprawling temples, while the worship of Shiva (Shaivism) and Vishnu (Vaishnavism) almost precisely reflected the hierarchical order of Hindu society, legitimizing and bolstering local rulers.

Religious texts accordingly tended to reflect the demands of such rulers, who projected themselves as divinely ordained, in many cases descended from the gods themselves. The *Ramayana*, for example, told of a mythical king, Rama, said to be a reincarnation of Vishnu, who undertook a journey the length of the country to modern Sri Lanka to free his wife, Sita, held captive by a demon, Ravana. It was a growing commonplace for Indian ruling families to identify themselves as direct descendants of Rama.

It was also in this period that the Puranas were written, some dating from as late as the twelfth century. A vast body of disparate works, they sought to explain not just the creation of the universe but the individual histories of an immense cast of gods, heroes, and kings, the whole covering an epic time span of millions of years.

ADI SHANKARA
☙

Adi Shankara (c. 788–820), preacher, scholar, founder of four major monasteries or *mathas*, and regarded by some Hindus as an incarnation of Shiva, was a key figure in the dissemination of what became known as Advaita Vedanta.

Sanjaya said:
To him who had been thus filled with pity, whose eyes were filled with tears and showed distress, and who was sorrowing, Madhusudana uttered these words:

The Blessed Lord said:
O Arjuna, in this perilous place, whence has come to you this impurity entertained by unenlightened persons, which does not lead to heaven and which brings infamy?
O Partha, yield not to unmanliness. This does not befit you. O scorcher of foes, arise, giving up the petty weakness of the heart.

Arjuna said:
O Madhusudana, O destroyer of enemies, how can I fight with arrows in battle against Bhisma and Drona who are worthy of adoration?
Rather than killing the noble-minded elders, it is better in this world to live even on alms. But by killing the elders we shall only be enjoying here the pleasures of wealth and desirable things drenched in blood.
We do not know this as well as to which is the better for us, [and] whether we shall win, or whether they shall conquer us. Those very sons of Dhrtarastra, by killing whom we do not wish to live, stand in confrontation.
With my nature overpowered by weak commiseration, with a mind bewildered about duty, I supplicate You. Tell me for certain that which is better; I am Your disciple. Instruct me who have taken refuge in You.
Because, I do not see that which can, even after acquiring on this earth a prosperous kingdom free from enemies and even sovereignty over the gods, remove my sorrow [which is] blasting the senses.

—Adi Shankara, *The Path of Knowledge*

Adi Shankara, also known as Bhagavatpada Acharya ("the teacher at the feet of Lord") traveled on foot to various parts of India to disseminate the teachings of the Vedanta.

India is a vast land of geological extremes, from the arid Thar desert in the northwest (below) to the high Himalayas in the north (inset, below), and the uniquely diverse Western Ghats in the west (right). At times in the subcontinent's storied past, the only common cultural feature was the shared heritage of Hinduism, with myths as rich and varied as their home country.

THE VEDANTA
☙

During this period the key Hindu doctrine, the Vedanta, was further developed, emerging as a dominant strand in certain schools of Hindu thought. To the extent that a religion as multifaceted and various as Hinduism can be codified at all, the Vedanta—literally the "end" or "culmination" (*anta*) of knowledge (*veda*)—holds that the fundamental nature of all living things is divine and that true spirituality is attained only when we have discovered the divinity within ourselves.

Characteristically, the means of discovering this inner divinity, the overarching cosmic consciousness of which we are all part, are not merely infinite but inform every aspect of our lives just as God—Brahman—takes infinite forms and informs every aspect of our lives. But prayer and ritual (*bhakti yoga*), recognizing God in everything (*jnana yoga*), selflessness (*karma yoga*), and attuning your mind to God through meditation (*raja yoga*), the whole allowing you in the end to recognize that God, however elusive, is the only reality and that the material world is an illusion, are in essence the core methods of reaching this state. Even so, the nature of Vedanta is such that it simultaneously held no one system inherently superior to any other, even no one religion superior to any other. If we can train ourselves to find God, we discover in the end that God is everywhere.

The Hindu Pantheon

Perhaps appropriately for a religion with no known founder and which at least until the nineteenth century called itself simply the *sanatana dharma*, or "eternal religion," Hinduism is simultaneously monotheistic—that is, it recognizes a single God, Brahman, coexistent with the universe and all living things—and polytheistic, in that Brahman takes multiple, in some senses infinite, forms. The nineteenth-century Hindu sage Sri Ramakrishna summed up this seeming paradox: "There can be as many spiritual paths as there are spiritual aspirants and as many gods as there are devotees."

At the same time, there is a clear hierarchy within the kaleidoscopic Hindu pantheon. Heading it is the trinity (*trimurti*) of Brahma, Vishnu, and Shiva, respectively the creator, preserver, and destroyer of the universe, and their consorts, the goddesses Saraswati, Lakshmi, and Kali.

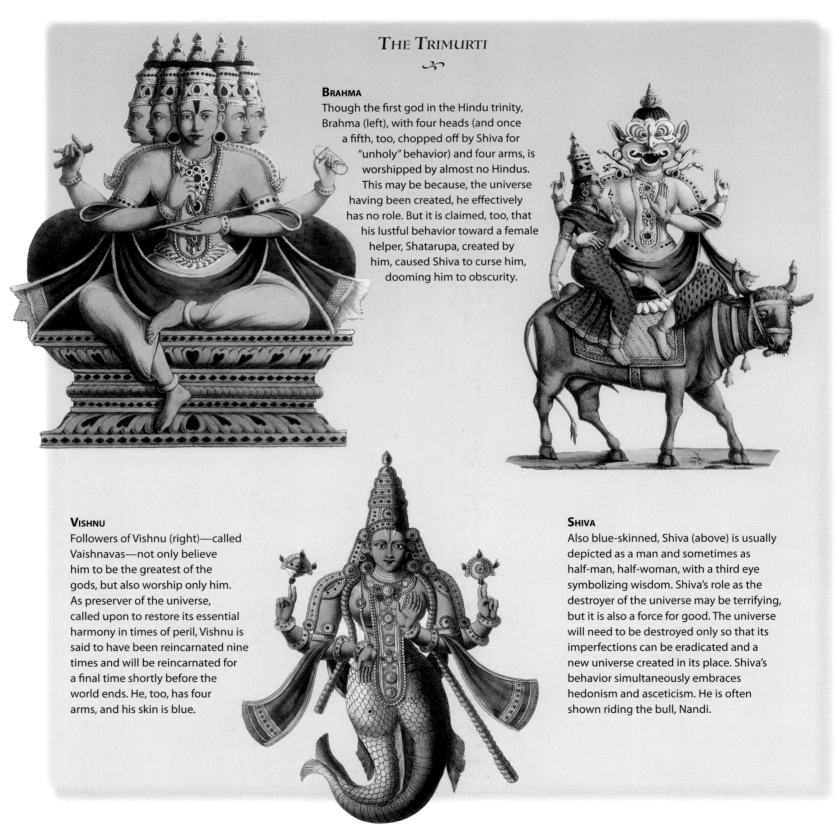

THE TRIMURTI
ॐ

BRAHMA
Though the first god in the Hindu trinity, Brahma (left), with four heads (and once a fifth, too, chopped off by Shiva for "unholy" behavior) and four arms, is worshipped by almost no Hindus. This may be because, the universe having been created, he effectively has no role. But it is claimed, too, that his lustful behavior toward a female helper, Shatarupa, created by him, caused Shiva to curse him, dooming him to obscurity.

VISHNU
Followers of Vishnu (right)—called Vaishnavas—not only believe him to be the greatest of the gods, but also worship only him. As preserver of the universe, called upon to restore its essential harmony in times of peril, Vishnu is said to have been reincarnated nine times and will be reincarnated for a final time shortly before the world ends. He, too, has four arms, and his skin is blue.

SHIVA
Also blue-skinned, Shiva (above) is usually depicted as a man and sometimes as half-man, half-woman, with a third eye symbolizing wisdom. Shiva's role as the destroyer of the universe may be terrifying, but it is also a force for good. The universe will need to be destroyed only so that its imperfections can be eradicated and a new universe created in its place. Shiva's behavior simultaneously embraces hedonism and asceticism. He is often shown riding the bull, Nandi.

The Consorts of the Trimurti

Saraswati

The consort of Brahma and goddess of love, music, and wisdom and the daughter of Shiva and Durga, Saraswati (right) also has four arms, representing the intellect, awareness, the self, and the mind. She is generally depicted playing a stringed instrument called a veena and dressed in white riding a swan, a symbol of purity.

Lakshmi

Lakshmi (right), the consort of Vishnu, is the goddess of prosperity in both senses: spiritual and material. Always shown with gold skin, she is invariably dressed in rich red robes—to symbolize effort—embroidered with gold coins cascading from her. She sits or stands on a lotus, also a symbol of purity.

Kali

A fierce consort of Shiva, the black-complexioned, three-eyed Kali (right) is the Dark Mother. Her immense tongue protruding from her mouth, she is the most fearful of the Hindu gods, a relentless slayer of evildoers and tireless protector of her children, her worshippers. Two of her four arms carry a sword and the severed head of a giant. She wears a necklace of skulls and a belt of human heads.

Other Major Hindu Gods and Goddesses

Ganesha

The son of Shiva and Parvati, Ganesha (below), with his elephant head and human body, is among the most enduringly popular of the Hindu gods, the "Lord of success" and god of learning. His head represents wisdom, his body the realities of human existence. He rides a lowly mouse as a symbol of his humility.

Krishna

The enigmatic and glamorous Krishna (above) is the ninth reincarnation of Vishnu and almost certainly the most popular Hindu god for the mass of India's peasantry, at once "hero, protector, teacher, and friend," the Brahman himself. He was born, it is claimed, perhaps 5,000 years ago, his purpose to exterminate the evil rulers then despoiling India.

Rama

The seventh reincarnation, or avatar, of Vishnu, Rama (below), a knightly warrior and hero of the *Ramayana*, became popular in Hindu worship only in the eleventh century. Yet this commanding figure, almost always shown armed with a bow and arrow and arrayed in princely garments, has since become one of the most widely worshipped of all Hindu gods.

Durga

Durga (right) is the supreme mother goddess, celebrated every autumn in ten days of fasting, feasting, and dancing. She has multiple manifestations, especially as Shiva's consort Parvati, but her role as the protector of the good and ferocious opponent of the wicked is unchallenged. In her many arms she wields a variety of weapons. She is normally shown as riding a lionlike beast.

Hanuman

Hanuman (right), "the wisest, swiftest, and strongest of all apes," was the companion, servant, and helper of Rama and popularly believed to be a manifestation of Shiva himself. His nobility of character, resoluteness, and faithfulness to his master have made him a symbol of endurance and loyalty.

HINDUISM
The Hindu Temple

ONE OF THE GREATEST ACCOMPLISHMENTS of Hinduism was the construction of a series of magnificent temples, fully the equal in size, splendor, and symbolic meaning of even the greatest of Europe's medieval cathedrals. Though two distinct regional styles developed from at least the fifth century—the Nagara in the north, the Dravida in the south—all Hindu temples embodied the same fundamental religious tenets.

Most important, whatever deity a temple was built to honor, the temple was more than just the deity's house: it was a representation of the god himself—or herself. So just as the supreme God, Brahman, is omnipresent, even in all lesser gods, any temple was meant to be a representation not just of Brahman but,

Thousands of Hindu temples decorate the subcontinent, from Sri Lanka to the Himalayas. Although many regional styles exist, they can be classified broadly into two major traditions, each of which developed from the fifth century through the fourteenth and beyond.

like him, of the cosmos itself. These were buildings in which the universe was intended to be made real, a manifestation of revealed, universal truth.

Complex schemes, based on square grids, which carry a profound religious meaning in Hinduism, were evolved to represent this truth. The heart of the temple was the *garbha griha* (literally, "womb chamber"), where a representation of the presiding deity was displayed. To approach this chamber, worshippers had to pass through a series of increasingly sacred spaces. Directly above the inner sanctum was a tower, the *shikhara*, often the most remarkable feature of these extraordinary buildings.

The Nagara style of the north favored a beehive-shaped *shikhara*, typically topped by a cushionlike stone known as an *amalka*, while the Dravida style of the south favored a pyramid-shaped and stepped tower. From about the fourteenth century, Nagara temples also began to be surrounded by ever more elaborate walls pierced by sumptuous gateways—*gopurams*—themselves crowned by towers, the whole creating the impression of a fabulous, celestial city.

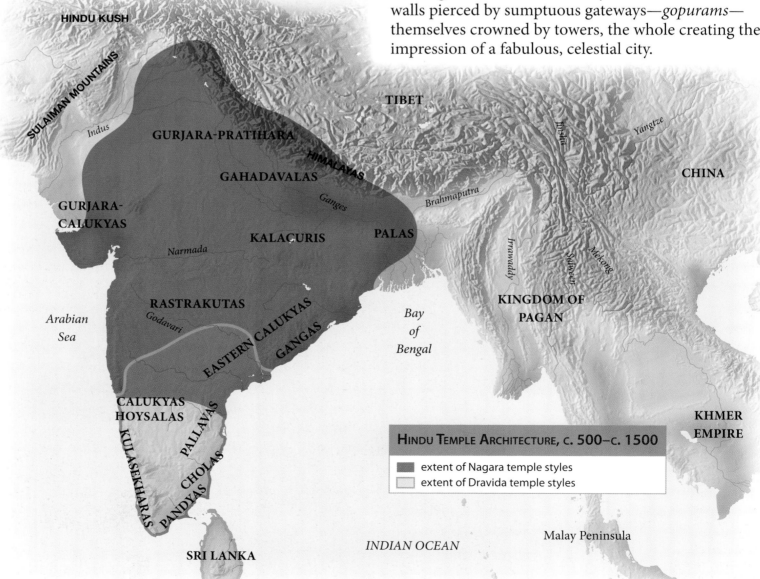

HINDU KUSH

HINDU TEMPLE ARCHITECTURE, C. 500–C. 1500

▇ extent of Nagara temple styles
▨ extent of Dravida temple styles

SULAIMAN MOUNTAINS

Indus

GURJARA-PRATIHARA

GAHADAVALAS

TIBET

HIMALAYAS

Ganges

Brahmaputra

Indus

Yangtze

CHINA

GURJARA-CALUKYAS

KALACURIS

PALAS

Narmada

Arabian Sea

RASTRAKUTAS

Godavari

EASTERN CALUKYAS

GANGAS

Bay of Bengal

Irrawaddy

Salween

Mekong

KINGDOM OF PAGAN

CALUKYAS
HOYSALAS

PALLAVAS

KULASEKHARAS

CHOLAS

PANDYAS

KHMER EMPIRE

SRI LANKA

INDIAN OCEAN

Malay Peninsula

Built in the eleventh century at Tanjore, southern India, Brihadeshvara Temple is a masterpiece of Chola architecture. The Dravida-style temple reaches more than 200 feet (70 m) high, all of its surface covered in elaborate carvings.

TEMPLES AND THE NATURAL WORLD

One of the most obvious characteristics of any Hindu temple is the profusion of exterior carving, with surfaces shimmering in apparently permanent motion, as though the building itself were alive. Hinduism's pleasure in the natural world is thus made manifest. Similarly, the temple had to be placed at a site that would please the god concerned, usually near water—the Ganges itself is said to have flowed from heaven—and near shade. Mountains, too, the original abode of many Hindu gods, carried symbolic significance. The *shikhara* was intended to suggest a mountain— often they were painted white, in imitation of snow-covered peaks.

This symbolism was carried into the interior. Reflecting the fact that the earliest Hindu shrines were in caves, the *garbha griha* was itself intended to resemble a cave. In stark contrast to the exuberance of the exterior, it was small, dark, and deliberately

The Nagara-style Vishwanath Temple, dedicated to Shiva, stands on the bank of the Ganges River. Although recent (the current structure dates to the eighteenth century), it is one of India's most famous temples.

unadorned, with massive, frequently crude, masonry. All this focused attention on the image of the presiding god, the *archa*, lit by dimly flickering candles, and richly perfumed by incense. It was a place for contemplation without distractions.

TEMPLE LIFE

The primary impetus and means for the building of Hindu temples in this period almost always came from ruling families. Their motives were straightforward: to demonstrate to the gods their own piety and so hasten the moment when they could achieve *moksha*, liberation from the cycle of reincarnation. That the resulting temples were built for the use and spiritual nourishment of whole communities only made such seemingly selfless gestures the more worthy.

The temple establishments, especially the largest, rapidly grew rich, in some cases astoundingly so, enjoying a steady stream of donations that ranged from small cash payments to grants of what were often huge tracts of land. As the temples prospered, so they exerted ever greater influence—economic and political as much as spiritual—over the territories they served. In the eleventh century the Chola Rajarajeswara (Brihadeshvara) temple in Thanjavur in southern India directly employed 600 people, among them conchblowers, parasol bearers, astrologers, and lamp-lighters, as well as a variety of tailors, water-sprinklers, and carpenters. These were worlds almost as varied and surprising as the Hindu pantheon itself.

Explicit carvings at the Khajuraho temple complex, a group of Nagara-style Jain-Hindu temples in central India, highlight the artistic abilities of tenth-century temple carvers. The carvings would later shock British aristocrats but indicate the depth of a cultural connection between eroticism and religion.

HINDUISM
The Muslim Supremacy

THE CHARACTER OF HINDU INDIA was slowly but surely changed after 1206, as Muslim invaders from Afghanistan and Persia spilled irresistibly into the subcontinent. The first series of Muslim dynasties, called the Delhi Sultanate, lasted for 320 years and was followed by the Mughal Empire, which under Babur, a descendant of Genghis Khan, defeated the last of the Delhi sultans in 1526. By the death of the greatest Mughal emperor, Akbar, in 1605, Muslim rule extended across the whole of northern India. Both the Delhi sultans and the Mughals were exceptionally self-confident rulers, militarily strong, culturally highly sophisticated, and introducing in their wake Persian traditions in the arts as well as politics that would leave an enduring legacy.

During this period Islam was imposed on substantial areas of northern India. Southern India, never under effective control by either the Delhi Sultanate or the Mughals, remained Hindu. For much of the fourteenth and fifteenth centuries, the south was ruled by the Hindu Vijayanagara Empire, which was engaged in a long and inconclusive series of struggles with the Muslim states to the north.

In the north, especially in the Punjab and Bengal, substantial numbers of Hindus converted to Islam, particularly among the poorer sections of society. Many of these conversions may have represented a genuine change of religious allegiance, as a means of escaping the repressive nature of the Hindu caste system. The consequences—the lasting establishment of Muslim majorities in much of the country—were momentous. But for the most part, the process of conversion was peaceful. Where conflict between Hindu and Muslim states existed, it generally took the form of conventional wars of conquest, not struggles for religious supremacy.

The early modern period saw India overrun by foreign demands on territory and religion. Although native traditions like Jainism and Hinduism never disappeared, the Christian and, especially, Muslim inroads made during this period became indelible features on the physical and the religious landscapes of India.

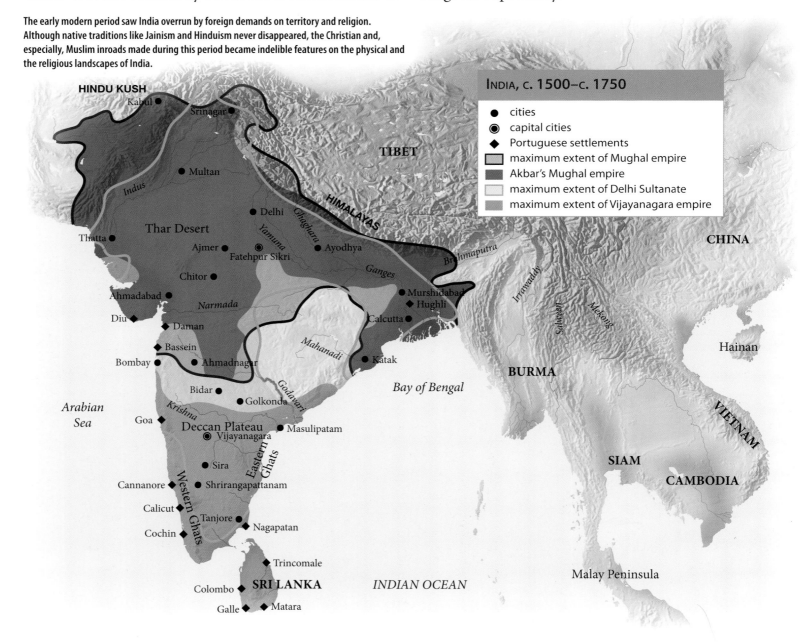

INDIA, C. 1500–C. 1750

- ● cities
- ◉ capital cities
- ◆ Portuguese settlements
- maximum extent of Mughal empire
- Akbar's Mughal empire
- maximum extent of Delhi Sultanate
- maximum extent of Vijayanagara empire

In this city you will find men belonging to every nation and people, because of the great trade it has, and the many precious stones there, principally diamonds.
—PORTUGUESE TRAVELER DOMINGO PAES,
ON THE HINDU CITY OF VIJAYANAGARA, C. 1520.

Shah Jahan, one of the Mughal Empire's most famous rulers, constructed Jama Masijid Mosque in Delhi in 1656. Still in use today, it is one of the most visible reminders of northern India's Muslim history.

A cow, sacred animal of Hindu tradition, wanders across the ruins of the once-great city of Vijayanagara, whose name somewhat ironically means "City of Victory" in Sanskrit.

In the Hindu south, where Muslim influence did not reach, the vigorous tradition of temple building begun earlier was continued on an even more astounding scale. At its height in the early sixteenth century, the temple complex of Vijayanagara was in effect a substantial city in itself, an emphatic statement of Hindu belief on an immense scale. Even though much was destroyed in a Muslim raid in 1565, enough remains to make startlingly clear the reach of the greatest Hindu state of the period.

THE HINDU-MUSLIM CONFRONTATION

Among the consequences of the Muslim conquests was that the subcontinent came to be integrated into the wider Asian world, in particular West and Central Asia—a process accelerated by the arrival of migrants fleeing the devastations of the Mongols. The result was an extraordinary and rich cultural synthesis, part Persian, part Muslim, part Hindu.

This synthesis was evident in the opulent courts of the Mughals, above all at Akbar's newly built capital, Fatehpur Sikri. It was also the result of a policy of toleration toward Akbar's Hindu subjects. Mughal architecture, though making clear its Persian origins, owed much to Hindu models. Of more lasting significance to the development of Hinduism were attempts to find common ground between Hindu and Muslim practices. If for many Muslims Hinduism and its multiplicity of beliefs and gods could never be reconciled with their belief in a single God and his prophet, others genuinely sought ways to reconcile the two faiths. One consequence was the emergence of new faiths, the most prominent being Sikhism, founded in the early sixteenth century by the Hindu mystic Nanak.

THE EUROPEAN ADVANCE

In 1579, as part of what would become an attempt to synthesize the world's religions, the emperor Akbar invited to his court Portuguese Jesuit missionaries from Goa, on the west coast of India. As an instance of religious toleration, it was a significant move. Perhaps even more significant was that there were European trading stations in India at all.

The Portuguese had first arrived in India in 1498, after Vasco da Gama had rounded the Cape of Good Hope and then crossed the Indian Ocean. Within twelve years, Goa had been made the capital of all Portugal's Indian possessions, which by the end of the century were scattered the length of the west coast, some in territories directly administered by the Mughals.

India had been fought over for millennia, a plethora of states large and small emerging, expanding, and contracting. But since the fall of Rome, European contact had been minimal. That had now changed. In the wake of the Portuguese would come other Europeans—Dutch, English, French, and Danish. It was a development fraught with significance for India.

Se Cathedral, built between 1552 and 1619 in Portuguese fashion, is one of Goa's oldest churches and is a reminder of the European—and Christian—presence in the early colonial period.

Buddhism, from India to Tibet

INDIA, THE BIRTHPLACE OF BUDDHISM, sent forth two great lineages during the early centuries of the common era: Theravada (sometimes called Hinayana) and Mahayana. Meanwhile Buddhism in India continued to develop, producing the two main branches of Mahayana Buddhism, the Madhyamaka and Yogacara schools. Madhyamaka elevates the importance of the middle path, or the negation of dualities. Its core teaching is *shunyata*, or emptiness. Yogacara was centered at Nalanda, the largest Buddhist university in northern India, in present-day Rajgir, Bihar. This tradition applied yogic practices and logic to philosophical questions of doctrine. The tradition of debate, still widely popular in many Buddhist traditions, originated in the Yogacara school.

Buddhism was all but obliterated in India during the course of the Muslim incursions of the eleventh century. Fortunately, a new form of Buddhism had arisen in Tibet in the eighth century, essentially safeguarding the Indian Mahayana traditions. The native Tibetan religion, called Bön, had fused with essential Mahayana teachings and Indian Tantric teachings. In this form, Tantra is known as *Vajrayana*—Diamond Vehicle or Thunderbolt Vehicle. Although officially classed as Mahayana, Tibetan Buddhism has so many unique practices, traditions, and lineages that many scholars see it as a school, or "vehicle" unto itself. Often Tibetan Buddhism is known simply as Vajrayana, though this is only one of its aspects. The word *vajra* itself refers to a ritual implement—in Tibetan a *dorje*—which is a small, two-headed scepter representing the thunderbolt, male energy, or skillful means. It is used in ritual with a bell or cup—a *ghanta*, representing female energy or wisdom.

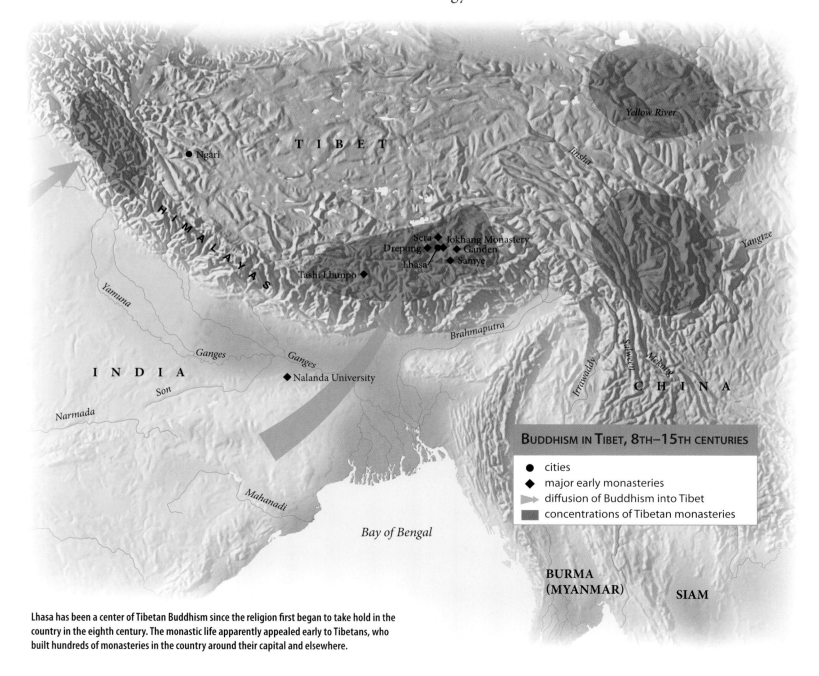

BUDDHISM IN TIBET, 8TH–15TH CENTURIES

- ● cities
- ◆ major early monasteries
- ➤ diffusion of Buddhism into Tibet
- ▨ concentrations of Tibetan monasteries

Lhasa has been a center of Tibetan Buddhism since the religion first began to take hold in the country in the eighth century. The monastic life apparently appealed early to Tibetans, who built hundreds of monasteries in the country around their capital and elsewhere.

EARLY TIBETAN BUDDHISM

The first great proponent of Buddhism in Tibet was King Songtsän Gampo (c. 617–49), who unified Tibet and forged peace with the Chinese emperors. Songtsän Gampo's two wives, the Chinese princess Wen Cheng, and the Indian princess or demigod, Bhrukti Devi were both devout Buddhists and are worshipped as incarnations of Drolma (Sanskrit: Tara), goddess of compassion. Songtsän Gampo's greatest legacy was the foundation of the Jokhang temple in Lhasa.

Roughly a hundred years after Songtsän Gampo, Buddhism got another boost from King Trisong Detsen. He constructed Tibet's first monastery, Samye, in present-day Shannan prefecture, under the spiritual guidance of the Tantric master Padmasambhava. According to legend, the king had invited Padmasambhava to Tibet to exorcise the local Bön gods and demons. Instead, the teacher brought the local deities into sympathy with Buddhism, effectively incorporating the indigenous religion into the new one. At the convocation of Samye monastery in 785, close to 3,000 monks were ordained, initiating the Nyingma order. Buddhism went into decline for several centuries after this, as succeeding kings were hostile toward the religion. There was a revival of Bön practices, and Buddhism was almost lost to Tibet.

The first Buddhist temple built in Tibet, Jokhang remains central to Tibetan Buddhism today. It has been renovated and expanded several times, most recently in the early twentieth century.

THE GOLDEN AGE OF TIBETAN BUDDHISM

Buddhism was revived in Tibet in the eleventh century, in what is sometimes called the "second diffusion." The man most responsible for this revival was Atisha (982–1054), an Indian prince born in present-day Bangladesh, in the region of Bikrampur, northeast of Bengal. Atisha renounced his worldly life and traveled around India, studying in the Mahayana, Theravada, and Tantric schools. He first came to western Tibet, to the Ngari region, then to central Tibet, to the region around Lhasa. Atisha brought together the study of *sutras* (texts) with the practice of Tantra. This and his numerous writings, especially "A Lamp for the Path" were his greatest legacy. Atisha is the founder of the Kadampa school, which later became the Gelugpa order.

The Gelugpa, or "Yellow Hat," school is the order of Buddhism to which the Dalai Lama belongs. Gelugpa translates as "the virtuous ones." Its most influential teacher was Je Tsongkhapa (1357–1419), a sage of wide learning in many Buddhist traditions, and follower of Atisha. He placed special emphasis on the *vinaya*, or code of practice.

A Dalai Lama, the highest teacher in the Gelugpa tradition, is considered to be an incarnation of Avalokiteshvara (Tibetan: Chenrezig), the bodhisattva of compassion and one of the most important deities in Mahayana Buddhism. Under Mongolian rule in the seventeenth century, political as well as spiritual power passed to the Dalai Lama with the installation of Lozang Gyatso (1617–82), often called the Great Fifth Dalai Lama. Lozang Gyatso was responsible for the construction of the current Potala Palace in Lhasa. His organization of Tibetan government, which divided power between religious and secular leaders, survived into modern times.

Almost immediately after Buddhism entered Tibet, Avalokiteshvara became the most important Buddhist deity there. Made in Ngari, this statue dates to the first half of the eleventh century and thus reflects the resurgence of Buddhism in Tibet at that time.

TANTRA

Tantra is a specialized and esoteric form of worship found in both Hinduism and Buddhism. The name derives from a set of texts called Tantras. As with other forms of Buddhism, the practitioners of Tantra seek to attain Buddhahood, with particular focus on *upaya*, or skillful means. Tantric Buddhist rituals include the chanting of mantras, the practice of yoga, and the contemplation of mandalas—circular diagrams depicting deities and the cosmos. The guidance of a guru, or teacher, is of utmost importance in Tantra. Initiation rituals are given only to those students deemed ready. Because access to teachings and rites is safeguarded, there is an element of secrecy, mystery, and even magic to Tantra.

Tantric practice seeks to unify all states of being. *Tantra* literally means "weaving," or "looming." This helps explain the prevalence of sexual symbolism in Tantra. Here, sexual union represents the union of dualities. A central symbol of Tantric Buddhism is the deity Hevajra, who is usually shown in union with his consort, Nairatmya. Hevajra owes much to the Hindu deity Shiva, who is often shown paired with his consort Shakti.

BUDDHISM
Southeast Asia: Theravada and Temples

THE LANDSCAPE OF SOUTHEAST ASIA is rich in Buddhist architectural treasures, many dating from the turn of the first millennium. Grand and golden temples, stupas, and pagodas—some hidden for centuries in deep jungles—dot the landscape of Myanmar, Thailand, Laos, Cambodia, Vietnam, and Indonesia. These structures bear witness to the early dominance of Buddhism in this region, in particular the Theravada school.

The Theravada school of Buddhism is the most ancient form of Buddhism. It is the only branch remaining from the eighteen schools that are said to have flourished in India after the death of Gautama Buddha. *Theravada* translates in Pali as "the teachings of the elders." Theravada is sometimes called the "southern school," because of its prevalence in Southeast Asia and its point of diffusion, Sri Lanka.

The jungles of Southeast Asia welcomed both Theravada and Mahayana Buddhism, with religious fortunes bound to political dominance. The magnificent temples, emerging from the dense vegetation like mountains grown wild, are enduring and astonishing reminders of the will of these civilizations to house both forms of Buddhism.

Theravada is occasionally referred to as Hinayana, or "lesser vehicle," when it is compared with the school of Mahayana ("greater vehicle") Buddhism, but this is viewed by most scholars as derogatory. One of the distinguishing features of Theravada is the use of the Pali language for its liturgy rather than Sanskrit, which is used in the Mahayana school.

Elaborately carved reliefs cover the walls of Angkor Wat, a twelfth-century temple built in the capital city of the Khmer Empire.

Map: Buddhism in Southeast Asia, c. 600–c. 1400

Ganges

CHINA

INDIA

KINGDOM OF PAGAN
Pagan

Hainan

Irrawaddy

Bay of Bengal

Mekong

South China Sea

Shwedagon Pagoda — Thaton

SUKHOTHAI KINGDOM

Philippine Islands

MON KINGDOMS

Angkor Wat

Ayutthaya

Andaman Sea

KHMER EMPIRE

AYUTTHAYA KINGDOM

Gulf of Thailand

PACIFIC OCEAN

Anuradhapura

Sri Lanka

Strait of Malacca

INDIAN OCEAN

Sumatra

Borneo

Celebes

SRIVIJAYA EMPIRE

Srivijaya

Java Sea

BUDDHISM IN SOUTHEAST ASIA, c. 600–c. 1400
- ● cities
- ◉ capital cities
- ◆ major Buddhist temple
- → spread of Theravada school
- → spread of Mahayana school

Borobudur   Java

THE PALI TIPITAKA

The scriptures of the Theravada school are known as the Pali canon and are contained in the Tipitaka (Sanskrit: Tripitaka), or "three baskets" of learning. Said to contain an exact rendition of the Buddha's teachings, the Pali Tipitaka was long transmitted orally. It was written down in stages, mostly in Sri Lanka during the centuries just before the common era. No early versions remain intact, having been lost to the humid climate of the region. The earliest printed editions date from the nineteenth century and fill dozens of volumes.

The three "baskets," or portions, of the Tipitaka contain both essential teachings and commentary. They also contain anecdotes or stories told by Buddha, in parable fashion, to illustrate some of the core precepts of his teachings. The three portions of the Tipitaka are

- Vinaya Pitaka, the code of conduct for members of the *sangha*, or worship community. The Vinaya contains a section of rules and precepts for monks and nuns.
- Sutta Pitaka, a collection of close to 10,000 *suttas* (Sanskrit: *sutras*), or discourses, delivered by the Buddha and his closest disciples.
- Abhidhamma Pitaka, a systematic and analytical set of discourses that expands on the teachings of the suttas. Scholars disagree on the origin of this portion of the scriptures; some attribute the teachings to Buddha himself, others to scholars of the third century BCE.

THE SHIFTING SANDS OF SOUTHERN BUDDHISM

Buddhism in Southeast Asia was subject to the rise and fall of kingdoms and empires. For century upon century in this fertile landscape, borders shifted, rulers fell, and religion followed suit. While Theravada Buddhism is the dominant school in Southeast Asia today, the Mahayana school once thrived here as well. Relations between the two schools were often strained, and warfare between kingdoms led to strife between branches of this largely peaceful religion. The geography of the region and the twin paths of Buddhist diffusion—the northern and southern routes—help explain these opposing traditions.

From the seventh to twelfth centuries, the Khmer ethnic group dominated the Mekong Valley, site of present-day Cambodia, southern Laos, and Vietnam. The Khmer practiced a syncretic blend of Hinduism, native animism, and Mahayana Buddhism introduced from China. Angkor Wat, the majestic stone temple in Cambodia, is the most famous product of this culture. Initially dedicated to the god Vishnu, Angkor Wat is designed to represent Mount Meru, center of both Hindu and Buddhist cosmology.

Farther west, in Thailand, closer to the Sri Lankan source of Buddhism, Theravada was the dominant school. In the twelfth century the powerful Sukhothai kingdom arose in Thailand, overthrowing the Khmer and bringing Theravada practice to Cambodia and Laos. The succeeding Thai kingdom, Ayutthaya, dominated the western Indochinese Peninsula until the eighteenth century.

The Indonesian archipelago was home to one of the largest Buddhist kingdoms in Southeast Asia, flourishing from the seventh to the fourteenth centuries. Coexisting with Hinduism, Indonesian Buddhism ranged from Theravadin to Tantric, or Vajrayana. Borobudur, the magnificent temple complex on Java, is a product of the Vajrayana tradition. A sprawling monument built of volcanic rock, Borobudur is fashioned as a massive stone mandala, or depiction of the Buddhist cosmos. After Islam was introduced to these islands in the fifteenth century, Buddhism rapidly declined in practice.

The massive temple of Angkor Wat is perhaps the most impressive remnant of the Khmer capital, Angkor. Built in the twelfth century as a Hindu temple, a century later, it had become a center of Buddhism and still attracts hundreds of monks a day.

THE TEMPLES OF MYANMAR

One of the oldest and grandest temples in Southeast Asia is the Shwedagon Pagoda in Yangon, Myanmar (Rangoon, Burma). Dating from the sixth century, the golden stupa is a testament to the early adoption of Theravada Buddhism by the Mon people, indigenous to lower Myanmar and parts of Thailand.

The Mon, whose capital was at Thaton, were later conquered by the Burmese, an ethnic group from the border of Tibet and northern Myanmar. The Burmese subsequently adopted Buddhism as well, following the lead of their king, Anawrahta (reigned 1044–1077). Based in Pagan (present-day Bagan, Myanmar), Anawrahta is said to have acquired Buddhist scriptures and relics by force—a claim probably meant to underscore Anawrahta's imperfect understanding of Buddhist precepts. Nevertheless, under the 200-year kingdom founded by Anawrahta, close to 5,000 temples and pagodas were built throughout the region, including the ornate, gilded Ananda temple in Pagan. Building these temples was believed to confer spiritual merit on the donor, to assure a more desirable rebirth, or ultimately attainment of *nibbana* (Sanskrit: *nirvana*)—freedom from rebirth.

More than 2,000 Buddhist temples cover some 16 square miles in Bagan, Myanmar (ancient Pagan). Sadly, thousands more temples have been lost over the centuries to human neglect and the ravages of nature.

The Golden Age of Chinese Buddhism

THROUGHOUT CHINA, massive stone statues of Buddha sit in silent contemplation, carved into mountainsides and overlooking great rivers. Smaller but no less impressive gilded statues of Buddhas and bodhisattvas fill museums and galleries. These national treasures date mostly from the Tang dynasty (618–907), Buddhism's golden age in China. During this period several schools of Buddhism were founded, and numerous temples and monasteries were built. Block printing was developed in order to preserve Buddhist scriptures, particularly the Lotus Sutra, the central text of the Tiantai, or Lotus school. Founded at Mount Tiantai, in modern Zhejiang Province, the Lotus school remains an important Mahayana Buddhist school throughout Asia.

One Chinese ruler was the particular champion of Buddhism during these centuries, and that ruler was also one of the most exceptional in Chinese history. The only woman to officially hold the position of emperor in China was Wu Zetian (625–705). Ruthless in her struggle for power but relatively stable in her rule, Empress Wu was patroness on a large scale for Buddhism. Her particular attention was given to the Huayang (Sanskrit: Avatamsaka), or Flower Garland or Flower Adornment school, after the sutra of the same name. The third patriarch of the school, Fazang, wrote extensive commentaries and devised now-famous demonstrations to explain sticky metaphysical questions to the empress. Many scholars point to a distinctly Daoist influence in the Flower Garland school. In Japan, the Huayang became the Kegon School.

Persecution was to follow shortly on the heels of these gains for Chinese Buddhism, however. In 845, under the rule of the Daoist Tang emperor Wu-Tsung, Buddhism came under attack, seen as a foreign religion. Monasteries and temples were destroyed, and monks and nuns were forced into hiding. Unity among Buddhist schools arose from these difficulties, however, and some scholars point to this period as one of great cross-pollination between the varied branches of Chinese Buddhism.

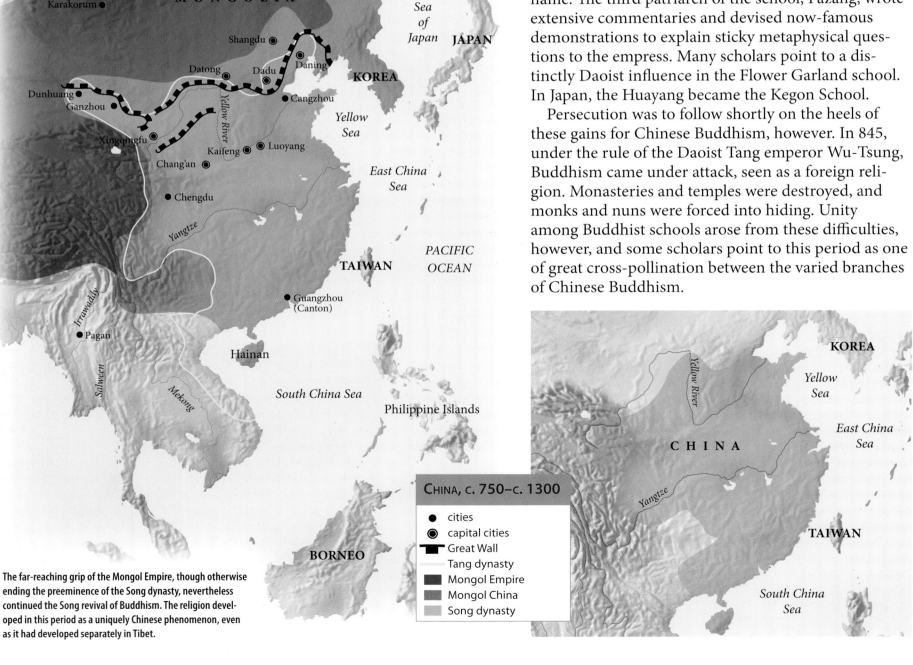

The far-reaching grip of the Mongol Empire, though otherwise ending the preeminence of the Song dynasty, nevertheless continued the Song revival of Buddhism. The religion developed in this period as a uniquely Chinese phenomenon, even as it had developed separately in Tibet.

CHINA, C. 750–C. 1300

- ● cities
- ◉ capital cities
- ▬ Great Wall
- Tang dynasty
- Mongol Empire
- Mongol China
- Song dynasty

THE PROSPEROUS SONG AND THE MONGOL YUAN

The turn of the first millennium was a prosperous time for China. Under the Song dynasty (960–1279), which succeeded the Tang, new rice cultivation techniques led to abundant food, and the population of China nearly doubled. Advances in architecture, movable-type printing, and engineering marked the rule of the Song. Buddhism was revived, but the destruction of so many Buddhist institutions made it difficult for the religion to regain its former vitality. In addition, Buddhism had been obliterated in India under Islamic rule, effectively cutting off the source of inspiration and the root of the faith.

Under Song rule, however, several important Buddhist documents were collected and penned. The Chinese Tripitaka, a translation of the Pali Tipitaka, or collected teachings of Buddha, was assembled during this period. Two other important collections, the Blue Cliff Record and the Gateless Gate, came out of this period as well. These contained *koans* (Chinese: *gong-an*), which are central to the philosophy and practice of Chan (Zen). Part riddle, part parable, koans are meant to be understood intuitively, as they often seem to make no rational sense. The best known example is: "When two hands clap, a sharp sound is heard. What is the sound of one hand clapping?"

As the Song ruled over a prosperous China, the great Mongol Empire was growing to the north and west. The discovery of gunpowder had allowed the Song to effectively keep the Mongols at bay. In the late thirteenth century, however, the Mongols under the rule of Kublai Khan, grandson of Genghis Khan, overtook first northern and then southern China, initiating the Yuan dynasty (1271–1368). China became a large puzzle piece in the enormous Mongol Empire, which reached as far west as eastern Europe. Buddhism was once again favored, in particular the Tibetan schools,

BUDAI, THE LAUGHING BUDDHA

Westerners are sometimes confused by the seemingly contradictory images of Buddha. The serene and restrained figure commonly seen around the world is countered by a laughing, bald character with a round, exposed belly. He carries a sack filled with an unending supply of food and bounty. This is Budai or Budai Luohan (Japanese: Hotei), commonly known as the Laughing Buddha.

Buddhists believe that a succession of Buddhas are born throughout the ages. The Buddha of our age is Shakyamuni Buddha, or Siddhartha Gautama. But in future there will be another Buddha, known as Maitreya. Budai is one representation of this future Buddha, and he is modeled after a Chan (Zen) monk said to have lived during the tenth century in China. He represents abundance and material pleasure and has become a popular figure not only in China but around the world. Some Buddhists view this figure as decadent and unrepresentative of the Buddhist precepts of poverty, asceticism, and the vow to end the world's suffering. For others, Budai represents generosity, lightheartedness, and prosperity. A folk belief holds that rubbing the belly of the Budai will bring good luck.

A stone Budai statue sits in Xian, China. Despite some Buddhist disapproval, the jolly figure and his obvious association with plenty have proven their appeal worldwide.

which some Mongol rulers had adopted. This was a period of religious openness, because trade and exchange of ideas between West and East was vigorous. Kublai Khan moved his capital to Tatu (present-day Beijing). A generation after his death, however, the Mongol Empire was fractured, and rule of China returned to the Han people.

MING: THE LAST HAN EMPIRE

The first Ming emperor, Zhu Yuanzhang, who took the name of Hongwu, was a member of the White Lotus society, a Buddhist sect. Chinese rule was returned to the Han, the largest Chinese ethnic group, and Hongwu initiated nearly three centuries (1368–1644) of growth and prosperity.

The Ming emphasized agriculture and land reform, military infrastructure, and widespread trade. Many of China's iconic landmarks were built or completed under the Ming—the Imperial City in Beijing and the Great Wall, to name just two. Buddhism was the dominant religion. Religious strife took back seat to cultural advances, however, and for the most part under the Ming, the three religious traditions in China—Daoism, Confucianism, and Buddhism—maintained a relative equilibrium.

GUAN YIN

The female incarnation of the bodhisattva of com-passion, Guan Yin is usually seen as the Chinese parallel to the Indian deity Avalokiteshvara, or the Tibetan Chenrezig. Also spelled Kwan Yin, Guan Shi Yin, or Quan Yin, Guan Yin is widely revered throughout Asia. In Japan, she is known as Kannon. Her name translates as "the one who observes the cries of the world."

Guan Yin first appeared in Chinese art during the Tang dynasty. She is depicted in white robes, sometimes seated on a lotus flower, symbolizing purity of heart even in the midst of impure conditions. Often shown with children, and called "the bestower of children," Guan Yin has been compared with the Virgin Mary of Christianity. In the Pure Land school of Buddhism, Guan Yin conducts the "bark of salvation," a boat that carries worthy souls to the western paradise of the Amitabha Buddha.

A delicately carved statue of Guan Yin, dated to the Ming dynasty, incorporates lotus blossoms and wavelike elements on the pedestal.

BUDDHISM
Japan Receives the Dharma

THE WORD *ZEN* has become so commonplace in contemporary speech as to have nearly been divorced from its original meaning. We speak of having a zen moment, we decorate our houses with zen-inspired furnishings, and drink zen tea. In modern usage zen has come to mean serenity, simplicity, and purity, implying an almost modernist lack of pretense and ornamentation. Yet Zen, the Japanese form of Buddhism, dates back to the eleventh century. It is perhaps the most widely known form of Buddhism in the West, but only one of a variety of Japanese schools. Its origins go back to the Chan school of Buddhism, brought to China in the fifth century by Bodhidharma, a traveling Indian monk.

Buddhism came to Japan by way of Korea in the sixth century CE. Legend says that a Korean delegation of monks visited Japan in 538, bringing gifts in the form of a Buddhist statue and scriptures. The gifts were received and appropriately housed in a shrine. But when natural disaster and disease struck, the Buddhist objects were promptly thrown into a canal. The understanding was that the new religious items had angered the native gods, or *kami*. So began the uneasy relationship—one that was eventually reconciled—between the new religion from China and the native religion of Japan, which had come to be known as Shinto, or the way of the gods.

Though largely derived from Chinese schools, Japanese Buddhism took on characteristics, beliefs, and practices all its own. Daoism and Confucianism also made inroads in Japan, and when the various traditions were filtered through native Japanese customs and spirituality, a new form of Buddhism arose.

Kiyomizu-dera is one of Kyoto's most famous temples. A Tendai temple built in 1633, it is a particularly lovely example of temple architecture in this period.

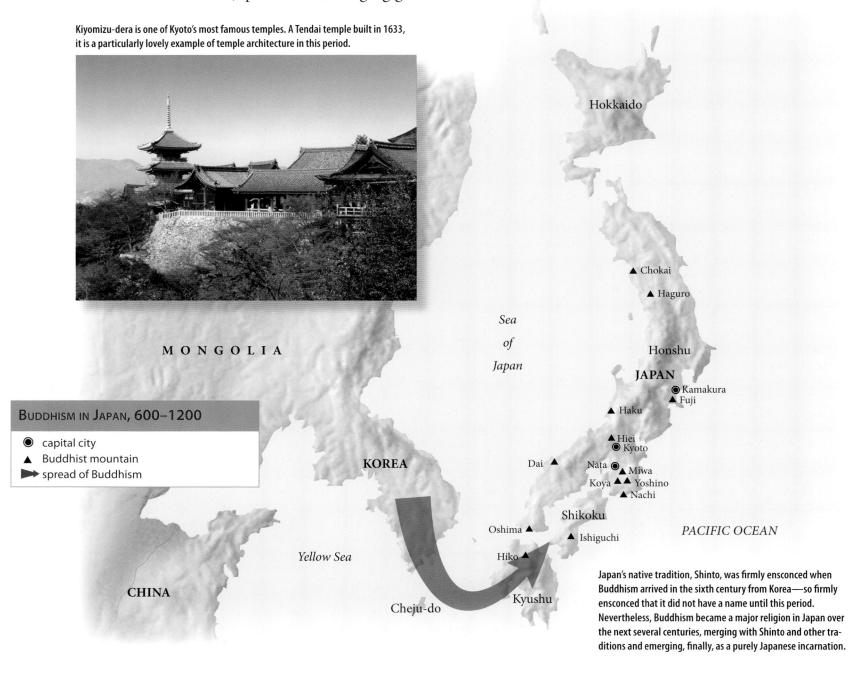

BUDDHISM IN JAPAN, 600–1200

- ◉ capital city
- ▲ Buddhist mountain
- ➤ spread of Buddhism

Hokkaido

▲ Chokai

▲ Haguro

Sea of Japan

Honshu

JAPAN

◉ Kamakura
▲ Fuji

▲ Haku

▲ Hiei
◉ Kyoto

Dai ▲

Nata ◉ ▲ Miwa
Koya ▲ ▲ Yoshino
▲ Nachi

MONGOLIA

KOREA

Shikoku

Oshima ▲

▲ Ishiguchi

PACIFIC OCEAN

Yellow Sea

Hiko ▲

CHINA

Cheju-do

Kyushu

Japan's native tradition, Shinto, was firmly ensconced when Buddhism arrived in the sixth century from Korea—so firmly ensconced that it did not have a name until this period. Nevertheless, Buddhism became a major religion in Japan over the next several centuries, merging with Shinto and other traditions and emerging, finally, as a purely Japanese incarnation.

THE NARA AND HEIAN PERIODS

Early Japanese Buddhism was largely a philosophical tradition for the aristocracy. During the Nara period of the sixth and seventh centuries, the six primary Chinese schools of Buddhism came to Japan, including the Huayan (Avatamsaka), or Flower Garland school (Japanese: Kegon). Incorporating many Daoist elements, Kegon focused on the teaching of dependent origination, or the interrelatedness of all phenomena.

Under the patronage of the seventh-century prince Shotoku, Japanese monks were sent to study Buddhism in China; they returned not only with Buddhist teachings, but with the Chinese script as well. In addition Chinese arts and sciences crossed the sea to the Japanese archipelago, in a wholesale influx of Chinese culture. In the eighth century Buddhism became the state religion of Japan.

During the Heian period (794–1185) the imperial capital was relocated from Nara to Heian-kyo (present-day Kyoto). Buddhism flourished during these years, resulting in two principal schools, each founded by a charismatic teacher. The first of these schools was Tendai, founded at Mount Hiei by Saicho (767–822). Saicho made several trips to China and returned with the core precepts of the Tiantai, or Lotus Sutra school. The emphasis of Tendai was on the essential Buddhahood, or Buddha nature, in all things and people. This concept was sympathetic with native Shinto belief in the all-pervading kami, or spirits. With this widely accessible approach to worship, Tendai was instrumental in bringing Buddhism down from the ivory tower of the ruling class and into the homes and shrines of ordinary Japanese people.

Tendai was followed closely by the founding of the Shingon, or "True Word" school. Originating with Indian Tantric practices and beliefs, this esoteric school of Buddhism is a form of Vajrayana, most widely practiced in Tibet. The founder of Shingon was Kukai (774–835), one of the more popular figures in Japanese Buddhist history. Kukai traveled in China as well, absorbing the oral teachings and mysteries of Vajrayana. He founded a monastery at Mount Koya and a school of arts and sciences, believing that Buddha nature is evident in all things of beauty. Kukai is credited with developing the Japanese script system based on syllables, called *kana*, and with penning the *iroha*, one of the best-known poems in Japan. To this day monks still bring food and drink to Mount Koya, believing that Kukai did not die in 835 but sits in a perpetual state of meditation.

A painting of a bodhisattva from Korea's Goryeo Dynasty. Artwork of the period often focused on Buddhist themes.

BUDDHISM IN KOREA

With a powerful neighbor like China to the north, it stands to reason that Korea would absorb much of that country's culture, language, and religion. But the Korean people have always had a strong independent identity. So the forms of Buddhism that naturally found their way to Korea—the principal Mahayana schools—took on a character of their own.

Wonhyo was a seventh-century Korean Buddhist who advocated for a gathering of traditions, to merge the various Mahayana doctrines into one comprehensive practice. This came as Korea was unified for the first time by the Silla kingdom. At about the same time, Chan (Zen) entered Korea, where it became known as Seon, and captured the attention of the people. Zen rose to prominence, and eventually a charismatic figure named Jinul (1158–1210), also called National Master Pojo, founded the Chogye Zen sect. Buddhism thrived during the Goryeo period (918–1392), with constant exchange between Korean Zen masters and holders of the Linji (Rinzai) lineage in China. Korean masters simplified the elaborate koan study process.

In the fourteenth century the Goryeo fell to the Joseon dynasty. Buddhism was suppressed in favor of a strict Neo-Confucianism. Numbers of Buddhist temples and study centers went into a sharp decline, but the tradition remained alive and continued to develop, until it was revived in the early twentieth century.

KAMAKURA AND BEYOND

Warring factions in Japan led to a militarized society in the late twelfth century—the Kamakura period—and Buddhism had to adapt to this new social order. Shingon, with its mystery and secrecy, did not fare as well as Tendai. But even this popular form became splintered. With the influx of new ideas from the Chan school in China, Tendai emerged in Japan as Zen. The two principal Zen lineages, still widely practiced today, are Rinzai and Soto. Rinzai, descended from the Tang-era Linji school in China, was founded in Japan by Eisai (1141–1215) and emphasized the study of koans to gain enlightenment. In Rinzai, the teacher is of primary importance, summing up a student's understanding based on the answers he gives to these philosophical riddles. Rinzai was favored by the growing samurai warrior class in Japan and retains some martial elements, particularly in its strict internal hierarchy.

Soto Zen (Chinese: Caodong), founded in Japan by Dogen Zenji (1200–1253), is now the largest Zen sect both in Japan and in the West. Soto emphasizes mindfulness, placing experiential spirituality over intellectual or philosophical pursuits. *Shikantaza*, or meditation that is "just sitting," is a hallmark of Soto Zen. Indeed, both Soto and Rinzai rely on *zazen*, or sitting meditation, as the primary means of gaining enlightenment. Soto Zen's simplicity made it a favorite of common people. In sitting meditation, one emulates the Buddha's own path in the purest and most pared-down way.

One more important Zen master and school arose during this period and has had lasting impact on Buddhist practice. Nichiren (1222–82) revered the Lotus Sutra and taught that repeatedly chanting one's devotion to the wisdom of the sutra "*nam myoho renge kyo*" could help practitioners achieve enlightenment. Nichiren Buddhists are one of the few evangelical Buddhist sects, and certain contemporary branches of the school have met with some controversy.

The Path to Moksha

Jainism gained a formal title and began as an organized religion in the sixth century BCE. Mahavira (c. 599–527 BCE), considered by Jains to be the twenty-fourth *tirthankhara*, was a contemporary of Buddha. Although he is not considered to be the founder of Jainism, it was with Mahavira's life that the religion took shape. Like Buddha, Mahavira was a member of the ascetic movement that flourished in northern India before the common era. He is credited with collecting the wisdom contained in the most sacred texts of Jainism, notably the *Tattvartha Sutra*, but the tradition of Jainism and its teachings is said to have originated millions of years ago. It centers on *ahimsa*, or nonviolence to all living beings.

Jainism is named for the *jinas*, a Sanskrit word that means conquerors, or ones who overcome. Jinas are also known as *tirthankaras*, or "ford builders," because they are said to be able to ford the river of rebirth.

These esteemed beings have conquered the passions and desires of this world during their lifetime, thereby accumulating enough merit to avoid being born again. The endless cycle of birth, death, and rebirth—with its attendant suffering—is central to Jain belief. The goal for a Jain is attain liberation from this cycle—a state known as *moksha*, similar to nirvana. Those who have achieved moksha are known as *siddhas*, and live in a realm inhabited by the tirthankaras.

After the death of Mahavira, his original twelve disciples, known as *ganadharas*, established a lineage of spiritual teachings. Jainism was favored during the Mauryan Empire, and by the turn of the common era, worship practices were well established. Jain worship includes meditation, fasting, and recitation of prayers. The foremost Jain prayer is the Navakar Mantra, which dates from the second century BCE. It pays homage to the five supreme beings of Jainism.

The Great Schism

About a millennium after the life of Mahavira, Jain adherents split into two sects. They are known as the Digambara, or sky-clad, and the Svetambara, or white-clad. The schism came in the third century CE, after a long-standing disagreement over central teachings, particularly the idea of clothing. Mahavira had been an ascetic who preached complete renunciation of all worldly possessions.

The Digambara sect understood Mahavira's call to renunciation to include clothing and believed that to truly live an ascetic life, one should go naked. In addition, the worldly emotions such as shame, symbols of attachment to self, must be disregarded. Monks in the Digambara sect practice complete nakedness, but the practice is not advocated for women for two main reasons. First, nakedness in women is considered a hindrance to the vow of *brahmacharya*, or sexual abstinence. Second, Digambara followers believe that women are not candidates for *moksha*, or liberation from karma. They must first be reborn as men, which is seen as a higher spiritual state.

The Svetambara, or white-clad sect, allows its monastic followers several possessions, including a set of white robes and shoes. In an effort to preserve all living beings, Svetambara adherents also wear a thin gauze panel over their mouths to avoid inhaling or swallowing any insects, and they carry a whisk to gently clear

The Udayagiri and Khandagiri caves, near Bhubaneswar, housed Jain monks in the second or first century BCE. They may have been constructed during the reign of King Kharavela, who ruled Kalinga as a devout Jain sometime in the same period.

insects from their path and the ground before sitting. Because Svetambara beliefs do not grant men an advantage in spiritual attainment, there are nearly twice as many white-clad nuns as there are monks. Lay Jain practitioners of either sect can wear any clothing.

In Jain art and architecture, Svetambara representations of enlightened beings have prominent eyes that appear to be staring intently. Digambara art and statues are naked and usually have downcast eyes, as if the subject were in deep meditation.

THE FIVE SUPREME BEINGS

When Jains pray, it is not to a deity but to idealized examples of human spiritual attainment. These spiritual masters, or *pancha paramesthin*, are divided into five groups, and each receives a bow and declaration of respect. Jains believe it is within the grasp of all humans to attain the highest state, a *siddha*. The five groups of supreme beings honored in the Navakar Mantra are:

- **ARHATS**
  Arhats are the "worthy ones," who have attained liberation from rebirth, or moksha, and who enable the salvation of others. These are the tirthankaras or jinas. Mahavira is venerated above all others but is not singled out by name in the Navakar Mantra.

- **SIDDHAS**
  Liberated souls who also have achieved release from rebirth but who may not be known to living beings, since this liberation occurs only after death.

- **ACHARYAS**
  Spiritual teachers, both past and present. Acharyas have mastered the Jain scriptures, have gained special insight into the doctrines and wisdom of the religion, and transmit this wisdom to others.

- **UPADYAYAS**
  Monks and nuns who have accumulated wisdom and merit through acts of compassion and adherence to Jain spiritual practices.

- **SADHUS**
  Monks who have renounced worldly pursuits and follow a spiritual path, according to the three jewels of Jainism—right belief, right knowledge, and right conduct. Monks also adhere to the five vows—nonviolence, honesty, not taking anything that is not given, sexual abstinence, and non-attachment. Nuns are known as sadhvis.

THE SPREAD AND RISE OF JAINISM

From its original home in the Ganges basin of northern India, Jainism spread to the south and the west. One of the first centers of Jain worship was Kalinga, in present-day Orissa. Magnificent stone carvings in caves outside the city of Bhubaneswar are one of the few surviving Jain monuments from before the common era. The main areas for Jain worship have historically been the regions of Gujarat, Rajasthan, and Maharashtra. Mohandas Gandhi, who was Gujarati, was a practicing

Hindu but was deeply influenced by Jain principles, especially *ahimsa*, or nonviolence.

The Middle Ages in India were a time of great religious strife, particularly between Hindus and Muslims in northern and central India. In southern India, however, where many Jains had settled, Jainism enjoyed royal patronage. One of the greatest Jain literary works, the *Adipurana*, was composed in the tenth century by the Kannada

poet Adikavi Pampa. Pampa lived in the southeastern state of Andhra Pradesh. The *Adipurana* retells an earlier Sanskrit work by the eighth-century Digambara monk Jinasena, adviser to the royal family in the southwestern state of Karnataka. And one of the largest statues in India, the figure of the Digambar saint Gommateshwara (also called Bahubali) is found in the Karnataka city of Sravanabelagola.

Map

SPREAD OF JAINISM IN INDIA, TO C. 1000

- ● cities
- ➤ spread of Jainism

PUNJAB

Indus

HARYANA

DELHI

SIND

RAJASTHAN — UTTAR PRADESH — *Brahmaputra* — ASSAM

GUJARAT — *Ganges* — BIHAR

MADHYA PRADESH — BENGAL

Arabian Sea

MAHARASHTRA — ORISSA (ANCIENT KALINGA)

Godavari — ● Bhubaneswar

BOMBAY — *Bay of Bengal*

Krishna — ANDHRA PRADESH

KARNATAKA

Sravanabelagola ●

TAMIL NADU

From its sixth-century origins near the Ganges delta, Jainism spread rapidly, reaching nearly all of India by the close of the first millennium and surviving—even thriving during—the massive political unrest of India's Middle Ages.

THE SVASTIKA: SACRED JAIN SYMBOL

The *svastika*, or *swastika*, is an ancient Indian symbol. The earliest representations are found on soapstone seals from the Indus Valley civilization, dating from the third or fourth millennium BCE. It is associated with many religious traditions, most notably Jainism. For millennia the symbol represented good luck, or the benevolence of nature. The Sanskrit name is a compound of *su* (good or well) and *asti* (the root of the verb "to be"), so the essential meaning is "well-being." Today, because the symbol was appropriated by the Nazi Party and became synonymous with intolerance and hate, it retains this stigma and is infrequently used in the West. Jains view the symbol with reverence, as it represents the seventh *tirthankara*. Jain svastikas are often shown with seven dots, four blue and three green. The open-hand symbol was adopted by Jains in 1975 to commemorate the 2,500th anniversary of Mahavira.

SIKHISM
One God, Many Gurus

SIKHISM WAS BORN IN INDIA, the fourth world religion to come from the great subcontinent. Next to Hinduism, Buddhism, and Jainism, Sikhism is a young religion. It was founded in the fifteenth century and stems from the inspiration and teachings of one man, known as Guru Nanak (1469–1539). Nanak was followed by nine more gurus, or teachers. During the life of the tenth and last of these, Gobind Singh, the

religion was officially established—Sikhs consider 1699 as the birth date of their religion. In Guru Nanak's native Punjabi language, a variant of Sanskrit, a *sikh* is a disciple or, literally, a learner. In the context of the religion, the Sikhs are those who seek the path to union with God.

Sikhism is distinguished from the other religions of India in that it is monotheistic, though it does incorporate some elements of the karmic religions. Its founder was a raised a Hindu, but the Sikh doctrine formally rejects Hinduism. At the time of Guru Nanak's birth, India was ruled by the Mughal Empire, and the official religion was Islam. Mughal rulers' policies toward Hindus alternated between open tolerance and violent persecution, and the country had seen many bloody clashes between the two religions. According to legend, Guru Nanak was visited by a divine revelation, leading him to declare, "There is no Hindu, there is no Muslim, so whose path shall I follow? I will follow God's path. God is neither Hindu nor Muslim."

A splendid *gurdwara* (Sikh place of worship) stands in modern Janam Asthan, Pakistan, marking the birthplace and childhood home of Guru Nanak.

Perhaps the most widely-traveled founder of a major religion, Guru Nanak's four journeys brought him from his homeland in the northwestern region of India known as Punjab to the edge of Southeast Asia and nearly the length of the Arabian Peninsula.

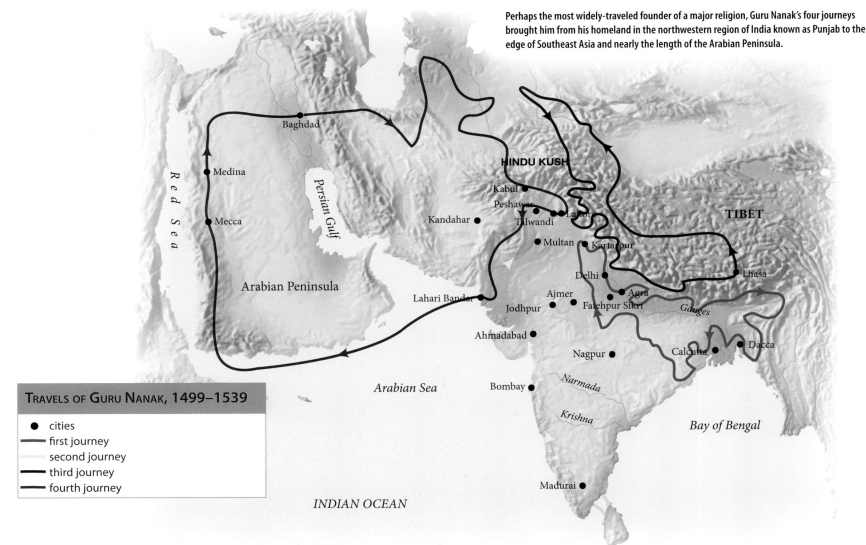

TRAVELS OF GURU NANAK, 1499–1539

- ● cities
- —— first journey
- —— second journey
- —— third journey
- —— fourth journey

As fragrance abides in the flower,
As reflection is within the mirror,
So does your Lord abide within you.
Why search for him without?
—GURU NANAK

THE LIFE OF GURU NANAK

The region known as the Punjab lies in the northwest of the Indian subcontinent and straddles what is now the border between Pakistan and India. Guru Nanak was born here in 1469 in a village called Talwandi, now known as Nankana Sahib, Pakistan. The Punjab had rich regional traditions and a large group who worshipped in the Sant tradition—a loose assortment of mystics and poets. Some Sants were *Vaishnava bhaktis,* or devotees of the Hindu god Vishnu. Others, like the poet Rumi, were Sufis, a mystical branch of Islam. This poetic tradition, with its individualistic and largely monotheistic beliefs, was a strong influence on Nanak. Deeply spiritual as a youth, the future guru sought a direct connection with the divine, which he believed was present in all people. The young Nanak spent hours in daily meditation, partly influenced by another growing spiritual group called the Nath, practitioners in the Hatha yoga lineage.

After Nanak's divine vision, which occurred while he was bathing in a river, he left home at age thirty and spent years in pilgrimage. Nanak's two companions were Bhai Mardana, a musician who accompanied the guru as he preached his poetic sermons, and Bhai Bala, who wrote semimythical accounts of these journeys. These stories, sprinkled liberally with miracles, are known as *Janamsakhis,* and were added to by later scribes and poets. They form the basis for the biographical information we have on Guru Nanak.

The five journeys of Nanak, called *udasis,* took him first in the four cardinal directions, then finally on a tour of his native Punjab. First he went east, as far as present-day Bangladesh, followed by a long trek as far south as Sri Lanka. Next Nanak traveled north into mountainous Tibet, followed by an extended journey west to Mecca, Medina, and Baghdad. In each of these places, Nanak debated matters of faith and practice, and

The lovely Punjab region, now divided between India and Pakistan, has a long and varied religious history, with Sikh, Jain, Hindu, Buddhist, and Muslim sites all sharing the holy landscape.

established worship centers. Upon returning home to the Punjab, Nanak settled at the town of Kartarpur on the Ravi River with his wife and two sons. Before dying, Nanak appointed a successor, who became Guru Angad, initiating the Sikh succession of divine authority.

GURU NANAK, THE TEACHER

Many colorful stories about Guru Nanak point to his skill in teaching, as he slyly shows skeptics the folly of their ways or the narrowness of their conception of the divine. According to legend, Nanak especially liked to undermine what he considered empty ritual or misplaced devotion—the worship of symbols of God rather than God in spirit.

One of the most popular stories recounts Nanak's pilgrimage to Mecca, where he arrived after a long journey and promptly lay down for a nap. A guard awoke him and severely admonished him—Nanak's feet were pointing toward the Ka'bah, or sacred shrine of the Great Mosque. Nanak is said to have replied, "Point my feet in the direction where God is not." When the guard moved Nanak's feet, the Ka'bah moved as well. After this exercise had been repeated several times, Nanak said to the dumbfounded guard, "You see, God does not live in one place; God lives everywhere."

An illustration of the just-awoken Guru Nanak explaining himself to Muslim guards in Mecca.

Sikh Worship and Community

GURU NANAK and his successors are seen by Sikh faithful as embodying the actual spirit of God. For this reason they are known as *satguru,* or true teachers. After the ten living gurus, the Sikh holy book of scriptures, the Guru Granth Sahib, is seen as the eleventh guru, an undying manifestation of God. It is only with the aid of a guru that one can attain divine union. Nanak likened the guru to a ship that helped the faithful cross the ocean of worldly desires to the other shore, where the soul can become one with God.

This nineteenth-century illustrated manuscript of the *Dasven Padsah ka Granth* (also called *Dasam Granth*), which consists of writings attributed to Guru Gobind Singh, is written in the Gurmukhi script developed by Guru Angad.

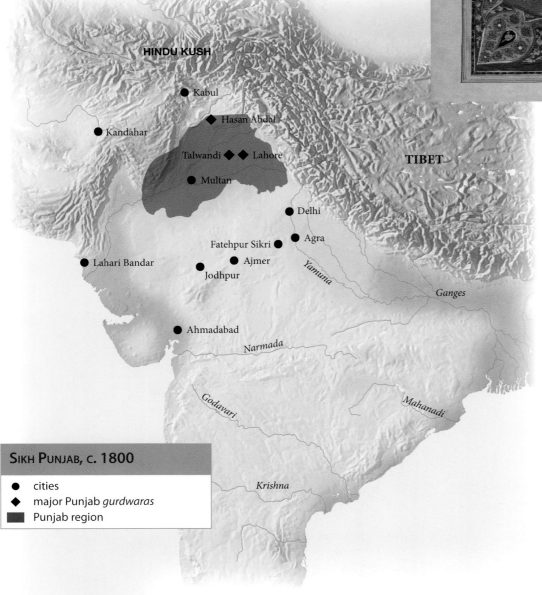

SIKH PUNJAB, C. 1800

- ● cities
- ◆ major Punjab *gurdwaras*
- ▨ Punjab region

Most Sikh holy sites—as well as most Sihks—are located in the same region of the Indian subcontinent where their religion formed. Their placement there, between strongly Hindu and strongly Muslim areas, is no accident (Sihkism specifically references both traditions), but it has led to periodic contention and even violence on all sides.

Gurus in the Sikh religion are not just holy leaders but head of the Sikh community as well. Guru Nanak instituted regular service and charity within the community, known as *seva*. A communal meal called a *langar* (literally "anchor") represents the ideals of the Sikh community—families or members bring whatever they can, and each takes according to need. One who has nothing to give is still welcome to join in the meal. This practice, where all sit on the ground, is meant to engender equality within the community—a notion close to Guru Nanak's heart, as it defied the traditional Indian caste system that he held in scorn.

Despite Guru Nanak's irreverence for many outward forms of worship, a set of rituals and formalities soon became central to Sikhism. The worship centers, or *gurdwara*, are often elaborate buildings that house the holy book, the Guru Granth Sahib. It is understood by Sikhs, however, that worship and rituals, such as the use of *amrit* (holy water or nectar) or reading of scriptures, does not negate the presence of God everywhere. Temple worship is merely a locus, while true devotion imbues all places and activities. Guru Nanak wrote, "The only temple that matters is within oneself."

The Sikh gurus, with Guru Hargobind on the far left, greet each other in an eighteenth-century painting of a fictional meeting.

Belief and Devotion

Omnipresent and formless, the God of the Sikhs is also without gender. Many English translations attach the male gender to God when translating Sikh scriptures, but this does not accurately represent the belief. Guru Arjan, the fifth guru, said, "Thou, O Lord, art my Father and Thou my Mother."

Nam simram (remembrance of the name) is a primary form of worship. A Sikh will meditate while repeating the name of God. Karma is a concept shared by Hindus, Buddhists, and Sikhs. Reincarnation, or the transmigration of souls, is key to karma, which is the accumulation of actions throughout life. One can be reborn in endless cycles, or, with the proper devotion, aid of the guru, and good works, one can merge with God.

Central to Sikh practice is the avoidance of the five evils, or cardinal vices. These are described as lust, anger, greed, attachment, and pride. It is thought that engaging in these evils blinds one to the true message of the guru, so that one lives in a state called *maya*—deluded by the material.

Guru Nanak's Successors

By choosing a successor who was not his son—one was deemed too ascetic, the other too worldly—Guru Nanak set the precedent for religious authority based on merit and spiritual fitness rather than blood. Several later gurus were related by blood, but the initial line of succession was not.

Guru Angad (1504–52), the second guru, carried on Nanak's literary tradition, composing hymns and poems. Angad also developed the Gurmukhi script in which the Punjabi language is written. This helped the Sikhs to gain an identity separate from Hinduism, whose scriptures are mostly in Sanskrit.

Angad was succeeded by Guru Amar Das (1479–1574), who became guru when already in his seventies. Legend says that at age sixty, he heard his brother's wife singing hymns by

A late-nineteenth century painting of the ten gurus, Guru Nanak center. Also visible are Guru Nanak's companions, Bhai Mardana below Guru Nanak's left knee and Bhai Bala above his left shoulder.

Guru Nanak and became entranced with their beauty and message. He went on a journey to meet Guru Angad, who appointed him his successor over his own son. Guru Amar Das established the worship center at Goindval in the Punjab.

The fourth guru, Ram Das (1534–81), was born in Lahore. He founded the holy Sikh city of Amritsar and oversaw the construction of the large pool, Harimandir, the future site of the Golden Temple. These first three successors were able to shepherd the teachings of Guru Nanak into an organized religion with an identity and growing tradition all its own, and to do so relatively free of persecution. This was to change by the turn of the seventeenth century, however, and the holy mission of Sikhism was to take on a new militancy, born of crushing persecution.

Women in Sikhism

The position of women in Sikhism is one of near-total equality, in stark contrast to the Muslim and Hindu traditions that were dominant during Guru Nanak's life. Rejecting the traditional Hindu four stages of life (student, householder, recluse, and renunciant), Nanak saw householder as the ideal state for a Sikh. In practical terms, this meant that Sikh faithful could have families and livelihoods along with devotion. One did not have to choose devotion or family, but could integrate the sacred into all aspects of life.

Beginning with Guru Nanak, Sikh women as well as men were educated, admitted into the *sangat*, or congregation, and given rights to own property. Guru Nanak forbade the practice of *sati*, whereby a widow is burned on her husband's funeral pyre. He also abolished *purdah*, or veiling and segregation of women practiced by Muslims and some Hindus. In the ideal Sikh marriage, said Guru Amar Das, husband and wife are equals and share "one soul in two bodies."

A Sikh woman rests across from the administrative center of Sikh temples in Amritsar, India.

DAOISM

The Origins of Religious Daoism

LEGENDARY DAOIST MASTER LAOZI is said to have lived in the sixth century BCE, making him a contemporary of the Buddha. For roughly a millennium after his life, the wisdom contained in his teachings was to have a profound influence on Chinese culture and thought. But the formal organization of Daoism into a religion did not begin in earnest until Buddhism was becoming well established in China, in roughly the fifth century CE. As Buddhism grew, and temples and monasteries were established, the ancient and complex beliefs of the Chinese seemed suddenly to be lacking in ceremony, form, and ritual. The presence of a thriving Buddhism effectively jump-started religious Daoism.

Laozi's followers had long considered him a deity, circulating ever more fantastic stories about his birth, life, death, and reincarnation—a principally Buddhist concept. The beginnings of religious Daoism go back to the years of the Han dynasty. It was a Daoist sect, the Yellow Turbans, or Taiping Dao (The Way of Supreme Peace) who toppled the Confucian Han regime early in the third century CE.

The first Daoist religious orders date from the Han period as well. The Celestial Masters sect, still an important Daoist lineage today, originated from a group called the Five Bushels of Rice society, under the charismatic leader Zhang Daoling. This growing Daoist movement flourished briefly during the turbulent few centuries between the Confucian Han era and the establishment of Chinese Buddhism.

The Celestial Masters sect assembled all the earmarks of a true religious order. These included a set of newly revealed sacred texts, most importantly the *Ling-pao* scriptures; a set of worship rituals that mostly centered on talismans; and a church hierarchy beginning with Zhang Daoling himself. Other branches of Celestial Masters arose in the north, and the Taiping Dao (Way of Supreme Peace) grew in numbers as well, favored by several passing emperors. The monastic Complete Reality school was a large sect that grew around the turn of the first millennium, the most important of the scores of monastic Daoist sects to emerge before the close of the Ming dynasty.

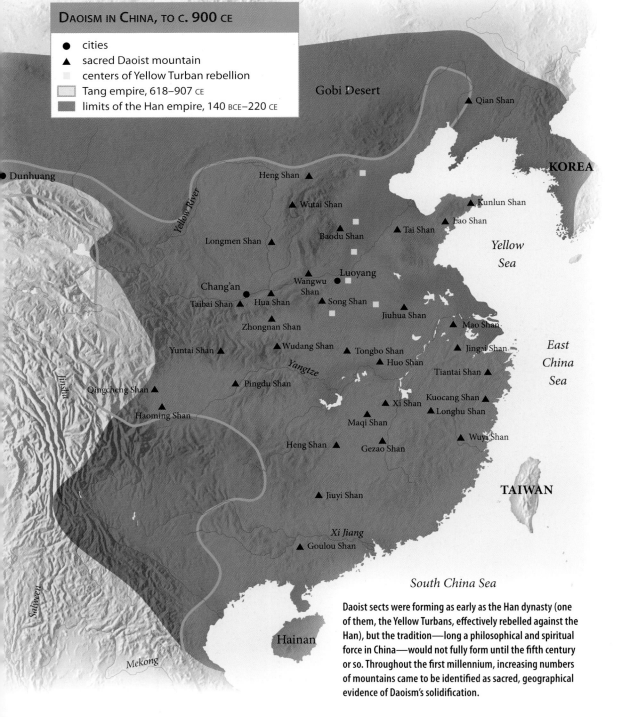

DAOISM IN CHINA, TO C. 900 CE

- ● cities
- ▲ sacred Daoist mountain
- ▢ centers of Yellow Turban rebellion
- Tang empire, 618–907 CE
- limits of the Han empire, 140 BCE–220 CE

Daoist sects were forming as early as the Han dynasty (one of them, the Yellow Turbans, effectively rebelled against the Han), but the tradition—long a philosophical and spiritual force in China—would not fully form until the fifth century or so. Throughout the first millennium, increasing numbers of mountains came to be identified as sacred, geographical evidence of Daoism's solidification.

A modern illustration of Zhang Daoling, a Daoist monk of the second century CE and founder of the Five Bushels of Rice society, so called for the requirement that society members and visitors each donate five bushels of rice every year.

Laozi the Deity

In the seventh century Laozi was officially deified. The emperors of the Tang dynasty (618–907), who shared the family name Li with Laozi (born Li Er), saw the advantage in tying their lineage to this divine being. Claiming direct ancestry between the imperial family and the founding sage of Daoism gave a new legitimacy to both parties, even at a time when Buddhism was declared the official state religion of China.

If Chinese Buddhism contains many Daoist elements in its philosophy—the concept of emptiness, for example—then religious Daoism in turn borrowed many of the outer trappings of Buddhism. Daoist temples, or guan, were established, and monastic Daoism began at this time—both hallmarks of Buddhist practice. Commentaries and texts relating to the Dao and essential Daoist scriptures were collected in the fifth century into a canon called the Daozang; like the Buddhist Tripitaka, the Daozang was divided into three sections, called "three grottoes," later supplemented by four minor sections.

In addition, the Buddhist notion of transmigration or reincarnation was effectively used by Daoists to claim the entire Buddhist tradition as their own. A fifth-century text from the Celestial Masters sect paints Laozi as an immortal master who had had three births to record: first, as the pure energy of the Dao itself; second, as the human philosopher Laozi; and third, in India as the Buddha himself. This was meant to show that Buddhism was born of the Daoist tradition, granting Daoism the superior role of mother tradition.

Daoist Temples

Before religious Daoism, there was no strictly Daoist form of worship. Zhuangzi, the greatest Daoist philosopher after Laozi, was a near-hermit, favoring a remote mountaintop for contemplation. Laozi himself viewed the workings of politics and society with a slightly bemused detachment. It is safe to guess that neither of them would have recognized as their own the temples that sprang up a millennium after their time, temples dedicated to the wisdom of their teachings.

Daoist temples roughly followed the plan of their Buddhist counterparts. The oldest ones were of modest design and were situated mostly on mountains, considered sacred places. Under the reign of Kublai Khan, great temples of ornate design sprang up, with elaborate images of Daoist deities prominently displayed. The best known of these is White Cloud Temple in Beijing, central to the Dragon Gate sect. Founded in 741 under the Tang dynasty, the temple was later expanded to its present size and design. As with Buddhist temples, a central area houses the essential Daoist scriptures. The founding philosophy of Daoism is shown in representations of the yin yang symbol and the eight trigrams of the I Ching (Yi Jing).

The Huang Mountains of Southern China form one of the country's most recognizable landscapes. Often the subject of Chinese art, with the act of painting itself a spiritual activity, the mountains host a number of Buddhist and Daoist monasteries; in the latter tradition especially, the mountains of China are held in high religious esteem.

Some historians see early religious Daoism as a melting pot of spiritual traditions. The life, legend, and teachings of Laozi provided the base, into which were added elements from Buddhism, Confucianism, and ancient Chinese shamanism. In creating this synthesis of form and belief, religious Daoism was almost guaranteed a permanent place in Chinese culture.

The Transformations of Laozi

A second-century CE text called the *Laozi bianhua jing* (*The Transformations of Laozi*) describes the emerging view of Laozi as the supreme deity:

> Laozi was at the origin of the Great Beginning
> Revolving in the Great Expanse.
> Alone and without companion,
> He was moving in the times of yore,
> before Heaven and Earth.
>
> Coming out of the hidden and returning thereto,
> Being and nonbeing,
> He is the First One.
>
> (Translation by Livia Kohn)

Daoist preoccupation with understanding the world's spiritual forces has endowed certain natural features with specific symbolic meaning; the crane, for instance, represents longevity, and frequently appears in Chinese art.

Alchemy and Immortality

If Buddhists were concerned with a positive rebirth, or with ending the cycle of death and rebirth, religious Daoists went a step further, seeking to eliminate death altogether. Immortality was the great quest of early Daoist practitioners, and alchemy was their principal tool. Alchemy is loosely defined as the transformation of base materials like lead into precious ones like gold. Daoist alchemists were searching for an elixir of immortality. Gold, it was reasoned, was an incorruptible material. By ingesting gold, or substances like cinnabar (mercuric sulfide) that could transform themselves—in this case, into poisonous mercury—Daoists hoped the physical body could also become incorruptible. Unfortunately, the results of such experiments often led to death, for alchemists and emperors alike. Many Tang dynasty rulers perished seeking the elixir of immortality.

Daoist alchemical experiments followed ancient Chinese beliefs that view the various body parts as correlated with the five basic elements: metal, wood, water, fire, and earth. The way that these elements interact in nature is seen as reflected in the human body. This system is the foundation for traditional Chinese medicine as well. Alchemical experiments yielded sometimes unlooked-for results; the use of sulfur and saltpeter, for example, resulted in the discovery of gunpowder—an ironic outcome for the search for immortality. The Daoist alchemists are seen as laying the foundation for modern chemistry.

THE EIGHT IMMORTALS

In addition to the gods of the Daoist pantheon, there are legendary humans said to have gained immortality. Each achieved this state in a different way, sometimes passing on the secrets to one another. Numerous legends are attached to each of the immortals. They are often shown together, either winged and flying through the air, or in a boat on their way to an Eastern Paradise. In popular Chinese culture, the luck attached to the number eight originates with the immortals.

HE XIANGU
Also called Ho Hsiang Ku. The only woman in the group of immortals, she carries a lotus, or sometimes a peach of immortality. She is a patron deity and protector of young women.

LAN CAIHE
Lan is of ambiguous gender; some legends paint Lan as a woman, others as a man "who didn't know how to be a man." He may have been a hermaphrodite, or simply a youth. He is sometimes shown wearing only one shoe, and he carries a flower basket.

HAN XIANG
Carries a flute and is the patron of musicians. Han was a disciple of Lu Dongbin.

ZHONGLI QUAN
Shown holding a feather fan and with an exposed belly. In life he was a general in the Han army. He represents the military and has the power to restore life.

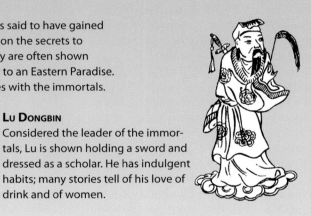

LU DONGBIN
Considered the leader of the immortals, Lu is shown holding a sword and dressed as a scholar. He has indulgent habits; many stories tell of his love of drink and of women.

LI TIEGUAI
Nicknamed "Iron Crutch," he carries a gourd full of life-saving elixir. He is the guardian of the sick or disabled.

ZHANG GUOLAO
Usually shown riding a donkey and holding a bamboo cylinder drum, he is the elder of the immortals and known for his eccentricity. He is the patron of the elderly.

CAO GUOJIU
Nicknamed Royal Uncle Cao, as he was said to have been an uncle to a Song dynasty emperor. Shown with castanets, or with a badge or tablet of royal office, showing his membership in the royal family.

The accidental invention of gunpowder by Daoist alchemists may be one of the most momentous discoveries in history. Here, the Chinese formula for gunpowder in its earliest known incarnation, from a military treatise dated to the mid-eleventh century CE.

INTERNAL ALCHEMY: THE WAY OF QI

During the Song dynasty (960–1279), the dangerous forms of "external" alchemy were mostly superseded by practices called "internal alchemy." Following principles inherent in the I Ching (Yi Jing), internal alchemists practiced breath control, physical and sexual exercises, and meditation. Daoist meditation, or "sitting and forgetting," outwardly resembles Zen meditation, but the aim for Daoists was to become unified with all natural phenomena—to become one with the Dao.

The foundation for these practices was the concept of qi (chi), the essential breath of life.

It was believed that if the qi, jing (life force), and shen (spirit) are in perfect balance, the body could be preserved indefinitely. Tai chi chuan (taijiquan) originated during this period as well; the martial arts practice was seen as cultivating both body and mind, balancing the energies of heaven and earth, and promoting the flow of qi.

Through the centuries, the Daoist search for literal immortality was directed instead into a focus on longevity, firmly rooted in observance of the Dao. To struggle against the immutable way of the universe eventually wears down body, mind, and spirit. Instead, Daoists believe the key to longevity is to live in balance and harmony, to observe the wisdom of wu wei, or "going with the flow."

The Eight Immortals crossing the sea to the Eastern Paradise, with the eccentric Zhang Guolao riding his donkey instead of sitting in the boat, and accompanied by the beneficent symbols of dragon and crane.

THE DAOIST PANTHEON

Daoism has a wide pantheon of deities and spirits. Another subset of revered figures are the Immortals, who were once human. Out of the thousands of Daoist gods, the principal ones are:

TAI-SHANG LAOJUN

The name for the deified Laozi. He embodies the principles of the Dao and is granted supreme honor above all other deities.

THE THREE PURE ONES (SANJING)

A trinity of deities, they embody the three pure realms of the Daoist cosmos. They are the Jade Pure One (Yuqing), the Supreme Pure One (Shangqing), and the Grand Pure One (Taiqing). They represent the energies of shen (spirit), qi (breath), and jing (life force), respectively.

THE JADE EMPEROR

An incarnation of the Jade Pure One, he was chosen by other deities to rule over all others and over heaven and earth. He sits in judgment over mankind, awarding longevity to those who merit it.

THE CELESTIAL EMPRESS OF THE WEST (XI WANG MU)

Sometimes called the Heavenly Queen or Queen Mother of the West, she tends an orchard of the peaches of immortality, which ripen only once every thousand years.

The Daoist trinity of the Jade Pure One (top), the Supreme Pure One (right) and the Grand Pure One (left).

A New Life for Confucianism

As China's imperial period matured at the close of the first millennium, the three religious traditions that had alternated influence for roughly a thousand years came to an uneasy but logical balance. If Daoism and Buddhism can be broadly classified as addressing the realm of the body, mind, and spirit of the individual, then Confucianism addresses the structure of society and the actions of the individual within society. While there is certainly overlap in the domains of China's three traditions, this broad division effectively allowed them to coexist. For most of the second millennium, Chinese worshipped according to Daoist or Buddhist beliefs (or a synthesis of the two) but lived in a state largely ordered by Confucianism.

Early state Confucianism had placed the Confucian scholar in the academy, or as adviser to the emperor, particularly under the Han dynasty (206 BCE–220 CE). In fact, during this period, the first Confucian academy was founded. The study of the five Confucian classics, culminating in an examination, became the basis for entry into civil service—a system that would endure until the reforms of the twentieth century.

Under the Song dynasty (960–1279), a political and social movement known as Neo-Confucianism arose. Its followers, who had come to revere Confucius as a near god, were steeped in ideals espoused by the sage over a thousand years earlier. But the Neo-Confucians had also absorbed many of the teachings of Buddhism and Daoism. Now the social and political lessons of the great master were infused with a new spirituality, while the metaphysical concepts of Daoism and Buddhism gained new, practical applications. By the eleventh century most cities in China had a Confucian temple, but none larger than the one at Qufu, birthplace of Confucius.

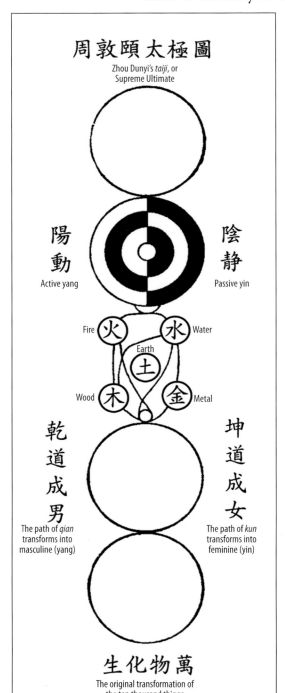

周敦頤太極圖

Zhou Dunyi's *taiji*, or
Supreme Ultimate

陽動
Active yang

陰靜
Passive yin

Fire 火   水 Water
Earth
土
Wood 木   金 Metal

乾道成男
The path of *qian*
transforms into
masculine (yang)

坤道成女
The path of *kun*
transforms into
feminine (yin)

萬物化生
The original transformation of
the ten thousand things

A pictorial representation of Zhou Dunyi's *taiji*, incorporating yin and yang with the traditional five elements of Chinese philosophy.

THE SUPREME ULTIMATE: NEO-CONFUCIANISM EMERGES

From the depths of the ancient Chinese text the *I Ching* (*Yi Jing*), or *Book of Changes*, arose a new concept for a new Chinese millennium. Building on the notions of yin and yang, negative and positive, light and dark, contained within the *I Ching*, the eleventh-century philosopher Zhou Dunyi wrote a treatise called *The Diagram of the Supreme Ultimate* (*Taijitu shuo*). Zhou Dunyi, born in Dao Zhou, Hunan Province, was sympathetic to both Buddhism and Daoism and is considered the pioneer of the Neo-Confucian movement.

The Supreme Ultimate, or *taiji*, integrated beliefs from the *I Ching*, yin yang, and the five elements. But rather than resting on the beliefs themselves, Zhou Dunyi turned a Confucian-trained eye on the practical application of these truths. Part of his treatise proclaimed, "The many are ultimately one, and the one is made manifest as many." This Daoist view of the unity of all things, however, is tempered by a Confucian emphasis on all things having their proper place: "The one and many, each has its own correct state of being. The great and the small, each has its definite function."

Two disciples of Zhou Dunyi, known as the Cheng brothers (Cheng Hao and Cheng Yi) furthered their master's teachings but were outwardly hostile toward Buddhist forms of worship. The monastic tradition in particular drew their ire; they favored a traditional model of Confucian filial piety. The Cheng brothers were positive about human nature, but they drew a line between the essential goodness of the original mind and the feelings and desires that can be aroused, which are seen as potentially evil. But the Cheng brothers' main focus was on the idea of a universal principle: "The mind of each human being is one with the mind of Heaven and Earth. The principle of each thing is one with the principle of all things." For the Cheng brothers this universal principle was *li*, or righteousness.

THE VINEGAR TASTERS

This well-known allegorical painting from the Song dynasty shows Confucius, Buddha, and Laozi all tasting vinegar from the same jar. It is frequently shown with the caption "The three teachings are one!"

Further commentaries focus on the facial expressions of the three masters, however, with some scholars pointing to a distinctly Daoist slant. Confucius makes a face that is sour, perhaps indicating his essential distaste of Chinese society during his lifetime, which he felt was in need of reform. Buddha is said to have a bitter expression, which some say stands for the first noble truth of *dukkha*, that all life is suffering. Only Laozi smiles sweetly, perfectly at peace with the laws of the universe.

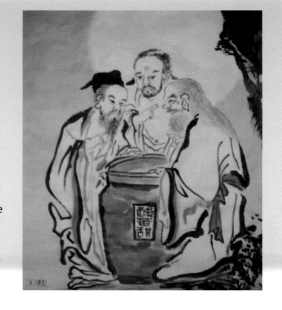

NEO–CONFUCIANISM IN THE SONG DYNASTY, 960–1279

● cities
◎ capital cities
◆ major Confucian temples
▰ Song China

Even as Buddhism did, Confucianism found new life in Song dynasty China. Unlike Buddhism and Daoism, whose temples and monasteries tended to perch on remote mountains, Neo-Confucianism found its most sympathetic homes in cities, encouraged perhaps by rulers eager for the tradition's hierarchical social structure.

QUFU: MONUMENTS TO THE SAGE
~

In the birthplace of Confucius, the life and teachings of the sage are celebrated with a grand complex of three monuments. This rural town in Shandong Province is the site of the world's largest Confucian temple, known as Kong Miao. Kong was the family name of Kong Fuzi, or Confucius—the latter being the anglicized version of the name. The temple itself is the second-largest historical complex in China, after the Forbidden City, and comprises 460 rooms. Kong Miao has been destroyed and rebuilt several times and stands as a testament to the esteem Confucius and his teachings enjoy in China.

In addition to the sprawling temple complex, Qufu is also site of the Kong family burial ground known as "the Forest," a parkland of thousands of mature and rare trees with Confucius's own tomb in the center. The Kong family mansion is the third attraction in Qufu. Descendants of Confucius still occupy this palatial compound.

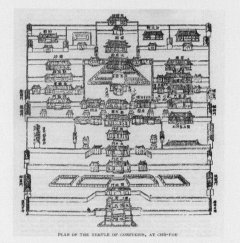

A 1912 map of the Confucian temple complex at Qufu.

Kong Miao is located at the center of a walled compound surrounded by the town of Qufu, the birthplace of Confucius. The largest Confucian temple in China, it is one of the country's most popular tourist destinations.

One Master, Many Schools

THE REVIVAL OF CONFUCIAN THOUGHT affected the religion, politics, and social fabric of China at the turn of the first millennium. But Neo-Confucianism was anything but unified in its beliefs. In fact, the variety of thinkers and writers who came under this banner was wide indeed. They were spurred on toward ever more precise renderings of their philosophy both by competition among themselves and by competition with the Buddhist and Daoist establishment in China. The twelfth and thirteenth centuries saw a prodigious outpouring of ideas in China. The old Confucian classics were closely examined with fresh eyes, gaining new relevance for a new millennium. If Buddhism had its golden age under the Tang dynasty, the Song dynasty was the moment for Neo-Confucianism.

Rulers of the Southern, or Later Song, dynasty modeled themselves on the successful Han dynasty, which had ruled a thousand years earlier. They adopted a Confucian model of governing, especially in the relationship between the court and bureaucratic officials.

This was a dynasty at war, however; the Song had just lost the central plains of China to the Jurchen people, who established the competing Jin dynasty (1115–1234). The Song especially wanted to defuse any dissent within their bureaucratic ranks. Song rulers looked toward Confucianism to bolster the sense of duty, propriety, and hierarchy among their officials. It is no surprise that they eventually favored the school of Neo-Confucianism that outwardly most resembled the old Confucian guard. This was known as the School of Rationalism. It became the dominant branch of Neo-Confucianism, competing directly with its more Daoist-influenced counterpart, the School of Idealism.

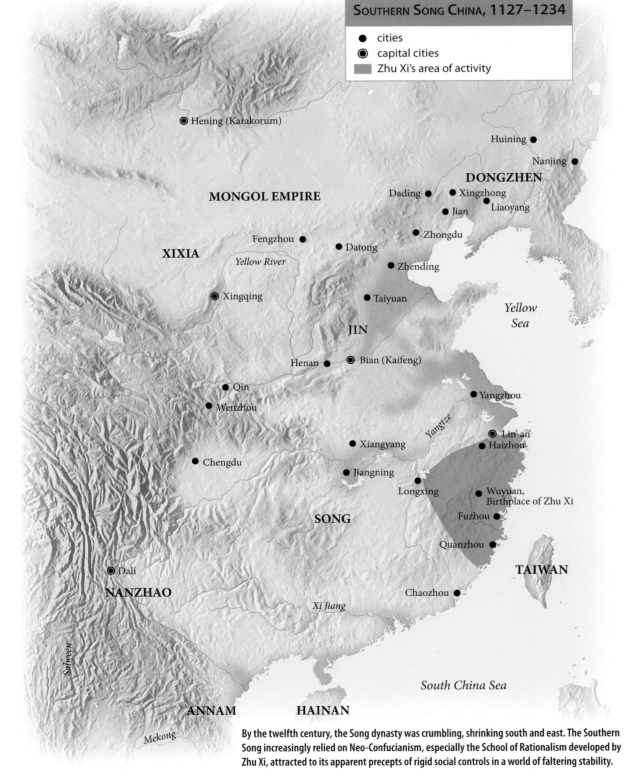

SOUTHERN SONG CHINA, 1127–1234

- ● cities
- ◉ capital cities
- ▓ Zhu Xi's area of activity

◉ Hening (Karakorum)

Huining ●

Nanjing ●

DONGZHEN

MONGOL EMPIRE

Dading ● ● Xingzhong

● Jian   Liaoyang ●

Fengzhou ●   ● Datong   ● Zhongdu

XIXIA   *Yellow River*   ● Zhending

◉ Xingqing   ● Taiyuan   *Yellow Sea*

JIN

Henan ●   ● Bian (Kaifeng)

● Qin   ● Yangzhou

● Wenzhou

Xiangyang ●   ◉ Lin'an

● Chengdu   ● Jiangning   ● Haizhou

Longxing ●   ● Wuyuan, Birthplace of Zhu Xi

SONG   Fuzhou ●

● Quanzhou

◉ Dali   **TAIWAN**

NANZHAO   Chaozhou ●

Xi Jiang

Salween

South China Sea

ANNAM   **HAINAN**

Mekong

By the twelfth century, the Song dynasty was crumbling, shrinking south and east. The Southern Song increasingly relied on Neo-Confucianism, especially the School of Rationalism developed by Zhu Xi, attracted to its apparent precepts of rigid social controls in a world of faltering stability.

Cheng Yi, a progenitor of the Neo-Confucian movement and particularly influential in the development of the School of Rationalism, favored by Song dynasty emperors.

ZHU XI AND THE SCHOOL OF RATIONALISM

The main architect of the Rationalistic school (*Li Xue*— sometimes translated as the School of Principle) was a philosopher named Zhu Xi (1130–1200), born in Fujian Province. Zhu Xi built on the guiding ideas of his Neo-Confucian predecessors Zhou Dunyi and the Cheng brothers, particularly Cheng Yi (1033–1107), but he added in Daoist ideas of self-cultivation. Zhu's main concern was the interaction between *qi* (cosmic life force) and the principle of *li*, widely translated as "righteousness," or "correctness of place," but here meaning simply "principle." In his prolific writings, Zhu defined the *li* as the principle for everything in the universe, or the form it takes, while qi is the matter or material by which things are produced. Both li (the metaphysical) and qi (the physical) are contained in the concept of the Supreme Ultimate, or *taiji*.

While he ably synthesized the thinking of his immediate Neo-Confucian predecessors, Zhu Xi's primary influence was the so-called second sage, Mencius, or Meng Zi (372–289 BCE). Like Mencius, Zhu believed in the innate goodness of humankind. He accounted for differences in temperament in two ways. First, a person could have an overabundance or imbalance of qi, and second, he could lack proper understanding of li, or his essential principle. Zhu Xi founded an academy to further the study of Confucianism. But his greatest legacy is his commentary and collection of classic texts known as the Four Books.

This Song dynasty painting, though possibly a reproduction from a Tang dynasty original, illustrates the high esteem the emperor held for scholars, who are shown dining at an imperially commissioned banquet.

THE SCHOOL OF IDEALISM

Not all Neo-Confucians agreed with Zhu Xi's reordering of essential Confucianism. Another influential school was known as the School of Idealism or of Heart/Mind (*Dao Xue*)—literally translated as Learning of the Way (Dao). As its name implies, this Neo-Confucian school had much more in common with Daoism and Buddhism than did the Rationalists. The main figures of the Idealistic school were Zhu's contemporary Lu Xiangshan (1139–93) and the later thinker Wang Yangming (1472–1529).

For the Idealistic school, the principle of li was interpreted as the essence of the mind; cultivation of the mind, then, was the main focus of practice. Borrowing freely from Zen (Chan)

Although the Song imperial court favored Confucianism, other traditions, such as Daoism and Buddhism—evinced here by a Song dynasty bodhisattva, carved of wood—continued simultaneously, all of them enriching the practice of the others.

meditation techniques, Wang in particular espoused a direct, intuitive experience of li through meditation, rather than the diligent study prescribed by the Rationalists. According to Wang, it is incumbent on the individual to maintain "clear intelligence," by which all matter and spirit can be apprehended. In a parable that sounds part Zen koan, part Daoist riddle, Wang Yangming writes:

> The Teacher was roaming in Nan-chen. A friend pointed to flowering trees on a cliff and said, "[You say] there is nothing under heaven external to the mind. These flowering trees on the high mountain blossom and drop their blossoms of themselves. What have they to do with my mind?" The Teacher said, "Before you look at these flowers, they and your mind are in the state of silent vacancy. As you come to look at them, their colors at once show up clearly. From this you can know that these flowers are not external to your mind."

THE FOUR BOOKS

Confucius spent years of study collecting and annotating a canon of learning that came to be known as the Five Classics. Zhu Xi refined this learning into an updated, streamlined Confucian canon called the Four Books. This collection formed the core curriculum for all Chinese civil servants until the twentieth century. They are:

• *The Analects of Confucius* (*Lunyu*)
This seminal text of Confucianism shows the master in conversation with students and contains the famously pithy and brief sayings for which Confucius is known. The guiding principle is *ren*, or benevolence, from which all other behaviors should stem.

• *The Book of Mencius* (*Mengzi*)
Written in the fourth century BCE, this book contains conversations between the sage and kings or leaders of his time. Mencius argues for the essential goodness of human nature, which can be corrupted by lack of moral cultivation.

• *The Doctrine of the Mean* (*Zhongyong*) and *The Great Learning* (*Daxue*)
Two sections from the *Book of Rites* (*Li Ji*), one of the five Confucian classics. The two sections together reinforce the idea of the heavenly mandate and propose that rulers and subjects alike must act according to a divinely prescribed set of virtues.

SHINTO
The Way of the Gods

JAPAN IS A COUNTRY OF SOARING MOUNTAINS, dense forests, and a seemingly boundless sea. An island nation composed of four main islands and thousands of smaller ones, Japan is geographically, ethnically, and culturally set apart from mainland Asia. An indigenous religion developed here over the course of millennia but was never given a particular name until foreign traditions such as Buddhism arrived. Then, in order to distinguish the ancient traditions from the new ones, the word *Shinto* was coined. The term derives from two Chinese words—*shin*, meaning "gods" or "spirits," and *dao* (tao), meaning "way" or "path."

In Shinto belief myriad sacred spirits, or *kami*, inhabit all things and all creatures. These spirits can embody the essence of a particular natural feature or phenomenon but may also be the spirits of ancestors. Some natural land formations are associated with particular kami. Mount Fuji, for example, is thought to embody the spirit of the goddess Sengen Sama; a shrine dedicated to Sengen stands at the summit of the mountain.

Kami, like humans, can be fickle and proud, or constant and benevolent. Shinto doesn't hold to an absolute separation between good and evil; rather, all kami possess both gentle and rough qualities. Demons called *oni* do exist in the Shinto pantheon, but they can sometimes act in benevolent ways. If misfortune befalls humans, it may be caused by a disruption in the natural order—an almost Daoist perspective—or it may be that the gods have been angered. Japanese mythology is also rich with stories of internal struggles between the gods themselves. And kami can certainly intercede on behalf of humans. When China under Kublai Khan twice tried to invade Japan, the spirits of the offshore winds, or *kamikaze*, were credited with driving off the invading fleet.

Surrounded by ocean, crowned with mountains, and bedecked with green and gold forests, Japan's native religion understandably invokes nature at every turn. The landscape, literally infused with Shinto gods, thus plays an enormous role in Shinto worship.

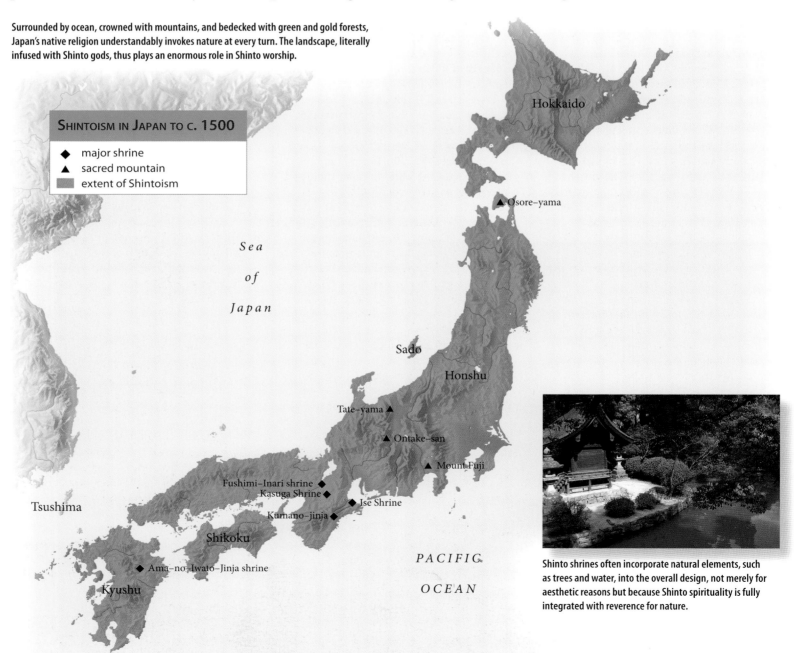

SHINTOISM IN JAPAN TO C. 1500

◆ major shrine
▲ sacred mountain
▬ extent of Shintoism

Hokkaido

▲ Osore-yama

Sea of Japan

Sado

Honshu

Tate-yama ▲

▲ Ontake-san

▲ Mount Fuji

Fushimi–Inari shrine ◆
Kasuga Shrine ◆
◆ Ise Shrine
Kumano–jinja ◆

Tsushima

Shikoku

◆ Ama–no–Iwato–Jinja shrine

Kyushu

PACIFIC

OCEAN

Osumi Islands

Shinto shrines often incorporate natural elements, such as trees and water, into the overall design, not merely for aesthetic reasons but because Shinto spirituality is fully integrated with reverence for nature.

One of the temple buildings at Ise Shrine, intended particularly for ritual dance and musical festivities.

SHINTO WORSHIP

In large public shrines or small ones at home, Shinto worship is mostly local, personal, and specific to a particular spirit. The kami can be petitioned for favors, or asked for guidance. Early Shinto shrines consisted of a simple space carved into a rock, or even simply a tree or grove that was designated as sacred. Worshippers could leave offerings of food or water, or pray to and communicate with the deity.

Shinto's oldest and most sacred shrine is in Ise, Mie Prefecture. It is dedicated to Amaterasu and is said to have been founded in 4 BCE by an emperor's daughter who was guided by the voice of the goddess herself. Ise today consists of a complex of shrines, which are systematically torn down and rebuilt every twenty years. This practice is thought to refresh the site for the gods and to renew the gods themselves. The ceremony reflects the Shinto reverence for the constant destruction and renewal inherent in the cycles of nature.

The *torii* is a well-recognized symbol of Shinto shrines. This large ceremonial gate topped by two crossbeams symbolizes a separation between the sacred space of the shrine and the profane world outside. Inside a shrine there is an inner sanctuary, or *honden*, a private space intended only for the kami. The public comes to pay homage to the gods at the outer *haiden*, or worship hall. Public ceremonies are held there as well.

Before entering a Shinto shrine, a worshipper must first be purified. A bowl of water stands outside the gate, which the worshipper uses to cleanse face and hands. Purity and cleanliness are of utmost importance in Shinto belief, with many rituals associated with purification. The five elements to purify are water, fire, salt, sand, and sake, or rice wine.

SHINTO IN BUDDHIST JAPAN

Native Shinto beliefs were not obliterated by the arrival of Buddhism but rather came to peacefully coexist with the new religion. Indeed, Japanese Buddhism has been infused with many Shinto qualities. The Buddha and bodhisattvas were merely held to be kami of a particular character. A reverence for nature and an emphasis on purity and ritual are hallmarks of both Japanese religions. In addition, the arrival of script from China, brought by Buddhist monks, allowed the long-held oral tradition of Japanese mythology to finally be committed to writing.

Two great historical works were composed shortly after the arrival of Buddhism, during the Nara period. First of these was the *Kojiki*, or *Records of the Ancient Matters*, completed in 712 by Ono Yasumaro. In addition to outlining the major kami pantheon, the *Kojiki* traced the ancestry of the present emperor back to Jimmu, the legendary first emperor. Jimmu, in turn, was descended from the sun goddess Amaterasu. Through this mytho-historical genealogy, the Japanese imperial family is traditionally considered divine. The second historical work of the Nara period was the *Nihongi*, or *Nihon Shoki*, usually translated as the *Chronicles of Japan*. The *Nihongi* was completed in 720 and traces Japanese history up until that time.

In building temples, Buddhists did not seek to tear down and replace the indigenous shrines with those of the new religion but simply built temples near the sites of shrines. Nowhere is this more evident than in Kyoto,

JIZO

One of the most beloved deities in Japan is the bodhisattva Jizo. Small statues of the deity, who is usually shown as a child monk, can be found all over Japan, particularly at crossroads and in temples and shrines. Jizo originates from the Buddhist Ksitigarbha, the bodhisattva who guards those in hell. In Japan, Jizo is more widely revered as the protector of children, including the unborn, and of children who have died. He also protects travelers and firefighters. This deity is widely popular with Japanese Buddhists and Shinto adherents alike.

A stone statue of Jizo, dressed with a traditional red cap and bib, stands beside a forest path.

where Shinto and Buddhist houses of worship are interspersed throughout the former capital city. And many early Japanese Buddhist temples were built on sites like mountains that were considered particularly sacred.

At 12,388 feet (3,776 m) Mount Fuji is both the highest mountain in Japan and one of Shintoism's most sacred spots. It is also considered sacred by Japan's Buddhist sects.

Abraham, Father of Three Religions

SOMETIME IN THE EARLY second millennium BCE, a shepherd named Abram (or Abraham) was living near the city of Haran in northern Mesopotamia, when, according to the Book of Genesis, he received a direct message from God. If he left his father and moved to a strange new land he would become the father of "a great nation." Abraham was then seventy-five years old and childless.

Years earlier Abraham had moved with his father to Haran from the Sumerian city of Ur. Both Haran and Ur were cult centers for the moon god Sin, but Abraham, the scriptures relate, worshipped only one God, the nameless God who made a startling demand and an amazing promise. A man of deep faith, Abraham gathered together his possessions and moved with his wife, Sarai (Sarah), and his nephew, Lot, to Canaan.

After many years in Canaan Abraham still had no children. So at Sarah's insistence he fathered a son by Hagar, an Egyptian servant. The son's name was Ishmael. Later, at the age of 90, Sarah miraculously bore a son of her own, Isaac. When Sarah became jealous of Ishmael, she had Abraham send him away with his mother to live in the desert.

Isaac became the father of Esau and Jacob (later called Israel). Jacob fathered a daughter and twelve sons, the ancestors of the twelve tribes of Israel who were to spread the traditions of Judaism throughout the land. Ishmael married an Egyptian woman and fathered twelve sons and a daughter who married Esau. Ishmael is recognized as the ancestor of the Arab people, who brought Islam into the world.

In effect, then, three of the world's major religions view Abraham as their holy patriarch: Judaism, Christianity (which branched off from Judaism), and Islam—the Abrahamic religions. All three religions were unusual in that they insisted on the existence of only one God.

A seventeenth-century Dutch depiction of Hagar's dismissal.

HAGAR

An Egyptian servant of Sarah's, who at Sarah's urging bore a child to Abraham. Later, Sarah and Abraham cast her and the child into the desert.

ABRAHAM

Considered the patriarch of three major religions and, in a historical sense, an early monotheist. His name either means "the father/God is exalted" or "the father of many nations."

SARAH

Wife of Abraham, portrayed in the bible as skeptical of God's promises because of her long-lasting barrenness.

Sarah, shown in a sixteenth-century Flemish engraving.

UNNAMED (ISHAMEL'S WIFE)

Unknown Egyptian woman chosen by Hagar for her son.

ISHMAEL

Son of Abraham and Hagar. He is considered to be the patriarch of the Arab people and the progenitor of Islam itself. Victimized by Sarah's jealousy, he is cast into the desert with his mother after the birth of Isaac.

A seventeenth-century Russian icon of Abraham.

ISAAC

Son of Abraham and Sarah, born miraculously to his ninety-year-old mother.

REBEKAH

Wife of Isaac and great-niece of Abraham; mother of Esau and Jacob.

TWELVE SONS
ONE DAUGHTER, WHO MARRIES ESAU

ESAU

Minutes older than Jacob, his twin, Esau would have received the greater of his father's blessings, but Jacob, with Rebekah's help, tricks Isaac into bestowing this favor on Jacob instead.

JACOB

Born clasping his brother's heel, Jacob manages to supplant his brother as the favored heir. Later, he is called Israel, an identification with the nation of Israel, as Esau is identified with Edom.

SACRIFICE OF ISAAC/ISHMAEL

Both Genesis and the Qur'an tell how God demands that Abraham offer his precious son as a human sacrifice but at the last moment sends an angel to substitute an animal. In the Hebrew account the son is Isaac, but in the Qur'an he remains unnamed, though some Muslims believe that the endangered son was not Isaac, but Ishmael, Abraham's firstborn son and their own ancestor. Whichever son was intended, the story signals God's disapproval of the human sacrifices that were common in Abraham's day.

A seventeenth-century Dutch painting depicts Abraham as he prepares to sacrifice his son Isaac.

TWELVE SONS

Ancestors of the twelve tribes of Israel (Judaism).

Later Christianity branches off from Judaism.

A nineteenth-century British painting of the birth of Jacob and Esau.

> "I will indeed bless you, and I will multiply
> your descendants as the stars of heaven and as
> the sand which is on the seashore. And your
> descendants shall possess the gate of their enemies."
> —Book of Genesis

The Three Religious Traditions

In addition to their staunch monotheism, Judaism, Christianity, and Islam share other beliefs. All three believe in prophets—men and women who speak for God. Hebrew scripture includes many prophets, including Abraham, Moses, and Isaiah, who made a covenant (contract) with God and urged his people to fulfill their part of it. Isaiah also predicted the coming of a Messiah who would bring God's promises of peace and justice to full completion. Christians consider the Hebrew scriptures as the early chapters in salvation history and see Jesus as both a prophet in his own right and the fulfillment of the Hebrew prophecies—he is the Messiah who announced the beginning of the reign of God, instituting a future era of everlasting peace. Islam sees itself as correcting Hebrew and Christian scripture and as building on it and completing it. It holds that Adam, Noah, Moses, Isaiah, and Jesus were all prophets, but Muhammad is the last prophet who gave us God's final revelation as found in the Qur'an.

All three traditions believe in a day of judgment, when God will punish the wicked and reward the good. In Judaism it is frequently referred to as the Day of the Lord, when a great king or leader, a Messiah, will take charge and make all things right. Both Christians and Muslims believe that God will return at the end of time to judge us all, though the specifics of that return differ.

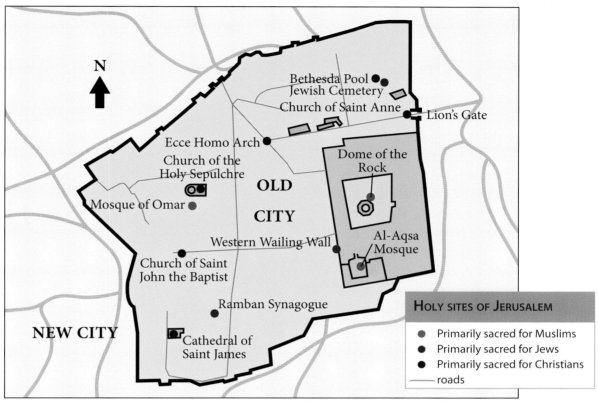

By virtue of its central importance to three of the world's major religions, Jerusalem's old city may be counted among the holiest places on Earth. Christian, Jewish, and Muslim holy places crowd together in barely a third of a square mile (0.9 sq km), a proximity both unavoidable and often contentious.

In the Beginning

The Hebrew book of Genesis relates that one God created the universe and all it contains and how the first humans, Adam and Eve, disobeyed God, bringing death into the world as a consequence. Another major passage tells how only Noah and his family survived a great flood by riding it out in a large boat, or ark, along with every species of animal. Following the flood story Genesis inserts a long genealogy (the Table of Nations) that traces the lineage of Noah down to Abraham and shows the origins of all the nations known to exist in Abraham's time. Christians later adopted the Hebrew scriptures as a whole, and Muslims incorporated much material from Genesis into their sacred Qur'an.

A depiction of the biblical flood, survived only by Noah, his family, and the animals that he saved by God's command, from the *Vienna Genesis*, an early-sixth-century illuminated manuscript. All three Abrahamic religions hold Noah sacred.

Many of the stories in Genesis resemble those of other religions of western Asia, but in place of multiple gods and goddesses, who were often feuding, Genesis focuses on one God, who creates all and rules over all. Genesis was written to convince its readers that all creation came from a single God, rather than a large pantheon. At the time, monotheism was unknown, and even Abraham probably believed in the existence of many gods, but chose to worship only one. In time, however, Abraham's descendants would come to believe that their God was the only God who existed, initiating true monotheism. Christians and Muslims embraced this strict monotheistic belief.

Medieval cartography in Europe relied heavily on Christian and Jewish traditions. A common map form, the T-and-O rendering depicts the oceans as a "T." Each continent is the domain of one of Noah's sons: Shem (Sem) in Asia, Ham (Cham) in Africa, and Joseph (Iafeth) in Europe.

Judaism in Palestine and Mesopotamia

EVEN AFTER THE DESTRUCTION of Jerusalem in 70 CE, Jews had continued to live in Palestine, where they established centers of religious studies. By the sixth century, scholars had compiled the Talmud, a collection of old traditions and discussions of Jewish law. The Talmud regulated every aspect of life and set the standard for Jewish living. Guided by the rabbis, Jews devoted themselves to study, prayer, and works of piety. They hoped for the coming of the Messiah who would reunite all Jews in a renewed kingdom.

The Palestinian Jews survived even under the Muslims, who respected them as people of the book. In the eleventh century, however, harsh living conditions and internal disputes led to widespread Jewish emigration. When Christian crusaders conquered the Holy Land in 1099, Palestinian Judaism virtually ceased to exist.

Many Jews emigrated to Mesopotamia, where a Jewish community that had existed since the end of

the exile in the sixth century BCE had compiled its own Talmud. The so-called Babylonian Talmud was disseminated by the *geonim*, the heads of the *yeshiva* (academy) who established and enforced Jewish laws and customs. Because Mesopotamia had only briefly been under the sway of the Roman Empire, the Mesopotamian Jews were not affected by Hellenistic or Roman ideas and developed independently of them.

The geonim ruled with a firm hand and so were challenged by dissident groups and self-proclaimed messiahs. Following a renewed interest in Greek philosophy in the ninth century, some Jews questioned basic Jewish beliefs about the creation and revelation. They were opposed by the geonim but made an impact nevertheless. In time, though, the Babylonian Talmud came to be preferred over the Palestinian Talmud, and so the regulations set by the geonim were eventually accepted by the entire Jewish world.

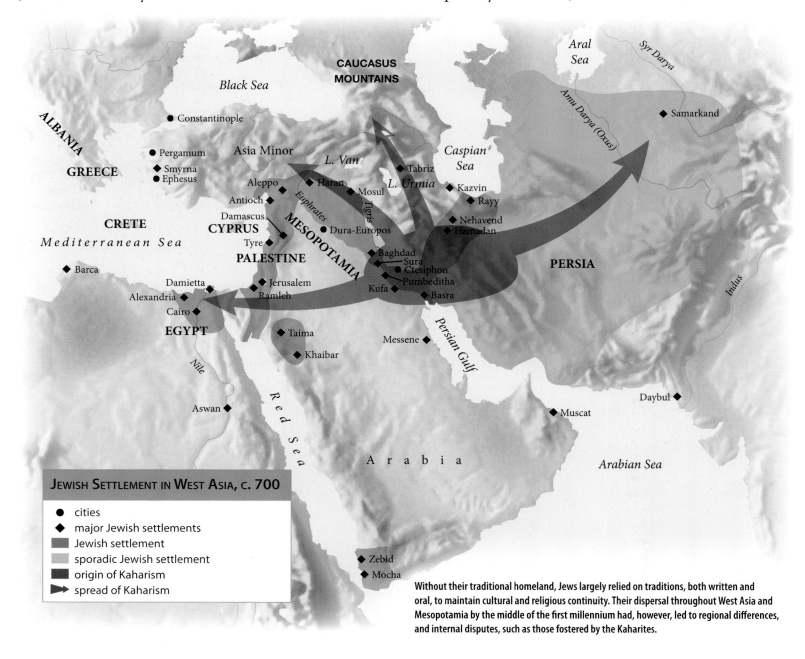

JEWISH SETTLEMENT IN WEST ASIA, C. 700

- ● cities
- ◆ major Jewish settlements
- Jewish settlement
- sporadic Jewish settlement
- origin of Kaharism
- ➤ spread of Kaharism

Without their traditional homeland, Jews largely relied on traditions, both written and oral, to maintain cultural and religious continuity. Their dispersal throughout West Asia and Mesopotamia by the middle of the first millennium had, however, led to regional differences, and internal disputes, such as those fostered by the Kaharites.

The Kaharites

Chief among the critics of the geonim were the Kaharites, who in the 760s advocated a threefold program: (1) to return to Palestine to hasten the coming of the Messiah, (2) to reject rabbinic law as human fabrication, and (3) to reexamine scripture to retrieve God's authentic law. The Kaharites also disagreed with the geonim on the date for Passover. The sect quickly spread throughout the Jewish world.

In response to the Kaharites' demand for scriptural scrutiny, over the next few centuries a group of non-Kaharite scholars, the Masoretes, developed a system for indicating vowel sounds in Hebrew texts. Because the Hebrew alphabet consists of twenty-two consonants but no vowels, the biblical texts were written without any indication of the vowel sounds, leaving room for misreading a text by supplying the wrong vowels. The Masoretes painstakingly produced manuscripts of the Hebrew scriptures, adding symbols of their own design to indicate vowel sounds. The Masoretic text, which was completed in the tenth century, continues to be the standard text for the Hebrew Bible.

False Messiahs

With no country of their own, the Jews anxiously awaited the expected Messiah, who would reestablish them as a nation ruled by peace and justice. Various false messiahs rose and fell. In eighth-century Persia Abbu 'Issa al-Isfahani founded a Jewish sect (the first under Islam) and claimed to be the last of five messengers from God after Abraham, Moses, Jesus, and Muhammad. He led a rebellion against the Abbasid rulers and was

Jewish Sabbath and Feasts

Jews have always celebrated Saturday as the Sabbath, a day of rest in honor of God, who is described in the book of Genesis as resting on the seventh day after six days of creating the universe. In addition there are two high holy days: Rosh Hashanah inaugurates the new year, and Yom Kippur is a day of atonement on which all Jews examine their lives and resolve to live better. Some other feasts originally related to agriculture but eventually took on new meanings. Passover marks the start of the agricultural year and celebrates the Jews' emancipation from slavery in Egypt. Pentecost is a harvest festival that also offers thanks to God for the Ten Commandments. The Feast of Tabernacles (or Booths) closes the agricultural year and commemorates the long years the Jews lived in the desert during the Exodus.

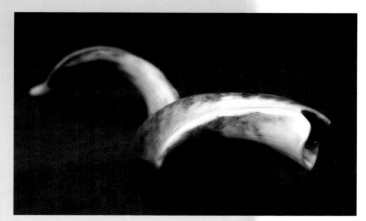

The shofar is a musical instrument, typically made from a ram's horn, used for millennia in Jewish rituals. Once used to announce the Sabbath, today it is most often sounded on Rosh Hashanah.

Retracing the steps of many of their ancestors, some of whom, like Abraham, occupied a place in their sacred text, many Jews of the first few centuries CE would have followed the Euphrates River as it made its long journey through Mesopotamia.

The world's oldest known synagogue, from c. 244 CE, still partially stands at Dura Europos and crowds together with other ancient temples, including a temple to Adonis (visible in the foreground), a Christian church, and a Mithraeum.

killed in battle. In the twelfth century David Alroy, a supposed descendant of King David, sent dispatches from Kurdistan to Baghdad inciting Jews to prepare for a miraculous return to Israel. Many waited on their rooftops for this messiah's arrival, but he never appeared. Finally, in 1648, Shabbetai Tzevi, a Jewish mystic from Smyrna, proclaimed himself Messiah. He traveled throughout Egypt and west Asia, attracting unruly mobs of enthusiasts, many of whom fell into financial ruin by selling their homes to follow him to Israel. After being imprisoned in Constantinople, he converted to Islam in order to save his life and was later banished to Albania, where he died in obscurity in 1676. Among many Jews, messianic hopes eventually settled into faith in an ultimately redeemed world of peace and justice, as opposed to a personal Messiah.

JUDAISM
Judaism in Medieval Spain

THE HISTORY OF JEWS IN MEDIEVAL SPAIN is one of extremes, including both full acceptance and total rejection. In 613 the Visigothic rulers of Spain made Jews choose between conversion to Christianity or exile, instituted surveillance of the converts, and prohibited the celebration of Jewish feasts. In 633, at the Fourth Council of Toledo, the Christian church condemned the practice of enforced baptism but allowed an already baptized child to be taken from its still-Jewish parents to prevent the child's reverting to Judaism.

In 711 Muslims invaded Spain and everything changed. Jews were free to practice their religion, engage in commerce, and travel freely. Many Jews held high positions, including army commander and court physician, and Jewish poets and philosophers thrived. In the Emirate of Córdoba, Jewish culture enjoyed a golden age under Caliph 'Abd ar-Rahman III (912–961), and Jews continued to play a prominent role in society, learning, and commerce until 1391.

The reconquest of Spain by Christians began in 1085, when Alfonso VI of Castile took Toledo; it continued for four centuries. To help them hold their ground, the Muslims of Spain joined with Muslims from northern Africa, who revoked all Jewish privileges. Muslims destroyed the Jewish community in Granada in 1090 and massacred Jews in Toledo and Burgos in 1109, prompting Jews to flee to northern Spain. Matters became worse in 1391, when Christians initiated anti-Jewish riots in all parts of Spain. These riots spelled the end for centuries of any kind of peaceful cohabitation of Jews, Christians, and Muslims in Spain. Christians resumed forced conversions and, in 1481, set up the Inquisition. In 1492 King Ferdinand and Queen Isabella completed the reconquest of Spain by capturing Granada and issued a proclamation expelling all Jews from their lands.

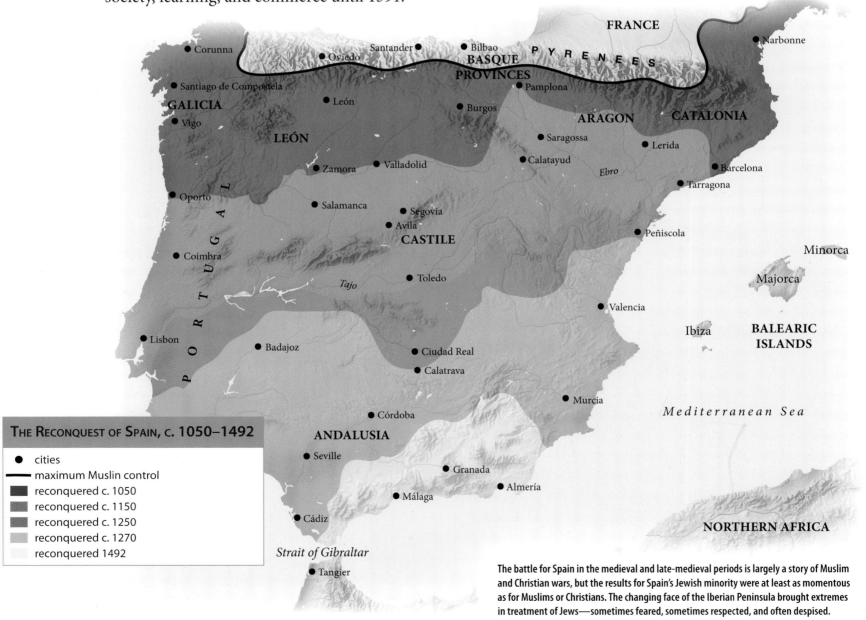

THE RECONQUEST OF SPAIN, C. 1050–1492

- ● cities
- ▬ maximum Muslin control
- reconquered c. 1050
- reconquered c. 1150
- reconquered c. 1250
- reconquered c. 1270
- reconquered 1492

The battle for Spain in the medieval and late-medieval periods is largely a story of Muslim and Christian wars, but the results for Spain's Jewish minority were at least as momentous as for Muslims or Christians. The changing face of the Iberian Peninsula brought extremes in treatment of Jews—sometimes feared, sometimes respected, and often despised.

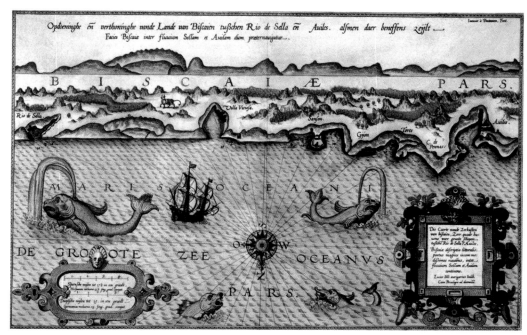
This Dutch map dates to 1586 and shows a portion of the Spanish Atlantic coast.

In our day when scholars are few and scholarship rare, I, Moses, the son of Maimon the Spaniard, am compiling a book on the entire Jewish law without discussions or debates, wherein all the laws are clearly explained.
—MOSES MAIMONIDES, MISHNAH TORAH

first fifty years of the Inquisition. In later years the Inquisition pursued other forms of heresy and other breaches of church law. It lasted for a total of 350 years.

FORCED CONVERSION

The Christians based their persecutions of Jews on religion, enacting measures that would convert Jews to the "true" faith. They pressured and even threatened Jews to convert, but also promised immediate acceptance into the Christian fold after baptism. In fact, many conversos, as converted Jews were called, rose to high political or ecclesiastical positions.

Some conversos were zealous in their new faith, but others made an outward show of being Christian while secretly holding on to their old faith. These so-called marranos (from the Spanish for "swine") aroused envy and suspicion in lifelong Christians, who began to characterize all conversos as wealthy, socially prominent, and treacherous. In time conversos were regularly attacked, and general disorder resulted. When the situation worsened, Pope Sixtus IV gave Ferdinand and Isabella the power to appoint inquisitors in Castile to deal with the problem.

THE SPANISH INQUISITION

The idea behind the Spanish Inquisition was that deviance from the Christian faith constituted a threat to political and religious unity and must be rooted out. Starting in 1478, inquisitors examined thousands of conversos for any signs of their reverting to Judaism. Tómas de Torquemada, a Spanish Dominican priest, was appointed inquisitor general, and he pursued his work with grim perseverance.

Torquemada encouraged the people to denounce marranos or anyone else not conforming to Christian practice, and he brought many suspects to trial, confiscating their belongings and often torturing them to elicit confessions. Those found guilty were turned over to the secular authorities and publicly burned at the stake. The inquisitors deliberately incited fear, holding that they were not trying to save the souls of the heretics but to keep others from falling into heresy. Thousands of conversos were executed in the

MAIMONIDES

One of the greatest figures in medieval Judaism was the physician and theologian Moses ben Maimon, or Maimonides (1138–1204). In about 1160 Maimonides and his family left their home in Córdoba to avoid the anti-Jewish atmosphere of the reconquest. Settling in Cairo, Egypt, Maimonides became court physician and adviser to the visir Al Fadir. As leader of a thriving Jewish intellectual community, Maimonides wrote several books. His *Mishnah Torah,* which interpreted Jewish law without including conflicting rabbinic arguments, as was traditional, became a classic and a major source for later law codes. In *The Guide for the Perplexed,* Maimonides addressed Jews who followed both philosophy and the Torah, attempting to reconcile the apparent contradictions between the two. Highly influenced by Aristotelian philosophy, Maimonides opposed the literal interpretations of some passages in favor of a more figurative and philosophical approach. The book caused a furor among Jews who accepted the Torah literally, but eventually it dominated the development of Jewish thought, and in time Maimonides himself was seen as a model of pure and authoritative Judaism.

Somewhat controversial in his own time, Maimonides is today regarded as the foremost Jewish scholar of the Middle Ages.

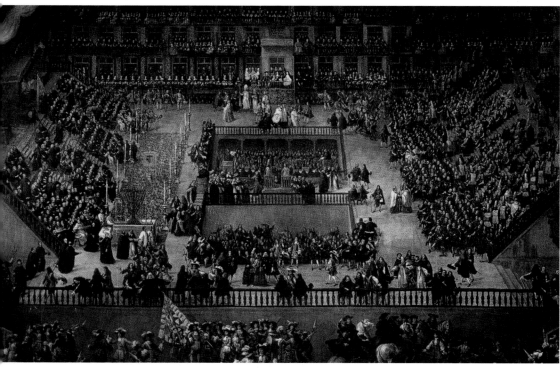
An auto da fé in Madrid, 1680, painted by Francisco Ricci. Sentencing of religious criminals—whose numbers counted Jews, condemned witches, and Protestant Christians—and the imposition of punishments were public and often drew enormous crowds.

Judaism in Medieval Europe

IN THE MIDDLE AGES Jews spread across Europe from Portugal to Russia. The earliest settlers were Jewish merchants who went to southern France, assured of protection by the Frankish kings who wished to encourage and control trade. In the tenth century, after the merchants had established a prosperous Jewish middle class in France, large families moved there as well, often led by rabbinical scholars. They also settled in Italy and the Rhine Valley, and later in England, Switzerland, and the Netherlands. In the eleventh century these communities grew and, led by the rabbis, developed disciplinary measures to prevent feuds between the various families.

Later known as the Ashkenazim, the Jews in central Europe followed customs different from those of the Jews of Spain, Portugal, and the Arab countries, who came to be known as Sephardim. (*Ashkenaz* and *Sepharad* are names from the Hebrew scriptures that were associated with Germany and Spain in ancient times.) The major differences between the two Jewish groups stemmed from their origins. The Sephardim traced their origins to Mesopotamia and northern Africa, lived according to the Babylonian Talmud, and—under the influence of Islamic culture—often wrote both religious and scientific works in Arabic. The Ashkenazim traced their heritage to Palestine, lived according to the Palestinian Talmud, and wrote almost exclusively in Hebrew—and only on religious topics.

The Ashkenazi rabbis held regional synods to enact laws on matters not covered by the Talmud. Among the measures they passed were prohibitions against polygamy and arbitrary divorce and severe economic penalties for abandoning wives. They also adopted severe disciplinary measures for Jews who informed against fellow Jews to the Christian authorities, for European Jews were constantly threatened by their non-Jewish neighbors and frequently subject to persecution. Many were expelled from the countries of their residence.

Ashkenazi and Sephardic Jews followed several different customs and settled in different areas of Europe, but both suffered dreadful treatment under harsh laws and popular fears. Generally less mistreated in Muslim countries, Jews in Europe were blamed (and punished) for natural catastrophes, various illnesses, infant mortality, and Christian impoverishment.

JEWISH SETTLEMENT IN EUROPE TO C. 1300

- ● cities
- ◇ major massacres of Jews
- ▨ Ashkenazi settlement
- ▨ Sephardic settlement

All souls must undergo transmigration and the souls of men revolve like a stone which is thrown from a sling, so many turns before the final release. . . . Only those who have not completed their perfection must suffer the wheel of rebirth by being reborn into another human body.

—THE ZOHAR

THE KABBALAH

In the early thirteenth century a mystical movement called the Kabbalah ("tradition") gained popularity among the Ashkenazi Jews as they sought ways to cope with the problems of being dispersed around the world. The main text for the movement was the *Zohar*, a compilation of theosophical theology, mystical psychology, anthropology, myth, and poetry. According to kabbalistic philosophy, God is unknowable except as he manifests himself through creation and scripture in ten sefirot, or aspects, including wisdom, love, power, and eternity. Meditating on the sefirot and performing good works creates a mystical ladder of ascent that the believer can climb to partake in the life of the Godhead. In an age when the lives of Jews were constantly being threatened, the Kabbalah offered a degree of comfort, and so the movement quickly spread from France to northern Spain. Today there is a renewed interest in the Kabbalah among Jews and Gentiles alike.

Medieval Christian art, such as this stained glass example from twelfth-century Germany, often depicted Old Testament characters, such as Daniel, in contemporary Jewish dress—in particular, the distinctive funnel-shaped cap that was commonly used to distinguish Jews from Christians.

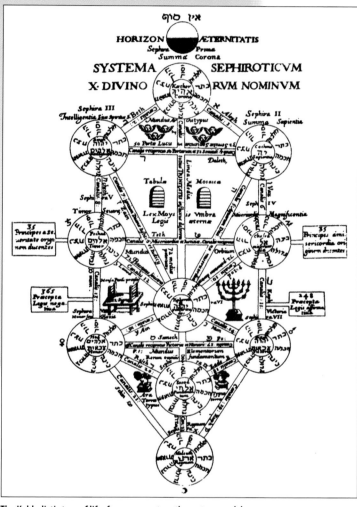

The Kabbalistic tree of life, from a seventeenth-century work by Athanasius Kircher, a Jesuit priest much fascinated by ancient Egypt and its presumed relationship to Christian theology and mysticism.

PERSECUTIONS AND EXPULSIONS

Separated from their Christian neighbors by religious practices, customs, and dress (occasionally imposed by Christian authorities) Jews were often viewed with suspicion and even regarded as Christ killers because the Gospels describe Jesus's crucifixion as prompted by a few Jewish authorities. During the Crusades (1095–1272) and in their aftermath, many Jews were massacred. Others were forbidden to own land or engage in trade. Because Christians were prohibited from charging interest on loans, Jews often became moneylenders and were then accused of merciless extortion. Jews were expelled from England in 1290 and from France in 1306.

When the black death broke out in 1348, the Jews were blamed, and in Provence, the number of Jews killed in a single massacre rivaled the number of deaths from the plague that year. In Chillon, France, some Jews were coerced into "confessing" that they had poisoned wells to start the plague and destroy Christianity. Even though Pope Clement VI denounced such accusations, persecutions grew worse, resulting in executions and collective imprisonments. In later years many

nations expelled the Jews or consigned them to ghettos. Great numbers of Jews moved eastward to Austria, Prussia, Hungary, Russia, and especially Poland, where some 150,000 Jews were living by 1648.

Rashi's commentary on the Torah remains influential today.

SEEKING SOLACE

To retreat from the horrors that were being committed against them, some Jews turned to mysticism, embracing asceticism, penitence, and martyrdom, or sought solace in the mystical movement of the Kabbalah. Others looked for spiritual guidance in liturgical poetry, the lives of scholars and saints, and Hebrew biblical tales as interpreted by the rabbis. The most popular and insightful of these rabbis was the French scholar Solomon ben Isaac (c. 1040–1105), known as Rashi—an acronym of his full name in Hebrew. His interpretations of the Hebrew scriptures gave precise definitions of obscure terms and accessible meanings to biblical stories, rather than allegorical readings. His commentaries were remarkably clear. Rashi also wrote a straightforward commentary on the Babylonian Talmud, which is unmatched in any period for its compact thoroughness and lucidity.

CHRISTIANITY

Christianity Spreads through Europe

WHEN CONSTANTINE BUILT his new capital, Constantinople, or the New Rome, some 800 miles to the east of the old Rome, he left the old city to immigrants from northern Europe, the "barbarians" who were already entering in large numbers. By the mid-sixth century, Rome was in a shambles. Its population was reduced to fewer than 50,000, and poverty was rampant. In 568 Germanic warriors known as the Lombards, or Longbeards, invaded Italy and soon controlled much of the peninsula. The city of Rome was left to the popes, who until then had enjoyed just a bit more authority over the Christian church than did the patriarchs of Antioch and Alexandria. But with the new imperial capital at Constantinople, that New Rome was threatening the power long wielded by the old Rome.

The greatest pope of the era was Gregory I, who provided food for the poor, concluded a peace settlement with the Lombards, and instituted vast reforms in the church itself. Gregory also sent missionaries to Britain in hopes of bringing the English into the church. Although Christianity had found its way into Britain in the second century, Germanic tribes—Angles,

The Book of Kells, probably produced on Iona in the late eighth century, is a masterpiece of the Irish illuminated manuscript tradition.

Saxons, and Jutes—had invaded Britain in the mid-fifth to early sixth centuries and imposed worship of their Norse gods on the populace, all but obliterating Christianity. Gregory's missionaries, led by a monk named Augustine, converted King Aethelbert of Kent and thousands of others to Christianity and set up a church at Canterbury, which remains the center of the English church today.

Meanwhile, Christianity was thriving in Ireland, and Irish monks went as missionaries to Scotland, northern England, and the European continent. Other monks followed suit, and soon Christianity had spread throughout Europe, and even to the Arctic and sub-arctic islands of Iceland and Greenland.

Formally crowned on Christmas Day, 1000, Stephen I of Hungary was canonized in 1083 and is today recognized as Hungary's patron saint.

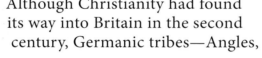

IRISH MONKS

From the fifth to the eighth century, when Germanic tribes were overrunning Europe, burning books, and otherwise destroying the culture of those they conquered, Ireland remained safely isolated on its far western island. Christianity thrived there, and the many monasteries served as the only schools. Some of the monks copied Christian works—many that might otherwise have been lost—into highly ornamented manuscripts, which are masterpieces of art.

A number of Irish monks traveled to distant lands to build new monasteries and convert the local people to Christianity. In 563 the Irish monk Columba and twelve others sailed a rickety wicker-covered boat to Scotland, where they established a monastery at Iona that would become a leading center of learning. Aidan established an equally famous monastery at Lindisfarne in northeastern England, and Columbanus brought Christianity to France and through his example respiritualized areas where Christianity was at a low ebb. Willibrord, a monk from Northumbria, traveled to Utrecht and became apostle to the Frisians, and then to Denmark. Finally, Boniface, another Briton, converted the Germans.

OTHER CONVERSIONS

In eastern Europe two Greek monks, Cyril and Methodius, went to Moravia (then overlapping what are now parts Slovakia and the Czech Republic) on the request of the prince. The brothers not only converted and ministered to the people there, but also developed an alphabet for the Slavonic language, which had none. They translated the Bible into Slavonic—though Cyril died before the translation was finished. Years later, when Slavonic was banned from use in the churches, Methodius and his followers scattered throughout eastern Europe, bringing Christianity and the Slavonic Bible to much of the Balkans and to Russia.

Christianity was not always spread by missionaries. In 997 Stephen, the first king of Hungary, who had been baptized a Christian in 985, set out to Christianize his nation after ascending the throne. Although his work was partially undone by his pagan successors, Christianity continued to thrive in Hungary. And in 1000 the farmers of Iceland voted at their annual assembly at Thingvellir to adopt a single "Christian law" rather than face the disruptive consequences of prolonged divisions between pagan and Christian families.

GREGORY THE GREAT

The pope who invigorated the Roman papacy, Gregory was the son of a senator and himself a city prefect but donated all his riches to the poor and lived as a poor monk. Soon, however, because of his brilliance, he was called to serve in the church hierarchy, and in 590, much to his consternation, he was elected pope.

As pope, Gregory put the city of Rome on its feet, spending vast amounts of money on charity and making changes that affected even civil administration and military defense. He had such a large hand in reforming church music that the resulting singing style came to be known as Gregorian chant, even though it went through further changes after his time. In his strained relations with the east, Gregory upheld the supremacy of Rome and refused the title of patriarch used by the head of the church in Constantinople. In all he did Gregory acted with firmness tempered with gentleness. Since his death in 604 he has been known as Gregory the Great.

Gregory the Great inaugurated the medieval age of papal authority, reestablishing Rome as a great secular power and cementing its religious eminence.

Christianity spread through Europe not as a unified force but as a patchwork quilt, with regional adaptations, chronological hiatuses, and occasional intrachurch disputes. Some missionaries reintroduced Christianity to areas that had reverted, and many countries were Christian in name but not in reality.

CHRISTIANITY IN EUROPE, c. 500–c. 1000

- ● Christian center
- ◆ Archbishopric

Missionaries:
- Columba
- Columbanus
- Willibrord
- Boniface
- Cyril and Methodius
- predominantly Christian, c. 1000

FINLAND
Viborg
NORWAY
SCOTLAND
Iona
Uppsala
Stockholm
ESTONIA
Novgorod
North Sea
SWEDEN
LIVONIA
Bangor
Whithorn
Lindisfarne
Lough Corib
Armagh
Monkwearmouth/Jarrow
Växjö
Baltic Sea
LITHUANIA
Smolensk
Clonard
Candida Casa
Whitby
Roskilde
Lund
IRELAND
Ripon
York
Königsberg
Vilnius
WALES
Burgh Castle
Dokkum
Hamburg
Lübeck
Schwerin
POMERANIA
PRUSSIA
RUSSIA
ENGLAND
Glastonbury
Rochester
Canterbury
Utrecht
Bremen
Ratzeburg
Magdeburg
Gniezno
Thorn
Dobrzyń
ATLANTIC OCEAN
Ghent
HESSE
THURINGIA
POLAND
Rouen
Corbie
Maastricht
Amöneburg
Geismar
Kiev
Lagny-sur-Marne
Mainz
Fulda
SAXONY
Rheims
BOHEMIA
MORAVIA
Tours
Sens
Annegray
Luxeuil
Reichenau
Kremsmünster
Lyons
Salzburg
Bourges
St. Gall
Chiemsee
BAVARIA
Gran
HUNGARY
BURGUNDY
CARINTHIA
Vienne
Aquileia
Pécs
FRANCE
Venice
Toulouse
Bobbio
Sirmium
Narbonne
Arles
Ravenna
CROATIA
Black Sea
PORTUGAL
SPAIN
Tarragona
Corsica
ITALY
SERBIA
Lisbon
Toledo
Rome
BULGARIA
Constantinople
Balearic Islands
Sardinia
Cagliari
Salonica
Sicily
GREECE
AFRICA
Mediterranean Sea

CHRISTIANITY
Medieval Monasticism

THE MISSIONARY MONKS who spread Christianity throughout Europe built monasteries in which to teach the people they converted. Monasticism thrived in Europe, though it took various forms. But in the early sixth century a man emerged whose influence would change and unify the nature of Western monasticism—Benedict of Nursia.

An Italian educated in Rome, Benedict retired from the outside world in about 500 CE to live as a hermit in a cave near Subiaco, to the east of Rome. When his lifestyle attracted followers, Benedict established monasteries for them. Then in about 529 he established a monastery at Monte Cassino, between Rome and Naples, where he remained the rest of his life.

Benedictine monks live in community, taking vows of poverty, chastity, and obedience to their abbot, or elected leader. They pray together and engage in every type of labor, from farming to washing dishes to copying and illuminating manuscripts—all offered as a prayer to God. Separate monasteries (convents) were established for women.

Benedict wrote a rule—or set of regulations—for all his monasteries. Addressing the monks in a paternalistic style, the rule tells them what they should and should not do. While many European monasteries used Benedict's rule, others created their own. In time, however, the Benedictine rule gained favor, and in the ninth century when Charlemagne called for all monasteries to have a uniform rule, Benedict's was chosen. By the eleventh century several thousand monasteries were following it with some variations.

In 909 the monastery at Cluny, France, elaborated on the communal prayer life of the monks, while neglecting manual labor. More than 1,000 monasteries followed Cluny's example. In 1098 monks at Cîteaux, France, responded by returning to a strict adherence to the rule and simplifying communal prayer. Over time further reforms followed and more monastic orders were formed.

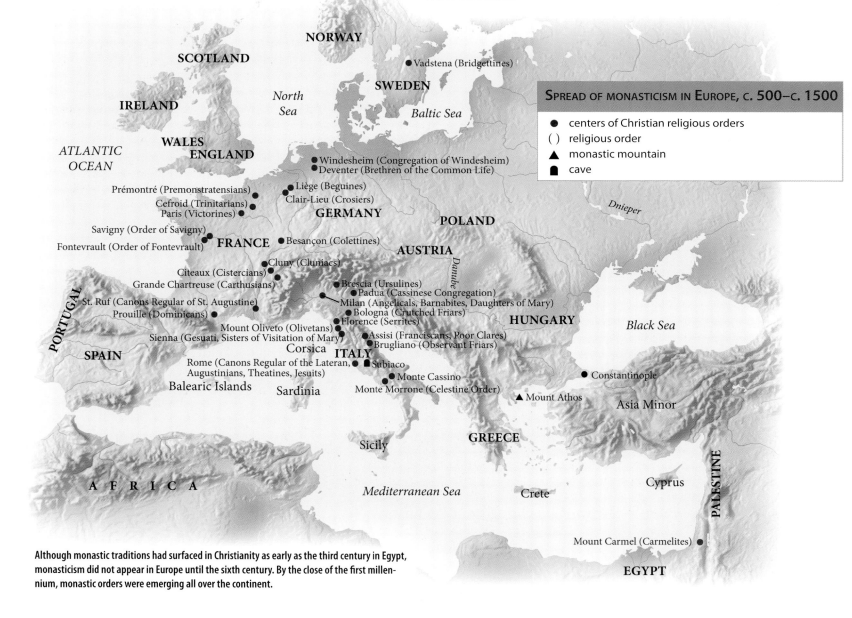

SPREAD OF MONASTICISM IN EUROPE, C. 500–C. 1500

- ● centers of Christian religious orders
- ( ) religious order
- ▲ monastic mountain
- ⬠ cave

Although monastic traditions had surfaced in Christianity as early as the third century in Egypt, monasticism did not appear in Europe until the sixth century. By the close of the first millennium, monastic orders were emerging all over the continent.

If you notice something good in yourself, give credit to God, not to yourself, but be certain that the evil you commit is always your own and yours to acknowledge.
—FROM *THE RULE OF SAINT BENEDICT*

OFFICE OF THE HOURS

Under the Benedictine rule the lives of the monks are centered on the office of the hours, or divine office, the communal prayer that is sung, chanted, and recited by the monks at various fixed times throughout the day and night. There were eight canonical hours in all: matins and lauds (long before dawn), prime (early morning), tierce (midmorning), sext (noon), none (midafternoon), vespers (evening), and compline (nightfall). Varying according to the time of year and the observance of the house, each hour included psalms, silent prayer, a hymn, and readings from the Bible or the church fathers. At the appropriate time the monks would stop their work or rise from sleep and gather in the chapel to pray. In addition, between lauds and prime the monks were encouraged to do spiritual reading on their own. Work, private prayer, and mealtimes were sandwiched between the daytime hours. Benedict himself referred to the office of the hours as the *opus Dei*, or "work of God."

The practice of rigorously following the canonical hours made its way into the laity with the book of hours, various forms of which became popular among the wealthy in the thirteenth to fifteenth centuries. These books, often lavishly illustrated, provided specific prayers to be intoned at the various canonical hours.

Benedictine monks adopted a uniform black robe, shown here in a fifteenth-century Italian fresco; other monastic orders chose different colors of similar austerity, such as gray (later brown) for the Franciscans or white for the Cistercians and Carmelites.

ALTERNATIVE TRADITIONS

Benedictine monasticism was a rural lifestyle. For more urbanized societies, a new form of religious life evolved with the mendicant orders, so called because their members lived in strict poverty and begged for sustenance. Although the mendicants lived in community, they also went out into the world, teaching, preaching, and tending to the poor and disabled. In 1209 the Order of Friars Minor was established by the charismatic Francis of Assisi, who strove in every way to be like Christ. In 1216 Dominic de Guzmán, a Spanish cleric, founded the Order of Preachers to fight heresy. Both Dominic and Francis also founded orders for women, and for men and women who lived devout lives while remaining with their families. Other early mendicant orders included the Augustinians and Carmelites.

In 1540 a former Basque soldier, Ignatius of Loyola, founded still another type of religious order, the Society of Jesus. The Jesuits, as they are known, devote themselves to teaching, spiritual direction, and spreading Christianity, and early missionaries went to the Orient and the Americas. Most later religious orders were based on the Jesuit pattern, which was characterized by private rather than communal prayer, authoritative leadership, inconspicuous clothing, and strict obedience to the pope.

EASTERN MONASTICISM

Monasticism flourished in the Eastern church, also, first in Greece and around Constantinople, and then—by the eleventh century—in Russia. Eastern monasteries do not divide into individual religious orders, like those in the West, nor do they follow a single rule. In some monasteries the monks are free to follow their own prayerful, ascetic way of life. Although monks in other monasteries do follow a strict common life, it is a lifestyle tailored for that one particular community. In 961 Athanasius the Athonite founded a monastery at Mount Athos on a peninsula in Macedonia. In time additional monasteries were founded on the peninsula, which was isolated from the world by forests and the Aegean Sea. To this day Mount Athos is the heart of Eastern monasticism.

Today, Mount Athos is the site of twenty monasteries and their dependencies. Pictured here is Gregoriou monastery, founded in the second half of the fourteenth century.

CHRISTIANITY

The Holy Roman Empire and the Papacy

WHEN PEPIN THE SHORT, son of Charles Martel, became king of the Franks in 751 he supplanted the old Merovingian regime and started a new dynasty—the Carolingians. Pepin went to the aid of Pope Stephen II by fighting the Lombards and handing over the exarchate of Ravenna to the pope to rule, thus creating the Papal States, which would grow and endure until 1870. In 800 Pope Leo XIII crowned Pepin's son Charlemagne emperor of the Romans in an attempt to recreate a central authority in Rome, which had lost much of its authority to Constantinople. Charlemagne vastly expanded his domain, known as the Holy Roman Empire, while offering the pope support and protection.

In 843 the empire was divided, and in the tenth century a smaller Holy Roman Empire emerged under the Saxon ruler Otto I. The close relationship between the emperors and popes ended, with both sides claiming the authority to appoint bishops and depose kings. In 963 Otto had Pope John XII deposed for conspiring against him and forced the election of Pope Leo VIII. In 1059 Pope Nicholas II decreed that popes must be elected by the cardinals (the church's top bishops), without interference from lay rulers. This led to the election of the antipope Honorius II in opposition to the canonically elected Alexander II. The struggle between rulers and popes intensified, and in 1076 Pope Gregory VII excommunicated and deposed the emperor Henry IV and forced him to perform public penance.

In the twelfth century the conflict between papal and civil authority continued unabated. With the accession of Innocent III in 1198, the papacy reached a pinnacle of power, and England, Bulgaria, and Portugal all became papal fiefs.

Despite the best efforts of Charlemagne and his successors, Europe continued to fracture and reform during the Middle Ages, impossibly pressured by both politics and religion—which became nearly completely entangled as popes and kings competed for lands and souls.

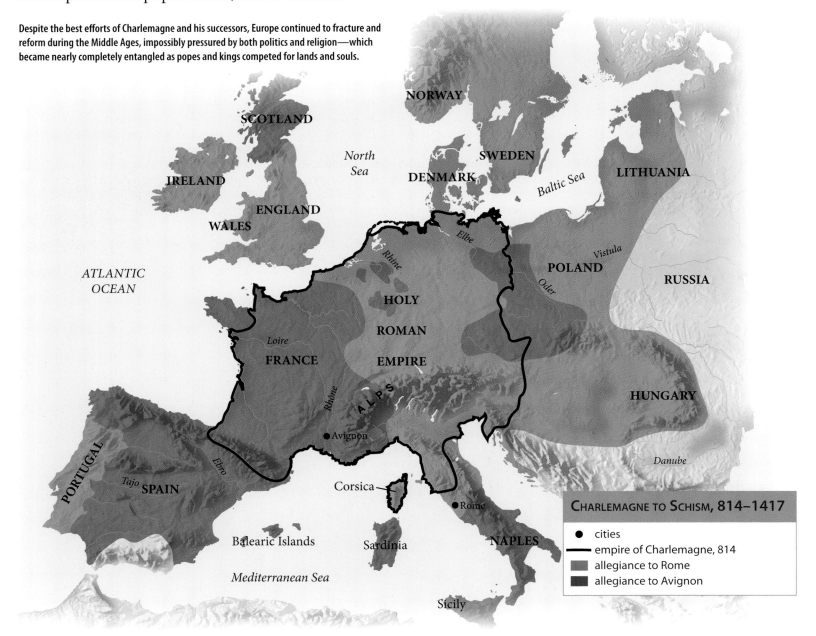

CHARLEMAGNE TO SCHISM, 814–1417

- ● cities
- ── empire of Charlemagne, 814
- allegiance to Rome
- allegiance to Avignon

An 1831 French map of Europe titled "A Map of Europe under Charlemagne, c. 800." Charlemagne's empire is outlined in red.

THE HOHENSTAUFENS AND THE PAPACY

The Hohenstaufen dynasty, which ruled the Holy Roman Empire from 1138 to 1208 and from 1212 to 1254, was constantly in conflict with the papacy as it vied for power. When Frederick I Barbarossa gained strength in Italy, Pope Alexander III used the Lombard League, an alliance of Italian cities, to fight him, forcing Frederick to grant the Lombards communal liberties and jurisdiction. Frederick II, Barbarossa's grandson, however, continued to pursue his dynasty's imperial policies against the papacy, even holding bishops prisoner to further his aims. In 1245 Pope Innocent IV called a church council in Lyon at which Frederick was deposed on charges of perjury, sacrilege, and suspicion of heresy. When Frederick died five years later, his son Conrad IV tried to reclaim his father's title but was stopped by the pope and eventually retreated to Sicily, where he reigned as king, never managing to reach an understanding with the papacy.

A sixteenth-century depiction of Charlemagne.

CHARLEMAGNE'S COURT

Charlemagne supported and protected the papacy, brought church leaders into his government, and sought to advance both the physical and spiritual well-being of his people. He was also a patron of learning and the arts and imported scholars from all over Europe to promote Christian learning. Poetry thrived in his empire, a notable example being the *Song of Roland*—a romanticized version of the exploits of one of Charlemagne's best warrior knights during a campaign against the emir of Córdoba, Spain.

Charlemagne also brought the most talented scribes and artists into his empire. Among them was Alcuin, an Irish monk. Alcuin perfected a new writing style known as Carolingian minuscule, which connected the letters in words rather than using block letters—and so allowed for more rapid writing. As director of the scriptorium at Tours, Alcuin produced a revised edition of the Vulgate (Latin) Bible and oversaw the copying and illumination of many spiritual and liturgical works.

The oldest extant Roman-script Slavic-language texts, the Friesing manuscripts date perhaps to the tenth century and were written in Carolingian script.

THE AVIGNON PAPACY AND ITS AFTERMATH

Distressed by the factionalism that constantly raged in Rome, in 1309 Pope Clement V moved the papal capital to Avignon in Provence. There, under the leadership of seven French popes, the cardinals gained a stronger role in church government. Reforms of the clergy were instituted, missionaries were sent as far as China, university education was promoted, and numerous attempts were made by the popes to settle royal rivalries and to establish peace, but to no avail. This "Babylonian Captivity" of the papacy lasted until 1377.

After Gregory XI moved the papal capital back to Rome, the cardinals selected a second pope, who assumed the vacant Avignon seat. This marked the onset of the Great Schism (1378–1417). A succession of "antipopes" were elected, resulting in increased authority for ambitious cardinals, who then attempted to wield their power over the pope through church councils. In 1409 a council at Pisa deposed the two reigning popes and elected a new one, but the first two refused to acknowledge the council's authority, and so there were three popes reigning at the same time. Unity was finally achieved by the election of Martin V in 1417.

The Palace of the Popes in Avignon housed popes and antipopes from the time of its construction, 1335–1364, until 1417.

Christianity in the East

AFTER CONSTANTINE MOVED HIS CAPITAL from Rome to Constantinople, the Latin (Roman) and Greek (Orthodox) churches started drifting apart. In 532, when the emperor Justinian began building the magnificent Hagia Sophia church as a symbol of Constantinople's position as the center of the Christian world, he further alienated Rome. Then, after the bubonic plague ravaged Constantinople in the mid-sixth century, the emperor all but forgot Rome, and the Roman church began to grow stronger and more independent.

In the East, church factions came to hold different positions on the nature of Jesus. Constantinople upheld the official view of the Council of Chalcedon (451) that Jesus was a single person with two natures, human and divine. Many Christians in Alexandria, Egypt, however, held that Jesus had only a single, divine nature—and so were known as Monophysites. Christians in Antioch, Syria, generally followed the view supposedly held by the fifth-century bishop Nestorius that in Jesus there were two distinct persons.

Efforts were made to reconcile the Monophysites with the Roman church, but positions hardened, resulting in separate Armenian, Ethiopian, Coptic (Egyptian), and Syrian Orthodox churches. Meanwhile, both Nestorians and Monophysites sent missionaries eastward, reaching China in the seventh century. But Muslim invasions soon weakened the Eastern church and cut it off from the West. In time the church in Russia (founded in 988) emerged as the largest of the Orthodox churches.

Meanwhile, relations between Rome and Constantinople grew worse. Reasons given for the tension were the Orthodox churches' use of leavened bread for the Lord's Supper, instead of unleavened bread, and Rome's addition of the word *filioque* ("and the Son") to the Nicene Creed in 589, which subtly changed the meaning of a key phrase. But the true reason probably lay in the East's resentment over the growing power of the pope.

Although Christian missionaries never discovered Eden—reputed in Europe to be located in distant Asia—they nevertheless pressed into Tibet, India, and China, even as Christendom split into western and eastern halves, with Constantinople and Rome glaring at each other over an increasingly hostile Mediterranean Sea.

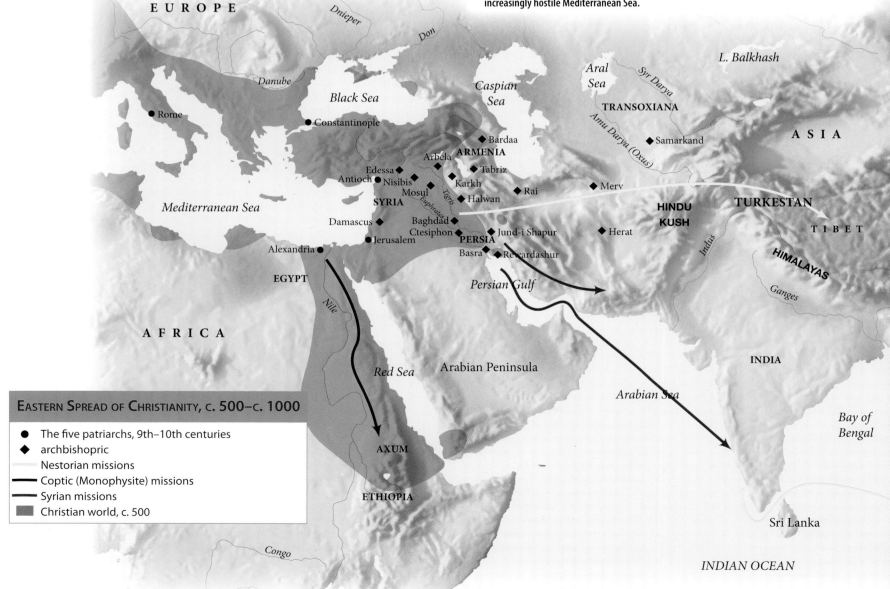

EASTERN SPREAD OF CHRISTIANITY, C. 500–C. 1000

- ● The five patriarchs, 9th–10th centuries
- ◆ archbishopric
- Nestorian missions
- Coptic (Monophysite) missions
- Syrian missions
- ▓ Christian world, c. 500

A depiction from a fourteenth-century illuminated manuscript showing the destruction of a church by iconoclasts.

THE LASTING RUPTURE

In the ninth and tenth centuries, Eastern church leaders held fast to the concept that the Christian church was ruled, more or less equally, by five "patriarchs"—the spiritual leaders of Rome, Alexandria, Antioch, Jerusalem, and Constantinople. However, Western Christians objected to the inclusion of Constantinople, holding that the city had no ties with the early church. The battle for power escalated, and in 1054 Michael Cerularius, the patriarch of Constantinople, banned Latin rites from his jurisdiction, while Pope Leo IX banned Greek rites in the West. Leo then sent delegates to Constantinople to officially refuse the title of patriarch and to demand that the Orthodox churches accept Rome's claim to be the "head and mother of the church." When the Orthodox churchmen refused to comply, the pope's legate laid a bull, or papal notice, on the altar of Hagia Sophia, excommunicating the eastern leaders. Cerularius responded by excommunicating the pope's legates. Although efforts were made at reconciliation over the next few decades, the split between the Eastern and Western churches was beyond mending.

An icon of Mary, the infant Jesus, two saints, and two angels, dating to c. 600.

THE JESUS PRAYER

Icons were not the only aids to prayer used in the East. A mystical movement known as Hesychasm ("Quiet") popularized the short Jesus Prayer, which could easily be prayed by anyone in any place. The Hesychasts advocated the continuous repetition of the prayer: "Lord Jesus Christ, Son of God, have mercy on me." They recommended reciting it with controlled breathing and eyes fixed on the place of the heart. Repetition of the Jesus Prayer was designed to bring the soul to a tranquil state of repose in communion with God. In the thirteenth century Hesychasm came to be associated with the monasteries on Mount Athos, but its roots extend back to the fourth or fifth century.

CHINA

Yangtze

PACIFIC OCEAN

THE ICONOCLASTIC CONTROVERSY

To add fuel to the fires of discontent, in the early eighth century a controversy erupted in the Byzantine church over the use of religious art, eliciting suspicion and disapproval in the West. In the Orthodox tradition it is common for people to pray before icons (images) of Jesus, his mother, and the saints. The idea is that the images offer physical help in meditating on abstract spiritual ideas and so improve the quality and depth of a person's prayers. The Monophysites, who minimized the human side of Jesus, found the icons offensive. Others claimed that icons supported the Nestorians by dividing the two natures of Jesus, only one of which could be portrayed. Icons of the saints were considered outright idols. In addition, some devout people began to believe that the icons themselves had magical powers.

In 726 the Byzantine emperor Leo III, deploring the overuse and misuse of religious art, ordered the destruction of all icons, which he characterized as idols, and persecuted anyone who resisted the destruction of their icons. Serious civil disturbances broke out across the empire, and many monks and other devout Christians were persecuted—against the objections of the popes. The "iconoclastic controversy" raged on for more than a century. It was finally settled when icons were returned to the churches by the empress Theodora in 843.

CHRISTIANITY
The Crusades

FOR CHRISTIANS, THE LAND where Jesus had lived—Bethlehem, Galilee, and Jerusalem—was the Holy Land, and pilgrims had traveled there for spiritual fulfillment since the second century. Pilgrimages continued even after the Holy Land was taken over by Arab Muslims in the seventh century, for the Muslims were generally supportive of the pilgrims. When the more warlike Seljuk Turks came into the region in the late eleventh century, however, their widespread battles blocked the roads to Jerusalem, effectively stopping pilgrimages. In the view of the Christians, their Holy Land was in the hands of "infidels" (a people unfaithful to the "one true church"). In addition, Turks were battling the Byzantine Christians, who appealed to Pope Urban II for help in 1095.

Urban responded by calling for a Crusade. Christian knights must stop fighting each other, he demanded, and fight the Turks instead. In so doing they would aid their eastern brothers in Christ, safeguard the pilgrim routes, take the Holy Land out of the hands of the Turks, and acquire new lands on which to settle and maintain a Christian enclave in the heart of Islam.

Eight major Crusades were fought between 1096 and 1291. There was also a tragic Children's Crusade in 1212, when large numbers of children as young as six years of age marched away to fight the Turks. Most never got out of Europe, but some managed to reach northern Africa, where they were sold into slavery.

In the end little was accomplished by the Crusades, though they may have spurred the reconquest of Spain (the Spanish drove the last of the Muslim conquerors from the Iberian Peninsula in 1492). In addition, the tolerance traditionally extended by Muslims toward Christians ended, due to the harsh treatment they had received at Christian hands during the Crusades. In 1453 Constantinople fell to the Turks.

Shocked into a semblance of unity by the rising tide of Islam, Europe's entanglement in wars to retake Palestine (the "Holy Land") was as politically motivated as it was religious. The First Crusade was instigated by Pope Urban II, indicative of the power of the papacy, but thereafter kings, nobles, and even children called for—and died in—repeated attempts to shake the Muslim grip on West Asia.

FIRST THROUGH FOURTH CRUSADES, 1096–1204

- ● cities
- —— First Crusade, 1096–1099
- —— Second Crusade, 1146–1148
- —— Third Crusade, 1188–1192
- —— Fourth Crusade, 1202–1204
- ····· Children's Crusade, 1212
- ┌─┐ Holy Roman Empire
- ▇ Muslim territory, 1095
- ▇ Roman Catholic territory, 1095
- ▇ Greek Orthodox territory, 1095
- ▇ Armenian Christian territory, 1095

KNIGHTS OF THE CRUSADES

Many of the knights who fought in the Crusades likely did so as much for prestige as out of any deep piety. Knighthood was a status symbol, and the knights had their own codes of chivalry and courtly deportment. They also often accrued vast wealth.

During the Crusades, however, a special type of knighthood emerged—members of religious orders who fought battles in the name of God. In all, there came to be more than two dozen such orders. The earliest ones, including the Hospitallers (or Knights of Malta), began by nursing sick or injured pilgrims in or on the way to the Holy Land. Others, such as the Knights Templar, protected pilgrims on the road. In time the type of service shifted to actually fighting in—and leading—battles. Although these warriors continually engaged in bloody combat, they otherwise lived as monks, taking religious vows and living in community. In time most military religious orders went out of existence, but the Knights of Malta still survive, providing ambulance service, running hospitals, and doing other charitable work.

INDULGENCES FOR CRUSADERS

In order to urge knights to fight in the Crusades, the popes granted them special indulgences—guarantees that God would not punish them for their sins. According to the Gospels, Jesus gave the power to forgive sins to Peter, the first bishop of Rome (or pope), and subsequent popes claimed to have inherited that power, which they could pass on to other bishops and priests. If a person's sins are forgiven, the church holds, that person does not suffer eternal punishment in hell, but might still endure punishment for a limited time after death in the realm of purgatory. The indulgences granted to the crusaders supposedly freed them from spending time in purgatory for sins they confessed, but in the view of most fighting men, earning an indulgence was like getting a free ticket to heaven.

As the costs of the Crusades grew, the popes also extended indulgences to anyone who paid a crusader's expenses or who built ships to transport the crusaders to the Holy Land, or left money in their wills for the Crusades. After the Crusades had ended, indulgences were still widely dispensed, and their eventual abuse spurred the young Martin Luther to seek reform in the church.

Nearly as imposing today as when it was built in 1142 by the Knights of Malta (the Hospitallers), the Krak des Chevaliers was the greatest of Crusader fortresses. It fell to Muslim forces in 1271, during the last crusade.

A fifteenth-century depiction of the violence of a crusade. The red-and-white tunics, decorated with crosses, identify the Christian knights.

FIFTH THROUGH EIGHTH CRUSADES, 1217–72

- ● cities
- — Fifth Crusade, 1217–1221
- — Sixth Crusade, 1228–1229
- — Seventh Crusade, 1248–1254
- — Eighth Crusade, 1270–1272
- ⌐ ⌐ Holy Roman Empire
- Muslim Territory, 1217
- Roman Catholic Territory, 1217
- Greek Orthodox Territory, 1217
- Armenian Christian Territory, 1217

No fewer than eight major crusades over 200 years pitted Christians against Muslims, but even as the balance of power seesawed between the religions, each faced internal fracturing; Christianity, already halved east and west, developed irreconcilable differences between its many regions and knightly orders.

Western European Spirituality

THE MIDDLE AGES WERE TURBULENT. Crusades were waged against the Muslims in the East, heresies arose and were violently put down by the Inquisition in the West, popes and emperors vied for power, the Eastern and Western churches split apart, and there was even a time when one pope ruled from Rome and another from Avignon. Later, reformers attempted to bring order to the church but in the process often instigated wars and persecutions. Understandably, individual Christians sometimes sought to retreat from the chaos and commune directly with God in a personal way. These men and women are called mystics.

Mystics generally seek a direct experience of God or a sense of union with the Divinity. They work toward that goal through lives of asceticism, prayer, and meditation. Many have described a threefold path of spiritual purgation, illumination, and perfection. The journey along this path is long and arduous, and along the way the mystic usually enters a period of depression fueled by a sense of abandonment, known as the dark night of the soul. Once beyond this dark night, however, union with God is seen as possible. Mystic experiences often take the form of ecstasy, levitation, visions, and seeming powers of healing.

Many of the medieval mystics were also writers. Hildegard of Bingen, a theologian, physician, and composer, described her visions of the cosmos and the joys and torments of the afterlife. Meister Eckhart distinguished between humankind's formal being as creatures in time and space, and its virtual being in God from all eternity. Richard Rolle held that the contemplative life is characterized by heat, sweetness, and angel song. An anonymous woman, known as Julian of Norwich, because she lived in the church of St. Julian in Norwich, England, related visions that emphasize God's love but also acknowledge the problems posed by sin and evil.

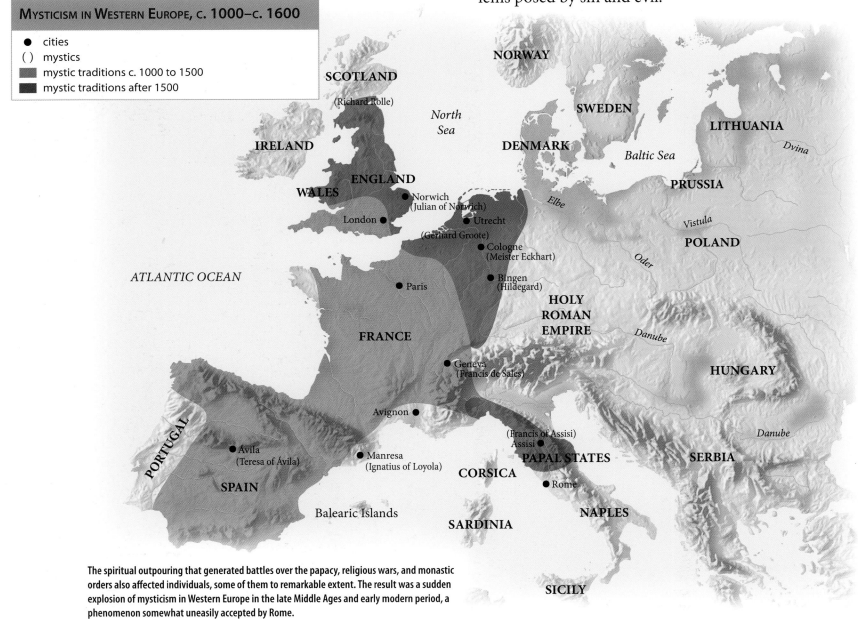

MYSTICISM IN WESTERN EUROPE, C. 1000–C. 1600

- ● cities
- ( ) mystics
- mystic traditions c. 1000 to 1500
- mystic traditions after 1500

The spiritual outpouring that generated battles over the papacy, religious wars, and monastic orders also affected individuals, some of them to remarkable extent. The result was a sudden explosion of mysticism in Western Europe in the late Middle Ages and early modern period, a phenomenon somewhat uneasily accepted by Rome.

> *When I tried to resist these raptures, it seemed that I was being lifted up by a force beneath my feet so powerful that I know nothing to which I can compare it.*
> —FROM THE LIFE OF TERESA OF JESUS: THE AUTOBIOGRAPHY OF TERESA OF AVILA (TRANSLATION BY E. ALLISON PEERS)

BRETHREN OF THE COMMON LIFE

Most Christians were unable to immerse themselves into mysticism, but there were alternatives. In the fourteenth century, Gerhard Groote, a preacher from Utrecht, traveled throughout the Netherlands calling Christians to lead spiritual lives. He attracted a large following, some of whom lived devout lives without taking religious vows, and others who adopted a monastic rule. By the mid-fifteenth century Groote's followers had established houses for men and for women throughout the Netherlands and Germany. Known as the Brethren (or Sisters) of the Common Life, adherents devoted their lives to meditative prayer and producing devotional literature for others. They also ran schools that offered general education at no cost to the students. Among their students were the future pope Hadrian VI, the philosopher, mathematician, and scientist Nicholas of Cusa, and Thomas à Kempis, who is credited with writing the devotional manual *The Imitation of Christ* (c. 1418).

Long one of the most widely read religious texts outside the Bible, *The Imitation of Christ* is a manual of practical methods for overcoming vice and growing in virtue. The emphasis is on the acceptance of suffering and on love, with the object of freeing oneself from worldly attachments so that one can more easily find oneself and God.

LATER SPIRITUAL WRITERS

Two remarkable mystics emerged in Spain during the sixteenth century. Teresa of Avila, founder of a reformed order of Carmelite nuns, wrote extensively on prayer and the mystical life, the basis of which she said was love of neighbor. In *The Interior Castle* Teresa described mystical life metaphorically as seven mansions, leading to betrothal to God in the sixth mansion and marriage in the seventh. Teresa's spiritual adviser, John of the Cross, was a poet and a mystic, who wrote of the threefold path to union with God, emphasizing the dark night of the soul.

Although not a mystic, Ignatius of Loyola, founder of the Jesuit order, wrote *The Spiritual Exercises* (1541), a program of self-examination, meditation, and prayer for attaining spiritual growth. Similarly, Francis de Sales, bishop of Geneva, wrote *Introduction to a Devout Life* (1609), a spiritual guide outlining meditations and instructions for growing in spirituality. Both books were highly influential.

Hildegard of Bingen is central to this engraving, enhanced with the kinds of mystical symbols developed in the late Middle Ages.

One of the primary female mystics, Teresa of Avila (later canonized) is shown here half-swooning as she gazes upon the crucified form of Jesus Christ.

VENERATION OF RELICS

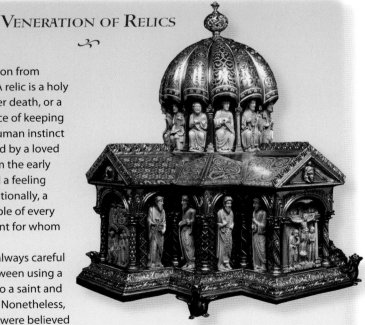

Many Christians drew consolation from venerating relics of the saints. A relic is a holy Christian's physical remains after death, or a personal belonging. The practice of keeping relics is based on the natural human instinct to treasure what was left behind by a loved one. Relics were venerated from the early days of Christianity and offered a feeling of contact with the saints. Traditionally, a relic was set within the altar table of every church—often a relic of the saint for whom the church was named.

Medieval theologians were always careful to point out the difference between using a relic to bring a believer closer to a saint and worshipping that saint as God. Nonetheless, because relics of certain saints were believed to work miraculous cures, the veneration of relics was abused, with charlatans hawking fake relics, and cults centering on churches and shrines that housed favorite relics. The fanatical use of relics became a prime target of the sixteenth-century reformers.

Medieval reliquaries were often quite elaborate—even decadent. This one, the Eltenberg Reliquary, dates to the twelfth century (possibly with more recent additions or restorations). In addition to theological protests of inappropriate veneration, such richly furnished reliquaries were targets of thievery and intra-church contention.

CHRISTIANITY
Times of Unrest

ALTHOUGH CALLED TO FOLLOW CHRIST, many church leaders used their offices to accrue power and wealth. A number of reformers emerged in the twelfth through the early fifteenth century, demanding that the church rid itself of its riches and stop trying to rule the world. The first was Arnold of Brescia, an abbot from Lombardy. In the 1130s he began preaching that church leaders should live in poverty, as the apostles did. He later led an open revolt against Rome and was eventually executed.

In 1170 Peter Waldo, a rich merchant from Lyon, inspired by the Gospels, sold all he had and traveled and begged while preaching Christian poverty. His lay followers did the same but were condemned by Rome for preaching without approval. They managed to survive, however, and are today called Waldensians. The son of another rich merchant, Francis of Assisi, also chose a life of poverty, along with many followers, but he first obtained permission from Rome in 1209, and his new Franciscan order prospered.

After studying the Gospels, John Wycliffe, an Oxford scholar, also condemned the church for its riches. Shocked by the struggle for power between a pope and an antipope, he declared that the Bible, not Rome, was the voice of God. His followers made the first English translation of the Bible in 1395, and his ministers traveled about reading it—incurring the unflattering name of Lollards, or "murmurers."

Inspired by Wycliffe's writings, Jan Hus, a priest from Prague, also preached against greed in the church and promoted the Bible as the supreme authority. He was eventually charged with heresy and burned at the stake in 1415. His martyrdom incited years of strife among his followers, the Hussites, and other religious factions in Bohemia. Reforms were still needed in the church and would follow.

Internal threats were troublesome to much of Christendom in the late Middle Ages. These included—for many worshippers—Jews, witches, and heretics, this last label often applying to the first two. Major movements deemed heretical popped up all over Europe, with disastrous results for many of their followers.

SCOTLAND

IRELAND

North Sea

DENMARK

Baltic Sea

LITHUANIA

RUSSIA

WALES

ENGLAND

Oxford ● ● London

Elbe

Vistula

Rhine

HOLY

Oder

POLAND

Dnieper

● Paris

ROMAN

● Prague

ATLANTIC OCEAN

Loire

EMPIRE

FRANCE

Danube

CARPATHIAN MOUNTAINS

Rhône

Lyons ●

A L P S

HUNGARY

● Avignon

Black Sea

PYRENEES

Danube

SPAIN

CORSICA

PAPAL STATES

SERBIA

BULGARIA

● Rome

● Constantinople

SARDINIA

NAPLES

HERESIES IN EUROPE, c. 1100–c. 1500

OTTOMAN EMPIRE

GREECE

● cities

SICILY

Mediterranean Sea

Hussite heresy

Bogomil heresy

Cathar heresy

Crete

Cyprus

Lollard heresy

If a temporal lord neglects to fulfill the demand of the Church that he shall purge his land of this contamination of heresy, he shall be excommunicated.

—FROM THE DECREES OF THE
FOURTH LATERAN COUNCIL (1215)

DUALISTIC VIEWS

In both eastern and western Europe, a number of religious groups adopted a dualistic theology. First, in seventh-century Armenia, a group known as Paulicians preached a doctrine of both a good God, who created our souls and ruled Heaven, and an evil God, who created our bodies and ruled the material world.

In the eighth century Paulicians settled in southeastern Bulgaria, and their preaching led to the development of the Bogomils (Bulgarian for "beloved of God"). Elaborating on Paulician views, the Bogomils held that true Christians ("the perfect") should renounce worldly possessions and abstain from marriage, meat, and wine. The ordinary faithful who sinned, but obeyed the Bogomil leaders, might receive spiritual baptism on their deathbed. The Bogomils spread though the Balkans and Asia Minor in the eleventh century, and in the twelfth century were a major influence on the Cathars.

The Cathars (from the Greek for "pure") first appeared in Germany in about 1140 and proclaimed their mission to restore the early purity of the church. By the twelfth century they had gained strength in Italy and France, where they were known as Albigensians (after the inhabitants of the city of Albi in southern France). Like the Bogomils, they believed in a good God and an evil God and the evil nature of the physical world. Redemption, they held, consisted of liberating the soul from the flesh and ending the "mixed state" that had been brought about by the devil.

The church condemned the Albigensians as heretics. The Dominican order was founded in 1216 especially to fight their advance in France, and the forces of the Inquisition were used against them. In addition, civil leaders were ordered to fight heresy in their lands or face excommunication. By 1300 Catharism had been suppressed.

ANTICIPATING THE END OF TIME

Throughout the Middle Ages some Christians saw the turmoil of their times as signs that the world was coming to an end. In the Gospels Jesus had promised to return following a series of ominous events and catastrophes. The biblical Book of Revelation elaborates on the theme, using frightening images of a seven-headed dragon and an Antichrist who would rule in terror just before Jesus returned to institute a reign of eternal peace. Although Jesus warned his followers that no one could know when the end would come, Christians kept trying to predict it. In doing so, they ignored the long-accepted view that Revelation was not a realistic prediction of the future but an allegory of the struggle between good and evil, with the eventual triumph of good.

Speculations on the end time abounded, including the popular views of Joachim of Fiore, a twelfth-century monk. Joachim divided history into three eras, relating to the Trinity. He also interpreted the seven-headed dragon in Revelation as representing seven rulers who would reign before Jesus's return. The sixth leader, he held, was Saladin, the current Muslim ruler of Jerusalem, who would be succeeded by the Antichrist.

Even the poor were infected with end-time fever. In 1525 some 8,000 ill-equipped peasants confronted a coalition of German military forces, believing them to be the evil ones whose destruction is predicted in Revelation. About 3,000 peasants were slaughtered.

Among other horrors of the Christian apocalypse, the Book of Revelation speaks of a seven-headed dragon, identified with the Devil, making war on the forces of Heaven. In the Middle Ages, the Devil was viewed as a real and terrible force, and such imagery doubtless helped inspire religious fervor.

Now a historic monument in France, the Chateau de Queribus in southern France became the last Albigensian (Cathar) stronghold to fall, when the French army took control of it in 1255. The takeover was bloodless, because the remaining Albigensians had already fled to friendlier territory.

John Wycliffe (c. 1330–84), one of the most influential theologians of the fourteenth century, foreshadowed later church reformers in his relentless and all-encompassing attacks on the Catholic Church.

CHRISTIANITY
The Reformation

IN 1506 POPE JULIUS II laid the foundation stone for the new St. Peter's Basilica and approved the sale of indulgences to finance the massive project. Indulgences were papal guarantees that a sinner would spend less time or no time at all in purgatory suffering for his sins. Peddlers wandered from town to town hawking their wares, and one such peddler, Johann Tetzel, always ended his sales pitch with the jingle, "As soon as the coin in the coffer rings, the soul from purgatory springs." In 1517 Tetzel was observed by the theologian Martin Luther, who went into a rage. A professor at the University of Wittenberg, Luther had recently come to believe in "justification by faith alone"—that God's forgiveness could be received only as a divine gift through faith in Jesus Christ, and that neither good works nor papal indulgences could buy it.

Luther wrote ninety-five theses condemning the sale of indulgences and other abuses, and nailed them to the church door at Wittenberg, instigating the

Protestant Reformation. He later rejected the authority of the pope and refused to recant his beliefs at a hearing in Worms. Taking advantage of the newly invented printing press, he distributed inflammatory pamphlets against the papacy and copies of the Bible, which he had personally translated into readable German. In 1537 a summary of his beliefs was presented to the emperor at Augsburg and became the official confession of beliefs of the new Lutheran church.

Many other reformers followed. John Calvin and Huldrych Zwingli reformed the Swiss church, replacing the trappings of Catholicism with more ascetic surroundings. Calvin stressed the doctrine of predestination—that souls were saved or condemned by God's design alone. After visiting Calvin in Switzerland, the Scottish priest John Knox returned home to lead the reform of the church in Scotland. All the reformers placed special emphasis on the Bible.

Few periods in European history were as definitive as the Reformation. For nearly 1,000 years, Roman Catholicism had held sway in Europe, facing down Muslims and those it deemed heretical or pagan. During the Reformation, however, its grip was irrevocably loosened, as Protestant elements appeared everywhere to challenge the Roman church.

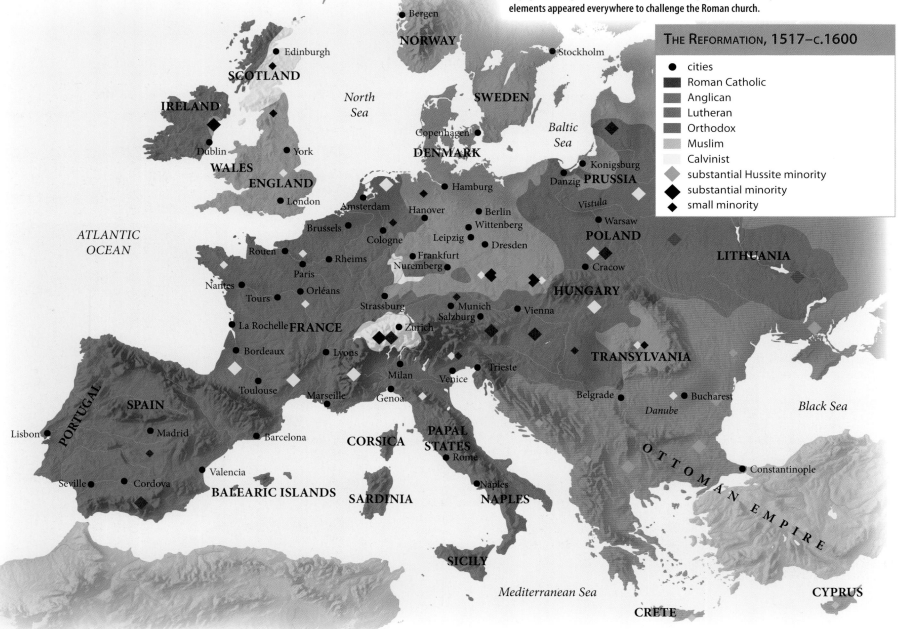

THE REFORMATION, 1517–c.1600

- ● cities
- Roman Catholic
- Anglican
- Lutheran
- Orthodox
- Muslim
- Calvinist
- ◇ substantial Hussite minority
- ◆ substantial minority
- ◆ small minority

Discontent with the excesses of the Catholic Church had been developing for a century or more, still Martin Luther (1483–1546) and his audacious act of nailing ninety-five theses on the Wittenberg church door is credited with starting the Protestant Reformation, one of the most momentous periods in Christian history.

WARS OF RELIGION

Calvin outlined his beliefs about God, grace, and church organization in *The Institutes of Christian Religion* (1536) and dedicated the book to King Francis I. At their first synod in Paris in 1539, the French Protestants, called Huguenots, formally organized into a Calvinistic body. They met fierce resistance, however, and from 1562 to 1594 the Catholics and Huguenots were at war with each other. The war reached its peak on the feast of St. Bartholomew, August 24, 1572, when thousands of Huguenots were massacred on the order of the Catholic king Charles IX. In the succeeding weeks more slaughter followed in Paris and other French cities. After the Protestant Henry IV became king in 1589, he granted the Huguenots religious freedom with the Edict of Nantes (1598). Forced to convert to Catholicism in order to keep his crown, Henry quipped: "Paris is well worth a Mass." Some believe, however, that Henry's conversion was genuine and not merely political. Toleration for the Huguenots soon eroded, and the Edict of Nantes was revoked in 1685. Some Huguenots converted to Catholicism; others went into exile.

Called the "worst of the century's religious massacres," the St. Bartholomew's Day massacre of 1572 took the lives of many of the Huguenots' aristocratic leaders, marking a turning point in the French wars of religion.

THE ENGLISH REFORMATION

The Reformation in England started when King Henry VIII, who had recently been named Protector of the Faith, broke with Rome because the pope refused to annul his marriage to Katherine of Aragon. In 1534 Henry proclaimed himself sole head of the Church of England. Though he made few doctrinal changes, he suppressed most of England's monasteries.

In 1549, during the short reign of Henry's son, Edward VI, the Book of Common Prayer was issued; as revised in 1662, it continues to be the official prayer book of England. Henry's daughter Mary I restored Catholicism to England, earning the nickname Bloody Mary for her persecution of Protestants. But on Mary's death Henry's other daughter, Elizabeth, came to the throne, and the kingdom reverted to Protestantism—this time with persecution of Catholics. Elizabeth I had a long and distinguished reign, however, and the new Church of England prospered.

THE COUNCIL OF TRENT

Faced with the spread of Protestantism, the Catholic church was forced to look into itself, acknowledge its faults, and initiate reforms by calling a general council. At the request of Emperor Charles V, Pope Paul III called a council at Trent, in northern Italy. It ran on and off from December 1545 until December 1563.

During its twenty-five sessions, the Council of Trent reaffirmed and clarified the church's traditional beliefs and practices, reiterating that the basis of faith was to be found in the Nicene Creed. The council rejected Luther's doctrine of justification by faith, insisting that good works increased grace and were also necessary for salvation. The council also established the first seminaries—schools with set curricula for training priests—and authorized a new catechism in the vernacular. Bishops were urged to hold regular synods and pay regular visits to their parishes to anticipate problems. Finally, the sale of indulgences was forbidden, though indulgences themselves could still be earned through prayer.

If I had to do without . . . either the works or preaching of Christ—I would rather do without his works . . . for the works do not help me, but his words give life, as he himself says.
—MARTIN LUTHER, PREFACE TO THE NEW TESTAMENT (1522)

Between them, Mary I (1516–1558), above, and her half-sister, Elizabeth I (1533–1603), below, represent the religious wars tearing through Europe in the sixteenth century. Two of the most famous of England's queens, the country swung first one way under the Catholic Mary and then entirely the other way under the Protestant Elizabeth.

Christianity in the Americas

AFTER CHRISTOPHER COLUMBUS reached the New World in 1492, many European explorers streamed into the Americas in search of a fortune. Generally, Christian missionaries accompanied them with the idea that the local "savages" needed to be converted and baptized. In 1493 Pope Alexander VI divided the undeveloped lands of the New World so that Brazil fell to Portugal and the rest of the Americas to Spain. Only a few missionaries ventured into North America before 1600, but Mesoamerica and South America were inundated.

In 1519 Hernán Cortés sailed to Mexico and quickly defeated the Aztecs, destroying their sophisticated culture. Franciscan and Dominican missionaries converted large numbers of the Indians but unfortunately burned Indian manuscripts, considering them to be the work of the devil. The conquistadors, led on by unbridled greed, exploited the local people, although a few missionaries tried to minimize the damage.

In South America the Inca had built up a vast empire in the Andes. Although they had no writing system, the Inca had managed vast resources and organized workers with astonishing efficiency, keeping tight control of the nation from their capital in Cuzco. Nonetheless, they crumbled quickly when the Spanish attacked in 1532, led by Francisco Pizarro. Although the Spanish had only 180 men, they defeated some 40,000 Inca. The Spanish found vast amounts of gold in the new land, which they pillaged, while missionaries were working to convert the Indians.

The Portuguese found no gold in Brazil, but they used the local people to plant and harvest sugar for export. When the Indian population was decimated through disease, the Portuguese imported black slaves from their African colonies to work the land. Starting in 1549 Jesuit missionaries ventured deep into Brazil, converting the local people, and in 1568 they set up Christian communities for Indians in Paraguay.

One of the most elaborate early maps of the Americas, this engraving resulted from the collaboration of a Spanish-Dutch team in 1562. They unhesitatingly included giants, mermaids, and other fabulous monsters, whose existence in the New World had been widely popularized by fantastic early rumors.

The Aztec calendar was a highly advanced system combining a cycle of ritual days (lasting 260 days in all) and a calendrical cycle of 365 days. The ritual, or sacred cycle, was divided into twenty 13-day months, each of which was dedicated to an Aztec god.

The astonishing ruins of Machu Picchu forcibly suggest the majesty of the Incan civilization. Spanish conquistadors, in their fervor for conversion or gold, largely destroyed the ancient Peruvian peoples but fortunately never discovered the "lost city of the Incas."

INCAN RELIGION

The Inca had a state-controlled religion that was designed to help the people. Although the Inca believed in numerous gods, including a creator god (Viracocha), they directed most of their attention toward the sun. The emperor, a descendant of the sun, was also a god. Priests offered sacrifices of llamas, consulted oracles, and conducted services.

The surrounding mountains also played a significant role in Incan religion. The Inca believed that when the sun rose each dawn it emerged from the inside of a mountain.

Similarly, their ancestors had emerged from inside Tampu T'oqo mountain before ascending to Cuzco ("the zenith"), where they built their capital. The Temple of the Sun at Cuzco displayed a great gold sun disk and gold images of maize and animals, mirroring the mountains, which were believed to contain stores of grain and animals.

Roads radiated from the Cuzco temple like the rays of the sun to local shrines that mirrored both the Cuzco temple and the surrounding mountains. The shrines included storehouses, and gifts and sacrificial offerings made at the shrines were systematically redistributed to the people throughout the empire as needed.

From him it began, from Quetzalcoatl it flowed out, all art and knowledge.
—REFRAIN SUNG IN AZTEC SCHOOLS

AZTEC GODS

The Aztecs considered themselves people of the sun, and though they worshipped many gods and goddesses, their chief deities were creator gods, and gods who represented different aspects of the sun. Quetzalcoatl, the feathered serpent god of earlier Mesoamerican peoples, was to the Aztecs a heroic creator god, the source of cosmic harmony, the calendar, agricultural abundance, the arts, and priestly ritual.

According to one legend, after fashioning humans from his own blood, Quetzalcoatl fed them by disguising himself as an ant and stealing a kernel of corn the ants had hidden in a mountain. Quetzalcoatl is also said to have joined with another god, Tezcatlipoca ("Smoking Mirror"), in creating and destroying four suns before settling on the current sun. Tezcatlipoca was eventually worshipped as the god of the sun, but he appeared in various aspects and colors. As the southern aspect of the sun, he was known as Huitzilpochtli ("blue hummingbird on left foot"), the god of war and the chief god of the Aztecs. It was Huitzilpochtli who directed the Aztecs to the ideal place to build their capital city of Tenochtitlán (now Mexico City).

An Aztec artifact of carved jade, depicting Quetzalcoatl.

As a sun god, Huitzilpochtli was thought to keep humans alive by following a regular routine. Each evening he died and rested in the bosom of mother earth. Each dawn he was born anew and fought the moon and the stars, driving them away with a shaft of light. However, to continue his daily battle to bring light and so sustain human life, the god needed sustenance in the form of human blood. Consequently, the Aztecs sacrificed prisoners to the god, and when prisoners were few, they fought wars to capture more humans to keep their god satisfied.

The Aztecs generally built their temples atop step pyramids. There are two temples atop the pyramid at Temple Major, or Serpent Mountain, in Tenochtitlán. One temple is dedicated to Tlaloc, the god of rain and fertility, and the other to Huitzilpochtli.

The Aztec practice of human sacrifice, here depicted in gruesome detail in the Codex Mendoza, a native-made but Spanish-commissioned manuscript of c. 1541, horrified the conquering Spanish and was quickly stamped out by Christian authorities.

Part Three: The Rise of the Major Religions ❧ 191

ISLAM
Muhammad: "Seal of the Prophets"

WHILE MEDITATING IN A CAVE near the Arabian city of Mecca, a forty-year-old man from the local Quraysh tribe is said to have received divine revelation, hearing a voice that summoned him to become a prophet. Thus, according to Muslim tradition, began the mission of the founder of Islam, who took the name Muhammad, "the praised one."

Muhammad (570–632) was illiterate, but he memorized the words of the recurring voice and recited them to those who began to follow him. He called upon his family, friends, and neighbors to worship only one god, and to be of upright, highly moral character. He attacked polytheism and criticized selfishness and greed. For the next twenty-two years of his life, Muhammad was a prophet, statesman, and military leader, and his following multiplied to number many thousands.

Muhammad's recitations were recorded by his closest companions and later collected in a book called, in Arabic, the Qur'an (Koran), considered to be the literal words of God as conveyed to Muhammad by the archangel Gabriel. The Qur'an—"recitation" in Arabic—is believed to be infallible, absolutely perfect as the word of Allah, "the God," or "the one and only God."

The term Islam is Arabic for "submission," and in this case, submission to God. A Muslim is "one who submits" to Allah. The faithful believe Muhammad is the final prophet in a line of prophets that reaches down from Adam through Noah, Abraham, and Jesus. Both Muhammad and Jesus are believed to be fully human, not divine, but with god-given powers of prophecy and instruction. Muhammad represents the closing of divine prophecy, and as such he was the "Seal of the Prophets."

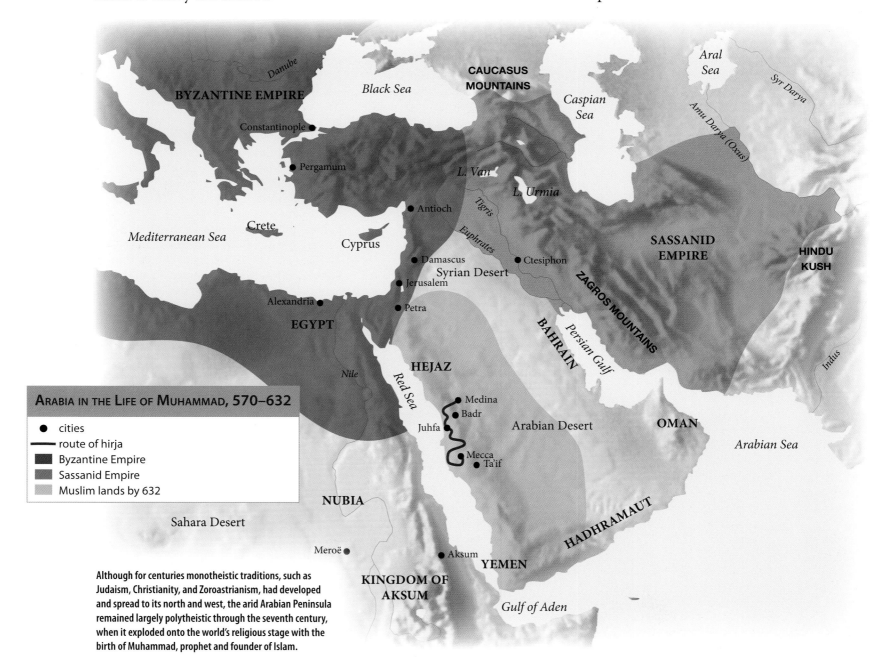

ARABIA IN THE LIFE OF MUHAMMAD, 570–632

- • cities
- — route of hirja
- ■ Byzantine Empire
- ■ Sassanid Empire
- ■ Muslim lands by 632

Although for centuries monotheistic traditions, such as Judaism, Christianity, and Zoroastrianism, had developed and spread to its north and west, the arid Arabian Peninsula remained largely polytheistic through the seventh century, when it exploded onto the world's religious stage with the birth of Muhammad, prophet and founder of Islam.

A medieval Persian manuscript depicts Muhammad, on the right, leading other prophets in prayer. These include Abraham, Moses, and Jesus, who in Islamic tradition are prophets like Muhammad, though with lower status (illustrated by the relative sizes of their flaming haloes).

ISLAM'S SWIFT GROWTH

For Muslims, Islam is not a new religion, but the continuation of the earlier "Abrahamic" monotheistic beliefs, Judaism and Christianity. Those religions, it is said, perverted or twisted the teachings of the prophets. The advent of Muhammad meant a renewal of divine prophecy, and the Qur'an is Allah's direct instruction in proper religious practice and way of life.

The Qur'an offers guidance in all aspects of daily life as well as religious life—which cannot be separated one from the other. Salvation requires that a Muslim surrender to the will of Allah, and faithful Muslims are considered to be united as one community. Muslims observe five duties—the Five Pillars of Islam—and also follow a strict legal system, known as *sharia*. These laws order the Muslim's life, addressing everything from diet to family, from war-making to finance.

Islam grew rapidly during the seventh century, even though deep schisms developed over interpretation of the Qur'an and over who should lead the faith. In the first

A late-nineteenth- or early-twentieth-century rendering of Mecca as it may have appeared during the lifetime of Muhammad. Visible at the left is the sanctuary of the Ka'bah, in Muhammad's time a major polytheistic temple and transformed by the prophet into Islam's holiest site.

decades of Islam's growth, Arabic often became the language of the faithful, who were increasingly to be found outside the

PIETY IN ISLAM

Muhammad recites the prescriptions of Islam, explaining the essence of piety.

True piety is this:
to believe in God, and the Last Day,
the angels, the Book, and the Prophets,
to give of one's substance, however cherished,
    to kinsmen, and orphans,
the needy, the traveler, beggars,
and to ransom the slave,
to perform the prayer, to pay the alms,
    And they who fulfill their covenant
when they have engaged in a covenant,
    and endure with fortitude
misfortune, hardship and peril,
these are they who are true in their faith,
    these are the truly god fearing.

—The Qur'an, II
(translation by A. J. Arberry)

Arabian Peninsula: in North Africa, the Levant, Mesopotamia, Persia, and as far east as China.

The Arabian cities of Mecca and Medina became sacred places because of Muhammad's sojourns, conversions, and conquests there. The nomads of Arabia became more settled and organized as the religion took hold there, and the faith became more important than the once-dominant bonds of family and tribe. Surrounded by the great empires of Persia and Byzantium, the Islamic Arabs prospered, dominating trade routes as seafarers and intrepid overland traders conducting camel caravans laden with the wealth of East and West.

Wherever they journeyed, to India and Southeast Asia, Anatolia and Mediterranean lands, Muslims brought their faith, which took root and flourished far and wide by the eighth century.

Quba Mosque, in Medina, modern Saudi Arabia, is built on the site of the world's oldest mosque. Its first stones were laid by Muhammad himself during the hirja.

MUHAMMAD'S ARABIA

Muhammad was born among the Arab people at a time of troubles and unrest, when foreign empires were striving to manipulate and control the Arabian Peninsula.

In response to outer pressure, the tribes were uniting as never before, and a common Arab culture developed. At the same time, monotheism was steadily replacing the traditional polytheism, with its local gods and goddesses. Muhammad's home city, Mecca, was the domain of an ancient warrior god, while other communities on the peninsula had influential monotheistic Jewish and Christian populations.

The prophet's inspiring message of social equality and the goal of selfless purity appealed to those who were without a tribe or poor, and especially to the idealistic young. For the most part, however, Muhammad's

teachings at first met strong resistance, particularly among the polytheists, and even among his own tribe.

Suffering severe persecution, Muhammad and a few score supporters left Mecca in 622, traveling through harsh countryside toward Yathrib (later to be called Medina, "city of the prophet"). This difficult *hirja*, or emigration, led to the beginning of Muhammad's success as a leader—religious, military, and political. His message was increasingly accepted around Medina, and an ever-growing number of Muslims began to face Mecca when they prayed.

Muhammad intended to return there one day, to begin again where he said that the divine message had first come to him from the angel Gabriel.

ISLAM
Mecca, a Holy City

AFTER HIS DEPARTURE for the oasis town of Yathrib in 622, Muhammad and his reorganized supporters conducted raids against Meccan caravans, harassing those who had persecuted him and eventually defeating them in open battle. At last, in 628, the Muslims won the right to return to Mecca, where they had long desired to perform the traditional pilgrimage, or *hajj*, leading to the Mount of Mercy and the site known as Arafat.

Muhammad's military and political power had so increased that he was able to forbid non-Muslims from entering Mecca, a holy city of long standing, and he ritually "purified" the Ka'bah, a former sanctuary of polytheist worship and a temple of the Arabic pantheon. For centuries, the Ka'bah—meaning "circle pit"—had been sacred to Arab tribes, some pagan and others Christian, and whose members annually made the *hajj* there. At this holiest of shrines

Arabs put aside tribal enmity; to them the Ka'bah was the center of the world.

Around the year 630 Muhammad removed or destroyed the 360 pre-Islamic idols of the Ka'bah and dedicated the ancient shrine solely to Allah, the god of Islam. In time, Muhammad supervised the reconstruction of the Ka'bah, overcoming resistance from former polytheistic Arab leaders, many of whom had been embroiled in longstanding feuds. With the obliteration of the idols and the rebuilding of the Ka'bah, the world's newest religion now claimed its most sacred site.

By the time of his death in 632, Muhammad had brought together the political, military, and proselytizing elements that spread Islam throughout much of the Arabian Peninsula. Islamic forces conquered Palestine, Syria, and Mesopotamia by 637, and in a few more years penetrated into Egypt, Persia, and North Africa.

Few religions have expanded as rapidly as Islam. Only a generation or so after its founder's death, Islam covered nearly the entirety of West Asia and had made significant inroads into Africa. Facilitated by weakened empires and tolerant policies, Islam's rising star would continue on the path started by the Four Rightly Guided Caliphs for centuries after.

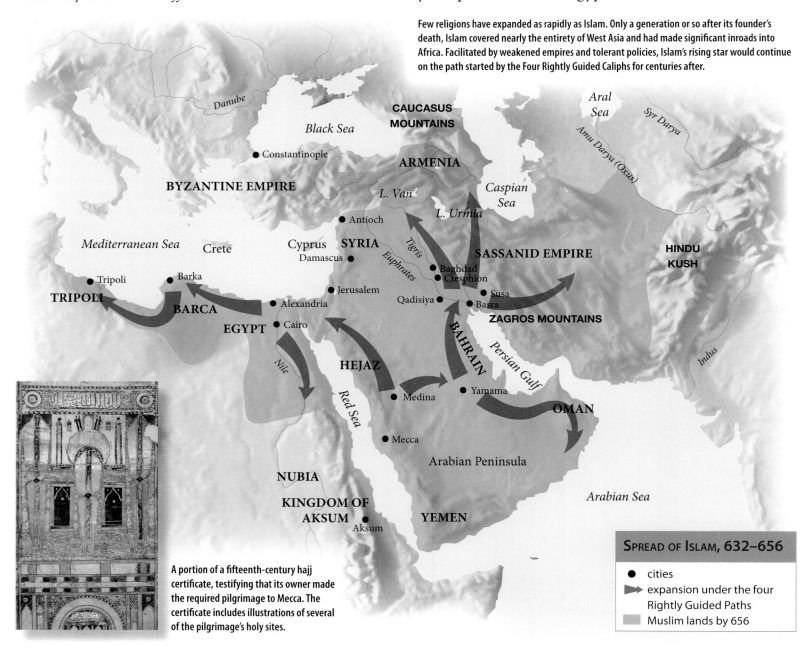

A portion of a fifteenth-century hajj certificate, testifying that its owner made the required pilgrimage to Mecca. The certificate includes illustrations of several of the pilgrimage's holy sites.

SPREAD OF ISLAM, 632–656

- ● cities
- ➤ expansion under the four Rightly Guided Paths
- ▮ Muslim lands by 656

ISLAM SPREADS BY CONQUEST AND CONVERSION

The once-powerful kingdoms of the eastern Mediterranean and Persia had been weakened by warfare, their populations ready for new rulers who could bring peace. Islamic conquerors did not generally force the peoples of their new domains to convert. Instead, Muslim officials were placed in charge of societies that essentially were allowed to continue on as before.

Naturally, the conquered peoples often saw a social or economic advantage to adopting the religion of the ruling class, which subsequently brought about many voluntary conversions. Further, Islam's religious tolerance—recognizing and integrating with its own concepts and philosophies those of other faiths—also facilitated conversions.

Muslims were forbidden from forcing Jews or Christians to convert, because those faiths shared many of the same traditions and scriptures as Islam. Polytheists might be forced to convert or else be persecuted, but members of the other Abrahamic religions were allowed the freedom to worship—as long as they paid the required taxes.

Many non-Muslim fighters were recruited for the armies of Islam and took part in continuous conquests that by the eighth century had reached the Iberian Peninsula in the west, Constantinople and beyond in the north, and Central Asia and the Indus River valley in the east. Muslim sultans and emperors ruled vast regions and became, in turn, adversaries who engaged in their own quarrels and wars while also battling Christians or Buddhists or Hindus.

The most famous Muslim ruling dynasties were the Arabic Umayyads and Abbasids and the mainly Turkic Mughals and Ottomans.

ISLAM'S TIDES OF CONQUEST

By the eleventh century Islam controlled much of Spain and southern Europe, had invaded the Hindu lands of South Asia, and was winning adherents in East Asia. Muslim seafaring colonies thrived in Southeast Asia, including the islands around the South China Sea. By the fifteenth century, Muslim sultans ruled much of Sumatra, Borneo, Java, and the coastlines of the Molucca Sea.

Relentless warfare eventually drove Muslim forces out of Spain by 1500, and in 1529 the advance of Muslim armies through Central Europe was turned back at the gates of Vienna. Despite defeats, by 1600 Islam was firmly established as the majority faith in many lands, from southern Europe to central Africa, and from the Arabian Peninsula to India and East Asia.

By 1600, the time Europeans were beginning to settle in the Americas, Islam (purple) had already spread from the west coast of Africa to the islands of Indonesia. Mecca and Medina on the Arabian Peninsula were holy cities and the destinations of pilgrimages for the world's Islamic population.

THE KA'BAH AND THE BLACK STONE

Muslims pray daily, facing Mecca and the Ka'bah, Islam's holiest shrine. A cube-shaped masonry building, the Ka'bah is constructed mainly of local granite and is approximately 43 feet (13.1 m) tall, 36 feet (11 m) long, and 12.6 feet (3.8 m) across. Its door is on the northeastern wall, 7 feet (2.1 m) above ground and accessible only by movable steps. The entire building is draped in black silk cloth embroidered with Qur'anic sayings written in gold thread.

The Ka'bah's four corners are approximately oriented to the four points of the compass. In the eastern corner is the sacred Black Stone, the al-Hajaru al-Aswad, long revered by pre-Islamic Arabs and reputed to be part of a meteorite. During reconstruction of the Ka'bah, Arab elders contended for the honor of placing the Black Stone as a cornerstone. In the ceremony, Muhammad arranged for leading tribal elders to raise, in unison, the Black Stone, held in a cloak, and he then placed it with his own hands.

Muslims believe that the Black Stone dates to the time of Adam and Eve, and during a *hajj* pilgrims hope to kiss it or at least point to it. The *hajj* involves walking counterclockwise around the Ka'bah seven times (the *tawaf*) before proceeding to the Mount of Mercy. On the way pilgrims visit other sacred sites. The *hajj* is a religious duty of every Muslim and is meant to reenact Muhammad's final pilgrimage in 632.

A late sixteenth-century Ottoman miniature shows Muhammad at the Ka'bah. The prophet's face is blank in accordance with an Islamic tradition, followed only sporadically through Muslim history, proscribing visual representations of Muhammad.

ISLAM

The Caliphate

IN THE FIRST DECADES AFTER MUHAMMAD, Islam was shaped by the qualities and fortunes of the individual who rose to succeed the prophet as the faith's political leader. Elected by principal Muslim religious and tribal figures, this leader was known as the caliph—khalifah in Arabic, usually interpreted as "successor" to Muhammad. The caliph was leader of the faithful, or ummah, the worldwide Islamic community.

This community grew rapidly as Islam expanded under the first four caliphs, known to most Muslims as the "Rightly Guided Khalifahs." Islamic forces crushed the armies of Persians, Sassanids, and Byzantines, in large part because of skillful Arab generalship and their fast-moving mounted tactics. One factor aiding Muslim victories was the war-weakened condition of those empires; another was the widespread plague that had wiped out many populations.

Accompanying their military conquests, the successive caliphs and their supporters were often embroiled in civil strife and rebellion. In the 660s, after the assassination of the fourth caliph, the Umayyad family took power, establishing a dynasty that ruled from Damascus for ninety years. Islam was now the religion of an imperial elite, and West Asian culture—including art, architecture, and science—permeated foreign lands as never before.

By 750 the Umayyads had been overthrown and the Abbasids became caliphs, their dynasty ushering in the Islamic golden age, a flowering of literature, art, science, and technological progress that lasted more than a century. In many places Christians, Jews, and Muslims freely mingled and exchanged ideas, cultures, and knowledge, as witnessed by the rise of libraries and educational institutions, none more impressive than those in Muslim-controlled Spain. Muslim cities such as Córdoba and Granada became hubs of intellectual and commercial intercourse between Western Europe and the Mediterranean lands.

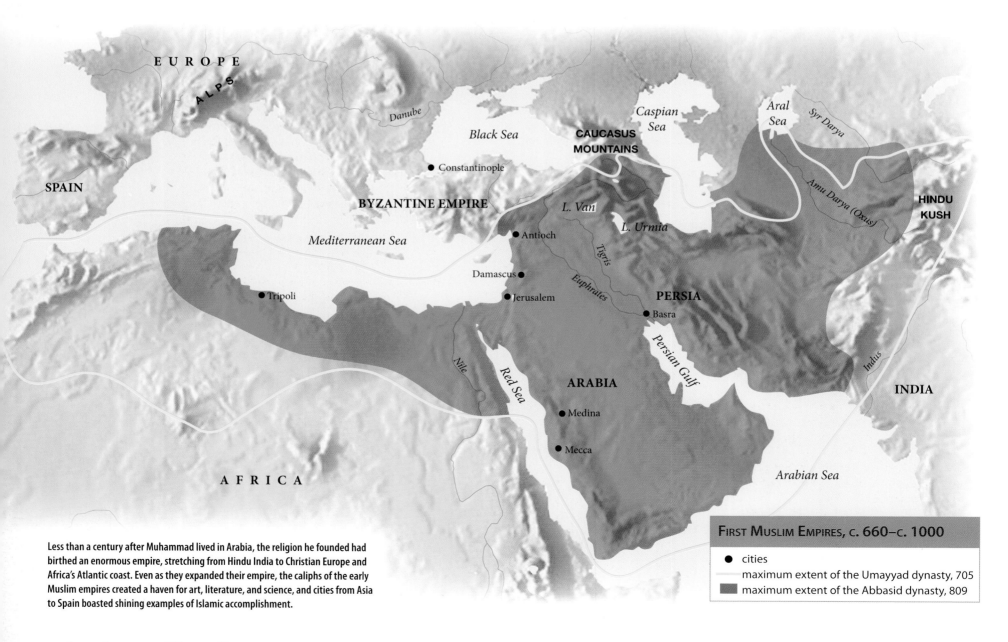

Less than a century after Muhammad lived in Arabia, the religion he founded had birthed an enormous empire, stretching from Hindu India to Christian Europe and Africa's Atlantic coast. Even as they expanded their empire, the caliphs of the early Muslim empires created a haven for art, literature, and science, and cities from Asia to Spain boasted shining examples of Islamic accomplishment.

FIRST MUSLIM EMPIRES, C. 660–C. 1000

● cities
maximum extent of the Umayyad dynasty, 705
maximum extent of the Abbasid dynasty, 809

Arches in the Cathedral-Mosque of Córdoba reflect the original Moorish design of the building, built in Umayyad Spain in 784 to 786. A masterpiece of Islamic Europe, the former mosque became a cathedral in 1236, during the Christian reconquest of Spain.

THE GUIDING FORCE OF ISLAM'S HOLY SCRIPTURES

The "Rightly Guided Khalifahs" produced the Qur'an as a published book, which in turn served to define and legitimize the authority of the caliphs. The rule of the first caliph, Abu Bakr, saw Muhammad's revelations—orally transmitted to his followers in recitations over twenty-three years—compiled into a volume; under the third caliph, the Qur'an was formally standardized into final form.

The Muslim holy book, composed in Arabic, contains 114 chapters, termed *suras*, with more than 6,000 verses, or *ayat*, many in rhymed form. Muslims believe the words in the Qur'an are exactly as Gabriel imparted them to Muhammad. Although there have been many translations, the Arabic version is considered the actual revelation.

The Qur'an is the ultimate source of guidance for Islamic religious and social principles and moral values. The earlier chapters come from the prophet's years at Mecca and are mainly concerned with spirituality and morality. Later chapters, from the Medina period, are concerned with issues that affect the daily life of the devout Muslim. Many subjects or events related in Judaic and Christian scriptures are also found in the Qur'an, although often interpreted differently.

While the Qur'an is the central Islamic religious text, other valued writings, known as hadiths, further discuss Islamic observances and customs. Among the most important observances interpreted by the hadiths are the

THE FIVE PILLARS
❧

By submitting to God's will, the devout Muslim follows the right path toward salvation, a path guided by the faith's most important precepts: the Five Pillars of Islam. These express the essence of most Muslim religious observance.

First is *shahada*, faith as expressed by the creed, or declaration: "There is no God but Allah, and Muhammad is God's messenger." Next is *salah*, ritual prayer that must be performed five times a day, facing the Ka'bah in Mecca. *Zakat* is the act of alms-giving for those in need. Fasting, or *sawm*, is required of every Muslim during Ramadan, the ninth and most holy month of the twelve-month Islamic calendar, when the faithful celebrate the original revelation of the Qur'an. The fifth pillar is the *hajj*, or pilgrimage, to Mecca, which all Muslims who are able are expected to make during their lives.

The Five Pillars are the key to worship for the Sunnis, the largest Muslim community, while the other major Muslim tradition, Shi'a, practices eight rituals, which integrate the five precepts.

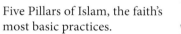

An excerpt from the Qur'an, dated to the Abbasid dynasty.

Five Pillars of Islam, the faith's most basic practices.

By the eleventh century the Abbasid caliphate was breaking up, losing its political unity, and local rulers were taking power, forming their own caliphates and independent states. The Qur'an remained the overarching and unifying force for Islam's faithful, although disputes over the choice of caliphs split Islam into rivalries that would last more than a thousand years.

The Umayyad Mosque, located in Damascus (modern Syria), is one of the oldest and most famous mosques in the world. Built between 706 and 715, it is the latest of several temples, dedicated to numerous gods, to have stood on the site.

Conflicts: Political and Religious

THROUGHOUT ISLAM'S FIRST MILLENNIUM, from the seventh through the sixteenth centuries, Muslim armies fought not only to conquer the lands of the kafirs (rejecters of Allah)—from the Hindu Kush to Hungary to France—but also were engaged in warfare between Islamic rulers.

Conflicts among Muslims were sometimes on a vast scale, such as the defeat of the Umayyad caliphate and capture of Damascus by the Abbasids in 750, or the sixteenth-century Ottoman Turk conquests of Muslim sultans (sovereign rulers) from Mesopotamia to Egypt and Algeria. Yet it was another conflict, involving the most profound principles of faith, that has caused Islam enduring strife: the dispute between Sunni and Shia, Islam's foremost denominations.

At the heart of this dispute is the issue of the right to be head of the ummah. The Sunni distinguish between secular and spiritual leadership—the caliph (originally elected by Muslim leaders) was the political authority, while the clergy and religious experts, or ulama, had religious authority. Shia holds that only an imam (guide), someone who is a direct descendant of Muhammad, can be the head of the faithful. This imam has both political and spiritual authority, according to Shia doctrine.

This controversy arose upon the death of Muhammad in 632. One faction declared 'Ali ibn Abi Talib, the prophet's cousin and son-in-law, as the rightful successor. Shia means "the party of 'Ali." The Shia candidate was not, however, chosen as the prophet's immediate successor. The majority of Muslims—"followers of the sunna," or Muhammad's example—believe the caliph should be qualified by ability, not by blood ties to the prophet.

After the death of the third caliph, 'Ali held the position for five years—a term that was torn with strife and that ended with his assassination.

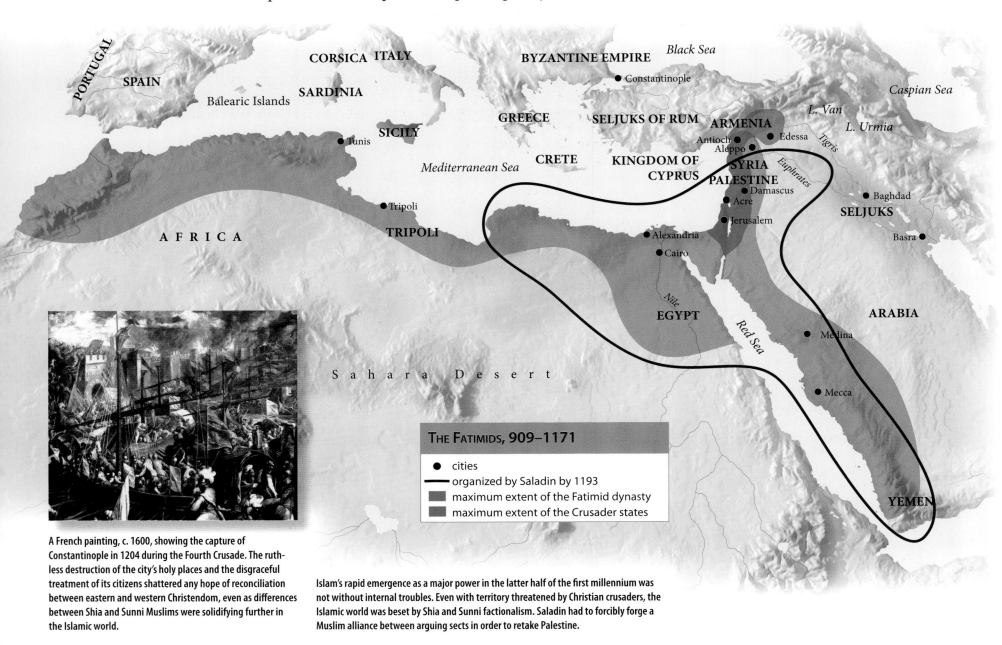

THE FATIMIDS, 909–1171

- • cities
- — organized by Saladin by 1193
- ■ maximum extent of the Fatimid dynasty
- ■ maximum extent of the Crusader states

A French painting, c. 1600, showing the capture of Constantinople in 1204 during the Fourth Crusade. The ruthless destruction of the city's holy places and the disgraceful treatment of its citizens shattered any hope of reconciliation between eastern and western Christendom, even as differences between Shia and Sunni Muslims were solidifying further in the Islamic world.

Islam's rapid emergence as a major power in the latter half of the first millennium was not without internal troubles. Even with territory threatened by Christian crusaders, the Islamic world was beset by Shia and Sunni factionalism. Saladin had to forcibly forge a Muslim alliance between arguing sects in order to retake Palestine.

Saladin united much of the Muslim world in the twelfth century, overthrowing Shia rulers in some areas and attracting unorganized armies to his cause. When he wrested Jerusalem from Christian crusaders in 1187, he ensured his place in history as a Muslim hero.

The latest mosque to stand on the site, Imam 'Ali Mosque in Najaf, Iraq, was built in 1500. It houses the tomb of 'Ali ibn Abi Talib and is one of the holiest Shia sites.

CRUSADERS SEEK THE HOLY LAND

The Sunni Abbasid dynasty found itself in frequent contests with rebellious sultans and emirs (princes, or generals) who declared for the Shia tradition as a way to challenge imperial rule. Several powerful leaders spread Shiism widely by the 1600s, although Sunni Islam remained the mainstream belief.

In the tenth century the Fatimids, a Shia dynasty, rose to power in Egypt, and for almost three hundred years they ruled from North Africa to the Levant. This dynasty claimed direct descent from Muhammad's daughter, Fatima, wife of 'Ali. In the early sixteenth century the Safavid ruler of Persia established a form of Shia as the state religion, thus adding a vast region to Shia influence. Shia Islam eventually achieved considerable political power, from Morocco in the west to Yemen and the Caucasus in the east.

Near the end of the eleventh century, European Christian forces landed in West Asia, determined to shake Islam's grip on Jerusalem and the "Holy Land," as Palestine was called. These "crusaders" also sought to compel Muslims to withdraw from parts of Europe, including the Iberian Peninsula and the Balkans. The First Crusade, which had been called by the pope in 1095, captured Jerusalem by 1099, as well as other major cities in the region. Crusaders established the Kingdom of Jerusalem, a Christian state that controlled some of Islam's holiest sites.

Muslim resistance was unified under the leadership of Saladin (1137–93), a Kurd from Mesopotamia, who besieged and recaptured Jerusalem in 1187. New Crusades were organized but achieved little. The Fourth Crusade, organized in the early thirteenth century, never reached the Holy Land but instead was diverted to take Christian Constantinople, in one of the bloodiest and most destructive plunders of the age. Churches and mansions alike were laid waste, and the cultural treasures of the former Eastern Roman Empire were pillaged or destroyed.

The fall of Constantinople weakened what remained of the Byzantine Empire, now vulnerable for conquest by Ottoman Turks, who would establish one of the world's three great Muslim empires.

BAGHDAD: THE CITY OF PEACE

In 764 the Abbasids founded Baghdad, near the Tigris and Euphrates rivers, to be the imperial capital, replacing the Umayyad capital of Damascus. A busy center for trade and blessed with bountiful water and a good climate, Baghdad was favored by generations of Abbasid caliphs. The city grew to be more impressive than even the former Persian capital, Ctesiphon, just a few miles away. With the remains of ancient Babylon also nearby, Baghdad became heir to the great heritages of Mesopotamia and Persia.

The new city grew during Islam's golden age, with world-famous libraries and institutions of science and learning. The ancient literature of Greece, Syria, and Persia were preserved, copied, and translated, as scholars came from Islamic and *kafir* lands alike. In the ninth century the Abbasids established the famed House of Wisdom, a great library and translation center. Ancient and contemporary Muslim science and philosophy were disseminated widely from this highly cultured Muslim metropolis.

In time Baghdad became one of the world's largest and richest cities, known for its waterways, parks, promenades, and handsome estates. Built in concentric circles and known as the "Round City," Baghdad had been designed by two Persians, one a Zoroastrian and the other a Jew. Its center held a mosque and the Golden Gate Palace of the Abbasids. The city's name was likely derived from Persian for "god-given," or "God's gift," but Baghdad was also called *Madinat as-Salam*—the "City of Peace."

ISLAM
Seljuks, Mamluks, and Mongols

IN THE ELEVENTH CENTURY the Turkish clan known as Seljuks, who had recently converted to Sunni Islam, fought their way to power, dominating the Abbasid caliph who ruled at Baghdad. The Seljuks captured Syria and Palestine, defeating Fatimid forces there, and victories over the Byzantines brought much of Christian Anatolia under Islamic control.

By the last decades of the eleventh century Seljuks governed from Central Asia to the Persian Gulf and west to the Mediterranean. Islam became the official state religion under the Seljuks, who increased the clergy's political authority. This essentially did away with the caliphate's governmental structure, as successive Seljuk generations assumed regional leadership as powerful sultans.

The Seljuks were patrons of the arts, sciences, and education, establishing universities and creating realms in which the likes of Persian astronomer and poet Omar Khayyám (1048–1122) and philosopher al-Ghazali (1058–1111) could work and thrive.

The Seljuk states were often fighting crusaders, with the famed Saladin taking the lead for the Muslims. Early in the twelfth century, the Seljuk empire declined, increasingly characterized as an agglomeration of independent states.

After warring with crusaders, Saladin continued his conquests, now against Muslim opponents, defeating the Fatimids in 1171 and capturing their capital city, Cairo. Saladin founded the Ayyubid dynasty, which gave increasing power to the Egyptian military order known as Mamluks. Created from foreign-born slave children—especially Christian Kipchak Turks from Byzantine regions and the Caucasus—Mamluk regiments had fought for various Muslim rulers over almost three centuries.

As children, Mamluks were converted to Islam and trained in chivalry and war. The Seventh Crusade of 1249, under Louis IX of France, was defeated by the Mamluks, who captured and ransomed the king himself. This triumph eventually brought the Mamluks to power as the Bahri dynasty, named after a Kipchak regiment.

In the twelfth century, the Islamic world became seriously threatened both by internal political struggles and by outside threats. Having fended off Christendom during the long years of the Crusades, a new enemy—the Mongols—appeared to the northeast, even as dynasties crumbled and new ones arose.

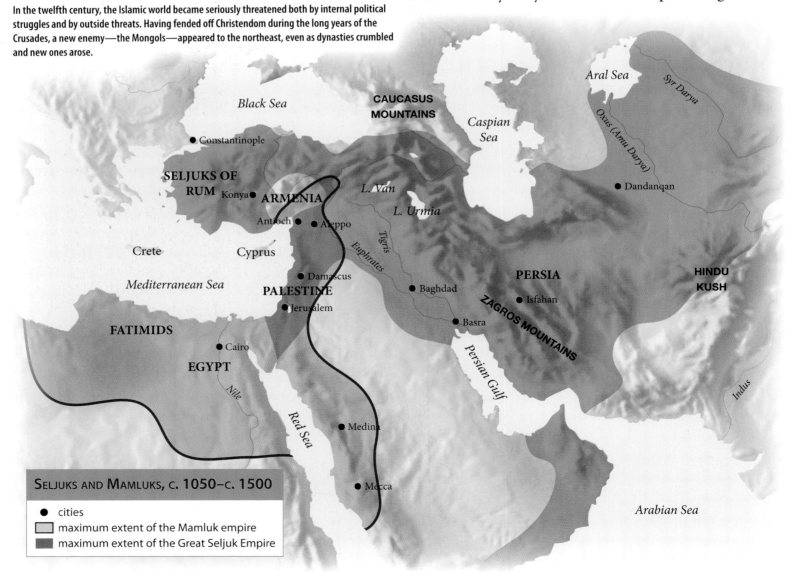

SELJUKS AND MAMLUKS, C. 1050–C. 1500

- ● cities
- ▢ maximum extent of the Mamluk empire
- ▢ maximum extent of the Great Seljuk Empire

MAMLUKS: CHAMPIONS OF ISLAM

The Mamluk sultanate at Cairo was a rival to the Abbasid caliphate at Baghdad. By the mid-thirteenth century, an irresistible Mongol invasion pressing down from the north and east spelled doom for the Abbasids. The Caspian regions had been conquered, and Persia was overwhelmed by 1250. At last Baghdad was destroyed in 1258.

The last Abbasid caliph at Baghdad was executed by the Mongols, and the once-spectacular city was left in ruins, even the magnificent House of Wisdom obliterated. It is said the Tigris River ran black for half a year because of the ink from the thousands of House of Wisdom books thrown into the water during the Mongol pillaging.

The Mamluks led the counterattack against the Mongols, defeating them several times over the following half century. In this time, the Mamluks installed a survivor of the Abbasids as caliph at Cairo. Since this was merely a ceremonial position, with no real authority beyond Mamluk territories, this line of caliphs was referred to as the "shadow caliphate."

The Mamluk empire expanded throughout North Africa and West Asia, and a leading thirteenth-century commander of Muslim forces invading India was a Mamluk. The rule of the Mamluks at Cairo was marked by constant struggles for power. Conspiracies, assassinations, and rebellions resulted in the average reign of a Mamluk ruler lasting only seven years.

The Mamluks were decisively defeated by the Ottomans in 1517.

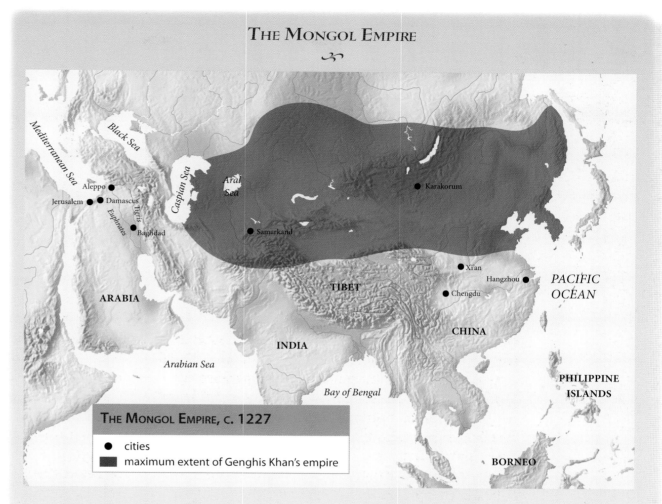

THE MONGOL EMPIRE

THE MONGOL EMPIRE, c. 1227

- ● cities
- ■ maximum extent of Genghis Khan's empire

In the first years of the thirteenth century a mighty military force burst out of Central Asia under the leadership of Genghis Khan (c. 1162–1227), a Mongol warlord. No people could withstand the shock and speed of Genghis Khan's hordes—mostly Turkic and Mongolian fighters—who were led by his sons and grandsons after his death.

By late in the century the Mongol domain was the world's largest contiguous empire, encompassing more than a fifth of the earth's landmass, with more than 100 million people. At its peak, the empire dominated most of China, Siberia, Russia, Central Asia, and eastern Europe, and reached down into Anatolia, Mesopotamia, and Persia.

For all their ruthlessness with any who resisted their authority, the mainly shamanist and animist Mongols were tolerant of the beliefs of others. A grandson of Genghis Khan, Berke (d. 1266) converted to Islam, as did many in his

army, known as the Blue Horde. Islam eventually became the major Mongol faith, although there were also Buddhists and Christians in their ranks.

While campaigning in Central Asia, Berke was infuriated when a force belonging to his non-Muslim cousin, Hulagu Khan, mercilessly destroyed Baghdad in 1258.

"He has sacked all the cities of the Muslims, and has brought about the death of the Caliph," Berke declared, according to a thirteenth-century Persian historian. "With the help of God I will call him to account for so much innocent blood."

Berke went to war against Hulagu (whose queen and main general were Christians), allying with the desperate Mamluks attempting to defend Palestine and the Levant. Thanks to Berke's alliance, the Mamluks stopped the Mongol advance toward Jerusalem and Egypt.

An illustrated manuscript of the Qur'an, with the graceful style and embellishments typical of Mamluk Egypt. This example was probably produced in the fourteenth or fifteenth century.

Persian poet, mathematician, and astronomer Omar Khayyám was raised a Shia Muslim, but he disdained religious fanaticism and close-mindedness:

Allah, perchance, the secret word might spell;
If Allah be, He keeps His secret well;
  What He hath hidden, who shall hope to find?
Shall God His secret to a maggot tell? . . .

The Koran! well, come put me to the test—
Lovely old book in hideous error drest—
  Believe me, I can quote the Koran too,
The unbeliever knows his Koran best.

And do you think that unto such as you,
A maggot-minded, starved, fanatic crew,
  God gave the secret, and denied it me?—
Well, well, what matters it! believe that too.

(Translation by Richard Le Gallien)

The Mongol Hulagu Khan imprisons the Muslim Caliph in Baghdad, shown in a fifteenth-century illustration.

Muslim Missionaries

Much of Islam's success converting and proselytizing, from Europe and Africa to East Asia and the distant islands of Southeast Asia, was the result of Muslim merchants and traders spreading the message of their faith far and wide. The seacoasts of South Asia and Africa had dynamic Muslim communities, the Silk Road linked Muslim lands with China and India, and caravan routes crossed the African deserts, reaching southward to sub-Saharan regions where the people were open to conversion.

Yet it was not only merchants and traders who brought Islam to the rest of the world. Perhaps Islam's best missionaries were the Sufis, as several orders (*tariqas*) of mystics were called. Achieving considerable importance by the twelfth century, the Sufis were mainly ascetics who chose poverty, humility, and moral purity in their quest to overcome the desires of the flesh and strengthen the relationship with Allah.

Sufis traveled widely along the trade routes, holding meetings and founding shrines to individuals considered to be holy, or saints. They carried Islamic teachings to distant places, where the faith was little known, particularly in Africa and Central Asia. Offering a spiritual example with their meditation and daily devotional exercises, Sufis held discussions with prospective converts, usually singing songs and reciting prayers. The Sufi order known as "whirling dervishes" was famed for dance and music intended to induce spiritual ecstasy. Dervishes also were known for skill in medicine and for their poetry and wit.

The most famous Sufi poet was Jalal al-Din Rumi (1207–73), a Persian-born theologian who lived most of his life in Anatolia and whose work was an inspiration to the dervishes.

Poets, merchants, and missionaries spread the culture and principles of Islam, but real dominion was achieved by force of arms. At the close of the sixteenth century, three powerful Muslim empires dominated much of the world.

Although Islam rarely endorsed official missionaries, the Sufi order dispersed so widely and attracted such attention (and conversions) that they may be called missionaries, carrying the word of Islam through Asia and Africa along well-established trading routes.

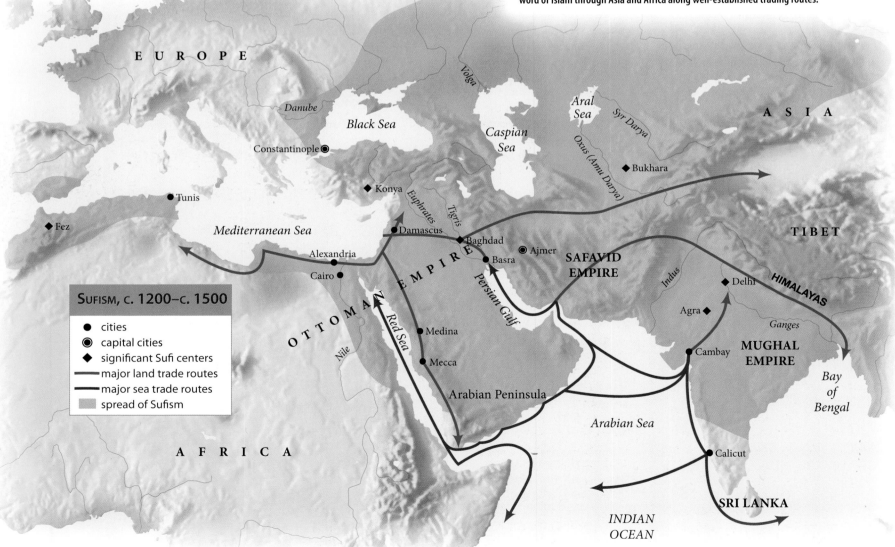

SUFISM, c. 1200–c. 1500

- ● cities
- ◉ capital cities
- ◆ significant Sufi centers
- —— major land trade routes
- —— major sea trade routes
- ▨ spread of Sufism

The twirling motion of the Sufi order known as the Whirling Dervishes is a ritualistic activity designed to induce a state of heightened spirituality. Although best known for this trademark activity, the dervishes were also champions of art, music, and poetry and had a lasting impact in many Islamic countries.

In the name of the One God (Allah) Pray for your Prophet and Servant Jesus son of Mary.
—ISLAMIC PRAYER INSCRIBED ON THE INTERIOR OF THE DOME OF THE ROCK

IMPERIAL ISLAM

As the year 1600 approached, the Ottoman, Safavid, and Mughal empires seemed unshakable. Their militaries were the finest, their wealth immense. All were successful, in large part, because of the skillful use of gunpowder, but also because of their effective civil administrations.

Although these three imperial courts were mainly Islamic, they were generally tolerant of other religions. This policy enabled the governing of many diverse and often-quarreling peoples.

The Ottoman Turks ruled from Hungary to the Horn of Africa and controlled three-quarters of the Mediterranean coast. The Ottoman Empire had Islam's most sacred sites, as well as the holiest sites of Jews and Christians. The ruling elite were mainly Muslims but included important Greek Orthodox clergy and wealthy Christians and Jews. For much of the sixteenth century Sufis were prominent in Ottoman administration and influenced policies, but eventually religious authorities were made subordinate to the central government.

To the east the Safavids of Azerbaijan united the Persians for the first time since the Sassanid era that ended in the seventh century. The Safavids were of mixed Azeri and Kurdish heritage and originally had been members of a Sufi order. Although most peoples of Persia had been Sunnis, Shia was established as the state religion and became the empire's predominant Islamic denomination.

The Turkic-Persian and Mongol dynasty known as the Mughals ruled most of the Indian subcontinent and parts of Afghanistan. Founded in 1526 as a culmination to generations of invasions from Central Asia—the founder, Babur, was a descendant of Genghis Khan—the Mughal Empire made a form of Sunni Islam the state religion. Still, all subjects were free to practice any faith. Hindu and Zoroastrian festivals were officially observed, even by the emperors.

THE SACRED HEART OF JERUSALEM

One of the most imposing sites in Jerusalem is the Dome of the Rock, a gold-painted shrine built by the Umayyad caliph between 685 and 691 to shelter Muslim pilgrims visiting the city. The dome stands on a broad man-made stone platform, a site that is of the holiest significance to both Islam and Judaism. Muslims named it the Noble Sanctuary, and to Jews it is the Temple Mount.

It was from here that Muhammad is believed to have made a miraculous journey to heaven, guided by the angel Gabriel. Here, too, according to Jewish tradition, was where the patriarch Abraham prepared to sacrifice his son Isaac. This was also the site chosen by David upon which King Solomon built his temple. That temple was destroyed by the Babylonians in the sixth century BCE, and a second temple was obliterated during the first century CE uprising against Rome. It is believed the Dome of the Rock and the nearby Al-Aqsa Mosque, built during the seventh and eighth centuries, are on the ruins of Solomon's temple.

The spiritual importance of the Noble Sanctuary makes Jerusalem Islam's third-holiest city after Mecca and Medina.

One of Jerusalem's most recognizable sites, the golden-crowned Dome of the Rock is an Islamic architectural masterpiece, remarkable not only for its deep religious meanings but also for its historical merit.

SUFISM'S GREATEST POET

Rumi composed in the "New Persian" vernacular, which had overtaken Arabic as the literary language of Islamic Persia. Widely translated, his poetry influenced Urdu and Turkish literature. Rumi's most famous work is *Masnavi-I Ma'navi*, six books on spiritual themes, totaling more than 50,000 lines of rhymed couplets.

Rumi described the *Masnavi* as "the roots of the roots" of Islam. Sufi ethics combine with Islamic faith in this excerpt:

Arise, O son! burst thy bonds and be free!
How long wilt thou be captive to silver and
    gold?
Though thou pour the ocean into thy
    pitcher,
It can hold no more than one day's store.
The pitcher of the desire of the covetous
    never fills,

The oyster-shell fills not with pearls till it is
    content;
Only he whose garment is rent by the vio-
    lence of love
Is wholly pure from covetousness and sin.
Hail to thee, then, O LOVE, sweet madness!
Thou who healest all our infirmities!
Who art the physician of our pride and self-
    conceit!
Who art our Plato and our Galen!
Love exalts our earthly bodies to heaven,
And makes the very hills to dance with joy!
O lover, 'twas love that gave life to Mount
    Sinai,
When "it quaked, and Moses fell down in a
    swoon."

—From the prologue to Book I of *Masnavi-I Ma'navi* (translated by E. H. Whinfield)

CHRONOLOGY OF WORLD RELIGIONS

c. 400,000 BCE

Homo erectus inhabits China, as evidenced by fossil remains known as Peking Man.

c. 300,000 TO 40,000 BCE

Middle Paleolithic period. Objects accompany burials in France, suggesting belief in an afterlife.

c. 100,000 BCE

Modern humans appear in the fossil record in Africa. Within the next 30,000 years humans migrate into Europe and Asia.

c. 60,000 TO 48,000 BCE

Australia and western Oceania become inhabited by humans.

c. 48,000 TO 38,000 BCE

Humans arrive in New Guinea and Tasmania.

c. 45,000 BCE

World's oldest known rock art created in South Australia.

c. 40,000 TO 12,000 BCE

High Paleolithic period. Cave paintings and sculptures from several locations, particularly the Iberian Peninsula, suggest religious traditions.

c. 30,000 BCE

Statuettes known as Venuses begin to appear, suggesting religious concepts of fertility and reproduction.

c. 20,000 BCE

The Venus of Willendorf, a famous example of the Venus statuette type, is created.

Humans reach North America via a land bridge and continue to South America.

c. 12,000 TO 300 BCE

The Jomon culture develops and flourishes in Japan.

c. 9000 BCE

A settlement appears at Jericho in western Asia.

Humans reach the southern tip of South America.

c. 9000 TO 8000 BCE

Rock carvings in Damaidi, China, seem to be proto-Chinese writing.

c. 8000 BCE

Neolithic period begins in Europe. Widespread evidence of burial customs indicates belief in an afterlife. Animal imagery may indicate some form of worship or propitiation.

The last wave of human migration into North America crosses the Bering Sea land bridge, before warming temperatures raise sea levels.

c. 6000 TO 5000 BCE

Sahara cave paintings depict animals.

c. 5000 BCE

Agricultural practices begin to spread through northern and western Europe.

c. 5000 TO 1500 BCE

The Yangshao culture appears in north and northwest China.

c. 4500 BCE

North America's first pottery appears in what is today the U.S. state of Georgia.

c. 4000 BCE

Egypt is divided into two kingdoms, Upper and Lower Egypt.

Pottery appears for the first time in South America, in modern Ecuador and Colombia.

c. 4000 TO 3000 BCE

Cities develop in Egypt, the Indus Valley, China, and Mesopotamia.

c. 4000 TO 2000 BCE

Persian plateau dominated by pastoral and nomadic peoples.

Arabian Semites establish a presence in Canaan-Phoenicia.

c. 3500 TO 1700 BCE

Harappan civilization flourishes in Indus Valley. The worship of Hindu gods, such as Shiva and Vishnu, begins.

c. 3500 BCE

The earliest known writing appears in western Asia. Agriculture begins to flourish, and early Mesopotamian religions based on a concord between king and god begin to form.

c. 3400 BCE

Hieroglyphs begin appearing in Egypt.

c. 3100 BCE

Village of Skara Brae on Orkney, northern Scotland, is occupied. Inhabitants likely involved in building nearby megaliths, such as tomb at Maes Howe and the Ring of Brodgar.

c. 3100 TO 3000 BCE

The Narmer Palette carved, an early example of Egyptian hieroglyphs.

c. 3000 TO 2000 BCE

Elam becomes a major power on the Persian plateau, influencing and absorbing Mesopotamian cultures and religions.

Mesopotamian kings begin to build ziggurats, massive brick-and-stone temples.

c. 3000 BCE

Egypt's two kingdoms united, purportedly by King Menes.

Phoenicians arrive in Canaan-Phoenicia, probably from Persian Gulf region.

Age of megalithic building begins in northwestern Europe.

China begins to produce silk, attributing technology to the legendary emperor Huangdi (the Yellow Emperor).

One of more than 350 stone heads recovered from the site of a Gaulish sanctuary, active in the first century CE. It is likely that the sanctuary honored a goddess of war.

THE CELTIC CULT OF THE HEAD

Classical authors reported that Celtic warriors decapitated slain enemies, preserving and displaying their heads. Although this cannot be specifically confirmed, archaeological evidence attests to a long tradition of mounting severed heads, real or carved, on the outside walls of temples and forts. Later Welsh and Irish literature also suggests this fascination with the decapitated head; severed heads produce prophecies, bless the waters of wells, and in one mythical instance—from the Welsh *Mabinogi*—guard the shores of Britain from foreign attack.

The Celtic "cult of the head" is thus attested to over a long period and a wide geographic range. A fundamental aspect of the cult seems to focus on the severed head's warding or guarding properties: when placed on temples, similarly to gargoyles on Christian cathedrals, they may have offered some protection to the sacred space within. In the later literature, heads provide a liaison with the Otherworld; perhaps in the early period, too, severed heads invited Celtic gods to make their presence known.

c. 3000 to 2180 BCE
Era of Egypt's Old Kingdom.

c. 3000 to 1000 BCE
Mesopotamian Bronze Age. Most peoples of the region practice polytheism. Judaism forms as a monotheistic religion.

2697 to 2598 BCE
Legendary reign of Huangdi, mythical first emperor of China.

c. 2550 to 2490 BCE
Three Egyptian pharaohs construct the three great pyramids at Giza in succession. The Sphinx likely constructed contemporaneously.

c. 2500 to 1700 BCE
The Langshan culture active in eastern China.

2334 to 2279 BCE
The lifetime of Sargon I, king who brought Mesopotamian empire of Akkadia to its height.

2333 BCE
Mythical founding of kingdom of Gojoseon in Korea by god-king Dangun Wanggeom.

c. 2100 to 1600 BCE
China's dynastic period begins with semilegendary Xia dynasty.

2040 to 1786 BCE
The Middle Kingdom of Egypt. Thebes becomes a major city.

c. 2000 BCE
Abraham—considered a holy patriarch in Jewish, Christian, and Islamic traditions—leaves the Mesopotamian city of Ur and travels throughout western Asia.

Sumerian versions of the *Epic of Gilgamesh* begin to appear.

Trade routes established in Europe, enabling cultural exchange.

Communal burial practices peak in north-central Europe.

Indo-European peoples migrate into Greece from the north and introduce new religious beliefs and practices. Island of Crete thrives as a separate region.

c. 2000 to 1300 BCE
Lapita culture appears in Melanesia and gradually spreads eastward, ultimately to Fiji.

c. 2000 to 1000 BCE
European cultures begin to develop a warrior elite, affecting religious practices.

c. 1800 BCE
Hyksos invasions defeat the kingdom of Egypt.

Scandinavian Bronze Age begins.

1792 to 1750 BCE
Hammurabi reigns in Babylonia; codifies laws in written form.

KING AHAB DIES AS PROPHESIED

According to the Hebrew scriptures, a group of flattering court prophets told King Ahab of Israel that he would win the battle he was to fight the next day, but Micaiah, a true prophet, told him that he would die if he fought. Ahab ignored Micaiah and died in battle.

In ancient times prophets who were believed to speak for their gods were common in West Asia. They could work independently or be attached to a temple or a royal court. King Ahab's wife, Jezebel, brought to court 450 prophets of the god Baal when she came to Israel to marry Ahab. Court prophets, however, tended to tell the king what he wanted to hear. The Hebrew scriptures include the writings of fifteen prophets who were considered true and recount stories about many more. In Israel, because they were thought to speak for God, prophets could generally tell a king he was wrong with immunity. Many prophets were persecuted, however, because they delivered a message that no one wanted to hear.

King Ahab dies in the midst of battle, as prophesied by Micaiah.

c. 1700 BCE
A new form of writing (Linear A) appears on Crete.

c. 1650 to 700 BCE
The Woodland culture flourishes in what is today the state of Louisiana, building large complexes for unknown purposes.

c. 1600 BCE
Scandinavian rock carvings seem to represent gods and religious beliefs.

1600 BCE
Hittites sack Babylon.

1600 to 1046 BCE
Reign of Shang dynasty in China. While imprisoned by the last ruler of Shang, King Wen of neighboring Zhou designs a sequence of the I Ching (Yi Jing) hexagrams, an expression of an ancient Chinese philosophy.

c. 1600 to 1200 BCE
Tumulus culture of central Europe is active, primarily known from burials in long tombs (*tumuli*).

c. 1500 to 1070 BCE
The New Kingdom of Egypt.

c. 1500 to 1200 BCE
Pyramidlike mounds begin to appear in Mesoamerica, suggesting development of established societal structure and religion.

c. 1500 BCE
Aryans migrate into northern India, bringing their Vedic religion. The oldest known Veda, the Rig Veda, may date to this period.

c. 1450 BCE
Greek invaders conquer much of Crete, ending Minoan influence but perhaps incorporating aspects of Minoan religion into Greek beliefs.

1400 to 1390 BCE
Pharaoh Thutmose IV of Egypt erects the "Dream Stele" at the foot of the Sphinx, recounting a dream in which the Sphinx spoke to him as a god.

c. 1350 BCE
Assyria rises to power.

c. 1350 to 1334 BCE
Pharaoh Akhenaten of Egypt institutes a monotheistic religion based on the sun god, but upon his death polytheism reasserts itself.

c. 1330 BCE
Elaborate tombs at Mycenae in Greece indicate a flourishing culture, aspects of which appear to influence later Greek myths.

1288 BCE
The Battle of Kadesh ends in stalemate between Egypt and the Hittites.

c. 1250 BCE
Moses leads the Jews out of Egypt and into Canaan. On this journey, according to Judeo-Christian tradition, Moses receives the Ten Commandments from God.

c. 1200 BCE
Canaanite religion, customs, and culture begin to be subsumed by Phoenicia.

Hebrews and Greeks appear in Canaan-Phoenicia.

c. 1200 to 1150 BCE
The Mycenaean culture disappears from Greece for unknown reasons.

c. 1200 to 800 BCE
Warring States period in Canaan-Phoenicia. The influx of various peoples from Egypt, Anatolia, and Mesopotamia influences the religious development of the region.

Urnfield culture of central and eastern Europe is most active, known primarily for interring cremated remains in urns.

c. 1150 to 300 BCE
The Olmec culture thrives in Mesoamerica, developing an elaborate religion in which rulers are apparently believed to be sacred.

Sovereignty Goddesses in Ireland and Wales

Emain Macha, a hill in modern County Armagh, Ireland, is named for the goddess Macha, and was considered a holy site of kingship in the pre-Christian period.

Before the Christian period, kingship in the Celtic countries of Ireland and Wales was a sacred office, dependent on the goodwill of Otherworldly deities. Most important of these in this context was the goddess of sovereignty. Major goddesses of this type include Rhiannon of Wales, Macha of Ulster (northern Ireland), and the promiscuous Medb, goddess of Connacht (western Ireland).

In the mythology, sovereignty goddesses choose kings by offering them a drink (a heavily symbolic act) and usually by marrying them. The theme occasionally appears prurient in the (Christian period) literature, but nevertheless accurately reflects the Celtic conception of land as female. Rightful kings were literally wedded to the land, and men watched the land for signs of their "wives'" displeasure, deposing the king if crops failed, too many storms arrived, or game vanished.

c. 1100 to 1000 BCE
Enuma Elish, a Babylonian epic poem, is written down, detailing Mesopotamian cosmogony.

1025 BCE
The twelve tribes of Israel in Canaan unite into a kingdom.

c. 1000 BCE
Indo-European peoples have migrated from the north into Italy, bringing religious traditions and the language that will become Latin.

The Mogollon people settle in what are today the U.S. states of Arizona and New Mexico.

Pottery first appears in South America's Amazon basin.

c. 1000 to 900 BCE
Fiji's Lapita people push eastward, ultimately to Samoa.

965 BCE
King David succeeded by son Solomon as ruler of Israel. Soon after, kingdom splits in two: Israel and Judah.

c. 1000 BCE to 0
Vedic traditions spread throughout northern India, influencing cultural and religious development. A strictly stratified social structure, still found today in Hindu India, begins to form.

c. 1000 BCE
Early representations of the svastika, or swastika, used on soapstone seals from the Indus Valley.

c. 900 BCE
One of the four Indian Aryan Vedas, the Atharva Veda, may have its origins in this period.

c. 900 to 800 BCE
Phoenician sailors explore the Mediterranean Sea, establishing a far-flung trading empire.

c. 900 to 200 BCE
Chavín culture emerges in South America's Andes.

c. 800 to 700 BCE
Jewish prophet Isaiah recounts the myth of the

leviathan, a theme also known in other Mesopotamian and West Asian religions.

Writing reappears in Greece, using a Phoenician script. The first Greek temples are constructed, and Greek settlers begin to colonize lands around the Aegean Sea. A cult surrounding the prophetess Sibyl develops in a Greek settlement in southern Italy. Delphi is associated with the oracular powers of a female priestess.

c. 800 to 600 BCE
A large tiered pyramid is built at Cuicuilco, in present-day Mexico, apparently for religious use.

c. 800 to 500 BCE
Archaic period in Greece. City-states develop along with regional religious practices.

c. 800 BCE
Phoenicia founds Carthage in North Africa.

776 BCE
The first Olympic Games held in Greece, honoring Zeus.

753 BCE
Traditional date of Rome's founding by the mythical brothers Romulus and Remus.

c. 750 BCE
Greek poet Hesiod writes the *Theogony*, a primary source of Greek religious concepts.

746 to 721 BCE
Assyria conquers northern Jewish kingdom, Israel.

c. 700 to 600 BCE
The *Epic of Gilgamesh* translated into Akkadian, its best-known form.

Ethiopia conquers Egypt; wars erupt in the region over the next two centuries.

c. 725 to 675 BCE
Homer's Greek epic poem *The Iliad* is recorded in written form.

701 BCE
Jerusalem repulses invading Assyrians.

650 BCE
The Greek city-state of Sparta establishes a military regime and a dual monarchy.

640 to 609 BCE
Josiah reigns in Judah and instigates religious reforms that forbid worshipping any other gods but Yahweh.

639 BCE
Assyrian invaders, led by King Ashurbanipal, destroy Susa, the Elamite capital.

c. 600 BCE
Beginning of six centuries of cultural development in Europe, Asia, and the Indian subcontinent; many religions come into being and others expand in this era, known as the Axial Age.

Zoroastrian teachings spread throughout the Persian plateau. The *Gathas* (a collection of hymns), later incorporated into the sacred Zoroastrian text the Avesta, date linguistically to this period. They are said to be the words of Zoroaster, whose actual lifetime remains undetermined.

Jainism becomes an organized religion in the sixth century BCE.

Mayas of Mesoamerica begin building ceremonial centers, incorporating pyramidal structures.

c. 600 to 500 BCE
Hebrew prophet Jeremiah preaches against polytheistic worship of nature gods.

Pythagoreans, members of a Greek mystery religion that delves into politics, mathematics, music, and other intellectual pursuits, become influential.

Athens, Sparta, Corinth, Thebes, and other Greek city-states emerge as major regional powers.

c. 600 to 300 BCE
Dao De Jing, the text from which the teachings of Daoism derive, is traditionally attributed to the fourth-century BCE Chinese sage Laozi, legendary founder of Daoism; but *Dao De Jing* may be a sixth-century BCE collection of writings by multiple contributors rooted in ancient Chinese beliefs.

According to tradition, the legendary Buddhist monk Bodhidharma travels to China and establishes the Chan school.

The sacred Vedic texts, the Vedas, are written down in India.

c. 599 BCE
Mahavira (c. 599–527 BCE), a holy man often called the founder of Jainism, born in the Ganges River valley.

c. 590 to 530 BCE
Approximate lifetime of Cyrus the Great, emperor of Persia, who extended Zoroastrianism throughout western Asia.

587 BCE
Nebuchadnezzar, king of Babylonia, captures Jerusalem and destroys the Jewish temple there. He exiles many Jews to Babylon, where they endure the "Babylonian captivity."

The Ellora Caves

ॐ

Constructed between the fifth and tenth centuries CE, the Ellora caves are part of a large complex of rock carvings near Aurangabad, India. The thirty-four caves together contain Buddhist, Jain, and Hindu art. The Hindu art dates mostly from the seventh century and shows events from the wealth of stories surrounding Hinduism's primary deities. The carvings were created at a time when Hinduism was enjoying a golden age, when the great epics were written, and the cults surrounding Vishnu and Shiva were gaining in influence.

Shiva and his consort Parvati are shown seated above Ravana, king of demons, who angered Shiva by shaking the god's mountain. Ravana become a devotee of Shiva after this transgression.

c. 569 BCE
Mahavira becomes an ascetic and begins teaching Jainism in India.

c. 563 BCE
Siddhartha Gautama, later known as the Buddha, born in Lumbini (now in Nepal).

553 BCE
Etruscans of Italy ally with Carthage, defeating Greeks in a major naval battle.

c. 551 BCE
Confucius born in China. Confucius's study of the ancient Chinese tradition of the I Ching becomes a primary Confucian text.

551 BCE
Egypt invades Kush, and the Kushites (Nubians) flee south to establish a new capital at Meroë.

539 BCE
Cyrus the Great of Persia captures Babylon and permits the Jews exiled there to leave, ending the Babylonian captivity. Many return to Jerusalem, others settle across West Asia and the lands surrounding the Mediterranean.

c. 534 BCE
According to Buddhist tradition, Siddhartha Gautama (Buddha) leaves his childhood home and begins his life as a holy man.

527 BCE
The Jain ascetic Mahavira dies, but the religion he helped found continues to spread through India.

525 BCE
Persia conquers Egypt.

510 BCE
Athens defeats Sparta in war.

509 BCE
Roman citizens depose tyrannical king Tarquinius (credited with bringing the divinatory Sibylline Books to Rome) and establish republican form of government.

508 BCE
Athenian statesman Cleisthenes leads Athens in establishing the first form of democratic government, with power shared by all male citizens.

c. 500 BCE
First structures of Monte Albán constructed in what is now Mexico; within a few centuries the Monte Albánites develop the Americas' first written language.

Adena culture in North America erects enormous earthen burial mounds as part of larger ritual complexes.

Ascetic religions, including Buddhism, Jainism, and Ajivika, take root in India. The first Buddhist nuns are ordained.

Drama begins to develop in Athens as a form of worshipping Dionysus.

Greeks, Etruscans, and Italic-speaking peoples cohabit on the Italian peninsula.

By this period North America is widely settled, with several distinct culture groups.

c. 500 TO 400 BCE
Nebuchadnezzar II restores Babylon as a major regional power.

Mystery cults spread through Greece dedicated to Demeter, Orpheus, Dionysus, and others.

c. 500 BCE TO 0
Sacred Hindu texts are written down for the first time.

Empires established by Greek city-states and by Carthage, Macedonia, and Rome. Trade routes and conquests spur cultural, linguistic, and religious blending.

490 BCE
Athens defeats a Persian invasion at Marathon.

c. 400 TO 300 BCE
Apparent ritual sacrifices performed in Denmark (the most famous victim is known as the Tollund Man), suggesting complex and well-established religious practices.

c. 483 BCE
The Buddha dies at Kushinagar in northern India. His closest disciples gather in Rajagaha at the First Buddhist Council and recite the Buddha's words to establish them in an oral tradition.

480 BCE
Athens defeats the Persians at Salamis, then allies with states in the eastern Aegean Sea and becomes a center of cultural, philosophical, and artistic development.

479 BCE
Chinese sage Confucius dies.

457 TO 221 BCE
Several Chinese philosophers, including Mozi, the Daoists Zhuangzi and Liezi, and the Confucian Mencius, are influential during this period in Chinese history. The important political philosophy of Legalism develops.

432 BCE
The Parthenon, a temple to Athena that today is considered a pinnacle of classical Greek architecture, is completed in Athens.

431 TO 404 BCE
Peloponnesian War between Athens and Sparta.

404 BCE
Egypt regains its independence from the Persian Achaemenid Empire.

c. 400 BCE

Jewish texts, including the Hebrew Bible, are being translated into Greek at Alexandria.

The Greek Temple of Apollo is constructed at Delphi.

c. 383 BCE

The Second Buddhist Council is held in Vasali to assess and formulate Buddhism's practices and traditions.

c. 371 TO 289 BCE

Lifetime of Mencius, called the "second sage" of Confucianism.

343 BCE

Artaxerxes III of Persia conquers Egypt, reincorporating it into the Achaemenid Empire.

337 BCE

Philip II of Macedon conquers Greece.

332 BCE

Alexander the Great of Macedon wrests control of Egypt from Persia. Received as a semi-deity, he founds the city of Alexandria near the mouth of the Nile.

330 BCE

Alexander conquers Persian Achaemenid Empire.

327 BCE

Alexander invades northwest India, reaching the Indus River, the farthest extent of his empire.

c. 325 BCE

Chandragupta ascends the throne of Magadha and begins a series of conquests across India.

323 BCE

Alexander dies in Babylon.

323 TO 185 BCE

The Mauryan Empire rules India.

312 TO 60 BCE

The Seleucid Empire controls Persia, Syria, and Babylonia, ensuring the dominance of Hellenic art forms and culture.

c. 300 BCE

The Zhuangzi, a primary Daoist text, is written.

The Yayoi people arrive in Japan from the Chinese mainland. Their Daoist religion merges with the indigenous Jomon religion.

c. 300 TO 200 BCE

The library at Alexandria, dedicated to the divine muses, is revered throughout the civilized world for its vast holdings.

c. 300 TO 100 BCE

A decline in classical religion in Greece coincides with the rise of Greek philosophy and mystery cults.

298 BCE

Chandragupta dies, having established India's first true empire and founded the Mauryan dynasty.

268 TO 232 BCE

Lifetime of Mauryan dynasty emperor Ashoka, who extends India's borders and converts to Buddhism, establishing its dominance in his empire; Buddhist missionaries journey far beyond India. The Vedic religion, already in decline, further subsides.

The Mon people of Myanmar (Burma) adopt Buddhism.

264 BCE

Rome consolidates its hold over the Italian peninsula.

264 TO 146 BCE

In a series of wars between Rome and the Punic Empire, centered at Carthage, Rome triumphs and becomes the dominant Mediterranean power.

c. 250 BCE

Third Buddhist Council is held in Pataljputra to assess Buddhism's religious practices and traditions. The

schism in Buddhism begins to crystallize into two schools, eventually called Theravada and Mahayana.

Buddhism and Jainism reach southern India; the Buddhist monk Mahinda arrives in Sri Lanka with 250 other monks. Buddhist temples and stupas appear in the Sri Lankan city of Anuradhapura, which is to enter Hindu mythology as home of King Ravana in the *Ramayana*.

247 BCE TO 224 CE

The Parthian Empire controls the Persian plateau.

233 BCE

Slave revolts contribute to the political instability of the city of Rome.

c. 224 BCE

The Sassanids overthrow the Parthians and establish an empire on the Persian plateau, endorsing Zurvanism—a form of Zoroastrianism—as the official state religion.

221 TO 206 BCE

The Qin dynasty unifies China as an empire for the first time. Emperor Qin Shi Huangdi tries to eradicate Confucianism, promoting Legalism instead.

210 BCE

Terracotta figures fashioned for the massive mausoleum of Emperor Qin of China.

206 BCE TO 220 CE

China's Han dynasty restores Confucianism, becoming the first Chinese government to officially adopt the philosophy.

c. 200 BCE

The Pueblo Indians (Anasazi) appear in the southwest of North America.

c. 200 BCE TO 0

The Gundestrup cauldron constructed, with scenes suggesting Celtic ritual or myths; deposited in a Danish bog.

c. 200 TO 100 BCE

Rome extends rule into Spain, northern Africa, and the Aegean; imports foreign beliefs and ideas such as the Greek pantheon of gods.

c. 200 BCE TO 200 CE

The Tamil region of southern India experiences its golden, or Sangam, age. Buddhism travels from this busy international trading center to various Southeast Asian lands.

The Ramayana is composed; a text on Indian history and Hindu mythology that is central to Hinduism, it is traditionally attributed to the poet Valmiki.

c. 200 BCE TO 500 CE

The Hopewell people, whose culture supplants the Adena culture in North America, build large burial mounds in the Ohio River region.

c. 200 BCE TO 600 CE

The Nazca culture flourishes in Peru. Enormous pictures are inscribed on the desert floor, presumably for religious or spiritual purposes.

c. 200 BCE TO 900 CE

The Teotihuacán and Mayan cultures flourish in Mesoamerica. The Maya construct enormous and

Commonly encountered in Mesopotamian mythology, the Akkadian lamassu (Sumerian lama) appears as a human-head winged bull. A protective deity, this lamassu guarded King Sargon II's palace door in the eighth century BCE.

elaborate temple-palace structures throughout their territory and develop a complex system of religious ritual.

196 BCE
Rome wrests Greece from Macedonian rule.

185 BCE
King Pushyamitra Sunga overthrows the Mauryan dynasty in India and embarks on a destructive campaign against Buddhism.

168 TO 164 BCE
The Maccabees lead a revolt in Judaea, winning independence from the Seleucid Empire and rededicating the temple in Jerusalem.

C. 150 BCE
Descendants of the Lapita begin to push eastward across the Pacific Ocean, setting out from Samoa and Tonga and reaching the Marquesas and Society islands.

C. 109 TO 91 BCE
The Chinese scholar Sima Qian writes *The Records of the Grand Historian*, which provides the only extant information on Laozi, legendary founder of Daoism.

C. 100 BCE
The Silk Road complex of trading routes links East and West.

The Fourth Buddhist Council held in Kashmir; unrecognized by the Theravada school, the council cements the formation of the Mahayana school.

C. 100 BCE TO 0
Medes and Parthians dominate the Persian plateau, their faiths featuring religious reverence for natural forces.

Rome dominates the Mediterranean world. The earliest Roman calendar dates to this period, identifying the religious aspects of each day as well as establishing holy periods dedicated to specific gods and celebrated with prescribed rituals.

COUNCIL OF JERUSALEM

The early leaders of the Christian Church had to decide whether to accept non-Jews as members and, if they did, whether these men and women should be expected to follow Jewish law. According to the Acts of the Apostles (a book in the Christian Bible), Peter, Paul, and others met in Jerusalem to discuss the matter. The most controversial issue was circumcision, which was required for all male Jews. If an adult Gentile (non-Jew) became a Christian, did he have to undergo the painful rite of circumcision? After heated discussion a compromise was reached. Gentile Christians would not have to be circumcised, but all Christians should observe certain Jewish dietary restrictions and marriage laws. The leaders then sent out to all the local churches a letter disclosing their decision.

The Council of Jerusalem was the first such Christian assembly, and it set the tone for the later ecumenical councils—gatherings of representatives from all parts of the world—that were to establish doctrine for the entire church.

HEROD'S TEMPLE IS DEDICATED
⁓

When the Jews returned to Jerusalem after exile in Babylon in the sixth century BCE, they rebuilt the temple the Babylonians had destroyed. It was not nearly as grand as the original temple, which had been built by King Solomon; nevertheless, it was used for some 500 years. When Herod the Great became king of the Jews in the late first century BCE he undertook the gargantuan task of restoring and greatly expanding the temple. Construction began in about 20 BCE and ended in 63 CE, sixty-seven years after Herod's death. Jesus taught in Herod's temple while it was still under construction. The completed temple was larger and grander than Solomon's original and included vast walled courtyards in addition to the main temple buildings. In 70 CE, however, a mere seven years after its completion, it was destroyed by the Romans when they put down a rebellion of Jewish Zealots. All that remained standing was a section of retaining wall, where Jews still come to pray.

A model of Herod's Temple before its destruction in 70 CE.

98 BCE
Tacitus, a Roman senator and historian, writes *Germania*, which provides information about religious beliefs and practices of Germanic and Celtic peoples.

C. 83 BCE
The canon of Theravada Buddhist beliefs (the Buddha's remembered words), called the Tipitaka, which existed as an established oral tradition, is written down.

68 BCE
Emperor Ming of China's Han dynasty welcomes back his envoys to India, who are accompanied by Buddhist monks and bring with them disassembled buildings and a Buddha statue.

59 TO 49 BCE
Roman general Julius Caesar conquers Gaul. He records his observations of the religious practices of the Germanic and Celtic peoples he encounters.

44 BCE
Caesar, who had ruled Rome as dictator for life, assassinated by senators.

30 BCE
Gaius Octavius defeats Mark Antony and Cleopatra, bringing Egypt under Roman rule as the province Aegyptus. The political situation encourages a blending of Roman and Egyptian religion in northern Africa.

C. 30 BCE TO 0
Migrations and expulsions result in the establishment of far-flung Jewish communities across Europe.

27 BCE
Gaius Octavius crowned as the first emperor of Rome, renaming himself Augustus Caesar. He deifies Julius Caesar, thus entwining Roman politics and religion. Augustus reasserts the primacy of Roman religion and declares Greece a Roman province, naming it Achaea.

12 BCE
Augustus Caesar declares himself pontifex maximus (high priest).

C. 7 BCE
Jesus of Nazareth born in Bethlehem, a town near Jerusalem.

4 BCE
According to legend, the most sacred Shinto shrine is built in Ise and dedicated to Amaterasu, the Japanese sun goddess important in the Shinto religion.

C. 0 TO 100 CE
Jewish scholars are recording oral traditions, primarily concerning biblical interpretation.

The Kingdom of Aksum (Ethiopia) is a regional power along the southwest coast of the Red Sea. According to biblical tradition, Philip the Evangelist baptizes an Ethiopian noble, who subsequently establishes Ethiopia as the first African Christian nation.

C. 0 TO 200
Images of the Buddha first appear. The tradition develops in northern India, particularly near Gandhara.

C. 0 TO 200
An Egyptian scholar of Hellenic Alexandria, Ptolemy makes great strides in astronomy, cartography, and mathematics. His theory of a geocentric universe has a major influence on Islamic and Christian cosmology for 1,300 years.

64
A severe fire in Rome devastates much of the city. Emperor Nero uses the fire to incite persecution of Christians. Martyred Christians probably include two of the most influential early church leaders: Peter, one of the twelve apostles of Jesus Christ, and the missionary Paul of Tarsus.

70
Emperor Titus of Rome puts down the revolt in Judaea, taking the city of Jerusalem and destroying the Jewish temple there. Many Jews flee to Alexandria, where they establish a thriving community.

c. 100

A fourth Christian Gospel written, attributed to an author named John.

Gnostic movements become a powerful philosophical and religious force in the Roman Empire, influencing (often by opposition) early Christian theology.

c. 100 to 200

The Mogollon culture peaks in North America.

The Christian church develops an episcopal system of organization, with bishops presiding over groups of churches.

The Ebionite sect, a group of ascetic Jewish Christians, develops in Palestine.

Valentius founds a Gnostic movement in Rome that spreads through the empire and provokes hostility and theological arguments from orthodox Christianity through the third century.

The Madhyamaka and Yogacara schools of Buddhism develop in India.

c. 100 to 300

Focusing on communal worship, Christianity develops the ritual enactment of Christ's Last Supper, and readings from various texts, many of which later become part of the New Testament.

c. 110

Bishop Ignatius of Antioch, later canonized, is martyred in Rome. His letters establish fundamental arguments of orthodox Christianity, and his embrace of martyrdom establishes martyrdom as a religiously responsible act for Christians.

132

Led by Bar Kokhba, Jews known as Zealots retake Jerusalem from Rome.

135

Rome retakes Jerusalem, killing Bar Kokhba and ending independent Jewish statehood in Palestine until 1948.

136

Inscriptions honoring the Persian god Mithra become extremely popular in the Roman world. Mithraism gains a large following throughout the empire, particularly attracting members of the Roman army.

184 to 205

A Daoist sect called the Yellow Turbans rebels against the Han dynasty in China. Although not immediately successful, the rebellion helps extinguish the dynasty and ends Confucianism's supremacy.

c. 200

Rabbis record oral traditions concerning religious interpretation of Jewish scriptures in a work called the Mishnah ("repeated study").

Christian authorities repress overt Gnosticism, although elements of the philosophy persist.

Construction of Tiwanaku, the center of a technologically advanced civilization in the Andes of South America, begins.

200

Jain adherents split into two sects: the Digambara, or "sky clad," and the Svetambara, or "white clad."

c. 200 to 300

Monatus, a priest of Cybele, converts to Christianity and founds the ascetic Monatist sect, which spreads throughout much of the Roman Empire.

Jewish scholars are writing down the Talmud, scholarly commentaries on the scriptures, laws, and other oral traditions.

200 to 700

The Avesta, the primary text of Zoroastrianism, is compiled from older manuscripts and traditions by the Sassanian kings.

c. 210 to 276

Lifetime of Mani, founder of the influential Manichean sect, dubbed heretical by Christian authorities; Manichaeanism spreads rapidly in the West, and as far east as China, and influences many sects and Christian heresies.

c. 215 to 272

King Shapur I rules the Sassanid Empire and supports Manichaeanism. The sect loses favor after his death, and Manichaeans are persecuted. Sassanid officials are believed to have put Mani to death.

220 to 280

During what is now known as the Three Kingdoms period of Chinese history, several distinct Buddhist schools develop in China, including the Pure Land and Chan schools.

250 to 336

Lifetime of Arius, a Christian priest in Alexandria who starts the widely popular Arian movement—eventually denounced as heretical by church authorities—that splits Egypt's Christians into hostile groups.

251 to 356

Anthony of Egypt, later canonized, lives as a hermit in Egypt. His retreat begins an ascetic custom often imitated throughout Christianity.

c. 300 to 400

Christian authorities compile the texts of the developing Christian scripture. By the end of the century, the New Testament had been established.

Faith in the ancient gods of Egypt fades almost entirely as Christianity rises in the region.

Frumentius and Edisius, two captured Phoenician Christians, preach Christianity to the Ethiopian court.

A Royal Pilgrimage

Since the second century, Christians have traveled to Israel to visit the places where Jesus walked. Perhaps the most famous of the early pilgrimages was that of Emperor Constantine's mother, Helena, who traveled to Jerusalem in 326. Already in her seventies, Helena had become an ardent supporter of Christianity, the religion her son had legalized about a dozen years earlier. According to the Christian writer Eusebius, Helena traveled around the region, identifying sacred sites and ordering the construction of churches and shrines to mark the locations.

A legend recounts that Helena went to Jerusalem specifically to search for the cross on which Jesus died and that she found it buried on the hill of Golgotha. On this hilltop and over the nearby grave identified as the place where Jesus was buried, Helena commissioned the building of the Church of the Holy Sepulcher. This church became the highlight of the millions of pilgrimages that were to follow in the centuries ahead.

A statue of Saint Helena, referencing her legendary recovery of Christ's cross, stands in Saint Peter's Basilica in Rome, Italy.

SANCTA HELENA

311 TO C. 700

Dissatisfaction with the election of Caecilian to the see of Carthage precipitates the Donatist schism. Led first by Carthaginian bishop Donatus, the Donatist church resists persecution by Roman and Christian authorities until Islamic conquest in the seventh century.

312

General Constantine of Rome receives a vision of the Christian cross before the Battle of the Milvian Bridge. Fighting under the cross, he wins a decisive victory and becomes emperor of the West. His subsequent conversion marks a crucial turning point in Christian history.

313

Emperor Constantine and Licinius, emperor of the East, together issue the Edict of Milan, ensuring religious freedom throughout the Roman world.

320

Pachomius, later canonized, establishes the first organized community of Christian monks in Egypt.

320 TO 550

Reign of the Gupta dynasty in India, a period of political stability and religious tolerance, during which Jainism and Buddhism flourish and Hinduism enters its classical period. The Hindu god Vishnu gains in eminence, and the Mahabharata, the great Hindu epic, is written down.

324

Emperor Constantine defeats Emperor Licinius, who had been persecuting Christians.

325

Emperor Constantine intercedes in Christian theological arguments, convening the Council of Nicaea. The ensuing Nicene Creed resolves, at least temporarily, the contentious issue of Jesus Christ's divine nature, concluding that he was both human and divine.

330

Emperor Constantine rededicates the Greek city Byzantium as the new capital of the Roman Empire. It acquires the name Constantinople and becomes a center of Christianity.

337

Emperor Constantine is baptized on the day of his death, formally accepting Christianity as his religion.

338 TO 422

Lifetime of Fa Xian, the Chinese pilgrim who seeks Buddhist sites in India.

C. 350 TO 400

The Palestinian Talmud (meaning "study or learning"), compiled in Caesarea and Tiberius, is written. Both the Palestinian and Babylonian Talmuds contain the Mishnah as well as the Gemara ("completion"), rabbinic commentary on the Mishnah.

C. 350 TO 750

The nine earliest Puranas, sacred Hindu texts, composed in India.

366

According to tradition, a traveling Buddhist monk envisions 1,000 golden Buddhas and begins the excavation of the Mogao Caves near Dunhuang, China.

ANIMALS IN NORTHERN EUROPE

Animals play large, vivid, and complex roles in the mythologies of northern Europe. Wolves appear regularly in Norse iconography; boars romp with impunity across Celtic carvings; and horses everywhere carry deities across worlds. Other favorites include bears, ravens, and cattle, each with deep mythical significance.

Christianity tends to impose a hierarchy upon the natural world, placing humans at the top and animals in descending order of use (thus sheep, as providers, were prevalent metaphors, while wolves became devilish hordes), but this was not the case in pre-Christian Europe. Animals were viewed as existing in both the human and divine realms, and there was no clear distinction between animal and god on the one hand and human and animal on the other. Reports of adaptation of animal characteristics may thus indicate rituals, designed to merge human and divine through the common medium of animal, and there is no shortage of shape-shifting in Celtic, Norse, or Germanic mythology or mythic iconography.

A bronze boar from a first-century Gaulish sanctuary in what is today Loiret, France.

380

Emperor Theodosius I of Rome proclaims Christian faith to be predicated on a belief in the Holy Trinity (the Father, the Son, and the Holy Ghost). Christianity becomes the official religion of the Roman Empire.

394

The last Olympic Games of the ancient world are held.

C. 400

Seafaring Polynesians colonize the easternmost and northernmost islands of the Pacific, including Hawaii and Easter Island, where they erect remarkable statues, seemingly with religious or spiritual intent.

The Kingdom of Ghana appears in northwestern Africa.

C. 400 TO 500

Worship of the remaining ancient Egyptian gods, notably Isis, disappears.

Christian missionaries arrive in Ethiopia.

Daoist teachings are organized into a formal religion. The *Daozang*, a collection of Daoist texts, commentaries, and scriptures, is compiled.

The Mogao Caves, near Dunhuang, China, become a holy site for many religions, including Buddhism, Daoism, Confucianism, and Christianity.

Though two distinct regional styles developed from at least the fifth century—the Nagara in the north, the Dravida in the south—all Hindu temples embody the same fundamental religious tenets.

405

Jerome, an early biblical scholar who is later canonized, completes the first major translation of the Christian Bible into Latin. It is known as the Vulgate, after the Latin word for common (referring to Latin as the common language).

410

Visigoth raiders sack Rome, ending the Roman Empire.

413–426

Bishop Augustine of Hippo Regius, later canonized, writes *The City of God*, a major Christian theological treatise.

C. 450

The Hopewell culture of North America goes into decline.

Saxons invade Britain.

C. 500

The Jewish Babylonian Talmud, which includes much of the earlier Palestinian Talmud and is usually referred to simply as the Talmud, is completed.

By this period, both schools of Buddhism (Theravada and Mahayana) have spread east as far as the Pacific Ocean.

C. 500 TO 600

The six primary schools of Chinese Buddhism appear in Japan.

500 TO C. 540

The Kingdom of Aksum (Ethiopia) becomes a significant center of Christianity.

511

The Gupta Empire is overthrown by the Hephtalites ("White Huns").

532

Emperor Justinian I begins construction of the Hagia Sophia church in Constantinople, which symbolizes Constantinople's centrality in the Christian world, and alienates Rome.

MID SIXTH CENTURY

The bubonic plague ravages Constantinople; the Roman church strengthens.

570 TO 632

Life of Muhammad; Islamic religion spreads over the Arabian Peninsula.

THE MABINOGI

The major corpus of Welsh mythology, the *Mabinogi* consists of four major tales (sometimes termed "branches") and several additional stories. None appear in manuscripts before the fourteenth century, but certainly the tales are centuries older. They offer a beguiling glance into the Welsh conception of gods, heroes, and the Otherworld—a place of indifferent geography and of enchantment.

Of particular interest in the *Mabinogi* is the role of magic and the supernatural, which constantly threatens disruption and interference. This likely reflects a very basic Celtic world-view, balancing (human) order and (Otherworldly) chaos through myths and ritual. Several episodes in the Mabinogi deal with the tension between human and Otherworld, order and chaos, invariably requiring carefully calibrated cooperation between the two worlds. For example, a misstep by a human king, Pwyll, nearly results in disaster when he offends the Otherworld king Arawn; but since he, as a mortal, is able to slay Arawn's supernatural foe, harmony is achieved and Pwyll's reign is blessed.

A modern sculpture by Ivor Robert-Jones depicts the mythological giant-king Bendigeidfran, hero of the second branch of the *Maginogi*, carrying the body of his nephew.

c. 600
The Teotihuacán culture of South America and its eponymous main city decline.

Hinduism is first adopted by Indian royal courts.

c. 600 to 700
Buddhism prospers in Tibet, where it blends with indigenous traditions.

Buddhism arrives in Indonesia and thrives.

Islam arrives in Ethiopia, supplanting Christianity.

Laozi, the originator of Daoist thought, is deified by the Tang dynasty, although Buddhism is China's official religion.

A dualist Christian sect emerges in Armenia, preaching a doctrine of a good and an evil God and rejecting much of the Bible and the established church. According to its teaching, an evil God created and ruled the physical world, while a good God ruled heaven.

Islam grows rapidly in North Africa, the Levant, Mesopotamia, Persia, and China. Major differences in the interpretation of the Qur'an emerge, as well as differing opinions regarding who should lead the religion. The predominant language of Islam is Arabic.

c. 600 to 1200
The Khmer ethnic group dominates the Mekong Valley. The Angkor Wat temple is built under King Suryavarman II in the early twelfth century.

613
Visigoth rulers of Spain force Jews either to convert or be exiled.

617 to 649
King Songtsän Gampo unifies Tibet and establishes Buddhism in the region. He founds Jokhang temple in Lhasa, and his two wives are worshipped as incarnations of a Buddhist goddess.

618 to 907
The golden age of Chinese Buddhism under the Tang dynasty. Confucianism's influence wanes.

622
Muhammad and a number of followers depart Mecca for Yathrib (Medina). This *hijra* (migration) marks the beginning of Muhammad's success as a leader and leads to the establishment of Islam as a religious and social entity. The *hijra* also marks the starting point of the Islamic calendar.

c. 630
Muhammad travels to the Ka'bah (shrine) in the temple at Mecca and orders all idols to be removed in order to restore the shrine's purity.

632
Muhammad makes the first *hajj* (pilgrimage) to Mecca, a symbolic event that Muslims replicate each year.

633
The Fourth Council of Toledo declares against the enforced baptism of Jews. Previously baptized infants are nonetheless kept from their Jewish parents.

637
Islamic forces conquer Palestine, Syria, and Mesopotamia. They soon penetrate Egypt, Persia, and North Africa.

c. 650
The South American Huari culture, based in the Andes, controls all of what is today northern Peru.

With the rise of Muslim power in Persia, Zoroastrians flee to surrounding countries.

c. 650
In the mid-seventh century, the powerful king Songtsän Gampo takes control of western China and parts of northern India.

655 to 705
The reign of Wu Zetian, China's only official female emperor. She is a patron of Buddhism as a whole, but particularly the Huayang school.

c. 660
After the death of the fourth caliph, the Umayyad dynasty begins its rule over many Muslim lands.

668
Korea united under the Silla kingdom, as Zen Buddhism, known as Seon, arrives in the country and rises in popularity.

685 to 691
The Dome of the Rock, a Muslim shrine built over a place sacred to both Muslims and Jews, is constructed in Jerusalem during the reign of an Umayyad caliph.

c. 700
The Mississippi culture rises in southern North America.

King Arthur appears in Welsh literature

c. 750
Three sects of Hinduism arise on the Indian subcontinent: the Palas in the northeast, the Gurjara-Pratiharas in the northwest, and the Rashtrakutas in the south.

c. 700 to 800
Tibetan Buddhism (often called Vajrayana) develops.

Abbu 'Issa al-Isfahani founds a Jewish-Islamic sect (the first of its kind) in Persia and leads a rebellion against the Abbasid rulers, claiming to be the last in a line of prophets that includes Jesus Christ and Muhammad.

710 to 784
Buddhism becomes Japan's official religion during what is known as the Nara period.

711
Muslims from North Africa conquer Spain, restoring freedom and social status to Jewish residents.

712
The *Kojiki*, or *Records of the Ancient Matters*, is completed. This book includes a genealogy that traces the ancestry of the Japanese imperial family back to Amaterasu.

720
The *Nihongi*, or *Chronicles of Japan*, is completed. The second historical work of the Nara period, it is an account of Japanese history until 720.

726 to 843
The Byzantine emperor Leo III orders the destruction of all icons, beginning the "iconoclastic controversy." Many dissenting Christians are persecuted in this controversy, settled in 843 when the empress Theodora allows churches to venerate icons.

741
The White Cloud Temple, central to the Dragon Gate sect of Daoism, is built under the Tang dynasty in Beijing.

750
The Abbasid dynasty overthrows the Umayyads and an Islamic golden age begins.

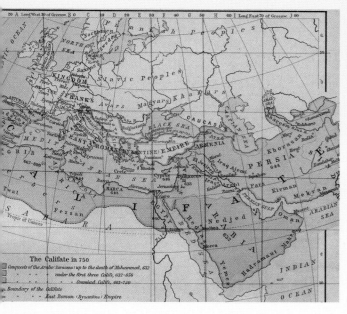

The Califate in 750
Conquests of the Arabs (Saracens) up to the death of Muhammad, 632
under the first three Califs, 632–656
Ommiad Califs, 661–750
Boundary of the Califate
East Roman (Byzantine) Empire

751

Pepin the Short, son of Charles Martel, becomes king of the Franks, beginning the Carolingian dynasty.

c. 750 TO 1000

Eleven Hindu Puranas are composed.

760 TO 770

The Karaites, a Mesopotamian Jewish sect, call for a return to Palestine and the rejection of rabbinic laws. Jewish religious authorities, known as the geonim, reject the movement.

764

The Abbasid dynasty moves the imperial capital to Baghdad, replacing the Umayyad capital of Damascus. This move is symbolic of their shift of focus from West to East.

c. 770 TO 1000

Jewish scholars called the Masoretes introduce vowels to written Hebrew, in an attempt to reduce linguistic ambiguity in Jewish texts. They retranscribe the Hebrew Bible at the end of this period, the result of which has since become the standard.

778 TO 850

The temple Borobudur is constructed under the Shailendra dynasty in Indonesia. This grand temple is a relic of the Vajrayana Buddhist tradition that prospered in Indonesia from the seventh to the fourteenth century.

785

King Trisong Detsen constructs Samye, the first Buddhist monastery in Tibet. The Nyingma order is founded.

794 TO 1185

During the Heian period, Buddhism flourishes in Japan. Two principal schools are founded: the Tendai, founded by Saicho, which makes Buddhism available to all people instead of just the ruling class, and the Shingon, founded by Kukai, which is a form of Vajrayana Buddhism.

788 TO 820

Adi Shankara (788–820), preacher, scholar, and founder of four major monasteries, or *mathas* is a key figure in the dissemination of what became known as Advaita Vedanta. Shankara is also regarded by some Hindus as an incarnation of Shiva.

KHAZARS

By the eighth century these seminomadic Turkic peoples of the steppe lands north of the Caucasus Mountains and the Caspian Sea had converted from shamanist religious practices to mainly Christianity and Islam. As their dominion grew over a vast region, the Khazars found themselves under intense pressure from Christian and Islamic political forces that demanded they become allies. Unwilling to be swept into open conflict with either camp, the Khazars—or at least their leaders—instead converted to Judaism.

793 TO 1066

The Viking Age. Much of the Celtic and Anglo-Saxon literature is written during this time.

800

Charlemagne crowned emperor of the West by Pope Leo XIII.

c. 800 TO 900

The Maya culture of Mesoamerica declines.

c. 800 TO 1000

Tibetan Buddhism declines under hostility from Tibetan kings.

830

Abbasids found the House of Wisdom, an important library and translation center in Baghdad.

843

The Holy Roman Empire is divided.

845

Chinese Buddhism comes under attack during the rule of the Daoist emperor Wu-Tsung. Monasteries and temples are destroyed, and monks and nuns are forced from religious life.

c. 900 TO 1000

The Jewish population in France, hitherto mostly merchants, begins to expand.

A smaller Holy Roman Empire emerges under the Saxon ruler Otto I.

The Fatimids, a Shia dynasty claiming direct descent from Muhammad's daughter, come to power in Egypt. They rule from North Africa to the Levant until the end of the twelfth century.

912 TO 961

Reign of Caliph Abd ar-Rahman III in the Emirate of Córdoba (Spain). Spanish Jewish culture peaks.

918 TO 1392

During the Goryeo period, both Buddhism and Confucianism are prominent in Korean society. Toward the Goryeo's end, Buddhism loses influence.

936

Zoroastrian refugees escaping persecution in Iran land on the Indian coast and establish a thriving enclave.

941

One of the greatest Jain literary works, the *Adipurana*, composed by the Kannada poet Adikavi Pampa.

c. 950

The southern dynasties gradually come to displace the previous hegemony of northern India, especially with the rise of the Cholas from the middle of the century.

Puranas are being written, some to date from as late as the twelfth century.

960 TO 1279

An era of prosperity begins for China under the Song dynasty. Buddhism revived but unable to flourish due to the destruction of its institutions under Wu-Tsung as well as its downfall in India under Islamic rule.

Confucianism resurfaces in an expanded form under the leadership of the philosopher Zhu Xi, synthesizing its core philosophy of ethical behavior with transcendent elements of Buddhism and Daoism.

A Chinese translation of the Pali Tipikata is assembled.

963

Otto I has Pope John XII deposed for conspiring against him and forces the election of Pope Leo VIII.

ALBIGENSIAN CRUSADE
ॐ

The Albigensian Crusade of 1209–29 was declared by Pope Innocent III (1161–1216) to wipe out the Cathar heresy in the Languedoc region of southern France. This highly cultured and prosperous country had close ties with Catalonia and little affinity for northern France. Innocent's promise to give the Cathar estates to crusaders appealed to many Catholic lords attracted by Languedoc's riches.

The Cathar church refused to bow to the doctrinal dictates of Roman Catholicism and instead preached a gospel inspired by Gnosticism and Manichaeanism. The Cathars believed human beings possess a divine aspect that is trapped in the material realm. The forces governing that realm can be transcended only by direct knowledge of the divine, of God.

The fighting was fierce in several campaigns, and Catharism was destroyed, in part because of an Inquisition that executed anyone who refused to recant their beliefs. As many as one million people, mostly noncombatants, died in the Albigensian Crusade.

The Siege of Carcassonne, in 1209, ended with humiliation for the Cathar stronghold when the victors allowed the city to empty peacefully—so long as they left all possessions, including clothing, behind.

982 TO 1054

Lifetime of Atisha, an Indian prince who begins a revival of Buddhism in Tibet, where he founds the Kadampa school (later the Gelugpa, or "Yellow Hat," order).

c. 1000

Athabascan Indians (the ancestors of today's Navajos) appear in North America's southwest, interacting with and eventually supplanting the Pueblo Indians.

The Tiwanaku and Hwari cultures of the Andes Mountains in South America decline; the Chimú take over much of their former territory.

c. 1000

The seventh reincarnation of Vishnu, Rama, a knightly warrior and hero of the Ramayana, becomes popular in Hindu worship.

c. 1000 TO 1100

The eastern and western halves of the Christian church decisively split over theological issues (primarily, the nature of Christ's divinity) and Church organization.

Muslim invasions of India nearly eradicate Buddhism from the subcontinent.

Jewish communities in central Europe continue to grow, developing a separate culture, later called Ashkenazi (as opposed to the Sephardic Jews of the Iberian Peninsula and the Arab countries).

The Turkish Seljuk clan, recent converts to Sunni Islam, fights its way to power, capturing Syria, Palestine, and much of Christian Anatolia.

The Eastern and Western churches split, becoming the Orthodox and Catholic churches, respectively.

Islam becomes the official state religion under the Seljuks, who govern from Central Asia and the Persian Gulf to the Mediterranean. The clergy gains political authority.

c. 1000 TO 1300

Pre-Christian myths of Scandinavia are recorded and interpreted by Christian scholars. Primary sources include the Poetic or Elder Edda, a compilation of poems composed between the eighth and tenth centuries, and the Prose or Younger Edda, written by the Icelander Snorri Sturluson in the thirteenth century.

c. 1000 TO 1500

The last group of the Hindu Puranas composed in India.

1040 TO 1105

Lifetime of Solomon ben Isaac (Rashi), an enormously influential French Jewish scholar.

1044 TO 1077

Reign of the Burmese king Anawrahta, who converts Burma to Theravada Buddhism. His kingdom is based in Pagan (now Bagan) and lasts for two centuries.

c. 1050 TO 1300

The Pueblo Indians (Anasazi) of North America's southwest construct impressive cliff dwellings, which include semi-subterranean kivas, or sacred rooms.

1054

In an escalating conflict between western churches and Constantinople, which the West felt had too large a role in the Christian church, the patriarch of Constantinople bans Latin rites in his Orthodox churches, while Pope Leo IX bans Greek rites in the West.

1059

Pope Nicholas II decrees that popes must be elected by cardinals rather than by lay rulers.

1070

A riot in Granada, Spain, destroys the Jewish community there.

1076

Pope Gregory VII deposes and excommunicates the Holy Roman emperor Henry IV.

1085

Alfonso VI of Castile conquers Toledo, beginning a long reconquest of Spain by Christian rulers. Spain's Muslims ally themselves with Muslim rulers of North Africa, who gradually impose strict rules on the Jews of Spain.

1095

Pope Urban II calls for a crusade to protect Christian pilgrimage routes and claim the Holy Land.

1099

Christian crusaders conquer Palestine; Palestinian Judaism nearly vanishes as many Palestinian Jews emigrate to Mesopotamia. The Kingdom of Jerusalem, a Christian state controlling some of the holiest sites of Judaism, Christianity, and Islam, is established by the crusaders.

c. 1100

Hopi Native Americans in what is now the state of Arizona found Old Oraibi, the oldest continuously inhabited settlement in North America.

c. 1100 TO 1200

The Buddhist Mon Kingdom of Burma reaches its zenith.

David Alroy, a Jew from Kurdistan, inspires a large Jewish following to believe in the imminent arrival of a messiah who will return them to Israel.

Sufis, an order of ascetic Muslims living in poverty and attempting to overcome earthly desires, gain importance as missionaries.

1109

Muslims massacre Jews in Toledo and Burgos, Spain, prompting Jews in the region to flee to northern Spain.

According to a Catholic legend, Cathar and Catholic books were collected during the Albigensian Crusade and subjected to trial by fire; although the Cathar books burned, the Catholic ones survived intact, thus demonstrating their orthodoxy.

CATHARS

The Cathars were a Gnostic Christian sect that flourished in southern France between the eleventh and thirteenth centuries until being wiped out by the twenty-year-long Albigensian Crusade. Considered a dangerous heresy by Pope Innocent III (1161–1216), who called for the crusade, Catharism traces its origins back to the Bogomils of eastern Europe, the Gnostic Christians, and Hermetic movements in Egypt, among others.

Those forerunners, too, were often ruthlessly persecuted by the established religious authorities as heresies to be eradicated. Although the Cathars were destroyed by the crusade and the subsequent Inquisition, their culture and beliefs influenced many later religious figures and philosophers. Cathar doctrine and teachings were banned, but much of its spirituality was conveyed to other lands by the veiled songs of the troubadours.

The symbolism of the troubadours' songs of courtly love has been described as the suitor (the seeking soul) loving the lady (the divine spirit) but having to contend with the jealous husband (the religious authorities).

c. 1130

Arnold of Brescia, an abbot from Lombardy and an early reformer, begins preaching that church leaders should live in poverty. He is eventually executed while leading an open revolt against Rome.

1138 TO 1204

Lifetime of Moses ben Maimon (Maimonides), a Spanish-born Jew who removes to Cairo, Egypt, during a period of persecution and becomes one of history's most influential Jewish scholars.

1140s

The Cathars, a heretical Christian group similar to the Paulicians, begin to gain strength in Germany, France, and Italy.

c. 1150 TO 1500

Theraveda Buddhism becomes the predominant practice in Cambodia and Laos as the Khmer lose power and Thai kingdoms take control of the area.

LATE TWELFTH CENTURY

The Tendai school of Buddhism changes and adopts new practices that become known as Zen Buddhism, which splits into two major sects: Rinzai, structured around a strict hierarchy and placing supreme importance on the teacher, and Soto, which values individual spirituality and meditation as the way to enlightenment.

Nichiren Buddhism appears. Placing faith in the Lotus Sutra, its founder (Nichiren) denounces other Japanese Buddhist sects as misguided.

c. 1170

A rich merchant from Lyon named Peter Waldo gives up his belongings and family and begins preaching in southern France. His followers, known as Waldensians, advocate freedom of conscience and respect for religious diversity. They are persecuted as heretics.

1171

Muslim sultan Saladin, a Kurd, defeats the Shiite Fatimids and captures their capital city, Cairo, returning Sunni Islam to Egypt.

1187

Saladin unifies Muslim resistance to Christian crusaders and recaptures Jerusalem.

1198

Pope Innocent III increases papal power, and England, Bulgaria, and Portugal become papal fiefs.

c. 1200 TO 1300

Kabbalism, a form of Jewish mysticism, gains popularity in Jewish thought.

The *Prose Edda* is written; it is one of the primary texts of Norse mythology.

1206

The character of Hindu India is slowly changed after 1206, as Muslim invaders from Afghanistan and Persia advance into the subcontinent.

1206 TO 1526

A series of Muslim dynasties, called the Delhi Sultanate, rules from northern India. They are supplanted by the Mughal Empire, which under Babur, a descendant of Genghis Khan, defeats the last of the Delhi sultans in 1526.

THE GREAT CATHEDRALS OF EUROPE

With roots in the Roman Empire, the great cathedrals were built during a span of centuries—with the heyday of building in the eleventh to sixteenth centuries. Scattered across the continent and the British Isles, there are breathtaking examples in a wide range of architectural styles, including the Byzantine St. Mark's Basilica in Venice, the Romanesque Worms Cathedral in Germany, the High Renaissance St. Peter's Basilica in Rome, and the Baroque St. Paul's Cathedral in London. It is the soaring Gothic-style cathedrals, however, that truly epitomize the cathedral spirit, with France's Chartres and Germany's Cologne Cathedral as notable examples. Above is one of the most famous of medieval cathedrals, Notre Dame de Paris, which epitomizes Gothic architecture and the fervent religiosity that inspired such grand, ornate buildings.

EARLY THIRTEENTH CENTURY

The Catholic Church condemns the French Cathars as heretics and begins a crusade (Albigensian) against them. By the 1270s the Cathar culture has collapsed.

1210

Pope Innocent III approves "the Rule of St. Francis" and the Franciscan Order, disciples of Saint Francis of Assisi.

1212

Thousands of children join the Children's Crusade in an attempt to gain back the Holy Land from the Muslims without force. It is a disaster, with many children sold into slavery before reaching their destination.

THE JEWISH-CHRISTIAN ALBA BIBLE

To fight anti-Jewish sentiment in fifteenth-century Spain, Don Luis de Guzmán, a Spanish nobleman, decided to publish a Spanish-language Bible that combined Christian and Jewish scholarship. In 1422 he asked Rabbi Moses Arragel to translate the Hebrew Old Testament and to include commentary to help Christians understand the Jewish perspective. The rabbi declined, afraid that the Jewish view of the Old Testament was different enough from the Christian view that the clash might spark even more tension. Guzmán persuaded the rabbi to comply by having two Christian monks work with him.

The result of this collaboration, completed in 1433 and known as the Alba Bible, was a masterpiece, lavishly illustrated and filled with commentary drawing from the ancient wisdom of Jewish rabbis. Unfortunately, it did not accomplish Guzmán's goal. In 1492 Jews who refused to convert to Christianity were expelled from Spain.

1258

Baghdad is destroyed by the Mongols.

1271 TO 1368

Under the Yuan dynasty, Buddhism is favored in a period of religious, intellectual, and commercial exchange across the Mongol Empire.

1290

England officially expels Jews.

c. 1300

In Nagara, India, Hindu temples begin to be surrounded by ever more elaborate walls pierced by gateways crowned by towers, the whole creating the impression of a fabulous, celestial city.

Utrecht preacher Gerhard Groote (d. 1384) travels through the Netherlands calling for Christians to lead spiritual lives, resulting in the creation of the Brethren of the Common Life. Followers (known as brothers and sisters) devote themselves to meditative prayer and run free schools for general education.

c. 1300 TO 1400

The 2,000-year-old ascetic Ajivika religion disappears.

1306

France expels Jews.

1309 TO 1377

Pope Clement V moves the papal seat to Avignon, in Provence.

1348

Europe is beset by the bubonic plague (the Black Death), which many Christians interpret as an example of God's wrath or else attribute to Jewish mischief. Many Jewish communities are subsequently destroyed.

1357 TO 1419

Lifetime of Je Tsongkhapa, famed Tibetan Buddhist teacher, founder of the Gelugpa school.

The Holy Grail
~

Literature presents many interpretations of the nature of the mysterious Holy Grail, described in Christian mythology as the vessel used by Jesus at the Last Supper, before he was arrested and crucified. The grail has also been described as the vessel used to catch Christ's blood. In Old French *san graal* means a sanctified dish or vessel (*graal*), but medieval writers often preferred the alternative term *sang réal*, meaning blood (*sang*) that is royal or kingly. The grail was also seen as the symbol of ideal perfection accessible only to the pure. It was also said to be a sacred stone that fell from heaven and was the sanctuary of angels. Some believe the grail symbolizes the prepared human soul, ready to accept the divine spirit.

In English folklore the grail—said to have miraculous religious or esoteric powers—is sought after by knights of Arthurian legend. Another legend claims the grail was secreted by the Cathar heretics of southern France to keep it from the religious authorities. Some grail legends hark back to pre-Christian mythology and also find new structures in modern suspense novels and popular films.

Saint Joseph of Arimathea lifts the Holy Grail in a modern stained glass church window. Arthurian legend credits Joseph with carrying the grail to England.

1378 TO 1418
In 1378 Gregory XI moves papal seat back to Rome, but dissenting cardinals select a second pope to fill the now-vacant Avignon seat, beginning the Great Schism of Western Christianity, resolved by the Council of Constance of 1414–18.

1380 TO 1381
English theologian John Wycliffe and his followers complete the first English translation of the Bible. Forerunners of the Protestant Reformation, Wycliffe's followers (Lollards) further his opposition to church tenets after his death in 1384.

1390 TO 1440
The Imitation of Christ is written, widely attributed to German monk Thomas à Kempis. The work emphasizes love and the acceptance of suffering, with the objective of freeing oneself from worldly matters in order to find oneself and God.

1391
Christians riot across Spain, destroying Jewish communities and massacring Jews. Christian rulers reestablish the practice of forcing conversion to Christianity.

1392
The Joseon dynasty, dominated by aristocrats, gains control of Korea. Neo-Confucian orthodoxy overtakes Buddhism as the dominant religion and ethical code.

c. 1400 TO 1500
Hermeticism, descended from an ancient form of spirituality with roots in Egypt, becomes popular in Europe.

Islam replaces Buddhism as the dominant religion in Indonesia.

Christianity arrives in sub-Saharan Africa when Portuguese missionaries convert the king of the Congo and his son.

After conquering Constantinople, Ottoman ruler Mehmed II assumes the title of Caliph of Islam as well as Caesar—claiming his domains to be the successor to the Roman Empire.

1409
As part of the controversy known as the Great Schism of Western Christianity, a council at Pisa attempts to depose the two reigning popes and elects a new one to replace them. The reigning popes refuse the council's decision, and three popes reign simultaneously.

1415
Jan Hus, an important Czech religious reformer, is burned at the stake for heresy.

1417
With the election of Martin V, the church is unified under a single pope, ending the Great Schism.

1428
The Aztecs rule Mexico.

THE RISE OF SATAN
Tirelessly working against God, Satan has a complicated history in Christian theology, but never was he considered so powerful as in the late Middle Ages and Early Modern period in Europe. His most feared subjects were witches, whose unspeakable acts threatened the very core of Christendom. The tragic result of this fear led to the torture and execution of hundreds of thousands of women and men.

1453
Constantinople falls to the Turks.

1457
Followers of Jan Hus organize the Bohemian Brethren or Unity of the Brethren, an early Protestant group that would become the Moravian Church.

1469
Guru Nanak born in what is now Pakistan.

1497
Vasco da Gama rounds the Cape of Good Hope and crosses the Indian Ocean.

1478
Pope Sixtus IV, encouraged by King Ferdinand and Queen Isabella of Spain, issues a bull allowing the monarchs to investigate converted Jews as possible heretics. The Spanish Inquisition begins.

1483
A full-scale investigation of the sincerity of forced Jewish conversions begins in Spain.

1492
Ferdinand and Isabella capture Granada, completing the reconquest of Spain from Muslim rulers. They expel all Jews.

c. 1500
Reformation: Lutheran churches spread throughout Germany and Scandinavia, where they are often decreed the state church.

EARLY SIXTEENTH CENTURY
The Safavid ruler of Persia establishes Shia Islam as the state religion.

1506
Pope Julius II lays the foundation stone for Saint Peter's Basilica, which would be completed in 1615.

1517
German monk and theologian Martin Luther writes his Ninety-five Theses, critical of the Catholic Church.

Ottomans defeat Mamluk dynasty in Egypt and Syria.

1519
Spanish conquistador Hernán Cortés invades Mexico.

1526
The Mughal Empire founded by Babur, a descendant of Genghis Khan; a form of Sunni Islam becomes the state religion.

1529
Muslim armies invading central Europe turned back at Vienna.

1529
Religious reformers known as Anabaptists settle in Moravia (now part of the Czech Republic), led by Jacob Hutter.

1530
Augsburg Confession, the primary Lutheran confession of faith, presented by German princes and free cities to the Diet of Augsburg, a conference of the Holy Roman Empire's leading authorities.

1532

Spanish conquistador Francisco Pizarro invades Peru.

1534

King Henry VIII breaks with Rome and proclaims himself head of the Church of England. England's monasteries are closed.

1536

French Protestant John Calvin publishes *Institutes of the Christian Religion,* criticizing Roman Catholicism. Later expanded and republished in several languages, it greatly influences Protestantism in Europe and North America.

1545 TO 1563

The Roman Catholic Church convenes the Council of Trent, which condemns Protestant heresies and defines church doctrine regarding scripture, sacraments, mass, and veneration of saints.

1548

The Spiritual Exercises, a book by Saint Ignatius of Loyola, founder of the Jesuit order, is approved by Pope Paul III and published. The text presents a program of self-examination, meditation, and prayer.

1549

The Anglican Book of Common Prayer published; the revised edition of 1662 becomes the standard Anglican liturgy in Britain.

Spanish Jesuit Francis Xavier introduces Christianity to Japan.

Portuguese Jesuit missionaries appear in Brazil and begin to convert indigenous peoples.

1556

Spanish missionaries make the first attempts at converting North American Indians by setting up missions along northern Florida's Atlantic coast.

Jalaluddin Muhammad Akbar inherits the Mughal throne. Known as Akbar the Great, he is an advocate of Sunni Islam but is tolerant of other religions. He founds his own belief system, "Divine Faith," which mixes Islam and Hinduism.

1559

The first synod of Huguenots (French Protestants), convened in Paris, formalizes their beliefs, aligning with Calvinist doctrine, thus changing from a Lutheran to a Reformed church.

1562 TO 1594

The Wars of Religion between French Huguenots and Catholics.

1568

Jesuit missionaries set up communities for Christian natives in Paraguay.

1571

The Church of England approves "The Thirty-Nine Articles of Religion," a statement of Anglican doctrine regarding the Reformation.

1572

Inca festival of the sun, Inti Raymi, banned by Spanish authorities.

AUGUST 24, 1572

Nearly all Huguenot leaders in Paris are killed in the St. Bartholomew's Day Massacre, and thousands more Protestants are slain throughout France in the following weeks.

1577

The fourth Sikh guru, Ram Das, founds a trading town that will become the holy city of Amritsar.

1579

Mughal emperor Akbar invites to his court Portuguese Jesuit missionaries from Goa, on the west coast of India.

1587 TO 1629

Reign of Abbas I, Safavid shah of Persia, who is instrumental in developing Persian arts and restoring sacred Muslim shrines. Abbas wins victories over the Ottomans (recapturing Baghdad in 1623), Kurds, and Uzbeks.

1585

Construction of the Harmandir Sahib temple (also known as Hari Mandir temple and the Golden Temple) begins in Amritsar.

1595

The king of Spain sends colonists to New Mexico, instructing the accompanying Franciscan priests to spread Catholicism to the natives.

1598

French Protestant king Henry IV issues the Edict of Nantes, granting Huguenots religious and political freedom.

1604

English Puritans petition King James I for church reform but are rejected.

1605 TO 1627

The reign of Jahangir, Akbar the Great's son, era of the creation of great Mughal architecture; also a time of persecution of Jains, Sikhs, and Hindus.

1610

The first English trading post established in India, at Surat on the west coast.

EARLY SEVENTEENTH CENTURY

The Ottoman Empire wars with the declining but still-powerful Safavid Empire for control of the Caucasus and Mesopotamia.

C. 1600 TO 1700

Southern Africa's Muslim population augmented by Malaysian and Javanese migrations. Islamic sultanates rule much of Indonesia.

1609

Introduction to the Devout Life, a spiritual guide by French priest Francis de Sales, bishop of Geneva, is published.

1609 TO 1616

Sultan Ahmed I builds the "Blue Mosque," one of the Muslim world's greatest houses of worship, in Constantinople.

1617 TO 1682

The life of Lozang Gyatso, the first Dalai Lama to assume political as well as spiritual power in Tibet. During his reign, the Potala Palace—seat of subsequent Dalai Lamas—is constructed in Lhasa.

DECEMBER 1620

The *Mayflower* reaches Plymouth harbor, and its passengers—called separatists for their wish to part from the Anglican church—establish the first permanent European settlement in New England. They later will be termed Pilgrims, and eventually Congregationalists.

1624

The Dutch colonize New Netherlands and establish the Dutch Reformed Church there.

ROSICRUCIANISM

A secret society of mystics, scientists, and philosophers announced itself in the early 1600s by the publication of anonymous manifestos calling for the "universal reformation of mankind." The members of the society were labeled "Rosicrucians," a term derived from their symbol—a cross affixed with a rose.

The Rosicrucians offered the model of "Christian Rosycross" (Christian Rosenkreuz, in German, his nationality), a pilgrim on the path that transcends the material world. The pilgrim seeks esoteric spiritual truths once known in the ancient past but which are concealed from anyone who does not seek for them.

The Rosicrucian cross can symbolize the material world (horizontal bar) as it is being transcended (vertical bar), and the rose symbolizes the human being's divine aspect. The rose is affixed at the point where the bars cross and is opening its petals to the divine light.

Rosicrucian philosophy contemplated the relationship between the physical universe and the divine ("as above, so below," it postulated). It was so influential among the educated classes of the day that its effect has been termed the "Rosicrucian Enlightenment."

The Rose Cross appears at the bottom of a "well of initiation," built in the early twentieth century in Portugal. Descent into the well references Christian Rosenkreuz's mysterious crypt "in the interior parts of the earth."

1624 TO 1691

The life of George Fox, founder of the Religious Society of Friends, or Quakers.

1627

Akbar's grandson, Shah Jahan, builder of the Taj Mahal, comes to the throne.

1632

Catholic nobleman, Cecil Calvert, Lord Baltimore, receives the royal charter for the colony of Maryland, which will be colonized by his brother, Leonard. Governing principles include religious toleration and the separation of church and state.

1633

The Daughters (or Sisters) of Charity of St. Vincent de Paul founded by Vincent de Paul and Louise de Marillac. The nuns of this order engage in charitable work outside their convents.

1636

Roger Williams founds Providence in New England. In 1639, he sets up the American colonies' first Baptist church.

1638

A short-lived colony of Swedes settles on the Delaware River and introduces Lutheranism to the colonies.

1640 TO 1859

Missionaries in Japan are prosecuted and martyred and Christianity is banned. Contact with the outside world is forbidden under the policy of *sakoku*, or isolationism, and all Japanese citizens are required to register at a Buddhist or Shinto temple.

1642 TO 1651

Puritans and Royalists engage in the English Civil War, which results in the overthrow and execution of King Charles I and leads to the establishment of a parliamentary monarchy.

c. 1645

Construction begins on Potala Palace, crowning the consolidation of Tibetan Buddhism as Tibet's national religion.

1646

The Westminster Confession drawn up at Westminster, England, outlines basic Presbyterian beliefs on such issues as worship, doctrine, and church government.

1647

The Society of Friends (Quakers) founded in England by George Fox.

1648

During the Khmelnytsky Uprising, in which Cossacks in Ukraine revolt against Polish rule and Polish gentry, many Jews, widely considered to be upper class, are killed.

1648 TO 1676

Period of activity for Shabbetai Tzevi, a Jewish mystic from Smyrna, who declares himself the Messiah. He attracts a large following in west Asia and Egypt but converts to Islam during imprisonment in Constantinople.

1650

Protestant John Eliot persuades many native peoples of the Massachusetts Bay colony to move to "praying-towns," in which they follow a biblical code of laws and live in European-style houses.

1650

Great Britain becomes a military threat to the Mughals as British colonial strength in India increases.

1658

Mughal emperor Shah Jahan imprisoned by his son, Aurangzeb, who embarks on unsustainable military campaigns.

SWEDENBORGIANISM

Emanuel Swedenborg (1688–1772) devoted himself to inventions and scientific studies until he was fifty-six, when dreams and visions initiated a new interest, the reform of Christianity. His theological writings, such as *Arcana Cœlestia* ("heavenly secrets"), maintained that humans could progress from a materialistic to a spiritual being, and influenced William Blake, Ralph Waldo Emerson, Carl Jung, and Johnny Appleseed. A "New Church" movement after Swedenborg's death resulted in today's General Church of the New Jerusalem and the Swedenborgian Church of North America.

1664

Great Britain takes over New Netherlands, renames it New York, and promotes the Church of England.

1673

French Jesuit Jacques Marquette travels down the Mississippi River, establishing missions along its banks.

1682 TO 1684

Wealthy English Quaker William Penn arrives in Pennsylvania, which he had recently established as a colony for Quakers and a place of religious freedom.

1685

French king Louis XIV revokes the Edict of Nantes, which established religious freedom for Protestants. More than 400,000 Protestants emigrate during the following years.

1693

The Amish, followers of Swiss Mennonite bishop Jakob Amman, separate from the Mennonites, a pacifist Anabaptist sect founded in the sixteenth-century.

EIGHTEENTH CENTURY

Christian missionary work increases in West Africa, especially around British, Danish, and Dutch trading posts along the Gold Coast.

Reacting to Enlightenment and its rationalist view of religion, Pietism—promoting a vigorous Christian life—spreads across Europe and North America.

The Ottoman, Mughal, and Safavid empires decline as European powers strengthen.

1703

Muhammad ibn Abd al-Wahhab, founder of Wahhabism, born on the Arabian Peninsula.

1704

In response to a lack of decorum on the part of Jesuit missionaries in China, the Catholic Church rules that mass must be in Latin. The Chinese emperor, offended by the pope's ruling, outlaws Christianity in China.

1708

The Church of the Brethren originates among religious dissenters in Schwarzenau, Germany. Many will emigrate to North America and settle in Pennsylvania.

1715

The tenth Sikh guru, Gobind Singh, murdered by Muslim assassins.

c. 1725 TO 1760

The Great Awakening (American Pietism movement) spreads through the colonies.

1729

The first American synagogue built in New York City.

REMEMBERING THE DEAD

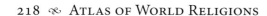

Lights to guide, commemorate, or ward off the dead feature widely in festivals of the dead. Here, a Polish cemetery on All Saint's Day.

Today in much of the Western world, October 31 is a popular secular holiday, but Halloween (from All Hallows' Eve) has its origins somewhere in the murky traditions of pre-Christian Europe. Particularly in Ireland, the end of October signaled the end of the year and the start of winter (usually only two seasons were recognized). Such transitional periods were considered dangerous, with the change from one year to the next, from summer to winter, belonging to all manner of supernatural creatures. To propitiate them, food and drink was left on doorsteps and crossroads, not unlike the Chinese Festival of Ghosts. So strong was the belief in wandering spirits that the Christian calendar marks two autumn days to commemorate the dead: November 1, or All Hallows' Day (also called All Saints' Day), remembers the saints, and November 2 is celebrated as All Souls' Day, a time to visit graves and remember the "faithful departed."

John Wesley organizes the Holy Club at Oxford University. Relying heavily on readings from the Bible to deepen faith, the club would soon develop into the Methodist movement.

1741

The first American community of Moravians established in Pennsylvania.

1750

Hasidic Judaism appears in Poland (now part of Ukraine), founded by Jewish rabbi and mystic Yisroel ben Eliezer, also known as Baal Shem Tov.

1761

An Afghani Muslim army destroys the Sikh temple, Harmandir Sahib, which is subsequently rebuilt.

1769

Spanish missionary Junípero Serra establishes the first Franciscan missions in California.

1770s

Black ministers in America begin serving as pastors for Baptist congregations of both slaves and free blacks.

1781

Holy Roman Emperor Joseph II issues the Edict of Toleration to free Jews from discrimination; later, French revolutionaries and several German principalities grant Jews citizenship. In Eastern Europe, however, persecution of Jews increases.

1787

Anglican churchmen buy land in Sierra Leone, western Africa, for a self-supporting Christian settlement of blacks. The settlement soon collapses.

1792

Black Americans who had sided with the defeated British in the American Revolution rebuild the settlement in Sierra Leone, where members of various Protestant denominations will thrive.

The popular American imagery of Santa Claus suggests his Scandinavian *nisse* origins in his red furs, snowy homeland, and Christmas timing.

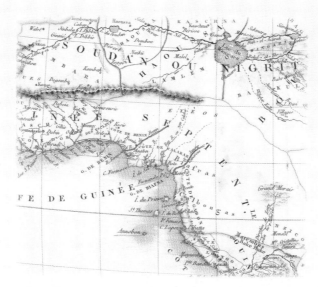

1793

The Universalist Church of America is formed, rooted in the doctrine of universal salvation.

1795

Protestants organize the London Missionary Society as a nondenominational organization to spread Christianity in non-European lands.

Methodists become a separate Protestant denomination that spreads quickly throughout Britain and the United States.

1799

King Ranjit Singh captures Lahore and establishes the first Sikh state.

1803

Delhi falls to the British.

NINETEENTH CENTURY

The Wahhabi-Saudi alliance attacks Shia cities and is temporarily suppressed by the Ottomans. Wahhabi adherents struggle to make the movement the dominant form of Islam on the Arabian Peninsula.

1807

Britain outlaws the slave trade, but not slavery itself.

HOUSEHOLD SPIRITS OF NORTHERN EUROPE

Innumerable Scandinavian legends tell of the *tomte*, or *nisse*, a small spirit of loyal but mischievous character who, usually attached to a single family, would help or hinder that family's prospects. Several of these focus on the tradition of feeding the spirit a bowl of porridge, with an appreciable pat of butter. Hiding the butter—a common plot device—invariably leads to disaster.

The *tomte* receives his porridge on Christmas Eve, and in appearance he is usually described as an elderly man with a full beard, dressed in furs and showing a penchant for the color red. The similarity to Santa Claus, the legendary saint who deposits gifts and is provided with cookies in the United States, is not coincidental. Other elements of the Santa Claus legend—his North Pole (Lapland) home, his reindeer sleigh, and his elf companions—are also most likely Scandinavian in origin, and some scholars believe his alignment with a Christian saint is simply another example of syncretism with pre-Christian mythology, in this case household gods or even Odin himself.

THE FULANI

In 1804–10 Islamic reformer and teacher Usman dan Fodio (1754–1817) led an army of Muslim followers from his people, the Fulani, in a rebellion against the powerful Hausa kingdoms of present-day Nigeria and Cameroon. After several military defeats, Usman's forces were victorious in this jihad, known as the Fulani War, and established the Fulani Empire in West Africa. Several such jihads were launched by other Islamic leaders in the region, which became overwhelmingly Muslim.

1809

Voodoo in New Orleans is influenced by Haitian immigrants to Louisiana after the Haitian Revolution.

1820 TO 1848

The American Board of Commissioners of Foreign Missions sends eighty missionaries to Hawaii to introduce Christianity and Western education to the islands.

1823

Evangelical preacher William Miller predicts the Second Coming of Jesus will occur in 1843 or 1844. Although his prediction is wrong, many Christians, known as Adventists, prepare for the Second Coming.

1824

Russian Orthodox missionaries convert Inuit and Tlingit Indians in Alaska.

1825

The American Unitarian Association established, influenced by theologian and preacher William Ellery Channing.

1830

The Church of Jesus Christ of Latter-Day Saints, known as Mormons, founded by Joseph Smith Jr. Scripture that Smith asserts was written on gold plates revealed to him by an angel named Moroni is published as *The Book of Mormon*.

1830

French philosopher Auguste Comte proposes the "religion of humanity"—with the goal of mankind being to worship itself.

1836 TO 1886

Life of Ramakrishna, Bengali mystic and ascetic who gained a large following through his intense devotion—particularly to the mother goddess Kali.

1838

Mormons settle Nauvoo, Illinois, with a charter virtually freeing them from political authority; Nauvoo soon becomes the state's fastest-growing settlement.

1840

Two bloody wars with the Sikhs in the 1840s bring the Punjab under British control.

1844

Mormon leader Joseph Smith Jr. arrested and imprisoned at Nauvoo, then murdered by a mob.

1847

Brigham Young leads most Nauvoo Mormons to Utah to settle in the Great Salt Lake area.

1848

The Christadelphians, who base their beliefs on the Bible, appear in Great Britain and the United States; movement founded by English surgeon John Thomas.

American Indians and Their Legends Are Diminished

American Indians were pushed out of their lands and often massacred by white settlers through the nineteenth century, so that at the start of the twentieth century fewer than 250,000 American Indians remained in the entire United States—an all-time low. Disappearing with the Indians were many rich tales of the origins of the land. Surviving stories give but a hint of what was lost. For example, the Plains Indians believed that the valley that rings the Black Hills was once a racetrack where the world's two-legged, four-legged, and winged creatures ran to establish their destinies. The two-legged creatures won the right to hunt buffalo. The Kiowa Indians believed that the monolith just north of the Black Hills that is now known as Devils Tower was created when seven sisters were chased by a bear and took refuge on a huge tree stump. From the stump they flew up to become stars in the constellation of the Big Dipper. The stump then petrified, and the claw marks of the bear can still be seen in it.

Known in Lakota as Mato Tipila (Bear Tower), Devils Tower has cultural links to many American Indian tribes.

1848
Islamic authorities imprison Persian mystic Bahá'u'lláh, an important leader of Babism, a religion that had broken away from Islam. He is eventually banished and journeys to Baghdad.

1853
The Humanistic Religious Association organized in London.

1854
The sakoku isolation of Japan's Edo period forcibly broken by American military incursion.

1854 to 1856
Britain and France ally with the Ottoman Empire against Russia in the Crimean War.

1857
Scottish Congregationalist missionary Robert Moffat translates the Bible into Tswana, a South African dialect.

Muslim and Hindu colonial soldiers rise against the British East India Company in the Indian Rebellion and capture Delhi. The soldiers install the Mughal Badahur Shah II as emperor, but the uprising is defeated and he is exiled.

1858
The advent of the British Raj, or rule, of India.

1860
Community of Christ, also known as the Reorganized Church of Jesus Christ of Latter Day Saints, organizes under Joseph Smith III, considered by followers the rightful successor to Joseph Smith Jr., his father.

1863
Bahá'u'lláh founds the Baha'i faith.

Seventh-Day Adventist church officially established.

1863 to 1902
Life of Hindu sage and social reformer Swami Vivekananda, Ramakrishna's most famous disciple.

1864
A Nigerian who had been freed from a slave ship and studied theology in London, Samuel A. Crowther is named bishop of the Niger region, the first black African Anglican bishop.

Swiss humanitarian Henri Dunant founds the Red Cross in Geneva to care for victims of war and natural disasters.

Pope Pius IX writes the encyclical (papal document) "Syllabus of Errors," condemning secularism, rationalism, nationalism, individualism, and liberalism.

1865
William and Catherine Booth found the Salvation Army, a Christian charity and church that is internally organized like a military service.

1867
The Free Religious Association established in Boston, led by Ralph Waldo Emerson and attracting religious liberals.

1868
Shinto declared Japan's state religion and Buddhist elements within it are outlawed (although people continue to practice popular aspects of Buddhism).

1869
Hindu spiritual leader Mohandas Gandhi born in India.

1869 to 1870
Pope Pius IX convenes the First Vatican Council at Rome, which reaffirms the pope's authority and issues the doctrine of papal infallibility.

The last of the Papal States absorbed into Italy.

1874
Hutterite groups come to North America.

1875
Theosophical Society founded in New York City by Russian mystic Madame Blavatsky (Helena von Hahn), with lawyer and journalist Henry Olcott and attorney William Q. Judge.

1876
Felix Adler founds the Society for Ethical Culture as a nontheistic religion.

1877
Blavatsky publishes first major work, *Isis Unveiled*.

1879
Mary Baker Eddy founds the Church of Christ, Scientist. Eddy's 1875 book, *Science and Health with Key to the Scriptures*, becomes a central text for the church.

1880s
American lay preacher Charles Taze Russell predicts the imminent return of Jesus. Taze's followers become known as Jehovah's Witnesses.

1881
The assassination of the liberal Czar Alexander II allows for frequent pogroms against Jews in Russia and Poland. Jewish mass emigrations begin shortly.

1882
Blavatsky and Olcott establish the Theosophical Society's international headquarters in India.

1889
In *Key to Theosophy*, Blavatsky summarizes the society's goals as promoting a "universal brotherhood of humanity," the study of the world's religions, and the investigation of the "hidden mysteries of nature," especially the "psychic and spiritual powers latent in man."

1890
The Mormon church forbids new polygamous marriages.

1891
Pope Leo XIII writes the encyclical "Of New Things" to defend workers' rights to form unions and to fight for living wages and humane working conditions.

1894
French Jewish army officer Alfred Dreyfus is unfairly convicted of treason. The novelist Émile Zola begins a public campaign to prove Dreyfus's innocence and expose the anti-Semitism behind the conviction. In response to the "Dreyfus Affair," Hungarian Jewish journalist Theodor Herzl starts the Zionist movement, claiming that Jews will be second-class citizens until they have a permanent home.

1896
The Olympic Games, once held in honor of the Greek god Zeus, are revived to foster international goodwill.

1905
The Baptist World Alliance forms in London, consisting of a fellowship of 214 Baptist conventions and unions, with a membership of 36 million.

1906
Indian Muslims establish the All-India Muslim League, a political party created to counter the erosion of Islamic culture under British rule.

1912
Abdul Bahá, the son of Baha'i founder Bahá'u'lláh, immigrates to the United States.

1913

Austrian philosopher, educator, and esotericist Rudolf Steiner (1861–1925) establishes the Anthroposophical Society with German members of the Theosophical Society.

1914 TO 1918

World War I rages over Europe.

1915

The Messianic Jewish Alliance of America is considered the world's largest association of Messianic Jews and non-Jewish believers in Yeshua (Jesus).

1917

Russian Revolution brings Communists to power and dethrones czar.

Britain approves establishment of a Jewish homeland.

1918

Nigerian Anglicans believing in divine healing and living by a puritanical code organize as the Aladura, or Prayer People. They soon split from the Anglican church; by the 1960s the Aladura spreads to Ghana and reorganizes as the Christ Apostolic Church, with around 100,000 members.

c. 1918

Ratana, a Maori religious movement, is initiated by faith healer Tahupotiki Wiremu Ratana

1919

The first school based on Rudolph Steiner's principles established at the request of the owner of the Waldorf-Astoria Cigarette Company in Stuttgart, Germany.

1919

United States approves establishment of a Jewish homeland.

1924

Turkish nationalists, having recently established the Republic of Turkey with a secular government, abolish the Ottoman caliphate and exile titular caliph Abdul Mejid II.

1927

Saudi Arabia recognized as a nation.

1928

Inti Raymi revived as Peruvian cultural-heritage display.

1930

The Rastafarian movement begins in Jamaica after the coronation of Ethiopia's Prince Ras Tafari Makonnen as Emperor Haile Selassie, believed by his followers to be God incarnate.

Anglican catechist Josiah Olunowo Oshitelu founds the Church of the Lord, the largest denomination in Africa's Aladura movement.

Aladura grows significantly when the prophet-healer Joseph Babalola leads an elaborate divine-healing campaign.

1933

The Humanist Manifesto written, calling for Humanism, an ethical doctrine of fifteen key points, to replace religion based on alleged supernatural revelation.

Early radio evangelist Herbert W. Armstrong founds the Worldwide Church of God.

1934

Missionary William Cameron Townsend establishes a school for training Bible translators, which becomes a major organization, Wycliffe Translators International.

1938

Anti-Semitic violence rages in Nazi-governed Germany, with synagogues, hospitals, businesses, cemeteries, and homes ransacked. More than 100 Jews are killed, and 30,000 arrested; concentration camps expanded to contain them.

1939 TO 1945

World War II results in more than 55 million deaths.

The Jewish population in Palestine, which had risen precipitously during the 1930s due to immigration from Europe, plateaus at nearly 500,000, with travel virtually halted by the war.

The American Humanist Association established to lead local and national Humanist organizations toward progressive social change.

1945

Discovery of Gnostic texts dating to the second century in Nag Hammadi, Egypt, reveals much about early Christian theology and prompts a resurgence of the Gnostic movement.

1945

At the end of World War II, the Buddhist sect Soka Gakkai emerges in Japan.

1945 TO 1949

Chinese civil war; ends with Communist victory.

THE SALVATION ARMY

A combination of evangelical Christianity and social service agency, the Salvation Army originated in 1865, when William Booth began preaching to the outcasts of London's streets, offering them food and shelter as well as aiming to save their souls. By the 1870s a thousand volunteers served "General" Booth and called themselves his "army" of "Salvationists," often performing music on street corners to attract attention. Today the Salvation Army's worldwide operations are in 111 countries and 175 languages.

1946

The White Identity Church of Jesus Christ–Christian founded by Wesley A. Smith, a former Methodist minister and Ku Klux Klan organizer; in 1957 it is renamed the Church of Jesus Christ Christian.

1947

India achieves independence. The subcontinent is soon divided into the Muslim Pakistan and East Pakistan (later Bangladesh) and predominantly Hindu India.

1948

The United Nations adopts the Universal Declaration of Human Rights (UDHR), which will in 1976 become part of the International Bill of Human Rights accepted by the U.N. General Assembly and given the force of international law.

The World Council of Churches formed to address concerns common to Christians and to promote unity among all denominations.

State of Israel officially established.

A coalition of five Arab nations attacks Israel the day after the partition of Palestine is announced by the United Nations. After months of fighting, Israel gains territory.

Mohandas Gandhi assassinated.

Commonwealth of Ceylon achieves independence (known as Sri Lanka since 1972).

1949

Dutch East Indies achieves independence as Indonesia, a mostly Muslim nation.

1950

The Islamic Association of China represents ten nationalities in the People's Republic of China.

China moves to annex Tibet, sending troops into the region.

Albanian-born nun Mother Teresa establishes the

Born on October 2, 1869, Mahatma Gandhi is now called the "Father of the Nation" in India for his tireless efforts to win independence from Great Britain.

Nonviolent Protest

ॐ

The concept of *ahimsa* (Sanskrit for "nonviolence") is firmly rooted in many Indian religions. Arguably it is most important in Jainism, where it is most rigidly prescribed and followed. Historically, Hindu practice has fluctuated on the concept, allowing exceptions in certain circumstances. However, it is also through Hinduism that the concept gained global attention, when leader Mahatma Gandhi strongly advocated nonviolent protest against British rule in India in the mid-twentieth century. The *ahimsa* concept, in both Hinduism and Jainism, rests largely on the notion of *karma*, and the religious necessity of avoiding negative *karma*. After Gandhi's success with nonviolent protest, the methods caught on, most notably in America in the 1950s. The civil rights movement—although essentially secular—largely adopted nonviolent tactics. Today, at least one entire species has Hindu *ahimsa* to thank for its very existence: the Asiatic lion has been driven to extinction everywhere except in the state of Gujarat, India—where Gandhi himself was born.

Missionaries of Charity, a community of thirteen nuns in Calcutta dedicated to caring for the disadvantaged.

1952
Evangelist Rex Humbard begins televising weekly services from his Cathedral of Tomorrow in Ohio.

International Humanist and Ethical Union founded.

1954
Scientology founded in Los Angeles by L. Ronald Hubbard, a science fiction writer and author of best-selling *Dianetics: The Modern Science of Mental Health*.

The Unification Church established in Seoul, Korea, under the leadership of Reverend Sun Myung Moon, who claims to be the second coming of Christ.

1955
Oral Roberts, reputed king of faith healers, is the national leader of neo-Pentecostal television broadcasters; in 1963 he will establish the Oral Roberts Evangelical Association, including the newly founded Oral Roberts University.

1956
Sister Cities International is created by President Dwight D. Eisenhower (1890–1969) to foster international human relations and municipal interaction without direct governmental intervention.

1958
Yoido Full Gospel Church founded by David Yonggi Cho in Seoul, South Korea.

1959
The Dalai Lama flees Tibet after a failed uprising against the Communist Chinese. Escaping to India, he sets up a government in exile and remains head of Tibetan Buddhism.

c. 1960
Kabbalism, a form of Jewish mysticism, gains popularity among various religious and spiritual groups.

1961
The American Unitarian Association and the Universalist Church of America consolidate to form the Unitarian Universalist Association (UUA).

1961 TO 1965
Pope John XXIII convenes Second Vatican Council for the Catholic Church to address modern political, social, economic, and technological developments.

1963
Kenyan Catholics unhappy with recent reforms establish a church called the Legion of Mary.

1965
Eckankar founded in Las Vegas by former Scientology adherent John Paul Twitchell, who describes himself as part of an ancient line of Eckankar masters.

1966
China's Great Proletarian Cultural Revolution launched by Mao Zedong undertakes systematic destruction of "liberal bourgeois" culture, and thousands of monasteries are turned to rubble; Confucianism and Daoism violently suppressed, as are the Uighurs, many of whom are Muslims.

Church of Satan, dedicated to the carnal nature of humanity, established by American occultist Anton Szandor LaVey.

New Order Amish is the collective name for less conservative groups that break away from the Old Order Amish Church.

Hare Krishna movement established in New York City by A. C. Bhaktivedanta Swami Prabhupada.

1967
The Third Arab-Israeli War, also known as the Six-Day War, begun with a preemptive Israel attack, routing the Arabs and capturing Arab-held territory, including eastern Jerusalem.

1968
Various American Methodist bodies unite to form the United Methodist Church, the principal Methodist Church in America.

David Brandt Berg leads the Children of God, part of the "Jesus People" movement.

The Beatles journey to India to study and meditate under Maharishi Mahesh Yogi, signs of a significant Western interest in Hinduism.

1970
Moishe Rosen, a Baptist minister who had been raised as an Orthodox Jew, begins missionary work among youth in San Francisco, targeting young Jews for his Jews for Jesus group.

1971
Organization of the Islamic Conference (OIC) promotes intergovernmental cooperation to benefit member countries and Muslims the world over.

1973
A second Humanist manifesto acknowledges overoptimism of its predecessor in light of the events of the intervening decades.

Egypt launches a surprise attack on Israel during the Jewish high holiday of Yom Kippur. A cease-fire is signed a month later, and a peace agreement in January, 1974.

1974
Aryan Nations, a white neo-Nazi nationalist group, forms from the White Identity Church of Jesus Christ–Christian.

1975
To commemorate the 2,500th anniversary of Mahavira, Jains adopt the open-hand symbol.

1978
Mediated by U.S. President Jimmy Carter, Israel and Egypt sign the Camp David Accords. Israel returns the Sinai peninsula to Egypt, and Egypt recognizes Israel's right to exist.

The Iranian Revolution begins and the following year deposes the shah.

1979
Iran's Islamic Revolution and the rise to power of the Islamic Shia clergy leads to increased persecution of the Baha'i and causes their mass exodus from Iran.

1980s
After the overthrow of Afghanistan's Soviet-backed government, the ultraconservative Taliban Islamist movement begins to wrest governmental control, harshly imposing sharia law.

The Sikhs fortify the Golden Temple, Harmandir Sahib, in Amritsar and man it with armed militants determined to establish a Sikh state.

1983
Sri Lankan ethnic Tamils, predominantly Hindu and known as the Tamil Tigers, launch a violent insurrection to establish a separate state in the island's northwest.

THE BRUDERHOF COMMUNITIES
The first Bruderhof community was founded in 1920 in Germany; its members escaped persecution there in the 1930s and moved to England and Paraguay, finally settling in the United States. Today the Bruderhof, known as Church Communities International, has branches in the United States, England, Germany, and Australia, with about 2,500 members. Community life and beliefs are based on the teachings of Christ and the example of the early Christian church: members share everything in common, do not serve in the armed forces, and assist humanitarian organizations.

1984

Indian army storms the Golden Temple and drives out Sikh militants. Later that year Sikh bodyguards assassinate India's prime minister, Indira Gandhi. Outraged Indians massacre at least ten thousand Sikhs in Delhi, leaving deep resentment on both sides.

1987

The Sakyadhita International Association of Buddhist Women established.

1989

Barbara Harris, the first female U. S. Episcopal bishop, is consecrated on February 11.

The Tenth Panchen Lama, Choekyi Gyaltsen, imprisoned and tortured in Beijing; after being freed, he continues to criticize Chinese destruction of Tibetan culture.

The Dalai Lama wins the Nobel Peace Prize.

1990

Organization of the Islamic Conference adopts the Cairo Declaration of Human Rights in Islam, which enumerates its member governments' positions on human rights and sharia law.

1991

Rajiv Gandhi, Indian ex–prime minister and son of Indira Gandhi, assassinated by a Tamil Tigers suicide bomber.

1992

Hindu zealots storm and demolish the sixteenth-century Babri Mosque in Ayodhya, claiming it had deliberately been built on the birth site of Lord Rama.

1992

A qigong system called Falun Gong is developed in China by little-known practitioner Li Hongzhi.

1993

Sri Lankan president Ranasinghe Premadasa assassinated by a Tamil Tigers suicide bomber.

1995

Construction begins on the East London Shri Swaminarayan Temple, to become the largest Hindu temple outside India.

The Dalai Lama announces the reincarnated Panchen Lama to be the six-year-old Tibetan-born Gedhun

Choekyi Nyima, whose whereabouts are unknown. The Chinese government claims superior authority and names a rival candidate, living in Beijing. To Tibetan Buddhists the rival is commonly known as the "Panchen Zuma," or "fake Panchen Lama."

The International Council of Unitarians and Universalists (ICUU) established.

1996

The Rastafari movement given consultative status by the United Nations.

The Reverend Sun Myung Moon combines his religious, commercial, political, and cultural organizations into the Family Federation for World Peace and Unification.

1999

The Communist Chinese government outlaws Falun Gong, stating that "the so-called 'truth, kindness and forbearance' principle preached by Li has nothing in common with the socialist ethical and cultural progress we are striving to achieve."

2001

The China Islamic Association created by the Communist Chinese government to oppose religious extremism while at the same time encouraging study of the Qur'an.

In response to devastating terrorist attacks on the United States, an American-led military coalition invades Afghanistan and overthrows the Taliban regime, accused of harboring a Muslim terrorist group known as al-Qaida.

2003

An American-led military coalition invades Iraq and overthrows secular dictator Saddam Hussein. Civil strife erupts between the Sunnis, Iraq's former ruling class, and the more numerous Shia.

The third Humanist manifesto offers the affirmation: "We work to uphold the equal enjoyment of human rights and civil liberties in an open, secular society and maintain it is a civic duty to participate in the democratic process and a planetary duty to protect nature's integrity, diversity, and beauty in a secure, sustainable manner."

The Nanakshahi calendar, developed by a Canadian Sikh, is officially introduced to the Sikh community.

The syncretistic faith Vodou is given official status as a religion by Haitian president Jean-Bertrand Aristide.

The United States Episcopal Church consecrates Gene Robinson, a gay man, as bishop of New Hampshire, drawing much worldwide animosity among believers.

2006

Guided by Buddhist principles, Bhutan's "Dragon King" Jigme Singye Wangchuk abdicates and hands rule of the nation over to its people.

2007

Myanmar's dictatorial regime brutally crushes antigovernment protests led by Buddhist monks.

2008

The Reverend Sun Myung Moon's son Hyung Jin Moon takes over leadership of the Unification Church.

SUZUKI AND SUZUKI: BRINGING THE DHARMA WEST

Buddhism was introduced to the West in part by a prolific Japanese scholar and translator named Daisetso Teitaro, or D. T. Suzuki (1870–1966). His landmark 1934 book, *An Introduction to Zen Buddhism* was an international success. The year of his death also marks the establishment of the first Buddhist training monastery in the West, Tassajara Zen Mountain Center in northern California. Coincidentally, the first abbot of this monastery was also named Suzuki. Shunryu Suzuki (1904–71) was a Japanese Soto Zen monk; the monastery he founded is part of the San Francisco Zen Center. In typically self-effacing style, Shunryu Suzuki was known to distinguish himself from his elder countryman by saying, "He's the big Suzuki, I'm the little Suzuki."

The *zendo*, or meditation hall, at Tassajara Zen Mountain Center in Northern California.

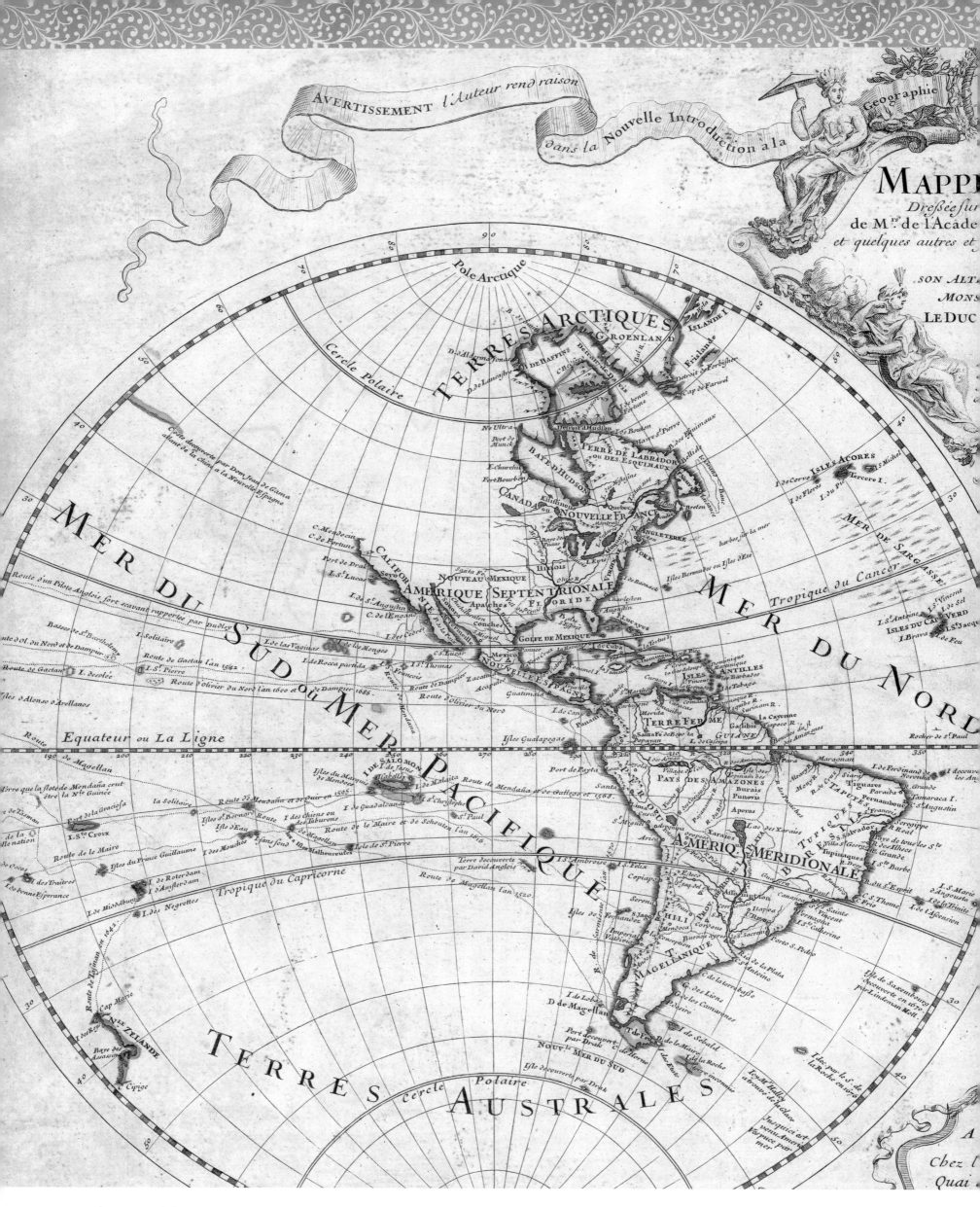

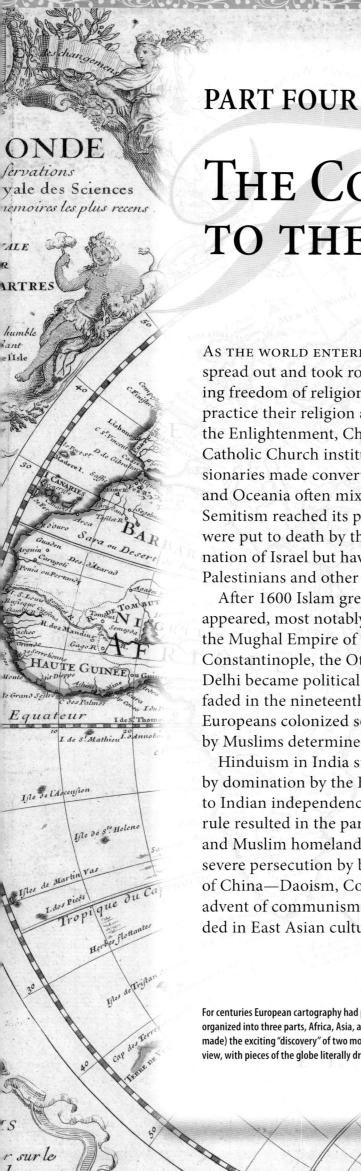

PART FOUR

THE COLONIAL ERA TO THE 20TH CENTURY

AS THE WORLD ENTERED THE MODERN PERIOD, the major religions spread out and took root in every continent. Christian dissidents, seeking freedom of religion, moved to North America, where they could practice their religion as they saw fit. In response to the rationalism of the Enlightenment, Christian Pietism surged worldwide, and later the Catholic Church instituted many reforms. Catholic and Protestant missionaries made converts in all parts of the world, but people in Africa and Oceania often mixed their Christianity with local beliefs. Anti-Semitism reached its peak during World War II, when six million Jews were put to death by the Nazis. After the war, Jews reestablished the nation of Israel but have been engaged in conflict with the surrounding Palestinians and other Arabs ever since.

After 1600 Islam grew steadily, and powerful Islamic empires appeared, most notably the Ottoman Empire based in Anatolia and the Mughal Empire of the Indian subcontinent. The great cities of Constantinople, the Ottoman capital, and the Mughal stronghold of Delhi became political and spiritual centers of the faith. Both empires faded in the nineteenth century, dismembered by European powers. Europeans colonized some of these lands—often oil-rich and populated by Muslims determined to win their political freedom.

Hinduism in India suffered persecution under Islamic rule, followed by domination by the British Raj, but emerged as a powerful catalyst to Indian independence in the twentieth century. The end of colonial rule resulted in the partition of India and Pakistan as primarily Hindu and Muslim homelands. Sikhism grew in numbers even as it suffered severe persecution by both Hindus and Muslims. The three traditions of China—Daoism, Confucianism, and Buddhism, were quelled by the advent of communism but remained alive nonetheless, deeply embedded in East Asian culture.

For centuries European cartography had placed Jerusalem at the center of a world neatly organized into three parts, Africa, Asia, and Europe. But by 1700 (when this map was made) the exciting "discovery" of two more continents required an entirely new world-view, with pieces of the globe literally drawn in bit by bit.

Hinduism and the Raj

THE DEATH OF AKBAR in 1605 began a slow decline of Mughal power in India. Though the empire continued its expansion southward throughout the seventeenth century, reaching its greatest extent only at the start of the eighteenth, the nature of Mughal rule was changing. The autocratic benevolence of Akbar was replaced by something much harsher. His grandson, Shah Jahan, the builder of the Taj Mahal, killed all his nearest relatives when he came to the throne in 1627. Declaring himself "Emperor of the World," he embarked on a round of reckless, vainglorious military conquest that came close to bankrupting the state. In 1658 he was the victim of a dynastic coup, hurled into prison by his son, Aurangzeb, who himself embarked on a further round of unsustainable military campaigns. His death in 1707 confirmed the obvious: that Mughal India was a spent force.

The long decline of Mughal power allowed the partial revival of Hindu dynasties, notably the Marthas. But from the mid-seventeenth century, the most serious military threat to the Mughals came from a much more distant rising power: Britain.

Even at their peak, the Mughals had no pretensions to naval power. Eighteenth-century Britain, by contrast, was clearly the rising naval power of the age. As early as 1610, the first English trading post had been established in India, at Surat on the west coast. By 1647 there were twenty-three such bases. English, later British, penetration of India continued at a relentless pace, bringing it into conflict not just with native states but with other European powers, chiefly the French, who themselves had designs on India's legendary riches.

This was not empire building as such. Trade was the goal, not territory. Further, it wasn't the British government that directed this expansion, it was the London-based East India Company. Yet such was the company's wealth that almost by itself it became a major military as well as commercial power. In 1757 it decisively defeated the Nawab of Bengal at Plassey. Granted control over Bengal's revenues in the 1760s, the company was able to field an army of more than 100,000. The British government capitalized on the company's gains, however, and in 1803 Delhi itself fell to a British army.

The East India Company directly controlled only a narrow strip of territories on the east coast and inland from Calcutta. Yet by 1803, when the Mughal emperor agreed to British protection, its effective rule was a fact.

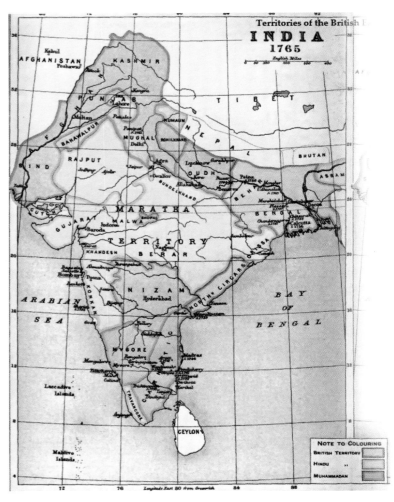

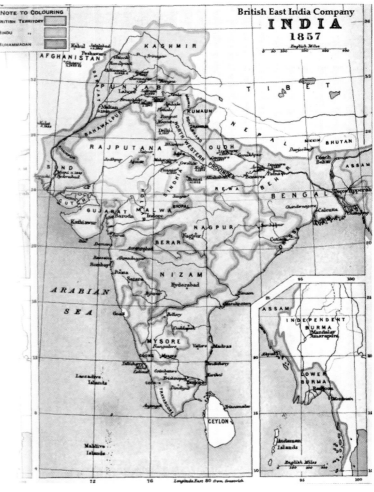

British holdings in India advanced to cover the entire east coast by the turn of the nineteenth century, as shown in these two period maps. British territory is shown in pink.

THE HINDU RESPONSE

As the British made their relentless way westward across India after 1803, they brought with them a set of fiercely held Christian beliefs that could not allow Hinduism to be regarded as anything other than idolatrous and hopelessly pagan, the product of what Winston Churchill would later call "a beastly people and a beastly religion."

In contrast, early European students of Hinduism had been notably sympathetic to the religion, recognizing its profound spirituality and eager to understand its origins and later history. It was not an attitude readily adopted by later generations of British colonizers. Suttee, or sati, in particular—the practice whereby a Hindu widow would voluntarily immolate herself on her husband's funeral pyre—was regarded as particularly barbaric. The discovery in the early nineteenth century of the temple complex at Khajuraho in Madhya Pradesh, its walls seething with carved figures of copulating couples, only reinforced British disdain.

It was in the face of these earnest Victorian attempts to coax the Hindus onto the path of Christian righteousness that the religion staged a remarkable comeback. What for millennia had been seen as a form of infinitely varied and dizzyingly spiritual worship, with no nationalist agenda, was transformed by a series of nineteenth-century Indian intellectuals and mystics into a growing focus of Indian national identity.

The complex of temples at Khajuraho, in north-central India, is ornately carved with gods and goddesses. Some of these are frankly erotic, and relate to Hindu Tantric practices.

SAINTS AND PATRIOTS

Two extraordinary men stand out in the swirl of influences and allegiances of late nineteenth-century India. Many modern Indians point first to Ramakrishna and then to Swami Vivekananda as the saviors of Hinduism, who elevated the religion in its darkest hour. Ramakrishna (1836–86) was a Bengali mystic and ascetic who gained a large following through his intense devotion—particularly to the mother goddess Kali—and his sometimes bizarre practices. Ramakrishna's primary contribution was a view of Hinduism that verged on the universalist, appealing to a wide spectrum of Indians.

Swami Vivekananda (1863–1902) was born in Calcutta and was Ramakrishna's most famous disciple. Charismatic and passionate, Vivekananda was also profoundly devout. He translated the inclusive message of his guru into a rallying cry for the people of India: "Awake, arise, and stop not until the goal is reached!" Vivekananda traveled in Europe and then America, where he was warmly received at the 1893 Chicago World's Fair. He is credited with introducing yoga and the teachings of the Vedanta to the West.

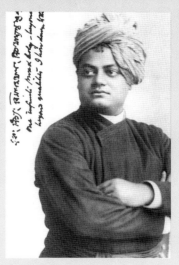

The highly regarded teacher and lecturer Swami Vivekananda is credited with introducing Hinduism to Westerners.

THE INDIAN REBELLION

No moment was more traumatic for Muslims, Hindus, and Britons alike than the Indian Rebellion, or Mutiny, of 1857–58. It was an event that shattered certainties on all sides. Its ostensible cause was the issue of new rifles, whose paper-covered cartridges had to be bitten open. These, it was claimed, were greased with fat, possibly pork, perhaps beef. The former was unacceptable to the East India Company's Muslim soldiers, the latter to its Hindu soldiers.

In reality, the causes of the mutiny were vastly more complex, though all could be traced to British hegemony, and all were an incoherent explosion of rage against it. The bloodshed was appalling as, painfully over fourteen months, Britain reasserted its control. The consequence was that the British government, in place of the East India Company, assumed direct responsibility for India. However benignly meant, British rule now virtually guaranteed future Indian resistance. And the form this would take was overwhelmingly an assertion of Hindu-inspired nationalism.

The bloody rebellion of 1857–58 saw both Hindus and Muslims in mutiny against the British East India Company. The uprising was quelled, but the fight for Indian independence would continue against a new ruling power, the British government.

HINDUISM
Toward Independence

IN 1876 THE AGING QUEEN VICTORIA was pronounced by her government Empress of India. In 1911 her grandson, George V, journeyed to India to be invested as Emperor of India in a ceremony, a *durbar*, deliberately modeled on Mughal traditions. For five days a succession of Indian rulers—from maharajas to humble local functionaries—paid homage to the monarch of the largest empire the world had ever seen, an empire, so proclaimed the *Times of India*, "unfaltering [in its] pursuit of peace, tolerance and progress."

This was not a view shared by a Hindu lawyer, Mohandas Gandhi. Gandhi, born in 1869, was a complex mixture of Hindu wise man and worldly sophisticate. Legal training in London may have familiarized him with the ways of British thinking, but it did nothing to stifle a latent spirituality or what would become a lifelong commitment to social justice. Gandhi railed against the oppression of the poor and India's teeming untouchables with as much vigor as he campaigned for *purna swaraj*—independence for India. He took for granted that in such a fully independent India there would be no discrimination between religions. Hindu and Muslim would be equal partners in every sense. This would be a single, united country.

The weapons he brought to bear in this struggle were unorthodox. The most important was *ahimsa*—nonviolence. British interests were to be undermined by noncooperation and civil disobedience. Whether weaving his own clothes to damage the British textile industry—it was in honour of this that a spinning wheel was subsequently incorporated in the country's flag—or defying Britain's monopoly on salt, he proved a brilliantly effective political campaigner, with several periods in prison to prove the point.

In this search for *satya*, or truth, he placed enormous emphasis on simplicity and humility. His struggle to achieve what he called *brahmacharya*—in essence celibacy, so as, as he put it, "to control the senses in thought, word and deed"—was as characteristic as his fasts, again intended to achieve spiritual purity by purging the body, and his insistence on remaining silent one day a week so as to attain *shanti*, or peace.

Mohandas Gandhi's efforts to lead India to independence by nonviolent means brought the Hindu concept of *ahimsa* into unprecedented focus. Rumblings of discontent and rioting throughout India were overshadowed by throngs of peaceful protesters, confounding the British and ultimately achieving Gandhi's goal.

INDEPENDENCE IN INDIA, TO 1947

- • cities
- — major riots, 1946–1947
- — noncooperation program, 1920–1922
- early riots and strikes
- British India
- princely states

PARTITION

❧

The eventual emergence in August 1947 of a fully independent Hindu India and a Muslim Pakistan, itself split between the Punjab (West Pakistan) and Bengal (East Pakistan), produced the greatest number of religiously inspired deaths of the twentieth century. The chaos, massacres, looting, and rioting were less the result of British intransigence—Britain had long since accepted it could not hope to continue to rule India—than of growing Muslim demands for a separate state.

It was not an eventuality that Hindu or Muslim campaigners would have foreseen in the 1930s, when a common desire for independence proved a powerful glue. It came about chiefly through the ambitions of the leader of the Muslim League, Muhammad Ali Jinnah, and it posed near insuperable difficulties. When the frontiers of the two states were finally determined, substantial Hindu and Muslim minorities were on the wrong the side of the borders. As many as 15

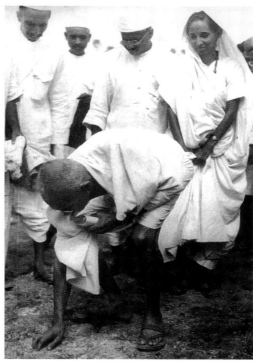

Mohandas Gandhi stoops to pick up salty earth at Dandi in western India, near the completion of the Salt March. This, the first major non-violent, organized campaign protesting British rule, resulted in few immediate concessions but brought Gandhi and his non-violent leadership international attention.

million people made the weary trek from one country to another. Up to 500,000 were killed. In October war broke out over the province of Kashmir, which was Hindu-governed but with a Muslim majority. Rarely has religious sectarianism proved more deadly.

GANDHI'S TRUTH

೨

Thus if I could not accept Christianity either as a perfect, or the greatest religion, neither was I then convinced of Hinduism being such. Hindu defects were pressingly visible to me. If untouchability could be a part of Hinduism, it could but be a rotten part or an excrescence. I could not understand the *raison d'être* of a multitude of sects and castes. What was the meaning of saying that the Vedas were the inspired Word of God? If they were inspired, why not also the Bible and the Koran? As Christian friends were endeavoring to convert me, so were Muslim friends. Abdullah Sheth had kept on inducing me to study Islam, and of course he had always something to say regarding its beauty.

—Gandhi, *The Story of My Experiments with Truth*, 1929

Above: Mohandas Gandhi is widely revered today in India and around the world for his practice of nonviolence. Left: British colonial rule reached an apex under the long reign of Queen Victoria, who in 1876 was named Empress of India.

Hinduism and Independence

THE CHALLENGES FACING the newly independent, largely Hindu India after 1947 were immense. At the stroke of a pen, it had become the world's largest democracy. After 150 years of British rule, India had to adjust quickly to a system of self-government, itself hastily worked out and ushered in by violence on a terrifying scale.

A series of urgent problems pressed in on the new nation. In the immediate short term was the need to house and feed those millions of suddenly impoverished Hindu refugees who had fled Pakistan. The population of Delhi alone almost doubled between 1947 and 1951, from 900,000 to 1.7 million. And there was the still unresolved matter of Kashmir. Sixteen months of bitter fighting between India and Pakistan over the province were ended only in January 1949 with a United Nations–imposed cease-fire. It would prove no more than a stopgap solution. Further fighting began in 1965,

when India accused Pakistan of infiltrating soldiers into the region. Even today the matter remains essentially unresolved.

The economic problems facing the new nation were hardly less daunting. Many parts of the country were desperately poor. The cities teemed with the dispossessed. Elsewhere, subsistence agriculture was all that could be hoped for: starvation was a fact of life for millions. What industry existed was inefficient, urgently in need of modernization.

India's avowedly secular, liberal government was trying to rule a country that was 80 percent Hindu yet riven by ethnic, linguistic, and religious faults. The complexity of these divisions was highlighted by the assassination in January 1948 of Gandhi. He was killed not by a Muslim, but by a Hindu nationalist, Nathuram Godse, who felt Gandhi had agreed too readily to the partition of India. It was a portent of further such disruptive Hindu extremism.

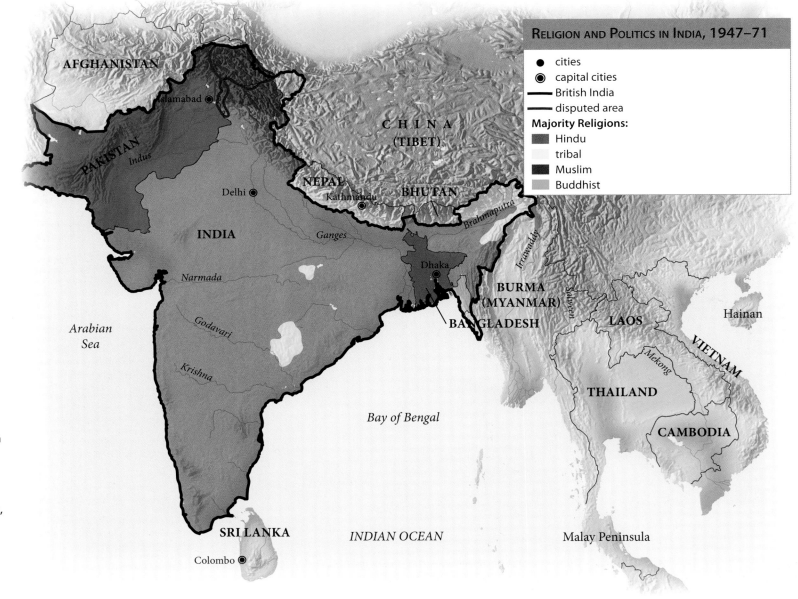

RELIGION AND POLITICS IN INDIA, 1947–71

- • cities
- ◉ capital cities
- —— British India
- —— disputed area

Majority Religions:
- Hindu
- tribal
- Muslim
- Buddhist

The religious differences on the Indian subcontinent, particularly between Muslim and Hindu but also concerning Sikh, Buddhist, and Jain minorities, have had drastic political consequences. Fragmentation into Pakistan, India, and Bangladesh came almost immediately after independence, and many boundary issues surrounding the partition are still unsettled.

RELIGIOUS INTOLERANCE

Sri Lanka, which achieved independence in 1948 as the Commonwealth of Ceylon (it has been known as Sri Lanka since 1972), presents a microcosm of the religious tensions bedeviling its vastly larger neighbor. Seventy percent of the island's population is Buddhist, and only about 15 percent Hindu. In 1983, ethnic Tamils, who are predominantly Hindu, launched a violent insurrection to allow them their own separatist state, Eelam, in the northwest of the island, where they constitute a clear majority. Reprisals followed, and it soon degenerated into a bitter conflict, one that saw the assassination in 1991 of the ex-prime minister of India, Rajiv Gandhi, and two years later that of the Sri Lankan president, Ranasinghe Premadasa.

Since the 1970s, India's Sikhs, though less than 2 percent of the country's total population, have also agitated for a separate Sikh state, Khalistan. In 1984 Indira Gandhi, mother of Rajiv (as well as daughter of the country's first prime minister, Jawaharlal Nehru), ordered the Indian army to storm the Golden Temple in Amritsar—the holiest shrine in the Sikh world—which had been occupied by armed Sikh separatists. The resulting gun battle lasted five days and left 300 dead. Retaliation came later the same year, when two of Indira Gandhi's Sikh bodyguards assassinated her, in turn sparking anti-Sikh riots that killed an estimated 3,000.

Hindu nationalists have not been free of this kind of extremism. In 1992, Hindu zealots, chanting that the fate of Muslims in

The site of Rajiv Gandhi's assassination in Sriperumbudur, India, is marked with a memorial. The popular prime minister was killed in by a Sri Lankan Tamil separatist.

India should be "Pakistan or Kabristan"— meaning Pakistan or the graveyard—stormed the sixteenth-century Babri Mosque in Ayodhya and demolished it, claiming that it had deliberately been built on the site of the birth of Lord Rama. The conflict over the site has never been resolved. In 2002, fifty Hindu pilgrims were burned to death on a train after visiting Ayodhya. In the rioting that followed, 2,000 Muslims were killed.

SUTTEE

The conflict between an India eager to modernize and fundamentalist Hindus is epitomized by the attitudes to suttee (sati), the ritual immolation of a widow on her husband's funeral pyre. It is a tradition whose origins and purposes are obscure. Britain's banning of the practice in 1829 has never been challenged by any independent Indian government. Even so, it is believed that around forty cases of suttee have occurred since 1947, none more notorious than that in

1987 in Rajasthan, when an eighteen-year-old widow, Roop Kanwar, committed sati.

It was a case that echoed around the world, sparking furious passions among those who denounced it, claiming that it degraded India and that the woman had either been coerced or drugged, and those fundamentalist Hindus who asserted it was the right of every Hindu woman. The case remains an uncomfortable reminder of the tensions between Hinduism and a secular, democratic India.

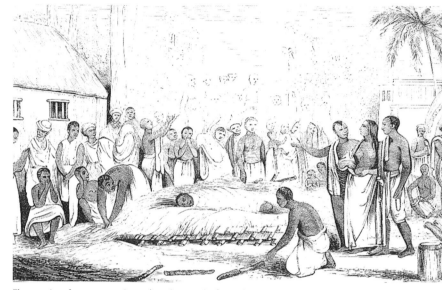

The practice of suttee, or sati, may have its roots in the ancient fire rituals of the Vedic period. This 1851 engraving shows the British view of the practice, which has since been banned.

JAWAHARLAL NEHRU

Jawaharlal Nehru (1889–1964), educated in England at Harrow and Cambridge, was the first prime minister of independent India. Notably liberal and strongly Western in outlook, he died still prime minister.

Long years ago we made a tryst with destiny, and now the time comes when we shall redeem our pledge, not wholly or in full measure, but very substantially. At the stroke of the midnight hour, when the world sleeps, India will awake to life and freedom. A moment comes, which comes but rarely in history, when we step out from the old to the new, when an age ends, and when the soul of a nation, long suppressed, finds utterance. It is fitting that at this solemn moment we take the pledge of dedication to the service of India and her people and to the still larger cause of humanity.

August 1947

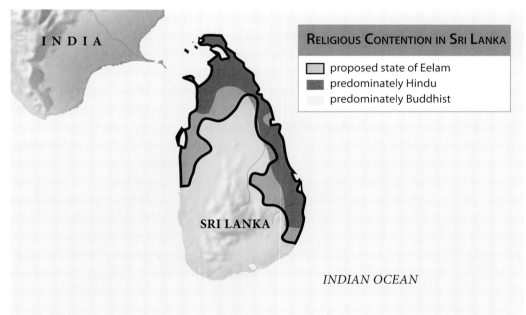

INDIA

RELIGIOUS CONTENTION IN SRI LANKA

☐ proposed state of Eelam
■ predominately Hindu
☐ predominately Buddhist

SRI LANKA

INDIAN OCEAN

Religious conflict on the Indian subcontinent has extended even to the independent island of Sri Lanka, where Hindus and Buddhists live in uneasy, unofficial segregation. Among the former, a separatist movement has pushed for a Hindu state it wishes to call Eelam.

BUDDHISM
Tibet's Buddhist Theocracy

FROM THE SEVENTEENTH to the nineteenth centuries, the tradition of Buddhism was carried on in lands where it had been established before the violent Muslim incursions into India had virtually exterminated the peaceful religion in its homeland. In places where Islam pressed beyond India, such as Indonesia and Java, Buddhism was similarly wiped out; but where the sword of the Qur'an did not reach, Buddhism continued and flourished.

The great barrier of the Himalayan Mountains protected the high plateau of Tibet from the burning tides of Islam's fervor. In the peace behind its lofty natural ramparts, Tibet developed a highly refined culture oriented completely around its religion, producing a distinctive Buddhist theocracy in which Buddhist values permeated every aspect of state and society. The highest governing authority rested with the nation's highest priest, the Dalai Lama, who ruled from Lhasa. This spiritual destiny was by no means obvious from Tibet's rugged beginnings.

In the early centuries CE, the Tibetans had been known as hardy warriors and successful conquerors of neighboring tribes. In the mid-seventh century, the powerful king Songtsen Gampo even took control of western China and parts of northern India. His conversion to Buddhism set Tibet on a new path, away from its martial ways, but it would take centuries for this religion to completely win the hearts of the people from their harsher native Bön animism. The Potala Palace built by the Great Fifth Dalai Lama in the seventeenth century crowned the consolidation of Tibetan Buddhism as the national religion.

As Tibetans accepted the new philosophy ever more deeply, they gradually shed their old fierceness, yet seemed to retain the tough determination that had been its core. Their strength did not leave them; it was merely applied in new and more subtle ways. Tibetans have gained a reputation for steadfast resilience and cheerful optimism in the face of tremendous difficulties. More than any other nation, Tibet came to reflect the Buddhist ideal.

MINGUN PAGODA
~

So pervasive was Buddhism in Myanmar (Burma) during this period that it was even used to express the power of a brutal and manifestly un-Buddhist ruler. King Bodawpaya acceded to the throne in 1782 after murdering his grandnephew, and then consolidated his power through bloody purges before he invaded the neighboring kingdom of Arakan, where he captured some 20,000 slaves.

King Bodawpaya considered himself the incarnation of Maitreya, or Arimittya Buddha, and to honor this blessed status he set about to build a colossal shrine called the Mingun Pagoda, north of Mandalay on the Irrawaddy River. Surviving portions of the complex include the beautiful and impressive Settawaya Pagoda. Built in 1811, it houses a footprint of the Buddha.

Had Bodawpaya's plan been completed, the huge main pagoda would have stood as the tallest Buddhist shrine in the world, but the dubiously Buddhist king died before his monument to himself was finished. An indication of the intended magnitude of Mingun Pagoda can be seen in the massive iron temple bell, which survives today. It is the largest undamaged bell in the world, weighing in at an astonishing eighty-seven tons.

Above: The Mingun Bell was begun in 1808 and took three years to complete. It was to have been the centerpiece to massive pagoda planned by Myanmar's King Bodawpaya. Right: Sited outside Mandalay, the Mingun pagoda was never completed.

A monk gazes out from Drepung monastery. Located near Lhasa, Drepung is Tibet's largest monastery, its training program structured like a university, and divided among seven on-site colleges. Such monasteries have long been crucial to Tibet's cultural and religious identity. At right is a dharma wheel, or dharmachakra.

THE MONASTERY SYSTEM IN TIBET

Tibetan society came to be organized around the unique national project of producing advanced souls. The monastery system combined education and government with Buddhist religion in a network that operated throughout the country. Nearly a quarter of all male Tibetans became trappa, or monks, for part of their lives, with perhaps 200,000 living in the monasteries at any one time. Candidates were drawn from throughout society on the basis of aptitude and merit. At the top of the system were the lamas, the highest clergy, regarded much like living saints.

The Tibetan monastery system was supported by the surplus produced by the rest of the populace. National surplus more conventionally goes to support the heavy cost of an army, but with no ambitions for conquest, and relying on its geography for defense, Tibet maintained only a tiny army of a few thousand barely equipped men. In advanced states, surplus is also typically invested in infrastructure such as roads. Tibet considered its ability to develop peaceful Buddhism a privilege of isolation from corrupting foreign influences, and deliberately sought to keep its roads difficult in order to discourage visitors and conquerors alike. Thus even in the cold and rocky land of Tibet, from which it was difficult to wring a living, there was sufficient surplus to sustain the monastery system—which itself minimized expenses by feeding its monks and lamas alike a bland diet of roasted flour tsampa and yak-butter tea.

The system was built on the premise that the best possible investment of the nation's surplus was the cultivation of spiritual advancement in its people, and governmental decisions to allocate resources were made accordingly.

SHWEDAGON PAGODA

Myanmar is rightly known as the "land of the pagodas." Devotion to Buddhism has raised a multiplicity of stupas and other shrines in this nation, many of them built to hold sacred relics. The greatest of these shrines towers over the very holiest relic: eight hairs believed to be from the Buddha's head lie deep within the heart of the stupa in Yangon (Rangoon) known as Shwedagon Pagoda.

The monument's exact age is uncertain, but it dates to at least the fourteenth century. Its later embellishments illustrate the continuing vitality of Burmese Buddhism during the nineteenth century. In 1871 King Mindon Min sheathed the entire ancient pagoda in several billion dollars' worth of gold. Glittering with rubies, emeralds, diamonds, and other precious stones, the spires soar heavenward, the central spire reaching 386 feet high, making Shwedagon Pagoda the tallest religious building in the world. Shwedagon Pagoda remains today a tremendous testament to the importance of Buddhism in Burmese society and culture, and devout pilgrims continue to embellish this spectacular shrine with contributions of gold.

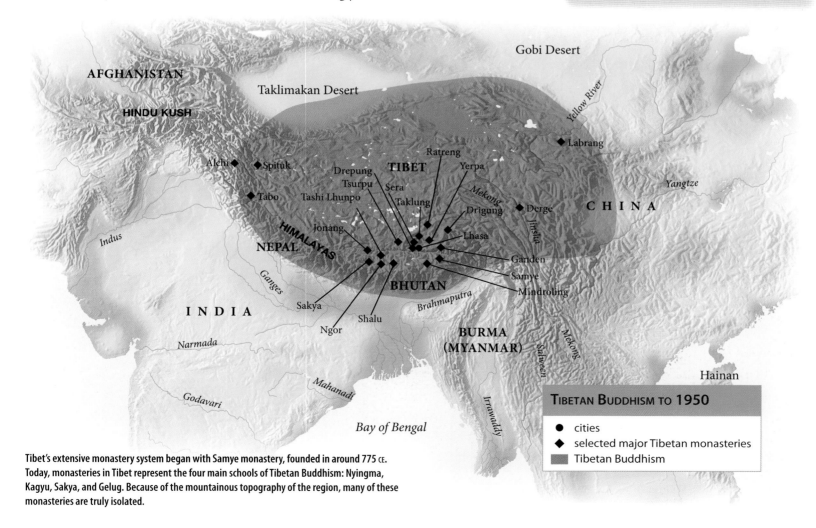

Tibet's extensive monastery system began with Samye monastery, founded in around 775 CE. Today, monasteries in Tibet represent the four main schools of Tibetan Buddhism: Nyingma, Kagyu, Sakya, and Gelug. Because of the mountainous topography of the region, many of these monasteries are truly isolated.

TIBETAN BUDDHISM TO 1950
- ● cities
- ◆ selected major Tibetan monasteries
- ▓ Tibetan Buddhism

BUDDHISM
China Invades Tibet

OVER THE LAST SEVERAL CENTURIES, Tibet's political status in relation to China has varied according to the stability and power of the Chinese government, which asserts authority over the region. Tibet enjoyed varying degrees of independence, relying primarily on its remoteness to keep it low on China's list of priorities. However, after World War II Mao Zedong's Communist government focused its attention on the annexation of Tibet and in 1950 sent troops into the region.

At first the Chinese occupation was peaceful, and in 1951 a Seventeen Point Agreement was drawn up allowing some Tibetan autonomy. However, it soon became clear that China would settle for nothing less than absolute control, and the occupation became increasingly forceful. Rebellion broke out in 1956, culminating in the Tibetan popular uprising of 1959. At this, efforts to make the occupation appear to be a welcomed liberation were dropped, and the Chinese troops unleashed their full force. Soldiers opened fire on the monasteries and killed monks en masse to take control of the nation.

Deep popular devotion to Buddhism throughout Tibet made the religion a rival to Communist authority, so China set about to eradicate Tibet's religious culture. The Chinese Cultural Revolution (begun in 1966) made systematic destruction official policy, and monasteries by the thousands were shelled into rubble. Libraries of sacred texts were burned, and religious artworks were smashed. Monks and nuns were tortured and slaughtered en masse, and all but a handful of the country's monasteries were left in ruins. Championing Marxist atheism, China maintained that it was freeing Tibet from a shameful and primitive heritage.

The young Fourteenth Dalai Lama fled for his life in 1959 and escaped into India, where he set up a government-in-exile and continued to serve as the head of Tibetan Buddhism.

Communist China's aggression toward Tibet, which began in 1950, was followed by forced annexation of the country a year later. Violence and destruction ensued; monks and nuns were killed, and monasteries were razed. The Dalai Lama fled in 1959, taking up residence in Dharmsala, India, where he maintains a government-in-exile.

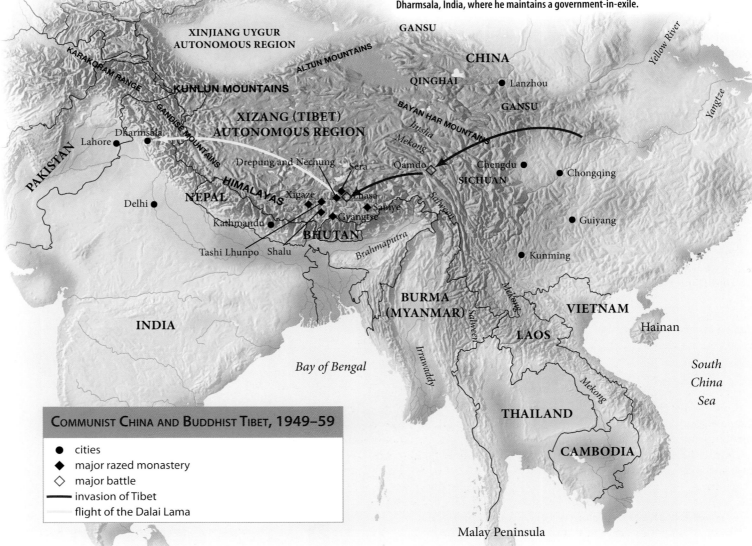

COMMUNIST CHINA AND BUDDHIST TIBET, 1949–59

- ● cities
- ◆ major razed monastery
- ◇ major battle
- ▬ invasion of Tibet
- ▬ flight of the Dalai Lama

The spiritual and cultural leader of Tibet, Tenzin Gyatso is the fourteenth Dalai Lama in a lineage that began in the fifteenth century.

A POLITICAL REINCARNATION

The second most important religious leader in Tibetan Buddhism is the Panchen Lama, the abbot of the monastery of Tashi Lhunpo. Like the Dalai Lama, he represents to Tibetan Buddhists the latest in an unbroken line of incarnations of the same holy man. Following his death, he must be recognized in a new birth.

The ritual process of recognizing the new incarnation of such an influential spiritual leader is complex and subtle. This identification is aided greatly by the fact that these two highest lamas identify and train each other in turn, making the Panchen Lama the final authority for recognizing each new Dalai Lama.

When the Dalai Lama fled Tibet in 1959, the Tenth Panchen Lama, Choekyi Gyaltsen, remained behind. He was imprisoned and tortured in Beijing and only allowed to return to his monastery in 1989, where he gave a speech in which he criticized Chinese destruction of Tibetan culture. He was reported dead five days later, of a heart attack at the age of fifty-one.

In 1995 the Dalai Lama announced the recognition of the reincarnated Panchen Lama as the young Gedhun Choekyi Nyima. The Chinese government claimed superior authority and named its own rival candidate, a boy raised and kept in Beijing. To Tibetan Buddhists he is commonly known as the "Panchen Zuma," or "fake Panchen Lama."

The six-year-old boy recognized by the Dalai Lama was quickly seized along with his family and has not been heard from since. Reports of the boy's death in prison have been met with steadfast refusal by the Chinese government to offer any evidence to the contrary.

The political disruption of this ancient religious lineage will doubtless leave the selection of the next Dalai Lama clouded with political controversy.

FALUN GONG

Through the centuries many Buddhist monasteries have taught physical disciplines to aid their monks in the cultivation of spiritual discipline. Some of these practices became martial arts self-defense traditions such as Shaolin Temple kung fu. Other Buddhist physical disciplines are nonmartial exercises, such as *qigong*, a practice combining structured breathing and stretching movements with meditation (*qi*, or *chi*, being the traditional Chinese concept of a spiritual life-force associated with breath, and *gong* being a discipline). Qigong practices are applied variously for physical fitness, stress reduction therapy, spiritual growth, or all of these.

The way of the oppressors is intimidation, coercion and the use of force. Ours is a belief in and reliance on truth, justice and reason.

—TENZIN GYATSO, THE FOURTEENTH DALAI LAMA

In 1992 a qigong practice called Falun Gong was developed in China by a little-known practitioner named Li Hongzhi. Falun Gong stresses the development of moral virtue on the three principles of truthfulness, compassion, and forbearance. Falun Gong grew rapidly into a popular movement with tens of millions of followers, who often practiced in public parks in the morning.

The Communist Chinese government outlawed Falun Gong in 1999, stating that "the so-called 'truth, kindness and forbearance' principle preached by Li has nothing in common with the socialist ethical and cultural progress we are striving to achieve." A massive crackdown followed, in which thousands of practitioners were imprisoned, tortured, or sent to labor camps as the government conducted an extensive propaganda campaign to discredit the movement. Periodic silent protests in Beijing were crushed by police beatings and arrests, and China's ongoing repression of Falun Gong has raised concern among international human rights organizations.

REPRESSION IN MYANMAR

Since 1962 Myanmar has been under the control of a socialist military regime, which changed the name of the nation long known as Burma. Supported by China, this state has asserted its power with deadly force, and government soldiers shot thousands of student protesters in 1988's pro-democracy "8888 Uprising." However, the regime faced a new challenge when Buddhist monks boldly led antigovernment protests in 2007.

Buddhist monasteries play a major role in Burmese society, which is largely Theravada Buddhist. Monasteries form the hearts of traditional villages, and the clergy command wide respect among the people. The socialist regime was reluctant to resort to the open killing of monks and nuns for fear of provoking a popular uprising and did not respond with immediate violence to the monks' demonstrations in 2007.

The Shwedagon Pagoda is a golden stupa in Yangon (Rangoon) that towers over 300 feet high. Considered the holiest shrine in Myanmar, the stupa has served as a focal point for popular movements. On September 24, 2007, some 20,000 monks and nuns began their march from this symbolic monument, emphatically putting the stamp of religious approval on antigovernment criticism. Government troops then crushed the protests, beating, imprisoning, and killing monks, closing off Shwedagon Pagoda and other Buddhist shrines, and assaulting and shutting down monasteries. In the end the violent tactics were effective. Protesters disappeared, and the monasteries were thereafter patrolled by troops.

The gilded Shwedagon Pagoda in Yangon, Myanmar, is one of Theravada Buddhism's most holy sites. The temple was the site of a standoff in September, 2007. Pro-democracy demonstrators and monks clashed with the military government, leaving several demonstrators dead.

A Tibetan Diaspora

CHINA'S VIOLENT AND REPRESSIVE occupation of Tibet drove some hundred thousand Tibetans to flee along with the Dalai Lama, and more have followed since. The primary Tibetan refugee community is in Dharamsala, India, where the Dalai Lama maintains his government-in-exile, but Tibetan communities are now found all over the world. The Dalai Lama has served as an active and visible leader of this dispersed community, winning a Nobel Peace Prize in 1989 and publishing and lecturing extensively on Tibetan Buddhism and the plight of his people.

In many respects the situation recalls that of the Jews in the time of the Roman Empire. The Jews were an ethnic group bound together by an unusual degree of devotion to their religion, whose practices were structured around the authority of a high priest and a central temple. Their revolt for independence was crushed by military might, their homeland was occupied, religious monuments were razed, and refugees scattered throughout the Roman world in

what is called the Jewish Diaspora. The parallels to the plight of Tibet are substantial.

China's Communist government has not destroyed Lhasa's Potala Palace as the Romans destroyed the Jewish Temple, but in driving out the Dalai Lama and his entourage they have left it largely a shell; it is no longer the vital hub of Tibetan Buddhism that it was before the invasion.

The dispersed Jewish communities faced the challenge of maintaining their ethnic and religious identity without a physical center or territorial community. The usual result of an ethnic diaspora is that the displaced people become absorbed into the culture of their new home. In the case of the Jews, however, the intense devotion to their faith maintained their distinct identity everywhere they went. The Tibetan refugees face a similar challenge, and only time will tell whether their culture and their distinct form of Buddhism can survive the Tibetan Diaspora.

BUDDHISM IN THE WEST

As refugee Tibetan Buddhist lamas took up residence throughout the West, they were welcomed by many eager students of Buddhism. After the cultural upheaval of the 1960s, North Americans in particular were open to the new perspective that Eastern religion offered—or at least to its novelty. The scattered lamas formed small communities of disciples and began to teach, but the wealth and comfortable environment of the West were far different from the life of a harsh Tibetan monastery, and the liberal Western mind far different from that of a dedicated Buddhist monk.

Many Westerners regarded the teachings as inspirational material from which they could freely pick and choose what they liked. Westerners tended to treat spiritual disciplines as optional, to regard commitments lightly, and to want quick results rather than to hear that some insights might require a lifetime of monastic dedication. Buddhism, and Tibetan Buddhism in particular, became not only popular but even fashionable in the West, but the authenticity of the tradition being received was much questioned.

By the end of the 1990s, the generation of lamas trained in Tibet had mostly died out and was being replaced by younger lamas raised outside Tibet, amid

The Japanese Tea Garden in San Francisco was built in 1894. California's location on the Pacific Rim made it one of earliest recipients of Buddhist teachings in the West, especially from Japan. Nearly every form of Buddhism is now represented in the region.

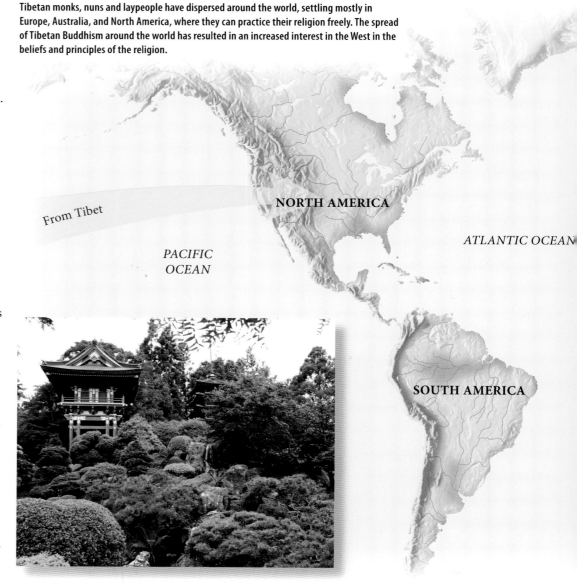

Tibetan monks, nuns and laypeople have dispersed around the world, settling mostly in Europe, Australia, and North America, where they can practice their religion freely. The spread of Tibetan Buddhism around the world has resulted in an increased interest in the West in the beliefs and principles of the religion.

From Tibet

NORTH AMERICA

PACIFIC OCEAN

ATLANTIC OCEAN

SOUTH AMERICA

the luxury and capitalist ethic of the modern world. Buddhism has enjoyed a new appreciation across a vast new audience and has offered a salutary balancing influence to the near-religion of Western consumer capitalism. But the great significance of the ancient Tibetan tradition is the refinement and integrity it attained over centuries of development. Whether the young new lamas can maintain their own depth amid the West's enthusiastic but often superficial embrace of Tibetan Buddhism will largely determine the legacy of this ancient religious culture.

BHUTAN: A BUDDHIST EXPERIMENT IN HAPPINESS

Isolated from the modern world by rugged Himalayan territory, the small Buddhist nation of Bhutan has preserved much of its traditional way of life. Bhutan has regarded the worship of material progress with a critical eye and has been slow to permit outside

visitors and adopt modern technology. The Bhutanese have reason to be conservative. One of the poorest nations, Bhutan is nonetheless one of the happiest, according to a 2006 British study, ranking it eighth in the world. Its citizens enjoy a stable and rewarding society that is the fruit of long development, shared cultural values, and restrained development under wise leadership.

The hereditary king of Bhutan spent the final decades of the twentieth century transforming his kingdom into a democracy, dispersing governmental authority slowly down through society, so that the people could learn to accept the responsibilities of self-rule. Guided by Buddhist principles, the "Dragon King" Jigme Singye Wangchuk abdicated his throne in 2006 and handed the nation over to its people.

Having taken its own time, Bhutan is now opening itself gradually to the outside world, inviting a growing number of tourist visitors and making its first connections to the internet. This small, tradition-bound country

Taktshang Monastery in Bhutan is precariously perched on a cliff that rises 10,000 feet (3,120 m) above the valley floor. Consecrated in the eighth century, the monastery is nicknamed "Tiger's Nest," for the legend that its founder, Padmasambhava, flew there on the back of a tiger.

is attempting to engage the modern world in a considered and deliberate fashion, cautiously preserving the best of its own traditions as it explores the benefits that modernism may offer. Bhutan's deeply Buddhist ideal of achieving national happiness rather than material progress at any emotional or spiritual cost has challenged nations of vastly greater wealth with the question of what such wealth is good for if it does not bring happiness.

Bhutan presents a remarkable picture, perhaps showing what might have become of Tibet if the Chinese had not invaded and forced the cult of development upon it—but that picture may soon change. Chinese troops entered the border region of Bhutan's Dolam Valley in November 2007 and destroyed empty military posts there. The Communist government in Beijing now lays claim to Dolam and is expected to extend its claims as its troops fortify positions deeper into Bhutan. The future of this small nation and its Buddhist experiment in democratic national happiness is gravely in doubt.

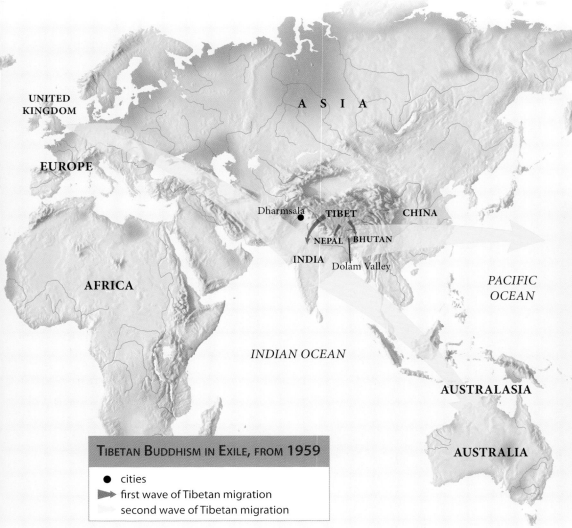

UNITED KINGDOM

EUROPE

AFRICA

ASIA

Dharmsala • TIBET CHINA

NEPAL BHUTAN

INDIA
Dolam Valley

PACIFIC OCEAN

INDIAN OCEAN

AUSTRALASIA

AUSTRALIA

TIBETAN BUDDHISM IN EXILE, FROM 1959

● cities
➤ first wave of Tibetan migration
second wave of Tibetan migration

A clapboard house in upstate New York, converted into a color-fully painted Tibetan Buddhist temple.

JAINISM
Jain Temple Worship

"THOU SHALT NOT MAKE for thyself graven images." The commandment Moses brought down from Sinai forbade the idol-worship practices that were comfortingly familiar to the Hebrews from their long sojourn in Egypt, where idols of Egypt's many gods were common. The book of Exodus describes the Hebrews as forging themselves an idol in the form of a golden calf, which infuriated Moses on Yahweh's behalf; but the Hebrews were not the only people to have trouble with this spiritual directive. The prohibition of idolatry has long proved challenging for individuals who prefer a tangible object upon which to focus their worship.

Rich ornamentation decorated traditional Jain temples in the exuberant Indian style that is widely familiar from Hindu places of worship. At the heart of a typical Jain temple's sculptural intricacy sat statues of the tirthankaras, the perfectly enlightened beings who had achieved the Jain ideal of *moksha*. A line of two dozen nearly identical statues might represent the lineage of the twenty-four tirthankaras. The statues represented role models rather than gods, but the idols served as a focus of reverence for generations of worshippers.

In the eighteenth century the Svetambara Jain monk Viraji concluded that the Jain custom of, in effect, worshipping idols violated the spirit of the faith. Viraji asserted that idolatry would not best serve the spiritual advancement of devout Jains, and that the more appropriate environment of worship would be a plain and unadorned building. This would allow worshippers to focus their meditation and prayer without the distraction of material objects or idols that might become objects of worship themselves, rather than instruments used to foster reverence toward abstract principles. So firmly did Viraji believe in his insight that a new movement appeared, distinct from the Svetambara. The new branch became known as Sthanakavasis, from the ordinary buildings, *sthanakas*, that served as their temples.

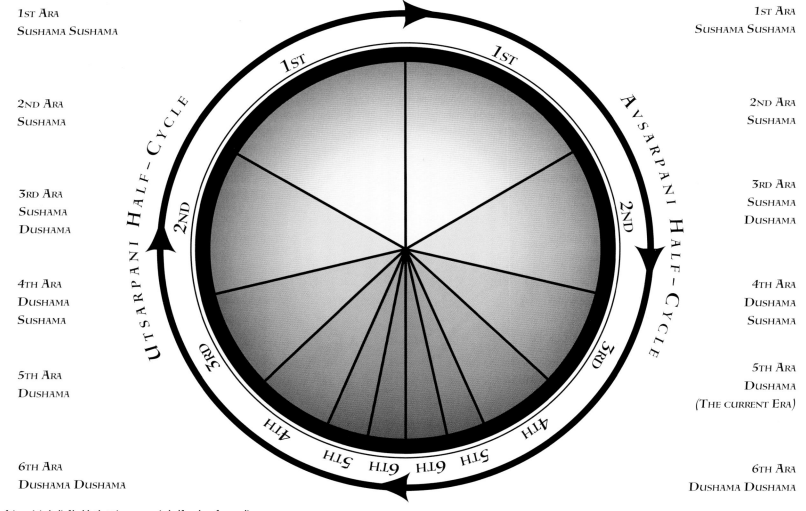

The Jain kalachakra, or wheel of time. Jain belief holds that time passes in half-cycles of ascending happiness, followed by half-cycles of ever-increasing sorrow and suffering. The large yellow triangles at the top represent the pinnacle of happiness, after which the wheel turns clockwise, entering a period of unhappiness. Our current time is the Dushama, the penultimate era of suffering.

Figures of two tirthankaras, Rishaba and Mahavira, from a Jain temple. These statues formed part of a group representing all twenty-four tirthankaras. In the eighteenth century, such figures were criticized as idolatrous by the Svetambara monk Viraji.

KALACHAKRA: THE JAIN WHEEL OF TIME

Behind the infinite pageant of the universe and all its forms of life Jains see the turning of the great *kalachakra*, the symbolic Wheel of Time. For Jains time is a cyclical phenomenon of vast scope, characterized by an ascending half-cycle and a corresponding descending half-cycle. The ascending half-cycle of *utsarpani* carries all life upward toward greater happiness, prosperity, and spiritual purity, through epochs of increasing duration. At the top is the first *ara*, called Sushama Sushama, the longest and happiest epoch, which ends the upward half-cycle. In this Edenic period people live to great ages, grow physically tall, and need little food, though the land provides bountifully. A second Sushama Sushama ara begins the *avsarpani* half-cycle, which descends through epochs of decreasing duration and increasing sorrow as the world gradually becomes harder to live in. Spiritual goodness is increasingly lost, and human society becomes progressively more violent and cruel.

Jains identify the current era as near the bottom of the descending half-cycle, locating the present day within the fifth ara, Dushama, a sorrowful period of 21,000 years, of which we have some 18,500 to go. The kalachakra cycle will carry time out of this ara through two further 21,000-year periods of even greater misery before its rise once again brings life toward the happiness known in the far past.

For Jains no divine hand operates the kalachakra cycle, which simply proceeds along inevitable trends according to natural laws no different from those that melt an ice cube. Within this mechanistic cycle, individuals are free to shape their own karma by their moral choices.

RANAKPUR TEMPLE

According to the Jain kalachakra time cycle, in order for beings to achieve spiritual advancement, times must be neither so happy and comfortable that people neglect the disciplines of faith, nor so miserable and difficult that people give up on hope and on the work of spiritual development. Likewise, within a given society, it is those people who have it neither too easy nor too hard who are most likely to have the discipline to work seriously at their spirituality along with the resources and support to pursue it.

Prosperous merchants and traders have always made up a large portion of the Jain population. Such individuals occupy what the Greeks might have called a Jain Golden Mean between the distracting hereditary ease of royalty and the crushing practical burden of poverty. Their situations gave them the means to study Jain philosophy and the inclination to appreciate the courage represented in its nonviolence.

Jain merchants patronized their faith and expressed their devotion by funding the construction of elaborate temples radiant with artistic symbolism. The fifteenth-century temple at Ranakpur presents uncarved exterior walls, but on venturing inside, the

First knowledge, then compassion. Thus does one remain in full control. How can an ignorant person be compassionate, when he cannot distinguish between the good and the evil?

—FROM THE DASAVAIKALIKA SUTRA

visitor finds a stunning profusion of ornate symbolic reliefs, with the beautiful white marble carved in such fine detail that in many places it becomes almost translucent. The entire building thus expresses the Jain belief that outward appearances are unimportant and that what matters is what lies within.

Above: Detail from carvings in the Ranakpur Jain temple, located in Rajasthan, India. Left: The ceiling of the Ranakpur temple, which is intricately carved in the form of a mandala, a representation of Jain cosmology, set inside a twelve-spoked wheel of life.

Foundation of Indian Sikhism

Not all of Islam's conquests in India were the work of the sword. The Muslim incursions into India exposed Hinduism to alternative concepts, including monotheism and equality before God, and a number of Hindu poet-philosophers called *sants* were won over by some of the Islamic ideas. By choice rather than compulsion, several of the sants came to advocate bringing Islamic elements into Hinduism.

Among these thinkers was Guru Nanak (1469–1539), who lived in northwest India's beautiful and verdant Punjab region. Nanak boldly rejected the entire vast Hindu pantheon of divinities in favor of the single mystical and formless God *sat*, or truth. Nanak dismissed traditional rituals, idol worship, and astrology as empty and foolish superstitions, preaching meditation instead. Nanak further rejected the powerful Hindu traditions of the caste system and its unfavorable treatment of women. With so many radical departures, he was clearly promulgating a distinct new faith in this land of extremely ancient religions.

Nanak emphasized the crucial role of holy gurus (teachers) in revealing God's nature. He chose his successor from among his disciples, and after his death Sikhism was carried on and developed by nine successive gurus over the next two centuries. This lineage of gurus ended with the tenth guru, Gobind Singh, who decreed in 1699 that the holy texts they had collected as the Granth Sahib would thenceforth fulfill the role of a living guru and from that point become the ultimate authority for this new religion, which was formalized as Sikhism.

Singh initiated the *gurpurb* baptism ceremony, which stripped away the burden of Hindu caste names. To permanently and distinctively mark Sikhs, to themselves and others, Singh instituted the strict adoption of symbolic accoutrements, which are worn by all baptized Sikh men, and the practice of never cutting one's hair. Sikhs are thus readily recognizable by their smooth turbans, which wind their long hair around their heads. This markedly un-Hindu religion developed a following that today numbers above twenty million, with most still living in the Punjab region.

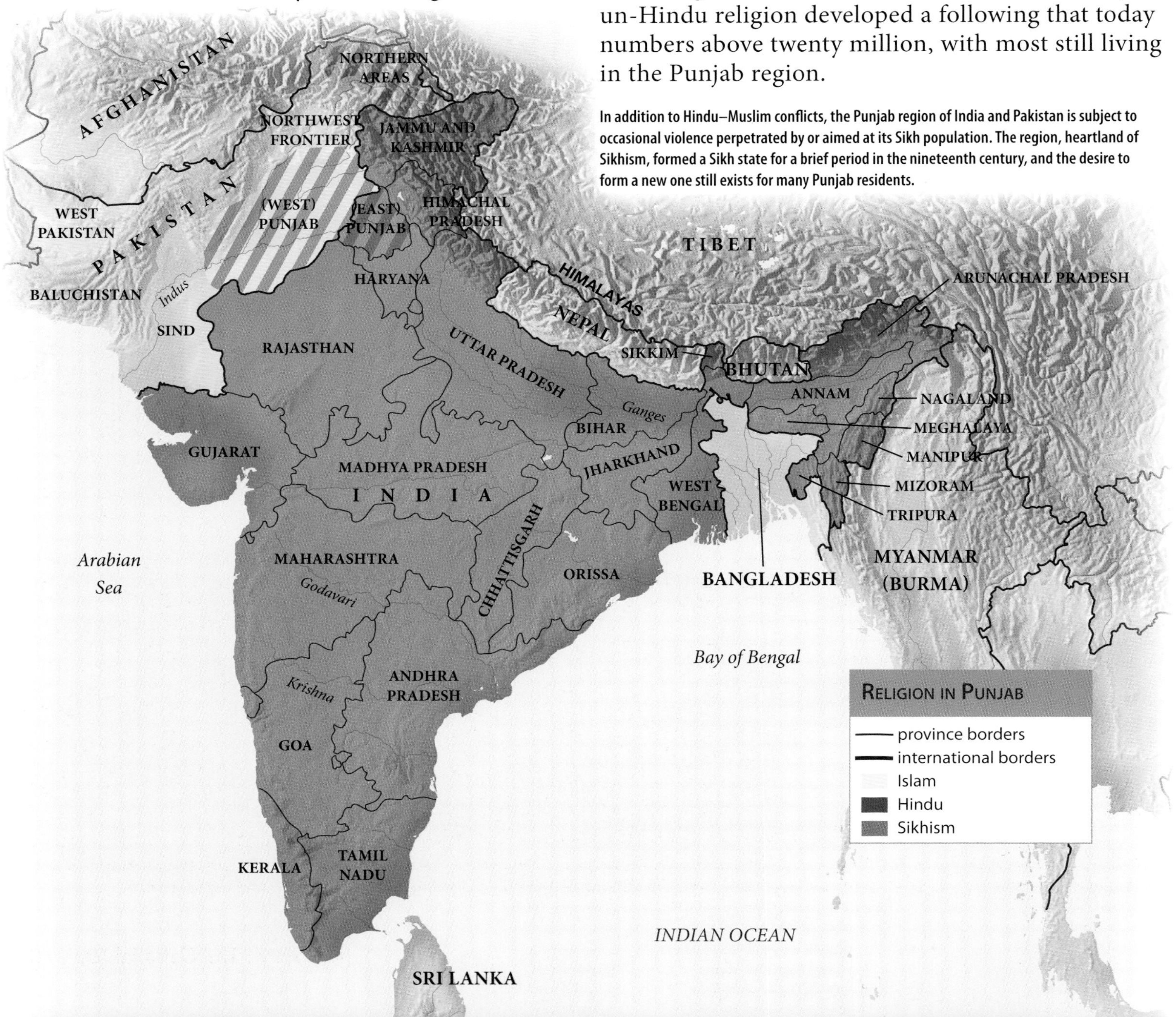

In addition to Hindu–Muslim conflicts, the Punjab region of India and Pakistan is subject to occasional violence perpetrated by or aimed at its Sikh population. The region, heartland of Sikhism, formed a Sikh state for a brief period in the nineteenth century, and the desire to form a new one still exists for many Punjab residents.

AFGHANISTAN
NORTHERN AREAS
NORTHWEST FRONTIER
JAMMU AND KASHMIR
WEST PAKISTAN
PAKISTAN
(WEST) PUNJAB
(EAST) PUNJAB
HIMACHAL PRADESH
BALUCHISTAN
Indus
HARYANA
TIBET
ARUNACHAL PRADESH
SIND
RAJASTHAN
UTTAR PRADESH
HIMALAYAS
NEPAL
SIKKIM
BHUTAN
ANNAM
NAGALAND
GUJARAT
Ganges
BIHAR
MEGHALAYA
MADHYA PRADESH
JHARKHAND
MANIPUR
INDIA
CHHATTISGARH
WEST BENGAL
MIZORAM
TRIPURA
Arabian Sea
MAHARASHTRA
Godavari
ORISSA
BANGLADESH
MYANMAR (BURMA)
Krishna
ANDHRA PRADESH
Bay of Bengal
GOA

RELIGION IN PUNJAB
— province borders
— international borders
Islam
Hindu
Sikhism

KERALA
TAMIL NADU
INDIAN OCEAN
SRI LANKA

A folio from the Sikh holy book, the Guru Granth Sahib. The book is seen as an incarnation of the wisdom and teachings of the line of ten gurus. As such, the Granth Sahib is worshipped as the eleventh and final guru of the Sikh religion.

KHALISTAN: A SIKH STATE

Sikh religious culture differs so strongly from that of Hindu India on one side and that of Muslim Pakistan on the other that Sikhs came to cherish the idea of the Punjab becoming an independent Sikh nation.

In addition to his other revisions of the faith, the tenth guru reformed the Sikh community into a military order in order to resist persistent abuse by the Mughal Muslims. Since the tenth guru, Gobind Singh, Sikhs have venerated militarism, and all Sikh men are required to carry the *kirpan*, a ceremonial steel sword. This martial rededication eventually produced significant Sikh military power. The king Ranjit Singh took Lahore in 1799 and established the first Sikh state. His kingdom encompassed the entire Punjab, and Singh became the Sikhs' national hero.

Singh's kingdom did not endure the tumultuous times that followed the king's death. When emboldened Sikhs made provoking incursions into neighboring British-protected territory, two bloody Sikh wars in the 1840s put the Punjab under British control even before the advent of the British Raj in 1858. Nonetheless, through the decades of colonial rule of India, the Sikhs continued to wish for Khalistan, a Sikh nation that would include all the territory once ruled by Ranjit Singh.

The Sikh dream of Khalistan rose anew with the independence of India in 1947, only to turn to bitter frustration when Nehru and Indira Gandhi each in succession declined to pursue promised talks. Tensions came to a boil in the 1980s, and the Sikhs fortified their central temple of Harimandir and manned it with armed militants determined to establish their Sikh state. In 1984 the Indian army attacked Harimandir and drove out the Sikh militants with violence. In October of that year two of the Sikh bodyguards who had been sworn to protect her assassinated India's prime minister, Indira Gandhi. Outraged Indians responded en masse by massacring at least ten thousand Sikhs in Delhi, leaving deep resentment on both sides and a problem that remained unresolved.

THE HOLY CITY OF AMRITSAR

In 1577 the fourth Sikh guru, Ram Das, founded a trading town that became the holy city of Amritsar. All Sikhs must make a pilgrimage at least once in their lives to this sacred site, which has grown into the largest city in the Punjab.

Within the heart of Amritsar lies an artificial lake known as the "pool of nectar," Amrit Sarovar. Pilgrims walk a route called the Parikrama around the water, visiting shrines that honor the Sikh gurus and pausing to read aloud from the Guru Granth Sahib.

An ornate golden temple seems to float on the glittering waters of the lake: this is the Harimandir, the center of Sikh worship. Begun in 1588 by the fifth Sikh guru, Arjan, the temple was gilded with 220 pounds of gold in 1830. Pilgrims reach the temple by a causeway called the Guru's Bridge.

The Harimandir houses a throne on which a huge copy of the Guru Granth Sahib sits in honor. All day long the temple rings with chants, songs, and readings aloud from the holy text. At night the book is ceremonially paraded to its nearby resting place in the Akal Takht, the sacred meeting place of the Sikh leadership.

The Golden Temple of Harimandir in the Sikh holy city of Amritsar appears to float over an artificial lake, known as the "pool of nectar." The site is the most sacred in the Sikh religion, which requires its adherents to make at least one pilgrimage here.

Daoism After the Ming and Mao

It has been said that Daoism "mirrors the social landscape of its adherents: there are as many meanings as there are vantage points." Confusing as this infinite diversity may be for those seeking to understand Daoism, it goes far toward explaining its survival after the fall of the Ming dynasty in 1644 and the even more traumatic convulsions China endured in the nineteenth and twentieth centuries. From having been in effect an officially sanctioned orthodoxy under a succession of Chinese dynasties, up to and including the Ming, Daoism was progressively shunted aside under the new Manchu Qing dynasty. The chaos into which Ming China descended before its final collapse—threatened by external attacks, weakened by crop failures and famines, its administration ever more corrupt—was blamed by some in Qing circles on Daoist influence.

Under the Qing, Confucian doctrines were accordingly promoted in a program known as *Hanxue* (National Studies). As China prospered, acquiring huge new territories in Central Asia and tripling its population (from 100 million in 1650 to 300 million in 1800), Daoism declined. The eighteenth-century imperial library contained almost no Daoist texts.

Late eighteenth-century China, despite a succession of uprisings and revolts caused by famines as the country struggled to feed its ever-larger population, was the largest state in the world, technologically assured and culturally rich. Its status, at least in its own eyes, was unquestioned. Yet within a century, China had in effect disintegrated, ripped apart by internal revolts and the hugely destabilizing impact of Europe's industrial imperialist powers, aggressively seeking to impose their commercial will.

China's history is punctuated by crises: foreign invasions, natural disasters, famines, and uprisings. Yet through them all, the essential nature of Chinese civilization endured, always resurfacing whatever the setbacks it had received. But the catastrophes that overtook China in the nineteenth century were on an entirely different scale. Furthermore, they were brought about by precisely those European peoples the Chinese had long regarded as inherently inferior—technologically backward and spiritually impoverished.

The disruption was not exclusively the result of foreign assaults. The Taiping Rebellion of 1850–64, made possible by a collapse in central authority, is believed to have cost twenty-five million lives. As a Christian-inspired uprising, led by a man who claimed to be the brother of Jesus Christ, it deliberately set out to ravage Daoism. Nonetheless, it was European penetration that was most destructive, as Russia, Britain, France, Germany, and Japan all carved out ever-larger spheres of influence within China as the country spiraled into what appeared to be irreversible decline.

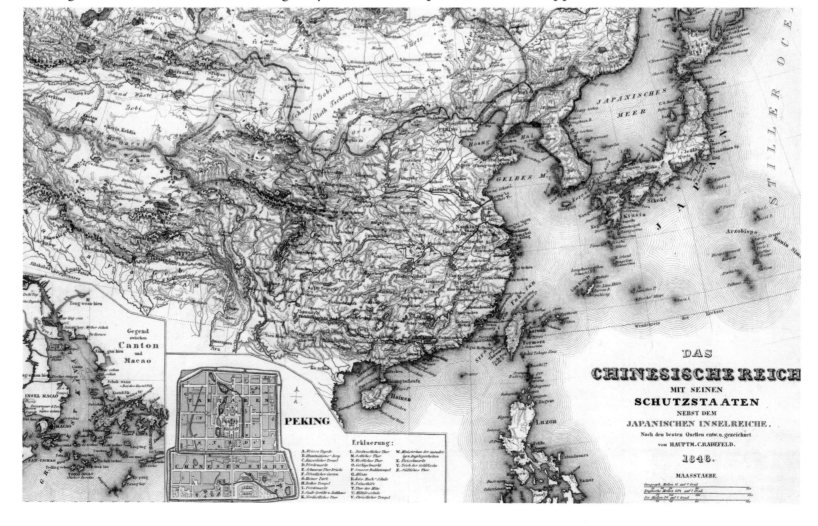

A map from 1846 showing the extent of the Chinese empire under the Qing dynasty. This Manchu-ruled empire was the last before the monarchy was deposed in 1912.

DAS
CHINESISCHE REICH
MIT SEINEN
SCHUTZSTAATEN
NEBST DEM
JAPANISCHEN INSELREICHE.
Nach den besten Quellen entw. u. gezeichnet
von HAUPTM. C. RADEFELD.
1846.
MAASSTAEBE

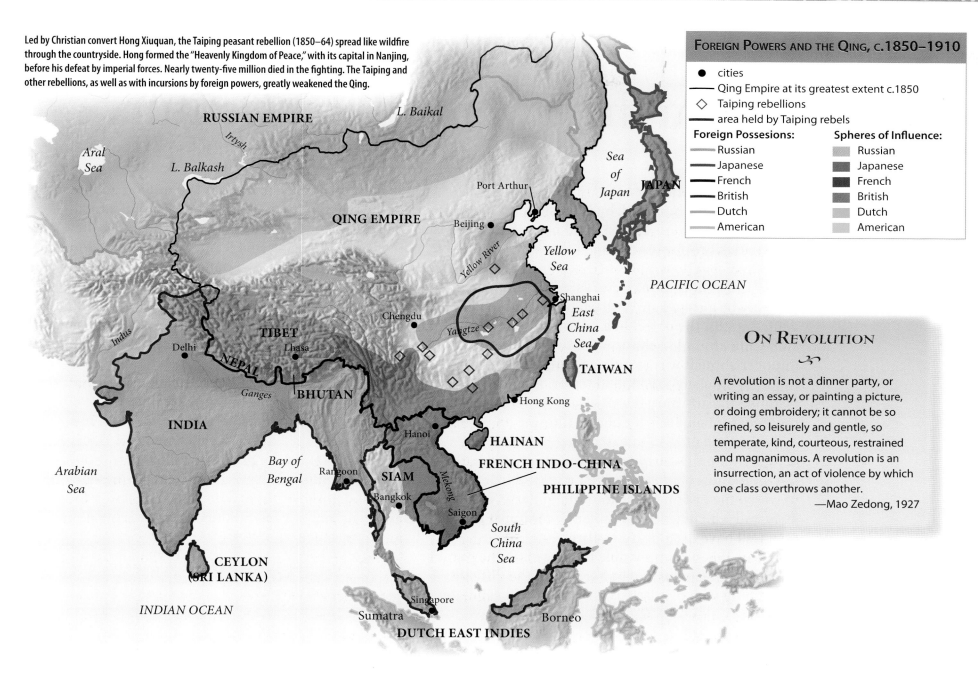

Led by Christian convert Hong Xiuquan, the Taiping peasant rebellion (1850–64) spread like wildfire through the countryside. Hong formed the "Heavenly Kingdom of Peace," with its capital in Nanjing, before his defeat by imperial forces. Nearly twenty-five million died in the fighting. The Taiping and other rebellions, as well as with incursions by foreign powers, greatly weakened the Qing.

ON REVOLUTION

A revolution is not a dinner party, or writing an essay, or painting a picture, or doing embroidery; it cannot be so refined, so leisurely and gentle, so temperate, kind, courteous, restrained and magnanimous. A revolution is an insurrection, an act of violence by which one class overthrows another.

—Mao Zedong, 1927

COMMUNISM AND DAOISM

In 1911, following yet another revolt, central authority collapsed. A system of imperial rule that had endured for 2,000 years was ended amid an orgy of bloodletting. China's government was now notionally under the control of Sun Yat-sen, leading a revolutionary, reformist party. In reality, large areas of the country were effectively controlled by warlords little different from gangsters. The appearance of the Nationalist (Kuomintang) Party in 1923 under Chiang Kai-shek made little difference. By now, too, the rapacious demands of Japan, which in 1931 would invade Manchuria, were clear. Into this volatile mix was also thrown the Chinese Communist Party, founded in 1920, and thereafter, however beleaguered, an increasing force to be reckoned with.

Even the defeat of Japan in 1945 did little more than prolong the agony, provoking a vicious civil war between the Kuomintang and the Communists that ended only in 1949 with a Communist victory under Mao Zedong.

Throughout this horror of slaughter and suffering, Daoism survived, however precariously. Mao then sought to destroy it for good. Communism was avowedly atheist, and Daoism was associated with an enduring Chinese social order that Mao aimed to crush, It was a natural target.

No reliable figures exist for the number of Daoist monasteries Mao destroyed, just as there are no reliable figures for the number of Daoist monks he put to death. But in both cases they were almost enough to ensure the obliteration of Daoism. In the end it survived—allowed, tepidly, to reestablish itself after Mao's death in 1976 and thereafter regaining lost ground with increasing speed and confidence. The rekindling of Daoism speaks volumes for a religion and a philosophy that was and is essentially inseparable from the underlying character of China itself, a country it has done so much to shape.

An engraving from 1858 showing a decisive battle in the Anglo-Chinese Opium Wars. These defeats at the hands of the British are seen as precursors to the Taiping Rebellion, which suppressed Daoism and installed Christianity as the state religion.

Daoism in the Twenty-First Century

THE DEATH OF MAO ZEDONG in 1976 amounted to a lifeline for China and, by extension, for Daoism. Under Mao, Daoism had not merely been systematically oppressed in the name of Communist orthodoxy, but its temples had been ransacked and destroyed, and its monks murdered in numbers that can only be guessed at. With Mao elevated to near deified status, the object of a relentless state-sponsored cult, China found itself turned into a country in which impoverishment was as much a daily certainty as random, officially sanctioned terror. Mao had wholly assumed the arbitrary life-or-death powers of even the most corrupt and self-indulgent Chinese emperor.

By the time of Mao's death, what had once been several million Daoist monks now numbered hardly in the thousands. Had Daoism not survived in Taiwan, to which the nationalist Kuomintang Party had fled in 1949 and which never fell under Communist rule, it may well have disappeared entirely.

Today, it is still impossible to determine the number of Daoists in China, in part because of the difficulty of defining who precisely is a Daoist. Most estimates suggest there may be around 400 million adherents of the religion in mainland China (out of a total population of 1.3 billion). In addition, it is believed that there are between 4.5 and 7.5 million adherents in Taiwan (out of a total population of 22.8 million) and a further 380,000 in Singapore (out of a total population of 4.5 million). Lingering Daoist influences can also be traced in those countries that historically have fallen under Chinese influences, chiefly Japan, Korea, and Vietnam.

As with many other Eastern religions, Daoism has won many champions in the West since the 1960s. The fact that it is almost a "godless" religion may make it more accessible to Westerners: many of Daoism's philosophical teachings can be followed without also having to embrace its religious elements or worship Daoist deities. Offshoots of Daoism, whether martial arts, feng shui, or meditation, have also contributed to its popularity in the West.

This feng shui compass, or *lo pan*, shows the eight primary trigrams of the I Ching, overlain with the five directions. In Chinese philosophy, the center is included with the four cardinal directions. These directions correspond with the five elements: wood, fire, earth, metal, and water.

China without Daoism would be a tree of which some of its deepest roots had perished.

—Joseph Needham, Science and Civilisation in China, 1954

Northern and Southern Schools

Beyond its multitude of sects and groups, Daoism today is divided into two principal schools: Southern, or Temple Daoism, and Northern Daoism (Quanzhen), also known as the School of Complete Perfection, or Complete Reality. As both have ancient origins, neither school can be considered "orthodox"; they simply reflect different paths of devotion, both stemming from the teachings of Laozi. In the same way, it is perfectly acceptable to meld different facets of Daoism, just as elements of Confucianism and Buddhism have infused Daoist practice. "The Way" remains an elusive concept, "observable in its manifestations" but "unknowable in its essence," as one scholar put it.

As its name suggests, Southern Daoism is practiced principally in the south of China,

as well as in Taiwan. It is liturgically based, its priests performing complex rituals with the aim of establishing harmony between worshippers and the cosmos. Northern Daoism, with its prime center of worship the White Cloud Temple in Beijing, was hardly known at all in the wider world until the 1980s, so close to extinction had Daoism come. Its prime focus is on personal purification through "moral and spiritual discipline."

Life in a Daoist monastery is exacting and rigidly hierarchical. The monks are expected to begin the day at 3 AM and then to follow a series of exactly prescribed activities, including extensive periods of meditation and prayer. Silence is expected at most times. The monks are also expected to work in the fields as humble farmers, as well as in the abbey's gardens. Artificial light is not depended upon, with the winter darkness—and cold—allowing time for more extensive contemplation. The day typically ends at 9 PM.

An aerial night view of Hong Kong, which along with Taiwan is an important center for Southern Daoism.

A Daoist priest in Macau, Philippine Islands. Religious Daoist worship and influence are widely practiced throughout East and Southeast Asia, especially in areas where there is a large Chinese population.

The two schools of Daoism in China are often called Northern and Southern Daoism. The Northern branch, whose influence extends into Korea, is centered in Beijing, at the White Cloud temple. The Southern School survived the Communist purges of the Cultural Revolution as it was centered in Taiwan.

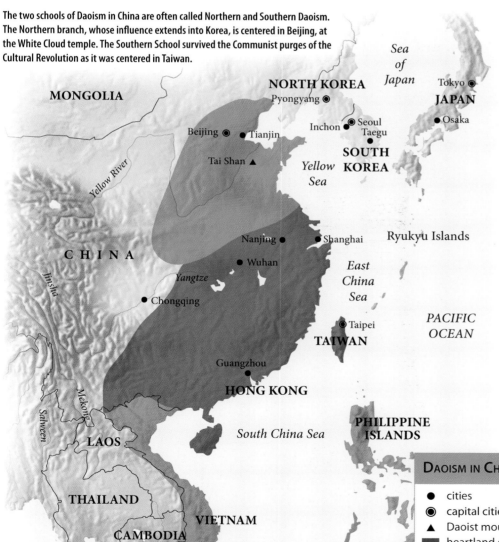

DAOISM IN CHINA, MODERN DAY

- ● cities
- ◎ capital cities
- ▲ Daoist mountain
- heartland of Southern Daoism
- area of Southern Daoist influence
- heartland of Northern Daosim
- area of Northern Daoist influence

CONFUCIANISM
Confucianism as State Ideology

BY THE SEVENTEENTH CENTURY Confucianism had become deeply entrenched as the national ideology of China. While Neo-Confucianism did reflect the influence of Buddhism and Daoism, it is significant that the centuries of Confucianism's rise in China were generally the centuries of Buddhism's wane. Both systems spoke much of endeavoring to live a life of virtue, and they held some definitions of virtue in common, but there were also fundamental differences in their philosophies.

In general, Buddhism looked inward toward the development of the individual spirit, whereas Confucianism looked outward and saw virtue primarily manifested in the context of society, through one's actions in relationship to others. If "right view" was an especially characteristic pillar of Buddhism, "propriety" was a characteristic pillar of Confucianism, which prescribed countless rites, or rules of formal etiquette that governed almost every form of social interaction.

The most advanced and devout Buddhists often practiced their faith in monasteries or as hermits.

Particularly in the Rationalist school of Neo-Confucianism, such separation from family and political service could be seen as violations of core Confucian values of filial piety (*xiao*) and devotion to the state (*zhong*); hence Buddhism sometimes fell into disfavor with Confucians, although Neo-Confucianism was so broad as to include different points of view on the matter.

Rulers of China faced the challenge of unifying a vast and populous nation, and the assertion of strong central control over the individual has long been the Chinese approach. Confucianism emphasized behavior according to rules, loyalty, and the constant acknowledgment of one's specific place in a strict social hierarchy. These qualities supported obedience to imperial rule, and imperial endorsement accordingly made Confucianism a bulwark of Chinese social stability through the end of the nineteenth century.

THE RISE AND FALL OF THE QING, 1644–1912

● cities

◆ unorganized rebellions, c. 1700–c. 1800

◇ British naval attacks in the first Opium War (1839–42)

▢ Ming China, c. 1600

■ Qing control, 1660

■ Qing control, 1770

The Qing Empire, the last of a long series of Chinese empires stretching into prehistory, controlled an enormous swath of eastern Asia at its greatest extent. Its Neo-Confucian ideology did much to support China's last era of imperialism, but internal rebellions and foreign powers slowly and irrevocably weakened the Qing throughout the eighteenth and nineteenth centuries.

CHINESE COMMUNIST REVOLUTION, 1934–49

- ● cities
- —— Communist campaigns
- ▨ Communist centers, 1934
- ▢ Communist (PLA) control, 1949

MONGOLIA

Harbin

Beijing
Tianjin
KOREA
Taiyuan
Jinan
Qingdao
Xining
Lanzhou
Luoyang
Xian
Nanjing
Shanghai
East
China
Sea
CHINA
Wuhan
Hangzhou
Chongqing
Nanchang
Changsha
Fuzhou
Guiyang
TAIWAN

South China Sea

The Communist advance through China left its centuries-old Confucian infrastructure in shambles, although the rigid totalitarian government of Mao Zedong may have been at least as regimented as the system it replaced.

THE IMPERIAL EXAMINATION SYSTEM

The Han emperor Wu Di (reigned 141 BCE–87 BCE), a man inclined to mass executions, was the first leader of China to establish Confucianism as official state ideology. Under Wu's reign began state-supported teaching of Confucian writings in order to inculcate Confucian social ethics in future administrators. Under the Sui dynasty in the sixth century CE, this education system matured into the formalized imperial examination system, by which candidates were evaluated according to standardized tests on their knowledge of the Confucian classics.

This imperial examination system would endure for thirteen centuries as the cornerstone of Chinese civil service. The system offered every man in China a chance, in theory, at entering the imperial bureaucracy. Passing grades were rewarded with government positions, which carried valuable prestige. Although candidates from lower-status backgrounds were disadvantaged by lesser access to study materials and tutors, in numerous cases merit nonetheless carried individuals from the lowest classes into high government office, and so the system functioned to encourage hope for all who aspired.

The system was greatly beneficial to China, not only to the government, which promoted loyalty through the tests' rewards and unity through the teaching of consistent values across the expanse of Chinese territory, but also to the Chinese people. Even aspirants who were not able to pass the exams learned much

and became better citizens by their improved knowledge and appreciation of Confucian values.

The imperial examination system represented a fulfillment of Confucius's ideal of a meritocracy, which he had argued should replace the traditional system of rule by hereditary aristocracy. Confucianism served as the foundation for this pioneering practice of advancement on the basis of equitably determined merit. Despite the ways in which the system inevitably fell short of perfection, it was a major step forward from earlier dynasties' practices of nepotism, cronyism, and the control of power by bloodlines regardless of merit.

CONFUCIANISM AND THE CHINESE REVOLUTION

Confucianism exerted a stabilizing influence and guided China through repeated upheavals. Its insistence on the superiority of strict tradition promoted a confident sense of Chinese identity that deepened with the passing centuries. However, what may have been an excessive reliance on Confucianism left China unprepared to cope with the rise of superior powers outside its static and unchanging worldview.

The Chinese court was utterly blind to the implications of modern Western technology, and unwisely added sneering insults to its dismissal of British gifts in 1793. Britain obliterated antiquated Chinese forces in the two Opium Wars of the mid-nineteenth century, and Japan followed suit in the Sino-Japanese War of 1894–95, delivering shattering blows that struck to the core of growing Chinese nationalism. At the beginning of the twentieth century, China found itself at the mercy of cultures it had despised as inferior, and the final imperial dynasty collapsed into chaos in 1912.

Emerging from civil war, the Chinese Communist Party took control of the nation in 1949. Under Mao Zedong this modern, totalitarian system banned and replaced aspects of culture that were seen to have

Respectfulness, without the Rites, becomes laborious bustle; carefulness, without the Rites, becomes timidity; boldness, without the Rites, becomes insubordination; straightforwardness, without the Rites, becomes rudeness.

—CONFUCIUS, ANALECTS

CONFUCIAN KOREA

Buddhism spread through Korea after its introduction from China in 372 CE and became well established throughout the country as the national religion, but it suddenly found itself in jeopardy with the accession of King Taejong in 1400. Taejong came to power amid the chaos of warring dynastic factions and the threat of local warlords, and to secure his rule he instituted major reforms designed to centralize government authority and assert the absolute dominance of the king. Buddhism constituted a rival power, and Taejong accordingly crushed its prominence in Korea, closing temples, seizing their ancient treasuries, and harshly repressing the Buddhist monastery system.

In its place, Taejong promoted Neo-Confucianism, which had long since succeeded Buddhism as the dominant ideology in China, and which was used very effectively by the Chinese emperors to support popular obedience to imperial rule. Under the leadership of Taejong's Joseon dynasty, Korea became a Confucian state on the Chinese model, and it remained so until the collapse of China's Manchu dynasty in 1912.

kept China backward and primitive. This movement culminated in the Cultural Revolution of 1966–76, which ordered a national purge of the "four olds": old customs, old culture, old habits, and old ideas. Under Mao's leadership, communist Red Guards led sweeping and brutal campaign of destruction that consumed temples, monasteries, books, and everything that might be identified as Confucian—along with millions of tortured, enslaved, or murdered people.

The Cultural Revolution was afterward determined to be "an error," but China continued to resort to bloody repression of any sign of variance from the dictates of the central government. In its desperate extremism and manic reversals, twentieth-century China exhibited what some saw as the effects of profound shock from suddenly abandoning the Confucian system that had for so long been the basis of its identity.

This image of Mao Zedong, with the hammer-and-sickle symbol of Communism, was widely circulated during the Cultural Revolution. Chairman Mao's dates shown at the top of the image are incorrect; Mao died in 1976.

Shinto's Rise over Buddhism

THE JAPANESE STATE SOUGHT TO CONSOLIDATE its fragile new unity at the beginning of the Edo period (1603–1868), and at first Buddhism was the religious beneficiary. In the early 1600s the shogunate moved to neutralize the perceived threat posed by Catholicism, suppressing this outsider's faith with mass executions of missionaries and converts and expelling Spanish and Portuguese embassies. By 1640 contact with the outside world was forbidden under the policy of *sakoku*, or isolationism, and all Japanese citizens were required to register at a Buddhist or Shinto temple.

However, in time the shogunate came to realize that in comparison with Buddhist ideals, Neo-Confucian principles were far more suited to the cultivation of obedience to centralized power. Neo-Confucian ethics were promoted to emphasize the individual's obligation to society and state. The Confucian focus on the state fostered the emergence in the late seventeenth century of *kokugaku*, or nationalist studies. Kokugaku led Japanese thinkers to seek their distinct national identity. They began to reject the foreign influences in Buddhism and Confucianism and championed in their place a "purified" version of the uniquely Japanese phenomenon that was Shinto.

Scholar Hirata Atsutane (1776–1843) summarized core beliefs of this new perception of Shinto: "The two fundamental doctrines are: that Japan is the country of the Gods, and her inhabitants are the descendants of the Gods. Between the Japanese people and [those of] other nations of the world there is a difference of kind, rather than of degree. . . . The Mikado [Japan's emperor] is the true Son of Heaven, who is entitled to reign over the four seas and the ten-thousand countries. . . . From the fact of the divine descent of the Japanese people proceeds their immeasurable superiority to the natives of other countries in courage and intelligence." With this development, Shinto had become the religion of Japanese nationalism.

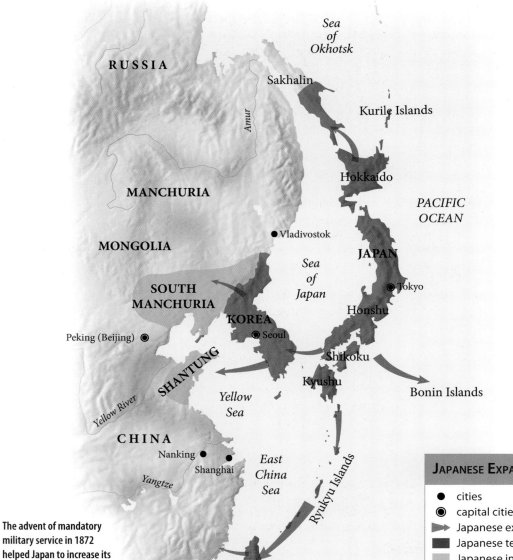

An 1852 Japanese map shows the coastal defenses of Tokyo Bay. A year later, these antiquated defenses, commanded by Samurai, would prove no match for the U.S. Navy's Commodore Matthew Perry. Under the threat of Perry's "Black Ships" and their modern guns, the shogunate agreed to end its policy of isolation and to open trade with the United States.

The advent of mandatory military service in 1872 helped Japan to increase its territories and win battles against much larger countries' forces.

JAPANESE EXPANSION, 1872–1918

- ● cities
- ◉ capital cities
- ➤ Japanese expansion
- Japanese territory, 1914
- Japanese influence, 1918

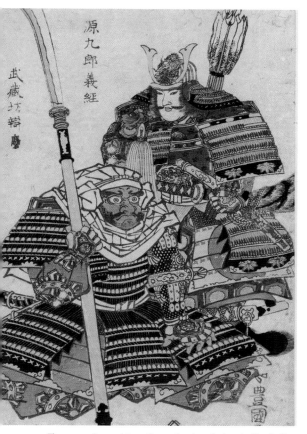

The samurai, an aristocratic warrior class during the first half of the second millenium, practiced *bushido*, a belief system rooted in the precepts and ethics of Shinto, and incorporating elements of other Japanese traditions, such as Buddhism.

STATE SHINTO

The *sakoku* isolation of the Edo period was forcibly broken by American military force in 1854, and the shock of encountering the technological power of the West destabilized the shogunate rule of Japan and precipitated a national crisis of identity. The solution to this crisis was found in a still deeper emphasis on Shinto, which had always claimed divine origin for the imperial family. The "Meiji Restoration" reorganized Japan as a Western-style constitutional state, but under the nominal rule of the emperor.

Shinto was declared the state religion, and in 1868 the Buddhist elements within it were outlawed (although people continued to practice popular aspects of Buddhism). The importance of the emperor at the center of Shinto was greatly amplified in new nationalist teaching, and submission to his divine authority became a spiritual duty of all Japanese people. The new national constitution promised religious freedom, but

The ties between Us and Our people have always stood upon mutual trust and affection. They do not depend upon mere legends and myths. They are not predicated on the false conception that the Emperor is divine, and that the Japanese people are superior to other races and fated to rule the world.
—EMPEROR HIROHITO, HUMANITY DECLARATION, 1946

Shinto was legally deemed to supersede mere religion as a universal truth.

Japan actively adopted Western industrial technology and institutions in the Meiji era, equipping the nation with a critical edge over its tradition-bound Asian neighbors. Exploiting this advantage, Japan's leadership expanded the imperial dominions into China and Russia by military conquest. By the eve of World War II, Shinto-based nationalism had intensified into an ultra-nationalist belief in the divine emperor and *hakko ichiu*, the destiny that Japan must rule the world, by holy war if necessary.

THE END OF STATE SHINTO

The later history of Shinto is inextricably bound up in the events of World War II, with the outcome of the conflict having a drastic effect on the religion.

Japan joined the other expansionist, nationalist nations of Nazi Germany and fascist Italy as part of the Axis powers in World War II. Japanese leaders believed absolutely in their inherent infallibility, aided in part by the newly nationalistic version of Shinto. This led them to make the colossal mistake of a sneak attack on the American naval base in Pearl Harbor. This provoked the entry of the United States into the war, culminating in the detonation of two atomic bombs over the major industrial cities of Hiroshima and Nagasaki. In the fire of these twin holocausts the national myth of Japanese superiority faced harsh reality. In their aftermath, the empire of Japan faced defeat.

During the ensuing occupation, Supreme Commander of the Allied Powers General Douglas MacArthur ordered that the Japanese government no longer take a role in religious matters. The emperor was required to deliver a statement admitting, to American satisfaction, that he was not a god, and state Shinto was abolished as the official faith of the Japanese people.

The Meiji Emperor's desire to buck the influence of Western nations led to an increase in nationalism and the practice of Shintoism, which emphasized his deitific status.

Japan's unconditional surrender forced a drastic realignment of national identity with liberal democratic principles. The punishment of its folly proved an extremely constructive experience for Japan, which went on to completely recover from the devastation it suffered from its aggressive military adventures, and by the later twentieth century the nation had become the second-largest economy in the world. Throughout this recovery, Shinto continued at the individual level, turning back into the folk religion of *kami* (spirit) propitiation and ancestor reverence that it had been before its adoption and transformation for nationalist purposes.

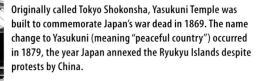

Originally called Tokyo Shokonsha, Yasukuni Temple was built to commemorate Japan's war dead in 1869. The name change to Yasukuni (meaning "peaceful country") occurred in 1879, the year Japan annexed the Ryukyu Islands despite protests by China.

JUDAISM

Jewish Migrations

IN THE SEVENTEENTH through the nineteenth century, western and eastern Europe differed in their attitudes to Jews. Western European nations increasingly came to welcome them, whereas eastern Europeans grew increasingly intolerant. Similarly, Judaism itself changed in different ways. Some Western Jews became more liberal and intellectual in their approach to religion, whereas Eastern Jews became more pious.

In 1781 the Holy Roman emperor Joseph II issued an Edict of Toleration, favoring Jews. The French revolutionaries gave Jews full citizenship, Napoleon freed the Jews in his empire from ghettos, and several German principalities granted Jews citizenship.

Meanwhile, Moses Mendelssohn, a Jewish intellectual from Berlin, encouraged the establishment of Jewish schools that taught secular subjects as well as Jewish law, holding that Jews needed to know the ways of the modern world to be true citizens. By 1871 restrictions on the rights of Jews had been removed or liberalized in Greece, Sweden, Denmark, Austria, and Italy.

Although Poland had welcomed Jews over the years, in 1648 there was a rebellion against the gentry, and the Jews—many of whom managed the estates of the nobles and were regarded as upper class—bore the brunt of the people's animosity. About a quarter of the Jewish population died in the uprising. Frightened by the animosity of their neighbors, some Jews retreated into a more pious form of Judaism. In time this led to the acceptance to a new form of worship known as Hasidism.

In 1795, when Russia annexed Poland, the Russian empire controlled the world's largest Jewish population. Most Jews lived in small towns, or shtetls, and centered their lives on their synagogue and family, practicing traditional Jewish rituals. However, after the assassination of the liberal Czar Alexander II in 1881, frequent and violent pogroms against the Jews began. Mass migrations followed, with Jews moving to all parts of the world.

State-sponsored pogroms killed thousands of Jews after the Russian czar's assassination, leading to waves of Russian Jewish migration; by 1920, the Russian empire had lost as much as a third of its Jewish population.

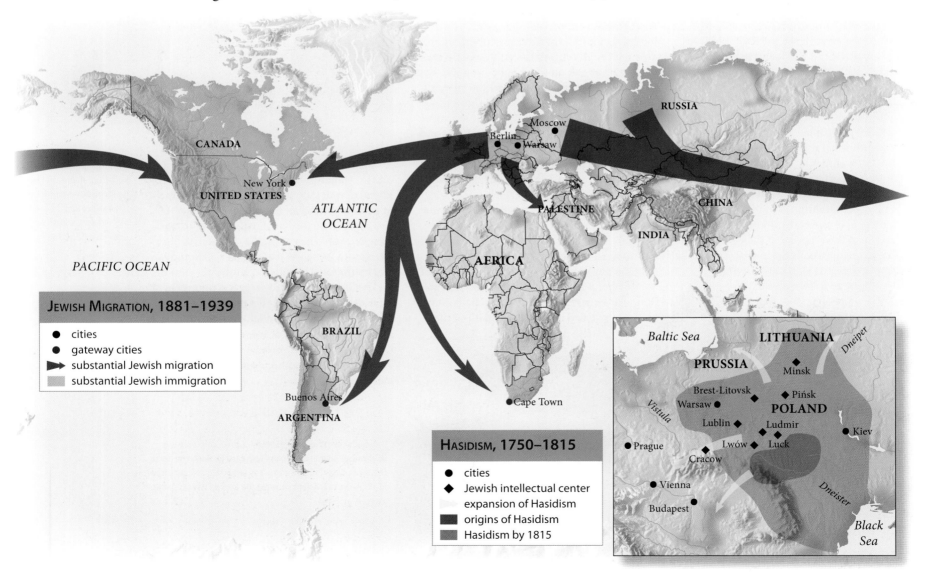

JEWISH MIGRATION, 1881–1939
- ● cities
- ● gateway cities
- ▶ substantial Jewish migration
- substantial Jewish immigration

HASIDISM, 1750–1815
- ● cities
- ◆ Jewish intellectual center
- expansion of Hasidism
- origins of Hasidism
- Hasidism by 1815

Considered the father of Jewish Enlightenment, Moses Mendelssohn (an observant Jew) introduced secular culture to those sequestered in their strict Orthodox Jewish existence while espousing religious tolerance on all sides.

JEWS IN THE AMERICAS
❧

Many of the Jews who fled the Inquisition in Spain and Portugal in the sixteenth century settled in England and Holland. Then, in the seventeenth century, when English and Dutch ships left for the New World, descendants of those Jews sailed on them. Some settled in the Caribbean, and others formed a flourishing Jewish community in Recife, which was then the capital of Dutch Brazil. When the Portuguese took back Recife in 1654, many of the Jews fled to the Dutch city of New Amsterdam (later to be New York), and other Jews settled in Newport, Rhode Island.

In the early years New World Jews gathered for prayer in one another's homes. The first synagogue in America was built in New York City in 1729. The second was built in Newport some thirty years later. Others followed soon in Savannah, Philadelphia, Charleston, and Richmond. By the end of the eighteenth century there were some 4,000 Jews in North America, including Sephardim from Spain and Portugal and Ashkenazim from other parts of Europe. Happy with their new freedom, they heartily supported the War for Independence.

In the early nineteenth century, Jews spread to the Deep South and the Midwest, settling in large American cities. In 1853 Isaac Mayer Wise of Bohemia settled in Cincinnati. A strong promoter of Reform Judaism, he set out to fashion American Judaism according to the Protestant pattern. When the American Civil War broke out, an estimated 10,000 Jews joined the military—about 3,000 of them in the Confederate army. The Union army even appointed Jewish chaplains.

Latin America was slow to get Jewish immigrants because the Inquisition was still in operation until Spanish colonialism ended in the first decades of the nineteenth century. Soon after that time, however, Jews arrived, settling in many parts of the land, from Mexico to Argentina. The first Jew to become a citizen in a Latin American country received his citizenship papers personally from Simón Bolívar, the liberator of Venezuela.

I am, therefore there is a God.
—MOSES MENDELSSOHN

The oldest standing Jewish house of worship in the United States, the Touro Synagogue still serves the Congregation Jeshuat Israel, which was first organized in 1658.

Ultimately Judaism thrived throughout the Americas, free of restrictions. Once the pogroms started in eastern Europe, the numbers of Jewish immigrants increased dramatically. By the 1930s there were nearly three million Jews in the Americas.

Immigrants, after a slow, arduous trip, still had to embark for clearance through Ellis Island. More than 11 million individuals were processed, many with new or shortened "Americanized" names.

HASIDISM
〜

The Hasidic movement was initiated in 1750 by a pious Jew known as Ba'al Shem Tov, or "Master of the Good Name." Hasidism avoided the elitism of Talmudic Judaism with its learned rabbis, and the kabbalists with their high asceticism, and spoke to the hearts of the people of the shtetls. It taught that God is present throughout the universe—even in the most unlikely places—and that believers need only train their awareness in order to see the sparks of divine light that are manifested everywhere. Instead of turning away from the world, Hasidism holds, a believer should embrace it and encompass it in a devotional life to channel the sparks in all things and reunite them with their source in God.

In its formative years Hasidism met heavy resistance, but by the early 1800s it had spread through most of eastern Europe. During World War II it was almost obliterated, but a remnant survived the Holocaust, and Hasidim continues to be influential.

JUDAISM
The Holocaust

WITH THE UNIFICATION OF GERMANY in 1871, many of the nation's Jews envisioned full integration into German society, as Jews were actively involved in the government and often defended liberal causes. When a wave of anti-Semitism emerged later in the decade, optimistic Jews considered it a onetime aberration that posed no real threat. Yet it was a hint of things to come.

In World War I vast numbers of Jews enlisted in the armies of Russia, Austria, and Germany and fought loyally to defend those countries. Jewish leaders were also influential in setting policy for all the major powers, but eventually their involvement led to distrust and anti-Semitism, and the Jews were openly accused of profiteering. When the war ended, most Germans considered the peace treaties unfair to them, and in the worldwide economic depression that followed, the Germans were particularly hard hit and used the Jews as their scapegoat. One individual in particular, Adolf

Hitler, voiced the feelings of many Germans when he advocated that the treachery of Jewish Socialists, liberals, and pacifists had led to the start of the late war and all the grief that had followed from it.

Hitler formed the Nationalist Socialist (Nazi) Party and took over Germany in 1933. He pledged to remove all Jewish influence from the government and to expand the German empire to the east. He did so with ferocious energy. Not only did he remove Jews from the government, however—he ultimately tried to annihilate them all. His anti-Semitic policies accelerated quickly. Jews were required to register with the government and wear badges. Later, Jewish businesses were disbanded or destroyed, and Jews were forced into hard labor. Many Jews were ordered to dig their own graves before being shot. When all these measures seemed insufficient, Hitler came up with the "final solution"—organized death camps.

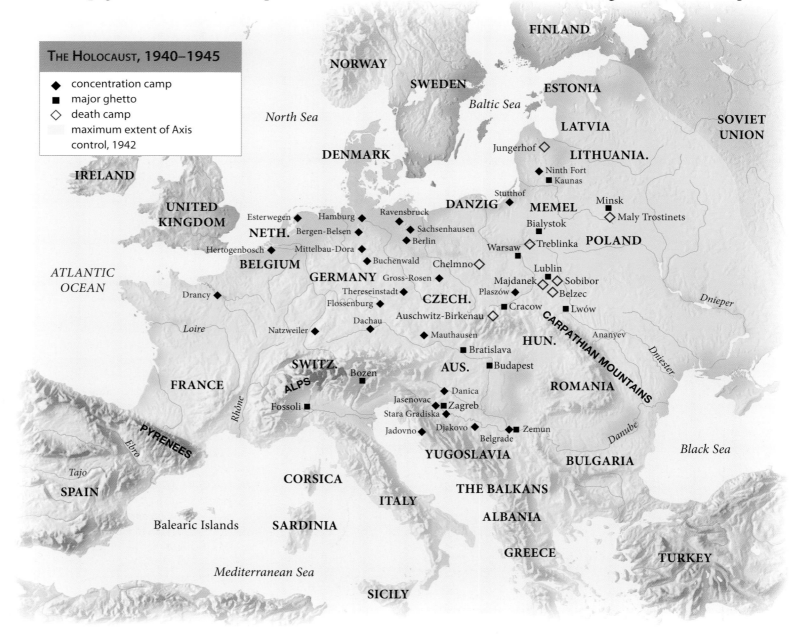

Concentration camps sprang up near factories and mines to provide labor for the Third Reich's war efforts. Almost half of all concentration deaths took place in the last year of the war.

As Hitler's army made advances on all fronts, conquering large swaths of the European continent, more recruits were being prepared with mandatory military training as members of the Hitler Youth.

I believe that I am acting in accordance with the will of the Almighty Creator: by defending myself against the Jew, I am fighting for the work of the Lord.
—ADOLF HITLER, MEIN KAMPF (1925)

KRISTALLNACHT

When a German diplomat was shot by a Polish Jewish student on November 7, 1938, the Nazis used the incident as an excuse to accelerate their anti-Jewish policy and begin working toward the final solution. After conferring with Hitler, Minister of Propaganda Joseph Goebbels pressured a gathering of storm troopers to instigate a network of violent reprisals under the guise of "spontaneous demonstrations." The police were advised not to stop these demonstrations but to arrest the victims.

On November 9 and 10, more than 1,000 synagogues were burned or otherwise damaged. Rioters ransacked and looted about 7,500 Jewish businesses, killing nearly 100 Jews, and vandalized Jewish hospitals, homes, schools, and cemeteries. Some 30,000 Jewish men were arrested, and to accommodate them, the concentration camps at Dachau, Buchenwald, and Sachsenhausen were expanded.

The pogrom came to be called Kristallnacht ("night of broken glass"), as it described the showers of broken glass that rained onto the streets and symbolized the final shattering of Jewish existence in Germany. Kristallnacht

had made Jewish survival in Germany impossible. Thereafter, the Nazis barred Jews from schools and authorized local authorities to impose curfews. Soon after Jews were banned from most public places in Germany. The methodical extermination of Jews in the death camps followed.

Auschwitz-Birkenau became the first Jewish death camp in 1942. After debarking from the cattle cars that brought them, Jews who were deemed unfit for labor were sent directly to the gas chambers.

DEATH CAMPS

The means of arriving at the final solution was carefully worked out by the Nazis. First they confined the Jews to ghettos, and from there they transported them to the east in crowded railway cattle cars. They unloaded the prisoners at death camps, the largest and most notorious of which was Auschwitz-Birkenau. On arriving at a camp the prisoners were taken from the trains and examined by doctors. Those who were strong were sent to work for the Nazis until they collapsed from exhaustion. The weaker prisoners and pregnant women—together with workers who were no longer able to work—were sent to gas chambers and killed. Their bodies were burnt in specially made furnaces.

When the Nazis lost the war in 1945, the concentration camps and death camps were liberated by Allied troops, who were appalled by what they found. By then some six million Jews had died at Nazi hands. Many of the Nazis who were responsible for these atrocities were convicted as war criminals.

JEWISH RESISTANCE

Before they were shipped east to concentration camps, the Jews were generally confined in overcrowded city ghettos where it was all but impossible to survive. Remarkably, while living in the poorest of conditions, many of the prisoners managed to hold on to their Jewish heritage and religion. Most resigned themselves to the inevitable and prayed for the strength to endure, but a few isolated groups of Jews actually tried

to resist their Nazi captors, though they had no hope of success. The most notable failed effort occurred in the Warsaw ghetto, where the people managed to collect stolen and homemade weapons. When the Nazis came in to lead the Jews to the trains, they were attacked on all sides. The fighting lasted for several weeks, but inevitably the Nazis subdued the Jews, many of whom committed suicide rather than fall into Nazi hands.

Taken by a Nazi soldier, this photo shows survivors of the Warsaw Ghetto uprising. When Ghetto denizens learned that deportation to Treblinka meant extermination, they resisted. It was the largest revolt of Jews during the Holocaust.

JUDAISM
Return to the Homeland

FOR MANY CENTURIES Jews scattered about the world dreamed and prayed that one day they would rebuild Jerusalem and reestablish the nation of Israel. Toward the end of the nineteenth century this longing for a homeland grew stronger. Although some Jews in western Europe and the United States felt comfortable, Jews in other parts of the world were suffering prejudice and persecution. Then, in 1894, Alfred Dreyfus, a seemingly innocent French Jewish army officer, was convicted of treason. Outraged, the novelist Émile Zola led a highly publicized campaign that showed that evidence had been forged and Dreyfus was the victim of anti-Semitism.

Alarmed by the implications of the Dreyfus affair, Theodor Herzl, a Hungarian Jewish journalist working in Paris, initiated a Zionist movement, holding that Jews would continue to be second-class citizens until they had a home of their own. Until his death in 1904, Herzl campaigned vigorously for a return to Palestine, but he met resistance from many Jews. Even so, by 1900 Jews had begun migrating to Palestine.

Meanwhile, the General Workers Union in Lithuania, Poland, and Russia was fighting to protect Jewish workers against capitalist oppression. Although the leaders of the union did not favor Zionism, the organization did much to consolidate Jewish identity in eastern Europe, and many Jewish Socialists joined Zionist organizations.

Support for Zionism gradually increased, and in 1917 and 1919 the British and then the U.S. government officially approved the establishment of a Jewish homeland. Immigration to Palestine increased, and by 1939 there were almost a half million Jews there. After the horrors of the Nazi Holocaust were revealed in 1945, resistance to Zionism ended, and the United Nations voted to partition Palestine into Arab and Jewish states. The state of Israel was officially established on May 14, 1948.

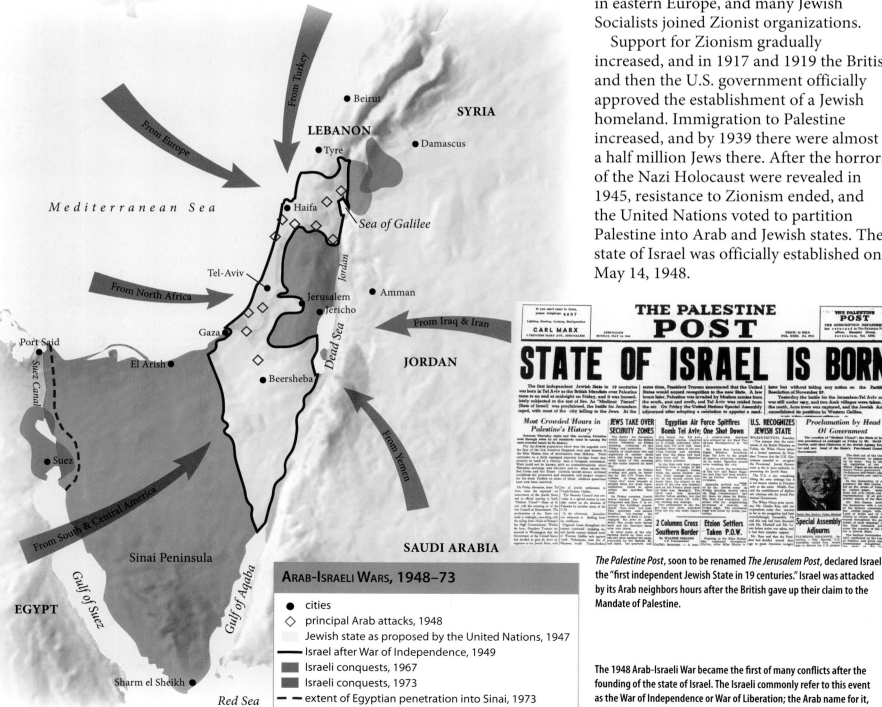

ARAB-ISRAELI WARS, 1948–73

- ● cities
- ◇ principal Arab attacks, 1948
- ▢ Jewish state as proposed by the United Nations, 1947
- — Israel after War of Independence, 1949
- ▨ Israeli conquests, 1967
- ▨ Israeli conquests, 1973
- – – extent of Egyptian penetration into Sinai, 1973
- ➤ Jewish immigration

The Palestine Post, soon to be renamed *The Jerusalem Post*, declared Israel the "first independent Jewish State in 19 centuries." Israel was attacked by its Arab neighbors hours after the British gave up their claim to the Mandate of Palestine.

The 1948 Arab-Israeli War became the first of many conflicts after the founding of the state of Israel. The Israeli commonly refer to this event as the War of Independence or War of Liberation; the Arab name for it, *al Nakba*, means "the Catastrophe."

*If I forget you, O Jerusalem,
let my right hand wither!
Let my tongue cling to the roof of my mouth,
if I do not remember you,*
—PSALM 137

advanced to Israel's borders with 100,000 men and 900 tanks. Faced with the threat of annihilation, the Israelis attacked, and a bitter, lightning war ensued in which the Israelis routed the Arabs and occupied the Sinai Peninsula and other territories that had formerly been held by Arab nations.

By 1973 Egypt had gathered enough strength to strike back at Israel and launched a surprise attack on the Jewish high holy day of Yom Kippur. After suffering an initial setback, Israel again defeated the Egyptians and gained still more territory. In 1979 Anwar Sadat of Egypt signed a peace treaty with Menachem Begin of Israel, but Sadat was assassinated two years later, and the other Arab countries remained in a state of war with Israel.

After witnessing anti-Semitic French mobs calling for death to the Jews after the notorious Dreyfus Affair, Theodor Herzl became an early proponent of a Jewish state. Herzl's 1902 novel *Altneuland* (German for The Old New Land) portrayed a Zionist state of the future as a utopia.

ARABS AGAINST ISRAELIS

On November 30, 1947, the day after the United Nations announced the partition of Palestine (which the Arab states had not approved), a coalition of five Arab nations attacked Israel. After months of fighting, the Israelis managed to survive and even gained more territory than originally granted them. Although the fighting stopped for a while, the refusal of the Israelis and the Arabs to recognize each other's claims resulted in a series of wars and border disputes that continue to this day.

Periods of fighting alternated with periods of relative quiet, as leaders tried to work out peace agreements. In 1967, however, a particularly brutal, six-day war erupted. Gamal Abdul Nassar of Egypt was determined to destroy Israel, and he formed alliances with most of the surrounding Arab nations, who

LIFE ON A KIBBUTZ

Even before Israel became a state, Jews in Palestine began living together in collective settlements known as kibbutzim. In a kibbutz, groups of families and individuals live together, pooling their resources and working together as farmers—or in some cases as manufacturers. All the wealth of the community is held in common, and profits are reinvested in the settlement after members have been provided with food, clothing, shelter, and social and medical services.

Adults living on a kibbutz have private quarters, but children are often housed together and educated and cared for as a group. Cooking and dining were originally always in common, though over time settlements have edged toward greater

privacy. On some kibbutzim Jewish festivals—notably Passover—are celebrated within the community without rabbis, cantors, or synagogues. Regular business meetings are held to determine policy and elect administrators.

By the late twentieth century more than 100,000 Israelis were living in some 200 kibbutzim in Israel and contributing more to Israel's economy and leadership than might be expected, given their relatively small numbers in comparison with the nation's total population. The kibbutzim played an important role in the pioneering of new Jewish settlements in Palestine, and their democratic and egalitarian character has had a strong influence on all of Israel.

Originally used to symbolize the Zionist movement, the flag of Israel predates the country's founding by more than fifty years. Based on the design of the Jewish prayer shawl known as the *tallit*, the flag also features the Magen David (the star, or shield, of David), Judaism's most well-known symbol.

CHRISTIANITY

Spreading Christianity Over the Earth

Christianity spread far and wide during the age of discovery, carried by explorers, traders, and missionaries. Both Catholic and Protestant branches of the faith found their way onto every continent, with particular early focus on the southern maritime regions. Christianity grew and developed, often assimilating the indigenous cultures of each new country it reached.

DURING THE AGE OF DISCOVERY, when ships left Europe to colonize or to trade in new lands, missionaries often went along to convert the native peoples to Christianity. And so the Spanish and Portuguese brought Catholicism to the Philippines and Indonesia respectively. Although India and China had been introduced to Christianity centuries earlier, new missionaries arrived around 1600. In India they intermittently met with success and resistance. (In 1990 about 1.5 percent of the population was Christian). In China, early Jesuit missionaries adapted themselves to Chinese culture to reach the people. However, more traditional missionaries objected that the Jesuits lacked decorum and were conducting the Mass in Chinese. In 1704 the pope ruled that the Mass must be in Latin, thus offending the emperor, who outlawed Christianity. Nineteenth-century missionaries converted many young Chinese men who wanted a Western education, but when the Communists took over in the mid-twentieth century, they closed most of the churches, and the missionaries were forced to leave. Christianity survived, but in small numbers.

The Spanish Jesuit Francis Xavier introduced Christianity to Japan in 1549, but later missionaries were persecuted and martyred, and Christianity was banned from 1640 to 1859. When the ban was lifted, Catholic, Protestant, and Orthodox missionaries worked in Japan with moderate success but were forced to leave when World War II broke out. (By 1990 only 1 percent of the population of Japan was Christian).

Although many missionaries simply accompanied European traders to new lands, this was not the pattern in the South Seas. Only a few Europeans had visited those islands, but the stories they told spurred the interest of Christians back home, who then sought a way to take Christianity to the exotic people described by the English explorer Captain Cook and the mutineers on Captain Bligh's ship, the *Bounty*.

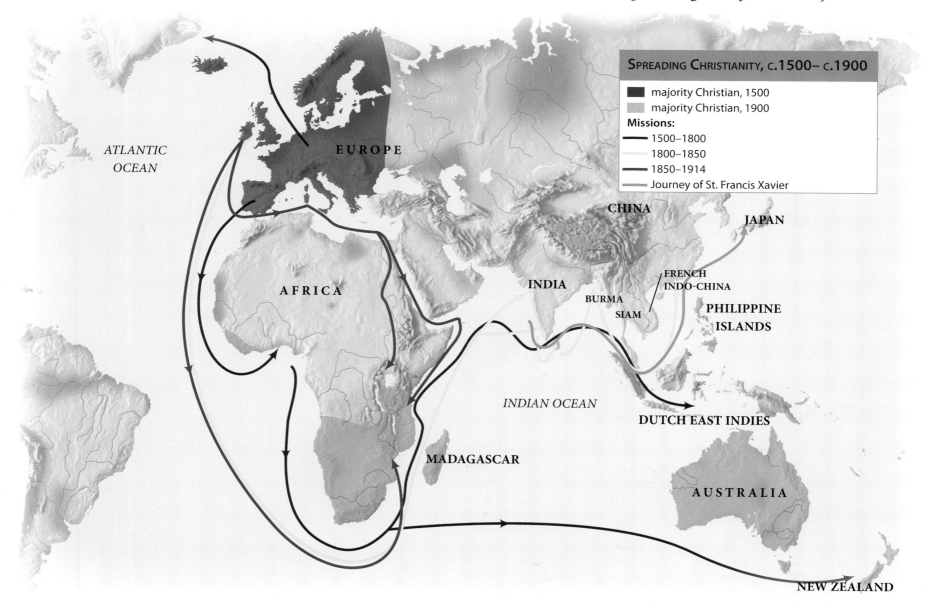

SPREADING CHRISTIANITY, c.1500– c.1900

- majority Christian, 1500
- majority Christian, 1900

Missions:
- 1500–1800
- 1800–1850
- 1850–1914
- Journey of St. Francis Xavier

ATLANTIC OCEAN

EUROPE

AFRICA

INDIAN OCEAN

CHINA

JAPAN

INDIA

BURMA

SIAM

FRENCH INDO-CHINA

PHILIPPINE ISLANDS

DUTCH EAST INDIES

MADAGASCAR

AUSTRALIA

NEW ZEALAND

HAWAII'S GODDESS OF FIRE

Native Hawaiian beliefs still inspire devotion in spite of Christianity's widespread practice on the islands. Here, offerings to Pele, the native goddess of fire, are laid at the rim of Kilauea Crater.

When the missionaries reached Hawaii they found the people celebrating a form of Polynesian religion that worshipped Pele, goddess of fire, among other deities. Pele is said to have come from Tahiti to Hawaii by canoe with her little sister, Hi'iaka, who had been born in the shape of an egg, tucked under her arm.

Pele was descended from the supreme beings Papa, or Earth Mother, and Wakea, Sky Father. She was among the first voyagers to sail to Hawaii, pursued, legends say, by her angry older sister, Na-maka-o-kaha'i, goddess of the sea, because Pele had seduced her husband. Pele debarked on Kauai, but every time she tried to dig a pit for her home, Na-maka-o-kaha'i would flood the pits—creating the water-filled volcanic craters still found on the islands. Pele moved down the chain of islands in order of their geological formation, eventually landing on Mauna Loa, a volcano with an altitude of 13,680 feet (4,170 m). There she made her home with her brothers, gods of the various forms of fire, and her sisters, goddesses of dance—including hula.

SOUTH SEA MISSIONS

In 1795 a group of Protestants from different denominations organized the London Missionary Society, which raised money, bought a ship, and sent thirty-nine missionaries to Tahiti, the Marquesas Islands, and Tonga. Progress was slow, and some of the missionaries met martyrdom, but in Tahiti the missionaries backed Chief Pomare II in a local battle and eventually converted him. The chief then threatened that if any islander refused baptism, he would remove the offender's intestines and put them out to dry in the sun. Once conversions began in this unorthodox manner, they continued throughout Polynesia. Other missionaries, both Protestant and Catholic, converted many of the islanders of Micronesia and Melanesia.

In 1788 the English had established a settlement for convicts in eastern Australia. Some of the settlement's chaplains worked individually with the Aborigines in the area, and one chaplain, Samuel Marsden, took the Gospel to New Zealand, despite the reputation of the Maoris there for cannibalism. Marsden arrived on Christmas Day, 1814, and eventually organized a string of missionary stations.

Still other missionaries sailed to Samoa, where the islanders said their god Nafanua

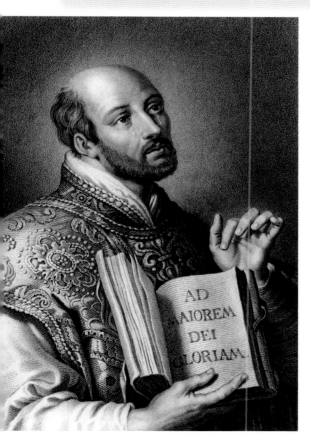

The Spanish Jesuit missionary Francis Xavier, who was later canonized, brought Christianity as far east as Japan during the sixteenth century. Christians in Japan were severely persecuted, and were forced to practice their faith in secret.

had predicted the coming of a newer, better, and stronger religion. The missionaries converted many Samoans, despite rivalry between two missionary groups. Christianity in all the islands tended to retain remnants of the myths and practices of the old religions. Once freed from missionary control, many South Seas churches became rigid and repressive, but Christianity continues to be the dominant religion of Oceania.

The American Board of Commissioners of Foreign Missions sent a group of missionaries to Hawaii in 1820. Queen Kaahumanu converted after she became deathly sick and a missionary wife nursed her back to health. Numerous chiefs and their subjects followed, and some of them made the Ten Commandments a rule of law, which all Hawaiians were mandated to obey. Within about ten years, more than 50,000 Hawaiians were enrolled in missionary schools, learning to read and studying the Bible.

The ruins of St. Paul's Cathedral in Macau are a reminder of the long rule of Spain in the Philippine islands. Today, the Philippines remain about eighty percent Roman Catholic—one of the largest Christian populations in the region.

CHRISTIANITY
Missions to Africa

ALTHOUGH CHRISTIANITY HAD THRIVED in northern Africa almost from the beginning, it did not reach south of the Sahara until the fifteenth century, when Portuguese missionaries converted the king of the Congo and one of his sons. Later the king's son became a bishop, and other missionaries worked in the Niger and Zambezi River deltas.

In the middle of the eighteenth century, missionary work in Africa began in earnest. British, Danish, and Dutch traders had set up forts along the Gold Coast, and missionaries were sent there by the Society for the Propagation of the Gospel and other groups. At the end of the century, missionary activity increased and evangelical and Catholic missionaries came to Africa. All worked tirelessly, establishing schools teaching catechism and looking after the health and welfare of the people. Soon competition between missionary groups grew so heated that colonial administrators had to allocate different areas to different mission groups.

There were different kinds of missionaries. Perhaps the single most famous missionary was David Livingstone, the Scottish explorer who led several expeditions deep into the heart of the interior and also wrote exposés of the slave trade. Other missionaries devoted themselves to translating the Bible, catechisms, and hymns into the languages of the people, generally having to develop new alphabets to do so. In 1857 Robert Moffat, Livingstone's father-in-law, translated the Bible into Tswana, a dialect of South Africa. The Anglican bishop of Natal, John William Colenso, published a harmony of the four Gospels in Zulu in 1857. Finally, there were missionaries who were themselves black Africans. Samuel A. Crowther, a Nigerian, was freed from a slave ship. After studying theology in London, he returned to Africa as a missionary and in 1864 was named bishop of Western Africa—the first black African bishop in the Anglican Church.

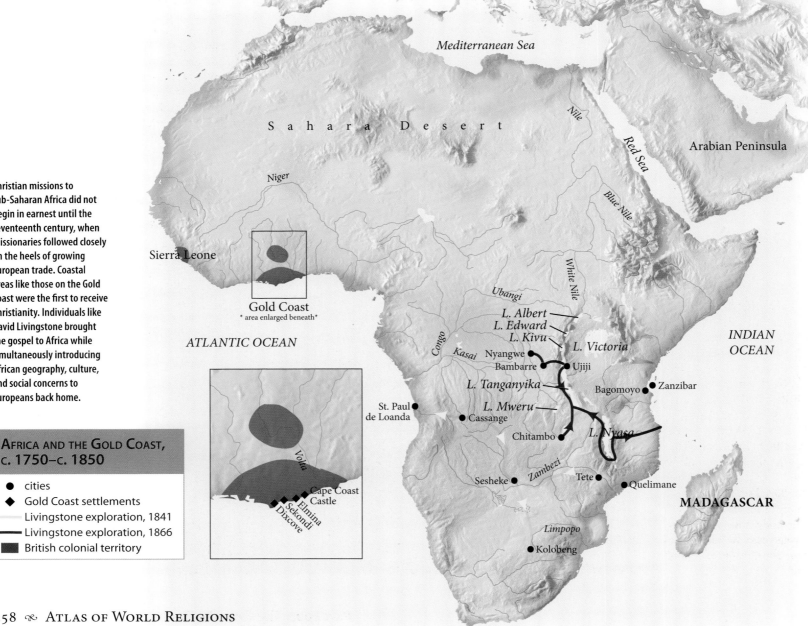

Christian missions to sub-Saharan Africa did not begin in earnest until the seventeenth century, when missionaries followed closely on the heels of growing European trade. Coastal areas like those on the Gold Coast were the first to receive Christianity. Individuals like David Livingstone brought the gospel to Africa while simultaneously introducing African geography, culture, and social concerns to Europeans back home.

AFRICA AND THE GOLD COAST, c. 1750–c. 1850

- ● cities
- ◆ Gold Coast settlements
- — Livingstone exploration, 1841
- — Livingstone exploration, 1866
- ■ British colonial territory

Wycliffe Translators

Spreading the holy word is hard to do if the people being addressed don't understand the words, and missionaries are often hampered by the lack of Bibles in the languages they need in the field. One frustrated missionary, William Cameron Townsend, did what he could to solve the problem. In 1934 he established a linguistics school for training Bible translators, and in time the school developed into a major organization known as Wycliffe Translators International—after John Wycliffe, who was the first to translate the Bible into English. Wycliffe translators work hard to identify cultures that have no written language, develop writing systems for them, and translate the Bible into those languages. Sometimes the people themselves request a translation. More often specially trained men and women drive and hike through remote areas of the world, interviewing people to determine who truly needs scripture in their own language. Translators are sent to those most in need.

So far, the Bible or at least parts of it have been translated into more than 2,400 languages, and translations into nearly 2,000 other languages are in progress. However, Wycliffe claims, just over 2,000 other languages are still waiting for translations of the Bible. Wycliffe translators hope that by the year 2038 they will have translation projects started—though not necessarily completed—in every language that needs one.

The Bible, printed in the Southern Min language—a dialect spoken in Taiwan. Scriptures in a people's native language go far to ease acceptance and understanding of a new religion. Wycliffe Translators is one company who has so far translated the Bible into hundreds of languages and dialects.

Now you have God's word in your own language. The word of God is like rain that brings forth growth. God brings new life. Put God first and everything will work better.
—BISHOP SENEMONA OF ZAIRE, 1996

The Post-Colonial Period

Missionaries benefited from colonial policies in Africa, though some dared criticize the abuses dealt out by colonial governments. After 1920 cooperation increased between the missionaries and the colonial governments in matters of education and health care. In some countries—notably Nigeria and South Africa—African Christians rejected the missionaries completely and formed their own churches. Some of these churches were mere copies of the ones they had split off from, while others centered on a "prophet" noted for preaching or supposed healing powers. Many of the new churches split into still other churches, and in time there were thousands of small churches. Many of these focused on spiritual healing and incorporated older African beliefs, including spirit possession and witchcraft. The major denominations that had been brought by the missionaries, however, continued to have the largest numbers of members. In the second half of the twentieth century, Christianity grew rapidly.

The southwest African country of Namibia is largely Lutheran; the country was a German colony during the nineteenth century. Christ Church, in the capital city of Windhoek, was begun in 1896.

Missionaries in Sierra Leone

A missionary project of a different sort appeared in Sierra Leone in 1787, when a group of Anglican churchmen bought land for a self-supporting Christian settlement of poor blacks. The settlement soon collapsed, but in 1792 it was rebuilt by black Americans who had sided with the British in the American War of Independence. Blacks of various Protestant denominations lived in the settlement and brought vitality to the practice of their religion. Then, after the British abolished the slave trade in 1807, Sierra Leone was used as a landing place for illegal slave ships that were intercepted. Many of the slaves who were freed joined the model society, which thrived in the following years. Residents who left to visit their home countries usually took Christianity with them.

Christianizing the North American Indians

American Indians were exposed to Christianity in random, isolated areas that roughly followed the patterns of exploration, trade, pilgrimage, and conquest. The earliest to convert to Christianity were probably those in northern Florida, where Spanish missionaries had established several small outposts. Later, French Jesuits spread Christianity through Canada, especially Quebec, while Jesuit Jacques Marquette journeyed along the Mississippi, founding missions along the way.

THE FIRST ATTEMPTS to convert the Indians of North America to Christianity probably occurred in northern Florida, where Spanish missionaries set up small outposts in 1556 and converted Indians along the Atlantic coast. Then in 1595 the king of Spain sent a military brigade to colonize New Mexico and instructed the Franciscan priests who went along to spread the Catholic faith and pacify the natives. By 1626 the Franciscans had converted some 30,000 Indians and built numerous mission compounds, where they taught practical skills. In time, however, the harsh treatment of the Spanish overlords and the strict discipline of the Franciscans, who also forbid the Indians to practice their old religions, began to wear on the Indians. When severe droughts were followed by epidemics of measles and smallpox, the Indians blamed the Spanish, and a revolt broke out. The Spanish were driven out for few years but returned and governed with more respect for the Indians and their customs.

The next area to attract missionaries was Canada. In 1625 a group of Jesuits arrived in Quebec and worked closely with the Indians. They hiked and canoed deep into the wilderness, fraternizing with the Indians, sleeping in their lodges, learning their languages, and sharing their hardships. Having earned the respect of the Indians, they converted many, but when an epidemic of disease broke out in Quebec and the Jesuits baptized the dying, the Indians believed that the missionaries were causing the deaths, and they tortured and killed some of the missionaries. Other Jesuits met similar fates. One of them, Isaac Jogues, was tortured and mutilated by Mohawks in 1642, escaped and returned to France, but then resumed his work and was killed by Mohawks in 1646. In spite of all the bloodshed, the missions endured. And farther south other missionaries were working with the Indians in the English colonies.

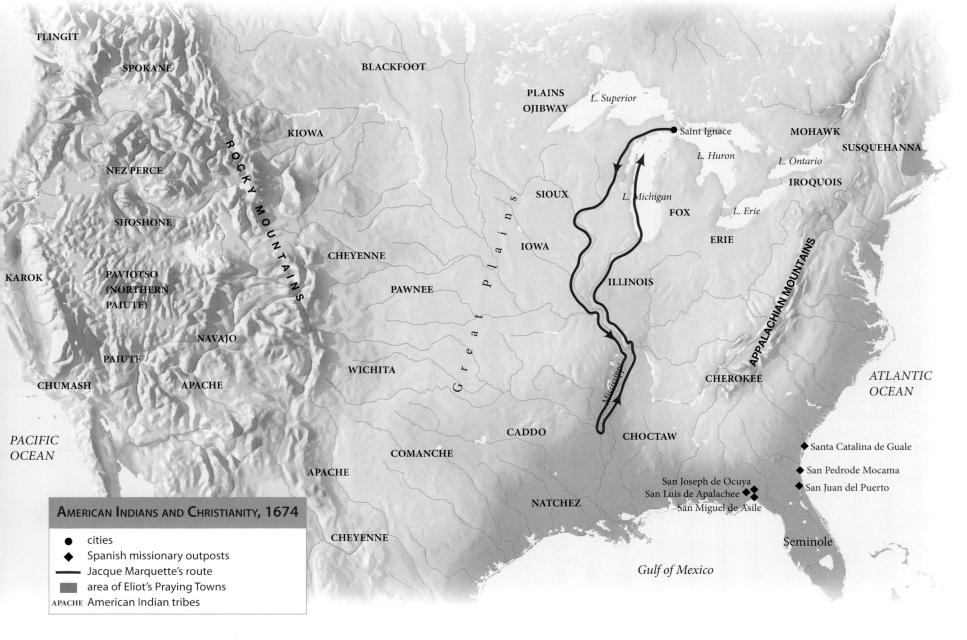

AMERICAN INDIANS AND CHRISTIANITY, 1674

- ● cities
- ◆ Spanish missionary outposts
- — Jacque Marquette's route
- ▪ area of Eliot's Praying Towns
- APACHE American Indian tribes

Artwork from 1901 shows a dramatized version of the baptism of Pocahontas, one of the most famous Indian converts to Christianity. Pocahontas lived in what is now Virginia.

> *This man was going to show the people how they could come back after they died. They thought he was some kind of medicine man. What he meant was that, if you led a good life, your soul would have eternal life....*
> —JIM WHITEWOLF, A KIOWA APACHE

INDIAN RELIGIONS

There is no one Indian religion, but hundreds, reflecting the myriad tribes, or nations, that were scattered throughout North America when the first Europeans arrived. On the whole, however, North American Indians tended to focus on the sacredness of nature. They saw all animate and inanimate nature permeated with spirits, and their shamans, or medicine men, would help the people communicate with these spirits to gain help or spiritual growth.

Indian creation myths often involve a woman and various animals. For example, the Seneca tell of a woman who falls from the sky and is caught by birds. The birds then direct a toad to pack dirt on the back of a turtle. When the dirt on the turtle's back grows large enough, the birds lower the woman onto it, where she lives and propagates.

Another of the common mythic types is the trickster, a shape-shifter who can instigate either good or bad. In a creation story told by the Maidu people of California, the trickster is a coyote. He watches as the first man and woman are created out of clay, then convinces the couple that it would benefit them to allow illness and death into the world. They follow his directions for doing so, and the first person to die is the coyote's son. So in the course of the story the coyote tells the first lie and sheds the first tears—over his son.

LATER MISSIONARIES

One of the first Protestants to work extensively with American Indians was John Eliot, pastor of a church in the Massachusetts Bay Colony. In 1650 Eliot persuaded some Indians who had heard him preach to move into a new "praying town," where they built and lived in European-style houses and followed a biblical code of laws. Eliot supplied the Indians with food and clothing while they tended gardens, raised cattle, and studied English, crafts, and the Bible. When they were ready, they were baptized Christians. Eliot was so admired for his work that supporters in England organized a missionary society to support it. By 1674 Eliot had established fourteen "praying towns," which housed some 4,000 Indians. The following year, however, war between the colonists and the Indians broke out. Because Eliot's Indians refused to fight, they were persecuted by both sides. The towns never fully recovered.

Mission work continued throughout the continent in similar fashion. In 1673 the French Jesuit Jacques Marquette sailed down the Mississippi River, establishing missions along its banks. In 1769 the Franciscan missionary Junípero Serra established the first of a series of missions in California. In 1824 Russian Orthodox missionaries converted the Inuit and Tlingit Indians in Alaska. In the 1840s Marcus and Narcissa Whitman crossed the country by wagon to work with the Indians in the Oregon country. At first they were well received, but when many other white families moved into the area, the Indians grew hostile and killed the Whitmans and fourteen others. In short, though some missionaries met their deaths, the majority managed to convert many Indians, look after their welfare, and often defend them from government officials who were often abusive in their treatment of the Indians.

A mosaic in the Cathedral Basilica of St. Louis showing Isaac Jogues, a French Jesuit who was killed by Indians after years of peaceful work. To the left is Kateri Tekakwitha, an American Indian girl who converted to Christianity but was persecuted by her own people. On the right is Rene Goupil, a Jesuit missionary who was killed by Indians. All three have been canonized by the Catholic Church.

A Miwok *hun'ge*, or roundhouse, in modern California. These structures were built partly underground and were used for various ceremonial or ritual purposes. The centers of sacred life, they were typically the largest of a village's buildings.

CHRISTIANITY
Colonial America

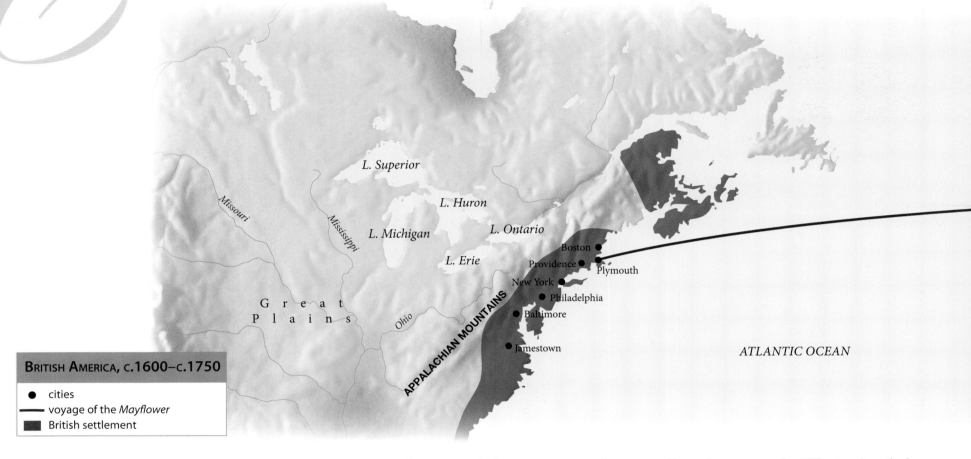

Map labels: Missouri · Mississippi · L. Superior · L. Huron · L. Michigan · L. Ontario · L. Erie · Great Plains · Ohio · APPALACHIAN MOUNTAINS · Boston · Providence · Plymouth · New York · Philadelphia · Baltimore · Jamestown · ATLANTIC OCEAN

The old meetinghouse of the Religious Society of Friends (Quakers) in Newport, Rhode Island was built in 1699. Rhode Island had passed a charter in 1644 guaranteeing religious freedom. By 1700, half the population of Newport were Quakers, a group that was widely persecuted in New England.

THE CHARTER FOR JAMESTOWN, North America's first permanent English settlement, stressed the need to evangelize the Indians for the Church of England. But few early English settlers were missionaries. Rather, especially in the colonies both north and south of Virginia, many were seeking religious freedom for themselves—having been prevented from freely practicing their religion in England.

The first religious refugees to arrive were thirty-five English Separatists—Puritans who had earlier fled to Leiden, Holland, to practice their Congregationalist form of religion, which was banned in England. These men and women (later known as the Pilgrims) sailed aboard the *Mayflower* with sixty-seven other people they had hired to protect their interests. The *Mayflower* reached Plymouth harbor in December 1620, and its passengers established the first permanent settlement in New England.

Ten years later the Massachusetts Bay Colony was founded by some thousand Puritans who had not openly separated from the Church of England and who wished to practice their religion freely. The churches in both the Plymouth and Massachusetts colonies were Congregationalist, setting the pattern for future New England Protestants. But the colonies established a harsh theocratic government that tolerated no dissenters.

Farther south the Dutch had colonized New Netherland in 1624 and established the Dutch Reformed Church there, but in 1664 the English took over, renamed the colony New York, and promoted the Church of England. In 1638 a colony of Swedes settled on the Delaware River near the site of the future Philadelphia and introduced Lutheranism to the colonies, but the Swedish colony was short-lived. In 1632, Leonard Calvert, a Catholic, carried out the plans of his late father George Calvert, Lord Baltimore, to found a colony where religious toleration and separation of church and state would prevail. In 1649 Maryland passed the first act of religious toleration in the English-speaking world.

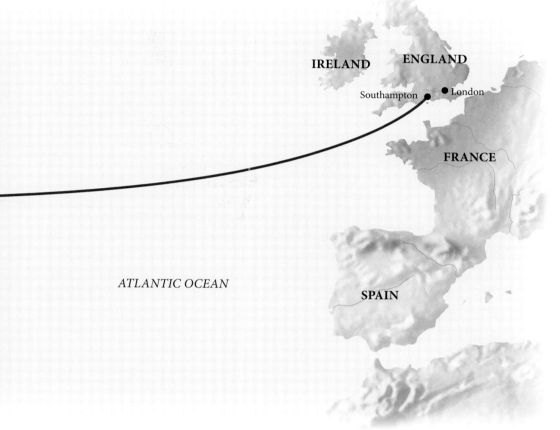

The *Mayflower* sailed from Southampton, England on September 6, 1620, arriving in Massachusetts on November 11. Among the passengers were 35 English Puritans who had been persecuted for their beliefs. This group founded Plymouth Colony, which was later joined by the Massachusetts Bay Colony. They were the two earliest New England colonies for religious refugees.

*They rush from Beds with giddy heads,
and to their windows run,
Viewing this light, which shines more bright
than doth the Noon-day Sun.
Straightway appears (they see't with tears)
the Son of God most dread;
Who with his Train comes on amain
to Judge both Quick and Dead.*
—MICHAEL WIGGLESWORTH,
THE DAY OF DOOM (1662)

England. Penn joined the Society of Friends (Quakers) in 1666 and was later imprisoned for his writings. In 1681 he sailed to America and established the colony of Pennsylvania to give Quakers a place to live their faith.

The Society of Friends had been founded in England by George Fox sometime around 1647. Friends believe in an inner light and a living contact with the divine spirit. At their meetings they remain silent until the spirit moves them to speak. Sometimes they experience a spiritual trembling at this point—possibly the derivation of the nickname Quakers. In their lives Friends strive for simplicity and promote justice, peace, and tolerance. They believe in allowing all people to practice the religion they feel compelled to follow.

New Amsterdam, shown here in 1660, was renamed New York when the city was transferred from the Dutch to the English in 1664. In the articles of transfer was a stipulation from the Dutch governor Peter Stuyvesant that its inhabitants "shall keep and enjoy the liberty of their consciences in religion" even under English rule.

BAPTISTS AND QUAKERS

Like Lord Baltimore, the Puritan clergyman Roger Williams was an advocate of religious freedom. When he discovered that limits on religious freedom were as restrictive in Massachusetts as in England, he set up a schismatic church and was ordered to leave the colony. He found refuge with some Indians and in 1636 founded a settlement that he named Providence. In 1639 he set up a Baptist church there—the first in the colonies. Williams managed to get a royal charter in 1663 and established what would become the colony of Rhode Island. Its constitution provided for wide religious latitude.

Another victim of religious intolerance was William Penn, who was expelled from Oxford University for opposing the Church of

THE EVOLUTION OF CONGREGATIONALISM

Puritanism, the driving force behind many of the early American colonists, began in England. During the reign of Elizabeth I a faction of strict Protestants complained that the Church of England was too popish and needed to be brought back to its original purity. These Puritans, as they came to be known, petitioned Elizabeth for reform, to no avail.

The Puritans upheld the primacy of the Bible and insisted that everything about their church should have a basis in scripture, including worship, decorations, and even the episcopacy—the church should not be led by bishops, they claimed, for Jesus Christ alone is the head of the church and will always be in the midst of any group of believers to guide them. Each of the "congregations" the Puritans set up was autonomous—free from regulation by outside churches, boards, or governments.

In 1604, a year after James I succeeded Elizabeth, the Puritans petitioned him for church reform along Congregationalist lines but were again rejected. Discouraged, some Puritans went into exile in Amsterdam and became the first English Baptists. Others went to Leiden, and some of them later sailed to America on the Mayflower. The remaining Puritans stayed in England and set up Congregationalist churches while claiming to be nonseparatists—in contrast to the exiles who were separatists. Some of the nonseparatists later sailed for America and founded the Massachusetts Bay Colony.

In 1642 the Puritans remaining in England were drawn into a civil war and eventually overthrew and executed King Charles I. After a repressive eighteen-year rule, the Puritans too were overthrown, and the monarchy was restored.

A nineteenth-century painting shows the Puritans' departure from Southampton, as the *Mayflower* is made ready in the background. Many did not survive the voyage to the New World; of those who survived the journey, many died during the first winter in America.

CHRISTIANITY
Christian Nurses and Nurturers

According to the Gospel of Matthew, Jesus said that whenever someone takes care of a sick person he is taking care of Christ himself, and every time he refuses to help the sick he is refusing Christ. Nursing and other forms of nurturing, then, are at the heart of the Christian message.

In the early church, nursing was undertaken by charitable individuals. Later, monks cared for the sick in their monasteries. In the era of the Crusades, the Hospitallers of St. John (Knights of Malta) nursed the sick along the roads to the Holy Land, and in Jerusalem they built a hospital (place of hospitality), one of the first ever. It accommodated 2,000 patients. More fell victim to illness, they found, than to military action.

In the seventeenth century, Christian nursing took a new turn. Vincent de Paul, a French Catholic priest, was committed to improving the intolerable conditions in the local hospitals. First, he established confraternities of charity—associations of wealthy laywomen who visited, fed, and nursed the sick poor and helped finance decent hospitals. In 1633 he worked with one of the confraternity women, Louise de Marillac, to found the Daughters (Sisters) of Charity of St. Vincent de Paul, an order of nuns patterned after the confraternities. Unlike the women of earlier religious orders, these nuns worked outside their convents, nursing, establishing and running hospitals, and caring for unwed mothers, the elderly, and the dying, as well as engaging in other charitable work. The order spread quickly through France and into other countries, and in the late twentieth century the Daughters of Charity constitute the world's largest congregation of nuns. The establishment of the Sisters of Charity had started a new trend in nursing, and similar orders quickly came into being.

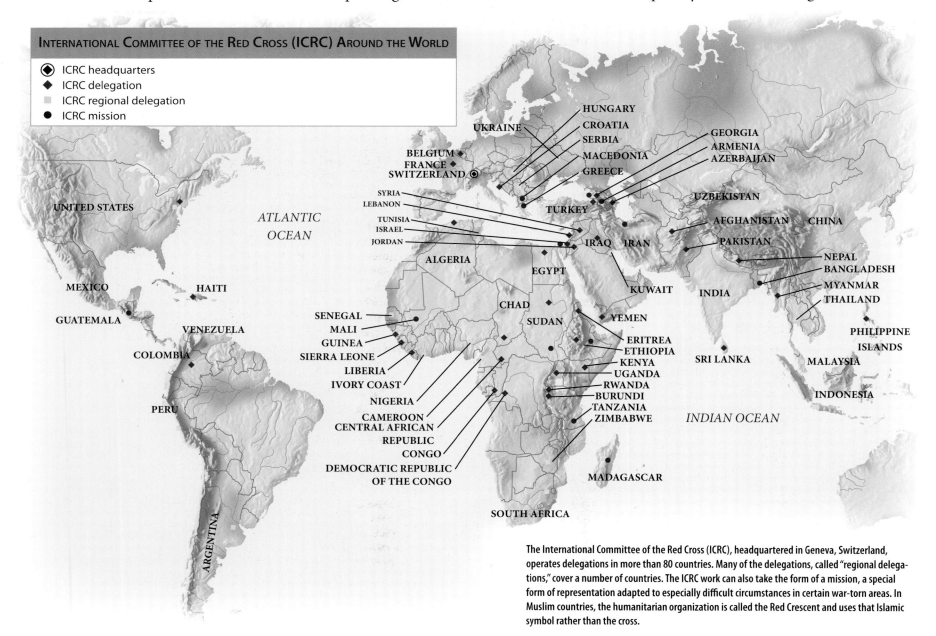

INTERNATIONAL COMMITTEE OF THE RED CROSS (ICRC) AROUND THE WORLD

- ⊚ ICRC headquarters
- ◆ ICRC delegation
- ▪ ICRC regional delegation
- ● ICRC mission

The International Committee of the Red Cross (ICRC), headquartered in Geneva, Switzerland, operates delegations in more than 80 countries. Many of the delegations, called "regional delegations," cover a number of countries. The ICRC work can also take the form of a mission, a special form of representation adapted to especially difficult circumstances in certain war-torn areas. In Muslim countries, the humanitarian organization is called the Red Crescent and uses that Islamic symbol rather than the cross.

PROTESTANT AND SECULAR CARE FOR THE SICK

Although Catholic Hospitals appeared all over the world, Catholics were not alone in ministering to the sick. Methodists, Baptists, and Quakers also played large parts in improving conditions in hospitals. They also supplied men and women who were willing to help as volunteers to care for the sick. In addition, in 1823 Amalie Sieveking, a German Lutheran, founded a sisterhood that was analogous to the Sisters of Charity, and these women worked hard in caring for cholera victims during a great epidemic at Hamburg in 1831. Impressed by the women's fearless labors, Theodore Fliedner revived the ancient order of deaconesses, which had been suppressed in the Middle Ages. Fliedner, however, reshaped the deaconate into a kind of religious order for women who would find and care for the needy sick. In 1836 he opened a hospital and center for training deaconesses in Kaiserswerth, Germany. One of

Nineteenth-century German reformer and Lutheran minister Theodor Fliedner founded a seminal training center for nurses and deaconesses. Florence Nightingale was among the graduates of his institute in Kaiserwerth, near Düsseldorf.

the women who trained at the Kaiserswerth hospital was Florence Nightingale, who went on to lead the major movement for nursing reforms in the nineteenth century.

Church hospitals and nursing orders still play a leading role in the twenty-first century, though local governments and private institutions are taking increasingly more responsibility for building and maintaining hospitals. Part of the reason for this trend is that there are fewer women in religious life today. Even in the Catholic hospitals that continue to function, nuns no longer fill all the nursing and maintenance jobs as they once did, but are more likely to be the administrators, leaving the hands-on work of caring for the sick to a secular nursing staff.

The biggest disease today is not leprosy or tuberculosis, but rather the feeling of being unwanted.
—MOTHER TERESA OF CALCUTTA

MOTHER TERESA OF CALCUTTA

Mother Theresa of Calcutta, an Albanian-born Roman Catholic nun dedicated her life to caring for the sick, destitute, and dying in India. She was awarded the Nobel Peace Prize in 1979.

The work of all the nursing sisters through the centuries could probably be summed up in the life of Mother Teresa of Calcutta. For more than forty years Mother Teresa devoted all her energies to caring for the poorest of the poor in India, the United States, and elsewhere.

Mother Teresa was born in Albania in 1910 and left home at eighteen to become a nun. After spending twenty years as a teacher in Calcutta, she felt called to work among the poor. In 1950, after receiving permission from Rome, she established a community of thirteen nuns, the Missionaries of Charity. The mission of the sisters was to care for "the hungry, the naked, the homeless, the crippled, the blind, the lepers, all those people who feel unwanted, unloved, uncared for throughout society, people that have become a burden to the society and are shunned by everyone."

The sisters did just that, and in 1952, with the help of Indian officials, Mother Teresa converted an abandoned Hindu temple, her first home for the dying, a free hospice for the poor. Her order grew quickly and expanded throughout the globe.

At the time of her death in 1997, Mother Teresa's Missionaries of Charity had over 4,000 sisters, an associated brotherhood of 300 members, and more than 100,000 lay volunteers, operating 610 missions in 123 countries. These included hospices and homes for people with AIDS, leprosy, and tuberculosis.

THE RED CROSS

An offshoot of the Christian dedication to caring for the sick was the Red Cross. Although not a clergyman, the Swiss humanitarian Henri Dunant grew up in a pious Christian family and developed a love for helping others. Shocked by the sight of the dead and wounded on the battlefield of Solferino, Italy, in 1859, he worked hard to establish an organization to aid wounded soldiers. In 1863

he managed to gain support at a meeting in Geneva on public welfare. The following year the first Geneva Conference was held, and Dunant met his goal by founding the Red Cross (using a Christian symbol to represent it). The Red Cross quickly grew and spread far and wide, caring not only for victims of war but also victims of natural disasters throughout the world.

A Red Cross emblem on a US military jeep. The Red Cross symbol links the organization to the ideals of Christian charity on which it was founded, caring for those in need regardless of nationality or creed.

CHRISTIANITY
Enlightenment and Pietism

The Pietist movement of the eighteenth century began in Germany and spread throughout Europe, reaching America where it became the Great Awakening. During this period, known as the Enlightenment, scientific inquiry and the pursuit of reason had come to challenge the view of the universe laid out in the Bible.

THE AGE OF ENLIGHTENMENT, which began in the seventeenth century and ran through the eighteenth, placed reason above faith and threw most devout Christians into an uproar. After Galileo, Newton, and others demonstrated that the universe was governed by natural laws, philosophers concluded that they could come to understand the workings of nature by close observation and the application of reason. Some of them concluded that since the universe is governed by strict laws, even God himself must abide by those laws and is therefore not all-powerful. Many Enlightenment thinkers became Deists, believing that God does not interact with humans or the world; others became agnostics or outright atheists. In addition, they regarded the Bible as fiction.

Reaction against the rationalist treatment of religion and the Bible led to a spread of Pietism—an intensification of the practice of Christian religion wound up to a highly emotional pitch. The movement began in Germany but moved quickly across Europe and into America. In England, between 1708 and 1712, the Presbyterian minister Matthew Henry attempted to counter the attacks on the Bible by publishing personally meaningful biblical commentaries, and small Bible study groups appeared throughout the West.

In 1729 John Wesley organized the Holy Club at Oxford University in England. Its members sought a deepening of their personal faith and relied heavily on readings from the Bible. The Holy Club developed into a number of overlapping groups throughout England and America. Charles Wesley, John's brother, helped found the club and composed rousing hymns to be sung at its meetings. In time the Holy Club developed into the Methodist movement.

A number of other popular movements also developed as reactions to Enlightenment views on religion and scripture. One of these was the so-called Great Awakening that swept through the American colonies.

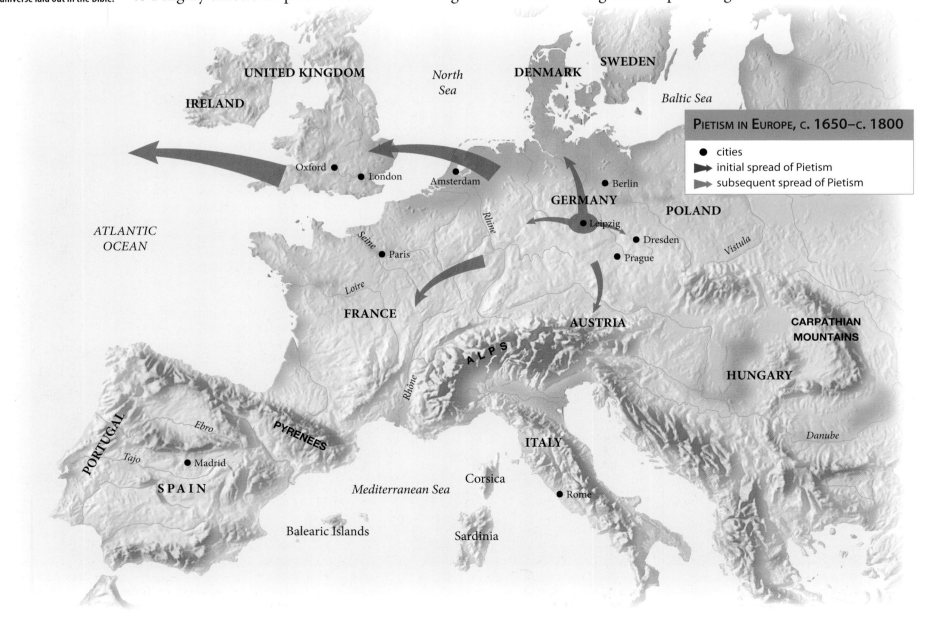

The modern evangelist preacher Billy Graham can be seen as the twentieth-century heir to the Great Awakening movement that swept America in the eighteenth century. Both the modern evangelist and the colonial Pietists aimed to revive beliefs they saw as threatened by rationalism or secularism.

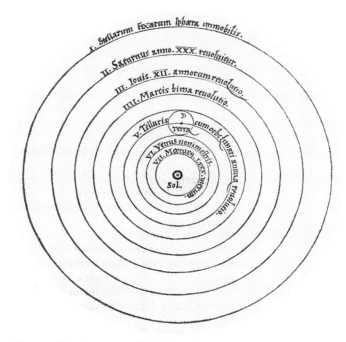

A diagram of the solar system published by Nicolaus Copernicus in 1530, showing the planets revolving around the sun. This discovery set in motion the conflict between science and religion, as it contradicted the Biblical explanation of natural phenomena. Galileo and Newton furthered the rational inquiry upon which the Enlightenment was founded.

EVANGELICAL PREACHERS

Fired by the need to react against the skepticism of Enlightenment thinkers, the Great Awakening spread across most of the American colonies south of New England from roughly 1725 to 1760. The British preacher George Whitfield, a follower of Wesley, preached to large crowds in Britain and then sailed to the American colonies in 1739 and traveled widely, preaching to crowds that were often so large they had to assemble in open fields. At these revival meetings Whitfield played on the emotions of his audiences, stressing the punishment in store for sinners and urging them to be reborn in Jesus Christ.

When criticism was directed at the emotionalism of the revival meetings, the Calvinist preacher Jonathan Edwards defended them as the work of the Holy Spirit, and he himself preached eloquently of the "surprising work of God." By midcentury the Great Awakening had spread to New England, and subsequent smaller revival movements recurred throughout the United States. After the Civil War the evangelist Dwight Moody left a successful business career to preach revivals throughout America assisted by Ira David Sankey, with whom he composed a popular hymn book.

Tent revivals were popular in the early twentieth century, and evangelist Billy Graham preached throughout the world through the entire second half of the century, reaching millions. Meanwhile, Catholics sent out teams of trained preachers to lead "missions" in parishes around the world. In recent times a number of popular evangelical preachers have reached unimaginably large numbers both in their own churches and through televised services and the Internet.

BIBLE SOCIETIES

The fight against rationalist interpretations of the Bible led many pious Christians to disregard the scholars of scripture and champion the cause of reading and interpreting the Bible themselves. Preachers urged all Christians to read their Bibles daily. Soon there were not enough Bibles in print to satisfy the demand for them. This led to the founding of societies devoted solely to distributing the Bible—which these groups considered to be the direct word of God—to as many people in the world as possible.

In 1710 the Canstein Bible Institute of Halle, Germany, was formed to produce inexpensive Bibles for the people. Similar organizations appeared later in the century. Then, in 1804, Christians of several denominations founded the British and Foreign Bible Society to print copies of scripture "without note or commentary" and to distribute them without financial gain. In the next ten years Bible societies sprang up in all parts of Europe and North America, and in 1816 the American Bible Society was formed.

At first individual workers went from door to door selling Bibles, traveling throughout their native countries and then venturing into foreign lands. By 1900 nearly 2,000 Bible salesmen were at work for various Bible societies in nearly all the countries of the world. Over time the societies used ever more sophisticated means to distribute Bibles and, when the need arose, made their own careful translations of scripture. At the start of the current millennium Bible societies were at work in more than 200 countries and territories, reaching more than 500 million people each year.

Eighteenth-century American minister and influential theologian Jonathan Edwards, whose Calvinist ideas and defense of Puritan ideals combined with an interest in science and metaphysics. Edwards was known for his fervent preaching style, and he became famous for his sermon "Sinners in the Hands of an Angry God."

CHRISTIANITY
Mormons, Mennonites, and Amish

TWO MAJOR CHRISTIAN DENOMINATIONS diverge sharply from the mainstream. One had its start in Europe but survives mainly in America, while the other is all-American in origin. They are the Amish and the Mormons.

The denomination with European roots is the Old Order Amish, an offshoot of the Mennonite movement, which was in turn an offshoot of the Anabaptists. The Anabaptists were among the earliest Protestants. They disapproved of infant baptism, insisting that only adult believers should be baptized, and they advocated a strict separation of church and state. Because of their outspoken ideas and the violence used by some groups, they were opposed by both Catholics and other Protestants. The Mennonites began as a branch of the Anabaptists, but because they stressed pacifism, they were named for their first leader, Menno Simmons, to distinguish them from more radical, militant Anabaptist groups.

The Mennonites hold that the Bible is the final authority in all matters of faith, and they advocate new birth in the form of adult baptism and separation from the everyday world.

The Amish themselves split off from a group of Swiss Mennonites in the 1690s under the leadership of Jakob Amman, opting for an even stricter lifestyle. They gained adherents in Germany as well as Switzerland, but most of them emigrated to the United States in the eighteenth and nineteenth centuries. Those who remained in Europe returned to the parent church, and the Amish survive almost exclusively in the United States and Ontario, Canada. The Amish believe that salvation can be gained only within the community, and they shun all worldly conveniences and pleasures. They take care of their own sick and educate their children in one-room schoolhouses. Many do not have electricity in their homes and use horse-drawn buggies instead of automobiles.

The followers of Joseph Smith came to be known as Mormons, or more formally the Church of Jesus Christ of Latter-Day Saints. Smith led his faithful from his home in western New York as far as Carthage, Illinois, where he was murdered in 1844. Brigham Young then assumed church leadership, and led his flock to the Great Salt Lake in Utah, still the center of the Mormon church. Altogether, the Mormons traveled 1,300 miles (2,092 km); their route is known as the Mormon Pioneer Trail.

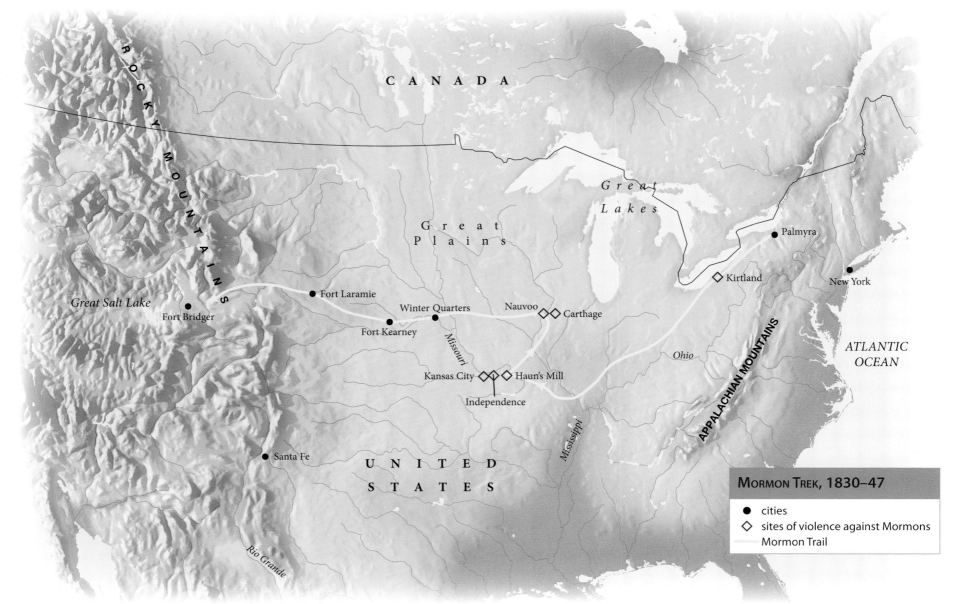

MORMON TREK, 1830–47

● cities
◇ sites of violence against Mormons
　 Mormon Trail

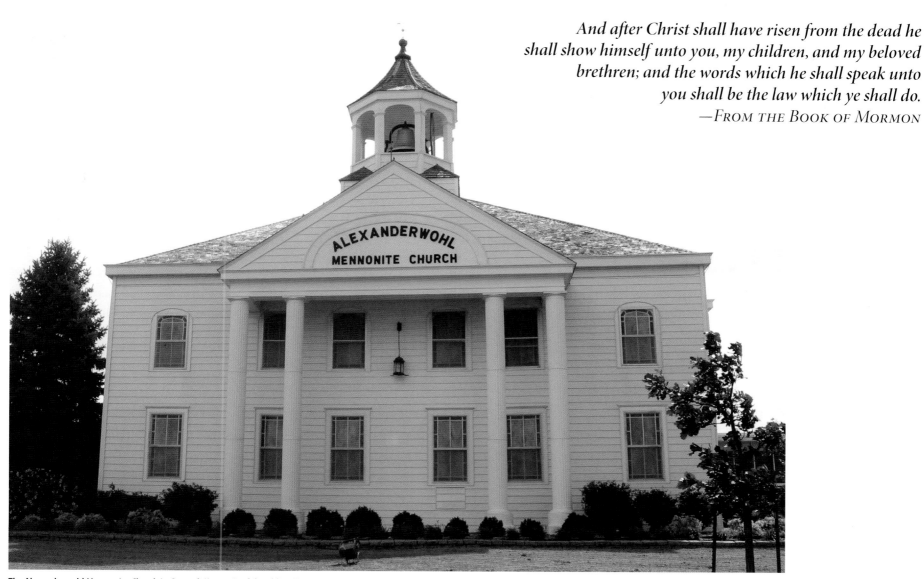

And after Christ shall have risen from the dead he shall show himself unto you, my children, and my beloved brethren; and the words which he shall speak unto you shall be the law which ye shall do.
—FROM THE BOOK OF MORMON

The Alexanderwohl Mennonite Church in Goessel, Kansas is of the oldest Mennonite groups in the United States. The Alexanderwohl congregation traveled as a group first from the Netherlands to Russia in the seventeenth century, then to Kansas in 1874.

THE MORMONS

In 1823 Joseph Smith, a young man from western New York, said he had a vision of the angel Moroni, a resurrected human, who told him where to find a long-lost book he had buried in a nearby hillside some 1,400 years earlier. The book, he said, contained formerly unknown revelations about Jesus Christ that had been made by a prophet named Mormon. It became the focus of a new religion, officially named the Church of Jesus Christ of Latter-day Saints, but commonly referred to as the Mormon Church, after the prophet.

In the early days the Mormons practiced polygamy and were persecuted wherever they went. Joseph Smith tried to establish headquarters in Ohio, then Missouri, and then Illinois, but always met fierce resistance. Even though many Americans considered Smith's teachings unorthodox, Smith announced his candidacy for president of the United States in 1844. When a group of Mormons, angered by his announcement, published a newspaper to attack him, he had the presses destroyed and was put in prison in Carthage, Illinois. A few weeks later a mob stormed the prison and shot him to death. Brigham Young, one of the church's administrators, then led the Mormons to the unsettled Utah Territory, where they established their church peacefully on the shores of the Great Salt Lake.

MORMON REVELATION

This depiction of the Angel Moroni's revelation to Joseph Smith was first published in 1886. The divine visitor was said to have delivered the inscribed metal plates that became the *Book of Mormon*.

The book that was revealed to Joseph Smith, which led him to found the Mormons, tells the story of a group of Israelites who had fled Jerusalem to escape the invasion of the Babylonians in 586 BCE and sailed to North America. In their new home, the book said, these Israelites experienced visions of the future ministry of Jesus, and they faithfully followed Jesus's teachings centuries before his actual birth in Bethlehem. In the first century, after Jesus rose from the dead, the book continued, he visited the exiles in America and instructed them personally. In the fifth century, wars wiped out these good people, but before the ultimate catastrophe a prophet named Mormon recorded their history on gold plates, and his son, Moroni, buried the plates. Smith borrowed the plates from the Angel Moroni and translated their contents into English as *The Book of Mormon* (1830).

Smith later wrote two other books. *The Doctrine of the Covenants* gives his followers instructions on how to live in the latter days (before Jesus's second coming) and warns others to repent before the end comes. *The Pearl of Great Price* is an anthology of Smith's pronouncements, revelations, and translations. The three books together with the King James Version of the Bible, as revised by Smith, constitute the Mormon scriptures.

Black Christians, Slave and Free

THE ESTABLISHMENT OF EUROPEAN COLONIES in Africa led to the initiation of a massive slave trade. Between 1500 and 1800, giant slave-trading franchises were set up, some by such established trading concerns as the East India companies. The largest markets for slaves were the Americas, with their huge plantations and mining companies. The Portuguese in Brazil were the first to import slaves, which they needed to work in the fields. Later the United States became the slave trader's most lucrative market. By the start of the American Civil War in 1861 there were some four million black slaves in the nation.

The Christians who bought and sold human beings used the Bible to justify their actions. Often they cited the book of Leviticus, which permits trafficking in non-Jewish slaves, and pointed out that the Jewish patriarchs themselves had slaves, as reported in the Bible. Even the story about the patriarch Jacob's son Joseph's being sold into slavery by his jealous brothers was used to justify the slave trade. The same story, however, was also used by the slaves themselves. Not only could they identify with Joseph's misery at being sold into slavery, but they could also gain hope from the end of the story, in which Joseph rises in the ranks of Egypt and heroically saves his people. Mostly, though, the slaves identified with the story of the Exodus, in which the Israelites are freed from slavery in Egypt and led by Moses to a land of their own.

Although most of the men and women who were brutally taken to the Americas in slave ships were not initially Christian, they converted to Christianity soon after they began their lives of slavery. Christianity offered at least a little solace to them in their plight.

Unmitigated by a Christian faith which advocated mercy, the slave trade displaced millions of Africans to the "New World," where they labored on fields, in mines, and in the houses of the rich for some 350 years. Over time, many slaves adopted Christianity, or blended it with African religions to form rich and unique spiritual traditions.

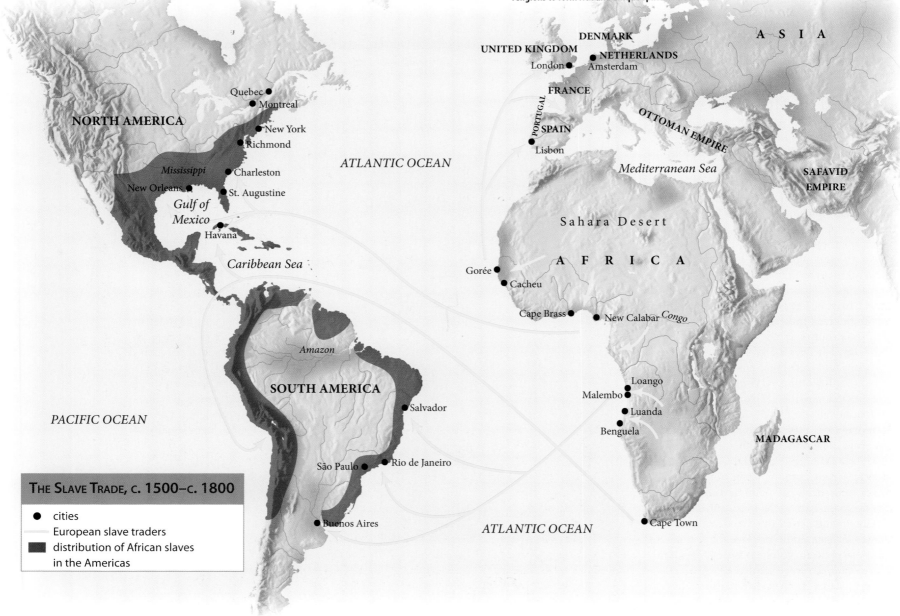

THE SLAVE TRADE, C. 1500–C. 1800

- cities
- European slave traders
- distribution of African slaves in the Americas

This image from 1880 is a somewhat softened depiction of the cruelty and harsh conditions that enslaved Africans endured on their voyage to America. After the Civil War and emancipation, Americans were only beginning to examine the brutal realities of slavery.

African slaves often incorporated elements of their native religions into worship services, which were nominally Christian and often held in their own quarters. Black churches did not grow in force until after the Civil War, though in the South, there were a number of black Baptist churches as early as 1770.

THE LIFE OF A CHRISTIAN SLAVE

It was not always easy for black slaves in America to learn about Christian faith or practice it. Some slaveholders refused to have Christianity taught to their slaves, because they were afraid that Christianity might make them less submissive. Other slaveholders offered their slaves limited religious instruction and had them attend their master's church, where they heard carefully selected Bible texts and sermons that would not disturb the status quo. Undoubtedly a Bible passage that was much used at these services was the apostle Paul's instructions that slaves should obey their masters.

On their own, however, many of the slaves looked for ways of learning about their new religion. Because they were not taught to read and write, they passed along stories from the Bible by word of mouth, and some slaves even memorized biblical passages. Often at night slaves grouped together and held their own secret worship services.

BLACK CHURCHES

In some parts of the United States blacks were able to run their own churches long before the Civil War. As early as the 1770s, black Baptists were acting as pastors of congregations of slaves and free blacks. After the Civil War all blacks were free to worship as they wished, but racism prevailed well into the twentieth century, and in the South blacks were required by law to sit separately from white worshippers. Meanwhile, the number of all-black churches grew rapidly, with many belonging to the evangelical and Adventist movements.

In the 1950s and 1960s, civil rights leaders fought valiantly to acquire equality for black Americans and ultimately succeeded to a large degree. One of the most beloved of all the civil rights activists was the black Baptist pastor Martin Luther King Jr., who was awarded the Nobel Peace Prize in 1964. He was shot to death by a sniper in 1968.

RELEASE THROUGH MUSIC

Black slaves in America often used religious music to release their tensions and defuse their anger over their lot in life. At Bible meetings, which were generally held at night, they danced and sang songs now known as spirituals. Some of the songs were mournful, but others were joyful and full of hope. Often the spirituals reflected a silent acceptance of the life of a slave by meditating on Jesus's suffering and death, as in: "They crucified my Lord an' he / Never said a mumblin' word." Often, though, the slaves sang of their yearning for freedom. One of the most popular spirituals was "Go Down, Moses," which evoked the Old Testament figure of Moses as he pleaded with Egypt's pharaoh to free his people from slavery. The original lyrics of this spiritual are as follows:

When Israel was in Egypt's land,
Let my people go;
Oppressed so hard they could not stand,
Let my people go.
Go down, Moses,
Way down in Egypt land;
Tell old Pharaoh
To let my people go.
"Thus spoke the Lord," bold Moses said,
"If not, I'll smite your firstborn dead."
Let my people go.

This 1845 title page for a folio of sheet music shows the great abolitionist and writer Frederick Douglass, himself an escaped slave. The title piece, "The Fugitive's Song" was dedicated to Douglass and to those still enslaved, for whom music was often a source of solace.

CHRISTIANITY
Pentecostalists and Adventists

Two movements within the Christian community gained force during the twentieth century and remain strong today. They are the Pentecostalists and the Adventists. Though the Adventists go back farther in time and have roots in the early church, the Pentecostalists have attracted larger numbers of adherents in more parts of the world.

The Pentecostalists strive to share the experience of Jesus's first followers on the Jewish feast of Pentecost. According to the Acts of the Apostles, before Jesus departed from his disciples he promised to send the Holy Spirit to guide them. Ten days later, when they were gathered together on Pentecost, they experienced a profound spiritual transformation and acquired the ability to speak in strange languages. They credited this new power (called glossolalia, from the biblical Greek) to the Holy Spirit, who they believed had descended upon them that day.

At the start of the twentieth century, individual Christian worshippers in Kansas and California acquired the gift of glossolalia, which they regarded as evidence of baptism in the Holy Spirit—a step beyond baptism by water. Subsequently, other gifts ascribed to the Holy Spirit, as mentioned in the Bible, were acquired, including prophecy and faith healing, and Christians sought to be rebaptized in the Spirit.

A Pentecostal movement developed quickly and spread like wildfire throughout the world. Pentecostal preachers were fervid, and their congregations, moved by the spirit, participated in worship services by singing, shouting, and hand-clapping. One of their most beloved leaders was Aimee Semple McPherson, founder of the Church of the Four-Square Gospel, who preached from 1915 until her death in 1943. She was also probably the first to preach on radio. Pentecostalism became so popular that it was even taken up in a moderate way by conservative Protestants and Catholics under the name the charismatic movement.

The Pentecostal movement spread quickly from its original centers in Kansas and California, especially through the central and southern states. One hallmark of the early movement was that both women and African Americans held prominent positions in Pentecostal churches, heading congregations and preaching with force and power.

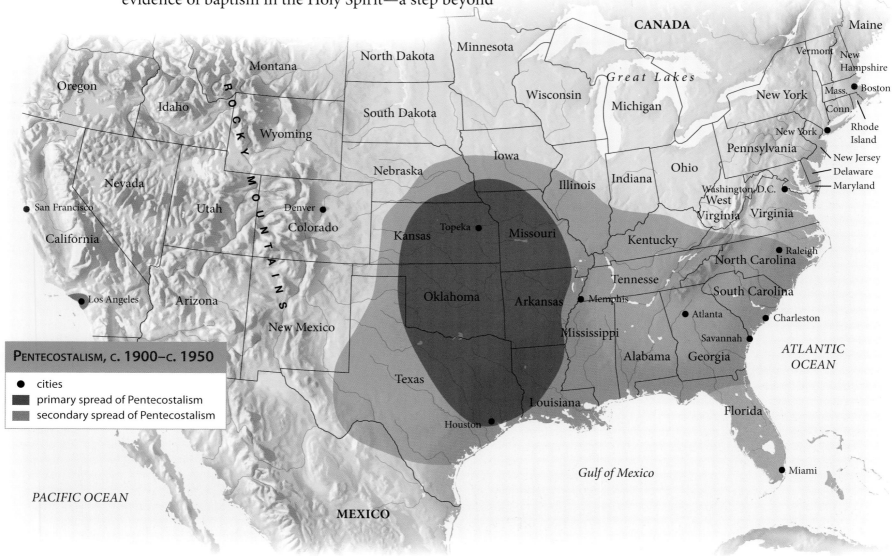

PENTECOSTALISM, C. 1900–C. 1950

- ● cities
- ■ primary spread of Pentecostalism
- ■ secondary spread of Pentecostalism

SEVENTH-DAY ADVENTISTS

In 1823 the evangelical preacher William Miller carefully studied dates in the Old Testament to anticipate the time that Jesus would return to earth as he had promised. Miller predicted that this Second Coming would occur in 1843 or 1844. He gained many supporters, and when nothing happened in the expected time, Miller admitted that his calculations had been mistaken but insisted that the Second Coming was still imminent. Many Christians since then have focused their attention on the Second Coming, preparing spiritually for the event. They are known as Adventists and are found in a number of Christian denominations, chief among them the Seventh-day Adventists.

The Adventist movement was not new to Christianity, of course, but had been present, under different names, since the early days of the church. Christians have always been quick to predict the end of the world and the Second Coming of Christ. As the new millennium approached in the 1990s, the end-time fever again grew intense, and in the new third millennium, fears aroused by awful wars and great natural disasters have brought more and more Christians to read the signs of an approaching end.

JEHOVAH'S WITNESSES

In the 1880s the American lay preacher Charles Taze Russell, like Miller before him and many others, predicted the imminent return of Jesus. But Russell claimed that Jesus Christ, a perfect man, had already returned invisibly to earth in 1878 to prepare for the

Kingdom of God, which would be inaugurated in 1914 after the Battle of Armageddon that is described in the biblical book of Revelation. Russell established the Watch Tower Bible and Tract Society to spread his message. He urged his followers to study the Bible and bear witness to others, warning them of the impending end of time so that they might survive God's judgment and be among the 144,000 people from all of human history who would be taken into heaven, according to Russell's reading of Revelation.

After 1914, when Armageddon did not occur, prophecies were reinterpreted and the society became theocratic, demanding the full commitment of its members, who are known as Jehovah's Witnesses. (Jehovah is an older English spelling of Yahweh, the name given to God in the Hebrew scriptures.) Later in the twentieth century, Jehovah's Witnesses focused on missionary outreach, enthusiastically proselytizing throughout the world and distributing copies of their biblically based magazines, *Awake!* and the *Watchtower*.

The popular and charismatic Pentecostal preacher Aimee Semple McPherson, active during the first half of the twentieth century. Known as "Sister Aimee," her passionate sermons drew standing-room only crowds and were broadcast nationwide over the radio.

GLOSSOLALIA

Speaking in tongues, or glossolalia, involves ecstatic, involuntary speech in a language that is either unknown or incomprehensible to the speaker. When a Christian engages in glossolalia, he or she must rely on a second person to interpret. In his first letter to the Christians of Corinth, the apostle Paul, who claimed to be proficient at speaking in tongues, referred to both glossolalia and its interpretation as spiritual gifts. Paul urged restraint, however, in the practice of glossolalia, because such a spectacular spiritual gift could be abused. He also considered it to be of less value than the gift of prophecy, which is also highly valued by Pentecostalists.

The Watchtower building in Brooklyn, New York, an arm of the Christian denomination the Jehovah's Witnesses, founded in the nineteenth century. The movement publishes several journals, the *Watchtower* and *Awake!* which are distributed as part of their proselytizing outreach.

CHRISTIANITY

The Catholic Church in the Modern World

AFTER THE COUNCIL OF TRENT ENDED in 1653, the Catholic Church worked to put its proposed reforms into effect. Then, like other Christian bodies, it was shaken by the anti-religious attitudes induced by the scientific revolution and the Enlightenment and by the democratic ideals promoted by the American and French revolutions. Church leaders resisted all such "modernism." In 1864 Pope Pius IX wrote the encyclical (papal document) "Syllabus of Errors," condemning secularism, rationalism, nationalism, individualism, and liberalism in general. Outside Rome, however, many Catholics responded to the new democratic ideals by working for social justice in their homelands.

Within the church, factions increasingly sought to place authority in the hands of councils of bishops rather than bowing to the sole authority of the pope. To address the issue, Pius IX called a churchwide council at Vatican City, which met in 1869–70. After much debate, the Vatican Council not only reaffirmed the authority of the pope but promulgated the doctrine of papal infallibility.

Although he retained his power, the pope lost his lands. The last of the Papal States were absorbed into Italy in 1870, although in 1929, with the signing of the Lateran Treaty, the tiny Vatican City was granted the political status of a city-state, in no way answerable to the Italian state that surrounds it.

By the late nineteenth century, popes began to look to their obligations toward everyday Catholics. In 1891 Pope Leo XIII wrote the encyclical "Of New Things" to defend the rights of workers to form unions and fight for living wages and humane working conditions. Subsequent popes and councils of bishops continued to promote social reforms, and in the 1960s such reforms played an important role in the overall reorganization of the church by the Second Vatican Council.

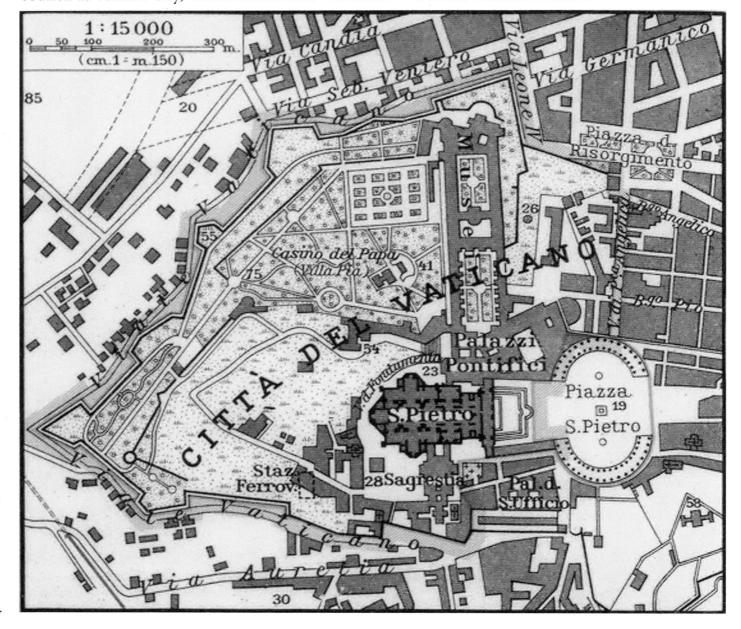

Tucked within a northwest pocket of Rome, Vatican City, here shown in a 1929 map (the year the Lateran Treaty was signed) is the center of the Catholic world. Less than 1 square mile in size, it nevertheless dominates the religious stage of more than 1 billion Catholics worldwide.

It is now for the Catholic Church to bend herself to her work with calmness and generosity. It is for you to observe her with renewed and friendly attention.
—POPE JOHN XXIII

The Basilica of St. Peter lies within the walls of Vatican City in Rome, considered by Catholics to be among the most sacred of places on earth. The church is believed to house the remains of St. Peter, one of the twelve disciples of Jesus, and the founder of the papal line.

THE SECOND VATICAN COUNCIL

Calling the Catholic Church to enter into dialogue with the modern world, Pope John XXIII called the Second Vatican Council (Vatican II), which held three sessions from 1961 to 1965 and ended by restructuring the entire church. The council was held in St. Peter's Basilica and attended by more than 2,600 bishops and at least 400 others, including theologians and non-Catholic clergy. When John died in the summer after the first session, the council was overseen by his successor, Pope Paul VI.

The changes made by Vatican II were numerous and far-reaching. To name but a few, Vatican II redefined the church as a mystery, or sacrifice, that was not simply an institution with a structured hierarchy, but a coming together of the whole people of God, including non-Catholics. The church's mission, the council fathers held, is not limited to prayer and preaching but should include work for social justice. Furthermore, members of the laity should also participate in the life of the church, bringing Christianity outside the walls of the church in order to renew the world. Indeed, the fathers contended, the church should embrace the modern world, not shun it as it had in the past. In so doing, they held, modernity can help the church, and the church can help modernity.

The council fathers also completely renovated the liturgy of the Catholic Church to encourage participation by the entire congregation. Furthermore, it was decided that worship services be conducted in the languages of the people instead of Latin, which had been used in church services since the fourth century (Greek was used before that time). Reversing the church's long-held position on scripture, the council fathers urged the use of modern critical methods for interpreting the Bible. Finally, invitations were offered to Orthodox and Protestant churches to discuss the possibility of future reconciliation.

THE AFTERMATH OF VATICAN II

In the years after Vatican II, its reforms were put into place, and the liturgy was greatly revised. The accomplishments of the council were applauded by many but opposed by others, most of whom preferred to retain the traditional attitudes of the church and especially the Latin liturgy. Rebel bands held Latin Masses in opposition to church regulations and continued to be so persistent that the church ultimately began allowing Latin Masses in certain circumstances. Church leaders met with separated Orthodox and Protestant church leaders in attempts to reconcile, and some progress was made, but no full reconciliation was imminent at the start of the new millennium.

PAPAL INFALLIBILITY

The infallibility of the pope as decreed by the First Vatican Council is very limited. It does not hold that the pope can never be wrong. It limits his freedom from error to statements on matters of faith and morals and then only if he makes an official pronouncement as pastor and teacher of all Christians in fulfillment of his high office. Vatican II added to this doctrine, stating that the college of bishops together with the pope could make infallible pronouncements, but that infallibility covers only interpretations of revelation and not entirely new concepts.

Catholic Mass is a weekly ritual usually occurring on Sundays, traditionally the holy day of rest in Christian belief. Conducted in Latin for centuries, priests today usually use the vernacular instead, in response to the dictates of the Second Vatican Council.

Muslim Commerce and the Ottomans

THE MILITARY, POLITICAL, AND CULTURAL influence of Muslim civilizations dominated seventeenth-century European, Asian, and African affairs. The emerging European countries were often at war with the expansive Ottoman Empire, but were also studying Muslim technology, science, medicine, and religious philosophy.

Muslim merchants and traders were crucial to European agricultural production, introducing important staple crops from Africa and Asia. Bananas, sugarcane, cotton, and sorghum were brought to Europe by Muslim merchants and seafarers. Another key Muslim commodity was the slave, taken from Slavic and Turkish regions defeated in battle, and from Iberia, Sicily, and North Africa.

Many male slaves sold to Muslim states were trained as youths to be mercenary soldiers, who usually converted to Islam. In the seventeenth century slaves from sub-Saharan Africa and Malaya became increasingly essential to European colonists developing agricultural

plantations in the Americas and South Asia. Muslim-dominated commerce on the African coast and interior saw caravans crossing the Sahara with thousands of black African slaves and as many as 25,000 camels.

The Byzantine Empire and its capital, Constantinople, had been one of the greatest centers for commerce before falling to the Ottoman Turks in the mid-fifteenth century. By 1600, however, European trading houses and mariners were actively seeking ways to circumvent Constantinople, where mainly Muslim middlemen—but also Jews and Christians—were profiting exorbitantly, especially from the spice trade. The Ottoman bureaucracy and its allies lorded over the former Byzantine trade routes, exacting high fees and commissions.

Muslim control of the Mediterranean and West Asian waterways and of overland trade routes spurred on European establishment of new sea routes to South and East Asia. Portuguese, Spanish, English, and Dutch explorers set out to make their fortunes, some seeking a fabled northwest passage in the Americas from the Atlantic to the Pacific.

Spanning the region from the Persian Gulf and Morocco in the south to Vienna in the north, the Ottoman Empire had reached its peak in the sixteenth century.

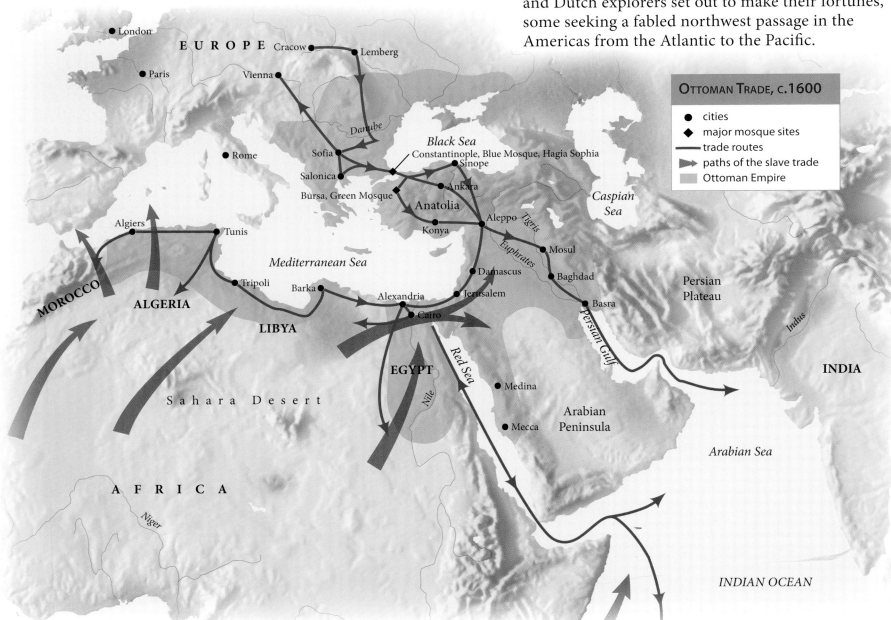

OTTOMAN TRADE, c.1600

- ● cities
- ◆ major mosque sites
- —— trade routes
- ▶ paths of the slave trade
- ▒ Ottoman Empire

The Sipahis were an elite cavalry force composed of ethnic Turks—landed gentry of the Ottoman Empire. Income from their fiefdoms was guaranteed in return for military service. In peacetime, their responsibilities included tax collection.

RESTORING THE CALIPHATE

The Ottoman Empire administered a vast region but could not capture Morocco, in northwest Africa. A Muslim nation, Morocco also defeated Portuguese invasions, fending off European colonization. One Moroccan sultan built an army of 150,000 slaves from sub-Saharan Africa, known as his "Black Guard."

With the Ottoman defeat of the Egyptian Mamluks in the fifteenth century, the empire had claimed caliphal authority, previously held by caliphs under the protection of the Mamluks. Ottoman ruler Mehmed II, conqueror of Constantinople, assumed the title Caliph of Islam, as well as Caesar—claiming the Byzantine mantle as (Islamic) successor to the Roman Empire. Ottoman rulers would only occasionally use the title of caliph—"sultan" was more common—but much of the Muslim world came to regard them as the leaders of Islam. Muslims in the Mughal domains of South Asia held the Ottoman caliphate in especially high regard.

Vested with religious and temporal authority, the Ottomans ruled from Constantinople—*al-Qustantiniyyah* in Ottoman Turkish. When referring to Constantinople, residents of nearby Anatolia and southern Europe commonly said "*is'tanbul*," which derived from a Greek phrase meaning "in the city" or "to the city." Most Muslims considered Constantinople Islam's capital.

Soon after his conquest of Constantinople, Mehmed ordered the magnificent Greek Orthodox cathedral, Hagia Sophia, converted into a mosque. Between 1609 and 1616 Sultan Ahmed I challenged the grandeur of Hagia Sophia by building, nearby, one of the greatest houses of worship in the Muslim world. Known as the "Blue Mosque" for the color of its exterior tiles, Ahmed's creation became a famed landmark for Constantinople and centuries later for Istanbul.

Although the Ottoman rulers always were male, influential women actually held the reins

[I]t is true that you have certain rights with regard to your women, but they also have rights over you.
—FROM MUHAMMAD'S FAREWELL SERMON

THE SULTANATE OF WOMEN

Royal Ottoman women, even some concubines in the imperial harem, wielded considerable influence throughout the history of the empire. Foremost among them were several concubines from the imperial harem whose sons became emperor while minors.

Muslim women in general, and Ottoman women in particular, had more rights than other women of the age. From the outset, Islam formalized the roles of the sexes as interpreted by sharia, or religious law, which definitively established Muslim women's rights to property, education, inheritance, and issues related to marriage. Writers of the period remarked that Ottoman women were held in unusually high regard.

Those members of the imperial harem who held power during the Sultanate of Women were guardians of their royal sons, seeing to their educations and shaping their policies. One source of influence for imperial concubines was their ability to take advantage of the custom of charitable giving to mosques, schools, and hospitals. These institutions greatly depended on these women, who also were responsible for creating water wells and fountains.

The great age of Ottoman conquests was ending, and there was a need to administer a far-flung domain with many different faiths and cultures. These women did not lead armies into battle, but they were instrumental in affairs of state and diplomacy, arranging advantageous marriages for their sons and corresponding with other powerful women in foreign lands.

The Turkish word harem is derived from the Arabic *haram*, meaning "forbidden." In addition to wives and concubines, the typical sultan's harem, or those living in women's quarters, included female relatives, as well as eunuch bodyguards and female servants.

of power for 130 years, until the 1650s. These were usually mothers of young sultans, who ruled as virtual regents. They were so assertive that this era became known as the "Sultanate of Women."

Sultan Ahmed I intended his "Blue Mosque" to have gold minarets, but due to a miscommunication with the architect, it instead became the first mosque with six minarets.

Religion in the Ottoman Empire

A DISTINCT OTTOMAN CULTURAL IDENTITY developed by the seventeenth century from the mingling of the empire's various ethnicities and religions. A crossroads of civilization, Anatolia had long been a dynamic brew of mingled faiths and ethnicities as Arab and Persian influences combined with Turkmen and Greek-Byzantine cultures.

The men of the ruling Osman family often took wives from different ethnic groups, so even the Ottoman emperors were of mixed heritage. To maintain civil tranquillity and prosperity, the government was obliged to balance the relations between its major religions.

Many faiths had their own inner tensions and disputes that had to be kept from boiling over into open conflict. The Eastern Orthodox had intense rivalries with Roman Catholics; Jewish expatriates from Spain differed from Jews of West Asia and Africa; and Shia Muslims of Mesopotamia diverged sharply from the majority Sunnis.

The Ottomans followed Muslim tradition and did not attempt to force conversions to Islam. Instead, they were remarkably tolerant, instituting a legal system based on the religious beliefs of various *millets*—Christian and Jewish confessional communities. There were three main court systems—one for Muslims, one for non-Muslims, and a third termed the "trade court." Muslims and non-Muslims were subject to their own courts, while commercial matters were addressed in trade courts.

Jews and Christians, as "People of the Book," had a somewhat higher status than other non-Muslims. They were known as *dhimmis*—those who traditionally were protected by the state and permitted freedom of religion. If dhimmis did appear in Muslim courts, they were subject to sharia law but could swear an oath different from that of the Muslims and thus not compromise their religious beliefs.

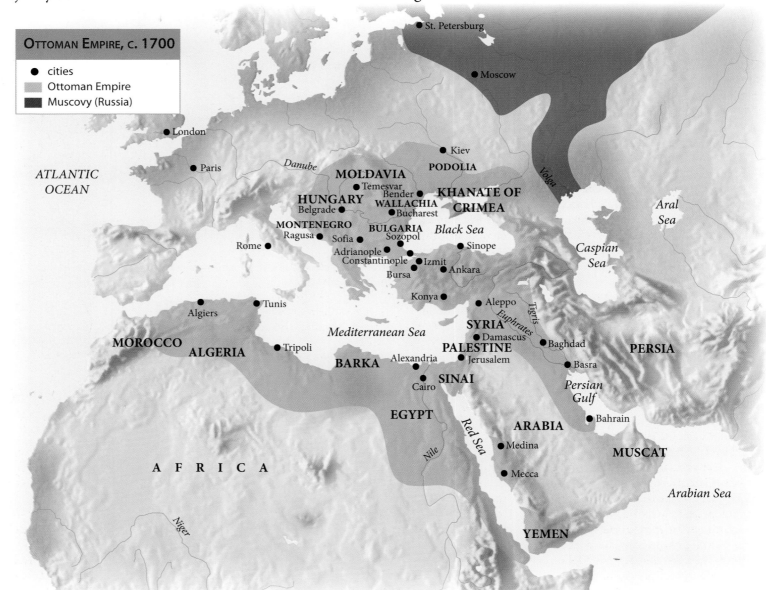

OTTOMAN EMPIRE, C. 1700
- cities
- Ottoman Empire
- Muscovy (Russia)

Unable to find European allies to wage war against the powerful Ottoman Empire, Orthodox Christian Czar Peter I of Muscovy, also known as Peter the Great, made a temporary peace to protect his southern border. He then attacked the Lutheran empire of Sweden.

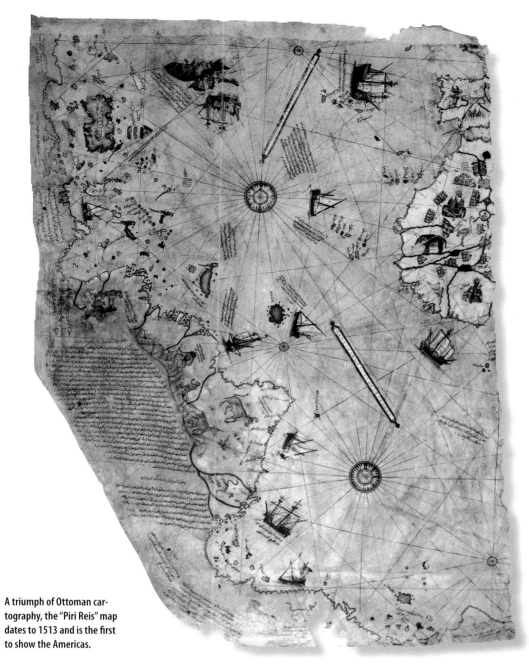

A triumph of Ottoman cartography, the "Piri Reis" map dates to 1513 and is the first to show the Americas.

MILLETS AND MADRASSAS

As relatively tolerant as the Ottomans were regarding religion, they maintained strict sharia law with Muslims. For example, voluntary conversion to Islam was welcome, but voluntary conversion from Islam to another faith was punishable by death. Education, too, was subject to religious control.

The millets had the right to run their own schools, while the Ottomans developed the system of madrassas (Arabic for "schools") established by the Seljuks in the eleventh century. Building mosques in conquered lands was a fundamental aspect of Ottoman administration, and usually those mosques had madrassas, organized from elementary to advanced levels. The Ottomans built many libraries, inheriting a longstanding tradition of Muslim study in natural science and technology, but madrassas were devoted mainly to the study of Islam and Muslim jurisprudence, including the reading of the Qur'an. Though many Ottoman students did not understand Arabic, they had to learn to recite and memorize the Qur'an if they wished to advance. Madrassas taught Islamic law, philosophy, mathematics, and astronomy, but much of modern science was shunned, since it diverged from the traditional beliefs of Islam.

As a result, Ottoman youth dared not delve into contemporary scientific developments, lest they be prosecuted for heresy. As late as the mid-seventeenth century, Ottoman Muslims were forbidden to use the printing press, considered an un-Islamic "devil's invention," even though Armenians, Jews, and Greeks in the realm operated presses.

The Ottoman madrassa system fell into decline during the seventeenth century, and some historians contend that the coincidental decline of the empire was in part the result of a failure to advance in science and technology—a legacy of madrassa education.

As the Ottoman Empire passed its apex in the early 1600s, wars recurred with Europeans, independent-minded Kurds, and with the declining but still powerful Safavid Empire to the east. The Ottomans fought the Safavids over control of the Caucasus and Mesopotamia, winning and losing Baghdad and eventually winning it again.

Another adversary arose to the north, the traditional source of Hun and Mongol outbreaks. This was the Russian state of Muscovy, growing in might and looking southward for expansion. The Russians, mainly Eastern Orthodox but with Roman Catholic allies, would be a force for both the Ottomans and Safavids to reckon with by the close of the seventeenth century.

The mandorla, a decorative motif, is used extensively in Islamic art to represent divinity. The word may be derived from *mandala*, Sanskrit for "circle" or from the Italian word for "almond," describing its shape.

ISLAM
Persia, Domain of the Shia

THE SAFAVID EMPIRE OF PERSIA was at its zenith in the seventeenth century. Since coming to power early in the previous century, the Safavids had championed a form of Shia Islam as the state religion. From the beginning of the dynasty, Sunnis were required, on pain of death, to convert to Shia. Many Sunni clergy were executed or sent into exile, replaced by Shia ulama approved by the Safavids. The shah brought Shia Muslims into Persia and gave them land and financial support, establishing a feudal theocracy and a new Persian monarchy.

Safavid policies enhanced the power of Shia *mujtahids*, recognized experts in Islamic law who could independently arrive at legal decisions. Intentionally or not, the Safavids set in motion a struggle between mainly urban Persians, who favored a secular government, and the Shia religious classes in alliance with the peasantry—"the

bazaar"—who demanded a government based on "pure" Islamic principles.

The Shia ulama grew in power and influence until it achieved such independence that it challenged the power of the Persian government. Even though the Safavids had originally been Sufis, all but one group from this order were banned from the Persian empire.

The Safavids were especially beholden to the Qizilbash, extremely conservative Shia Turkmen who had been a key military force during the Safavid rise to power. These "imperial guards" or "men of the sword" considered the Safavid shah to be their spiritual leader. In time, however, Qizilbash came to dominate the governments of several shahs, brought about assassinations, and deposed Safavid generals. In spite of their perceived religious obligations to the shah, the Qizilbash were loyal to their tribes before the king or empire.

Founded by a Sufi order, the Safavids combined military might and Islamic fervor to wage holy war against both the Ottomans to the west and the Mughals in the east. Safavid forces were further strengthened by the addition of Shia Ottoman soldiers who defected after Shia Islam was outlawed in their homeland.

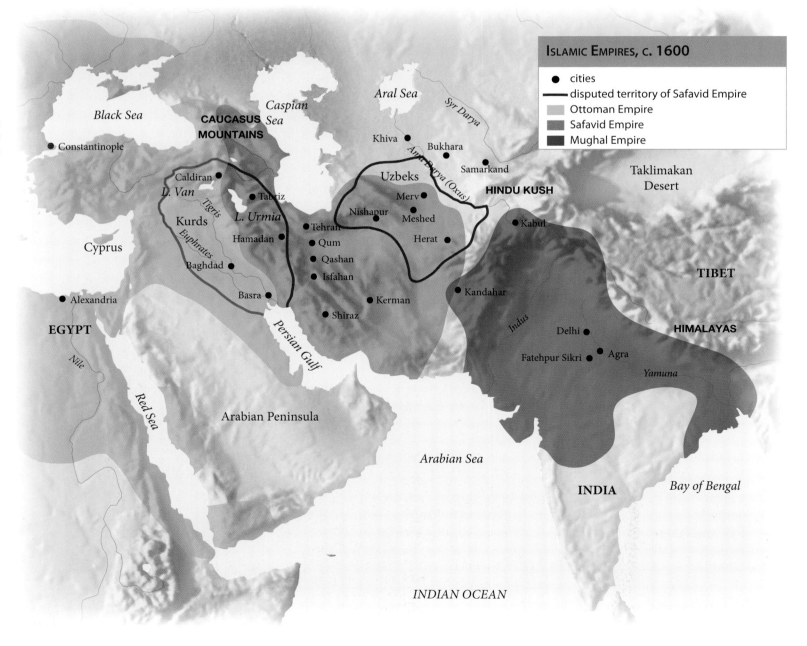

Along with nurturing Persian culture, Shah Abbas I organized the military into a disciplined force and introduced modernized forms of weaponry, creating a fighting force that recaptured lost territory.

TWILIGHT OF THE SAFAVIDS

Considered the greatest Safavid monarch, Shah Abbas I (1587–1629) was instrumental in developing Persian arts and restoring and refurbishing sacred shrines to Muslim saints. During his reign, carpet making became a major industry in Persia. Abbas promoted arts and artisans, whose work—carpets, tiles, pottery, and textiles—became leading exports. Another legacy of the rule of Abbas was Naqsh-e-Jahan Square, the twenty-acre plaza built in his capital, Isfahan, the largest such square in the world.

At first Abbas did not fare well in battle against the Ottomans and the Uzbeks to the east, so he brought in English military experts to put his forces on a modern footing. Abbas then won victories over the Ottomans (recapturing Baghdad in 1623), Kurds, and Uzbeks. The frequent battles for Baghdad in the Safavid era between Shia Persians and Sunni Ottomans laid the groundwork for enduring future hostility between these Islamic traditions in Mesopotamia.

As in the Ottoman Empire, commerce through Persia declined severely as European merchant mariners rose in influence, opening new routes and trading ports. Abbas improved his empire's seaports and welcomed Dutch and English merchants, thus establishing a thriving trade with Europe. As the empire prospered, a newfound pride in being Persian grew up among the people.

Abbas's modern military also allowed him to break the political hold of the Qizilbash, who were no match for a standing mercenary force carrying modern firearms.

When Abbas died with no son to follow him, a period of uncertainty and decline began, as most successor shahs were more interested in living lavishly than in governing the empire. Persia's frontiers came under frequent

SHARIA LAW

The body of Islamic religious law known as sharia (in Arabic the "way to the water source") is more a legal framework than an inflexible set of regulations. Sharia is considered a system of divinely ordained law, a way of belief and practice. It governs a Muslim's private and public life, from business and politics to family, hygiene, and social and sexual matters—sharia bans the use of alcohol and defines marital obligations.

Based on interpretations of the Qur'an and the recorded deeds and messages of Muhammad and his closest companions, sharia also relies on a consensus between those interpretations and the opinions of the ulama, as well as on reasoning by analogy, or comparison.

Sunnis and Shia follow different schools of legal thought. Shia rely on the Qur'an and the judgments of their imams but reject the concept of consensus and reasoning by analogy. Local customs also inform sharia and its interpretation and implementation.

Although most Islamic legal issues are brought before jurists who are members of the ulama, certain accomplished scholars with mastery of sharia law may reach their own independent interpretations of what is permissible for themselves. Known as a *mujtahid*, and generally associated with Shia Islam, these scholars arrive at their own rulings without consulting the ulama.

A detail of what is known as the Mantes carpet of the late sixteenth century represents the pinnacle of Safavidian carpet weaving. Other intricate artisanal achievements of the time included the creation of illuminated manuscripts and silk textiles.

assault and were often penetrated by mostly Sunni invaders: peninsula Arabs attacked Mesopotamia, Pashtuns rose up in Afghanistan, and troubles with the Ottomans and Kurds were unending. To the southeast the powerful Mughals moved into Afghanistan and captured the city of Kandahar.

The days of the Safavid Empire were numbered.

ANGELS IN ISLAM

One of the most important Islamic requirements is belief in angels—entities created by Allah from light in order to serve him. Angels do not possess free will but can assume any form, travel by wing faster than light, and appear real to human beings. Angels are often Allah's messengers, with archangels being the highest order and Gabriel and Michael the closest to Allah.

An angel facilitates the separation of the soul from the body, an angel is responsible for Hell, and an angel is responsible for Heaven.

Though unnamed in the Qur'an, the archangel Israfel, or Israfil, is described as the angel of the trumpet. According to Islamic lore, the dust he collected on a quest to one of the four corners of the Earth was used to produce the world's first human.

Akbar: Greatest of the Mughals

ISLAM HAD BEEN GAINING TERRITORY in northwest India since the eighth century, progressively overcoming Hindu, Jain, and Buddhist civilizations as it moved south and east. In the 1600s the most powerful South Asian Muslim rulers were the Mughals, whose empire would become the largest in the world by the eighteenth century. Reaching from the Hindu Kush in the northwest and Assam in the east, it would control most of the Indian subcontinent and as many as 130 million people at its greatest extent.

The greatest Mughal king was Jalaluddin Muhammad Akbar (1542–1605), who inherited the throne at thirteen in 1556. Known as Akbar the Great, he was a military hero, diplomat, architect, and artisan (blacksmith and lacemaker, among other skills), as well as an inventor and theologian. Akbar was tolerant of other religions and believed in "rulership as a divine illumination." He even founded his own belief system, known as the "Divine Faith."

Although Akbar was a champion of Sunni Islam, his own syncretic doctrine merged what he considered to be the best aspects of Islam and Hinduism. Mainly an ethical system, Divine Faith held that piety, prudence, abstinence, and kindness were essential virtues. Akbar organized debates between Muslims and Sikhs, Hindus, Jesuits, and even atheists. When he asserted that no single religion had a monopoly on the truth, Muslim clerics accused him of blasphemy.

Although Akbar was an art collector and founder of magnificent libraries with books in many languages—some of which he commissioned himself— he was also a military conqueror who extended his dominion across northern India. He defeated three major enemies and secured the Mughal realm before he was fifteen years of age. An accomplished warrior, strong and courageous, Akbar was compared to Alexander the Great as a field commander and leader of men on campaign.

Attaining the throne at age thirteen enabled Akbar I to achieve sustained expansion of the Mughal Empire over his almost half-century reign. Though a practicing Sunni Muslim, Akbar I maintained a good relationship with the Hindu majority while building the largest army in Mughal history and left his successor, Prince Jahangir, a stable kingdom.

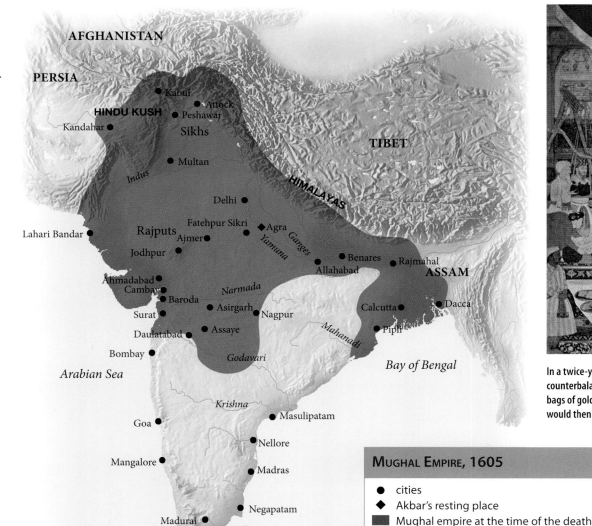

In a twice-yearly tradition started by his father, Akbar, Jahangir counterbalances the weight of his son Prince Khurram with bags of gold. The accumulated treasure equal to the weight would then be distributed to the poor.

MUGHAL EMPIRE, 1605

- ● cities
- ◆ Akbar's resting place
- ■ Mughal empire at the time of the death of Akbar

*O Soul, thou art at rest. Return to the Lord
at peace with Him, and He at peace with you.*
—CALLIGRAPHY DECORATING
THE GATE OF THE TAJ MAHAL

THE TAJ MAHAL

Considered one of the eight wonders of the world, the Taj Mahal was constructed by a force of 20,000 workers over a period of more than two decades. Ustad Ahmad, also known as Isa Khan, has frequently been credited as the Taj's chief architect.

One of the world's foremost architectural wonders, the Taj Mahal in Agra, India, is the mausoleum of Mughal queen Mumatz Mahal, a Muslim. The daughter of Persian nobles, she died in 1631 while giving birth to her fourteenth child with emperor Jahangir, for whom she was the third, and favorite, wife.

Architecture is at the forefront of the legacy left by the more than 300-year rule of the Mughals. The "Taj" is the most perfect example of Mughal architecture, combining Islamic, Persian, Turkish, and Indian design, building methods, and materials.

Completed around 1648, the Taj Mahal is built of white marble and tile and decorated with calligraphy that quotes the Qur'an.

CONVERSION: BY CHOICE OR THE SWORD?

While Muslim growth in most of the world was achieved without directly forcing conversions, the nature of Muslim advances in the Indian subcontinent remains a sensitive and controversial subject. Key issues are hotly debated and remain the source of bitter contention.

For example: Was Islam the "religion of the sword," as some contend, or did South Asian converts make their choice with heartfelt sincerity, or for the sake of improved social mobility in the Muslim state? Did lower Hindu classes convert en masse to Islam in order to escape oppression from Hindu caste structure? Or did they convert out of fear, or to escape onerous taxes waged on non-Muslims?

Opponents of the theory of forced Islamic conversion assert that the heartlands of some former Muslim empires contain non-Muslim majority communities that survived to modern times. Yet the legacy of hatred, hostility, and open conflict that defines so much of the subcontinent's Muslim-Hindu history is an enduring legacy of Muslim conquest and empire.

UNITY AND SLAUGHTER

Akbar's imperial policies built an efficient administration and revenue-collection system that would serve the Mughals for another two centuries. One means of uniting his diverse peoples of different faiths was to encourage intermarriage between Muslim and Hindu aristocrats. For his own part, Akbar included a number of Hindu princesses in his royal harem and took for his queen a Hindu princess of the powerful Rajput kingdom, which then became his lifelong ally.

Akbar reputedly drank from the Ganges River, sacred to India's Hindus and personified as the goddess Ganga, raised in heaven by Brahma, the Hindu god of creation. Vessels of Ganges water, which he called "the water of immortality," were brought to Akbar by special servants whenever he was traveling.

For all his diplomatic approaches to Hinduism in times of peace, in war there was another side to Akbar. Ruthless to his enemies, he destroyed Hindu temples or converted them to mosques, and slaughtered 30,000 unarmed civilians after taking one Hindu stronghold. Akbar ruled supreme until his death in 1605, but enemies among the Hindus so despised him (and Islam) that they raided his mausoleum at Sikandra, looting it and scattering his bones on the ground.

Akbar at times compelled conversion to Islam, a policy that was intensified by his son and heir, Jahangir (1605–27). Jahangir's rule was characterized by political stability and the creation of monumental Mughal architecture, but also by regular persecution of Jains, Sikhs, and Hindus. The next king, Shah Jahan (1592–1666), carried on with magnificent monument building—including the Taj Mahal, created in 1648 as a mausoleum to his wife. Shah Jahan faced increased warfare on his borders, with the Persians capturing territory in Afghanistan. His expanded military campaigns almost exhausted the imperial treasury.

After Shah Jahan fell ill and was deposed, subsequent kings continued to enlarge Mughal territory at the expense of both Muslim sultans and Hindu rajahs (princes). Enmity between Muslims and Hindus on the Indian subcontinent persisted and deepened throughout the rule of the Mughals, whose empire was in irreversible decline by the early eighteenth century.

A decorated Mughal dynasty dagger made with carved jade, inlaid gold, and fine steel speaks to the wealth and prestige of the Indian Islamic empire.

ISLAM
Islam Influences Culture and Trade

ALTHOUGH BITTER HATRED AND BLOODSHED define much of the 1,400-year history of Muslims and Hindus in the Indian subcontinent, Islamic culture profoundly influenced South Asian life in many positive ways. Architectural, artistic, and agricultural innovations were widely disseminated, and Islamic culture, from dress to music and cuisine, influenced all aspects of life and society.

In the subcontinent, bookbinding, paper making, carpet making, and ceramics all were developed with Muslim influence. One of the main languages, Urdu, combines Persian, Arabic, and Turkish influences and is written in Perso-Arabic script.

For South Asia one of the most important influences of Islam was the subcontinent's incorporation into an organized commercial network that controlled trade with the wider world. By the eighteenth century, Muslim merchants—mainly Arabs—had been instrumental in expanding trade, which stretched from Morocco to Indonesia, West Africa to Mongolia and China. Muslim legal structure and sharia governed and unified a far-flung mercantile realm where Islam was the main official religion. Prosperity stimulated the building of major roads and opening of ports—all promoting trade that was generally protected by the authorities in Muslim lands.

Islam was dominant in most of Africa by the eighteenth century, from East Africa's Zanzibar—"coast of the blacks" in Persian—to West Africa's emerging Fulani Empire and North Africa's Semitic Berbers. By the sixteenth century, Muslim sultanates and kingdoms in Africa had become major military and trading states. Central African and upper-Nile sultanates were regional powers, with the Muslim Songhai Empire one of the strongest, funded by controlling the Sahara gold trade.

On the east coast, ports such as Mogadishu, Mombasa, Mozambique, and Zanzibar had communities of Sunni Arab Muslims who traded with the interior and then shipped the commodities to Egypt, Persia, and India. East African Islam was administered by the Sultanate of Zanzibar and an ulama.

Muslim influence in Africa increased significantly between 1500 and 1800, with the Ottoman Empire controlling all of North Africa except Morocco. After the 1580 attack against the Muslim kingdom of Songhai, Morocco dominated the region for the next two centuries. Trans-Saharan trade was in gold, textiles, and other commodities.

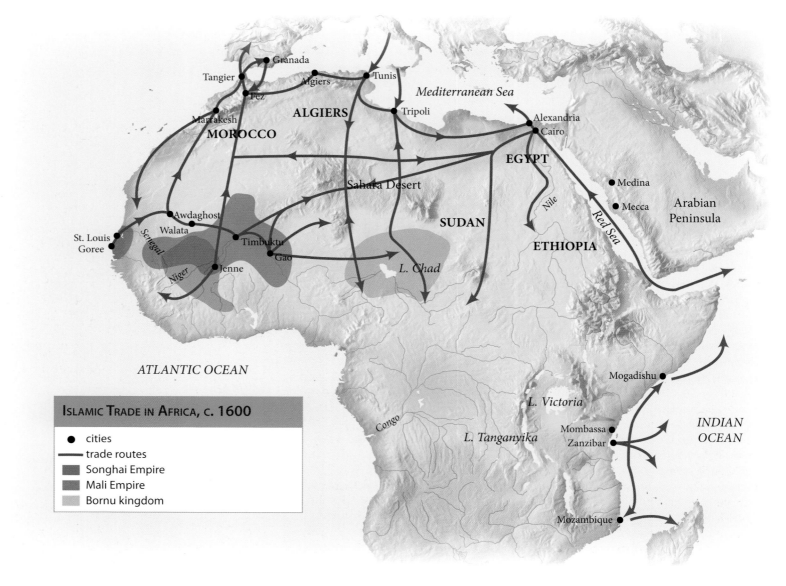

ISLAMIC TRADE IN AFRICA, C. 1600

- • cities
- — trade routes
- Songhai Empire
- Mali Empire
- Bornu kingdom

CONVERSION AND COLONIALISM IN SOUTHEAST ASIA

The Muslim population of southern Africa had been augmented by migrations of Malays and Javanese by the seventeenth century. Many of these people had been forcibly brought there as slaves or servants by the Dutch East India Company, which controlled much of Africa's southern coast. Many Malays and Javanese had been Islamicized since the fourteenth century, often in mass conversions.

In Indonesia's many islands, Sufi missionaries undertook most of the proselytizing, which had been started by Indian Muslim traders. Sufis translated Islamic literature from Arabic and Persian into Malay, which became an important Islamic language, with its own religious literature.

As in other lands, traditional Southeast Asian customs mingled with Islamic practices to produce unique indigenous belief systems. Even remote island peoples incorporated the rule of sharia into their lives, thus participating in an established system of laws that regulated culture and commerce in a vast portion of the known world.

By the seventeenth century Islamic sultanates ruled much of Indonesia, including Aceh, the most powerful state, and Malacca (Melaka), the region's most important trading center and the base for Islam's dissemination. Borneo's coastline and the Moluccan Islands were also Islamic, as was much of the southern Philippine island group, Mindanao.

The process of conversion to Islam was peaceful in these islands, as people followed their princes and chiefs. Many leaders became Muslim when the influential prince of Aceh, in northern Sumatra, converted in the fourteenth century.

Islam in southern Asia met competition for converts in the sixteenth and seventeenth centuries. European Christian priests went to work as soon as the Portuguese penetrated the region in the 1500s and took control of the Moluccas, known as the Spice Islands. By the mid-seventeenth century the English were establishing forts and trading posts on the coasts of India, and the Dutch occupied Java.

Europeans founded mercantile operations and church missions in their fortified "factories," as trading posts were called. They intended to challenge the dynamic growth of both Muslim commerce and religion.

Catholic Spain controlled most of the Philippines, except for Mindanao, with its people known as Moros, or "Moors"—Muslims, in Spanish. Fiercely independent and faithful to Islam, the Moros resisted the Spanish but would have to fight for liberty and religious freedom for the next five centuries.

Most cities in Java have mosques. As elsewhere, peaceful means rather than warfare were used to convert the populus.

ISLAM IN SOUTHEAST ASIA, c. 1600
- ● cities
- ◆ cities with major mosques

THE RELIGION FROM MALI

By 1600 the leading figures of West Africa's Bornu kingdom had accepted Islam, and their people began to be converted from traditional religions. The king established mosques and Islamic courts and built a hostel in Mecca for Bornu pilgrims on the hajj.

In this time considerable Islamic influence also emanated from the West African empire of Mali, which thrived from the thirteenth to the eighteenth centuries. Mali reached from the Atlantic to Timbuktu and Songhai, a domain larger than western Europe. Mali's laws and customs were adopted by most peoples of the Niger River, and in some lands Islam was thought to have been from Mali originally. The Yorubas called Islam *Esin-Mali*, or the religion from Mali.

On the former site of a palace, the Great Mosque of Djenné ranks as the largest adobe building in the world. The original mosque was constructed in the thirteenth century, but the current building dates from 1907.

One way Islam expanded was through trade caravans, making particularly significant inroads in West Africa and the Sudan.

The Demise of Imperial Islam

FOR ALL THE WEALTH and cultural splendor of the three great Muslim empires, they were falling apart as states by the 1700s. The Ottomans, Mughals, and Safavids were being outpaced by leading European powers in technological progress and civil administration. The Ottomans, in particular, had contributed to the rise of those new powers.

Since the sixteenth century, Ottoman aspirations to conquer southern Europe had ignited many wars with the Hapsburg monarchy, hereditary holders of the title of Holy Roman Emperor. The Ottomans maintained alliances with European adversaries of the Hapsburgs—France, Britain, and the Netherlands—giving them favored trading status in Ottoman lands, thus promoting their development as mercantile powers.

The global successes of those countries brought the ultimate demise of the Muslim empires. All three empires were diminished by rebellious regional leaders breaking away and establishing independent states—some allying with the powers of western Europe. Recurring wars resulted in Ottoman losses of territory and in financial troubles that set the stage for the empire's decline.

The Safavids of Persia also were fatally weakened, despite defeating the Mughals and sacking Delhi in 1739. Revolts and assassinations ended Safavid rule by the 1760s. The Mughals likewise suffered from frequent, costly wars, disastrous to the economy and sapping the vitality of the ruling class. External threats from Hindus and Sikhs were exacerbated by the government's war against the northern Pashtuns—the very people who traditionally made up the core of the imperial army, which as a result was irrevocably weakened.

By the close of the 1700s the British had waged several military campaigns in India and controlled much of the subcontinent.

By the nineteenth century, the mighty Ottoman Empire was in decline. Ottoman forces could no longer defend their vast territory against modern European militaries and the growing power of Russia to the north. World War I (1914–18) finally brought on the complete collapse of the Ottoman Empire.

COLLAPSE OF THE OTTOMAN EMPIRE, 1798–1914

● cities
Ottoman Empire, 1914
areas lost by the Ottoman Empire, 1798–1914

*Every group of Muslims that transgresses Islamic law ...
must be combated, even when they continue
to profess the credo.*
—Ibn Taymiyya, thirteenth-century Sunni scholar
whose work inspired the Wahhabis

Muslim Unitarians

Muhammad ibn Abd al-Wahhab, founder of Wahhabism, was born in 1703 in the fertile heartland of the Arabian Peninsula and studied Islam in the holy city of Medina. Al-Wahhab traveled abroad until 1736, studying and teaching and taking a stand against many Sunni practices. He opposed any custom that diverged from asserting the oneness, or "unity," of Allah. His book, *Kitab At-Tawhid* (*Book of Unity*), the primary text of Wahhabi doctrine, stresses that "polytheistic innovations" such as the adoration of saints, the visiting of tombs, and decoration of mosques should stop. Only the prophet Muhammad's original principles should guide Islam.

The term *Wahhabi* was originally derogatory and is generally used only by non-Muslims. Members of the movement call themselves *Muwahiddun*, or "unitarians." Wahhabism is also known as Salafism, or "predecessors," indicating reverence for the founders of Islam.

Campaigns by the Ottomans in the early 1800s temporarily suppressed the first Wahhabi-Saudi alliance, which had attacked Shia cities such as Karbala. Renewed Wahhabi struggles made the movement the dominant form of Islam on the Arabian Peninsula in the nineteenth century.

Abdul Aziz al Saud of the House of Saud waged war in the early twentieth century to form the nation of Saudi Arabia, becoming its first king in 1932, and the foremost leader of the Arab world. The rulers of the House of Saud have been followers of Wahhabism since the eighteenth century.

Protectors of the Faiths

By the close of the eighteenth century, European powers such as France, Great Britain, and Russia were racing to fill the vacuums left by the decaying Muslim empires. Protectorates and colonies were set up under the guns of European warships, and with the control of seaports came control of sea routes, trade, and natural resources.

Each power, whether Catholic, Eastern Orthodox, or Protestant, set up its own missionary network to win over native peoples and ease the path to colonialism. Missionary diplomacy opened many doors for foreign colonists, but in some regions the people resisted. Much of the force of Muslim opposition took root within Islam itself, as discontent stirred up calls for reform and renewal.

Movements to strengthen the orthodoxy of the majority Sunnis caught fire wherever Muslim territory was compromised by foreign colonialism. Shiism, too, became the object of orthodox Sunni hostility, and unrest roiled throughout the Muslim world. The influential and worldly Sufis were denounced by conservative Shia clerics for being un-Islamic. At the same time, some Sufi theologians in Delhi were calling for a return to fundamental Islamic principles, demanding that those principles and sharia be the basis for renewing Muslim government and society.

In central Arabia, where Ottoman authority was weak, strict fundamentalist Sunnis led by the Arab Islamic scholar Muhammad ibn Abd al-Wahhab allied with the House of Saud emirate to fight the empire, which they considered morally decadent. By 1805 the Saudis and "Wahhabis" had taken control of Mecca and Medina and were raiding into Mesopotamia.

It was not just Muslim holy cities that were objects of contention, however, for

Rather than the usual four minarets, the spectacular Blue Mosque, built in the early seventeenth century in Istanbul, had six; the Wahhabi movement criticized elaborate decoration of mosques.

Christian Europe still longed to control the Holy Land and Jerusalem, which belonged to the Ottomans. By now the former crusader mentality had been replaced by imperial appetites for exclusive domination. That appetite was repressed for a time when the Ottomans agreed to giving European powers the authority to "protect" the religious rights of non-Muslims in the empire. Russia would defend the Eastern Orthodox, Britain the Jews and Protestants, and France the Catholics.

This gave Europeans extraterritorial claims to intercede when they deemed they must defend non-Muslim houses of worship, in particular those in the Holy Land. These treaties brought about predictable disputes between the European powers themselves—disputes that ultimately led to the Crimean War of 1853–56.

As British governor-general of Bengal, Francis Rawdon-Hastings, 1st Marquess of Hastings, waged a decisive campaign in 1817 against the Maratha people, establishing British dominance in India. By the eighteenth century, the Hindu Maratha had moved into the power vacuum left by a crumbling Mughal Empire. The last Mughal emperor, Bahadur Shah II, was defeated by the British in 1857 and exiled to Burma (Myanmar).

Muslims: From Empire to Rebellion

THE CRIMEAN WAR (1854–56) was in large part the result of European powers vying to gain control over the weakened Ottoman Empire. At the core of the dispute was France's demand that Christians in the Ottoman-controlled Holy Land—Palestine—be brought under French "protection."

The Russians countered with their own demands on the Ottomans, who had already lost considerable territory to the czar. The British joined the fray as allies of the French. One point of contention was the French assertion of control over—"holding the keys" to—Bethlehem's Church of the Nativity, the reputed site of Christ's birth. Until then, the Eastern Orthodox Church had been responsible for this church.

Although the underlying reasons for the war were geopolitical rivalries joined with the desire to dismember the Ottoman Empire, the public declarations were claims of religious rights. Most of the fighting was on the Black Sea's northern shores, on the Crimean

Peninsula. After less than two years and an appalling half-million casualties (most from disease), peace negotiations did little more than set the stage for future wars.

The Ottoman Empire suffered economically and militarily, with subsequent nationalist and religious rebellions costing the empire territory from the Balkans to North Africa. The jealous European powers kept one another from completely dismantling the weakened empire, soon to be labeled the "Sick Man of Europe."

The Crimean War would be the last major war between "modern" states in which the ostensible sparks were religious issues in the Holy Land. As for the Church of the Nativity, its administration now came under Eastern Orthodox, Roman Catholic, and Armenian Apostolic authorities.

Through the rest of the nineteenth century, the growing European empires battled mostly Muslim rebellions in struggle after struggle.

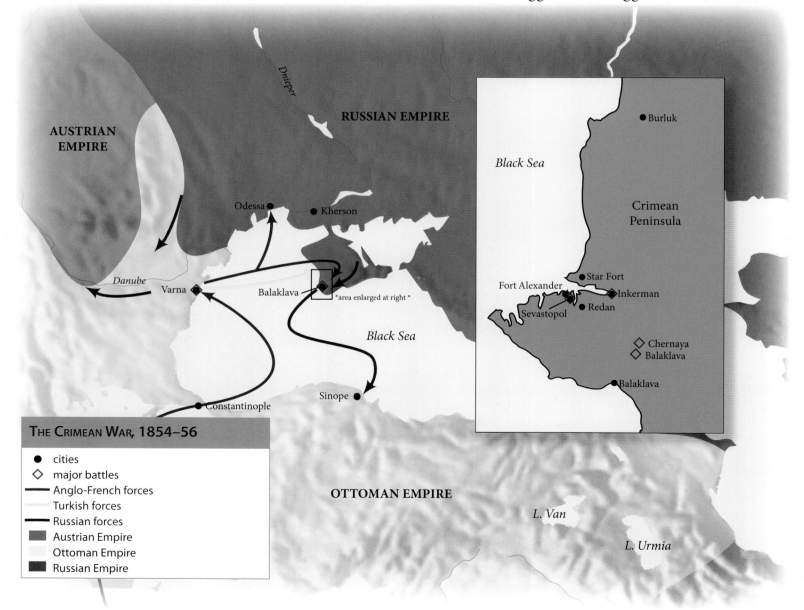

The Crimean War, 1853–56, featured campaigns on the shores of the Black Sea, with most of the fighting taking place on the Crimean Peninsula. Russian forces suffered decisive defeats at Inkerman and Balaklava in 1854. In a major setback, the key Russian naval base on the Black Sea, Sevastopol, was taken in 1855 after a yearlong siege.

THE CRIMEAN WAR, 1854–56

- ● cities
- ◇ major battles
- —— Anglo-French forces
- —— Turkish forces
- —— Russian forces
- ■ Austrian Empire
- □ Ottoman Empire
- ■ Russian Empire

Once a flourishing Black Sea port, Sevastopol was ruined by a year of warfare and artillery bombardment during the Siege of Sevastopol (1854–55). The siege resulted in the capture of this strategic Russian naval base on the Black Sea; upon defeat, Russian forces were forced to scuttle most of their Black Sea navy.

The Khalifa has no power or position except as a nominal figurehead.
—FIRST TURKISH PRESIDENT, MUSTAFA KEMAL ATATÜRK, REFUSING TO ALLOW THE TRADITIONAL OTTOMAN CEREMONY INAUGURATING ABDUL MEJID AS CALIPH

COLONIAL UNREST

The British depended on "native" troops to fight colonial wars, but those troops at times turned against them.

In the 1857 Indian Rebellion (also called the Indian Mutiny) Muslim and Hindu colonial soldiers rose up against the ruling British East India Company and captured Delhi. They reinstated a Mughal as emperor, Badahur Shah II, whom the British had confined to a Delhi fort. The rebels hoped a Mughal could unite Muslims and Hindus. The rebellion failed and the emperor was exiled, to be remembered as the last Islamic leader in India before the 1947 birth of the Muslim state of Pakistan.

During the late 1800s and into the twentieth century, imperial Britain, France, and the Netherlands variously battled Muslim uprisings in the Sudan, Afghanistan, North and Central Africa, and Indonesia. Russia also faced Muslim revolts, mainly in her Central Asian possessions. A few years after victories in the Spanish-American War (1898) and the Philippine-American War (1898–1902), the United States brutally repressed the rebellious Muslim Moros of Mindanao, killing an estimated 100,000.

In 1906 Indian Muslims established a political party designed to oppose what was perceived as the erosion of Islamic culture under the British, who were seen as favoring the Hindus. The All-India Muslim League would remain powerful on the subcontinent throughout the century.

The Ottoman alliance with Germany and Austria-Hungary during World War I (1914–18) spelled doom for this last Islamic empire, as Allied campaigns supported Arab revolts against the government.

During the war the Ottoman government accused Armenian Christians of collaborating with invading Russian forces. In the heat of conflict, millions of Armenians were deported or displaced by the government, and many hundreds of thousands killed, in what has been termed the Armenian Genocide. Turkey vehemently denies any genocide occurred and

JIHAD: STRUGGLE, ARMED OR SPIRITUAL

One of the most controversial Islamic concepts is *jihad*, Arabic for "struggle," used to mean both an inner spiritual struggle, or striving, and a Muslim armed action. One who struggles is a *mujahid*, with *mujahideen* as the plural. In the nineteenth and early twentieth centuries, Muslim uprisings against colonial empires were jihads of armed combat. Jihad in the sense of armed struggle can also mean going to war in order to preserve and protect an Islamic state. It can also mean wars of conquest in order to spread Islam.

Many Sunni and Shia scholars consider the requirement to undergo jihad in the non-violent, spiritual sense of moral struggle as a sixth pillar of Islamic doctrine. Muhammad is quoted as saying, after a military campaign, "We have returned from the lesser jihad to the greater jihad." He explained that the "greater jihad" is "the jihad against the lower self." There is considerable controversy in Islam about this quote's meaning, or whether Muhammad actually said it.

A statue of Saladin in Damascus, Syria, pays homage to a military leader considered by many to be the greatest of Muslim history. Saladin waged jihad to reconquer Crusader cities, including Jerusalem in 1187.

asserts there was never a government plan for organized persecution of Armenians.

The treaty that ended the war gave Great Britain and France immense influence in the region, now called the Middle East, which reached from Anatolia to northeast Africa. Mesopotamia, the Levant, and Palestine were mandates, quasi-colonies, administered by these powers. Independent Egypt and the Sudan were British protectorates, and parts of Anatolia were occupied by foreign troops— British, Italian, French, and Greek.

After World War I, Turkish nationalists led a revolution that drove the occupiers out of Anatolia and established the Republic of Turkey, with a secular, rather than Islamic, government. The republic abolished the Ottoman caliphate in 1924 and sent the caliph, Abdul Mejid II, into exile.

Palestine remained dominated by foreign Christian nations.

Armenian refugees in 1922. The Ottomans displaced millions of Armenians, contributing to the "Armenian diaspora." Today an estimated one third of the worldwide population lives in Armenia, while the rest of Armenians live abroad.

Twentieth-Century Resurgence

MUSLIMS WERE AT THE FOREFRONT of twentieth-century independence movements against colonial powers such as Britain, France, the Netherlands, and Portugal. Other Muslims, mainly in Central Asia, chafed under the iron rule of Communist China and Soviet Russia.

While Muslim politicians, writers, and poets called for independence from British rule in India, other Muslims took up arms. A number of insurgents were executed for their rebellious ways, some as late as the 1940s, when British India was in its final throes. The memories of British retribution after the 1857 uprising remained especially fresh in the minds of Muslims, whose forebears had been executed by the thousands near a Delhi fortress entrance known as the "bloody gate."

Muslims were important companions of Hindu holy man Mohandas Gandhi (1869–1948), the independence-movement leader who taught nonviolence. Hindus and Muslims cooperated closely in the movement until the 1930s, when rifts increasingly deepened between them. Indian independence was achieved in 1947, but by then hostility between Muslims and Hindus was so irreconcilable that the subcontinent was partitioned into Muslim Pakistan and East Pakistan (later to be independent Bangladesh) and majority-Hindu India.

In 1949 the former Dutch East Indies, after wartime occupation and a subsequent revolution, achieved independence as Indonesia, joining the ranks of new Muslim nations. Soon it would become the world's most populous Muslim-majority nation.

International destabilization caused by World War II (1939–45) spurred many such independence movements around the world. Armed struggles took advantage of Cold War geopolitics, placing many liberation movements in the Communist camp. Communism sought to destroy colonialism and its attendant capitalist doctrines, and developing nations were caught up in balance-of-power diplomacy. Many developing nations were rich in oil, making them desirable prizes for the industrial powers. One of the richest of the new Muslim nations was Saudi Arabia, recognized in 1927 and ruled by the Saud family, which after World War II was to become steeped in fabulous oil wealth.

After the winning of Indian independence from Britain in 1947, trouble flared between Muslims and Hindus leading to the formation of predominantly Muslim West Pakistan (present-day Pakistan) and East Pakistan (present-day Bangladesh), and majority-Hindu India. In West Asia, in 1927, the new Kingdom of Saudi Arabia, led by the Wahhabi House of Saud, was recognized. Growing Islamic power in West Asia was soon to be balanced by a new force: in 1948, on the eve of World War II, the Jewish state of Israel was founded.

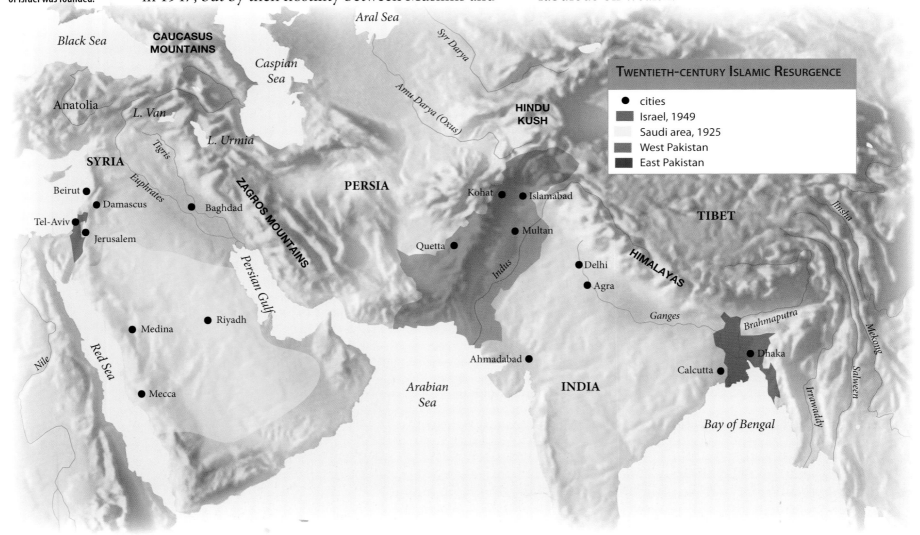

TWENTIETH-CENTURY ISLAMIC RESURGENCE

- ● cities
- Israel, 1949
- Saudi area, 1925
- West Pakistan
- East Pakistan

Malcom X (1925–65) was an influential crusader for black civil rights in the early 1960s and a spokesman for the Nation of Islam. After breaking with and renouncing the Nation of Islam in 1964, Malcom X converted to Sunni Islam, taking the name el-Hajj Malik el-Shabazz. He was assassinated by Nation of Islam gunmen in 1965.

Soviet combat vehicles roll through Afghanistan during the Soviet-Afghan War (1979–89). The superpower's military was not able to defeat insurgent mujahideen fighters. Although outgunned by the Soviets, the Afghan mujahideen were funded by the United States and Islamic nations. Especially effective were supplies of U.S.-made shoulder-mounted anti-aircraft missile systems.

ISLAM AND THE COLD WAR

The developing Muslim states after World War II were militarily and economically weak and soon found themselves ensnared in another "Great Game"—as one drawn-out phase of the nineteenth-century contest between major powers of East and West was called.

As former mandates and protectorates became truly independent nations—notably Iraq, Palestine, Syria, Egypt, and Algeria—Muslims yearned for strong leadership that would enable them to resist foreign interference and aggression. That leadership often came in the form of totalitarian dictators who founded their rule on nationalism and Muslim identity.

The Jewish state of Israel, founded in 1948 by a United Nations partition of Palestine, immediately became the center of international controversy and a key player in the Cold War. Backed by the United States and Britain, Israel fought several wars against its Arab neighbors, who were armed and supported by the Soviet Union. Israel was populated by Jewish immigrants from western Europe, the United States, and the Soviet Union and thus to Arabs symbolized foreign oppression of Arabs in general and Islam in particular.

In militarily strong Israel, the world had a new flashpoint of conflict between Muslims and nonbelievers, a conflict intensified by the forced relocation of millions of Palestinians (many of

them Christian) from their former homes. The American government's unequivocal support of Israel over the Arabs earned the United States the enduring resentment of Muslims around the world.

In 1979 the Iranian Revolution deposed the tyrannical shah, long propped up by the United States. Young revolutionaries occupied the U.S. embassy in Tehran, causing America international embarrassment and sparking pride among Muslims who admired such audacity.

In the 1980s, Muslims (who had secretly received arms from the United States) led the violent overthrow of a Soviet puppet government in Afghanistan, resulting in the takeover by the ultraconservative Taliban. The Taliban harshly imposed sharia law on a people who had been undergoing a process of modernization and liberalization.

Defeat in Afghanistan exposed the Soviet Union's political and economic weaknesses and triggered its breakup in 1989, opening the floodgates to independence for several Islamic Soviet republics in Central Asia. Meanwhile, the Muslims of Communist China, mostly ethnically Turkic, remained subject to brutal repression. Subsequent civil strife in formerly Communist Yugoslavia resulted in its

dismemberment, largely into Muslim and Christian states.

At the same time, Islam was growing rapidly around the world, establishing communities from western Europe to the United States. In America, a dynamic following developed for the Nation of Islam, also known as Black Muslims, who had substantial influence on African American culture and politics.

ISLAMIC REVIVAL

In the late nineteenth and early twentieth centuries, Muslim social movements worked to overcome colonialism while at the same time encouraging technological and social modernization. These movements often called for a revival of traditional values, with the object of reinvigorating Islam, to restore its former elevated status in the world.

Throughout this period a theme ran through the writings of independent-minded Muslim scholars and philosophers: the people of Islam are one nation, morally and spiritually superior to all others.

The quest for Islamic modernism and Islamic revival often were at odds with each other when it came to interpreting just what were the "original" values and just how modern a Muslim culture should strive to be. Nationalism, too, came into the mix, inciting passionate debate between modernist rulers and their conservative ulama.

By late in the century, much of Islam's effort to shake off persistent foreign control was driven by the conservative elements, one of the most dynamic of which was the Wahhabi movement, funded by the Saudis and instrumental in supporting the Taliban victory over the Soviets. Wahhabi was at the heart of a potent radicalism that demanded a return to Islamic values as defined by the Wahhabis.

Americans who had been taken prisoner during the Iran hostage crisis arrive at Andrews Air Force Base, Maryland, in 1981. The U.S. diplomats were held for 444 days, from November 4, 1979 to January 20, 1981.

INDIGENOUS RELIGIONS
First Nations and the Living Hopi

THE OLDEST CONTINUOUSLY INHABITED settlement in North America is Old Oraibi, a Pueblo village atop a small dry mesa in Arizona. Hopi Native Americans founded the community around 1100 CE and have lived there ever since. Oraibi's inhabitants maintain much of their traditional culture and still practice the ancient Hopi religion. Oraibi thus offers an unbroken, living connection back to the time of the Pueblo Indians, the builders of spectacular Pueblo ruins throughout the Southwest.

Hopi religion is built around a detailed mythology with a philosophical depth and sophistication unique in Native American culture. Spirituality permeates every aspect of Hopi life, and complex religious considerations can lie behind every choice—to speak or not to speak, to sit or to stand. Devoted to peace and ascetic spiritual discipline, the Hopi have long fascinated scholars, but the culture's great subtlety has often confounded study. The heart of this religion is generally lost on outsiders,

because the masked dancing gods of the Hopi make such a spectacular impression. Known as Kachinas, these colorful figures are manifestations of gods and spirits in Hopi cosmology. In the form of elaborately costumed masked dancers, they regularly visit Hopi villages for celebrations and festivals. The many specific Kachina types can be recognized by their distinctive attire, from the beloved Corn Mother to the clownlike Mud Heads, who entertain the audience with antics between the serious portions of the ceremonies.

The trauma of European invasions and forced conversions to Christianity devastated most Native American cultures, who were generally overwhelmed by the technology of Western civilization. By contrast, the Kachina religion has given the Hopi resilience through a strong identity. Since the foundation of a Catholic mission at Oraibi in 1629, every attempt to offer the Hopi a different way of life has failed, and their culture remains vital and healthy today.

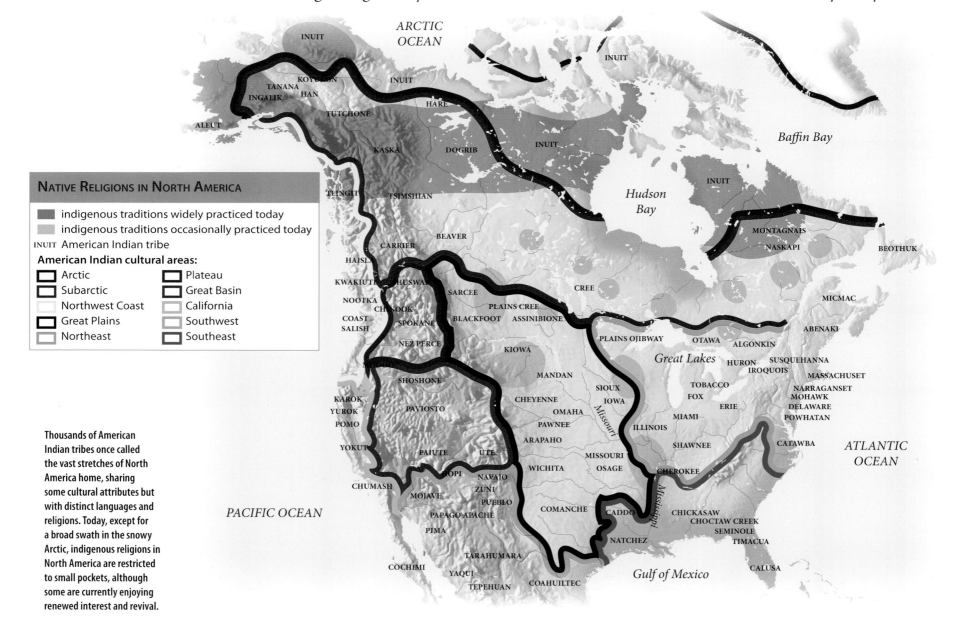

Native Religions in North America

- indigenous traditions widely practiced today
- indigenous traditions occasionally practiced today
- INUIT American Indian tribe

American Indian cultural areas:

- Arctic
- Subarctic
- Northwest Coast
- Great Plains
- Northeast
- Plateau
- Great Basin
- California
- Southwest
- Southeast

Thousands of American Indian tribes once called the vast stretches of North America home, sharing some cultural attributes but with distinct languages and religions. Today, except for a broad swath in the snowy Arctic, indigenous religions in North America are restricted to small pockets, although some are currently enjoying renewed interest and revival.

One of the most widely publicized Hopi religious ceremonies, the snake dance occurs annually in August. Dancers perform in ceremonial dress, sometimes holding live snakes in their mouths; these are released after the event as messengers to the gods and spirits.

THE GEOGRAPHY OF PROSPERITY: PACIFIC NORTHWEST COAST TRIBES

Native peoples have generally fared much better in Canada than in the United States, although Canada has its own checkered history as well. Indian tribes of the continental Canadian mainland are known today as "First Nations" peoples.

In one instance, unique economic prosperity allowed a First Nation culture to survive the arrival of European colonization with far greater success than was usually seen. The tribes of the Pacific Northwest Coast, such as the Tlingit and the Haida, are famous for their totem poles and their distinctive animal-based iconography, an impressive material culture that was made possible by the rich environment in which they lived. Heavy rainfall supported luxuriant vegetation (including the only rain forests in North America), and the coastal rivers and shore waters teemed with salmon and shellfish. Unlike other indigenous groups, the native peoples on the Northwest Coast found that making a living was relatively easy, leaving plenty of time for leisure. Leisure produced arts and wealth, and wealth gave rise to rare cultural sophistication. The famous potlatch parties involved complex interplay of social and economic issues and acquainted these First Nations with concepts such as exchange value, as with their "coppers"—decorated objects of no practical use, which functioned almost like money.

Their familiarity with economic principles and the exchange of goods positioned the Northwest Coast peoples to respond to the imposition of "white" culture with a far lesser degree of shock than normally occurred. Despite inevitable upheavals, many native

peoples successfully operated within the economic system of the Canadian colonists. Today Northwest Coast tribes are some of the wealthiest native groups in the Americas. The elders are still shrewdly managing their assets, presently developing tourist properties with an eye to long-term sustainability and the preservation of their own land and cultural integrity.

Animals, real or mythical, are nearly ubiquitous features of Pacific Coast totem poles. Frequently they signify ancestors or ancestral spirits, but since each pole is unique to the family which created it, they are difficult for outsiders to accurately identify or interpret.

INUIT TRADITIONAL CULTURE

The Inuit live in a world of snow, ice, and rocky islands. This harsh environment has long discouraged modern development, which is only now beginning to make inroads on the southern edges of the Canadian Archipelago. Within this comparatively less disturbed environment, both ecologically and culturally, the Inuit have maintained their traditional religious beliefs in many locations.

Responding to the risky and dangerous environment, the shamanistic and animist Inuit religion includes numerous taboos and rituals designed to avoid offending any of the animal or environmental spirits that the Inuit see as responsible for the catastrophic dangers that always threaten survival in polar seas. Inuit mythology also features heroic tales of whale and walrus hunts, celebrating the courage and the traditional knowledge—called *qaujimajatuqangit* in the Inuktitut language—that allows brave hunters to sustain their communities.

Global warming is melting the polar ice and dramatically affecting the animal populations hunted by the Inuit. Killer whales no longer kept out by sea ice are decimating beluga whale populations, for example. Alarmed scientists have asked the Inuit to reduce their hunting quotas. However, according to qaujimajatuqangit, the missing whales are merely "somewhere else," no overhunting is taking place, and beluga hunts are vital for the inculcation of traditional values among Inuit boys, so they must continue.

The Canadian government has yielded much of its former power over wildlife management to aboriginal tribes, and many Inuit communities have the power to decide the key issues that affect their interaction with polar animals. Only time will tell whether the scientists or the bearers of qaujimajatuqangit see the current situation more correctly. Either way, it will certainly be a test of how well traditional Inuit religion serves its people in the twenty-first century.

Very many North American religious ceremonies make use of masks. Their meaning depends on the specific culture and ritual, but they often provide a means of communicating with the spirit world by transfiguring the wearer into the spirit or its representative. Many masks include animal characteristics; this purely human, Inuit example, may represent an ancestor spirit.

The Conversion of Latin America

FROM THE BEGINNING of the Spanish conquest of Latin America, Catholic priests accompanied conquistadores such as Hernán Cortés and Francisco Pizarro, joining their military expeditions into Mexico and Peru in order to convert the indigenous populations to the Catholic religion. As the preserved writings of many missionary figures such as the sixteenth-century bishop Bartolomé de Las Casas attest, this conversion had multiple motivations.

On the one hand, many of the Catholic pioneers in post-conquest Latin America were sincere in their belief that they were helping to raise the native peoples from "superstitious ignorance" and liberate them from "devilish and infernal practices." Many priests undertook tremendous hardships as they ventured on their own into remote and impoverished areas to spread the word of God, and there is no doubt that pressure from Catholic authorities like Las Casas

The Spanish and Portuguese conquistadors of the fifteenth and sixteenth centuries converted—often forcibly—millions of South and Central American Indians to Catholicism, which is still the region's most prominent religion. However, indigenous traditions are still widely practiced in the jungles of the Amazon. It is also not always easy to distinguish between Catholic and indigenous beliefs.

sometimes eased the brutality of and slavery imposed on natives by their Spanish conquerors. Las Casas lamented the extermination of native peoples, documented abuses, and protested that Spain's atrocities would bring divine retribution.

On the other hand, the increase of church power was an important political motive behind funding the work of conversion, and despite critics such as Las Casas, the priests' cooperation with the conquerors provided Spanish rulers such as Philip II with a ready moral justification for their often brutal imperial expansion in the New World. The Spanish authorities certainly viewed conversion as a powerful aid to breaking native adherence to existing religious rulers and bringing conquered populations under Spanish cultural control.

With "the Bible in one hand and the sword in the other," Catholicism would be carried by the conquistadores throughout the length and breadth of Latin America, profoundly transforming the religious geography of the New World.

SUCCESS THROUGH SYNCRETISM

The Catholicism that emerged in Latin America richly expresses its composite origins. Spanish Catholic priests and missionaries did not generally attempt to eradicate native religious culture, but rather to transform it.

Like the Romans before them, Catholic fathers used deliberate syncretism to make their religion more readily acceptable to conquered indigenous peoples. They substituted their Christian saints for each of the various local deities such as Inca *apu* spirits, built shrines at Inca *huaca* (sacred sites), and linked the annual celebration of patron saints' days with traditional seasonal rituals that the natives observed near those dates. The result might be an ancient harvest festival superficially disguised as a Catholic feast day.

The continuance of indigenous worship practices was often tolerated around the fringes of public Catholic observance. In many cases, natives might still make animal sacrifices for the fertility of their flocks, or ask the Inca earth goddess Mama Occla to bless their crops, as long as they did it quietly and showed up at church for Mass on Sunday. Catholic churches were almost always built on the sites of native temples.

Higher Catholic authorities did not necessarily approve of the practical syncretism that priests resorted to, nor was the policy universal throughout Latin America. At various times and locations, stricter adherence to Catholic orthodoxy was pursued and enforced,

Gulf of Mexico

MEXICO
CUBA
JAMAICA
DOMINICAN REPUBLIC
BELIZE
HAITI
GUATEMALA
HONDURAS
EL SALVADOR
NICARAGUA
COSTA RICA
VENEZUELA
GUYANA
SURINAM
FRENCH GUIANA
PANAMA
COLOMBIA
ECUADOR
Amazon
BRAZIL
PERU
BOLIVIA
PACIFIC OCEAN
PARAGUAY
CHILE
Paraná
ARGENTINA
URUGUAY
ATLANTIC OCEAN

CATHOLIC AND INDIGENOUS TRADITIONS IN SOUTH AND CENTRAL AMERICA TODAY

— indigenous traditions widely practiced
strength of Catholicism, most to fewest number of worshippers (as a percentage of the total population)

using measures such as the burning of sacred Aztec codices in Mexico, the persecution of individuals revered as native spiritual leaders, and the banning of cultural customs or even foods that carried indigenous religious overtones.

The three major regions of Latin America broadly illustrate three different outcomes of this syncretism. In Mexico the Aztec religion's central focus on human sacrifice had to be eliminated, and so Catholicism asserted the primary role of worship, while accommodating acceptable native beliefs. In Central America the agrarian remnants of traditional Maya religion remained primary, incorporating Catholic elements. In Peru a complex synthesis between Catholicism and Inca religion was reached, making the most of similar elements, such as reverence shown for ancestors on certain feast days.

Where Spanish influence was strongest, the conversion to Catholicism was more thorough. In major cities such as Lima and Mexico City, great cathedrals were the site of magnificent formal Masses and elaborate rituals worthy of comparable communities back in Spain, with Catholic orthodoxy taught and practiced in great detail. In progressively remoter districts, conversion tended to be progressively less complete, resulting in greater persistence of ancient native practices.

By focusing their efforts prudently where they would achieve the greatest effects, and compromising when necessary, the Catholic Church succeeded in the effective conversion of the whole vast territory Latin America, repeating the similar success of ancient Rome by using similar techniques.

INCA ECHOES IN CUZCO'S CORPUS CHRISTI

Cuzco served as the capital of the Inca Empire, and the massive temple called Corincancha was the center of Inca religion. In one of the annual festivals, each of the communities around Cuzco would bring its local temple's primary sacred idol to Cuzco to show reverence and obeisance to the universal sun god, Inti. The carrying of the idols from their own temples to the capital was a grand and festive event, and it served to foster unity among the religious congregations in the area.

Early in the post-conquest era, Catholic authorities recast this ancient Inca festival as the Christian observance of Corpus Christi. The Inca idols came to be replaced by statues of Catholic saints. These statues, many wrought with precious metals just as the Inca idols had been, were large and heavy, to make the procession an intensely physical group effort. The saints were now carried from the

INTI RAYMI AND TOURISM

The greatest festival in the Inca realm was the Inti Raymi, a spectacular annual rite celebrated at the massive fortress of Sacsayhuaman in Cuzco. June 24 marks the winter solstice in South America, the day when the sun's light has decreased to its minimum. The Inti Raymi festival was conducted in order to pray for and ensure Inti's return to full brilliance. Inti Raymi was banned by the Spanish authorities in 1572, but in 1928 it was revived as a cultural heritage display. Today it has grown to become Cuzco's largest annual event, attracting over 100,000 spectators and involving hundreds of participants in traditional Inca garb.

Inti Raymi was originally focused around a central llama sacrifice, and the removal of the animal's beating heart.

Guinea pigs and additional llamas were also ritually killed for the ceremony. Today such blood rituals are omitted, primarily to avoid offending tourists, although such sacrifices are still sometimes performed privately.

The revival of Inti Raymi is celebrated as a resurgence of indigenous identity, but its popularity brings a challenge: will the performance of sacred rites in order to gain tourist income threaten to undermine their genuine religious content and turn them into mere show? From Hawaiian hula festivals to Hopi Kachina dances, native religious ceremonies have become popular tourist attractions around the world, and local spiritual leaders must each face the challenge and opportunity that tourism presents.

The fortress of Sacsayhuaman, now in ruins, may have represented the head of a puma (cougar) to its Inca builders. The animal, held in sacred esteem in Inca mythology, only compounds the holiness of the site, which is today again the location of the ancient festival of Inti Raymi.

nine neighboring Catholic parish churches into to the Cuzco cathedral, not to greet Inti, but to symbolically greet the body of Christ, sixty days after Easter Sunday. As they enter the cathedral, the saints pass its heavy wooden doors, carved with traditional Inca sacred pumas. The emotional and positive atmosphere of the event is still used to foster good relations among community leaders, who meet at this time to discuss problems.

Cuzco's feast of Corpus Christi presents an example of successful Catholic syncretism in Latin America and continues to express the strength of both traditional Inca beliefs and Christian faith in today's Peru.

Carnival, the riotous period of festivities before Lent, is particularly popular and vibrant in South and Central America. Although outwardly a Catholic holiday, the costumes, parades, and activities of carnival show elements of indigenous religions, from Africa as well as America.

Oceania's Semi-Christian Cults

AFTER CHRISTIAN MISSIONARIES began working in the South Pacific, islanders who came under their influence did not always fully accept Christian teachings. Often they formed independent churches that mixed Christianity with local beliefs. This phenomenon spread throughout Oceania, and in New Zealand alone Maoris founded some sixty independent religious movements, though many were short-lived. Hauhauism, one of the earliest of these movements, was founded by the Maori prophet Te Ua Haumene, who was schooled in a Methodist mission.

Te Ua claimed that the Angel Gabriel instructed him and granted him powers to perform miracles. According to Te Ua, Jehovah had sent angels upon the four winds (*hau*) to enter the bodies of believers through streamers attached to a pole of worship. During religious services worshippers held these streamers and marched around the pole to chants of mixed nautical, military, and biblical origin.

Promising eternal salvation, Te Ua predicted that all non-Hauhau believers would be destroyed and then the Maori sick and crippled would be cured, the Maori dead would rise from the grave, and believers would be taught all the best in European culture. To fulfill his prophecies Te Ua led his people into war but failed to achieve his goals.

The largest Maori movement was initiated by the faith healer Tahupotiki Wiremu Ratana in the 1920s. This movement rejects the use of medicine, relying only on healing through faith. Ministers who conduct worship services are known as apostles, but others, called disciples, can stand in for them. In time the names Jesus and Christ were eliminated from worship services, and Ratana himself, considered to be the mouthpiece of God to men and men to God, was praised instead. The movement quickly became involved in politics, and its adherents continue to represent Maoris in New Zealand's parliament today.

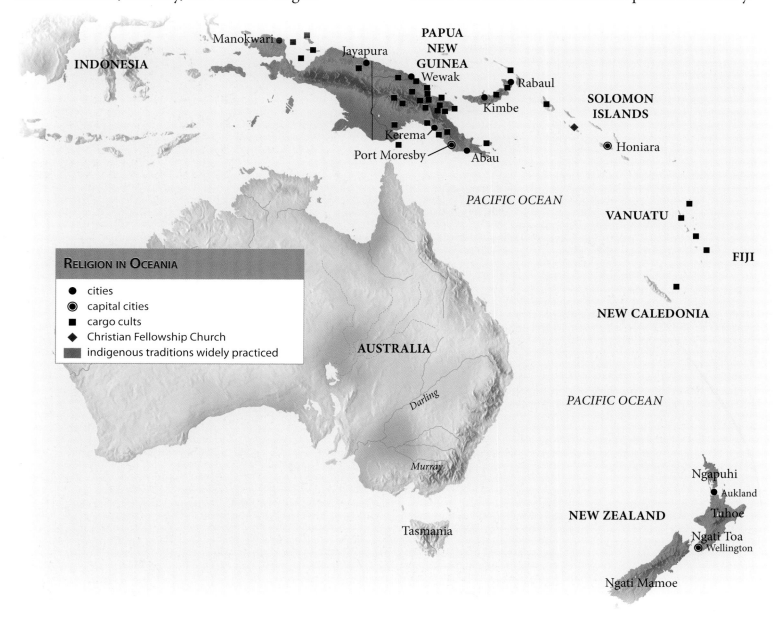

RELIGION IN OCEANIA

- ● cities
- ◉ capital cities
- ■ cargo cults
- ◆ Christian Fellowship Church
- indigenous traditions widely practiced

Beset throughout the modern period by Islamic empires, Christian missionaries, and European traders, many cultures of Oceania nevertheless retain their indigenous traditions. As elsewhere, Christian and indigenous religious elements occasionally blended, produced a vivid tapestry of belief systems through the South Pacific.

MELANESIAN CARGO CULTS

When European settlers arrived in the islands of Melanesia, they brought with them huge amounts of material goods, or "cargo." The islanders vainly sought through magic to acquire equivalent wealth in order to be on equal footing with the colonists. Many found refuge in special "cargo cults" that held that one day an ancestral spirit or tribal god would come to their island by ship—or plane—bringing cargo that would initiate an age of prosperity, justice, and independence. To prepare for this day, they built docks for ships, runways for planes, and storage sheds for the anticipated cargo. Between 1860 and 2000, more than 200 cargo cults emerged in the islands.

When the expected cargoes failed to arrive, disillusioned cult members often turned to the revivalist Christian churches that had been brought to their island by missionaries. However, as elsewhere in Oceania, many Melanesians did not accept all the teachings of Christianity but formed their own churches that incorporated local myths and traditions. Among the Melanesian Christian churches still active today are the Boda Kwato Church, the United Royal Church, and the Christian Fellowship Church.

A roughly-made wooden cross marks a ceremonial spot of the John Frum cargo cult on Vanuatu. The movement began in the 1930s and combined elements of indigenous worship and American culture brought by U.S. Army members during the second World War. It remains a powerful movement today.

CHRISTIAN FELLOWSHIP CHURCH

The largest of all independent churches in Melanesia, the Christian Fellowship Church has had a positive political impact. It was formed in 1960 by Silas Eto, a former Methodist, after a number of visionary experiences. Eto, the "Holy Mama," spoke of himself as the fourth member of the Trinity, and some of his church members described him as having superseded God. Following Eto's death in 1984, the church continued to grow, and because members relinquish ownership of their property to the church, the church owns enough real estate to give it almost complete control over land use. It has used this power to promote community-based forestry with a strong emphasis on reforestation.

Maori dancers perform a traditional dance. Indigenous Polynesian religions often incorporate dances in their rituals, many of which are currently experiencing a revival after centuries of suppression.

REVIVAL OF HAWAIIAN RELIGIOUS CULTURE

The *kahuna* shamans of Hawaii's native animist religion recognized numerous gods and spirits such as the volcano god Pele, taught the rigid ritual separation of the spiritually clean from the unclean through *kapu*, or taboos, and identified sacred places called *heiaus*—prayer locations that could range from giant stone platforms to small altars to unmarked natural sites. Like most religions, Hawaiian traditional beliefs involved concepts that are properly expressed only with their own particular words—there is, for example, no real English equivalent for *heiau*. Accordingly, the drastic decline in the use of Hawaiian language in the time since the islands were annexed by the United States

has led to a general decline in awareness and understanding of the old Hawaiian religious words and concepts. As of the year 2000, speakers of Hawaiian amounted to only about 0.1 percent of the islands' population.

However, since 1950, the historical decline has reversed, with improved appreciation fostered in part by a new Hawaiian dictionary published in 1957. Today children can learn in Hawaiian-language immersion schools, which was unheard of in 1950. Along with the language, more and more people of native Hawaiian descent are taking the time to learn their own history and to understand the customs and words that express respect for the ancient religion of their ancestors.

Ku'Emanu heiau, on Hawaii's "Big Island," was (and is) dedicated to ritual surfing. Today a popular Hawaiian sport, the heiau still accepts regular visitors, with a mix of religious and secular motives.

Indigenous Religions of the Arctic

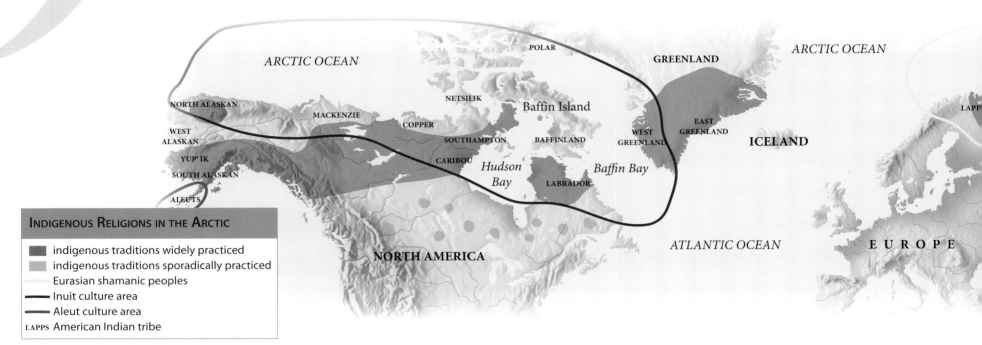

INDIGENOUS RELIGIONS IN THE ARCTIC

- ■ indigenous traditions widely practiced
- ■ indigenous traditions sporadically practiced
- □ Eurasian shamanic peoples
- —— Inuit culture area
- —— Aleut culture area
- LAPPS American Indian tribe

RELATIVELY UNAFFECTED BY THE REST of the world because of the harsh climate they live in, many of the indigenous people of the Arctic retain their ancient religious beliefs. However, even they are feeling the homogenizing effects of the modern world. While traditional religious festivals are still celebrated in remote regions, they are on the wane in more populous areas.

Arctic peoples can be broadly divided into three categories. Those who live in Alaska, Canada, and Greenland are generally called Inuit (meaning "true human beings"). They include the Yup'ik, Netsilik, and Aleuts. The Lapps of northern Scandinavia are not included with the Inuit because their beliefs were influenced first by Nordic mythology and later by Christianity, yet they still share many elements of Inuit religion. Finally, the indigenous peoples of Siberia (Tungas, Yakuts, Samoyeds, and others) are generally classified as Eurasian shamanistic peoples, but they too are sometimes considered Inuit. Although the indigenous Siberians are specifically labeled shamanistic, all the Arctic religions share this one dominant characteristic, which is also possibly the most ancient.

Because Arctic peoples hunt and fish to survive, they consider it essential to establish proper relationships with the animal world. They believe that every animal has an independent humanlike spirit, or *ina*,

and they rely on shamans to keep a balance between the people and the spirit world. Believing that an imbalance creates the people's problems, a shaman will seek to solve a problem by going into a trance, during which he is believed to travel through space to seek help from one of the supernatural beings that own the animals—the Moonman in the sky, or Sedna, who lives at the bottom of the sea. Shamans also attempt to appease the spirits by conducting rituals that involve singing, dancing, masking, and storytelling.

A Lapp family from northern Scandinavia, complete with dog, poses in front of a traditionally built home in the last decade of the nineteenth century. Because Lappish societies were until recently semi-nomadic, permitting them to follow herds of caribou for sustenance, traditional Lappish homes are impermanent creations.

We felt that all things were like us people, down to small animals like the mouse, and the things like wood. The wood is glad to the person who is using it, and the person is glad to the wood for being there to be used.

—JOE FRIDAY, A YUP'IK

With their cultures somewhat protected from foreign advance by the Arctic climate, peoples in the northern parts of the world have historically practiced indigenous religions with less interference than elsewhere. As the modern phenomenon of globalization continues, however, and environmental concerns train the world's eye on the northern ice, instances of collision are becoming more frequent.

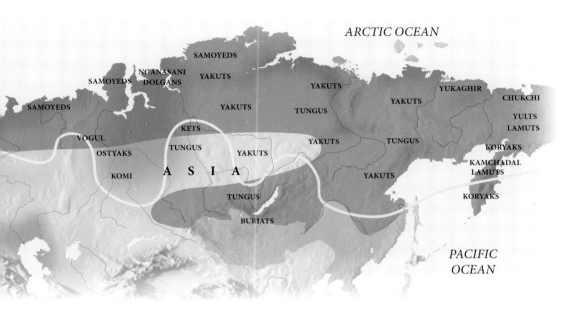

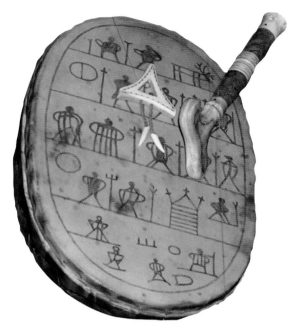

A seventeenth-century example of a Lappish drum used in shamanistic rituals. The drum is decorated with figures of gods or spirits.

Recent pressure from global or external communities—such as the push to save humpback whales from overhunting—has run head-on into local traditions, resulting both in increased cultural awareness and concern.

LAPP CULTURE

The Lapps are nomadic herders of reindeer who inhabit the Arctic regions of Scandinavia. Their gods generally represent elements of nature, such as Pieve, the sun. The Lapps offer sacrifices of white reindeer to Pieve on large platforms located near spectacular rock formation or ancient trees. Their daily lives are ruled by taboos, and the taboos surrounding the bear (their largest prey) amount to a separate cult, including a special bear language and elaborate rituals for hunting a bear or using its skin.

Like other Arctic peoples, the Lapps have a deep respect for the spirits of the animals, and so shamanism is prominent. Frequently Lapp shamans use a drumbeat to work themselves into an ecstasy. Often these drums are decorated with images of the gods.

ALEUTIAN BLADDER FESTIVAL

Every December at the time of the full moon, Aleutian villagers of western Alaska hold a festival to appease Sedna and honor the spirits of the seals and other marine mammals. The Aleuts believe that these spirits reside in bladders, and that if they treat the bladders properly, the spirits will be reincarnated, producing abundant game for the villagers.

In anticipation of the festival, the Aleuts collect the bladders of whales, seals, walruses, and polar bears and keep them inflated. In December they paint the bladders and hang them on stakes at the center of the village for the duration of a weeklong festival. During the festival the people respectfully offer food and drink to the bladders and then sing and dance, play games, make wood and ivory carvings, wear masks, play drums, and put on marionette shows. At the end of the week the men deflate the bladders with spears and push them into holes in the ice. Then they light a fire on the ice, sending the spirits from the bladders to the realm of Sedna at the bottom of the sea. In the spring, it is believed, the spirits will produce game for the village.

THE MYTH OF SEDNA

The ruler of the undersea world, Sedna, is the subject of many myths. In one, while she is escaping a seducer in a boat with her father, the seducer's followers send a storm to sink the boat, and her father throws her out of the boat in fear for his own life. When Sedna tries to cling to the sides of the boat, her father cuts off her fingers, which turn into seals, walruses, and other sea animals. Soon after, Sedna retreats to the bottom of the sea, which becomes her new home.

The name Sedna originated in the Baffin Islands and means "the one down there." The Netsilik know her as Nuliayuk, "the lubricious one," and the polar peoples know her as Nerrivik, or "the meat dish." She lives under the sea in various dwellings or (in Greenland) at the horizon. Numerous rituals are held to honor Sedna so that she will release marine animals for the people to hunt. The Siberian Chukchi believe in a similar figure, known as the mother of the walrus.

Most Sedna myths associate her with marine creatures such as seals, which are one of the most important sources of food, implements, and warmth (from their fur) in Arctic territories. Integrating animals into sacred myths and rituals reflects the perceived integration of human and animal life.

African Indigenous Religions

ALTHOUGH MODERN AFRICA is mainly Christian or Muslim, some seventy million Africans (about a tenth of the population) still practice traditional religions that date back centuries. There are literally hundreds of such religions, and all of them are different in many aspects. However, there are a few common qualities.

Most indigenous African religions recognize a principal god, generally a creator, and they revere the sacred ancestors of humans. In the beginning, some myths tell us, the creator god lived on earth with the ancestors, but something caused a rift between them. As a result, the god went up to heaven, where he remains, while the ancestors, remaining earthbound, were transformed into humans.

Olorum, the Lord of Heaven, is the god of the Yoruba of Nigeria, but he is little worshipped. Instead, the Yoruba pay tribute to an assortment of spirits. For the Zulus the creator is Unkulunkulu, meaning the

aged, or first, or most revered one. He is responsible for thunder and lightning. The ancestors, who live under the earth, cause illness and other troubles. However, if rituals are performed and sacrifices are made to the ancestors, they extend their protection in return. Often the rituals include dancers who wear elaborate costumes to impersonate the spirits of the ancestors

The spirits of ancestors are of primary importance in many African religions, and often the spirits of dead kings and priests are revered as deities. Normally, elaborate post-funerary rituals must be performed before a deceased person is given full status as a sacred ancestor. In some West African societies, ancestors are believed to be reincarnated as descendants. In the Akan religion of Ghana, the ancestors and the living meet at the sacred stool of the tribe, and stool festivals are held every twenty-one days and to bring in the new year. A new tribal chief is inaugurated while sitting on the stool.

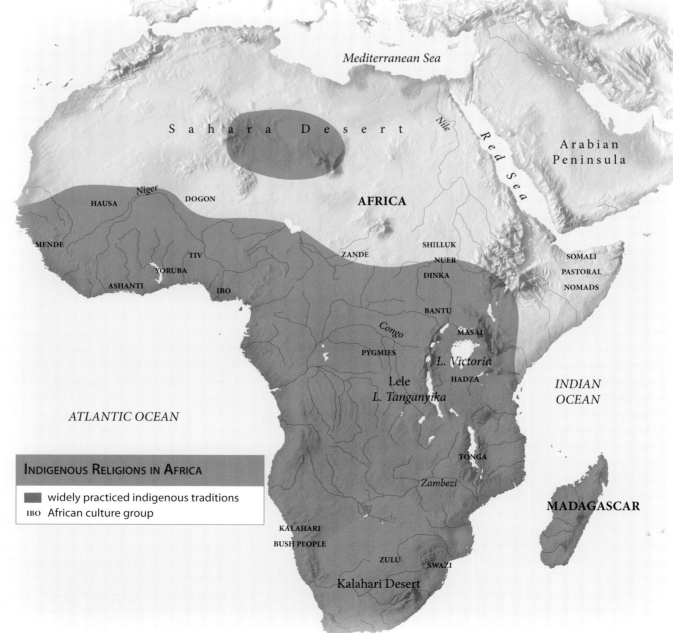

African religion is as varied as the African landscape, differing between cultures, language groups, and tribes. The regional prevalence of Christianity and Islam has also left its mark on Africa, and many religions today display elements of these as well as indigenous traditions.

INDIGENOUS RELIGIONS IN AFRICA

widely practiced indigenous traditions
IBO African culture group

Masks representing gods, spirits, animals, or ancestors (and often a combination) feature in many African religions. This horned example may have been used in initiation ceremonies of the Ivory Coast, and dates to the nineteenth century.

A Namibian holy man leads a ritual dance. Dances are nearly ubiquitous features of African religion and culture, used in ceremonies of prayer, healing, weddings, and many others.

WITCHCRAFT AND WITCH DOCTORS

The causes of illness or other misfortunes, when not attributed to neglected ancestors, is generally believed to result from witchcraft or sorcery. According to the Zande religion of Sudan and the Democratic Republic of the Congo, certain mysterious powers are at work in people and things, powers that can be manipulated by a witch to bring about misfortune or death. However, a witch or sorcerer has an identifiable substance in his body that provides his power, and he can be detected through divination by a skilled witch doctor. Sorcerers do their harm by using certain substances they claim are magic to work a spell on an enemy. To help someone in distress, a witch doctor needs to learn what trees and herbs provide the right magic substance, or *benge*, to counteract such a spell. Basically, good and bad magic use the same methods and are distinguished only by the intent of the person using them. A witch doctor may use a benge to stop an evil spell, but the witch can

use another one to counteract the cure. And so it becomes a battle of wits.

There are many methods of divination. In addition to the Zande method of finding the right magic substance, the most common is what the Yoruba people call *ifa*. It involves manipulating sixteen palm nuts or tossing out a chain and observing the patterns created. The diviner—always a man—is carefully trained to read the sixteen possible patterns and recognize the 256 possible figures that are associated with them. Each figure is assigned a verse that provides guidance—such as offering a sacrifice. The diviner, who has memorized all these verses, recites the ones associated with the pattern at hand until the client chooses one. He then follows the instructions given in that verse.

The other method of divination is through the use of a medium (usually a woman), who communes with the spirits to find a solution to a problem or a cure for a disease. Some Africans use both methods.

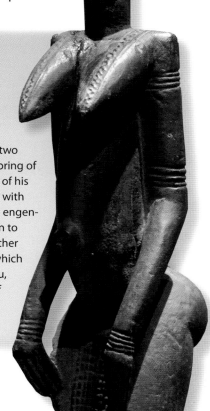

A Dogon carving from Mali, dated to the seventeenth or eighteenth centuries. The figure stands about two feet (59 cm) high and was likely intended to house the spirit of an ancestor.

DOGON CREATION MYTH

There are many different creation myths among the indigenous people of Africa, and the one professed by the Dogon people of Mali is typical. It holds that at the beginning of time a cosmic egg was shaken by the movement of the universe and divided into two placentas. Each placenta contained male and female twins, the offspring of the creator and father god, Amma. When the twin Yeruga broke out of his placenta, a piece of it fell and became the earth. Yeruga then mated with the earth, which was actually his own maternal placenta, in order to engender humans. When he failed, Amma sent the other set of twins down to mate with each other, and humans were born of their incest. In another version of this myth it is Amma himself who mates with the earth, which he had earlier created. The child born of this relationship was Yorugu, who brought evil and chaos into the world. Yorugu in this version of the myth later mated with his own mother, resulting in the birth of evil spirits.

PART FIVE

RELIGIONS OF THE WORLD TODAY

RELIGION IN THE NEW MILLENNIUM has developed into a widely varied landscape of belief and practice. Ancient faiths yet survive, some diminishing and others thriving, just as some steadfastly hold to tradition while others transform with the changing times. At the same time, new religious movements and systems of belief have arisen around the world, answering to the spiritual needs of their adherents.

By the start of the twenty-first century, Judaism was divided into Orthodox, Reform, and Conservative branches. Many Jews lived in Israel, but many more were scattered around the world. Christianity had splintered into hundreds of different denominations. The largest branches of Christianity were Roman Catholics and Eastern Orthodox. All other Christians, characterized as Protestants, were myriad. Megachurches reached out to vast crowds of worshippers and preached to millions by means of television and the internet.

The close of the twentieth century saw a migration into Europe of Muslims from former colonies. Western values often clashed with Islamic cultures, and Muslims worldwide resented the Western powers allying with Israel in the ongoing Arab-Israeli struggle. The twenty-first century had just dawned when destructive terrorist attacks, allegedly masterminded by Islamic extremists, struck New York City, London, and Madrid. War soon broke out between western powers and Islamic jihadists, with Afghanistan and Iraq the early battlegrounds.

The religions of Asia hold fast to ancient traditions, even as modernization and economic success bolster the fortunes of India and China. Natural disasters such as tsunamis, earthquakes, and floods have thrown old beliefs into sharp relief as the people of Asia rebuild—sometimes turning toward religion for solace, sometimes turning away. As globalization appears to shrink our world into an ever more tightly knit community, our varied religions remain an integral force. Venerable or modern, they offer a glimpse of the transcendent, a path to self-realization, a way to find meaning in a confusing world.

Nighttime lights in a composite satellite image are a visual reminder of humanity's expanding global community. Our diversity of faiths as we develop this community has the potential to enrich, inform, and enlighten, as well as the potential to divide, disrupt, and even destroy. As sensitive an issue as it is critical, religion promises to continue to be a fundamental aspect of human life.

Hinduism and the Wider World

THERE ARE PERHAPS 1.1 BILLION HINDUS in the world today, making it the world's third-largest religion, behind Christianity and Islam. Overwhelmingly the largest numbers of Hindus are in South Asia. Hardly surprisingly, India leads the way, its numbers dwarfing those elsewhere, with an estimated 880 million Indian Hindus. By comparison, Nepal, the country with the next largest number of Hindus, has only 22 million, though they make up 81 percent of the population. Thereafter, only Indonesia, with 17 million, and Bangladesh, with 15.5 million, have more than 10 million Hindus. Pakistan and Sri Lanka both have 3 million, Malaysia and the United States 1.5 million. In Britain there are just under 1 million Hindus.

India and Nepal aside, as proportions none of these numbers are particularly impressive. Sri Lanka's 3 million Hindus make up just 15 percent of the island's total population; Bangladesh's 15.5 million, 10.5 percent. Pakistan's 3 million Hindus account for only 1 percent of that country's population.

Yet if the global figures are modest, what is nonetheless striking is the growth in the numbers of Hindus outside the religion's homeland in the subcontinent. In part this is the result of immigration. Britain presents the most obvious case. The overwhelming majority of its 900,000 Hindus are arrivals from South Asia or their children who left the subcontinent in the wake of decolonization, drawn to the former colonial power in search of economic opportunity. (It is striking to note, however, that at 1.6 million, Britain's Muslim population is close to double the size of its Hindu community).

The other factor driving the growth in numbers, above all in the West, is the appeal of Hinduism itself as a religion preaching (if not always practicing) toleration, spurning materialism, and championing the search for spiritual enrichment. Since the 1960s, most famously when the Beatles journeyed to India to study and meditate under Maharishi Mahesh Yogi, a significant Western interest in Hinduism has developed. That the Maharishi later proved to be at least as interested in materialism as meditation—he suggested that the group donate 25 percent of its future earnings to him—did nothing to change the fact that the counterculture had discovered and embraced Hinduism, providing it with a modest but lasting foothold in otherwise predominantly Christian worlds.

The spread of Hinduism around the globe is the result of colonialism, migration, and conversion in the West. Many Hindus migrated from India to the United Kingdom and Australasia after independence was established. Significant numbers of Hindus live in South America, many having ancestors who arrived there in the nineteenth century as indentured laborers.

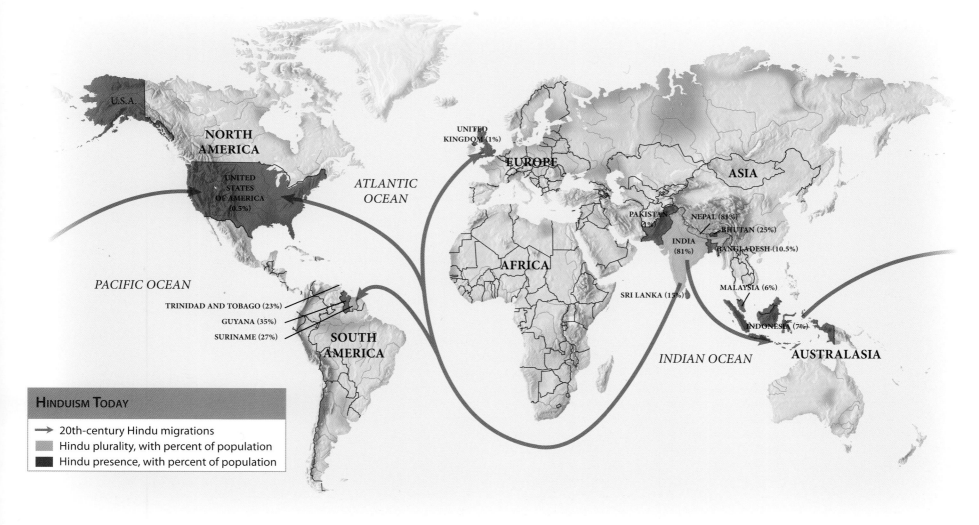

HINDUISM TODAY

→ 20th-century Hindu migrations
Hindu plurality, with percent of population
Hindu presence, with percent of population

In fifty years, the world would be under the hegemony of the USA, but in the 21st century, as religion captures the place of technology, it is possible that India, the conquered, will conquer its conquerors.
—Arnold Toynbee, Civilization on Trial and the World and the West, *1952*

Lingaraja Temple, built around 1000 ᴄᴇ, is the largest of the temples at Bhubaneswar, and a spectacular example of ancient Hindu temple architecture. Thousands of Hindu pilgrims as well as secular tourists make their way here every year.

A modern Indian *saddhu*, or holy man. Hinduism has remained a constant in the lives of modern Indians, in spite of modernization and an economic boom.

Hinduism in the Twenty-First Century

The challenge facing today's Hindus is clear: reconciling a sprawling and deeply spiritual ancient religion with an increasingly secular and modernized India. The country whose religion draws its precepts from a distant past is now embarked on a dizzying pursuit of economic growth. Despite the seeming disparity between its ancient roots and its modern flowering, however, India's native beliefs are not incompatible with its newfound prosperity.

Mohandas Gandhi had a vision of India as a rural, self-sufficient state whose citizens live simple, near-ascetic lives founded in Hindu devotion. Such a notion was not to be, however, as the reality of human self-interest emerged from the self-sacrifice of Gandhi's revolution. Yet Hinduism has remained a constant throughout these shifts in India's

self-identity. Indeed, the ancient religion's very diversity has long made it possible for even the most devout to reconcile faith with the pursuit of material wealth. Well before European dominance, an opulent and primarily Hindu civilization flourished in India. It was this promise of riches that initially drew Europeans to the subcontinent.

It is certainly plausible to imagine a future in which India emerges as a preeminent world power, although such a future is far from assured. Indian hegemony faces real dangers, both from within and without its borders. Tamil and Sikh separatist groups threaten India's unity, while conflict with Pakistan and an increasingly militant Muslim world are sharpened by the addition of nuclear capabilities both in India and Pakistan. Hinduism cannot afford to be complacent, but it has weathered close to four millennia of history. It may be that Hinduism's inherent resilience has also been its lasting strength.

Hindu Temples Abroad

One of the most striking manifestations of the slow spread of Hinduism into countries where it was almost wholly unknown even a few decades ago has been the growth in the number of Hindu temples. These vivid outposts of Indian spirituality and its exuberant architecture often stand out in surroundings far removed from those that gave rise to the originals.

In the United States there are almost 400 Hindu temples, 54 of them in California alone. In Britain the unlikely surroundings of the north London suburb of Neasden are the site of the largest Hindu temple outside India, the Shri Swaminarayan Temple, begun and completed in 1995. The interior is of Italian marble and the exterior, Bulgarian limestone, a material durable enough to endure London's winters but easily carved. Once quarried, the stones were sent to India, where 1,500 craftsmen in Rajasthan and Gujarat carved them. More than 26,000 carved stones were then sent back to England for assembly. The completed building lays claim not only to an under-floor heating system for the marble floors, but two fire escapes built of marble. The whole extends over 1.2 acres. By any measure it is a structure as impressive as it is unexpected—Eastern exoticism transported to a prosaic suburban setting to startling effect.

The largest Hindu temple outside India is the spectacular marble and limestone edifice in Neasden, a suburb of London. The temple is a testament to the large numbers of Hindus living in the United Kingdom.

HINDUISM
Ethics and Festivals

As DIFFICULT AS IT IS to make generalizations about a religion as diverse and inclusive as Hinduism, there are nonetheless clear ethical codes all Hindus attempt to honor. These codes broadly stem from the belief in *dharma*, a Hindu's "righteous duty" or "virtuous path." With compassion and forgiveness at the heart of Hindu teaching, it follows that Hindu ethical codes place consistent emphasis on acts of charity (*dharmik*) and on nonviolence (*ahimsa*). It is a further central tenet that all life—animal as much as human—is sacred.

Hindus do not specifically worship cows, but they do venerate them as they venerate the lives of all animals. Yet the cow—placid, docile, and a provider of milk, though never meat—enjoys a unique status, for no Hindu would kill a cow to eat it. At the same time, Hindus, most of whom are vegetarians, generally consider animals inferior to humans, and animal sacrifices are permitted.

In much the same way, though today many Hindus are not opposed to abortion if it is necessary to save the mother's life, abortion is otherwise strongly disapproved of. This is more than a matter of the sanctity of life, even of the traditional Indian belief that large families are a blessing. It is above all a question of the fetus's being seen as a soul, which, in accordance with the fundamental Hindu belief in reincarnation, would be denied the opportunity to improve whatever karma it inherited from its previous life and so delay the moment when it attains *moksha* and passes beyond the cycle of successive lives and deaths.

Contraception, however, is not banned: no new soul is at stake if conception has not taken place. However, more-traditional Hindus view contraception with something approaching horror, largely again the result of the belief that a large family, especially one with many boys, is a good in itself, both to provide for the parents in old age and to continue the family line. At the same time, faced with the country's booming population—357 million in 1950, 1.1 billion in 2007—successive Indian governments have encouraged birth control. In 1976 Indira Gandhi tried to institute a family-planning campaign that coerced—or effectively forced—thousands of poor men and women to become sterilized. This highly unpopular initiative contributed decisively to her election defeat the following year, the first time in thirty years the Congress Party had not been in government.

Suicide is regarded as wrong, not merely because it breaches the principles of ahimsa, but because it unnaturally separates the soul from the body, ensuring that when the former is reincarnated it will be plagued by bad karma. There is one exception: *prayopavesa*. This is a ritual fasting to death, undertaken by the very elderly and very spiritual, but only once it is clear that death is imminent anyway. It must also be public. As it is a gradual process, it induces a sense of serenity and release, as opposed to the violence of conventional suicide. It is exceptionally rare.

The Hindu attitude to killing is contradictory. On the one hand, it clearly does not accord with ahimsa and the belief in the sanctity of life. Gandhi himself asserted that there were many causes for which he would be prepared to die, but none for which he would be prepared to kill. Yet Hindu teaching has long taught that killing in self-defense is acceptable, indeed that it can be a moral duty. One of the most senior of the Hindu castes was the Kshatriyas, warriors whose duty it was to fight.

Also unresolved is the attitude to capital punishment, which is increasingly seen as wrong yet still resolutely defended by some Hindu teachers. India itself is one of the seventy-six countries in the world that retains the death penalty, however sparingly it is used. Just how controversial the practice remains was highlighted by the execution in 2004 of Dhananjoy Chatterjee, held on death row for fourteen years after being convicted of murder in 1990. The final, tortuous decision that he should die raised howls of protest across the Hindu world.

Indira Gandhi, prime minister of India for four terms from the 1960s to the 1980s, meeting with Tamil Nadu minister M. G. Ramachandran. India's first and only female prime minister, Gandhi was the daughter of Jawaharlal Nehru, the country's first prime minister.

FESTIVALS

The Hindu calendar is crowded with festivals. By no means all are celebrated by all Hindus. Many are also regional. The following, in calendar order, are some of the most important.

Makar Sankranti
Observed in a wide variety of ways across the Hindu world, it celebrates the beginning of the sun's return to the Northern Hemisphere. *January.*

Mahashivratri
Principal festival dedicated to the Lord Shiva. Always held on the night of the new moon. *March.*

Holi
The Hindu spring festival—the Festival of Colors—celebrated with immense zest. *March.*

Rama Navami
The birth of Rama, the signal for mass outpouring of piety, above all at Ayodhya. *March/April.*

Hanuman
The birth of Hanuman, the servant of Rama. *April.*

Raksha Bandhan
Celebration of love and universal brotherhood. *August.*

Janmashtami
Marks the birth of Shiva. Two-day festival during which the faithful should not sleep.

The first day is traditionally one of fasting. *August/September.*

Ganesh Chaturthi
Hugely important festival to mark the most popular of Hindu gods, Ganesh. At its most opulent it lasts ten days. *September.*

Navaratri
Part harvest festival, part celebration of the "Mother Goddess," Druga. Can last up to nine days. *September/October.*

Diwali
In some ways the most important Hindu festival, the "Festival of Lights," a riotous five-day celebration of the triumph of light over darkness and knowledge over ignorance. *October/November.*

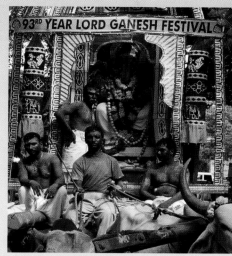

A celebration of Ganesh Chaturthi, one of the most joyous of Indian festivals. It honors the popular elephant-headed god, Ganesh, son of Shiva and Parvati.

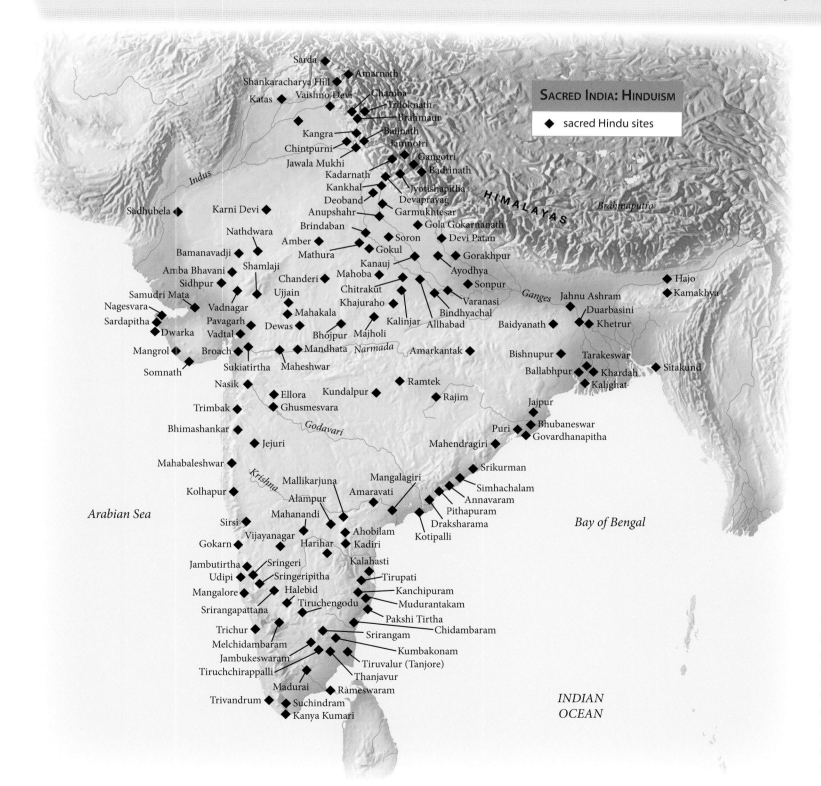

The Indian subcontinent is fettered with a network of sacred Hindu sites, some of which are well over 1,000 years old—and some of which, like the Ganges River, are simply timeless. Temples, shrines, and a variety of other sacred sites make up the holy Hindu geography of India.

Worldwide Buddhism

A view from a hilltop in Langtang, Nepal. Buddha was born in this remote mountainous region, and his teachings have now spread across the continents of the world.

BUDDHISM BEGAN WITH ONE MAN'S great spiritual journey toward enlightenment. Seeing the disparity between his own sheltered existence and the harsh reality of life, Siddhartha Gautama (born c. 563 BCE) left his wealthy home in a North Indian village (now in present-day Nepal), turned his back on his family and his life of ease, and embarked on the ascetic life of a holy man. Siddhartha eventually achieved enlightenment through meditation on the nature of existence and assumed the title Lord Buddha (the enlightened one). He devoted the next forty-five years of his life to teaching the path to enlightenment—the dharma—and his influence spread far and wide.

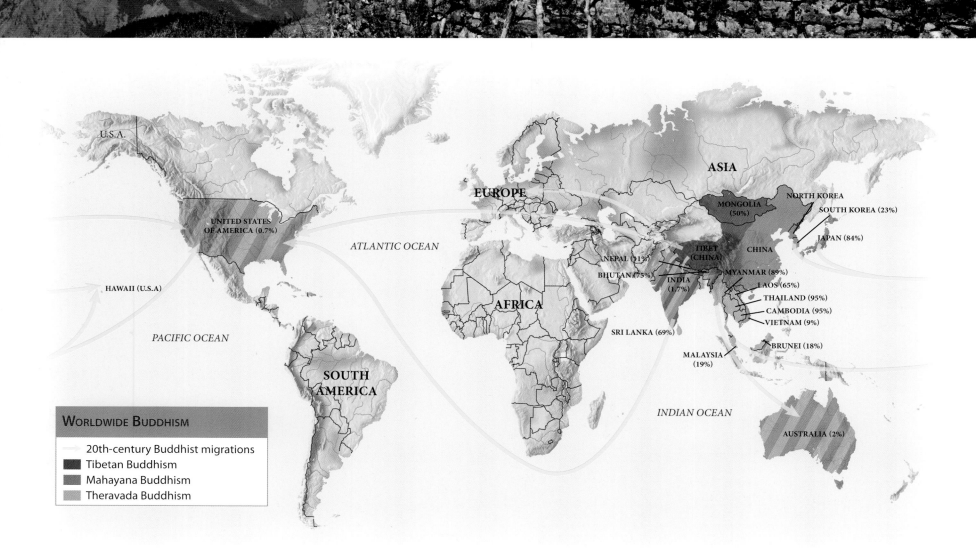

WORLDWIDE BUDDHISM

—— 20th-century Buddhist migrations
▬ Tibetan Buddhism
▬ Mahayana Buddhism
▬ Theravada Buddhism

Buddhism has spread around the world and is today increasingly practiced outside Asia, with Buddhist centers growing throughout the West. Tibetan Buddhism was carried abroad as a result of repression in its homeland, while the flow of other forms of Buddhism was the result of migration and overall cultural cross-pollination.

MODERN BUDDHISM IN JAPAN

At the end of World War II in 1945, a vigorous modern sect of Buddhism called Soka Gakkai emerged in Japan. Derived from the thirteenth-century Japanese Nichiren school of Buddhism, it teaches that happiness and success can be achieved by chanting the mantra *nam myoho*

renge kyo twice a day. Central to Soka Gakkai philosophy is the desire for world peace, an issue that was of particular relevance in postwar Japan. Soka Gakkai has established a sophisticated network within Japan with its own educational and cultural institutions. Its political offshoot, the Komeito (Clean Government Party), formed in 1964, plays an active role in Japanese government. Soka Gakkai is noted for its use of mainstream marketing and advertising strategies and for its proselytizing and outreach programs—not usual in Buddhism—and it reflects a very modern face of Buddhism. Soka Gakkai has grown rapidly to become an international movement with followers in more than 120 countries. It is estimated to have as many as 10 million followers in Japan and 1.26 million outside Japan, an estimated 300,000 of whom are in the United States.

Soka University, a private liberal arts university in Southern California, was founded by Tsunesaburo Makiguchi, the founder of the Soka Gakkai Buddhist organization, and is dedicated to the pacifist principles inherent in the religion.

No one saves us but ourselves. No one can and no one may. We ourselves must walk the path.
—BUDDHA

international community contains many different practices, common to all groups is the veneration of the Buddha or qualities the Buddha exemplified. Modern Buddhism can be broadly divided into two large groups. The Theravada school (called the Way of the Elders) is found mainly in Sri Lanka, Myanmar, Cambodia, Thailand, and Laos; while the Mahayana ("great vehicle") school, the most common form of Buddhism, is practiced in Japan, Korea, Taiwan, China, Nepal, Vietnam, Tibet, Mongolia, and in some parts of Siberia and India. Within these broad distinctions, however, are other Buddhist traditions that have been shaped by historical events or developed out of cultural change, such as Tibetan Buddhism and the Japanese Soka Gakkai

BUDDHISM AROUND THE WORLD

Today Buddhism is the fourth-largest religion in the world, practiced by over 350 million people (although its decline and later resurgence in Communist countries have made the numbers hard to quantify). From its beginning Buddhism spread rapidly, southward and eastward to Sri Lanka, Myanmar (Burma), Thailand, and other countries in Southeast Asia, and north and east through the Himalayan region into China, Korea, and Japan. While Buddhism waned in India in the eleventh century and was suppressed by communism in the twentieth century, it persisted as the leading religion in Japan, Korea, Myanmar, and Sri Lanka. Modern Buddhism thrives in Europe and North America and in some parts of India, Pakistan, Bangladesh, and Nepal.

Buddhism's growing popularity around the world today may be in part due to its combination of ancient traditional beliefs—karma, transmigration, and enlightenment—and its emphasis on personal spiritual growth and the timeless challenges of living in the world. Although it has an ancient monastic tradition, Buddhism is not deity-based and is as much a philosophical system as it is a religion. Its fundamental goal is the transcendence of suffering and the spiritual enlightenment that comes of that liberation (nirvana). The Buddha's fundamental teachings, the Four Noble Truths, the Eightfold Path, and the ethical code of the Five Precepts, have been effectively incorporated by a wide range of nationalities and cultures and continue to be as relevant to human beings in the twenty-first century as they were to Buddha's contemporaries 2,500 years ago.

THE THREE JEWELS

Official commitment to Buddhism is made through reciting the Three Jewels (or Three Refuges, as they are also known): "I take refuge in the Buddha, I take refuge in the dharma, I take refuge in the sangha" (respectively the Buddha, his teachings, and the wider enlightened Buddhist community). This is carried out in a formal ceremony performed in a Buddhist temple.

A symbol representing the Three Jewels of Buddhism: the Buddha, the dharma, and the sangha, or worship community.

BUDDHISM TODAY

Twenty-first-century Buddhism is a diverse and varied practice. All Buddhists adhere to the fundamental Buddhist philosophy, but they may differ in their interpretation and traditions. And while the increasingly diverse

school. Mahayana Buddhist practice places a greater emphasis on ritual, prayer, chanting, and devotional offerings than does the Theravada school, and the image or form of the Buddha takes a central place in the home and temple. The Theravada school, or Southern Buddhism, as it is sometimes called, is the oldest branch of Buddhism and considers itself the closest to the Buddha's original teachings. Theravada Buddhism has a strong monastic tradition and stresses the importance of meditation and personal responsibility for spiritual growth. Monastic life is regarded as an ideal among Theravada Buddhists, and monasteries are supported entirely by charitable donations from the lay community.

The sixteenth-century Erdene Zuu monastery was the first Buddhist monastery to be established in Mongolia, during the second diffusion of Tibetan Buddhist teachings.

Buddhist Festivals and Customs

Buddha encouraged communal gatherings as a way to promote unity among his followers, and festivals and ceremonial traditions are an integral part of modern Buddhist life. The Buddhist year contains a large number of festivals, from major events celebrated by all Buddhists to smaller regionally defined festivals and customs. In addition each country or region brings its own particular traditions to these celebrations. Buddhist festivals celebrate all aspects of the life of Buddha. They are joyful occasions, typically a mixture of reflection, celebration, rituals, and charitable giving.

Statues of Buddha and bodhisattvas are decorated with paper flowers on the Japanese holiday of Hanna Matsuri, a festival honoring the infant Buddha.

A Chinese carving depicts the myth of the infant Buddha bathing in perfumed waters. On Buddha Day, Buddhists bathe statues of Buddha to purify themselves.

Buddha Day

The most important Buddhist festival is Wesak, or Buddha Day, which commemorates Buddha's birth, enlightenment, and death. Buddha Day is celebrated in many different ways across Asia, is known by several names, and even takes place on different dates. Buddha Day is traditionally a time of renewal, houses are cleaned and repainted, new clothes are worn, offerings of (vegetarian) food, candles, and flowers are made to monks, and special Wesak lanterns made of paper and wood are lit. Often caged birds and animals are ceremonially released. During this time Buddhists attend the temple, and the Buddhist flag is raised. In many countries Buddha Day includes the Bathing the Buddha ritual, a symbolic purification ceremony in which fragrant liquids are poured over statues of the infant Buddha. In Japan the flower festival Hanna Matsuri, which takes place on April 8, similarly honors the infant Buddha. Legend has it that perfumed waters bathed the infant Buddha and his mother, and participants of the festival decorate the statues with flowers and pour scented tea over the statues to commemorate the miraculous event.

On Buddha Day in Thailand, shrines and statues are festooned with flowers, and statues of the Buddha are carried outside, where participants holding lit candles circle the Buddha three times, while in China unique cultural elements like the dragon dance are incorporated into the festival.

Holy Days and Festivals

On Magha Puja, or Sangha Day, the spiritual Buddhist community of the enlightened is honored. This is a joyful festival in which gifts are given and lamps are lit to symbolize commitment to Buddhism.

Asalha Puja, or Dharma Day, occurs during the full moon in July. A quiet, reflective festival spent in meditation and in reading from the

scriptures, Dharma Day celebrates Buddhist teachings and is an expression of gratitude that he shared his knowledge with the world.

The end of the monsoon in October and November is marked with the Kathina festival. This is a formal ceremony celebrated by Theravada Buddhists in Thailand, Sri Lanka, and Myanmar, in which cloth is donated to the monastic communities to be made into robes. In Thailand the Loy Krathong festival is celebrated by floating bowls made of leaves and containing lit candles, flowers, and incense sticks along the rivers, taking away bad luck as they go.

Indian Buddhists celebrate the Madhu Purnima festival, commemorating Buddha's time in the wilderness when he was sustained by foods brought by an elephant and a monkey (who brought him honey). Participants honor this occasion by presenting offerings of honey to the monasteries.

Buddha's death in a state of perfect enlightenment is celebrated by Mahayana Buddhists in the Parinirvana festival (also called Nirvana Day). This is a day for meditation and reflection on mortality and a time to remember the recently deceased.

The Buddhist Calendar

With the exception of Japanese Buddhism, which follows the Western calendar, the Buddhist year is organized around the lunar calendar, which begins each month at the new moon. A month therefore lasts twenty-nine or thirty days, and each year on the Buddhist calendar is ten days shorter than the Western year. New-moon days are of special significance to Buddhists and are usually chosen for festivals and religious ceremonies. The Buddhist New Year occurs at different times from country to country, according to tradition. The Tibetan New Year, Losar, takes place in February and is the most important festival in the Tibetan Buddhist calendar. Losar is both a family affair and a public holiday involving the entire Buddhist community. Cleansing and purification rituals are performed, houses are cleaned and whitewashed, new clothing is worn, and gifts are exchanged. Special ceremonies are held in the monasteries, which are lavishly decorated for the occasion, and there is feasting and dancing. Tibet's largest religious festival, the Monlam prayer festival, used to draw thousands of monks and pilgrims to celebrate at the Jokhang Temple in Lhasa, where on the last day the Dalai Lama would perform the Buddhist service. The festival is banned today by the Chinese authorities but is being revived in India, where newly established monasteries carry on the tradition.

Saffron-robed Buddhist monks watch a Cham dance, a ritual enactment of holy events or a moral lesson performed on the Bhutan festival of Tsechu.

Modern Buddhism

LIKE ALL BELIEF SYSTEMS based on ancient scriptures, Buddhism faces the challenge of reconciling its teachings and codes of conduct with the complexities of contemporary life. The emphasis on personal responsibility and individual growth provides Buddhists with a greater degree of freedom than more prescriptive religions might allow, but tradition and cultural context also play a major role in the practical application of Buddhism in the modern world. Buddhist attitudes vary considerably from region to region, especially between the more orthodox Buddhist countries and Buddhists in the West.

Although Buddha himself lived in India, the religion named after him is dominant today only in certain neighboring areas, particularly Bhutan, Nepal, the Tibetan region of China, and most of Southeast Asia. Japan also appears predominately Buddhist, although the tradition has blended there with Shinto. Elsewhere, Buddhists are a minority, with three different schools reigning in different regions.

A Japanese zen garden. Zen gardens have become popular in the West, so much so that many non-Buddhists use them for simple aesthetic reasons; as such, they represent both Buddhism's growing appeal worldwide and the challenges such popular appeal can raise for the tradition's integrity.

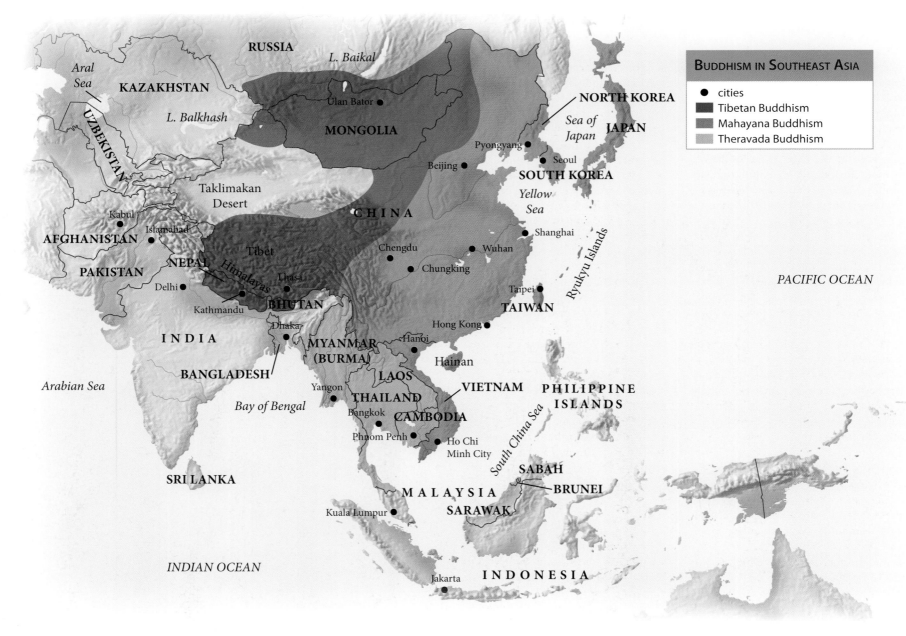

BUDDHISM IN SOUTHEAST ASIA

- • cities
- Tibetan Buddhism
- Mahayana Buddhism
- Theravada Buddhism

Buddhist monks pray together in a temple. While red robes are usual among Tibetan monks, yellow is more common in East Asian Buddhism; both colors traditionally indicate cheap cloth in their respective areas and thus the Buddhist's desire to transcend worldly concerns.

What is the appropriate behavior for a man or a woman in the midst of this world, where each person is clinging to his piece of debris? What is the proper salutation between people as they pass each other in this flood?
—BUDDHA

BUDDHIST ETHICS IN THE TWENTY-FIRST CENTURY

The Buddhist moral code is built upon the Five Precepts defined by Buddha 2,500 years ago. Stated simply, these are

Do not kill
Do not steal
Do not misuse sex
Do not lie
Avoid intoxication

Monks and nuns adhere strictly to the Five Precepts, but for the laity they serve more as a general guide to living a spiritually healthy life. Attitudes toward social issues such as abortion, the death penalty, homosexuality, adultery, and euthanasia, for example, vary considerably from country to country. There is no single official Buddhist position on these issues and no country in which Buddhism functions as a state religion. In strongly Buddhist countries, this can lead to the conflict of having state laws—capital punishment, for instance—run directly counter to Buddhist

precepts, such as "Do not kill." This first and foremost precept characterizes Buddhist life and is applied to all issues surrounding contraception, birth, and death, but it is not absolute. Buddhists consider life to begin at conception, so preventive contraception methods are approved, since they do not kill at a cellular level. On the other hand, the Dalai Lama has publicly stated that abortion should be considered case by case. There are, of course, no direct teachings by Buddha with regard to modern science.

"Do not kill" applies to all sentient beings, and for this reason many Buddhists are vegetarian. However, Buddhist are not necessarily opposed to scientific experimentation on animals for the purpose of alleviating human suffering, and in general they hold positive views on modern scientific advancements such as organ donation. An important factor in shaping Buddhist views on difficult issues is the belief in karma and in reincarnation. Questions of suicide and voluntary euthanasia, for example, are considered from the perspective of the negative effects on karma and their implications in the next incarnation, as well as from a strictly moral standpoint.

WOMEN IN THE BUDDHIST WORLD

Buddha's unprecedented inclusion of women into the monastic order ran counter to the patriarchal Indian culture he lived in, one in which women were regarded as inferior to men. Regardless of this, Buddhist nuns (*bhikkhunis*) have historically taken second place to monks (*bhikkhus*). The Sakyadhita International Association of Buddhist Women, established in 1987, attempted to address the inequality and hardships faced by Buddhist nuns, particularly those living in traditional patriarchal societies. Since then, greater emphasis has been given to the education and welfare of Buddhist nuns, and a vigorous international Buddhist women's organization has emerged, promoting equality for women

among all cultures and traditions. The rules for Buddhist nuns are more stringent and numerous than those for monks, but like monks, the nuns shave their heads and lead a life of strict celibacy. Their robes come in a wide variety of colors, although in Theravadan countries nuns are discouraged from wearing the traditional saffron robes of monks. Tibetan nuns are excluded from full ordination as bhikkhunis and are permitted only as novices. Full ordination is still opposed in some countries, such as Thailand, but is practiced in China, Taiwan, and increasingly in the West. Life as a Buddhist nun varies according to region and custom and ranges from the ascetic contemplative life to active community involvement and leadership roles. American Buddhism is particularly distinctive for the high number of women among its members.

Despite the cultural constraints experienced by women in some Buddhist countries, many significant contributions to society have come from innovative Buddhist nuns and laity alike. One example is Mae Chee Khunying Kanitha Wichiencharoen, a Buddhist nun who for over twenty years provided shelter and safety for tens of thousands of abused women and children in Bangkok, Thailand. In addition she used her training as a lawyer to help introduce legislation in Thailand furthering women's equality and co-founded of the Association for the Promotion of the Status of Women.

A Nepalese nun. Like Buddhist monks, Buddhist nuns shave their heads upon ordination.

DALAI LAMA

Although he is the spiritual leader of Tibetan Buddhism, the Dalai Lama is for many the human face of Buddhism today. Tenzin Gyatso (born Lhamo Dhondub in 1935) is the Fourteenth Dalai Lama and head of the Tibetan government-in-exile. He fled to India after the failed uprising in Tibet against Chinese rule in 1959 and has been living in exile ever since. As the first Dalai Lama to travel to the West, he is responsible for increased interest in Buddhism and raised awareness of Tibet's political crisis. He was awarded the Nobel Peace Prize in 1989 for his contribution to world harmony and to interfaith dialogue, and he is an important voice for tolerance and compassion around the world.

JAINISM
The Sanctity of Life

Two women, members of the Svetambara sect of Jainism, participate in the ritual ceremony of eightfold puja, laying out rice, fruit, and other goods.

CENTRAL TO JAINISM from its earliest conception to its modern-day form is the practice of nonviolence of all kinds (*ahimsa*)—physical, mental, and verbal. Jains believe that every living thing has a soul and that it is therefore sacred. The five core vows, together with the supreme guiding principle of *ahimsa*, are adhered to by both the laity and monks and nuns alike, though for practical purposes the vows practiced by the laity are of a moderated, less demanding form. Jain monks and nuns today still practice an austere ascetic lifestyle based on the renunciation of desires and the attainment of spiritual detachment from all worldly possessions and from physical discomfort. They do not wear shoes (some Jains forgo clothes completely), they reject all forms of mechanical transportation, and every part of their daily life is spent exercising the greatest care not to harm or disturb any living thing. Monks and nuns sweep the ground before taking each step, wear a muslin mask over their mouths to prevent accidental swallowing of insects, fast regularly and for lengthy periods, practice celibacy, and depend entirely on charity for their food.

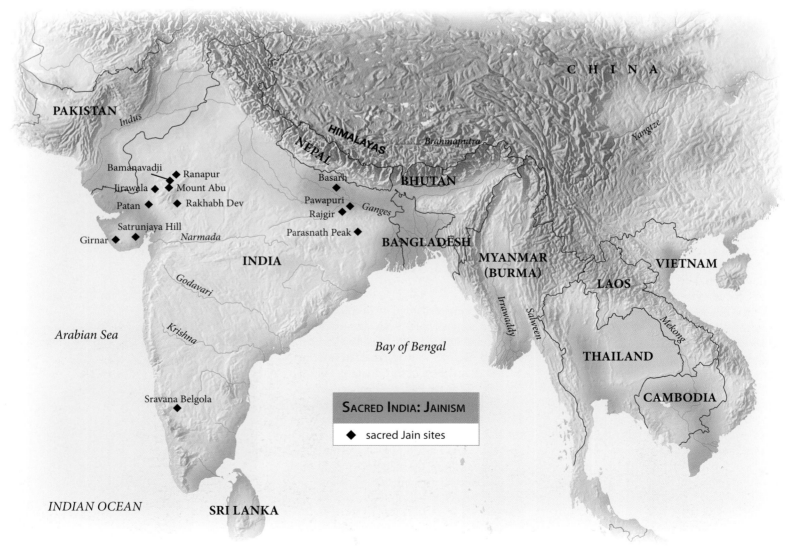

Although Jainism has spread beyond the Indian subcontinent, it is in its traditional homeland that most Jains, and all the most significant Jain holy sites, can be found.

SACRED INDIA: JAINISM
◆ sacred Jain sites

JAINISM TODAY

For modern-day Jains, adherence to nonviolence in all forms means keeping a strict vegetarian diet and a broad outlook on life based upon doing no harm. In practical terms this extends to avoiding clothing or food that in its production has caused harm to living things, and to not working in industries that harm or exploit living beings or whose by-products or intended use could cause injury. For contemporary Jains this often translates into working with organizations that aim to make positive change in the world, as long as it is through nonviolent means. Jainism also promotes equality among living things. For this reason it is relatively gender neutral, with the exception of the Digambara sect. Digambar Jains believe that nonattachment to temporal possessions extends to clothing, and so they practice total nudity. Because nakedness among Jain women would lead to distraction of men and possible sexual abuse, and because women raise children, they are considered less likely to attain the detachment required for enlightenment and therefore occupy a lower position than men.

WORSHIP AND FASTING

Jainism does not recognize a supreme creator or a single founding prophet, and it has no living figurehead. The twenty-fourth *tirthankara*, Mahavira, born in 599 BCE, is the most recent in a long succession of tirthankaras and is the founding teacher of Jainism in its current form. Jains revere the tirthankaras ("ford builders," because they ford the river of rebirth) for their teachings and exemplified virtues, not for their embodied form. The long, difficult path to enlightenment is regarded as an individual journey, and worship at Jain temples is purely personal. Jain temples serve to strengthen community bonds as much as they offer a place to focus on spiritual practice. For most Jains their religion is an integral part of daily life, governed by their core beliefs of helping others, doing no harm, controlling one's desires, having minimum possessions, promoting tolerance, and practicing forgiveness, and

each day is punctuated by prayer, meditation, and reading of the scriptures. Fasting among Jains is commonly practiced as a purification rite and also as penance for transgression or mistakes. An extreme form of this is *santhara*, fasting until death. This is usually practiced by elderly Jains who feel death is approaching and who stop taking all food and water. This is a cause for joy and celebration among Jains, who view the practice as a purification and greater spiritual readiness for death, but it is a subject of controversy in India today, where over 200 people die each year from this practice. Suicide and euthanasia are illegal in India, and members of the legal profession who believe santhara belongs to these categories have attempted to outlaw the practice.

JAINISM WORLDWIDE

Jainism is one of the smallest important world religions. However, its contribution to the development of Indian culture and philosophy is profound. Unlike Buddhism, Jainism did not become widespread and remains largely contained within India, where Jains account for less than 2 percent of the population. There are approximately six million followers of Jainism

worldwide. The largest Jain communities outside India are in East Africa, North America, and western Europe. Jains in the United States number over 75,000; in Europe Jainism is concentrated largely in England, which has about 30,000 followers and the largest temple built for Jain worship outside India.

THE WHEEL OF TIME

Jains do not believe in a supreme creator, but instead view the universe as having no end and no beginning. Time is conceived as a cycle, a wheel spinning endlessly, in whose momentum periods of time known as ages or *aras* are brought to the fore, and then diminish again as the momentum continues the cycle downward; this motion is known as the progressive time cycle and the regressive time cycle. The wheel of the time cycle turns very slowly. The Jains believe we are now living in the fifth ara and that we will not enter into another rotation for approximately 19,000 years. Like followers of many Eastern religions, Jains believe in reincarnation, and the ultimate goal of Jainism

In addition to the swastika, the open hand called the *chakra* is a primary symbol of Jainism. It is intended to represent the nonviolence principle of ahimsa.

is to escape the endless cycle of transmigration and to transcend to eternal disembodied bliss. The revered tirthankara Mahavira (b. 599 *BCE*), is the last in the present rotation containing twenty-four tirthankaras. Jains believe this is just one in an infinite number of rotations containing infinite incarnations of tirthankaras.

A statue of Mahavira, the primary holy figure of Jainism, sits in Delhi, India. His meditative pose suggests he has attained *moksha* (complete peace or liberation), the ultimate goal of Jain belief.

SIKHISM
Modern Sikhism

A Sikh man in Delhi, India, displays some of the "five Ks" that announce his faith: the *kesh* (his hair is tucked into his turban), a *kirpen*, sheathed on his chest, and a *kara* around his left wrist.

Although it is the youngest of the major religions to emerge in northern India, Sikhism is today one of the most widely dispersed. During the colonial period, British aristocrats brought Sikhs to other parts of the British Empire in Africa and Southeast Asia, as skilled laborers; since then Sikhs have traveled on their own accord to nearly all parts of the globe.

ONE OF YOUNGER RELIGIONS OF SOUTH ASIA, Sikhism was founded at the dawn of the sixteenth century by Guru Nanak (1469–1539) in the Punjab area of northern India that now straddles India and Pakistan. To a large degree Sikhism was born out of a rejection of Hinduism and has a distinct credo of a very different nature. Guru Nanak's teachings were further developed by nine successive gurus over a period of approximately 200 years until 1699, when, under the leadership of the tenth guru, Gobind Singh, Sikhism emerged as a fully formed independent religion.

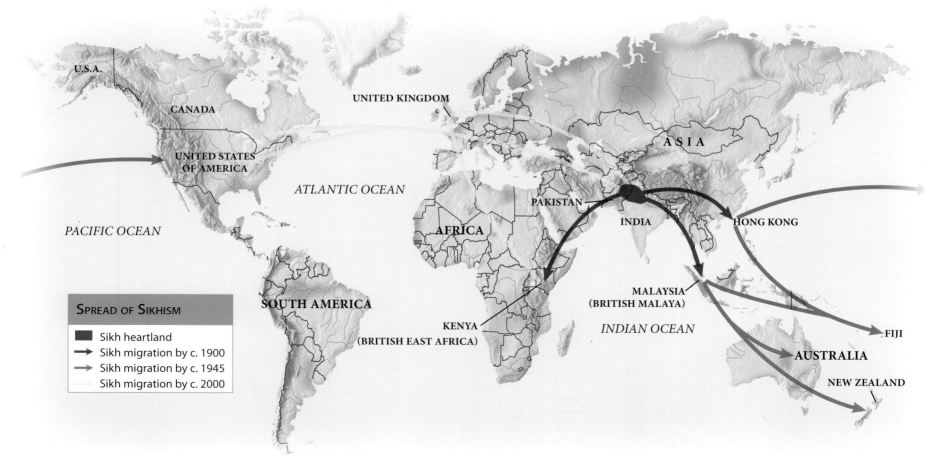

SPREAD OF SIKHISM

- ■ Sikh heartland
- → Sikh migration by c. 1900
- → Sikh migration by c. 1945
- → Sikh migration by c. 2000

U.S.A.

CANADA

UNITED KINGDOM

UNITED STATES OF AMERICA

ATLANTIC OCEAN

PACIFIC OCEAN

ASIA

PAKISTAN

INDIA

HONG KONG

AFRICA

SOUTH AMERICA

KENYA
(BRITISH EAST AFRICA)

MALAYSIA
(BRITISH MALAYA)

INDIAN OCEAN

FIJI

AUSTRALIA

NEW ZEALAND

Worshippers flock to the Golden Temple in Amritsar, India, holiest of holy places of Sikhism and in the religion's heartland: the Punjab region.

The lord can never be established nor created; the formless one is limitlessly complete in Himself.
—GURU NANAK

SIKH BELIEF

Like Hindus, Sikhs believe in reincarnation and adhere to the notion of karma, but thereafter the two religions follow very different paths. Sikhism is a strictly monotheistic religion. Furthermore, Sikhs believe God is without form—human or otherwise—and is neither male nor female. Sikhs believe that God is essentially unknowable and that God is present in nature and in all living things; therefore, prayer and practicing universal love are the only ways to achieve closeness to God. Sikhs try to uphold three duties: to always remember God; to live a life of honesty and integrity; and to share with others. The Sikh founder, Guru Nanak, rejected the Hindu caste system, and the Sikh religion is based on equality among all people, and between men and women. The main thrust of Sikh practice, after reverence for God, is good conduct in life. Sikhs attach great importance to positive contribution to society and to selfless devotion to others, and charitable giving is written into the religion. Selflessness and overcoming the ego are integral to Sikhism and are considered necessary as the only way to move toward a union with God. To this end, Sikhs practice a from of meditation called *mukti*.

FESTIVALS AND CEREMONIES

Sikhs are dismissive of "empty" rituals and superstitions, but their religion is rich with festivals and traditions. Major festivals in the Sikh calendar are Diwali (shared by Sikhs, Hindus, and Jains), Vaisakhi (the Sikh New Year), Hola Mahalla, and the Gurpurbs, which commemorate the lives of the gurus. Diwali is the biggest festival and is especially meaningful to Sikhs, as it also celebrates the release from prison in 1619 of the sixth guru, Hargobind Singh, along with fifty-two Sikh princes. The Golden Temple in Amritsar was lit up in celebration of Guru Hargobind's release. At Diwali—also known as the Festival of Lights—Sikhs spring-clean their homes, buy new clothes, give gifts, celebrate with fireworks, and decorate their homes with lights, continuing the tradition inaugurated centuries earlier at the Golden Temple. Attendance at a Sikh temple or *gurdwara*, "house of the guru," is unstructured, since worship can be either a communal or private affair. There are no iconographic or ritual objects in the temple, and no priests. Both men and women, depending on qualification and the nature of the ceremony, perform Sikh ceremonies.

THE FIVE KS

Baptism into the Sikh faith occurs at the age of awareness. The Amrit Sanskar, or Amrit ceremony, is central to becoming a true member of the Sikh faith and is when Sikh men take on the five Ks (symbolic objects each beginning with the letter *K*) that identify them to the world as Sikhs. These are: *kesh*, long hair wrapped under a turban (Sikh men and women are forbidden to cut any hair on their bodies); *kanga*, a small wooden comb symbolizing care and cleanliness; *kara*, a plain steel bracelet symbolizing the eternal nature of God; *kachera*, cotton shorts that represent chastity; and the *kirpan*, a ceremonial steel sword symbolizing the Sikh's duty to defend the faith. The five Ks identify the Sikh as a true member of the Khalsa Panth—the community of "soldier saints" conceived and initiated by the tenth guru, Gobind Singh, in 1699.

THE WRITTEN GURU

The holy lineage of Sikh gurus ended with the tenth guru, Gobind Singh, who decreed that from thereafter the Sikh holy book, the Guru Granth Sahib, also known as the Adi Granth, would fulfill the role of a living guru and be the ultimate Sikh authority. Although not worshipped as an idol, the book is venerated by Sikhs as an eternal guru.

THE SIKH CALENDAR

The Nanakshahi calendar, developed by a Canadian Sikh and officially introduced in 2003, is a very new component of the Sikh religion and an important step in asserting Sikh independence from Hinduism. It is a solar calendar, which marks year one as the year of Guru Nanak's birth. There are as many as 20 million Sikhs in the world today, and Sikhism constitutes the fifth largest religion. The separatist movement calling for an independent Sikh state in Punjab has strong support from Sikhs in Britain and North America.

THE TEN GURUS OF SIKHISM

1. Guru Nanak (1469–1539)
2. Guru Angad (1504–52)
3. Guru Amar Das (1479–1574)
4. Guru Ram Das (1534–81)
5. Guru Arjan (1563–1606)
6. Guru Hargobind (1595–1644)
7. Guru Her Rai Sahib (1630–61)
8. Guru Harkrishnan Sahib (1656–64)
9. Guru Tegh Bahadur (1621–75)
10. Guru Gobind Singh (1666–1708)

The first great guru and founder of Sikhism, Nanak, was born to Hindu parents in the village of Talwandi. At thirteen he rejected the traditional Hindu caste system, and in later life he traveled across India spreading the fundamental Sikh tenets of love for all and devotion to one God. The fifth guru, Arjan, laid the foundation of the Golden Temple at Amritsar and was the first Sikh martyr, tortured to death on charges of blasphemy against the Hindu and Muslim faiths. At five years old, Guru Harkrishnan Sahib (eighth guru) was the youngest appointed guru, who died three years later at the age of eight. The ninth guru, Tegh Bahadur, was the second Sikh martyr, publicly beheaded on the orders of the Mughal emperor Aurangzeb. The tenth, last, and most influential guru, Gobind Singh, was a warrior guru who introduced the five Ks to the Sikh religion and in 1699 created the Khalsa Panth, which is commemorated as the official birth date of the Sikh religion.

DAOISM
Daoism Today

DAOISM CAME INTO BEING IN CHINA around the same time as Confucianism, and together with Buddhism it is one of the three great religions of China. Its teachings are derived from a text called the *Dao De Jing*. For many years authorship of the *Dao De Jing* was attributed to a fourth-century BCE sage, Laozi, a figure compared to Confucius, and whose birth and life are shrouded in legend. (Laozi, which translates as "Old Master," is an honorary name.)

Scholars today, however, generally believe that the *Dao De Jing* derives from an earlier period, possibly the sixth century BCE, and is a collection of writings by more than one person. Its teachings are rooted in the most ancient of Chinese beliefs, originating many centuries earlier.

Despite twentieth-century persecution, Daoism is still concentrated in China and, to a lesser degree, in countries historically influenced by Chinese culture. In many places, including China itself, Daoism is merely one element of a complex, organic spirituality, making precise accounting of Daoist practices—not to mention Daoists themselves—difficult.

A Daoist priest in China. Candles and the color red—to which is ascribed positive qualities like luck and longevity—often figure in Daoist rituals.

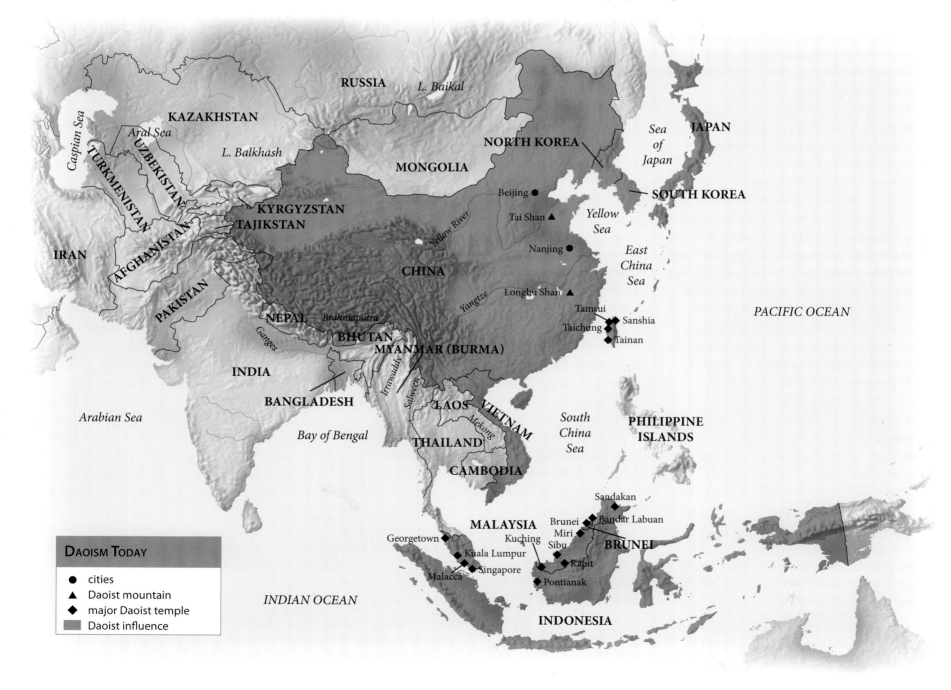

DAOISM TODAY

- ● cities
- ▲ Daoist mountain
- ◆ major Daoist temple
- ▬ Daoist influence

*The way that can be spoken of
is not the constant Way;
The name that can be named
is not the constant Name.
The nameless was at the beginning of heaven and earth;
the named was the mother of myriad creatures.*
—DAO DE JING

THE WAY

Dao literally means "path" or "way," but this is where literalness ends. The concept of Dao is at heart paradoxical, and its first rule is that it cannot be described, cannot be named, and cannot be discussed with words. Dao is an unknowable force that permeates and gives life to the world and all living things contained within it. It can be felt, but it is without form and cannot be known or grasped. Dao as a concept has at its core the mystery of life and connection to that mystery. The practice of Daoism acknowledges the harmony and duality in the universe and the unifying presence of a life force or cosmic energy known as *qi*. Central to Daoism is the concept of yin yang, symbolized by two opposite forms locked together in harmony within a greater whole. Daoists regard this duality as a universal dynamic, a relationship based on complementary forces and balance. The goal of Daoism is the attainment of harmonious union with nature and balance within the body and spirit. Another important aspect of Daoism is *wu wei*, "nonaction" in which one adopts a nonaggressive approach to all aspects of life, letting things take their natural course without interference and allowing for the natural flow of qi.

EASTERN AND WESTERN DAOISM

Daoism in the East is quite different from that practiced in the West. Followed in China for two thousand years, Daoism was relatively unknown in the West until the twentieth century. Daoism's growing popularity in the West is based mainly on its holistic philosophy and on the personal benefits that exercise like tai chi and qigong can offer in promoting health and well-being. However, in China and Southeast Asia, Daoism retains the framework of a large and complex religion, with strong ties to ancient traditions and folk culture, and it is structured around a strong monastic tradition and regular worship in Dao temples. The spiritual aspect of Daoism is integral to the practice, and there are many rituals, ceremonies, and talismans. Chanting and reciting sacred texts as a way to bring spiritual growth and good fortune has always been an important part of Daoist life, beginning in ancient times when most Chinese could not read, and continuing today. Daoism does not recognize a creator god, only the all-pervasive life force of Dao, and the many gods worshipped in Daoism are considered equally governed by this mysterious, intangible force. One of the most popular gods still worshipped today is the Kitchen God, who protects the home and the family.

WORLDWIDE DAOISM

There are an estimated 20 million Daoists worldwide, and 30,000 Daoists live in North America. Daoism is increasingly popular in the West, but the vast majority of adherents live in China, Taiwan, or Southeast Asia. Daoist practice and traditions in northern and southern parts of Southeast Asia have distinct identities, and within the religion as a whole there are many small groups and sects. The rise of communism in China ushered in a new period in China's spiritual life, and Daoism, together with other religious practice, was violently suppressed during the Cultural Revolution of 1966–76. Religious rituals and ceremonies that had been an integral part of Chinese culture for two thousand years were banned and the population "reeducated." Daoism was revived after the Cultural Revolution in a period of renewed religious tolerance, in part because of its philosophical nature and lack of religious authority, but during that time the number of Daoists in China had been greatly reduced. Many people in China today practice a combination of Daoism, Confucianism, and Buddhism.

YIN YANG

The yin yang symbol encapsulates Daoist philosophy, based on the appreciation of natural laws of balance and of the interdependency of opposites. Traditional opposites of masculine and feminine, for example, are awarded equal status, and Daoism is a gender-neutral religion. The black half—yin—is negative, empty, dark, cold, moon, passive, feminine; the white half—yang—is positive, full, light, warm, sun, active, masculine.

The beguilingly simple yin yang symbol embodies the subtle philosophy of Daoism.

DAOISM AND THE BODY

In Daoism the body and spirit are not regarded as distinct, separate entities. Daoists regard the human body as governed by the same dynamics as the universe—as a series of positive and negative forces held in unison by the cosmic life force or energy, qi. Daoists believe that what happens in the body will affect the spirit, and vice versa. Dao mind/body practices are intended to enhance a fluid interconnectedness of the whole self, creating space for cosmic energy to flow and allowing for a greater understanding of the Dao. The physical expression of Dao philosophy comprises a range of rituals and practices, which include breathing exercises (*qigong*); meditation; abstinence from certain foods, alcohol, and negative or harmful emotions; and the ancient practice of tai chi chuan (*taijiquan*). Tai chi emphasizes a balance between the physical and the spiritual through a series of fluid movements that cultivate balance, strength, and calm in the individual. Tai chi is practiced as part of a daily routine throughout China today.

Tai chi, performed alone or in groups, is a regular part of life for millions of people around the world. Its semi-spiritual, semi-physical functions illustrate the depth to which Daoist beliefs have influenced even mostly secular lives.

CONFUCIANISM

The Survival of Confucianism

Since its establishment in China in the sixth century BCE by Kong Fuzi, or K'ung Fu-tzu (whose name was Latinized to Confucius by early Jesuit missionaries), Confucianism has remained a cornerstone of Chinese philosophy. It was cruelly suppressed by the Qin dynasty (221–206 BCE), only to be reinstated and institutionalized by the succeeding Han dynasty (206 BCE–220 CE). As the state orthodoxy, Confucianism permeated all levels of Chinese society. Its influence waned during the Tang dynasty (618–907), when Buddhism reached a peak in China, but resurfaced in an expanded form under the leadership of the philosopher Zhu Xi in the Song dynasty (960–1279). Zhu Xi reenergized Confucianism, synthesizing its core philosophy of ethical behavior with transcendent elements of Buddhism and Daoism, creating a broader form of Confucianism known as Neo-Confucianism. The

Confucianism practiced today derives from this second major school created by Zhu Xi.

Confucianism continued to dominate Chinese thinking up until the twentieth century, but with the founding of the Republic of China and the rise of Chinese communism in the middle of the century, essential Confucian values such as the importance of family, ritual, and propriety were thrust aside. Symbolic of China's ancient feudal system, Confucianism was violently suppressed by the Cultural Revolution of 1966–76, and although it underwent a revival after the Cultural Revolution, it is unlikely that Confucianism will ever again contribute directly to Chinese political life. Despite this, Confucian ideals of social obligation, collective good, and filial obedience continue to exert a powerful influence on contemporary Chinese society.

Spreading far beyond its origins in Qufu, Confucianism has exerted its influence all over eastern Asia, from Japan to Indonesia. Passing through phases of both official sanction and repression in the course of its long history, Confucianism has left an indelible mark on China and many other countries currently or formerly under Chinese influence.

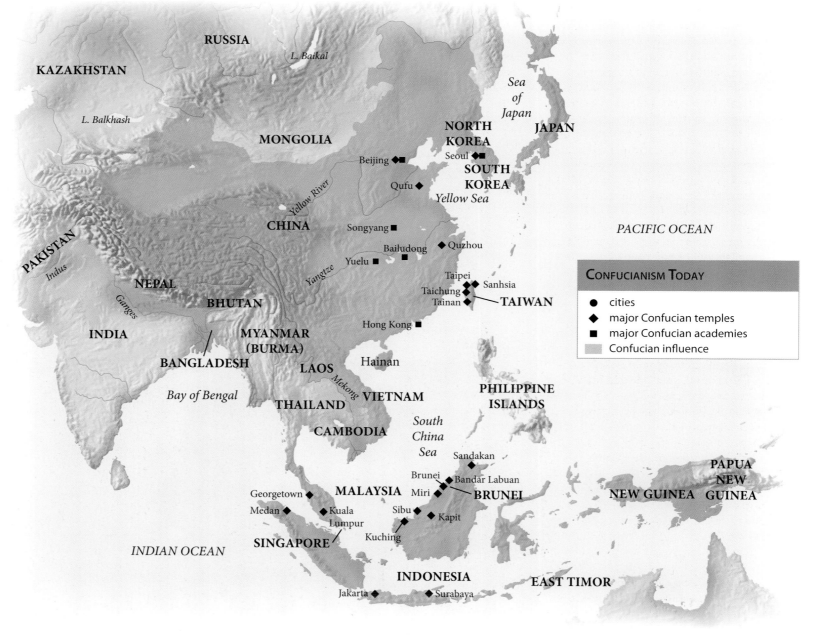

If a man withdraws his mind from the love of beauty, and applies it as sincerely to the love of the virtuous; if, in serving his parents, he can exert his utmost strength; if, in serving his prince, he can devote his life; if in his intercourse with his friends, his words are sincere—although men say that he has not learned, I will certainly say that he has.

—ANALECTS OF CONFUCIUS

CONFUCIANISM TODAY

The legacy of Confucius in China is profound, and it spread beyond Chinese borders across East Asia and into South Asia. Its revival after the Cultural Revolution meant the return in 1990 of the spectacular annual ceremony honoring the birth of Confucius, and other rituals and ceremonies. Reading aloud from the *Analects of Confucius* is once more a daily routine for some elementary school children in China, and the teaching of Confucianism has begun to be reinstated in universities across the country. Confucianism is practiced by an estimated six million people, primarily in China, Korea, Vietnam, and Japan, and by East Asian diasporas around the world.

VISITING A CONFUCIAN TEMPLE

Confucian temples have no priests and offer no spiritual guidance; they function today more as repositories for historic Confucian artifacts than as sacred sites. Early worshippers offered sacrifices to Confucius and performed rituals in his honor, but visitors today attend the temples simply to honor the memory of a great sage. The oldest Confucian temple was constructed soon after his death and is located in his hometown of Qufu in Shandong Province. Many extensions were added to the original structure, and it is today the largest Confucian temple in existence. Preserved as a national heritage site in China, the temple is visited by three million people a year from all over the world. Outside China the majority of temples dedicated to Confucius are located in Korea.

VIRTUE AND WISDOM

Confucianism's complex system of ethics has at its heart the individual pursuit of virtue and wisdom. The aim of Confucianism is to lead a life of virtue exemplified through the practice of its core values:

Li: propriety, ritual, etiquette
Xiao: love for the family, filial piety
Yi: righteousness
Xin: honesty, sincerity, integrity
Ren: benevolence toward others
Zhong: filial obedience and loyalty to the state

A statue of Confucius is enthroned inside the Confucian temple at Shanghai. Silks, gold, and other precious materials honor him as the founder of the tradition and one of China's greatest philosophers.

CONFUCIUS

Confucius was born into a poor family of the upper class, and he knew hardship early on. His father died when he was a small child, and he was raised in poverty. Devoted to learning from an early age, he became famous for his teaching while still a young man. He was dismayed by the moral laxity he saw in his contemporary China, and he traveled the country promoting a set of values that combined ancient teachings with his own ideas about the merits of virtue. There is no discussion of an afterlife in Confucianism, and he stressed the importance of loving virtue for its own sake, without promise of reward or retribution. Confucius believed that humans are born good and that all wickedness and bad behavior are the result of ignorance and a poor environment. He believed deeply in the power of good example of family and of rulers, and that education was the key to virtuous behavior. Instead of asking for intercession by spirits or deities, Confucius promoted self-reflection and self-discipline—moral and physical—in order to improve one's character and to transcend life's difficulties.

Doasan Seowon, a Confucian academy in South Korea built in 1547 and now serving exclusively as a ceremonial facility.

Dragons and the Kitchen God

NEARLY EVERY CHINESE HOME has a shrine to a most important couple—the Kitchen God and his wife. Zao Jun or Zao Shen (Tsao Chun), literally the god of the hearth or stove, is believed to return to heaven once a year to report on the affairs of the household. Families engage in an annual ritual during the lunar New Year as they try to seal the Kitchen God's lips with offerings of sticky sweets. A bad report will engender punishments from the high deity, the Jade Emperor, while a good report, or at least a sweetened version of the truth, will bring prosperity and luck in the coming year. To speed the Kitchen God on his way, his paper effigy is burned and firecrackers give him a festive send-off.

Such exuberant rituals express a deep strain of traditional belief in much of East Asia and form a part of what is commonly called popular religion. Communism dealt a decisive blow to organized religion in the Asian countries where it was established, but in many cases the blow was not decisive enough. Religious practices that had been cherished for millennia in China, Korea, and Vietnam remained alive and are an integral part of daily life.

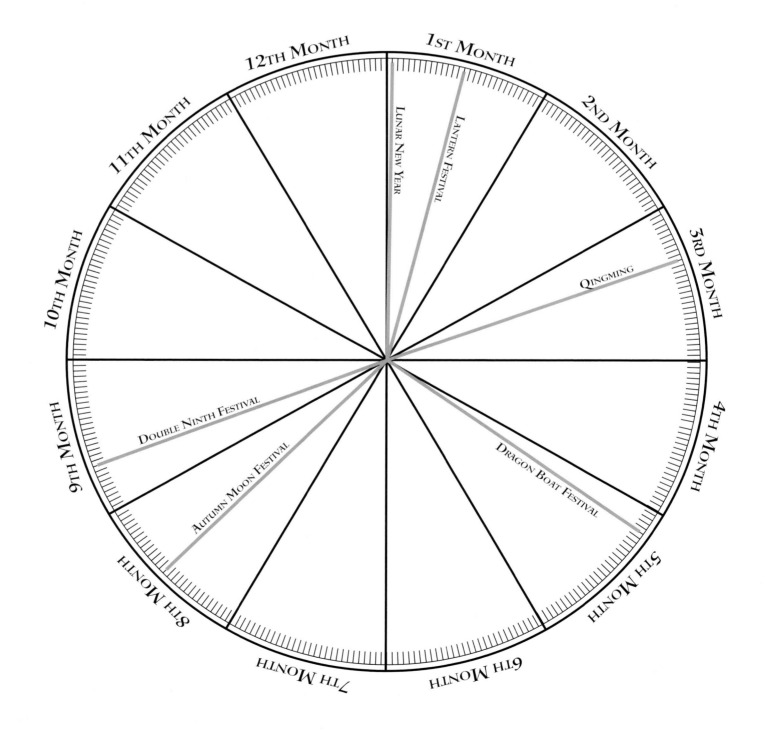

The Chinese calendar is dotted with several major festivals, some of which do not correspond exactly to a purely solar calendar, as the date depends on the lunar cycle. As a result, observance of some of these festivals occurs on different days in different parts of the world.

Legend has it that the emperor was descended from dragons. Looked upon as malevolent in Western lore, dragons were and are considered auspicious in traditional Asian culture, and it is thought to be wrong to depict their harm.

GODS, ANIMALS, AND ANCESTORS

East Asian popular religion incorporates ancient beliefs that also figure in the teachings of Confucianism, Daoism, and Buddhism. In their popular form, these truths are presented in simple, allegorical forms drawn from mythology, often using animals to represent various concepts. The forces of yin and yang are shown as a dog and a rooster, respectively. The dragon represents the power of Shangdi, or the god of heaven, while the tiger embodies potent yang energy. Evil or demonic forces take the form of five commonly reviled creatures—the spider, snake, toad, centipede, and lizard. Mythical birds, dragons, fish, and other animal spirits abound, especially in Chinese folk religion.

The pantheon of popular deities is long and varied and includes the demon-catcher Zhong Kuai (Chung K'uei). Household gods are also numerous, and each city or town has a protector deity, called a Cheng Huang. The gods of happiness, wealth, and longevity are often depicted as a threesome. The latter, Shou

Xing (Shou Hsing), also called Shou Lao, is a particular favorite. White-bearded Shou Xing is usually shown with a long gnarled staff, a bald, bulging forehead, and holding a peach, a Daoist symbol of immortality.

FESTIVALS AND RITUALS

The cycles of the year are celebrated in East Asia with great color and fanfare. Of the many festivals, the following are the most important.

- **Lunar New Year** (also called the Spring Festival)
  Falling on the first day of the first lunar month (usually in late January or early February), the festival is celebrated with family reunions, meals planned around symbolic foods, and parades that include lion dances.

- **Lantern Festival**
  On the first full moon of the lunar New Year, people light colorful lanterns and eat sweet rice dumplings, which symbolize reunion. This festival marks the end of lunar New Year.

- **Qingming (Ching Ming), or Tomb-Sweeping Day**
  A day to honor and mourn ancestors and to offer sacrifices to the dead. Usually falling around April 5, this spring celebration is sometimes called Pure Brightness Day.

- **Dragon Boat Festival (Duanwu)**
  This festival falls on the fifth day of the fifth lunar month, usually in June. Dragon-boat races and sampling of zongzi, pyramid-shaped dumplings, are favorite activities for this summer celebration.

- **Autumn Moon Festival**
  This harvest festival falls in lunar midautumn, usually in September. Lantern parades under the full moon and eating fancy moon cakes are among the many activities on this popular holiday.

- **Double Ninth Festival**
  The ninth day of the ninth lunar month is set aside to honor and care for the elderly. In order to dispel the dangerous yang energy believed to fall on this day, families hike up mountains and drink chrysanthemum tea.

The Land of the Kami

JAPAN IS A COUNTRY that takes great pride in its ceremonial traditions and ancestral heritage, so it is not surprising that its ancient Shinto rituals are preserved in its modern-day society. Early Shinto saw no distinction between human life and the wider natural world, viewing them as equally sacred, and this philosophy of harmony and reverence for nature played a crucial role in shaping Japan's spiritual identity. In Shinto belief the invisible world is occupied by *kami*—spirits or deities—which are worshipped still in shrines throughout Japan. The husband-and-wife deities Izanagi and Izanami are believed to have given birth to the island nation of Japan, and their descendants are by legend myriad. The kami are viewed as having a generally benign attitude toward people, although some are considered wicked.

The practice of Shinto is inextricably related to the physical features of Japan, and as such it is not a religion that travels easily. Hundreds of shrines on Japan's islands tie the physical world to the divine world, with some of the most major, like those on Mount Fuji, mere pinpricks on a much larger holy landscape.

SHINTO IN MODERN JAPAN

- ● cities
- ◆ Shinto shrines
- ▲ sacred mountains

Sea of Okhotsk

Ainu festivals
■ Abashiri
Asahikawa ■
Sapporo ●
Hokkaido

▲ Osore-yama

Iwaki-san ▲

Sea

of

Japan

Haguro-san ▲

SADO

Tosho-gu ◆

Tate-yama ▲   **Honshu**

JAPAN

Tokyo ● ◆ Meiji-jingu
Mount Fuji ▲

Isumon-no-Oyashiro ◆

Kyoto
Fushimi-Inari ◆   ● Kasuga Shrine
Hiroshima ●   Nara ●
Omme-yama ◆ Ise Shrine
Omme-yama ▲ ◆ Kumano-jinja
Koya-san ▲
Matsuyama ●   Mount Miwa

Tsushima

Kyushu   **Shikoku**
Ama-no-Iwato-Jinja ◆
▲ Aso-san

▲ Kirishima-yama

Korea Strait

PACIFIC OCEAN

Emperor Hirohito with his family in 1941, four years before he was forced to step down as part of Japan's surrender in World War II. The last Japanese emperor, Hirohito had been recognized as semidivine, the descendant of the gods as outlined in Shinto tradition.

There is no place on this wide earth,
Be it the vast expanse of ocean's waste,
Or peak of wildest mountain, sky-caressed,
In which the ever-present power divine,
In even/force of nature's not a shrine.
—FROM THE SENGE-TAKAZUMI-IZUMO SHRINE

SHINTO AND THE JAPANESE IDENTITY

Shinto has no god or founder, no scriptures or commandments, no structured worship or doctrine, and it has no absolutes of right and wrong, believing that humans are born pure and that wicked spirits are the cause of "badness" or impurity. Because Shinto is ritual-based, not belief-based, many Japanese do not consider it a religion at all, but rather a traditional custom based on common practice and shared belief. The arrival of Buddhism and Confucianism in the sixth through eighth centuries, and Christianity later in the sixteenth century, did nothing to weaken early Shinto practice, which incorporated ideas from Buddhism and Confucianism and was able to coexist happily with other religious practice. (It is telling that in 1936 the Vatican issued a declaration allowing Japanese Catholics—a tiny percentage of the population—to practice Shintoism as well as Catholicism, because it viewed Shinto as fulfilling a purpose more civic than religious.) During the Meiji Restoration in the nineteenth century, the status of emperor was elevated to that of a divinity. The Shinto sun goddess Amaterasu, daughter of the creator deities Izanagi and Izanami, was raised to prominence as the emperor's ancient ancestor, thus making Shinto the official state religion. Today approximately 84 percent of the population practices a combination of Buddhism and Shinto.

During the Allied restructuring of Japan after World War II, Emperor Hirohito was forced to renounce his divine status, and all official connection between state and religion was severed. However, Shinto was inseparable from Japanese national and cultural identity, and Shinto worship and rituals are still an integral part of Japanese life. Shinto ceremonies are performed not just in relation to spiritual life, but for secular and practical matters too, such as work, sports, art, politics, and ethics. Shinto is a uniquely Japanese religion, difficult to adhere to outside the country. The vast majority of followers therefore live in Japan, and those who do practice Shintoism overseas are overwhelmingly of Japanese descent. However, challenges raised by the rapid industrial development of the twentieth and twenty-first centuries have brought unprecedented developments in Shinto practice. Concern for the environment, for example, has led Shinto leaders to reach out beyond their borders, seeking international and interfaith dialogue and cooperation.

SHINTO RITUALS

Ritual cleansing is an important aspect of visiting a Shinto shrine. Earlier worshippers washed their bodies in a river before entering a shrine, but today visitors are required only to wash their hands and mouths at specially prepared water troughs outside the shrines. Although Shinto is based on reverence for nature and sees humankind as essentially good and the spirit world as essentially benign, death is considered unclean. For this reason, while a Shinto priest will attend all other rituals and festivals, funerals are performed by Buddhist priests, and there are virtually no Shinto cemeteries. There is no regular schedule or structure to shrine attendance, either; however, it is customary to visit a shrine at significant stages in life and before important events. Each shrine is dedicated to a particular deity. There are many Shinto festivals (*matsuri*) throughout the year, and these are centered on the shrines. Many of these festivals have rural agricultural origins and celebrate the changing seasons and the harvest; others mark the passage of time from childhood into adulthood. Shinto ceremonies are joyful, boisterous, and colorful and include a surprising mix of solemnity and seeming irreverence.

A water trough and ladle designed for the purification ritual, required for entry into many Shinto shrines. Usually, visitors wash only their hands and faces in fulfillment of the requirement.

TRADITIONAL SHINTO WEDDING CEREMONY

Although not as popular today among modern urbanized Japanese couples as it was for previous generations, the traditional Shinto wedding ceremony is still performed. Early Shinto weddings took on various forms, but the ceremony was standardized after the Shinto wedding of Crown Prince Yoshihito and Princess Sado in 1900. The ceremony is small and private, in contrast to the more extravagant and increasingly popular Western-style weddings. It takes place in a shrine and is performed by a Shinto priest, who begins by purifying the couple. The bride wears a traditional plain white silk kimono (*shiro-maku*) and distinctive Shinto headdress adorned with flowers, ornaments, and combs. The large white hood worn over the headdress is called *tsuno-kakush*—literally, "hiding the horns"—and symbolizes the bride's obedience to her husband. The groom wears a similarly plain montsuki kimono and a short haori overcoat bearing the family crest. The couple join in a ceremonial drink of sake (*san san kudo*) and offer sacred *sakaki* twigs to the gods. The ceremony is attended by *miko* bridesmaids dressed in white with red skirts, and by musicians playing traditional Japanese flutes.

A modern wedding ceremony in Japan. The bride wears white and a traditional headdress and can be seen directly behind the bridesmaid, who wears a red skirt.

JUDAISM
World Judaism

ACCORDING TO JEWISH TRADITION, a person is a Jew if his or her mother is Jewish. Statistics, then, count all offspring of Jewish women and have nothing to do with religious beliefs. Some "Jews" may even profess other faiths, and many are agnostics or atheists. The total number of Jews, technically speaking, is about 13.3 million. Of these, 5.5 million live in Israel. The country with the second-largest number of Jews is the United States, with some 5.3 million.

Jews who do profess their faith generally belong to one of several branches: Orthodox (including the Hasidic), Conservative, Reconstructionist, Reform, Humanist, or Liberal. Israel is officially Orthodox, but many Israelis have no religious affiliation.

Orthodox Jews believe that Moses received the entire body of Jewish law, or Torah, from God on Mount Sinai, and they feel obligated to fulfill that law faithfully. Other Jews believe that the law evolved over time in response to historic events. The Orthodox Jews rely on Orthodox rabbis to interpret the Jewish law for them and to adhere to traditional Jewish beliefs. No organ music is allowed during synagogue services, and men and women must sit separately. Furthermore, the Orthodox disapprove of the other branches of Judaism and refuse to recognize their marriages, divorces, or conversions. Some Orthodox groups, such as Hasidic Jews, adhere more strictly to the law than others. Hasidic Jews also follow charismatic rabbis who share the spirit of their founder.

Only a small number of Hasidic Jews survived the Nazi camps of World War II. Characterizing themselves as the "few brands plucked from the fire," they immediately began publishing writings inquiring into the causes of the Holocaust, generally blaming assimilated Jews, Reform Jews, and Zionists. They soon relocated to the United States, where they attracted large numbers of followers through a widespread educational program, and the community has grown significantly.

Only two countries, Israel and the United States, have a Jewish population of more than five million, with numbers falling off sharply in other countries where Jews constitute a significant presence. Nevertheless, Judaism—one of the world's oldest religions—exists now worldwide, and has been at the forefront of major international politics since the early twentieth century.

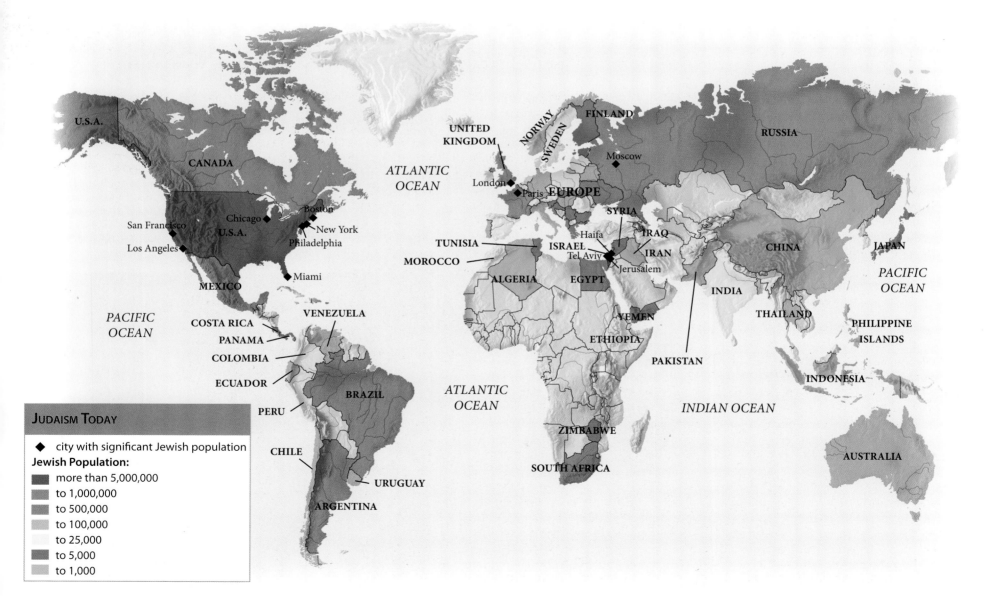

JUDAISM TODAY

◆ city with significant Jewish population

Jewish Population:

- more than 5,000,000
- to 1,000,000
- to 500,000
- to 100,000
- to 25,000
- to 5,000
- to 1,000

And you shall make a lampstand of pure gold. The base and the shaft of the lampstand shall be made of hammered work; its cups, its capitals, and its flowers shall be of one piece with it.... And you shall make the seven lamps for it; and the lamps shall be set up so as to give light upon the space in front of it.

—BOOK OF EXODUS

NON-ORTHODOX JUDAISM

In the early nineteenth century, many western European Jews became dissatisfied with the traditional means of observing their religion and grouped together under the leadership of the German Orthodox Jew Israel Jacobson, who modernized worship services in local synagogues. Subsequently, in 1818, the first official Reform Temple was established in Hamburg, Germany, where the congregation engaged in choral singing, prayed in German as well as Hebrew, and used modern scientific methods to study scripture: instead of assuming that Moses had given them the entire body of Jewish law, they carefully analyzed the texts to trace the probable history of their tradition. Reform Judaism quickly spread throughout Germany and North America. In some places it is known as Liberal or Progressive Judaism.

Conservative Judaism is an outgrowth of the Historical Movement of nineteenth-century Germany that sought a middle path between Reform and Orthodox Judaism. Conservatives emphasize the religion practiced by the people from generation to generation. They see Jewish law and thought as the means to conceive of and worship God, and not simply the heritage of the Jewish people as some more liberal groups hold. Although Jewish law is binding for Conservative Jews, changes can be made—mainly through their Committee of Jewish Law and Standards. Many of the recent changes have expanded the rights of women, including the right to be ordained as rabbis. Conservative Jewish communities are found mainly in the United States.

Reconstructionist Judaism, an offshoot of Conservative Judaism, was initiated by the American rabbi Mordecai Menahem Kaplan

in 1922. It views God not as a supernatural being but as an evolutionary process. Reconstructionists seek to honor traditional Jewish values, yet adapt them to the needs of contemporary society. The community is foremost, and decisions are made collectively rather than by rabbinic rule.

Humanistic Jews view Judaism as a cultural creation and rely on reason, not revelation, for discovering the truth. They believe that human beings can solve their own problems and

derive ethical guidelines from their pursuit of renewal, justice, and happiness. Humanistic Jewish communities are found in the United States, Israel, and Europe. Although they are served by certified leaders, they stress co-operative activities and celebrate traditional holidays and life-cycle rites as secular rather than religious events.

A synagogue in Munich, Germany, which opened its doors in 2006, reflects both the ancient and modern impulses in Judaism in its inspired architecture.

The menorah plays a central role in the celebration of Hanukkah, a yearly festival celebrating the sacred flame in Jerusalem's temple, which lasted for eight nights on a single day's worth of oil. Each evening for a period of eight days, one more candle is added to the menorah and the candles are lit, a ritual reenactment of the myth.

SYMBOLS OF JUDAISM

The star of David, or shield of David (*Magen David*), a figure consisting of two superimposed triangles, is today recognized as a symbol of Judaism, but it originally had nothing to do with either David or Judaism. Originally it was used for decoration or as a magical sign in various ancient civilizations and appears as a strictly decorative design on Jewish tombs and in synagogues. It was probably first associated with David (or rather his son Solomon) in Islamic magical manuscripts. The star was first used to represent Judaism in seventeenth-century Prague and gained popularity only in the nineteenth century, when European Jews were looking for a simple sign to represent Judaism, as the cross represents Christianity. A more ancient symbol of Judaism is the menorah—the lampstand, or candelabrum, with seven lamps that God instructed Moses to place in the Temple, according to the book of Exodus.

Branches of the Christian Church

ALTHOUGH THERE IS PURPORTEDLY only one Christian Church, over the centuries it has been divided into various branches and denominations. All Christians claim to be orthodox, in the general sense that they consider themselves true believers, and also catholic, in the sense that they strive to share their beliefs with all the peoples of the world. However, when the Eastern and Western churches split in the eleventh century, the Eastern Church came to be known as Orthodox (with a capital *O*), while the Western Church took the name Catholic. To these two major branches of the Christian Church a third was added when reformers of the sixteenth century broke away from the Catholic Church. This breach resulted in the third major branch, known as Protestantism because it was originally made up of reformers who protested certain policies and practices of the Catholic Church.

Within each of these three branches are many smaller divisions. Churches loosely characterized as Protestant are by far the most diverse, with an estimated 25,000 faith groups at the end of the twentieth century. One of the reasons for the high number of Protestant Churches is the tendency of Christian groups—especially in Africa and South America—to found local churches that are dissociated from any overseeing body. Other churches result from a splitting of the larger denominations themselves. Protestant Churches are also hard to characterize because many are built on theological beliefs, while others are distinguished by the style of their church governing structure. Among the most prominent denominations, though, are the Anglicans, Lutherans, Presbyterians, Baptists, and Methodists, all of which, in turn, are divided into various subgroups.

WORLD COUNCIL OF CHURCHES

In response to concerns of the wide diversity of Christian bodies, the World Council of Churches was formed in 1948. The council strives to address common concerns of Christians everywhere and promote reconciliation and union among its members. Over the years the council has grown in size and prestige. Currently all the major Protestant and Orthodox bodies are members. The Catholic Church, though not a full member, participates in many of the council's programs. In addition to unity, the council deals with issues of education, human rights, peace and justice, the resettlement of refugees, and emergency relief. Its headquarters are in Geneva, Switzerland.

A small Protestant church in a German immigrant area of Brazil—a country that otherwise is decidedly Catholic. Tension between groups of Christians has fallen since the days of the Reformation, and the Christian community continues to diversify.

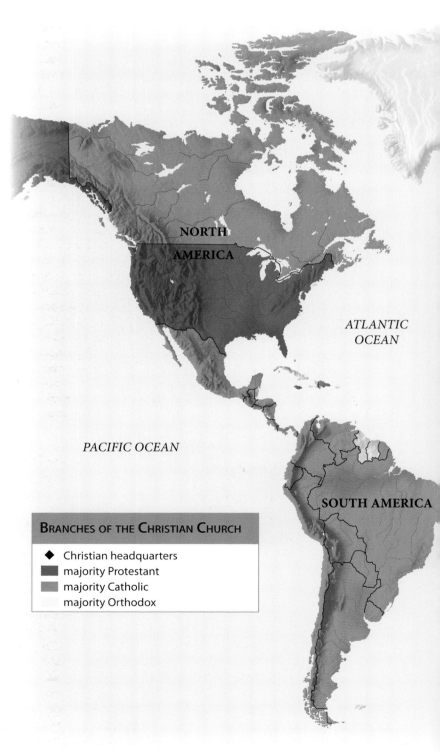

NORTH AMERICA

ATLANTIC OCEAN

PACIFIC OCEAN

SOUTH AMERICA

BRANCHES OF THE CHRISTIAN CHURCH

◆ Christian headquarters
■ majority Protestant
■ majority Catholic
□ majority Orthodox

CHRISTIANITY
The Catholic Church

*There is one body and one Spirit, just as you were
called to the one hope that belongs to your call, one
Lord, one faith, one baptism, one God and Father of us
all, who is above all and through all and in all.*
—From the Letter to the Ephesians

The Roman Catholic Church is the world's largest Christian Church and represents over half of all Christians and one-sixth of the world's population. It is a highly structured institution with a hierarchy made up of priests and bishops. Bishops overseeing major dioceses are known as archbishops, and a certain number of men (mainly archbishops) are given the title of cardinal, elevating their status and giving them the right to vote for the election of a new bishop of Rome—the pope. The pope is considered the successor to the apostle Peter, the first bishop of Rome, and exercises enormous powers in the church. The church looks to him as its highest human authority in matters of faith, morality, and church governance.

In addition to the priests and higher officials, there are large numbers of men and women who belong to religious orders—taking vows to lead a life consecrated to God as teachers, nurses, or contemplatives. Lay Catholics also have some part to play in the church as teachers and ministers of minor rites not reserved to ordained priests.

Pope Benedict XVI, elected to the papacy upon his predecessor's death in 2005, has expressed his interest in reinvigorating Catholicism, especially in regions—notably Europe—that have been in a long period of what the pope considers to be religious decline.

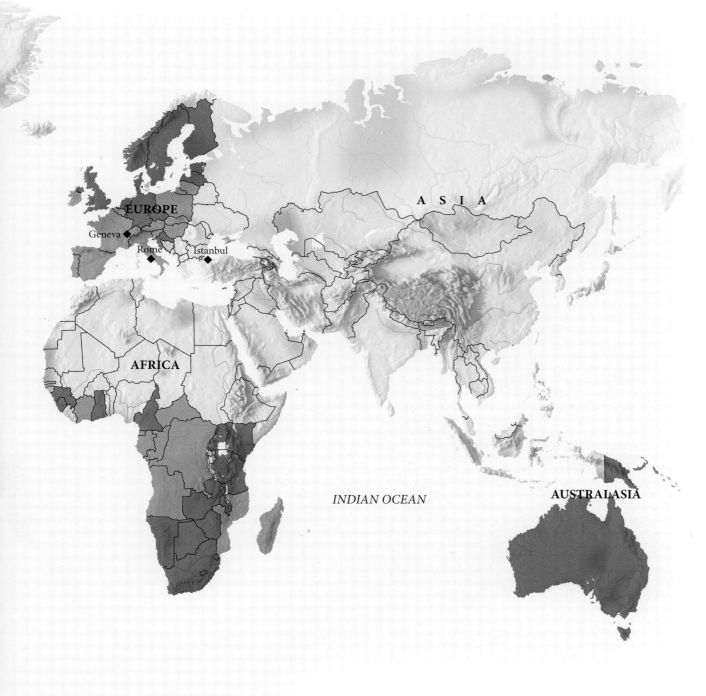

Christianity is the world's largest religion, with more than two billion worshippers worldwide. The religion is split into three major groups—Roman Catholic (or just Catholic), Eastern Orthodox, and Protestant.

Eastern Catholic Churches

Although there is basically only one Catholic Church, it is composed of the Western, or Roman, Church and a number of much smaller Eastern Rite Churches, which have their own administration and distinctive rituals but still fall under the authority of the pope. These churches developed in the early days of Christianity but later separated from the Roman tradition. When they later reconnected with Rome, they were allowed to keep their own rites and customs. For example, Roman Catholic priests are not permitted to marry, but Eastern Catholics do have married priests with families.

There are seven main Eastern Churches, though some of these are further subdivided. The largest, the Byzantine, consists of eleven Eastern European Churches, including Greek and Russian. The other Eastern Churches are Coptic (from Alexandria, Egypt), Armenian, Ethiopian, Maronite (from Antioch), and West and East Syrian.

CHRISTIANITY
Orthodox Churches

THE CHURCHES OF EASTERN EUROPE, Egypt, and Asia that had split off from Rome by the eleventh century are known as Orthodox or Eastern Orthodox. In their worship services they follow the Byzantine Rite, a liturgy that was developed in Constantinople during the days of the Byzantine Empire. All the Orthodox Churches recognize the primacy of the patriarch of Constantinople, although he is not their supreme leader but merely holds an honorary title as head of the Orthodox Churches. In fact, the Orthodox Churches do not obey any common governing figure, but each of the churches has its own head—patriarch, catholicos-patriarch, or archbishop. According to Orthodox theology, the purpose of the Christian life is to attain *theosis*, the mystical union of man with God.

The principal Orthodox Churches are the four Eastern patriarchates—Constantinople, Alexandria, Antioch, and Jerusalem—and the Church of Cyprus, which has been independent since the Council of Ephesus in 431. Since the split with the Roman Catholic Church, nine national churches have been added, most of them carved out of the once vast Patriarchate of Constantinople. They are Russia, Georgia, Greece, Serbia, Romania, Bulgaria, Poland, the Czech Republic and Serbia, and Albania.

Finally, there are some dozen autonomous churches. In an autonomous church the highest-ranking bishop or metropolitan is appointed by the patriarch of the mother church but is self-governing in all other respects. The total number of all the Orthodox Christians in the world is estimated to be anywhere from 100 million to 300 million.

An Eastern Orthodox Church in Ukraine from the second half of the twentieth century. The Soviet Union did not treat its churches kindly, but religious tradition was never eradicated and has now recovered.

ECUMENICAL COUNCILS

For Orthodox Churches the highest authority in matters of both faith and church discipline is not an individual leader, but joint decisions made in ecumenical church councils. These councils are conferences with representatives of all Christian Churches (therefore, ecumenical, from the Greek meaning "the whole inhabited world"). The basis for Orthodox theology comes from dogmatic definitions coined by the seven ecumenical councils held in the third through the eighth centuries in what is now Turkey—three in Constantinople, two in Nicaea, and one each in Ephesus and Chalcedon. Although not considered truly ecumenical, a few councils of Orthodox churchmen in the fourteenth through the seventeenth centuries played an important role in clarifying issues that had remained cloudy.

Most major Eastern Orthodox holy sites are now in Muslim countries, the result both of the collapse of the Byzantine Empire and Muslim supremacy in the region since the fifteenth century. Nevertheless, the Eastern Orthodox Church remains dominant in much of the territory it won in the first millennium and today is one of the three major forms of Christianity.

THE EASTERN ORTHODOX CHURCH

- ● Eastern patriarchies
- ◆ ancient council site
- Eastern Orthodox
- Catholic
- Lutheran
- Muslim

The Anglican Communion

The Church hath power to decree Rites or Ceremonies, and authority in Controversies of Faith: and yet it is not lawful for the Church to ordain any thing that is contrary to God's Word, written.

—*From article twenty of the Thirty-nine Articles of the Church of England*

AFTER KING HENRY VIII SEPARATED his kingdom from the Catholic Church, the English Parliament declared him and his successors head of the Church of England. An official Book of Common Prayer was first published in 1549 (though later revised), and the Thirty-Nine Articles, a statement of doctrine, was approved in 1571. The articles establish guidelines on matters of faith and steer a course between Catholicism and Protestantism. The archbishop of Canterbury is religious leader of the Church of England, though the reigning monarch is still considered its head.

As England pursued its policies of colonialism, the Anglican faith was taken to many parts of the world. This led to the formation of the Anglican Communion, an affiliation of Anglican Churches throughout the world. Some of these churches are known as Anglican, but others, such as the U.S. and Scottish Episcopal churches and the Church of Ireland, prefer separate names. Each church operates autonomously but is in full communion with the Church of England and recognizes the archbishop of Canterbury as the symbolic head of the worldwide communion. Some forty different churches are part of the Anglican Communion, which has some 77 million members.

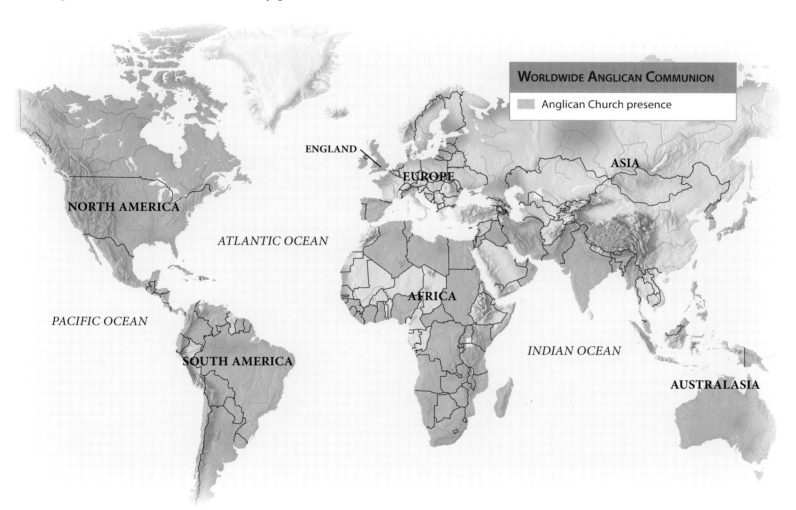

WORLDWIDE ANGLICAN COMMUNION

Anglican Church presence

ENGLAND

EUROPE

ASIA

NORTH AMERICA

ATLANTIC OCEAN

PACIFIC OCEAN

AFRICA

INDIAN OCEAN

SOUTH AMERICA

AUSTRALASIA

Although Anglicans can claim a majority nowhere except in England, Anglican churches can be found all over the world. Currently, the Anglican community is in an uproar over the issue of homosexuality in the clergy, and the church shows signs of fracturing.

The Most Reverend and Right Honorable Rowan Williams, Archbishop of Canterbury and current head of the Anglican Church, has been the mediator and occasional focus of the debate over homosexuality in the church.

HOMOSEXUALITY AND THE CHURCH

Over the past decade or two, many churches in the Anglican Communion have been liberal in accepting homosexual unions and gay clergy, but in recent years the matter has come under fire. In 2003 the Episcopal Church in the United States consecrated Gene Robinson, a gay man, as bishop of New Hampshire, but Anglicans in a number of provinces responded with animosity. The most negative reactions came from central Africa, but a few surfaced in Asia and South America as well—churches together constituting about half of the world's practicing Anglicans. Sides were taken, and the church was in danger of splitting over the matter, but as of 2008 Bishop Robinson had not been removed from office. Some disgruntled Americans withdrew from the U.S. Episcopal Church and realigned themselves with the Churches of Uganda and Rwanda, which initially opposed the appointment. Passionate discussions about the church's position on homosexuality are ongoing.

Lutheran Churches

I ask that men make no reference to my name, and call themselves not Lutherans, but Christians. What is Luther? My doctrine, I am sure, is not mine, nor have I been crucified for anyone.
—MARTIN LUTHER

MARTIN LUTHER'S ATTEMPTS to reform the Catholic Church in the sixteenth century resulted in a separation from the Roman Church and its pope and the formation of a new Christian Church, generally known as Lutheran. During the period of the Reformation, Lutheran churches spread through Germany and Scandinavia, where they were often decreed the state church. Later, Lutheranism spread throughout Europe, and missionaries took the faith to all the major areas of the world. In 1947 most Lutheran bodies were affiliated with the unifying Lutheran World Federation, a global communion of 140 Lutheran churches in 78 countries with nearly 70 million members. Lutheran churches form the largest communion of Protestant churches in the world.

Lutheran doctrine is based on the *Book of Concord* (1580), a compilation of sixteenth-century documents, including the Augsburg Confession of 1577, which outlines the denomination's basic beliefs, and a number of later clarifications of doctrines, and two catechisms written by Luther himself. The basic Lutheran tenets are the importance of scripture and justification by faith alone—that is, a person cannot be saved from the consequences of his sins by performing good works or in any other way, but only by placing his faith in Jesus. Church governance is in the hands of lay leaders, for Luther stressed the idea of a priesthood of all believers. Lutheran churches have retained some Catholic liturgical practices but place more stress on preaching the word of God, as embodied in the Christian scriptures.

LUTHERANS IN NORTH AMERICA

The first Lutherans came to America in the seventeenth century, but their numbers remained small until after 1730, when large numbers of German emigrants brought Lutheranism with them. From then on the Lutheran Church grew rapidly, and many Lutherans were caught up in the Pietistic movement that produced the Great Awakening.

In time America's Lutheran communities began to splinter into many different communions, and this disintegration challenged many Lutherans to make unity a priority. By the late twentieth century, the unity movement showed results, as numbers of smaller communions joined together in reconciliation. By 1988 there were only three major Lutheran church bodies in North America: the Evangelical Lutheran Church in America, the Evangelical Lutheran Church in Canada, and the Lutheran Church–Missouri Synod (one of the few Lutheran bodies not associated with the Lutheran World Federation).

A Lutheran church in Windhoek, capital of Namibia. Named for the primary instigator of the Reformation, Lutheranism developed first in Germany in the sixteenth century but today is a worldwide Christian denomination.

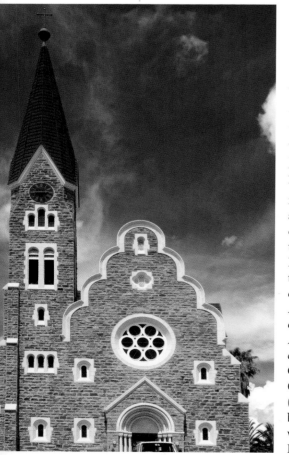

GREENLAND

ICELAND

U.S.A.

CANADA

UNITED STATES OF AMERICA

PACIFIC OCEAN

ATLANTIC OCEAN

SOUTH AMERICA

WORLDWIDE LUTHERANISM AND PRESBYTERIANISM

- Lutheran majority
- substantial Lutheran minority
- Presbyterian majority
- substantial Presbyterian minority

With more than 65 million Lutherans worldwide, the denomination named for the instigator of the Protestant Reformation, Martin Luther, ranks as the second-largest Protestant group (bested only by Baptists). Presbyterianism, founded by another major Reformation leader, John Knox, is significantly smaller, with a majority only in Scotland.

CHRISTIANITY
Presbyterian Churches

Man's chief end is to glorify God, and enjoy Him forever.
—FROM THE WESTMINSTER CONFESSION OF FAITH (1646)

PRESBYTERIANISM IS A FAMILY of Protestant Christian denominations named for the form of church government they favor. As introduced in Scotland by John Knox in the sixteenth century, Presbyterianism was a form of Calvinism; but even though some modern adherents still hold to the theology of John Calvin, today's Presbyterians cover a wide range of theological views. Generally, however, Presbyterian theology emphasizes the authority of God over everything and the necessity of grace through faith in Christ.

Over time the Presbyterians have split into diverse groups based on doctrinal controversies and disagreements about how closely those ordained to church office should agree with the Westminster Confession of Faith. The Westminster Confession, as it is called, is a document that was drawn up in 1646 at Westminster, England, outlining basic Presbyterian beliefs on such issues as worship, doctrine, and church government. A Larger Catechism and a Shorter Catechism were also published at that time. After the Bible, which is considered the supreme authority, the confession and the catechisms are held to present the standard doctrine of the Church of Scotland, and they have been influential within Presbyterian churches worldwide.

John Knox, a contemporary and acquaintance of John Calvin, was a leader in the Protestant Reformation and is widely considered the founder of Presbyterianism.

The Church of Scotland is the mother church for Presbyterians everywhere. North American Presbyterians are affiliated with either the Presbyterian Church (Canada) or with the Presbyterian Church (USA), which works with partner churches and organizations in more than one hundred countries and has missionaries in nearly seventy countries. Worldwide membership in Presbyterian churches is estimated at some fifty million. In addition, many Presbyterian groups have combined with other Protestant groups to form united churches of various types.

PRESBYTERIAN CHURCH STRUCTURE

John Calvin believed that Christ calls a local church to be a community that ministers in his name, and therefore each community must select its ministers by means of a governing council, or presbytery, composed of elected elders. These elders should be lay representatives of good character who are chosen from the congregation. They partake in local pastoral care and in decision-making at all levels. The same conciliar approach is followed for higher levels of decision-making in general assemblies that affect large groups of Presbyterian congregations. Theoretically, Presbyterians are to have no bishops. In actuality, though, some groups in eastern Europe, and a few ecumenically minded groups, do have bishops.

Baptist Churches

Baptists are Christians who believe that only men and women who are prepared to make a personal confession of faith in Jesus Christ should be baptized. Although they have certain links to the Anabaptists of the early Reformation, today's Baptists mainly derive from Christians in seventeenth-century England and Wales, many of who immigrated to America. In the eighteenth and nineteenth centuries the Baptists spread all through the southern United States, finding favor especially among the black population. In the beginning blacks and whites were members—even if on unequal footing—of the same Baptist churches, but by the end of the Civil War the congregations were generally either all black or all white. Black Baptist churches played an important role in the civil rights movement of the 1950s.

Baptist churches are generally autonomous, but individual congregations often link together in associations and unions. The Baptist World Alliance, which was formed in London in 1905, is a fellowship of 214 Baptist conventions and unions, with a membership of 36 million baptized believers. Its stated goals are to unite Baptists worldwide, lead in world evangelism, respond to people in need, defend human rights, and promote theological reflection.

Because Baptists do not have a central governing authority, beliefs are not totally consistent from one church to another. For example, Baptists are divided on whether to accept the Calvinist doctrine of predestination. However, all Baptists agree that scripture is central.

Worship services include prayers and lots of music, but the focus is on the sermon. Baptist preaching is generally impassioned. One of the most eloquent Baptist preachers of the twentieth century was Billy Graham, who preached to gigantic crowds throughout the United States and abroad for more than fifty years.

The most influential Baptist denomination in the United States, the Southern Baptist Church is based, as the name suggests, in the American South, where up to a third of the population identifies itself as Baptist. Southern Baptist adherents have spread well beyond the South, however, with most states counting at least a small percentage.

Perhaps the only holy river in Christianity, the Jordan River is a popular spot for baptism. According to the Gospels, it was in the Jordan's waters that John the Baptist recognized and baptized Jesus Christ himself.

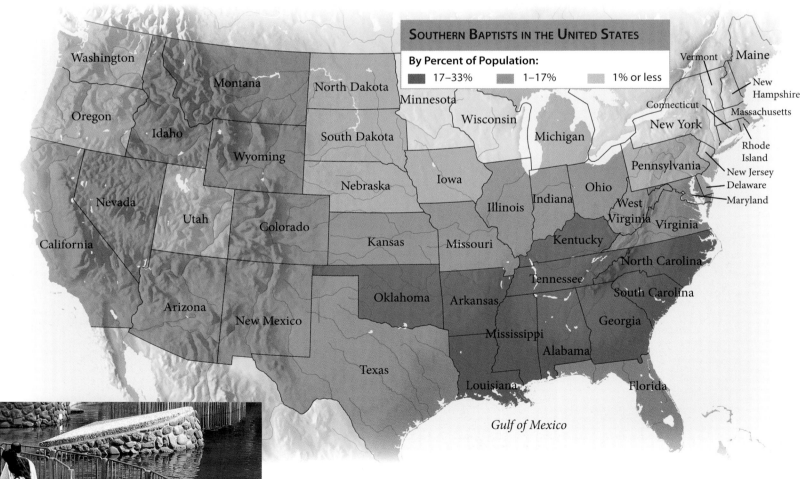

SOUTHERN BAPTISTS IN THE UNITED STATES

By Percent of Population:

17–33%	1–17%	1% or less

Gulf of Mexico

THE BAPTIST VIEW OF BAPTISM

Baptists reject infant baptism because they believe that for baptism to be meaningful, a person must choose it freely. Among Baptists the rite always involves total immersion in water, representing the baptized person's death and rebirth in Christ. This death and rebirth, the Baptists hold, reflects Jesus's own death and resurrection. But baptism is not necessary for salvation, according to the Baptists, although it is important for Christian believers to observe. They refer to baptism as a teaching of the Bible that Jesus intended his followers to observe. Even though a person chooses to be baptized, he or she does not make the spiritual change, they say, but is transformed by God himself.

CHRISTIANITY
Methodist Churches

*Do all the good you can,
to all the people you can,
at all the times you can,
in all the ways you can,
by all the means you can,
as long as ever you can*
—POEM USED BY JOHN WESLEY TO
TEACH ABOUT HUMAN PERFECTION

METHODISM STARTED as an evangelical movement within the Church of England under the leadership of John Wesley. In 1795 (after Wesley's death) it became a separate Protestant denomination that spread quickly throughout Britain and the United States. In America doctrinal disputes caused divisions that spread to Britain as well. British splits were healed in 1932 with the formation of a Methodist Church that reunited most English Methodists. In the United States various Methodist bodies united in 1968 to form the United Methodist Church, currently the principal Methodist Church in America. The World Methodist Council, an association of churches in the Methodist tradition, helps coordinate the efforts of the many Methodist Churches throughout the world. It has a membership of 76 denominations in 132 countries representing about 75 million people.

Methodist Churches are episcopal in form, and bishops have the power to appoint clergy to individual parishes. Methodists make use of tradition as a source of church authority, though they do not place it on the same level as holy scripture; tradition serves mainly as a lens through which scripture is interpreted. Methodist doctrine is based on Wesley's sermons and notes on the New Testament and on his Articles of Religion. The articles, an official doctrinal statement created by Wesley for American Methodists, are merely an abridgment of the Thirty-Nine Articles of the Church of England, with their Calvinistic statements excised.

ARMINIANISM AND CALVINISM

Protestant churches are often said to be either Calvinistic or Arminian. Calvinists believe in predestination—that God predetermines who will be saved and who will be damned and that humans have nothing to do with their destiny. Arminians, following the teachings of the sixteenth-century Dutch Reform theologian Jacobus Arminius, hold that while humans are naturally unable to make any effort toward salvation, Jesus died on the cross to save all people, and so God gives us the grace to be saved if we believe in Jesus. God also gives us free will so that we might reject his grace by rejecting faith in Jesus and so fail to achieve salvation. Traditionally, Methodists have accepted the Arminian view of free will, through God's grace, rather than Calvin's predestinarian determinism.

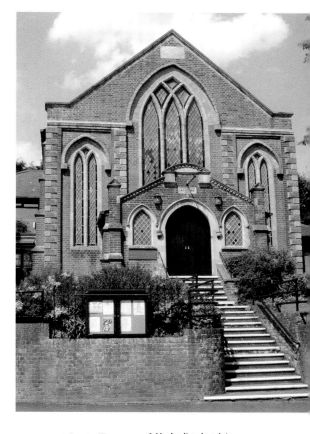

A Methodist church in Buckinghamshire, England.

UNITED STATES METHODISTS

By Percent of Population:
- 5–10%
- 1–5%
- 1% or less

In the United States, Methodist congregations can be found in every state, although nowhere do they constitute a majority. The denomination is strongest in the South and Midwest and weakest in the West.

CHRISTIANITY

The Mormon Church

THE LARGEST RELIGIOUS GROUP native to America, the Church of Jesus Christ of Latter-day Saints, more popularly known as the Mormon Church, is by some accounts the fourth-largest Christian denomination in the United States, as well as one of the fastest-growing Christian faiths in the world. "LDS" membership in the United States is currently estimated at six million; internationally, thirteen million members are in 176 countries and territories, with 124 temples and 27,475 congregations. Contributing to church growth are the more than 53,000 full-time volunteer LDS missionaries serving throughout the world. The Church of Latter-day Saints is headquartered in Salt Lake City, Utah; U.S. members are concentrated there and in nearby states, though they are found throughout the country.

The official name—the Church of Jesus Christ of Latter-day Saints—refers to the Mormon belief that they have restored the true church in the "latter days" after Christ's ministry on earth and the apostolic period. The term "saint" means a member of the church. The unofficial name, or nickname, for members—Mormons—comes from the sacred writings of the ancient prophet Mormon as revealed to and translated by Joseph Smith, the founder of the church.

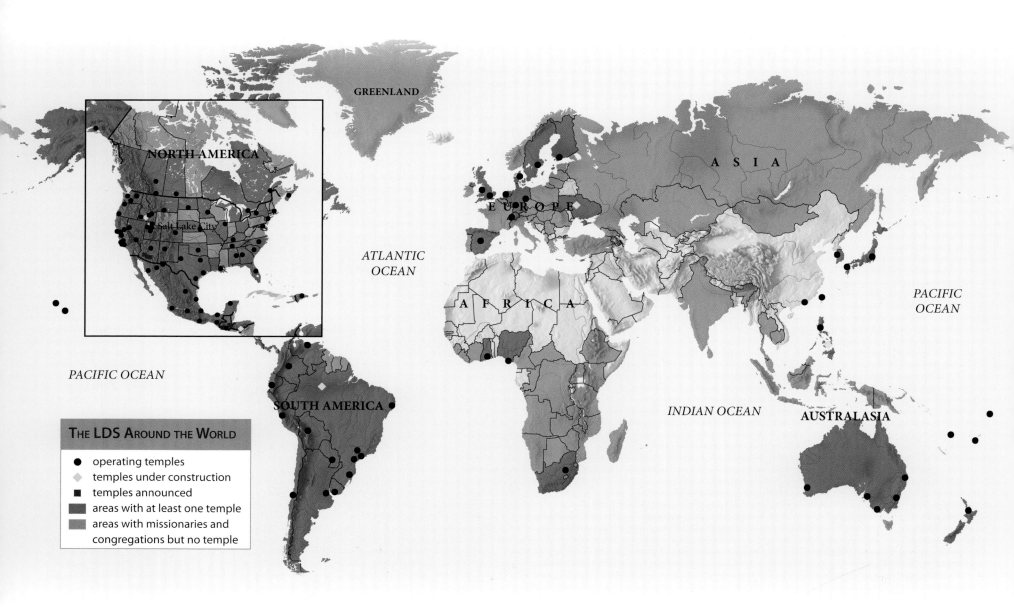

GREENLAND

NORTH AMERICA

Salt Lake City

ATLANTIC OCEAN

PACIFIC OCEAN

SOUTH AMERICA

ASIA

EUROPE

AFRICA

INDIAN OCEAN

AUSTRALASIA

PACIFIC OCEAN

THE LDS AROUND THE WORLD

- ● operating temples
- ◇ temples under construction
- ■ temples announced
- ▬ areas with at least one temple
- ▬ areas with missionaries and congregations but no temple

From its headquarters in Salt Lake City, Utah (United States), the Mormon Church has become a worldwide phenomenon, with temples on every continent and more on the way.

Becoming the leader of the Mormon Church after Joseph Smith's violent death, Brigham Young led an advance contingent of 143 men, 3 women, and 2 children to the Salt Lake Valley.

The Salt Lake Temple is the largest Latter-day Saint church. Dedicated in 1893, three years before Utah became a state, the temple took forty years to complete.

DIVINE REVELATIONS AND EARTHLY ZIONS

In 1820 "two personages" appeared to the young farmer boy Joseph Smith; they were, he believed, God the father and son. In subsequent visions, an angel named Moroni told Smith of gold tablets bearing God's revelation, hidden by prophets centuries earlier. According to Smith's account, he found them buried on a hill in Palmyra, New York, and his translation, *The Book of Mormon: Another Testament of Jesus Christ*, published in 1830, became the central text of the new religion he founded in that year. Smith and his followers dedicated themselves to restoring the "pure religion" described in the Book of Mormon.

Throughout the next decade, the gathering believers moved from Ohio to Missouri to Illinois, seeking to establish an "American Zion"—a community of like-minded believers. Their 1838 settlement in Nauvoo, Illinois, with a charter virtually freeing them from political authority, soon became the state's fastest-growing settlement; Mormon missionaries were sent to Canada and England and won thousands of new converts. However, dissension within the Nauvoo community and neighboring towns' suspicion of their increasing influence and unorthodox beliefs resulted in Smith's arrest, imprisonment, and mob murder in 1844.

Smith's confidant Brigham Young (1801–77) led most of the Nauvoo Mormons to Utah, which was then Mexican territory, and settled in the Great Salt Lake area in 1847. Here they transformed much desert into arable land and sought to create their own state, Deseret. Once the government of the United States gained control of the area, however, opposition to Mormon prominence and to their controversial beliefs, especially polygamy, resulted in a federal law against the practice. The church forbade new polygamous marriages in 1890. The idea of a separate Mormon state faded, especially as the new transcontinental railroad brought in many non-Mormons.

LATTER-DAY SAINTS TODAY

LDS members consider both the Bible and the Book of Mormon to be statements of Christ's ministry and divinity and of God's ongoing revelation. Commitment to marriage and to family, as the basic unit of church and society, is also emphasized, along with a strong work ethic, self-reliance, and community service. Church members volunteer at their own expense to serve for eighteen to twenty-four months throughout the world in humanitarian work or full-time missionary service and other church assignments. Male LDS members share the responsibility for individual congregations as a nonprofessional priesthood. The leader of the church is termed president and is considered a "prophet, seer, and revelator" who, as a successor to Joseph Smith, may still receive revelation.

LDS adherents believe in the coming of Christ's eternal kingdom on earth, open to all through repentance and baptism, including those who await in the spirit world after death. So that deceased ancestors may be identified to receive eternal blessings, the LDS church gathers genealogical records from all over the world and makes them available to the public in the Family History Library in Salt Lake City and in 4,000 family history centers throughout the world.

POLYGAMY AND THE MORMON CHURCH

Founder Joseph Smith endorsed "plural marriage"—polygamy—after a vision in 1843; the practice became doctrine a few years later and was followed for about fifty years by a minority of Mormons. Current LDS teaching rejects polygamy and maintains that anyone practicing it is neither LDS nor Mormon.

However, groups termed "Mormon fundamentalists" have split off from the main church, some to keep the practice of polygamy. Most of these groups are isolated, with no central authority. The largest entity is the Fundamentalist Church of Jesus Christ of Latter Day Saints (FLDS). This group emerged in the 1930s and is currently estimated to have 8,000 to 10,000 members in Utah, Arizona, Colorado, South Dakota, British Columbia, and Texas, where a FLDS group was the subject of a controversial raid in April 2008.

MORMON TABERNACLE CHOIR

One of the oldest and largest choirs in the world, the Mormon Tabernacle Choir is composed of 360 volunteer church members, ages twenty-five to sixty; a 110-member orchestra also volunteers. The choir's home is the historic 1867 "tabernacle" of the Church of Jesus Christ of Latter-day Saints, in Salt Lake City, Utah, west of the LDS temple. Church lore maintains that its unusual design was inspired by Brigham Young's contemplation of an eggshell cracked lengthwise.

Christian Science

IN 1879 MARY BAKER EDDY FOUNDED the Church of Christ, Scientist, to "reinstate primitive Christianity and its lost element of healing." Eddy and her followers believed that regeneration, spiritual growth, and the healing of both physical illness and sin came from the divine love and mind of God. Their guideline for the study and practice of Christian Science was Eddy's 1875 book, *Science and Health with Key to the Scriptures*, still a central text for the church's worldwide membership.

The Church of Christ, Scientist, is one of the few religious movements originating in the United States. A decade after its founding, almost a hundred Christian Science congregations had been established throughout America, mostly in the Atlantic states and the Midwest. The "Mother Church" was built in Boston, Massachusetts, in 1894, with Mary Baker Eddy as the first pastor. By the time of her death in 1910, there were more than 1,200 congregations worldwide. Membership reached a peak in the 1930s, with about 2,400 congregations internationally. Today, Christian Scientists are in 139 countries, and an estimated 1,800 to 2,000 branch churches are in 80 countries. Recent estimates of Christian Science adherents in the United States give a figure of fewer than 200,000.

Christian Science churches exist in sixty-eight countries. The world headquarters, known as the Mother Church and considered a Boston landmark, was built in 1894.

Now, as of old, Truth casts out evils and heals the sick.
—MARY BAKER EDDY, SCIENCE AND HEALTH

A quintessential feature of the Church of Christ, Scientist, about 1,900 reading rooms worldwide offer books, magazines, and other publications, along with audio and video materials, for the exploration of spiritual healing and other Christian Science practices and beliefs. They function as both a library and a bookstore and also sponsor special events.

A HEALING SYSTEM

Christian Scientists, in explaining the name of their church, maintain that as Christians they follow the teachings of the Bible and the ministry of Christ. The "science" of the title refers to a set of spiritual principles, or laws relating to the nature of God and creation, that they believe form a scientific system of Christian healing.

In Christian Science both mind and spirit are eternal and real; the material world is a kind of illusion, as is evil. Sin and ignorance of this truth can prevent an understanding of God's goodness. However, through prayer and spiritual development, these false beliefs can be corrected, resulting in health and happiness.

Sunday services at branch churches include music from the church's official hymnal, prayers, and readings from the Bible and Science and Health. Wednesday meetings feature testimony about how Christian Science has healed illnesses and solved other problems. Smaller organizations are called Christian Science Societies.

Church membership is not a prerequisite for the practice of Christian Science, though many Christian Scientists are members of the Church of Christ, Scientist. Unlike most churches, there is no ordained clergy. However, Christian Science practitioners complete a course in spiritual healing given by an authorized teacher and devote themselves to helping others through prayer. Christian Science nurses provide nonmedical physical care for those who rely on Christian Science for healing.

This Mary Baker Eddy monument is located in Mount Auburn Cemetery, in Cambridge, Massachusetts, Eddy's final resting place.

CURES AND CONTROVERSY

Christian Scientists are known for their refusal of standard medical treatment, relying instead on prayer to heal illness, disease, and injury. The official church stance, however, is that health-care decisions are a matter of individual choice; neither the church nor the Bible forbids medical intervention, but in most cases healing prayer will render it unnecessary, Christian Scientists maintain.

Nevertheless, both the concept and practice of healing by prayer are controversial, especially when children are involved. In well-publicized cases in recent years, children of Christian Science parents have died from lack of medical treatment for potentially curable ailments, leading to convictions of manslaughter in some instances.

CHRISTIAN SCIENCE MONITOR

"To injure no man, but to bless all mankind" was Mary Baker Eddy's mandate for the newspaper she founded in 1908. Since then the international Monday-through-Friday daily has won several Pulitzer Prizes; in covering worldwide events the *Monitor* relies on its own writers based in eleven countries, instead of wire services. Though the *Monitor* is not a religious publication, one article about religion is published daily, another of Eddy's stipulations. The *Monitor's* print circulation is relatively small—reported at 71,000—but its Web site has attracted a significant online readership.

MARY BAKER EDDY

Born in New Hampshire in 1821 and the youngest of six siblings, Mary Baker was a sickly child in a strict Congregationalist home. She married at twenty-two, in 1843, but in less than a year she was a widow; her health grew worse after her son was born. In the following years she sought relief through various unorthodox cures—including magnetic healing, hydropathy, and homeopathy—and through constant Bible study. In 1866 she fell on an icy sidewalk and apparently suffered life-threatening internal injuries. However, according to her account, after reading in her Bible about Christ healing the sick, she not only recovered her health but also had a profound insight into the spiritual laws of Christian healing. In the decades after she established the Church of Christ, Scientist, she wrote countless articles on Christian Science practices and beliefs, and at the age of 87, two years before her death in 1910, she founded the *Christian Science Monitor*, an international daily newspaper.

The founder of Christian Science, Mary Baker Eddy published her seminal work *Science and Health with Key to the Scriptures* in 1875. Decades later, at age eighty-seven, she started the *Christian Science Monitor* newspaper, which is still published today.

Modern Issues, Ongoing Conflicts

WHILE MAJOR MIGRATIONS SET OFF from nineteenth-century Europe, the second half of the next century saw a surge of migration into Europe, especially from Muslim countries.

Those later migrations were the result both of colonial attachments—such as Spain and France with Africa, and Britain with South Asia—and of the need for "guest workers" to fill employment shortages. Many of these guest workers faced unemployment and poverty at home. In the 1960s and '70s thousands of Turkish men went to the Netherlands for work, others to Germany and Belgium. Many later brought their families for permanent residency. Since the 1950s large numbers of Indians, Pakistanis, and Bangladeshis have moved to the United Kingdom.

By the twenty-first century, the West had increasing Muslim populations that often did not assimilate with the majority culture. France had 7.5 million Muslims (10 percent of the population), Germany 3.3 million (4 percent), the United Kingdom 1.6 million (2.8 percent),

and Spain 1.3 million (1 percent). Anti-immigrant prejudices developed as the newcomers gained in political and cultural influence. This prejudice was exacerbated by a sharp increase in Islamic radicalism.

Europe, from the Atlantic Ocean to the Balkans and the Ural Mountains, has 130 million Muslims in a total population of 728 million. Among the twenty-seven member states of the European Union, with a total population of 493 million, there are 16 million Muslims. In a great swath from Kazakhstan, south of Russia, back westward to Azerbaijan, Turkey, and Albania, Islam is the majority religion. In at least eight countries of western Europe Islam is the largest minority religion. With Muslim birth rates considerably higher than those of other European ethnic groups, the percentage of Islamic population is steadily increasing.

Japan has 1.2 million Muslims (1 percent), while the Muslim population of the United States is variously estimated at 4 million to 8 million (1.3–2.6 percent), including 2.1 million native-born African Americans.

Muslim migration has been economically motivated as well as an avenue to escape persecution during civil unrest in the emigrants' homelands. Some Muslims assimilate to their new culture, while others adhere more closely to traditional doctrines.

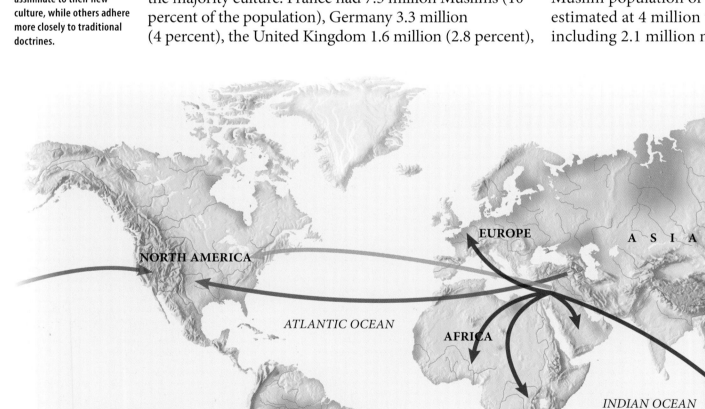

MAJOR MUSLIM MIGRATIONS, c. 1945–TODAY

➤ Lebanese migrations
➤ Palestinian migrations
➤ Kurdish migrations
➤ Philippine migrations

Tradition dictates that Muslims pray to Mecca, the birthplace of the prophet Muhammad, five times throughout the day. If finances and health permit, the faithful are obligated to make a pilgrimage to Mecca at least once in a lifetime.

The Almadiyya Mosque, Berlin's oldest mosque, was completed in 1928. At the time of the mosque's building, the Berlin Muslim Mission thought that the country might embrace Islam after the German defeat in World War I.

JIHADISTS AND HEAD SCARVES

In the first years of the twenty-first century the world, including Islam, was shaken by large-scale terror attacks blamed on international Muslim resistance movements. The 2001 destruction of New York's World Trade Center towers was allegedly perpetrated by an association of radical Muslims called Al-Qaeda, "the Base." The reasons for this attack were variously ascribed to anti-Americanism, anti-democratic "Islamist" jihadists, and retribution for Israeli repression of Palestinians.

Although most Muslims condoned armed resistance against oppressors, the vast majority deplored indiscriminate terrorism. Nevertheless, Islam was widely characterized as radical, reactionary, and violent.

With ultraconservative, radical Islamic movements taking root in the fertile soil of anticolonialism, the coinciding growth of Islam around the world laid this latest international struggle at the door of almost every country. The seething issues—and negative consequences—of Western and Islamic clashes were no longer contained in faraway Muslim lands, but were brought into Western cities—in part through immigration and in part through terrorist attacks, such as those in Madrid (2004) and London (2005), blamed on Islamic radicals.

At the same time, conservative Islamic traditions were being challenged by a new wave of modernism born of increased interaction between cultures. Muslim migration and the growth of migrant communities brought many issues to the fore, especially those related to women, traditionally required in public to wear the *hijab*—a veil or cover—and kept segregated from and subordinate to men. Several European countries forbade the wearing of

The traditional Muslim head scarf, or *hijab*, covers the hair and neck. In most Muslim cultures, young girls are not required to wear the hijab until they reach puberty.

head scarves in schools and the workplace; the scarves came to be considered a Muslim statement of defiance.

The status and roles of Muslim women in modern society came under scrutiny in many circles. For example, Muslims have long debated whether women may serve as *imams*, authorized to lead a congregation in *salat* (prayer). One opinion is that women may lead only all-women congregations—as did certain early Muslim women, including, it is said, Muhammad's wife. Although the Qur'an does not directly address this issue, others contend that certain hadith (statements attributed to Muhammad) permit women to lead mixed congregations. Medieval sexism, they say, brought about prohibitions of women as imams.

The majority of Muslim denominations allow women to serve as imams for all-female congregations, while a small minority has permitted women to lead mixed congregations. Although these are isolated cases, in modern times women occasionally have led mixed congregations in South Africa, Spain, Canada, and the United States. China has a unique system of mosques that are for women only, with female imams who are specially trained for their tasks.

THE MUSLIM CALENDAR

The Islamic calendar begins the Muslim era with Muhammad's *hirja*, or migration, to Medina in 622 CE: year 1 AH (*Anno Hegirae*—in the year of the hirja).

This dating system is used in most Muslim countries, except Turkey, which uses the Gregorian calendar accepted by the rest of the world. Also, while the standard Muslim calendar is based on a lunar year, the Iranians use a calendar based on a solar (or seasonal) year.

The Muslim calendar has twelve months, each beginning with the new moon. The first eleven months are alternately thirty and twenty-nine days long, with the twelfth month alternating between these lengths in order to synchronize with the moon's phases. The calendar has a thirty-year cycle, with nineteen years of 354 days and eleven years of 355 days. The twenty-first century CE is the fifteenth century AH.

ISLAM
State Religion, State Adversary

ISLAM IS THE STATE RELIGION in more than a dozen countries, the most prominent being Pakistan, Bangladesh, Iran, Egypt, and Malaysia. Many other countries call themselves Islamic states, or republics, and are guided by Muslim principles and sharia law. Authoritarian religious leadership in some Islamic countries has resulted in other faiths being discriminated against and freedom of speech suppressed.

The rise of international Islamist terrorism, aimed at establishing ultraconservative Muslim states, spurred a number of Western politicians and commentators to accuse many Muslim countries of fostering intolerance by denying human rights and the right of individual expression. They point to the generally subordinate position of women in Islam as proof of such repression. Further, the requirement that in many of those countries Muslim women must veil and cover themselves in public is sexist to Westerners. Muslims reply that Western culture is actually more sexist because women are expected to expose their bodies in public to be considered attractive.

Instances of official Muslim hostility to those who publicly disagree with orthodox Islam or who call for religious reform have further chilled relations between Islamic and secular societies. Aggression against "secularists," considered by ultraconservative Muslims as dangers to society, has resulted in state executions, internationally publicized death sentences issued by leading clerics, and assassinations.

Several Islamic countries wield considerable power because they possess the world's greatest oil fields. That power is formidable when unified, as demonstrated in the late twentieth century when Muslim governments, angered by American support for the state of Israel, placed brief oil embargos on the United States and western Europe, creating social disruption and widespread anxiety.

One concern broadly discussed in circles suspicious of Islam is the belief that most Muslims long for political unification under a reinstated caliphate. That event, say those who dread such "pan-Islamism," would lead to Muslims waging wars of conquest against non-Muslims. Other observers deride the notion of pan-Islamism, noting the wide differences in Muslims' ethnicity and cultures, and even in their interpretations of Islam.

Roughly one-fifth of the world's population practices the Muslim faith. In addition to formally designated Islamic republics such as Iran and Pakistan, many nations claim Islam as their state religion.

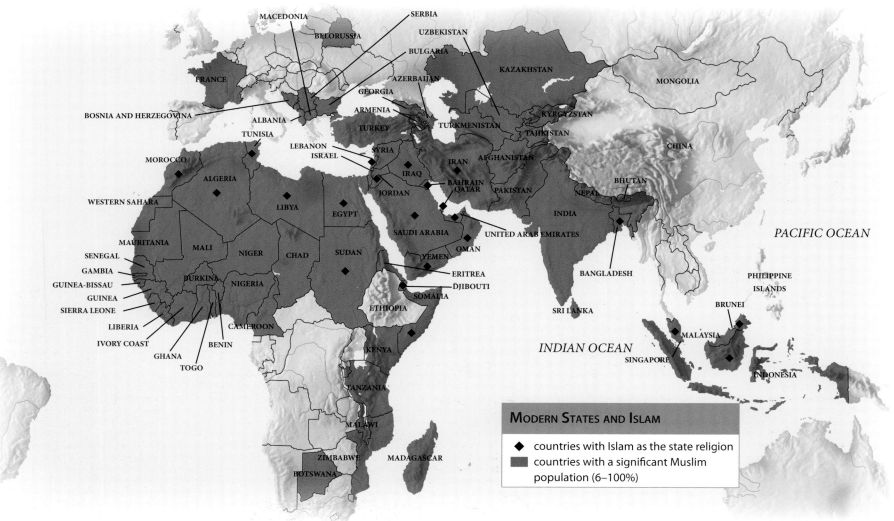

MODERN STATES AND ISLAM

◆ countries with Islam as the state religion

▮ countries with a significant Muslim population (6–100%)

Islam was introduced into China more than a thousand years ago. Kashgar, in the northwest, is predominantly Muslim, a legacy of its former Uighur rulers who converted in the late tenth century.

Those who preserved the language and written culture of Central Asia were the Uighurs.
—FERDINAND DE SAUSSURE, SWISS LINGUIST OF THE NINETEENTH AND TWENTIETH CENTURIES

A Saudi oil field. Though China ranks as fifth in world oil production, its booming economy increasingly relies on oil from Islamic states to sustain growth.

MOROS AND UIGHURS

At the start of the twenty-first century, Southeast Asian and Chinese Muslims were less prominent in world affairs than the Muslims of more volatile West and South Asia, where wars, terrorism, and petro-politics dominated mass media. Yet oil-rich Indonesia and Malaysia, the largest Muslim-majority countries in Southeast Asia, are dynamic states grouped with Asia's fast-growing "tiger economies," with stable governments based on European models.

Major migrations in the twentieth century often sent Muslims from distant lands through this region. Turks, Lebanese, Bangladeshis, Pakistanis, and Malays migrated to Japan, Australia, New Zealand, and Oceania. Japan has more than a million Muslims, while Australia has approximately 19,000 and New Zealand 38,000.

One of the enduring tribulations in the region is the ongoing insurrection of Moro Muslims in the southern Philippines. With a history of fighting occupiers ever since Spanish colonization, the Sunni Moros continued their struggle for independence through the twentieth century, fighting Americans and the mainly Roman Catholic Filipino government. Antigovernment guerrillas, known as Huks in the mid-twentieth century, were superseded by the more politic Moro National Liberation Front. A jihadist splinter group, the Moro Islamic Liberation Front, maintained an antigovernment insurgency into the twenty-first century. The insurgents contend the government is attempting to do away with their Muslim faith.

Similar grievances are voiced by ethnically Turkic Muslims, known as Uighurs, living in the People's Republic of China. Of China's estimated twenty-six million Muslims, the ten million Turkic-speaking Uighurs are one of the largest groups. They are found mostly in the Xinjiang Autonomous Region of Central Asia.

The Uighurs took part in nineteenth-century Muslim rebellions, with disastrous consequences, and were persecuted during the Cultural Revolution of 1966–76. The government remained wary of Islamic unrest in the region and cracked down harshly on suspected dissidents.

The Uighurs, whose name means "Confederation of Nine Tribes," had an extensive Islamic empire in the eighth and ninth centuries, achieving a high degree of culture. Contemporary Chinese visitors noted the beauty of temples, statues, wall paintings, gardens, and houses, and they admired skillfully made objects of silver and gold.

Historically, many Uighurs have been well educated, and they have a long-established literature, including original works and translations from regional languages. Uighurs often served on diplomatic staffs and as government ministers and were respected teachers and military officers.

In the twenty-first century Uighur nationalism is a strong current in the region, which Uighurs refer to as Chinese Turkestan. While most Uighurs want peaceful, and secular, progress toward ethnic recognition, radical Islamists advocate independence from China. They are often imprisoned, even executed. China has been accused of using the "war on terror" to justify destroying Uighur culture and repressing its Muslim faith, with one key tactic being to move ethnic Chinese emigrants into the region.

ISLAM IN COMMUNIST CHINA

China's long Muslim tradition began as early as 650 and included important cultural, economic, and military contributions, among them several Ming dynasty (1368–1644) generals. Most Chinese Muslims, predominantly Sunni, live in the western regions, with the rest mainly in the southwest.

Ethnic Chinese Muslims known as Hui number about ten million and generally speak Tibetan or Mongolian. The Hui had been Buddhists and Manicheans until converting to Islam in the tenth century.

Although the Communist government looks on religion with disfavor, almost 11,000 Chinese Muslims have been permitted annually since 2001 to make the hajj pilgrimage to Mecca. Islamic education is also permitted, with mosque schools, public and private Islamic colleges, and programs that allow Muslims to study in foreign lands.

The Islamic Association of China, founded in the 1950s, represents ten nationalities in the People's Republic of China. Another organization, the China Islamic Association, was established by the government in 2001 in order to oppose religious extremism while at the same time encouraging study of the Qur'an.

The creators of the Xian Great Mosque employed traditional Chinese architecture, forgoing Arab domes and minarets, to help keep the structure inconspicuous from its predominantly Buddhist and Daoist neighbors.

ISLAM

Terrorism, Invasion, Insurgency

THE ARAB-ISRAELI CONFLICT that began with the founding of Israel in 1948 continued into the twenty-first century. Israel's repeated victories in several twentieth-century wars with her mostly Islamic neighbors only exacerbated hostility and resentment among the world's Muslims, who decried the walling-in of impoverished Palestinians living in territories under Israeli guns. Western—especially American—support of Israel created enduring anger that came to a head with Al-Qaeda's violent terrorist operations in the West.

In response to the devastating September 11, 2001, attacks on the United States, an American-led coalition of nations immediately invaded Afghanistan and overthrew its Taliban regime, which was accused of harboring Al-Qaeda. Next, Iraq was charged by several Western governments with developing weapons of mass destruction (WMD) and of supporting terrorists. In March of 2003, a coalition force of more than 300,000 troops led by the Americans and British invaded Iraq, overthrowing its government. No Iraqi WMDs or direct links with terrorists were found.

Over the next several years those invasions turned into occupations and anti-insurgency conflicts. Hundreds of thousands of Iraqis died, mainly in civil strife between their majority Shia and minority Sunni populations. In Afghanistan the Taliban regrouped to fight on. Meanwhile, Osama bin Laden, a Saudi adherent of Wahhabi doctrine and nominal leader of Al-Qaeda, was a fugitive.

The so-called "war on terror" declared by U.S. leaders further incensed Muslims against the West, especially as Americans arrested, and at times tortured, suspected terrorists—virtually always Muslims—who for the most part were not tried in open court but languished in prison. The United States, and to a lesser extent the United Kingdom, increasingly came to be seen as anti-Islamic aggressors by the one-fifth of the world's population who share Islam as an ethical tradition.

Forty-nine of the world's countries have Muslim majorities, with the population based predominantly in northern Africa, Southwest Asia, and South Asia. Though closely associated with Islam, the region known as the Middle East holds only 15 percent of the world's Muslim population.

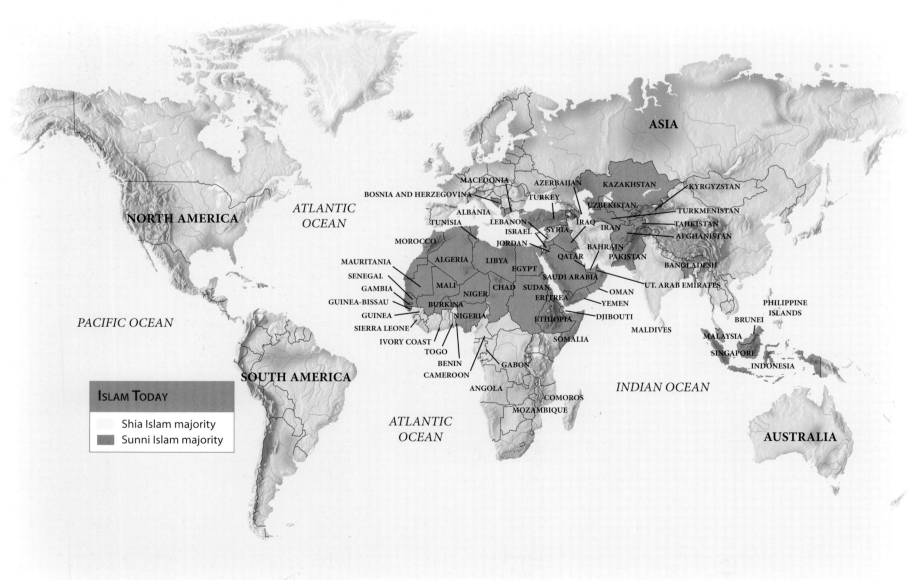

Islam Today

- Shia Islam majority
- Sunni Islam majority

The Arab world also won the Nobel with me. I believe that international doors have opened, and that from now on, literate people will consider Arab literature also. We deserve that recognition.
—NAGUIB MAHFOUZ, EGYPTIAN NOVELIST AND SOCIAL COMMENTATOR, WINNER OF THE 1988 NOBEL PRIZE FOR LITERATURE FOR HIS "ARABIAN NARRATIVE ART THAT APPLIES TO ALL MANKIND"

Israeli military forces are strengthened by the mandatory service of all Jewish and Druze citizens; more than 16 percent of the government's 2008 budget was spent on defense.

DEMOGRAPHICS AND GLOBALISM

Although estimates of the world's Muslim population vary, there are as many as 1.8 billion, with Muslim majorities in forty-nine countries. Ethnically diverse Muslims speak approximately sixty languages. Among the largest ethnicities are Indians, Arabs, Javanese, Malays, Turks, Persians, Kurds, sub-Saharan Africans, Slavs, Tamils, Tatars, Sudanese, Berbers, and Uighurs.

Asia has more than a billion Muslims, Africa 412 million, Europe 44 million, North and South America 9.7 million, and Oceania 372,000. Indonesia has the largest Muslim population, at 207 million; Pakistan, 159 million; India, 151 million; Bangladesh, 132 million; Egypt, 70 million; Turkey 68 million, Nigeria

THE CAIRO HUMAN RIGHTS DECLARATION

In 1948 the United Nations adopted the Universal Declaration of Human Rights (UDHR), which became part of the International Bill of Human Rights accepted by the U.N. General Assembly in 1976 and given the force of international law. Muslim countries objected to the UDHR, asserting it was based on secular Judeo-Christian values that contradicted Islamic law.

In 1990 the Organization of the Islamic Conference adopted the Cairo Declaration of Human Rights in Islam, articulating freedoms and rights in accordance with sharia. The Cairo declaration accepted most of the thirty UDHR articles, ranging from the protection of nonbelligerents in wartime to forbidding discrimination on the basis of race, color, gender, religion, or social status, as well as guaranteeing freedom of movement, expression, and due process and equality under the law.

The Cairo declaration is criticized, however, for not asserting fundamental freedom of religion or endorsing equality between women and men. Another objection stems from its failure to oppose the practice in many Muslim countries of having multiple wives.

and Iran, 64 million. At least eighteen countries are 97 percent or more Muslim, with Saudi Arabia and Somalia 100 percent Muslim.

Many of the world's great cities are majority Muslim. The largest (in order of population) are Karachi, Pakistan; Istanbul, Turkey; Jakarta, Indonesia; Lagos, Nigeria; Tehran, Iran; Cairo, Egypt; Lahore, Pakistan; Dhaka, Bangladesh; Baghdad, Iraq; and Riyadh, Saudi Arabia. Three of the world's top twenty metropolitan areas are majority Muslim: Jakarta, sixth; Cairo, sixteenth; and Karachi, twentieth.

Several international organizations represent the countries with large Muslim populations. The twenty-two-member Arab League, formed in 1945, promotes the interests of its states with political, economic, cultural, and social programs.

An international oil cartel, the Organization of the Petroleum Exporting Countries (OPEC), took form in 1960; nine of the thirteen current member states are Muslim. OPEC influences international oil prices.

The largest Islamic political association is the fifty-seven-member Organization of the Islamic Conference (OIC). Founded in 1971,

OIC promotes intergovernmental cooperation to benefit its member countries and Muslims the world over. In 1990 OIC adopted the Cairo Declaration of Human Rights in Islam, which enumerates its member governments' positions on human rights and sharia law.

In the face of a climate of suspicion between many non-Muslim and Muslim peoples, one notable initiative toward understanding has established approximately a hundred "sister cities" relationships between Muslim and Western metropolitan areas. Sister Cities International, founded in 1956 by President Dwight D. Eisenhower (1890–1969), fosters human relations and municipal interaction without the need for governmental diplomacy. Paired cities work together with programs for arts and culture, youth and education, humanitarian assistance, and sustainable economic development.

Among the "sister" partnerships are New York with Cairo; Los Angeles with Tehran and Ardabil, Iran; Baltimore with Egypt's Alexandria and Luxor; Houston with Baku, Azerbaijan, and Abu Dhabi, the United Arab Emirates; and San Diego with Jalalabad, Afghanistan.

The 2001 terrorist attack on the World Trade Center in New York City provoked a U.S.-led invasion of Afghanistan, which was accused of harboring 9/11 mastermind Osama bin Laden. In 2003, the global "war on terror" was continued when the United States and allied nations invaded Iraq.

BAHA'ISM

A New Faith from Persia

One of the world's seven Baha'i temples, the House of Worship in Wilmette, Illinois, may also be one of the world's most unusual and lovely temples. It serves administratively as the North American Baha'i headquarters.

ESTABLISHED LESS THAN 150 YEARS AGO, Baha'ism is the youngest, most diverse, and one of the most progressive independent world religions. It was founded in Iran, then called Persia, by Bahá'u'lláh (born Mírzá Husayn Alí Nuri; lived 1817–92). Bahá'u'lláh was one of the important leaders of Babism, a Persian religion that had broken away from Islam in 1848. At the heart of Babism was the prediction of the coming of a new messiah who would unite the world's religions. Bahá'u'lláh was said to fulfill this prophecy in 1863, when he proclaimed himself the Messiah and founded the Baha'i faith. He positioned himself as the descendant of a single continuous "family" of messiahs from the world's major religions—Jesus, Muhammad, Krishna, and so on—and adopted the name Bahá'u'lláh ("Glory of God" in Arabic). Bahá'u'lláh's leadership was continued by his son, Abdul Bahá (1844–1921), and his successors, and eventually a permanent central administrative base was established at the site of Bahá'u'lláh's tomb on Mount Carmel, Haifa, in Israel.

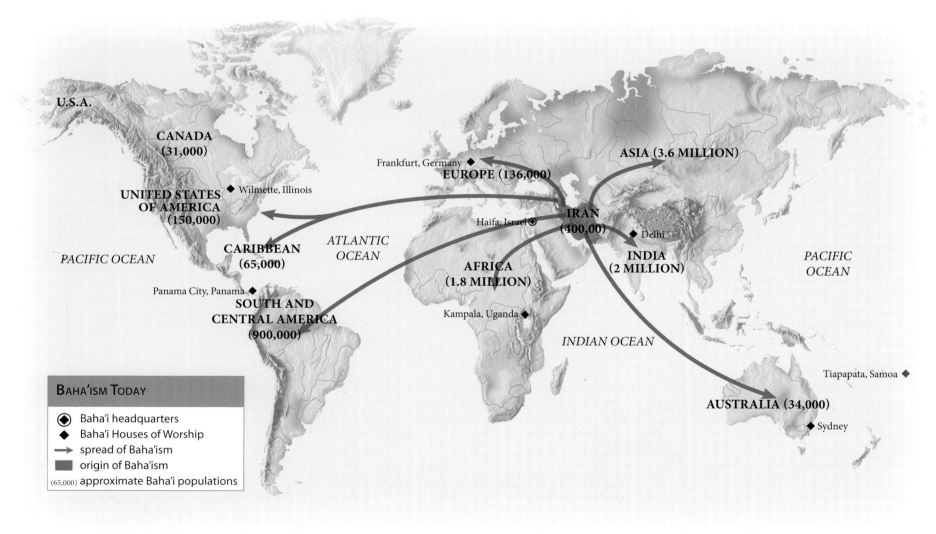

Although no country's population is more than 1 or 2 percent Baha'i, Baha'ism is truly a global religion, with worshippers on every inhabited continent and a worldwide population in the millions.

A simple nine-pointed star serves as the symbol of Baha'ism. It represents the Baha'i belief that all religions are fundamentally one—a unique position among the world's religions and one that draws many new faithful to its optimistic cause of peace and unity.

THE BAHA'I FAITH

There is no original sin in the Baha'i religion, but a belief that humans are born perfect and that humankind is still on a path of maturity toward a higher form. The Baha'i worship one God but do not follow a patriarchal hierarchy, as God is neither man nor woman, and men and women are considered equal. Baha'ism maintains traditional views on sexuality, however, and is opposed to homosexuality and abortion. Heaven and Hell are conceptual places defined by closeness to or distance from God, and religious worship is organized along democratic, collective lines. Babist and Baha'i writings in the early part of the twentieth century prophesied cataclysmic worldwide events preceding peace on earth, with a utopian conviction that that peace would be attained within the century. Modern Baha'i leaders face the challenge of reconciling this optimism with the violent reality of the world today.

From an abiding conviction that the success of future mankind lies in unity, the Baha'i call for "unity of nations" was built into their faith long before the official establishment of the United Nations in 1945. The main goals of Baha'ism are to live in tolerance, to do good in the world, and to strive for peace. The Baha'i advocate closing the gap between extremes of poverty and wealth and building a unified world that will share an international language, scripture, currency, and security force.

A "GREEN" RELIGION

The Baha'i hold the optimistic view that it is possible for human behavior to improve, both in relation to one another and to the environment. Living a simple life and making a positive, nonpolitical contribution to the planet is essential to Baha'i practice, and one of the most important tenets is care of the environment. The Baha'i are vocal and active in their opposition to the destruction of wilderness areas by commercial development. In fact, they were the only religious nongovernmental organization to attend the United Nations Conference on Environment and Development, the Rio Summit, in 1992.

PERSECUTION IN IRAN

From its early association with Babism in the mid-1800s, the minority Baha'i population in Iran has suffered prejudice and persecution, initially a consequence of the Babis' unsuccessful attempt to overthrow the ruling Islamic government of the day. As a doctrinal offshoot of Babism, Baha'ism was the target of continued enmity from Iranian authorities, despite its peaceful nonmilitaristic philosophy. The Islamic Revolution in 1979 and the rise to power of the Islamic Shia clergy led to increased persecution of the Baha'i and initiated a mass exodus from Iran.

A RELIGION OF DIVERSITY

Central to Baha'ism is the advocacy of tolerance, racial diversity, and the belief that all religions are equal. In an increasingly polarized world, this appealing message accounts in large part for the growing popularity of the Baha'i faith. The twentieth century saw the spread of Baha'ism around the world, and today there are between five and six million followers internationally. The majority live in India and Iran, but Baha'ism is also practiced in over 200 countries and territories among a hugely diverse population encompassing over 2,000 ethnic and racial groups. In 1912 Bahá'u'lláh's son, Abdul Bahá, emmigrated to the United States, and a large following exists there today. The Baha'i headquarters for North America is the large and beautiful House of Worship in Wilmette, Illinois, one of only seven Baha'i temples in the world. The Baha'i advocacy of racial diversity has meant that it has maintained unity among its great diversity of followers and has not subdivided into sects or branches. Part of its success as a global religion is its decentralized administration, democratically elected representatives, and its willingness to cooperate with communities at a grass-roots level.

The Baha'i House of Worship in Delhi, India is known as the Lotus Temple and attracts four million visitors from around the world each year.

Zoroastrianism Today

ONCE THE FAITH of the vast ancient Persian empire, based on the teachings of the prophet Zoroaster, or Zarathustra, and a form of monotheism predating and influencing Christianity, Judaism, and Islam, Zoroastrianism has been described as the major religion nearest extinction. Generally estimated to number fewer than 300,000 worldwide, Zoroastrians nevertheless can still be found in several countries, where they are often among the best-educated and most influential and economically successful groups.

After the rise of Muslim Arabs in Persia in the mid-seventh century CE, Zoroastrians who did not convert to Islam fled to surrounding countries or to isolated areas of Iran. Despite intermittent conversion, persecution, and discrimination, an estimated 30,000 to 100,000 Zoroastrians remain as Iran's oldest surviving religious community. They live in Tehran, the capital of Iran, and in the regions of Kerman and Yazd, the Zoroastrian spiritual capital.

Another large group, estimated at 75,000, lives in India, Pakistan, Sri Lanka, and Afghanistan. Known as Parsis, or Parsees ("Persians") they are descendants of the seven boatloads of Zoroastrian refugees who landed on the coast of India in 936 to escape continuing

persecution in Iran. They established a thriving enclave and by the nineteenth century dominated the commercial life of Mumbai (Bombay). Also living in India and Pakistan are Zoroastrians known as Iranis, later immigrants from the past two centuries.

Zoroastrian communities also can be found in Britain (5,000 to 7,000, concentrated in London) and Canada (about 6,000, with a significant population in Toronto, which today has the third-largest congregation of Zoroastrians after Mumbai and Pune, India). An estimated 2,700 live in Australia, 2,200 in Persian Gulf nations, with smaller groups in Hong Kong, Singapore, and East Africa; 11,000 to 15,000 live in the United States, with the largest centers in San Jose, Houston, Chicago, and New York.

Some statistics give a much higher number of Zoroastrians worldwide, with estimates of up to 3.5 million. Though surveys by official Zoroastrian organizations tend to agree with lower estimates, the higher numbers are thought to reflect some lessening of discrimination and therefore less need to hide a Zoroastrian identity, and even to indicate a new respect for this ancient Persian religion.

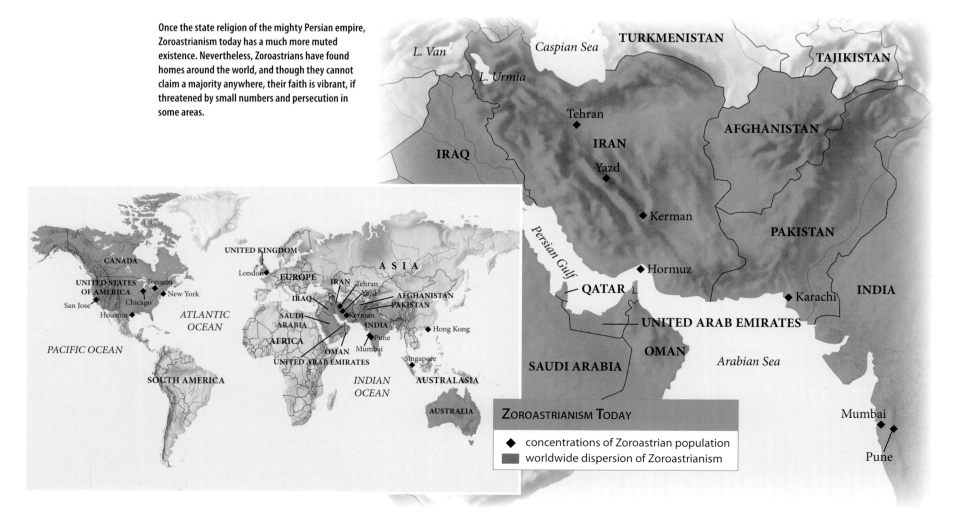

Once the state religion of the mighty Persian empire, Zoroastrianism today has a much more muted existence. Nevertheless, Zoroastrians have found homes around the world, and though they cannot claim a majority anywhere, their faith is vibrant, if threatened by small numbers and persecution in some areas.

ZOROASTRIANISM TODAY

◆ concentrations of Zoroastrian population
   worldwide dispersion of Zoroastrianism

The winged disk with a man's upper body, known as the *faravahar*, is a Zoroastrian symbol. The winged disk has long represented the divine right of a benevolent monarchy, and the three rows of feathers on the wings stand for good thoughts, good words, and good deeds.

KEEPING THE SACRED FIRE ALIVE

Though the practice of Zoroastrianism today differs throughout its world communities, key beliefs and values are universal, especially the importance of "good thoughts, good words, good deeds." In the lifelong struggle between good and evil, these basic principles are guidance along the path of *asha*, or righteousness and truth; their observance honors Ahura Mazda, the "wise lord," creator of the world, embodiment of good, and the source of light, and whose spirit is represented by fire, the symbol of the Zoroastrian faith.

Major Zoroastrian houses of worship are known as fire temples, where a constant flame is tended five times a day, and where adherents gather on holy days for community worship and ritual. Sacred writings, collected in the Avesta, include the teachings of Zarathustra and his followers. In a ceremony called the *navzote*, children are formally initiated into the religion and then can wear the *sudra*, a white undershirt with a pocket near the heart as a symbol of gathering good deeds, and the *kusti*, a woolen cord around the waist.

Today's Zoroastrians face challenges to the perpetuation of their faith. Adherence to traditional practices, some by their nature exclusive, are currently in conflict with new and more inclusive ideas. For example, intermarriage is increasing, but some priests, particularly in India and Iran, do not accept converts from another religion or the children of a marriage where the father is not a Zoroastrian. Also, according to Zoroastrian tradition, prayers are recited in their original ancient languages; some reformers suggest that translations into English or the language of the believer would promote better understanding.

The main fire temple in Yazd, Iran, contains one of the world's nine *atash adaran*, or "fire of fires," the highest grade of Zoroastrian's three types of sacred fires. *Atash dadgah*, the lowest level flame, can be found in most Zoroastrian homes.

THUS SPOKE ZOROASTER

Claimed by some as humanity's first prophet, Zoroaster (the Greek spelling) or Zarathustra (sometimes Zarthushtra and other variants based on the Avestan dialect of Old Iranian) also appears in fictional form in Western culture. Sarastro, the wise high priest in Mozart's opera *The Magic Flute*, is thought to be based on Zoroaster; ancient Persia was considered a source of Freemasonry, which the opera references throughout. German philosopher Friedrich Nietzsche used Zoroaster as the central figure in what he considered his magnum opus, *Also sprach Zarathustra (Thus Spoke Zarathustra)* where the prophet is a mouthpiece for the author himself. The book inspired the tone poem of the same title by composer Richard Strauss.

A detail of Raphael's *The School of Athens* (1509) depicts Zoroaster in white vestments, still the common wear of modern-day Zoroastrian priests.

Quakers

Walk cheerfully over the world,
answering that of God in everyone.
—GEORGE FOX, JOURNAL, 1647

THE RELIGIOUS SOCIETY OF FRIENDS, or Quakers as they are more widely known, believe in an individual sense of the divine, which they call the "Inner Light" or the "Christ within." Quaker founder George Fox (1624–91) defied the beliefs and rituals of the established religion in England and sought to experience God directly. Those attracted to his ideas and powerful preaching called themselves Friends in the Truth, or simply Friends; the title Religious Society of Friends dates from the eighteenth century. One explanation of the term Quaker is found in Fox's journal: charged with blasphemy in 1650, Fox admonished his judge to "tremble at the word of the Lord." The justice responded by deriding Fox and his followers as "quakers." Other accounts cite the members' shaking caused by religious fervor.

Despite persecution in England and its colonies, the movement grew. Quaker William Penn's Province of Pennsylvania, established in 1681, was a safe haven for Friends and other victims of intolerance. In the nineteenth century, Quakers were active reformers, particularly in the abolition of slavery; however, divisions arose over forms of worship and modernizing influences.

Today Quakers are found worldwide. Official statistics cite 359,000 members, with 43 percent in Africa, 30 percent in North America, and the remainder in the Caribbean and Latin America (17 percent), Europe, the Middle East (6 percent), and Asia–West Pacific (4 percent). Members in the United States officially number 87,000, though the American Religious Identification Survey (2001) lists 217,000 who consider themselves Quakers.

Dutch Quaker Functionaries in Amsterdam by Gerbrand van den Eeckhout (1621–74). The origins of the Quaker meeting are unknown, but this form of worship was known to have exist before Fox organized them in England.

Quaker preacher Edward Hicks, a sign painter by trade, is best known as the artist of *The Peaceable Kingdom*. Hicks completed more than a hundred versions of this acclaimed work, which was based on the chapter in the Bible: "The wolf also shall dwell with the lamb, and the leopard shall lie down with the kid, and the calf and the young lion and fatling together; and a little child shall lead them" (Isaiah 11:6).

INWARD LIGHT, OUTWARD SERVICE

Though various branches of Quakers have divergent beliefs and practices, their central inspiration is the "Inner Light," an unmediated revelation of divine truth. In a traditional Friends worship service, known as an "unprogrammed meeting," a group will sit silently in "expectant waiting" until someone is moved to speak. In a "programmed" meeting, Friends follow an order of worship, led by a pastor; a period of silent worship is usually included. The teachings of Christian scriptures also receive varying emphasis, as does religious evangelism.

The Quakers' inward convictions are manifested in their social activism, particularly in human rights, social justice, and world peace.

QUAKER TESTIMONIES

Though without a formal creed, Quakers have traditionally followed a general set of principles called "testimonies." These stem from Fox's understanding of the essential teachings of Christ, especially the admonition to "love thy neighbor as thyself." Best known is the peace testimony: Quakers are opposed to war and military service, seeking instead nonviolent solutions to conflict. The testimony of integrity, or truth, means that Quakers do not swear oaths, pay unfair wages, or set dishonest prices. Through the testimony of equality, women have always participated as Quaker leaders, and slavery was opposed. The testimony of simplicity meant that many used "plain speech" (avoiding titles or other class distinctions and using "thee" and "thou," which in early days was less formal), did not flaunt material wealth, and wore "plain dress" or dark, undecorated garments, some up to the twentieth century.

Unitarian Universalism

Universalists believe that God is too good to damn people, and the Unitarians believe that people are too good to be damned by God.
—Thomas Starr King (1824–64), Universalist and Unitarian minister

Unitarian Universalism combines a heritage of liberal Protestantism with expressions of spirituality from other faiths and from secular traditions. Despite their historical roots in the two Christian denominations that form their name, most Unitarian Universalists do not seek an exclusively Christian identity and affirm many ways of leading an ethical life.

The religion's largest organization is the Unitarian Universalist Association (UUA), established in 1961 in Boston from a consolidation of the American Unitarian Association and the Universalist Church of America. Recent statistics estimate 683,000 Unitarian Universalists in the United States, with 24 percent belonging to a congregation. The worldwide total is estimated to be 800,000 adherents, in Australia, Belgium, Canada, France, Mexico, New Zealand, and the Philippines, as well as the United States, and more than 1,000 "UU" congregations. In 1995 the International Council of Unitarians and Universalists (ICUU) was established.

An 1856 engraving from the *Illustrated London News* depicts abolitionist Boston preacher Theodore Parker addressing a crowd in New York. Parker was considered a maverick extremist and even a heretic by the more conservative Unitarian elements of the time.

A Community of Individuals

Without adherence to specific creeds, beliefs, or rituals, Unitarian Universalists encourage the personal search for truth and a diversity of practices. However, the UUA's set of "principles, purposes, and sources" summarizes their shared values: the worth of every human being, the importance of justice and compassion, respect for the environment, and the goal of worldwide peace and liberty. Religious observance usually includes Sunday worship services, as well as celebrations of holidays from various faith traditions, and of life events, such as coming of age and marriage. Unique to UU congregations are the spring "flower communion," when single offerings of different flowers are combined in one bouquet, and the fall "water communion," when water collected from participants' various travels is poured together—both symbolizing the formation of community from individuals.

Unitarian Universalists are sometimes faulted for borrowing sacred elements from other faiths without real context, and for seeming to believe only in not committing to any belief.

Divine Unity, Divine Love

Both Unitarian and Universalist ideas date from early Christianity, developed and often drew persecution to those who professed them throughout the Protestant Reformation, and flourished in eighteenth- and nineteenth-century America. Unitarianism denies the deity of Jesus and thus orthodox Christianity's view of the Trinity: God as Father, Son, and Holy Spirit. In 1819 Boston preacher William Ellery Channing protested the doctrine of the Trinity as irrational and unscriptural and proclaimed his conviction that "the Father alone is God." His sermons and influence helped consolidate the Unitarian ideas of the day, resulting in the establishment of the American Unitarian Association in 1825. Universalism is the doctrine of universal salvation, a reaction to the idea that the God of love would redeem only a select few. The Universalist Church of America was formed in 1793; circuit riders spread the movement throughout the new nation's rural areas.

Both denominations advocated for social reform, including women's rights and the abolition of slavery; such activism is a hallmark of Unitarian Universalists today.

UNITARIAN CHAPEL, BLACKWATER S.ᵗ

The Blackwater Unitarian church in Rochdale, England, was the site of the town's oldest "non-conforming" church. After being dismissed as Catholic Bishop of Middleton, Reverend Thomas Assherton came to Rochdale and held what are thought to be the earliest Unitarian services in 1512.

Amish, Mennonites, and Hutterites

DESCENDANTS OF THE ANABAPTISTS, sixteenth-century radical religious reformers, the Amish, Mennonites, and Hutterites share several beliefs and practices, some of which set them apart from modern culture. Many groups among them are called "Plain People," from their simple old-fashioned dress and resistance to technological change, epitomized by the use of horse-drawn buggies. Some continue to speak the language of their European origins and to live within the physical boundaries and social restrictions of their close-knit communities, shunning nonbelievers and even others of their faith whom they consider in error. Others, however, enter more freely into mainstream life, while still upholding the shared values of pacifism, separation of church and state, and the importance of the family.

THE AMISH

The Amish people originated in the followers of Jakob Amman, a seventeenth-century Swiss Mennonite bishop, separating from the Mennonites in 1693. Though Amish communities spread throughout Europe, today none remain there; their members rejoined the Mennonites or began emigrating to North America in the eighteenth century, settling first in eastern Pennsylvania, where a large group remains today. Most Amish live and work in farming communities, though younger members sometimes find other jobs in nearby factories, shops, and restaurants as available farmland becomes scarcer. Education rarely continues beyond the eighth grade.

The largest group is the Old Order—the quintessential model of the bearded Amish farmer behind his horses and plow. Most Old Order Amish don't use electricity, own cars or mechanized farm equipment, or have home telephones. They speak a dialect of German among themselves and High

A traffic sign in Illinois advises drivers to be alert for Amish horse and buggies, which travel between five and ten miles per hour (8 to 16 km/h). All Amish buggies in central Illinois are black, sometimes making them hard to see in the dark.

The centuries-old tradition of communal barn-raising is still alive in Amish circles. Participation in such events is considered an essential part of Amish living.

AMISH VOCABULARY

English, Englisher, Yankee, or **High People** are Amish terms for the non-Amish.

A **Grandpa house** or **Doddy house** is a small house for grandparents next to the larger house once a daughter or son marries and begins a new family there.

Meidung, or **shunning,** is expulsion from the Amish community for breaking religious rules, such as marrying outside the faith.

The *Ordnung* dictates the rules of Amish life and faith, from appearance to farming methods, and is specific to each community.

Pennsylvania Dutch (actually *Deutsch,* or German) is the dialect spoken by Amish at home; the term also describes the residents of central Pennsylvania from a German background, including but not limited to the Amish.

Rumspringa, or "running around," refers to Amish adolescence as young people sample life outside the community and its strictures.

German at worship services, which are typically held in each other's homes and are sometimes four hours long, with prayers, Bible readings, sermons, and singing from the 1564 Ausbund, their hymnal.

Old Order Amish live in twenty-three U.S. states and in Ontario, Canada, with more than 1,200 church districts and a baptized membership (which does not include children) of about 75,000. Actual population is estimated at about three times the membership; the Old Order is one of the fastest-growing religious groups in the United States, as a result of their high birth rate—an average of seven children in a family—and their retention of children within the Amish community. In the United States, Ohio has the largest population, followed by Pennsylvania and Indiana; other significant groups are in Iowa, Illinois, Kansas, Wisconsin, Missouri, Minnesota, and New York State.

Even more conservative are smaller Amish groups—Swartzentruber, Andy Weaver, and the Nebraska Amish of central Pennsylvania—some of which do not allow indoor plumbing or battery lights.

New Order Amish is the collective name for less conservative groups that broke away from the Old Order in the mid-1960s; they generally live in Pennsylvania and Ohio. They are less restrictive about modern technology and about the practice of "shunning," or excommunicating erring members. Another less conservative group is the Beachy Amish Mennonite Church, established in 1927 and named for Bishop Moses M. Beachy. Today, the "Beachys" have about 11,000 U.S. and Canadian members in 144 congregations, along with locations worldwide through their international missions and relief work.

THE MENNONITES

The Mennonites are Anabaptist denominations named for their early religious leader Menno Simons (1496–1561). Today, in contrast to the Amish, Mennonites are as likely to live among and look much like the surrounding population as they are to stay within a separate community and conform to

And be not conformed to this world: but be ye transformed by the renewing of your mind, that ye may prove what is that good, and acceptable, and perfect, will of God.
—From the Epistle to the Romans
(King James version)

Amish women work communally in such handiwork as quilting bees. The Amish are revered for the high quality of their quilts, with styles varying by community. The double wedding-ring variety ranks as one of the most popular patterns and one of the most difficult to make. The widely held belief that Amish women purposely make mistakes in their quilting to show humility because "only God is perfect" is spurious. Such an action, it is argued, would be lacking in humility, as it implies that the maker considers herself otherwise perfect.

The Amish separated from the Mennonites in the late seventeenth century, but maintained the tradition of simple dress and rejection of modern technology.

its restrictions. The most distinctive in appearance and practice are Old Order Mennonites, with their buggies and plain clothes.

Mennonites are established worldwide, numbering 1.5 million in seventy-five countries on six continents. Large populations are in the United States, Mexico, the Democratic Republic of the Congo, and Canada. Significant groups are the Mennonite Brethren (300,000 members on six continents); the Meserete Kristos Church in Ethiopia (120,600 members and 126,000 followers); the Mennonite Church USA, with more than 109,000 members in forty-four states; and Brethren in Christ, with 100,000 members worldwide. The total for Mennonites in the United States is estimated to be between 236,000 and 323,000. Though no one organization represents all Mennonites, the Mennonite World Conference includes the Mennonite Brethren, the Mennonite Church USA, and the Mennonite Church Canada, with a combined total membership of at least 400,000, or about 30 percent of Mennonites worldwide.

The Mennonites' varied beliefs and practices have a common basis in the authority of biblical teachings, particularly as found in the New Testament. The history of their early days, when their pacifism and ideas of radical reform resulted in punitive taxation and other persecution, is reflected in their continuing sense of community and their simple way of life with few possessions, plain architecture and clothing styles, and even the simplicity of their traditional church music, unaccompanied German chorales. Mennonites today bear witness to their religious convictions through their commitment to nonviolence and voluntary service, especially through worldwide disaster relief.

Hutterites

Like the Amish and Mennonites, the Hutterites originated in the Anabaptists of the sixteenth-century Reformation. Fleeing persecution in Switzerland, Germany, northern Italy, and southern Austria, some Anabaptists settled in Moravia (now part of the Czech Republic). In 1529 Jacob Hutter, or "hat maker," gathered followers there. After centuries of alternating discrimination and prosperity, Hutterite groups came to North America in 1874. Also like Amish and Mennonites, the Hutterian Brethren, or Hutterites, believe in adult baptism, pacifism, and the separation of church and state. A significant distinction is Hutterite communal life, with all material goods held in common and shared equally, modeled on Jesus and his disciples and the early Christians. Earning personal spending money (*Aagnutz*) is discouraged.

About 460 Hutterite colonies, with an estimated 45,000 members, are in the northwest United States, in North and South Dakota, Minnesota, Washington, and Montana; and in Canada, in the provinces of Manitoba, Saskatchewan, Alberta, and British Columbia. Hutterites also sponsor a mission in Nigeria. Hutterites attend a daily church service in the evening (*Gebet*, or prayer) and on Sunday (*Lehr*, or teaching), and for religious holidays and events. The men typically wear beards once married, buttoned shirts, and dark trousers; the women wear below-the-knee dresses and head coverings. Young girls' dresses are in bright colors; they also wear a *mitz*, or bonnet.

Anabaptist Churches

For the glory of God and my neighbors' good.
—EARLY BRETHREN MOTTO

ADDITIONAL GROUPS WITH ANABAPTIST ORIGINS or similarities also sought a return to the simplicity of the early Christian Church: the Church of the Brethren, the Moravian Church, and the Christadelphians. Their hallmarks are pacifism, the centrality of biblical teaching, and community.

Above: Diebold Schilling the Older's *Spiezer Chronik* of 1485 depicts a stylized rendering of the execution of Czech reformer Jan Hus. Accused of heresy, Hus was tried, condemned, and burned at the stake in 1416. Right: A monument to Jan Hus, in Prague, Czech Republic.

CHURCH OF THE BRETHREN

The Church of the Brethren originated in a group of religious dissenters who found refuge in Schwarzenau, Germany, and organized under Alexander Mack, a miller, in 1708, calling themselves "brethren." Their Anabaptist ideas brought persecution, and most of them emigrated to North America, beginning in 1719; their first congregation was established in Pennsylvania in 1723. From there, missionaries of the German Baptist Brethren, as they were known, expanded their settlements to the West Coast by the 1880s. They split into three groups, the largest taking the name Church of the Brethren in 1908.

Current membership in the United States and Puerto Rico is 127,500; Brethren churches are also in Brazil, India, the Dominican Republic, Haiti, and Nigeria, which has the largest Brethren population worldwide, about 150,000.

The Brethren's only creed is the Bible's New Testament. They are one of the three historic peace churches, along with Quakers and Mennonites, and seek to follow Christ's teachings through community service and disaster relief.

Another offshoot of the original Brethren group is named the Brethren Church. Organized in 1883, it now has about 13,000 members in 118 congregations, mostly in Ohio, Pennsylvania, and Indiana.

THE MORAVIAN CHURCH

Czech religious reformer Jon Hus (1369–1415) strove to return the church in Bohemia and Moravia (now the Czech Republic) to the simplicity of early Christianity. His followers organized as the Bohemian Brethren or Unity of the Brethren (Unitas Fratrum) in 1457, one of the earliest movements against Roman Catholicism. In the early eighteenth century a small Moravian group of Brethren began a series of settlements embracing a simple, communal way of life. The first U.S. community was established in Pennsylvania in 1741; western and Canadian expansion followed.

Today the Moravian Church has more than 750,000 members in nineteen provinces throughout the world. Their motto is "In essentials, unity; in nonessentials, liberty; and in all things, love." One highlight of Moravian worship is the "lovefeast," a music-filled service open to all where food is served to the congregation; it is meant to recall the gatherings of the early Christians.

CHRISTADELPHIANS

Another group drawing from Anabaptist traditions is the Christadelphians, founded in 1848 in the United States by English surgeon John Thomas (1805–71), who sought to reclaim the teachings of Jesus and his first-century apostles. Christadelphians meet, often in their homes, in local groups called "ecclesias," the name of early Christian congregations. Instead of ordained clergy or church hierarchy, leaders are elected male volunteers called lecturing, managing, or presiding brethren. Their interpretation of the Bible provides guidance and creed, and many Christadelphians follow a plan that directs a read-through of the Old Testament once a year and the New Testament twice.

Christadelphians reject the divinity of Jesus but look for his return to establish God's earthly kingdom in Jerusalem. Members do not vote, hold political office, or participate in the military. In the United States these "brethren in Christ," as the name translates, number about 6,500; worldwide membership is 50,000, with significant groups in Canada, Great Britain, Australia, and New Zealand.

Because of persecution in Germany, nearly all Brethren migrated to the New World in the eighteenth century.

Seventh-Day Adventists

THE IMPORTANCE OF OBSERVING the Sabbath and of the Second Advent of Christ is embodied in the name Seventh-Day Adventist Church, a religious movement originating in the United States and now established worldwide. The Sabbath, or day of rest, was originally Saturday—the seventh day in Judeo-Christian tradition—and Adventists follow this tradition for their day of worship.

Based on his study of the Bible, Baptist preacher William Miller (1782–1849) predicted that Christ's Second Coming would occur between 1843 and 1844. When this failed to happen—known as the "Great Disappointment"—some followers concluded that instead Christ had entered into heaven's "Most Holy Place," where his judgment of sins determines salvation; from there he will return soon for his second advent. Believers gathered to form the beginnings of the Seventh-Day Adventists, officially taking the name in 1860; the church was formally established in 1863, in Battle Creek, Michigan, with a membership of 3,500.

Today the church is one of the world's fastest-growing, with more than fifteen million members worldwide and a presence in well over 200 countries; fewer than 10 percent of Seventh-day Adventists live in the United States. Church headquarters have been in Silver Spring, Maryland, since 1989. The church also operates 7,200 schools, colleges, and universities, with an enrollment exceeding 1.4 million students, and its international relief and development efforts are in more than a hundred countries.

FUNDAMENTAL BELIEFS

Though most Adventist doctrines today are similar to those of other Bible-following evangelical Protestants, some teachings are distinctive. Among the church's "28 Fundamental Beliefs" is the idea of a "remnant" of the universal church, which keeps the commandments of God, even in the end-time days of widespread apostasy, and which will herald Christ's second coming; the remnant traditionally is thought to be the Adventist church. Also, Christ's heavenly work of "investigative judgment" reveals who among both the dead and the living are worthy of salvation. Another belief is that "spiritual gifts" are bestowed on church members, including the "gift of prophecy" manifested by Ellen White (1827–1915), Seventh-Day Adventist co-founder. However, the authority of her visions and writings is controversial among members today. The doctrine of the "great controversy," which explains how the world is the arena for the cosmic battle between Christ and Satan, is based on White's teachings.

In 1863, Mrs. White introduced the concept of spirituality having a direct link to physical well-being and a healthful diet that espoused vegetarianism—a significant component of Seventh-Day Adventism.

HEALTH AND HOLINESS

In accordance with their church teachings, Adventists regard both body and spirit as holy and therefore seek a pure lifestyle. In addition to wearing conservative clothing styles and rejecting entertainment and recreation that fail to meet "the highest standards of Christian taste and beauty," Adventists typically abstain from alcohol and tobacco and avoid caffeine and unhealthy foods; a vegetarian diet is recommended by the church. The Adventist Church also operates one of the largest non-profit health-care systems in the world.

LIVING THE GOOD LIFE

A recent study of 34,000 Seventh-Day Adventists in Loma Linda, California, determined that their lifestyle habits contributed to a longer-than-average life expectancy. The healthy practices of these Adventists included their vegetarian diet, regular exercise, appropriate body weight, no smoking, and a small helping of nuts a few times a week. Also considered signficant was their strict observance of a weekly day of rest and the social support of their close-knit community. The result within the Adventist population was a high rate of centenarians, much less disease, and more healthy years of life.

In addition to creating and distributing the periodical *The Present Truth*, Elder James and his wife, Ellen, created the Review and Herald Publishing Association. More than one hundred titles authored by Ellen James are still in print.

Theosophical Movement

Theosophy, Greek for "god wisdom" or divine wisdom, has been a religious philosophy from antiquity through the present. Called the Wisdom Tradition, the Perennial Philosophy, or Timeless Theosophy, its ancient version referred to mystical insight into the nature of God and the soul. The writings of Jakob Böhme (1575–1624), a German mystic whose visions he believed showed him the spiritual structure of the world, are an early inspiration for modern theosophy.

Theosophy today originated in the teachings of Helena Petrovna Blavatsky (1831–91), who sought spiritual paths to the enlightenment of the individual and the perfection of humanity. Today the members of the major Theosophical societies are thought to number about 40,000 worldwide, plus 5,000 in the United States, and thousands more as unaffiliated followers of its tenets and practices.

Though Helena Blavatsky cofounded the Theosophical Society (where she held the title of corresponding secretary), her initial claim to fame resulted from publication of her writings about paranormal phenomena.

Before cofounding the Theosophical Society, Henry Steel Olcott worked as a journalist reporting on spiritualistic phenomena. Serving as president of the Society for the rest of his life, Olcott accompanied Blavatsky on her travels to India.

QUEST FOR HIDDEN WISDOM

The original Theosophical Society was founded in 1875 in New York City by Madame Blavatsky, as she was known, with Henry Olcott, a lawyer and journalist, and William Quan Judge, an attorney. Russian by birth, Blavatsky had traveled the world seeking the meaning of life, delving into ancient Western teachings and Eastern spiritual thought. The initial goal of the society was to explore the metaphysical world through spiritualism, or psychic mediums, to gain access to hidden knowledge; however, Blavatsky soon aimed to change the Western religious world. The Theosophical Society encompassed ideas from Buddhism and Hinduism, such as reincarnation and spiritual evolution, or the ascent to higher planes of existence, not well known in the West then.

In 1877 Blavatsky published her first major work, *Isis Unveiled*, which demonstrated how theosophic ideas are based in ancient and modern religions, as well as in nature. Soon after, Blavatsky and Olcott moved to India, continuing the pursuit of Eastern beliefs with further study of Western mystical traditions such as Freemasonry, Gnosticism, the Kabbalah, and Rosicrucianism. In 1882 they established the Theosophical Society's international headquarters in Adyar, Chennai, in India. In her 1889 work *Key to Theosophy*, Blavatsky summarized the society's goals as promoting a "universal brotherhood of humanity," the study of the world's religions, and the investigation of the "hidden mysteries of nature," especially the "psychic and spiritual powers latent in man." The society's adherents sought to connect with the teachers of humanity from many religions, "ascended masters," formerly on earth but now in spiritual realms.

THEOSOPHY TODAY

The modern theosophical movement promotes the unity of existence and the progress of consciousness in perceiving it; today's theosophical beliefs offer a way of looking at life rather than a creed. Among these ideas are reincarnation, karma or moral justice, the existence of worlds of experience beyond the physical, the evolution of spirit and intelligence as well as of physical matter, and the possibility of conscious participation in evolution.

Three theosophical organizations formed after Blavatsky's death. The largest and most diverse group is the Theosophical Society Adyar, in India, with American headquarters in Wheaton, Illinois. The Theosophical Society Pasadena, in California, and the independent United Lodge of Theosophists, founded in 1909, emphasize the writings of Blavatsky. Some followers believe that the ideas developing subsequent to Blavatsky's should be termed "neo-theosophy."

UNIVERSAL INVOCATION

O hidden Life, vibrant in every atom,
O hidden Light, shining in every creature,
O hidden Love, embracing all in oneness,
May all who feel themselves as one with thee
Know they are therefore one with every other.

—Universal Invocation, Annie Besant, second president of the Theosophical Society

Anthroposophy

Anthroposophy is a path of knowledge aiming to guide the spiritual in the human being to the spiritual in the universe.
—RUDOLF STEINER, ANTHROPOSOPHICAL LEADING THOUGHTS, *1924*

FROM THE GREEK for "human wisdom," anthroposophy refers to "knowledge of mankind." Though the word was used by German philosophers in previous centuries, its current meaning is associated with Rudolf Steiner (1861–1925), as the name for his teachings about spiritual knowledge, especially as a distinction from Theosophy, the belief system of Madame Blavatsky and her followers beginning in the late nineteenth century.

While many Theosophists were increasingly embracing Eastern beliefs, Steiner was drawn instead to ideas gleaned from both Christianity and natural science. He broke away from the Theosophical Society, despite his important position in it, and helped establish the Anthroposophical Society in 1913.

Since then the Anthroposophical Society has aimed to foster both the spiritual development of its adherents and of society, through involvement in education, agriculture, medicine, the arts, and architecture. Today national branches of Anthroposophical Societies are in fifty countries, with smaller groups in an additional fifty countries. About 10,000 Anthroposophical institutions are worldwide, with 50,000 members. The General Anthroposophical Society's international center, founded by Steiner in 1923, is in Dornach, Switzerland.

SPIRITUAL RESEARCH

The basis for Anthroposophy was Steiner's belief that the scientific method could be applied to the life of the soul and to knowledge of "higher worlds," as he termed them. Religious mysticism alone was not sufficient for true spiritual understanding, since the knowledge gained through it was not exact; natural science was also limited, confined by its application to the outer world. Through Anthroposophy, however, a combination of both approaches, enhancing intellect with imagination, inspiration, and intuition, would help individuals find their own path to spiritual understanding without depending on external authority. These higher levels of consciousness could be attained through meditation, observation, and moral development. Steiner also taught that humans are reincarnated, with each life guided by their karma, or experiences in a spiritual realm between lives.

Today Anthroposophy continues to emphasize a spiritual view of human beings and their place in the universe. Thinking and knowledge are primary, as opposed to faith; the wisdom resulting from spiritual perception leads not only to the betterment of the individual but also of society.

The Goetheanum in Dornach, Switzerland, is the international headquarters of the Anthroposophical movement. Described as a masterpiece of twentieth-century expressionist architecture, the cast-concrete building was made to Steiner's design and features a thousand-seat auditorium. The building's name comes from German author Johann Wolfgang von Goethe, whose writings influenced Steiner.

STEINER SCHOOLS AND WALDORF EDUCATION

Rudolf Steiner extended the principles of Anthroposophy to many other fields, including a significant education system. The first school based on Steiner's principles was established in 1919 at the request of the owner of the Waldorf-Astoria Cigarette Company in Stuttgart, Germany—hence the now trade-marked name Waldorf for the worldwide schools and teaching methods, often adapted as well by teachers outside the system. Interdisciplinary learning is emphasized; academic, artistic, and practical subjects are integrated. An estimated thousand independent Waldorf schools and 1,400 kindergartens are in about sixty countries worldwide, along with Waldorf-based public and charter schools, special-education schools, and homeschooling information. Some Steiner schools have successfully brought together students of usually segregated races or beliefs and also offer community services to poor areas.

Though parents generally praise the schools' instructional techniques, some are wary of the Anthroposophical ideas behind them.

Simplicity is one of the keystones of the Waldorf philosophy. Though there were no plastic toys when Waldorf schools were first started, the emphasis was still on handmade toys and imaginative play.

Perhaps best known for his Waldorf School legacy, Rudolf Steiner studied mathematics, science, and philosophy. The scientific writings of Goethe, which he edited, influenced his own work. After his views on theosophy differed with the founders of the Society, he started a new German offshoot of the organization.

Humanism

Humanism will affirm life rather than deny it, seek to elicit the possibilities of life, not flee from it, and endeavor to establish the conditions of satisfactory life for all, not merely for the few.
—HUMANIST MANIFESTO I, 1933

AS A SYSTEM OF BELIEF, humanism means a philosophy of life that affirms the human ability to lead an ethical life without divine or supernatural guidance, and a commitment to the betterment of humanity through reason and science, as well as justice and compassion.

This definition of humanism should not be confused with the academic term referring to the Renaissance intellectual movement based on a new interest in the culture of ancient Greece and Rome. However, the origins of modern humanism can be found in the turning away of Renaissance thinkers from medieval theological concerns to seeking inspiration in human achievement.

Today humanism encompasses a range of definitions and meanings. Sometimes humanism is equated with secular humanism, which emphasizes nonreligious ethics and is also the term used by some conservative Christians to describe what they see as the sinful godlessness of modern society. In contrast, religious humanism can refer to humanism as a form of religion or as a nontheistic approach that accepts some religious beliefs and rituals while focusing on humanity. An official humanist "life stance" is known as Humanism, capitalized, to emphasize that it is a specific philosophy.

French philosopher Auguste Comte is considered the founding father of sociology. He believed that human actions should benefit society and raise everybody's quality of life. His book, *A General View of Positivism*, proposes replacing religion with humanism.

HUMAN PROGRESS, HUMAN RIGHTS

French philosopher Auguste Comte (1798–1857) proposed what he called the universal "religion of humanity"—the goal of mankind was to worship itself. His theory of positivism held that science would supersede theology and metaphysics, and that knowledge from sense perception was superior to dogmatic teachings. Positivist societies formed to consider how these principles applied to the issues of the day. Also in the mid-nineteenth century, the Humanistic Religious Association was organized in London; its members proclaimed their emancipation from "ancient dogma, myths, and ceremonies." In 1867 the Free Religious Association was established in Boston, led by Ralph Waldo Emerson and attracting religious liberals.

Reformer and educator Felix Adler founded the Society for Ethical Culture in 1876 as a nontheistic religion; its emphasis on ethical behavior encouraged social reform and the development of social work as a profession.

In the early twentieth century, members of Positivist and Ethical Culture groups began using the term "humanism" to mean a belief in human effort, and it became widely accepted among liberal religious congregations as well as academics and freethinkers.

Today the American Humanist Association, established in 1941, aims to lead local and national Humanist organizations toward progressive societal change. The International Humanist and Ethical Union, founded in 1952, represents an estimated four million Humanists organized in more than a hundred organizations in forty countries. The mission of the IHEU is to defend human rights and promote the dignity of all people.

Images such as these, from the revised edition of Jacob Riis's seminal *How the Other Half Lives*, helped to expose the poor conditions that the less fortunate were subjected to and led to social reforms, including the closing of poor houses.

THE HUMANIST MANIFESTOS

Three "Humanist Manifestos" have been composed as consensus statements by leading Humanists. The first, written in 1933, was the proclamation of a "new philosophy out of the materials of the modern world." In 1973 a second manifesto acknowledged the overoptimism of its predecessor in light of the events of the intervening decades, but offered hope while "reaching for vision in a time that needs direction." The third, written in 2003, offers this affirmation: "We work to uphold the equal enjoyment of human rights and civil liberties in an open, secular society and maintain it is a civic duty to participate in the democratic process and a planetary duty to protect nature's integrity, diversity, and beauty in a secure, sustainable manner."

Religions of the African Diaspora

AFRICANS TAKEN FROM THEIR HOMELAND as slaves brought nothing with them to the New World, with an important exception: their cultural and spiritual traditions. Nurtured in secret, African religious beliefs and customs were disguised or combined with the imposed teachings and rituals of the strange new lands. In this way, beliefs and believers persisted, adapted, and survived. The process is called syncretism, and the result among the Africans enslaved in the Caribbean came to be known loosely as Vodou, or "voodoo." Vodou practices have little to do with the voodoo of popular culture, a sensationalized black magic of zombies and human sacrifice.

Yemayá, considered the mother of all living things in the Santería and Candomblé belief systems, is often portrayed as a water nymph or mermaid. Because the legacy of the African traditions were largely transmitted orally, the goddess's name has numerous spelling variations.

HAITIAN VODOU: FAMILY SPIRITS

Haitian Vodou originated in Vodun, the religion of coastal West Africa, which is followed today by an estimated sixteen million people in Benin, Togo, Ghana, and Nigeria. Vodun is a form of monotheism, with one divine creator and the *vodun*, a host of other sacred deities and spirits of varying powers.

The West Africans brought as slaves to Haitian plantations retained elements of Vodun; they also adopted ideas from the native Indians they encountered. The concepts of one God and the intercessory saints and angels of Catholic Christianity, as taught by priests, were seen to be compatible with the remnants of the Africans' original beliefs. The result was a belief system that is widespread in Haiti today.

Haitian Vodou adherents generally believe in one creator God; however, more important in Vodou practice are spirits—*miste* or "mysteries," saints, and ancestors—who connect the human and the divine. They are honored and summoned with food, drink, and other offerings. Especially important are the family spirits,

or *loa*, who may appear to family members in dreams or trances. Mediating Vodou specialists are the male *houngan* and female *manbo*.

Though Vodou has been misunderstood and persecuted, it was given official status as a national religion in 2003 by Jean-Bertrand Aristide, then Haitian president. He identified Vodou as an "ancestral religion" and considered it "an essential part of national identity." This gave legal authority to Vodou ceremonies such as baptism and marriage. Despite the lack of reliable statistics, Vodou adherents in Haiti are thought to number in the millions.

CANDOMBLÉ: DANCING FOR THE GODS

A similar religion is Candomblé, practiced in Brazil. In response to attempts to suppress their traditional beliefs and to institute Catholicism, African slaves—Yoruba, Fon, and Bantu peoples—would seem to be honoring saints but were simultaneously praying to their own corresponding deities, or *orishas*. Candomblé managed to survive in a variety of forms for centuries, and in Brazil is now an established religion with an estimated two million adherents and thousands of temples. "Candomblé" means "dance in honor of the gods" and dancing is an important part of spiritual ceremonies; rituals may also involve healing and drumming, as well as seeking possession by orishas.

SANTERÍA: THE WAY OF THE SAINTS

Also combining African and Catholic elements is Santería, which originated mainly in Cuba and has spread primarily among Hispanic populations in the United States, South and Central America, and a few countries in Europe. The orishas of the Yoruba and Lukumi people of Nigeria were identified with

saints; the devotion they inspired in African slaves was mocked by Spanish Europeans as *santería*, the way of the saints. Today, many "santeros" in Cuba regard themselves as Catholic, though they sometimes have separate rituals for the orishas.

Naña Buluku ranks as the supreme being of the Yoruba belief system. Called the grandmother of all other deities by some, Naña is considered androgynous by others and goes by a variety of different names depending on the African tribal affiliation of worshippers.

LOUISIANA VOODOO

Voodoo dolls and gris-gris—African amulets—are items associated with "New Orleans voodoo" but are more likely to target tourist dollars than an unsuspecting victim. However, an authentic tradition of voodoo in New Orleans was influenced by Haitian immigrants to Louisiana starting in 1809, after the Haitian Revolution. The beliefs and practices of African-descended Haitians mingled with those of the French- and Creole-speaking African Americans. The related term "hoodoo" refers to African American folk magic.

FAITH GROUPS AND COMMUNITIES

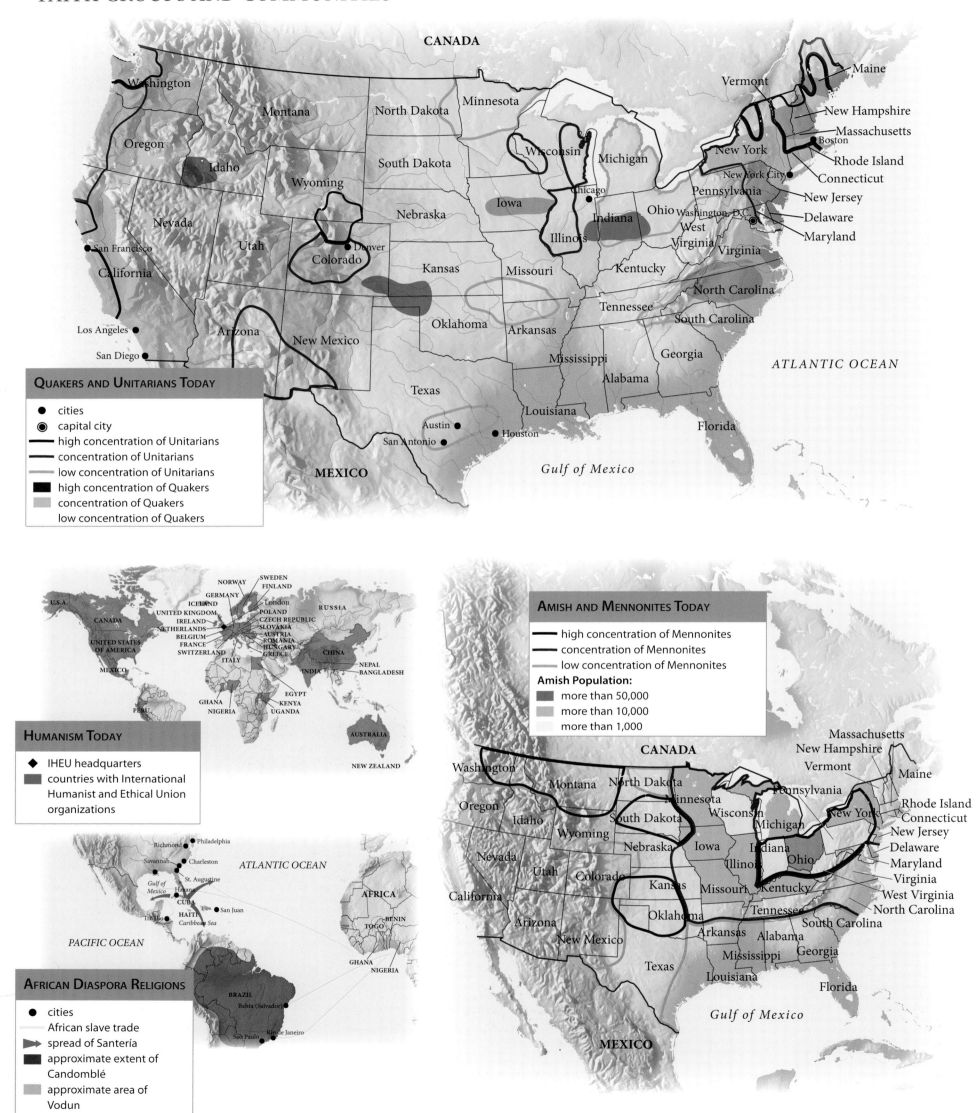

QUAKERS AND UNITARIANS TODAY

- ● cities
- ◎ capital city
- ▬ high concentration of Unitarians
- ▬ concentration of Unitarians
- ▬ low concentration of Unitarians
- ■ high concentration of Quakers
- concentration of Quakers
- low concentration of Quakers

HUMANISM TODAY

- ◆ IHEU headquarters
- countries with International Humanist and Ethical Union organizations

AFRICAN DIASPORA RELIGIONS

- ● cities
- African slave trade
- ➤ spread of Santería
- approximate extent of Candomblé
- approximate area of Vodun

AMISH AND MENNONITES TODAY

- ▬ high concentration of Mennonites
- ▬ concentration of Mennonites
- ▬ low concentration of Mennonites

Amish Population:
- more than 50,000
- more than 10,000
- more than 1,000

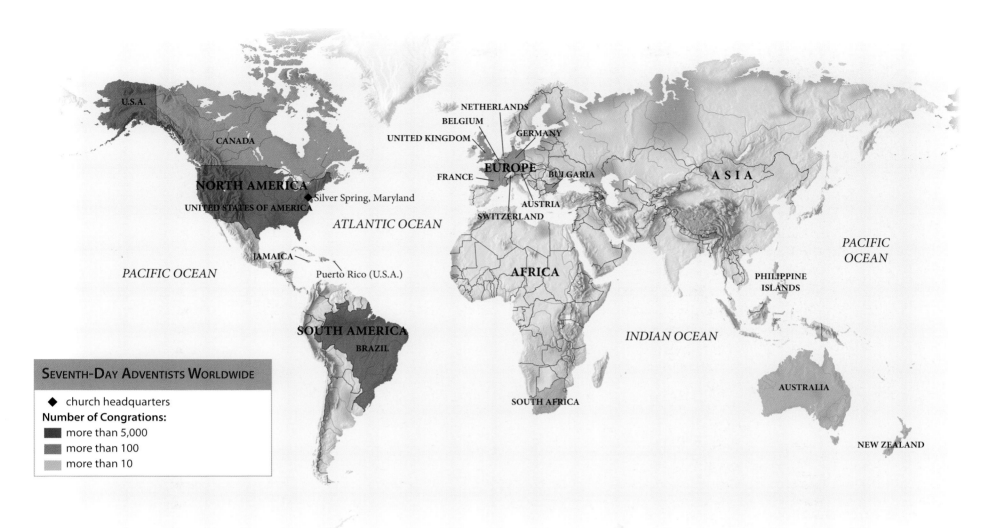

SEVENTH-DAY ADVENTISTS WORLDWIDE

◆ church headquarters

Number of Congrations:

■ more than 5,000
■ more than 100
■ more than 10

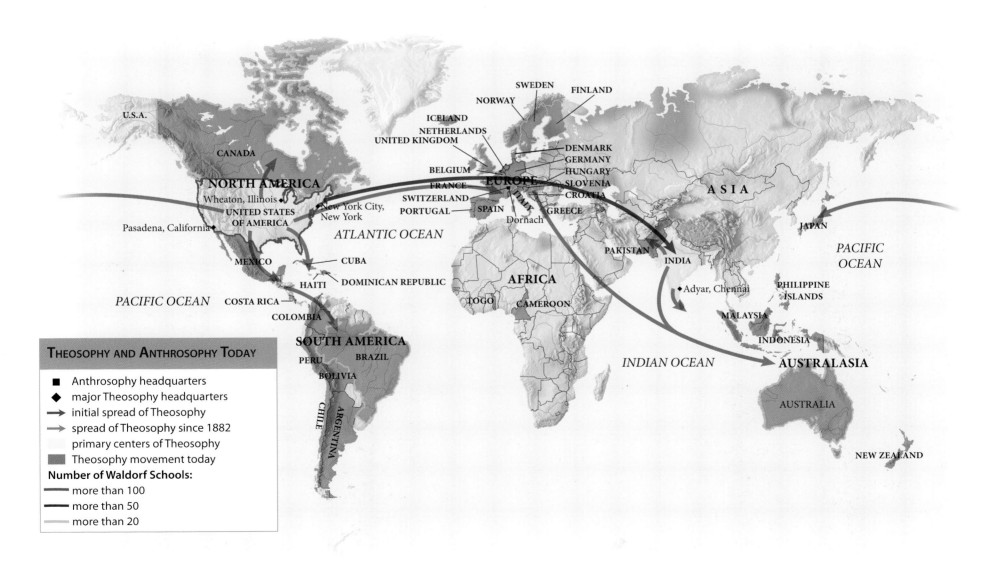

THEOSOPHY AND ANTHROSOPHY TODAY

■ Anthrosophy headquarters
◆ major Theosophy headquarters
→ initial spread of Theosophy
→ spread of Theosophy since 1882
□ primary centers of Theosophy
■ Theosophy movement today

Number of Waldorf Schools:

— more than 100
— more than 50
— more than 20

New Religions in the Modern World

TWENTIETH- AND TWENTY-FIRST-CENTURY religious movements are as diverse as their founders and followers. Some discover roots in ancient Eastern beliefs, some look for stronger connections between Christianity and Judaism, others are drawn to larger-than-life leaders. Movements may find inspiration in a transformative moment in time, such as the youth culture of the 1960s and '70s, or in specific interpretations of traditional scriptures, seeking to justify oppression or to be free from it. What they have in common is a way of explaining and guiding the human relationship to the divine and to the world.

Defining religious movements requires caution: the difference between denominations, sects, and cults can be debated—not only their specific definitions but also how they are applied. In general, however, a sect is considered a religious group, especially one that has separated from a larger denomination or official body of congregations; a cult is usually described as an extremist or false sect with an authoritarian, charismatic leader.

JEWS FOR JESUS

Jews for Jesus grew out of the "Jesus Movement" of the 1960s and '70s, when many young people found meaning in evangelical Christianity expressed through the hippie culture of the day. In 1970 Moishe Rosen, a Baptist minister who was raised as an Orthodox Jew, began missionary work among the youth drawn to San Francisco, particularly targeting young Jews. His creative evangelizing methods—rallies, drama and musical groups, broadside-style tracts—gained many followers and national media attention. Today Jews for Jesus continue their outreach worldwide through intense campaigns of street witnessing, when staff and volunteers distribute tracts in major international cities.

Jews for Jesus assert that Jesus is the fulfillment of the Jewish prophecy of the Messiah. New followers are usually baptized into Christianity and refer to themselves as "Hebrew Christians" or "Messianic Jews," retaining their Jewish religious identity. Many Jews, however, dispute this claim.

MESSIANIC JUDAISM

Messianic Jews believe that Jesus, called Yeshua, is the promised Jewish Messiah and Savior. While Messianic Jews consider themselves Jewish, some Jews disagree that the movement is Judaism in any form. Many Christians accept them as Christian.

Recent statistics give an estimate of 250,000 adherents of Messianic Judaism in the United States; in Israel, the number of Messianic Jews is estimated as 12,000. The Messianic Jewish Alliance of America, founded in 1915, is considered the largest association of Messianic Jews and non-Jewish believers in Yeshua in the world.

Jews for Jesus is sometimes described as a significant organization within the Messianic Judaism movement; however, some Messianic Jews disapprove of its theology and tactics.

The Jews for Jesus headquarters in New York City incorporates a star of David in its name, highlighting the group's identification with Jewish religion.

In recent years some Jews have come to reexamine Jesus Christ from the traditionally Christian viewpoint that he is the expected Messiah—fundamentally the same issue that divided Christians from Jews some 2,000 years ago.

CHILDREN OF GOD, THE FAMILY

To the hippies of Huntington Beach, California, David Brandt Berg (1919–94) was a missionary and prophet of Christian love. His radical religious group, the Children of God, was established in 1968, part of the "Jesus People" movement. Its members lived in communes and evangelized in the streets, sometimes with a technique called "flirty fishing," when women used sex appeal to attract male converts; "FFing" was officially discontinued in 1987. This practice and allegations of mind control and child abuse prompted the first organized anticult organization in 1971, Free the Children of God.

After several reorganizations, the group became The Family, an international Christian fellowship dedicated to spreading the message of God's love. The Family estimates that 10,000 full-time and associate adult volunteer members work in more than 1,100 centers or communities in 100 countries.

Hare Krishna, Hare Krishna,
Krishna Krishna, Hare Hare,
Hare Rama, Hare Rama,
Rama Rama, Hare Hare
—CENTRAL MANTRA OF ISKCON MOVEMENT

Abhay Charanaravinda Bhaktivedanta Swami Prabhupada founded the International Society for Krishna Consciousness to spread the Gaudiya Vaishnavism of Hinduism throughout India and the world while fighting accusations that his organization was a cult.

ECKANKAR

A modern religious movement emphasizing "soul travel" through spiritual exercises, Eckankar was founded in Las Vegas in 1965 by John Paul Twitchell (c. 1908–71), previously a Scientology adherent, who described himself as the 971st in an ancient line of Eck masters. "Eck" is defined as Life Force, the Holy Spirit, or Audible Life Current. Eckankar draws from a variety of traditions, including Sufism, Sikhism, and Hinduism.

The Temple of Eck, dedicated in 1990, in Chanhassen, Minnesota, is the worldwide headquarters, though the largest Eck temple is in Nigeria, with a total capacity of 10,000. The movement does not publish official membership figures but claims active adherents in more than one hundred countries in North America, Europe, Asia, and Africa. As of 2004, 36,700 members were estimated in the United States, with 50,000 worldwide, though a peak of 500,000 worldwide has been reported. The current leader, since 1981, is Sri Harold Klemp, the living Eck master, or Mahanta.

Eckankar teaches that the journey of "self- and God-realization" can be enhanced though meditation, prayer, past-life discovery, conscious dreaming, and mantras, especially singing or chanting "hu," said to be the ancient name of God. These techniques help the soul travel beyond the body to spiritual worlds. Eckists can advance to higher states of consciousness through successive stages of initiation.

Critics of Eckankar have alleged plagiarism in the movement's writings and deception by Eckankar leaders for personal profit, and explain adherents' spiritual experiences as psychological phenomena.

INTERNATIONAL SOCIETY FOR KRISHNA CONSCIOUSNESS (ISKCON) OR HARE KRISHNA

The Hare Krishna movement was established in 1966 by A. C. Bhaktivedanta Swami Prabhupada (1896–1977) in New York City. Two years later he began the first Hare Krishna commune, "New Vrindavan," in West Virginia. The Hindu-based movement spread rapidly, one of the most popular expressions of a new interest in Eastern religions in the 1960s and '70s. Adherents attracted attention with their colorful appearance, the women in bright saris and the men dressed in saffron or white robes with a shaved head and topknot.

Worldwide, ISKCON has more than 350 centers, 60 rural communities, 50 schools, and 60 restaurants in North America, Africa, Asia, Europe, and Great Britain; the fastest growth in recent decades has been in Eastern Europe and India. Official estimates cite 250,000 adherents plus 10,000 full members, called temple devotees; other estimates are as high as a million.

The central practice is the frequent daily recitation of the Hare Krishna mantra, to achieve "Krishna consciousness"—a higher state of being dedicated to the Hindu god Krishna, one name of the one Supreme God. The reform of society through a simple and natural way of life is the goal of Hare Krishna evangelism, which employs public singing and dancing and distribution of materials. "Congregational members" of ISKCON live a normal home and work life while practicing Krishna consciousness and worshipping at temples. "Temple-based" or full members live in temples and follow an ascetic lifestyle: celibacy except for procreation within marriage; meat, fish, eggs, alcohol, and drugs are prohibited. Charges of cult activity in the 1970s and '80s cited brainwashing, isolation from family and friends, and abuse of children at ISKCON schools.

The Palace of Gold, originally intended as the residence for A. C. Shakivendanta Swami Prabhupada, became a place of pilgrimage and popular tourist attraction in its unlikely location in Marshall County, West Virginia.

The Unification Church

A controversy surrounding the appointment of Josette Sheehan as the eleventh executive director of the UN World Food Programme was her fifteen-year affiliation with the Unification Church as both a member and an employee of News World Communications, its media arm.

ESTABLISHED IN SEOUL, KOREA, IN 1954 as the Holy Spirit Association for the Unification of World Christianity, or the Unification Church, this religious sect and its global enterprises were under the leadership of the Reverend Sun Myung Moon through 2008, when his son Hyung Jin Moon took over.

The Unification Church evangelizes in two hundred countries; though the number of believers is confidential, the church estimates three million adherents worldwide, the majority in South Korea and Japan. Other sources estimate 250,000 throughout the world, with 5,000 to 10,000 dedicated members in the United States. Membership peaked in the 1980s.

In 1996 Moon combined the many organizations he had established—religious, commercial, political, and cultural—into the Family Federation for World Peace and Unification, with a stated purpose of promoting family values and faith in God. National FFWPU headquarters is in Washington, D.C.

The city of Seoul was the birthplace of the Holy Spirit Association for the Unification of World Christianity, more commonly known as the Unification Church. Membership has now spread to more than 150 countries.

THE DIVINE PRINCIPLE

According to Moon's account, Jesus appeared to him on Easter morning in 1936, when Moon was 15, and asked him to help establish the kingdom of God on earth. In 1945 Moon gathered followers in northern Korea; by the late '50s he had founded thirty churches in South Korea and sent missionaries to Japan and Europe. In 1959 Moon's adherents came to the United States, considered a key country for world influence. Moon himself followed in the early '70s and launched a major recruitment effort.

The church's fundamental teaching is known as the Divine Principle: the sin of Adam and Eve, the first parents, and therefore of all humanity, has prevented God's earthly kingdom. However, the world will be restored to its perfect state once a second Adam and Eve pay an "indemnity" for sin. This new Adam or Messiah was not Jesus, but a "Lord of the Second Coming" who will arise in Korea, complete the indemnity, marry the new Eve, and bring about a sinless humanity. Moon and his present wife, the "True Parents," are considered by believers to be fulfilling this prophecy.

PRACTICES AND POLITICS

Early criticism of the church focused on its high-pressure recruitment practices and its alienation of church members from their families and from the outside world in general. An important church ritual, the mass wedding ceremonies of thousands of couples whose marriages were arranged by the Moons, is described as coercive and a means of extorting high fees. The Moon family's commercial empire and alliances with political organizations worldwide have also come under scrutiny, while revelations of problems within the Moon dynasty have undercut their image as the perfect family.

MOONIES

In the 1970s young members of the Unification Church selling carnations on the street to raise funds were called "Moonies" after their leader Sun Myung Moon, whose name means "word of shining light." Though considered a derogatory term, the name has persisted, referring to Moon's followers in general.

THE WASHINGTON TIMES

"Simply put, I founded the Washington Times in order to fulfill the Will of God."
—Sun Myung Moon, June 16, 1997

Established by Moon and his assistant Bo Hi Pak in 1982, the Washington Times is a daily newspaper in the United States capital. Along with wire service United Press International, purchased in 2000, the newspaper is part of the Unification Church's media conglomerate News World Communications Inc. Times circulation is about 100,000, or one-seventh that of D.C.'s other daily, the Washington Post. The Times is both commended and criticized for its politically conservative slant and is heavily subsidized by Moon.

Scientology

We seek no revolution. We seek only evolution to higher states of being for the individual and for society. We are achieving our aims.

—L. RON HUBBARD, THE AIMS OF SCIENTOLOGY (1950)

SCIENTOLOGY WAS FOUNDED IN 1954 in Los Angeles, California, by Lafayette Ronald Hubbard, a science fiction writer and the author of the best-selling book *Dianetics: The Modern Science of Mental Health*. Emerging from the book's self-improvement concepts was Scientology, described by its believers as "an applied religious philosophy." According to Scientology teachings, the word means "the study of truth," from the Latin *scio*, "knowing in the fullest sense of the word," and the Greek *logos*, meaning "study of."

As the Church of Scientology International, the organization claims to be the fastest-growing religion in the world, with more than 6,000 churches, missions, related organizations, groups, and activities ministering to more than eight million people in 159 countries in over 66 languages. Other estimates suggest 500,000 members worldwide; according to the 2001 census, self-identified Scientologists numbered 55,000 in the United States.

The Church of Scientology in Los Angeles, on L. Ron Hubbard Way off Sunset Boulevard, was the first Scientology church to be built, in 1954. The mother church of Scientology International is headquartered in Hollywood, as is the church's Celebrity Centre International. Spiritual headquarters is in Clearwater, Florida. The current worldwide ecclesiastical leader is David Miscavige, a second-generation Scientologist.

The West Coast headquarters of the Scientology religion is housed in a former hospital. Los Angeles, California—also home to Bridge Publications (the church's publishing arm)—has the highest concentration of Scientologists in the world.

FROM ENGRAMS TO ENLIGHTENMENT

The ultimate goal promoted by Scientology is spiritual enlightenment and freedom for the individual, or "thetan." Through the Scientology process called "auditing," negative experiences from this and past lifetimes, recorded in "engrams," can be discovered by measuring with an electropsychometer, or "E-meter," and discharged to eliminate self-defeating behavior; this is known as "going clear." Higher levels of auditing offer further liberation of the soul and the status of OT, or "Operating Thetan." Only after many years of study and practice can the "Bridge to Total Freedom" be attained.

CELEBRITIES AND CRITICS

Scientology has been endorsed and publicized by several high-profile adherents, such as film and television stars Tom Cruise, John Travolta, and Jenna Elfman. However, from its founding through the present, the organization has come under criticism for harmful practices and fraudulent claims. Members unable to pay the high fees for Scientology information and resources—a full course of auditing is estimated at $300,000 to $500,000—must recruit new members or work for the organization without pay. Members are forbidden contact with family and friends who question the group, in a policy called "disconnect." Threats, harassment, and prolonged litigation have been directed at former members, reporters, and prosecutors publicly criticizing the organization as a cult or as a business empire claiming to be a church for purposes of tax evasion.

In 2008 the internet-based group Anonymous organized protests at Scientology buildings in several major cities to call attention to such abuses. Many protestors wore masks to avoid identification and retribution from Scientology's lawyers, they claimed.

DIANETICS: MODERN SCIENCE OR SCIENCE FICTION?

According to Scientology, the science of Dianetics—"the modern science of mental health"—provides techniques for a happier, healthier life. Though its creator L. Ron Hubbard claimed that "Dianetics is a milestone for man comparable to his discovery of fire and superior to his inventions of the wheel and arch," in the late 1940s mainstream publishers and the medical establishment showed no interest in publicizing its principles. As a result, the first published explanation of Dianetics was in the magazine *Astounding Science Fiction*, May 1950.

Scientology has attracted numerous Hollywood celebrities, including Tom Cruise, John Travolta, and Kirstie Alley. It is alleged that the Church has offered Cruise special treatment, including a private chef and free landscaping.

Satanism and Christian Identity

NOT TO BE CONFUSED WITH POPULAR IMAGES of devil-worship in days of yore, or with goth youth subculture, Religious Satanism finds inspiration in the concept of Satan as a life force and as an adversary of hypocrisy. Far from deifying Satan, most Religious Satanists affirm their own individual liberty and reject the idea of any supernatural being or guidance.

The movement's largest and best-known organization is the Church of Satan. It was established in 1966 (Year One, *Anno Satanas*) by Anton Szandor LaVey (1930–97), American musician, public speaker, and writer. For the church's founding principles he admittedly synthesized ideas about seeking meaning and purpose through individual happiness from writers such as Ayn Rand and Friedrich Nietzsche.

Church of Satan adherents reject the "unreason of organized religions and mystical philosophies" and promote their form of Satanism as a way to enhance their members' lives. In their view, Satan represents indulgence instead of abstinence, wisdom instead of self-delusion, kindness to those who deserve it, and physical, mental, and emotional gratification.

Though the Church of Satan does not release membership figures, estimates of adherents are in the tens of thousands, with additional unaffiliated Religious Satanists.

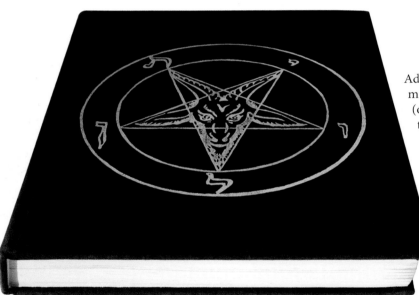

In print since it was written in 1969 by Anton LaVey, *The Satanic Bible* is divided into four parts exploring different aspects of Satanism: the Book of Satan, the Book of Lucifer, the Book of Belial, and the Book of Leviathan.

CHRISTIAN IDENTITY

Adherents of the Christian Identity movement believe that white "Aryans" (or non-Jewish Caucasians) are the true chosen people of God and that modern Jews are not Israelites or Hebrews but are actually descended from the Biblical Eve and Satan. The race war between Aryans and Jews throughout history, identified as the battle between good and evil, will culminate in apocalypse. These views are said to be based on interpretations of the Bible, of historical documents, and of archaeological discoveries, and are also influenced by British- or Anglo-Israelism, the idea that the ten "lost" tribes of Israel became the ancestors of the Anglo-Saxon race, the true Israelites.

This view was promoted in the United States by Herbert W. Armstrong, an early radio evangelist, through the Worldwide Church of God he established in 1933. (However, in 1995, the church officially rejected this doctrine. Currently, the Worldwide Church of God has 42,000 members in about 900 congregations in almost 100 nations and territories.)

In 1946 the White Identity Church of Jesus Christ–Christian was founded by Wesley A. Smith, a former Methodist minister and Ku Klux Klan organizer; in 1957 it was renamed the Church of Jesus Christ Christian. Its political wing was established in 1974: Aryan Nations, a white nationalist group. In the 1980s and '90s, government confrontations with right-wing extremists and white nationalists brought attention to these groups' connections with the Christian Identity movement.

Though it lacks an overall organizational structure, Christian Identity serves as a unifying belief system for several white separatist or supremacy groups. Some use its teachings as a religious basis for racism, even to the point of violence. Membership estimates vary from 2,000 to 50,000 members in the United States; statistics are unknown for worldwide adherents.

In 2007 a new Christian Identity group was formed, the United Church of YHVH. As a gathering of "Israelite (Adamite/Anglo-Saxon)" people they believe that as the chosen race they are destined to restore the truth of God's word, that spiritual warfare is inevitable, and that they are the holy remnant that will be saved exclusively.

The Ku Klux Klan, considered the nation's first terrorist group, combined racism, anti-Semitism, and anti-Catholicism with Christian fundamentalism. The founding of the White Identity Church of Jesus Christ–Christian seemed a likely extension of highly segregated church society.

The Rastafari Movement

*Princes shall come out of Egypt;
Ethiopia shall soon stretch out her
hands unto God.*
—PSALM 68

THE RASTAFARIAN MOVEMENT (or Rastafari or Rasta, preferred by adherents) began in Jamaica in 1930, its impetus and name a response to the coronation of prince Ras Tafari Makonnen as Emperor Haile Selassie of Ethiopia. However, its roots are in earlier efforts by impoverished black Jamaicans to reclaim and celebrate their African identity. Today it has branched out as a worldwide cultural and political movement, as well as a form of religious expression.

Biblical prophecies that were thought to foretell the emancipation of African people exiled by slavery, combined with the 1927 prediction of black nationalist leader Marcus Garvey that a black king would redeem them, led many Jamaicans to regard Selassie as God or "Jah" (a shortened form of the biblical Jehovah), a Messiah sent to lead them to their destiny—repatriation to Africa. They also believed that Selassie was descended from the son of the Queen of Sheba and King Solomon, son of David, ancestor of Jesus. The charismatic and highly regarded Selassie, who ended slavery in Ethiopia and initiated many other reforms, denied any divine status.

In 1996 the Rastafari movement was given consultative status by the United Nations. Today 5 to 10 percent of Jamaicans, or 139,000 to 278,000, identify themselves as Rastafarians. The more than one million Rastafaris worldwide have official branches in England, Canada, the Caribbean islands, and the United States and members in many more countries.

POWER AND PEACE

Black Jamaicans' social and political yearnings found expression in early Rastafari teachings: that blacks are the reincarnation of the biblical Israel, in exile in Jamaica as the Israelites were in Babylon, that the white man is inferior to the black man, who will rule the world.

However, Rastafaris today emphasize political reform and personal spirituality as a people chosen by God to promote his power and peace. Thus a return to African origins need not be actual repatriation but can be symbolic or cultural, through the rejection of oppressive Western systems or values—today's Babylon. Though some Rastafaris still esteem Selassie as the black Messiah, others seek divinity within every person, by showing respect for humanity and the environment.

Worship meetings are called reasoning sessions; marijuana, or ganja, is often used to enhance spirituality. Both inclusion and black self-determination are reflected in the Rastafari dialect, called Iyaric, which uses the personal pronoun "I" to replace the first letter or syllable of many words, and "I n I" to mean "we," "us," and "our." Some Rastafarians eat only what they consider natural and pure foods, a diet based on Old Testament laws and called "I-tal," from the word "vital."

Though the Rastafari movement in general is loosely defined, there are three main branches, or "mansions": Bobo Ashanti, whose members carry brooms to signify cleanliness; the Nyabinghi order, seeking a global theocracy; and the Twelve Tribes of Israel, the largest and most liberal branch.

RASTAFARI MUSIC

Awareness of the Rastafari movement throughout the world is often attributed to the widespread appeal of reggae music, especially as it was performed by musician Robert Nesta Marley. Originating in Jamaica, its name derived from "rege-rege," or ragged clothing, reggae joins elements of calypso and rhythm and blues, with a strong offbeat. However, the traditional music of Rastafari is Nyabinghi, the chanting and drumming of "reasoning sessions" or worship, which combines gospel music from nineteenth-century American evangelists and traditional African drumming to enhance participation and spirituality. Whatever the style, Rastafari music and lyrics emphasize liberation, redemption, and unity.

The term Rastafarian is derived from the word *Ras*, which is an Ethiopian title meaning "head" or "king," and the precoronation name of Emperor Haile Selassie of Ethiopia.

Early Rastafari, regarded as revolutionaries by Jamaican authorities and forced underground or into isolated communes, grew their hair and beards long and twisted into ropelike coils. These dreadlocks not only refer to the Rastafaris' separation from society but are also a response to biblical injunctions to leave hair uncut and a reference to the mane of the Lion of Judah, a Rastafarian symbol.

Neopaganism

Eight words the Wiccan Rede fulfill:
An it harm none, do what ye will.
—FROM WICCAN CREDO

NEOPAGANISM, SOMETIMES SIMPLY PAGANISM, is a modern revival of ancient religions, generally pre-Christian and European. The term "pagan" originally referred to a country dweller (Latin *paganus*), considered more likely than the urban followers of the "new" Christianity to cling to old beliefs; then it came to mean any non-Christian; and later, in some usages, it acquired connotations of anti-Christian practices.

Some Neopagans seek to reconstruct ancient beliefs as accurately as possible from historical sources, while others combine and interpret spiritual practices from a wide range of influences. The largest Neopagan movement is Wicca ("wise ones"); next in size is Neodruidism, based on the practices of ancient Celtic priests. Other Neopagans follow Asatru, the pre-Christian Norse religion; Hellenismos, from ancient Greece; and Kemetism, from ancient Egypt. Other traditions that Neopagans draw from are the occult, magic, and alchemy.

Estimates of the number of Neopagans throughout the world vary widely; an approximation is one million. The strongest movements are in the United States, Britain, the Baltic States, Scandinavia, and Ukraine. According to the American Religious Identification Survey (2001), 140,000 U.S. adults identified themselves as Pagan, 134,000 as Wiccan, and 33,000 as Druid.

Neodruids have journeyed to Stonehenge for more than a century. Visitation to the site reaches its height at the summer solstice.

The horned god is often represented in Wiccan culture, and such depictions are frequently derived from the ancient Celtic god Cernunnos. Other belief systems, however, also feature horned deities such as the Greek god Pan.

NATURE AND RITUAL

Neopagans revere the natural world, celebrating seasonal cycles and conducting their rituals outside whenever possible. They are often duotheistic or polytheistic, recognizing a god and goddess or several deities. Many Neopagans practice alone or in small groups, known by several names, such as garths, circles, groves, and covens; this is usually the extent of any organizational structure. Some Neopagans are wary of being misunderstood or criticized by other religions as Satanic, and so avoid practicing publicly.

Rituals are an important form of religious expression for Neopagans, connecting participants not only with the divine but with nature, their community, and the inner self. To create a frame of mind called "between the worlds," or between the sacred and the mundane, Neopagans may symbolically define their ritual space by cleansing it with salt water or incense, or by marking the area with a chalk circle on the ground or knife blade through the air. Deities or spirits are summoned to the space to be honored or supplicated; music, dance, or guided meditation aid the experience.

WICCA

The most familiar and widespread Neopagan movement is Wicca, a polytheistic nature religion based on pre-Christian beliefs from western Europe. Wiccans are known for the use of herbal magic and benign witchcraft; their central deity is a mother goddess.

Wiccans claim a heritage originating in the Stone Age. Modern Wicca, dating from the 1940s, was influenced by the English occultist and writer Gerald Gardner (1884–1964) and branched into several versions. American Wicca is considered a more feminist form.

New Age

Many minds are now questing for deeper meaning and a new understanding of the great one-ness of life.
—Sir George Trevelyan, 1983

MORE A BROAD CATEGORY OF BELIEFS and practices than a conventional religion, the New Age movement seeks the transformation of the individual and society through spiritual and holistic inspiration, thereby creating a "new age."

New Age communities, conventions, and informal groups, found worldwide, provide some structure for adherents in the absence of clergy, places of worship, scripture, and dogma. The movement is thought to attract more women than men because of its respect for feminine aspects of spirituality and lack of male-oriented hierarchy. "New Agers" also tend to be of the "baby boomer" generation—born in the later 1940s through the early 1960s—who grew up as new social movements and a newfound interest in Eastern thought contributed to the trend away from mainstream religion. The 2001 American Religious Indentification Survey lists 68,000 as the number of self-described New Age followers.

WEST MEETS EAST

Many New Age concepts originated in nineteenth-century ideas of spiritual evolution and constructive thinking, such as Theosophy and New Thought, which were influenced by the earlier theories of experimental physician Franz Mesmer and mystic Emanuel Swedenborg. These views contributed to the development of the human potential movement in the 1950s and '60s, based on psychologist Abraham Maslow's theory of self-actualization; both these schools of thought promote cultivating and unleashing the individual's capabilities and powers. In the 1970s and '80s these ideas combined with an increasing fascination with Eastern religions and philosophy, such as Hinduism and Daoism, and with elements of the Western esotericism, including astrology, mysticism, and herbalism. These concepts have been applied not only to personal empowerment and fulfillment but also to business management, to promote efficiency and productivity.

BODY, MIND, AND SPIRIT

New Age adherents typically select a set of practices from among many. Some embrace integrated or holistic ways of healing for body, mind, and spirit, such as yoga, meditation, macrobiotic diets; other alternative wellness techniques include acupuncture, crystal and psychic healing, homeopathy, reflexology, and iridology (the study of the iris of the eye). Divination, channeling, and astrology, as means of foretelling the future or contacting a higher plane of existence, are also attractive to many New Age adherents but not limited to them. In the background for many of these activities is New Age music: gentle and repetitive, and usually performed with synthesizers, acoustic and ethnic instrumentation, and soothing vocals.

New Age eclecticism sometimes engenders criticism of the movement's followers as faddish or credulous. Channeling and the belief in the powers of crystals have been denounced, as have seminar or group leaders who have made considerable fortunes from New Age participants.

An unlikely combination of scientist, philospher, and theologian, Emanuel Swedenborg founded the New Church, followers of whom were known as Swedenborgians. His writings include the twelve-volume *Heavenly Mysteries* (1747–58).

Amethyst is a popular crystal in New Age circles; it is believed by New Agers that this mineral can give a person greater clarity and increased energy. Clear and colorless, the stone has hexagonal facets.

A NEW AGE COMMUNITY

In 1962 in the Scottish seaside village of Findhorn, Peter and Eileen Caddy and their friend Dorothy Maclean started a vegetable garden in their trailer park. In its poor soil they grew an abundance of herbs, flowers, and spectacular forty-pound cabbages, a result, they believed, of working in harmony with nature and understanding the plants' spirituality. As the fame of the garden spread, a community of like-minded people gathered there. Today the Findhorn Foundation includes holistic businesses and initiatives sharing a positive vision for humanity and the earth and a "deep and practical nondoctrinal spirituality."

One of the Findhorn community's founders was New Age pioneer Sir George Trevelyan (1906–96). In 1971 he established the Wrekin Trust, an educational charity based in Gloucestershire, England, as part of the worldwide movement toward personal and planetary transformation.

NEW RELIGIOUS MOVEMENTS, SECTS, AND CULTS

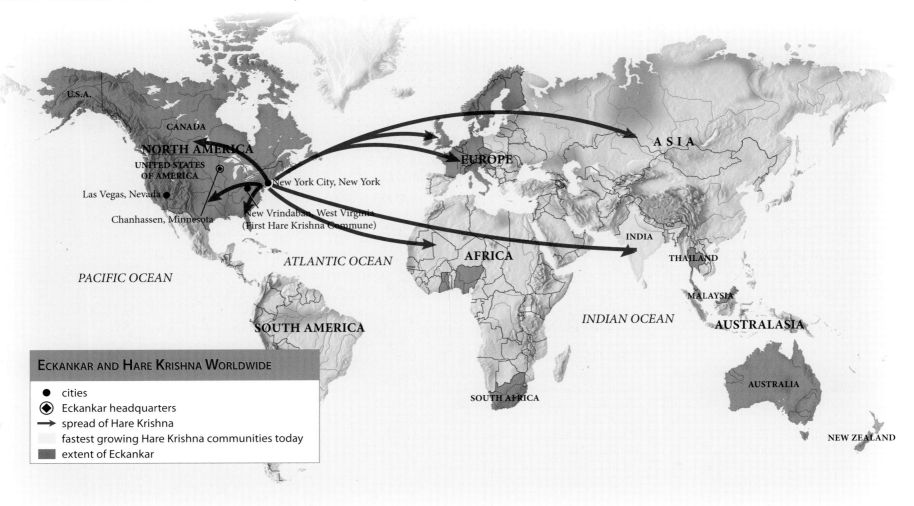

ECKANKAR AND HARE KRISHNA WORLDWIDE

- ● cities
- ◉ Eckankar headquarters
- → spread of Hare Krishna
- ▢ fastest growing Hare Krishna communities today
- ▢ extent of Eckankar

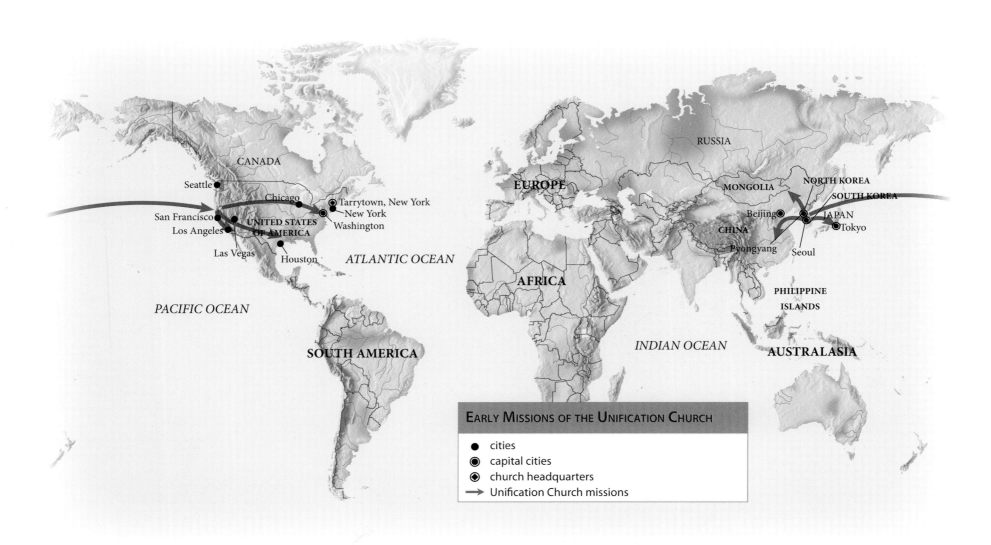

EARLY MISSIONS OF THE UNIFICATION CHURCH

- ● cities
- ◉ capital cities
- ◉ church headquarters
- → Unification Church missions

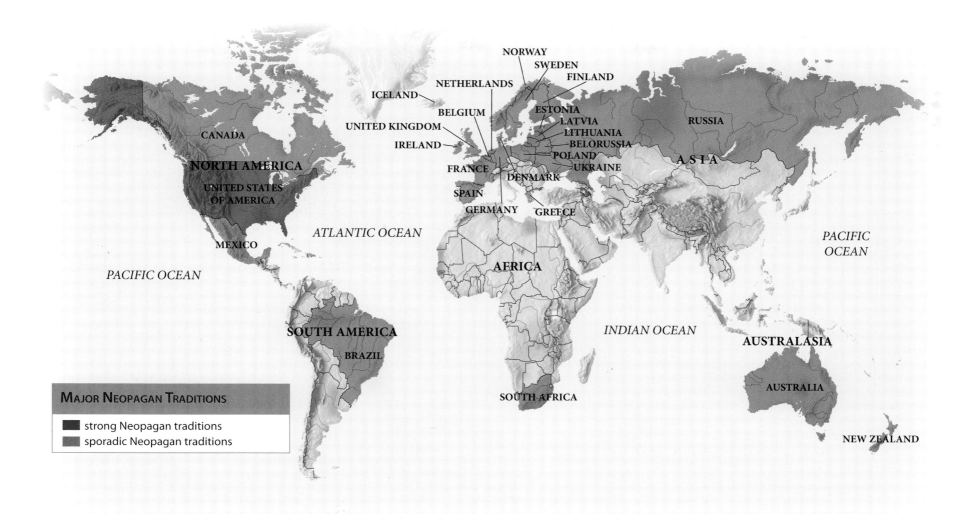

MAJOR NEOPAGAN TRADITIONS

- ■ strong Neopagan traditions
- ■ sporadic Neopagan traditions

NORWAY
SWEDEN
FINLAND
NETHERLANDS
ICELAND
BELGIUM
ESTONIA
LATVIA
UNITED KINGDOM
LITHUANIA
IRELAND
BELORUSSIA
POLAND
FRANCE
UKRAINE
DENMARK
SPAIN
GERMANY
GREECE
RUSSIA
ASIA

NORTH AMERICA
CANADA
UNITED STATES
OF AMERICA
MEXICO
ATLANTIC OCEAN
PACIFIC OCEAN

SOUTH AMERICA
BRAZIL

AFRICA
PACIFIC
OCEAN
INDIAN OCEAN

AUSTRALASIA
AUSTRALIA
SOUTH AFRICA
NEW ZEALAND

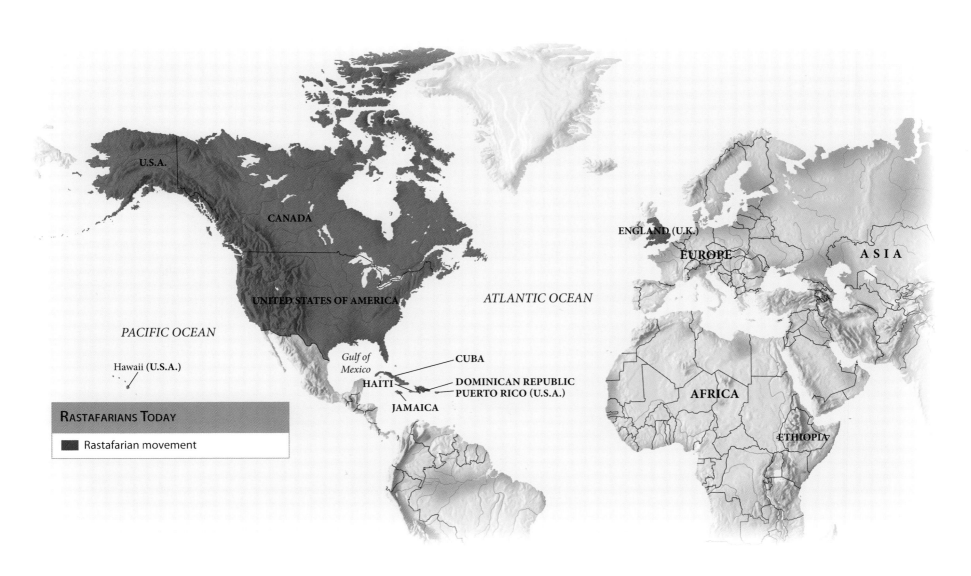

RASTAFARIANS TODAY

- ■ Rastafarian movement

U.S.A.
CANADA
UNITED STATES OF AMERICA
PACIFIC OCEAN
ATLANTIC OCEAN

Hawaii (U.S.A.)

Gulf of
Mexico
CUBA
HAITI
DOMINICAN REPUBLIC
PUERTO RICO (U.S.A.)
JAMAICA

ENGLAND (U.K.)
EUROPE
ASIA

AFRICA
ETHIOPIA

Devotion vs. Fanaticism

THE ANCIENT EGYPTIANS dedicated a tremendous portion of their society's resources to the worship of their gods, with an elaborate mythology and a vast body of ritual stewarded by a hierarchy of priests. Spiritual beliefs were woven throughout Egyptian life, earning the Egyptians a widespread reputation as "the most religious people in the world," in the words of the Greek historian Herodotus. The modern Hopi living in the American Southwest likewise practice a religion that permeates virtually every aspect of their lives, and they have also developed a reputation for extraordinarily profound spirituality. Both these cultures are known for the unusually intense degree of their religious devotion, and yet they are not characterized as extremists or fanatics. These examples highlight the fact that well-regarded *devotion* and negatively regarded *extremism* are two distinct matters in religious culture.

Globalization has brought the issue of religious extremism squarely into the spotlight of popular concern, as different religious cultures now come into constant contact with one another. The question of what exactly counts as devotion versus what counts as extremism provokes widely differing opinions that tend to be colored by the viewer's cultural perspective.

Western democracies have come to champion secular government as the societal ideal. In contrast, many non-Western states celebrate their governmental alignment with a particular religion with equal or greater zeal. Many Arab countries are organized as Islamic states. Similarly, Buddhism is the state religion in many Asian countries, and Israel is officially a Jewish state. Such basic differences in perspective on the place of religion in society ensure that religious extremism will continue to be defined in different ways by different observers. One view accepts as desirable the infusion of religion into every aspect of life, while the other sees it as suspect—even extreme.

RELIGIOUS CONFLICT AND TERRORISM

◇ sites of religious conflict or terrorism

Incidents of conflict and terrorism are often attributed to religious extremism. Acts of violence done in the name of a god are only the latest in a long series of religiously motivated violent acts, which have occurred throughout the course of human history.

A 2,000-year-old temple in Kom Ombo, Egypt, shows the ancient falcon-headed god Horus. Ancient Egypt expended massive resources into the creation of religious monuments.

Our Lord would say that in the end the positive thing that can come is the spirit of forgiving, not forgetting, but the spirit of saying: God, this happened to us. We pray for those who made it happen, help us to forgive them and help us so that we in our turn will not make others suffer.

—ARCHBISHOP DESMOND TUTU

EXTREMISM: RELIGION OR POLITICS?

The blending of religion and state blurs a distinction between political and religious motivations for controversial events such as conquest and violence. Patriotic extremism looks much like religious extremism when both are carried at the point of a sword. While conversion certainly accompanied the military conquests of the conquistadores and the armies of Muhammad, the degree to which the religions involved may have fostered these actions is difficult to ascertain.

No less difficult to determine is the degree to which religious feelings may lie behind contemporary terrorism. Spectacular acts of violence such as the suicide attacks on the World Trade Center and the bombings of trains, nightclubs, and street markets are zealously justified by their perpetrators and supporters as religious acts condoned by their respective faiths. Scholars and apologists distance such acts from the faith and characterize them as the deeds of political fanatics whose religion is an incidental matter, not a motivation.

RELIGION AND VIOLENCE

Religions differ widely in their official positions on violence. Under various conditions, the Qur'an sanctions holy war as *jihad*. In contrast, "holy war" is an inconceivable concept in Jainism, which condemns all forms of violence without exception. Buddhism likewise has no term that can be used to justify the killing of other human beings, and neither Jainism nor Buddhism is historically associated with physical conflict.

Christianity's founder demonstrated and preached radical nonviolence, exhorting his followers to "turn the other cheek" even when faced with physical assault. Christianity, however, has, generally found exceptions to this directive. The crusader armies marched out of Europe in the Middle Ages at the behest of the pope himself to conduct warfare in the name of Christianity, and historically Christian countries have not distinguished themselves as the most peaceful.

Whether Christianity, Islam, or any other faith condones, condemns, or encourages certain kinds of violence is a matter that may be debated as endlessly as other matters of scripture throughout the world of religion. However, the fact of violence and intolerance suffered in the real world demands more than academic concern as, on a shrinking globe, the ideal of an open society and free speech seeks somehow to blend with the alternative ideal of a religious society where faith, for some, is a matter of life or death. Whether a peaceful accommodation is possible remains to be seen; the question is one of the most pressing issues of our age.

Modern Iraq suffers from sectarian violence between Sunni and Shia Muslims, among other groups. Here, a Blackwater Security Company (a U.S.-based firm) helicopter investigates the scene of a car bombing.

Megachurches

WHEN LARGE-SCALE REVIVAL MEETINGS enjoyed a comeback in the twentieth century, many Christians were attracted to them because they were more lively and spirited than what was offered in the traditional small Protestant churches. Consequently, by the mid-twentieth century, individual churches with charismatic pastors began to draw thousands of people to Sunday services. Churches with more than 2,000 members came to be known as megachurches. Many are independent, and some call themselves nondenominational.

The largest megachurch in the world is the Yoido Full Gospel Church in Seoul, South Korea, with a membership of 830,000. It was founded in 1958 by David Yonggi Cho, who attracted members by preaching that physical health and financial prosperity are as much a part of God's will for Christians as the salvation of the soul. As the congregations grew too large for the original church building, Cho divided the city into zones, with church members in each zone meeting independently in small cells under an appointed leader. When a cell grew too large, it was split into two. This cell concept

was later adopted by many other megachurches. In 1973 Cho built a large church across from Korea's National Assembly. It can seat 26,000 people, and any overflow crowd can follow the services on television screens in nearby buildings.

At the City Harvest Church in Singapore, some 24,000 people attend Sunday services, more than half of them under twenty-five years of age. The attraction is partially the rock music that is provided by a large audio and video crew and blasted through a sixty-channel console. The church is housed in a gigantic $26.6 million titanium-clad building that contains waterfalls, gardens, playgrounds, a putting green, and coffee kiosks.

In the United States, the states of California, Texas, Georgia, and Florida have the largest number of megachurches, with combined congregations of more than 100,000 in each state.

Megachurches are scattered throughout the United States, with concentrations in parts of the South, but due in part to the technological advances of television and radio, megachurches cater to millions of Americans all over the country.

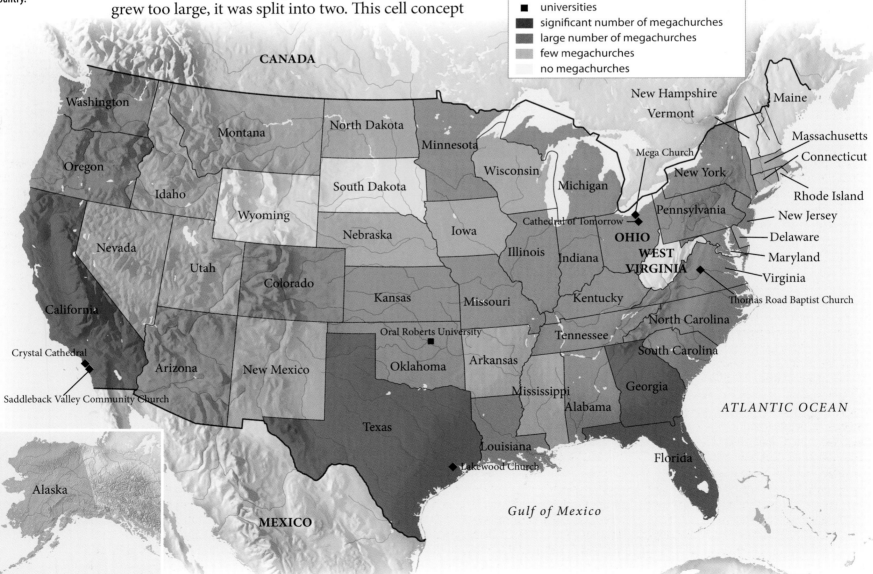

MEGACHURCHES IN THE UNITED STATES

- ◆ selected megachurches
- ■ universities
- significant number of megachurches
- large number of megachurches
- few megachurches
- no megachurches

*A thousand thousands served him,
and ten thousand times ten
thousand stood before him.*
—FROM THE BOOK OF DANIEL

Joel Osteen, senior pastor of Lakewood Church, preaches to members of his congregation both inside the church and, thanks to television broadcasting, many more at home.

SOME U.S. MEGACHURCHES

Rick and Kay Warren, fresh out of seminary, founded the Saddleback Valley Community Church in Lake Forest, California, in 1980 to attract people who had never before gone to church. The pastor kept the focus on the five biblical purposes of the church: worship, fellowship, discipleship, ministry, and evangelism. By 1980 the church had more than 16,000 members, and the average attendance at services was 20,000.

A church in Cleveland, Ohio, is actually called the Mega Church. Its Pentecostal congregation is distinguished by the diversity of ethnic groups it embraces.

Joel Osteen is known to many because he telecasts his services from the 16,000-seat sanctuary of his Lakewood Church in Houston, the nation's largest nondenominational congregation. The church has padded theater seats instead of wooden pews, a stage instead of an altar, and video projection screens instead of stained-glass windows. Its Web site features streaming video, which allows followers to watch services online, and anyone who registers can download free pod-casts. The Lakewood Church, like many others, also sponsors special groups that minister to every type of churchgoer, including youth, single mothers, men only, married couples, children, students, recovering alcoholics and addicts, and senior citizens. There are even groups that give financial and income tax advice.

TELEVANGELISM

When television became widely available in the 1950s, evangelists saw it as a new way to reach vast numbers of people. In 1952 Rex Humbard began televising weekly services from his Cathedral of Tomorrow in Ohio. His programs delivered personalized Christian messages, emphasized family life, and included lots of singing.

Many evangelists followed suit. Programs that ranged from televised sermons to talk shows stressed Bible reading and urged viewers to be born again in Jesus Christ. Messages ranged from inspirational with little theology to overtly sociopolitical.

The most popular early televangelist was Oral Roberts, known as the king of faith healers. By 1955 Roberts was the national leader of religious television, and in 1963 he used his success to establish the Oral Roberts Evangelical Association, which included the new Oral Roberts University. On his show, *The Hour of Power*, televangelist Robert Schuller stressed positive thinking to help Christians change their lives. In 1980, with donations from viewers, he built the $16 million Crystal Cathedral, an all-glass church in Garden Grove, California.

Jerry Falwell, pastor of the Thomas Road Baptist Church, a megachurch in Lynchburg, Virginia, used television to preach politics. In 1979 Falwell founded the Moral Majority, a conservative political lobbying group championing a "pro-family" platform. Benefiting from Falwell's telecasts, the Moral Majority is credited with delivering two-thirds of the white evangelical Christian vote to Ronald Reagan in the 1980 presidential election.

While televangelism was at its peak, Jimmy Lee Swaggart, who attracted an estimated eight million viewers each week, and Jim Bakker, who financed a large Christian community and theme park from viewer donations, were accused of sexual misconduct and, in Baker's case, illegal financial dealings. In the aftermath of these scandals televangelism declined somewhat, but it did not disappear. The televangelist Pat Robertson continued to draw large numbers of viewers, and he even instituted a new television network, the Family Channel, which enables him to reach vast numbers of people with programs that reflect his ministry's conservative Christian values.

The Crystal Cathedral, in Garden Grove, California, can accommodate nearly 3,000 worshippers at a time, not including a complement of 1,000 musicians and singers, and is constructed with more than 10,000 windows of glass. Despite its name, it is not technically a cathedral, as it belongs to a Protestant denomination that does not recognize or seat bishops.

Homeland and Diaspora

NOT UNTIL AFTER THE DEVELOPMENT of agriculture in the Neolithic period did human populations gain the ability to settle permanently. It was therefore not until the advent of cultivation that societies first encountered the experience of having a homeland. Of course, this development also set the stage for the ensuing discovery of the unique pain of being forced to leave one's homeland. Raiders might drive a settled people away from their community and once more into the wilderness. The walls of Jericho, the earliest known city defenses, testify to the determination that rooted communities developed to hold on to the identity that their location had given them.

Settled living brought a great increase in the material manifestations of religious practice and belief. Nomadic bands had to be able to carry any sacred objects with them as they traveled—hence the small, hand-size sculptures known from Paleolithic times. Neolithic peoples could establish permanent sacred sites, build altars, and construct dwellings for their gods. Temples,

altars, and idols commonly became the most significant physical expressions of a people's identity.

Idols, the symbols or even manifestations of deities, were often the most fiercely defended elements of an ancient city in time of invasion. They could represent the sacred identity of the whole community. In the *Iliad* Homer recounts a daring Greek commando raid on the city of Troy to steal the Palladium, Troy's most ancient religious icon, since the Greeks knew that such a loss would dishearten the Trojan defenders. Many classical Greek cities had their own palladia sculptures. When overpopulation pressures or other factors caused some citizens to leave and settle new colonies, colonists would often carefully copy the palladium icon of their mother city, to carry the core of their religious identity with them to their new land. The making of these icons is one of the earliest documented religious responses to the phenomenon we now call *diaspora*—the scattering of a people from their home territory.

From its initial diaspora nearly 2,000 years ago, Judaism has spread over the globe, maintaining a fundamentally similar culture regardless. Here, a Hasidic Jew in New York City.

After their home territory came under the control of Communist China in 1950, many Tibetan Buddhists followed their leader, the Dalai Lama, into exile. A large number fled to Europe, where they have founded new monasteries and developed communities.

TIBETAN DIASPORA

◆ Tibetan Buddhist monasteries
■ countries sheltering Tibetan Buddhist exiles

FINLAND
NORWAY
SWEDEN
ESTONIA
RUSSIA
LATVIA
UNITED KINGDOM
LITHUANIA
Eskdalemuir (Kagyu Samye Ling) ◆
North Sea
DENMARK
Baltic Sea
RUSSIA
IRELAND
BELORUSSIA
NETHERLANDS
ATLANTIC OCEAN
GERMANY
POLAND
BELGIUM
LUXEMBOURG
CZECH REPUBLIC
UKRAINE
FRANCE
SLOVAKIA
Rikon (Tibetan Monastic Institute) ◆
Le Bost (Dhagpo Kundreul Ling) ◆
SWITZERLAND
AUSTRIA
HUNGARY
Feldkirch (Der letzehol) ◆
LIECHTENSTEIN
SLOVENIA
ROMANIA
Lavaur (Nalanda) ◆
CROATIA
SERBIA
PORTUGAL
BOS. AND HERZ.
SPAIN
Corsica
ITALY
BULGARIA
Balearic Islands
MACEDONIA
Sardinia
ALBANIA
Mediterranean Sea
GREECE
Sicily

The Dalai Lama, a leader in exile, dedicated the main hall of the Chuang Yen monastery in Putnam County, New York, in 1997. The Dalai Lama's flight from Tibet was followed by the migration of tens of thousands of Tibetan Buddhists, many of whom settled in Western nations.

THE JEWISH DIASPORA

The destruction of the great temple by Roman troops in Jerusalem inflicted a tremendous calamity upon the Jewish people but also set in motion an important development in the history of religious geography.

Like most faiths, Judaism was initially tied closely to the land where it had developed. From the Egypt of Moses's Exodus to the Ur of Abraham's birth, the ancient Fertile Crescent was filled with landmarks significant to the faith. The Promised Land of Canaan, where the Jewish kingdom arose, was particularly rich with memories of the history that had shaped the Jewish people and their complex relationship with their God. Of all these landmarks associated with carefully preserved history, the holy city of Jerusalem stood highest, as the preeminent sacred center of the Jewish faith, the seat of kingship, and the site of their great temple.

When the Jewish nation came under the expanding authority of the Roman Empire, the foreign occupation was tolerated at first, but Jews were eventually provoked by disrespect for their religion into revolt in 66 CE. The Jews' resistance was firmly crushed by Roman military power. The temple was destroyed in 70 CE by the legions of the future emperor Titus, and Judaea became a province under direct Roman administration. Fleeing the occupiers' violence in their homeland, Jews scattered throughout the Mediterranean world.

This great scattering of ethnic refugees is called the Jewish Diaspora. Especially well-attested historically, the Jewish Diaspora has served as a reference example for the study of the many processes that affect ethnic communities forced to leave their homelands.

DIASPORA SURVIVAL STRATEGIES

The icons taken by Greek colonists offered a symbolic link with the homeland and its religious culture, but a statue alone could not prevent the development of a separate, colony culture isolated far from the mother territory. Where diaspora communities were not absorbed into dominant local populations, they typically developed distinct identities of their own over time, until the new land had become home.

The Jews scattered by the Romans faced similar prospects of assimilation or fragmentation, but they had a special asset: unlike other ancient religions of the time, the Jewish faith was centered on a core text, the Tanakh. This body of scripture allowed the Jewish hierarchy of religious authorities to maintain unity and integrity of faith. Almost two thousand years later, the Jewish people continue to maintain their cultural and religious identity in societies around the world.

Tibetan refugees from the Chinese invasion of their homeland have experienced a modern diaspora. The "palladium" of Tibetan Buddhism is not a sacred text nor a statue, but the person of the Dalai Lama. This spiritual leader has taken steps to preserve the unity of the Tibetan people in the face of their dispersal across the entire world, such as moving to organize the several major branches of Tibetan Buddhism more directly under his spiritual authority than they were in traditional Tibetan society. A charismatic and responsible leader like the present Dalai Lama can serve as a powerful unifying force for a diaspora culture, especially with the support of modern telecommunications. However, reliance on such an individual tends to place the community at risk of fragmentation upon the passing of that leader. The Tibetan Buddhist community has begun to express and discuss concerns about what will happen next to their faith as the fourteenth Dalai Lama enters his eighth decade of life.

A Greek vase from the fourth century BCE, showing the theft of ancient Troy's Palladium.

Pilgrimages

The world is full of pilgrimage sites, both holy and secular. Some of the most major, such as Jerusalem in Israel or the Ganges River in India, draw millions of faithful every year. The cities of Mecca and Medina, in Saudi Arabia, are central to Islam, and pilgrimage there (called the *hajj*) is required by every Muslim.

A JOURNEY TO A SACRED PLACE: pilgrimage is a concept common to many religions throughout history. In most religions, even those that see divine energies as permeating the whole universe, some places are considered more sacred than others, and thus the act of traveling to them from one's customary dwelling can become a facet of worship. Pilgrimages may be undertaken in order to show reverence, to advance one's spiritual development, to make atonement, or to earn religious merit. A pilgrimage may serve as a test and a demonstration of a worshipper's commitment to the faith. In this connection, the more difficult the journey, the more it accomplishes its purpose. Some pilgrimages require what may involve tremendous effort and sacrifice on the part of the traveler. Where a pilgrimage seems too easy, determined pilgrims may add deliberate difficulties, such as prostrating themselves after every step forward.

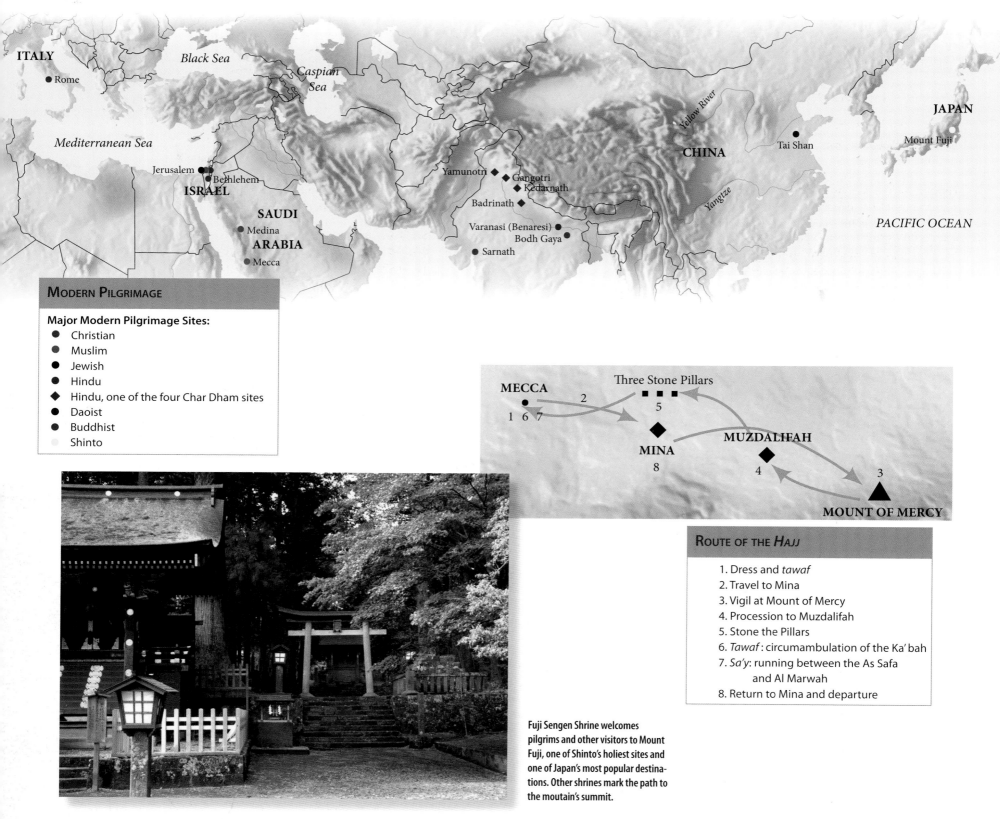

MODERN PILGRIMAGE

Major Modern Pilgrimage Sites:
- ● Christian
- ● Muslim
- ● Jewish
- ● Hindu
- ◆ Hindu, one of the four Char Dham sites
- ● Daoist
- ● Buddhist
- ○ Shinto

ROUTE OF THE *HAJJ*

1. Dress and *tawaf*
2. Travel to Mina
3. Vigil at Mount of Mercy
4. Procession to Muzdalifah
5. Stone the Pillars
6. *Tawaf*: circumambulation of the Ka'bah
7. *Sa'y*: running between the As Safa and Al Marwah
8. Return to Mina and departure

Fuji Sengen Shrine welcomes pilgrims and other visitors to Mount Fuji, one of Shinto's holiest sites and one of Japan's most popular destinations. Other shrines mark the path to the moutain's summit.

The Western Wall, the only remaining element of the Second Temple in Jerusalem, is a common place of pilgrimage for Jews. Because Jewish law requires the visitor to express grief at the sight of the destroyed temple, the wall is popularly known as the Wailing Wall.

SACRED PLACES

Sites typically acquire sacred status in one of the following ways:

Divination. A religious figure such as a shaman or priest may identify a place as holy by interpreting divine signs, by the ability to sense subtle qualities not apparent to laymen, or through prayer communication with a deity. Such locations are regarded as having been made sacred by divine action or will, with human involvement being only that of recognition. The sacred groves of Celtic druids and Classical polytheism, for example, were identified via divination.

Sanctification. A religious figure may pronounce a location sanctified, typically with some form of ritual ceremony, the successful performance of which establishes the place as having a new sacred status. Sanctification produces a holy site through human action that is considered to invoke divine blessing. The sites of historic Catholic churches, for example, were normally sanctified by priests before construction began.

Association. Sites often acquire sacred status through association with religious history or even mythic history. The places where events occurred that were of special significance to a faith may take on sacred status through divination or sanctification. Faiths that trace their origins to founding figures such as Mohammed or Jesus commonly regard locations associated with key events in the lives of those figures as sacred. The Dome of the Rock in Jerusalem marks the place where Muhammed ascended to heaven, according to Muslim tradition. The same location is revered by Jews as the site where the patriarch Abraham prepared to sacrifice his son Isaac. Great acts of personal sacrifice or piety by a religion's followers may also hallow a site. In 1749 the Roman Colosseum was declared a Catholic sacred site by Pope Benedict XIV in recognition of the Christian martyrs who had died in that arena for refusing to renounce their faith. Places where followers encounter the divine, or where healing is experienced that is attributed to miraculous intervention, may also become sacred. The small French city of Lourdes attracts some five million Catholic pilgrims every year to its shrine marking the grotto where a fourteen-year-old girl reported apparitions of the Virgin Mary in 1858.

SOME OF THE GREAT PILGRIMAGES

Islam
Islam famously enjoins all able-bodied Muslims to journey to the holy city of Mecca at least once in their lives, if at all possible, in the sacred pilgrimage called the hajj. So well-known is this tradition that any place that attracts large numbers of visitors is now commonly called a "mecca." The Muslim faith has long comprised far-flung territories thousands of miles distant from Mecca, making this pillar of the faith a formidable prospect, both physically and financially, for many pilgrims.

Christianity
Many Christians regard the whole region of the Holy Land as suffused with sanctity, for its myriad associations with Old Testament history as well as with the ministry and crucifixion of Jesus. The city of Jerusalem was traditionally the primary focus of Christian pilgrimage. Here stands the Church of the Holy Sepulcher, built to mark the sites where Jesus was believed to have been crucified (the hill Golgotha), interred, and resurrected.

Buddhism
Four locations rank as the holiest sites in Buddhism, all related to the life and spiritual development of the faith's founder. These sites were recommended by the Buddha himself as suitable destinations for pilgrimage. In Nepal lies Lumbini, traditionally identified as the place where Buddha was born and where he lived as a young man. Northern India holds the other three locations: Buddha achieved his enlightenment sitting under a tree that grew at Bodh Gaya, gave his first sermon at Sarnath near Benares, and died at Kushinagar.

Hinduism
A great many sites are sacred to Hinduism, and this faith sends streams of pilgrims out across the Indian subcontinent to pay their respects in numbers that grow every year as more and more Hindus become able to afford such journeys. The most revered pilgrimage of Hinduism is the Char Dham, a circuit through the Himalaya Mountains connecting four principal temples that mark special sites, including the ancient source of the holy Ganges River at Gangotri. Drawing the largest number of pilgrims is the temple at Badrinath, which is venerated as the seat of the god Vishnu.

Sikhism
Sikhs are required to visit their holy city of Amritsar at least once, to pay their respects at the Golden Temple, which houses the Guru Granth Sahib, the book of sacred writings that serves as the center of this faith.

Shinto
Considering the reverence of Japan's Shinto religion for the beauty and majesty of nature, it is no surprise that the magnificent Mount Fuji is considered to be deeply sacred to Shinto kami. The climb of Mount Fuji is the most famous and most popular Shinto pilgrimage, drawing many thousands of Shinto practitioners every year.

The source of the holy Ganges River, high in the Himalayas, draws Hindu pilgrims every year as they complete the Char Dham circuit.

RELIGION AND MODERN SOCIETIES

GREENLAND

ICELAND

UNITED STATES
OF AMERICA

CANADA

THE NETHERLANDS
BELGIUM
UNITED KINGDOM
IRELAND
FRANCE

PORTUGAL   SPAIN

ATLANTIC
OCEAN

MOROCCO

ALGERIA

WESTERN
SAHARA

MAURITANIA   MALI

UNITED STATES

OF AMERICA

PACIFIC
OCEAN

U.S.A.

CUBA
JAMAICA
HAITI
DOMINICAN REPUBLIC
PUERTO RICO (U.S.A.)

MEXICO

BELIZE

GUATEMALA
EL SALVADOR
HONDURAS
NICARAGUA
COSTA RICA
PANAMA

VENEZUELA

COLOMBIA

ECUADOR

PERU

BRAZIL

GUYANA
SURINAME
FRENCH GUYANA

SENEGAL
GAMBIA
GUINEA-BISSAU
GUINEA
SIERRA-LEONE
LIBERIA
IVORY COAST
GHANA
BENIN
TOGO
NIGERIA

BURKINA

RELIGION IN THE WORLD TODAY

Majority Religions:

- Protestant Christianity
- Catholic Christianity
- Orthodox Christianity
- Shia Islam
- Sunni Islam
- Hinduism
- Judaism
- Daoism/Confucianism
- Theravada Buddhism
- Mahayana Buddhism
- Tibetan Buddhism
- Secular
- Indigenous

BOLIVIA

PARAGUAY

CHILE

ARGENTINA

URUGUAY

ATLANTIC
OCEAN

Viewed in terms of religion, the world is a vibrant patchwork quilt, a bold and
complex pattern of human faith. Religious belief continues to be, as it has been
from the beginning, a fundamental aspect of human society, and appreciating its
ubiquity and complexity can only become more important as humanity continues to
develop and explore.

ARCTIC
OCEAN

NORWAY
SWEDEN
FINLAND

ESTONIA
LATVIA
DENMARK
LITHUANIA
BELORUSSIA
GERMANY
POLAND
CZ. REP.
SLOVAKIA
UKRAINE
AUSTRIA
HUNGARY
SLOVENIA
CROATIA
ROMANIA
ITALY
SERBIA
BULGARIA
BOS.
AND
MACE.
ALBANIA
GREECE
HERZ.

RUSSIA

KAZAKHSTAN

MONGOLIA

N. KOREA

TUNISIA

TURKEY

GEORGIA
AZERBAIJAN
UZBEKISTAN
KYRGYZSTAN
S. KOREA
JAPAN
ARMENIA
TURKMENISTAN
TAJIKISTAN

LEBANON
ISRAEL
SYRIA
JORDAN
IRAQ
IRAN
AFGHANISTAN
PAKISTAN
CHINA

PACIFIC
OCEAN

LIBYA
EGYPT
KUWAIT
QATAR
SAUDI
U.A.E.
NEPAL
BHUTAN
TAIWAN

ARABIA
OMAN
BANGLADESH
NIGER
CHAD
ERITREA
YEMEN
INDIA
MYANMAR
(BURMA)
LAOS
VIETNAM
SUDAN
THAILAND
PHILIPPINE
ISLANDS

CAMEROON
CENTRAL
AFRICAN
REPUBLIC
ETHIOPIA
SOMALIA
CAMBODIA

EQU. GUINEA
UGANDA
KENYA
SRI LANKA
BRUNEI

GABON
CONGO
RWANDA
MALAYSIA

DEM. REP. OF
CONGO
BURUNDI
SINGAPORE

TANZANIA
INDONESIA

PAPUA NEW
GUINEA

ANGOLA
MALAWI
INDIAN OCEAN
EAST TIMOR

ZAMBIA
Oceania

ZIMBABWE
MOZAMBIQUE
MADAGASCAR

NAMIBIA
NEW CALEDONIA

BOTSWANA
SWAZILAND

SOUTH
AFRICA
LESOTHO
AUSTRALIA

NEW ZEALAND

GLOSSARY

Adventists: Christians who expect the imminent end of the world, when Jesus will return to earth to judge everyone. There are numerous Adventist denominations among Protestant Christians.

agnostic: One who neither accepts nor denies the existence or nature of the divine.

ahimsa: The principle of nonviolence, one of five core ethical virtues in Jainism and widely respected among Hindus and Buddhists as well.

animism: The belief that all objects possess a natural life or vitality or are endowed with indwelling souls.

aparigraha: The principle of nonpossession, one of five core ethical virtues in Jainism and accepted in some strands of Hinduism and Buddhism as well. Some Jains believe aparigraha ideally calls for no human possessions at all; practically, many simply aspire to owning as little as possible.

apocalypse: A cataclysmic event signaling the destruction of the world. In a specific sense it usually refers to the Christian end-of-the-world event as foretold in the book of Revelation; in a general sense, several religions include similar catastrophic beliefs.

asceticism: The practice of renouncing physical needs or desires as a method of worshipping a god, or as a means to mystically connect with a god. Ascetics can be found in many major religions, both past and present, including Buddhism, Hinduism, Jainism, Christianity, and Islam.

Ashkenazi: Jews who settled in central Europe and followed customs different from the Sephardim—the Jews of Spain, Portugal, and the Arab countries.

asteya: The principle of not stealing, one of five core ethical virtues in Jainism and a principal virtue in Hinduism as well. Other religions—such as Judaism—also specifically prohibit theft.

Babylonian captivity: The deportation and exile of the Jews to Babylon from the Kingdom of Judah by Nebuchadnezzar in the sixth century BCE.

baptism: A sacrament in many Christian denominations, often performed at birth, that initiates a new member into the church. Water is either sprinkled onto the forehead or the person is fully immersed in water.

bhakti: Hindu concept of devotion, specifically between a god and a worshipper. Bhakti traditions have developed for all major Hindu deities.

bodhisattva: A semidivine person in Buddhist belief who is expected to attain the status of the Buddha (that is, reach nirvana).

brahmacharya: The principle of celibacy, one of five core ethical virtues in Jainism. Also espoused by Hindus and some Buddhists, brahmacharya specifically advocates sexual chastity but has been taken in a more general sense of basic morality.

Byzantine rite: An order of worship, or liturgy, that was developed in Constantinople during the days of the Byzantine Empire. The rite is used by the Orthodox churches and many Eastern Catholic churches. Although it was originally written in Greek, the Byzantine rite is also celebrated in other Eastern European languages, notably Russian.

caliph: The head of the Muslim ummah, or Islamic community; the successor to Muhammad as ruler of the Islamic world, also known as the caliphate.

Calvinism: School of theology named for its primary formulator, John Calvin (1509–64); also refers to derivative and ancillary theologies. Generally, Calvinist doctrines stress human depravity and unworthiness, contrasting human failings with the power and grace of God.

catechism: A teaching manual of the basic beliefs of a religious body, often in the form of questions and answers. Martin Luther wrote two, a shorter and a longer, and the Catholic Church published a catechism after the Council of Trent—in response to the Reformation—and a new one in 1992. Many other religions have catechisms as well.

Cathars: A Christian Gnostic sect that flourished in Europe from the eleventh to the thirteenth centuries. In France they were known as Albigensians; declared a heresy and suppressed by the church through preaching, reforms, a military crusade, and the prosecution of the Inquisition.

Catholic: A member of the Roman Catholic Church, which adherents believe was founded by disciples of Jesus in the first century. In the eleventh century the eastern branches of the Christian church (now known as the Orthodox) broke away from the Roman church, which retained the name Catholic, from the Greek word meaning "universal."

chi: See *qi.*

communion: A body of Christians sharing the same beliefs and church government. Also, as part of the Eucharist, a Christian rite in which bread and wine are consumed, representing the body and blood of Christ.

confession: An outline of a religious group's beliefs or an organized religious body professing the same beliefs. Also, a rite in Christianity wherein one's sins are confessed to a priest and absolution is received.

congregation: A worship community, or members of a church.

Congregationalism: a type of Christian church structure in which each Christian community, or congregation, is autonomous and free from regulation by outside churches, boards, or governments.

Coptic Christians: An Egyptian Christian denomination for Copts, or descendants of the ancient Egyptians.

Crusades: A series of at least nine military campaigns between the eleventh and thirteenth centuries, launched by European Christians against non-Christians, especially Muslims, in West Asia; also included the thirteenth-century capture of Constantinople.

Dalai Lama: The spiritual leader of Tibetan Buddhists and temporal leader-in-exile of Tibet; viewed by Tibetan Buddhists as a living incarnation of Avalokiteshvara, the bodhisattva of compassion.

Dao (Tao): Literally, the "way"; the basic principle of Daoism. A metaphysical concept that expressly denies definition, Dao may be construed as the fundamental nature of all things.

Deism: A movement originating in England in the seventeenth century that argued that religious principles should derive from reasonable inquiry rather than divine revelation or theology.

denomination: A religious organization that unites congregations of the same beliefs.

dharma: A fundamental concept of Hinduism, Buddhism, and Jainism, each of which perceive it slightly differently. Generally, it refers to a universal or spiritual truth or received divine wisdom.

diaspora: In Greek, a scattering or sowing of seeds; generally refers to the forced dispersion of a people from their homeland, as with the sixth-century BCE and second-century CE Jews of Israel and Judaea and the twentieth-century Armenians of Anatolia.

dogma: An officially sanctioned religious belief or body of beliefs.

Dreaming, the: Australian Aboriginal concept of mythological time, an eternal spiritual existence that is closely tied to the natural world and can be accessed through rituals.

dualism: The doctrine that the world is under the dominion of good and evil, two opposing principles, or forces.

Eastern Orthodox Church: The communion of Christian churches that split from the Roman Catholic Church in 1054 and that follow Byzantine rites.

ecumenical: All-inclusive. In Christianity, church councils that included the participation of representatives of all the world's Christian bodies were considered ecumenical, from the Greek meaning "the whole inhabited world." The Orthodox Church considers only seven church councils (in the third through the eighth centuries) to have been ecumenical, and it bases its theology on the proclamations of those seven councils.

episcopal: Having to do with the type of Christian religious leader known as a bishop. The word comes from the Greek for "overseer." Churches that have hierarchies that include bishops sometimes include the word in their names, such as the Episcopal Church in the United States of America, the U.S. branch of the Anglican Communion.

evangelism: A movement among Protestant Christians to spread the teachings of Jesus Christ (the gospel, or *evangelion* in Greek) to nonbelievers and to revitalize the faith of baptized Christians.

feng shui: An ancient Chinese principle of recognizing confluences of spiritual or heavenly laws with earthly designs; practically, feng shui involves making geographical decisions in order to maximize positive qi.

Five Pillars of Islam: Five duties or practices that unite Muslims into one universal community. Preceded by the basic creed that there is one God and Muhammad is his messenger, these include ritual prayer, alms-giving, fasting, and pilgrimage.

Four Noble Truths: One of the primary precepts of Buddhism, the Four Noble Truths were laid out by the Buddha. They outline human suffering: its existence, its causes, and the way to overcome it.

Gnosticism: A system of belief in which knowledge is imparted to an elect few. There were many forms of Gnosticism, but the most extreme believed in two Gods—a Supreme Being of light and knowledge and an inferior God who created the physical universe, which is all evil. Christian authorities considered Gnosticism heretical.

Guru: Specifically, any of the first ten leaders of Sikhism, including its founder, Guru Nanak, and its holy book, the Guru Granth Sahib. More generally, the term means "teacher" or "leader."

hajj: The Muslim pilgrimage to Mecca, which should be made at least once in the individual's lifetime and is one of the Five Pillars of Islam.

heretic: One who subscribes to a heresy—a religious belief or opinion contrary to the authorized standards of a religious organization.

humanism: A broad movement beginning in the sixteenth century stressing human ability to reason above theological disputation in determining ethical behavior. It also stresses empiricism in human development, disavowing the need for divine or spiritual guidance.

idol: An image or figure representing a deity and used as an object of worship.

imam: Islamic leader, often of a mosque; one who leads the prayer at Islamic gatherings; also, in Shia Islam, a descendant of Muhammad chosen to lead the faithful.

indulgences: Guarantees granted by the pope in the name of the Catholic Church that a person would spend less time or no time at all in purgatory suffering for sins he or she had committed. Indulgences were commonly seen as tickets to heaven and were often sold. In response to Martin Luther's campaign against them, indulgences are no longer sold in the Catholic Church but are still offered in recompense for saying certain prayers or performing specified works of piety.

Inquisition, the: An office established by the Roman Catholic Church, which worked in cooperation with secular authorities to force conversion to Christianity, detect heretics, or otherwise enforce the primacy of Roman Catholicism in participating countries.

jihad: In Arabic, jihad means "strive" or "struggle" and is an Islamic duty, sometimes described in the Qur'an as "striving in the way of Allah." A person engaged in jihad is a mujahid; the plural is mujahideen.

Ka'bah: Arabic for "circle pit," referring to a cube-shaped building at Mecca that is Islam's holiest shrine.

Kabbalah: A mystical Jewish movement in which meditation and good works are believed to create a spiritual ladder of ascent that a believer can climb to partake in the life of the Godhead. Kabbalah means "tradition."

karma: Hindu doctrine of action and how it affects one's destiny and future reincarnations; good karma will help result in rebirth as a "higher" life-form, while negative karma may result in rebirth as a "lower" life-form. The belief in karma is also fundamental to Buddhism, Jainism, and Sikhism.

liturgy: The rites, including prayers and music, used in public worship services of a given religion.

ma'at: One of the fundamental concepts of ancient Egyptian religion, broadly meaning "order." Maintaining ma'at was a basic spiritual function of ritual and worship and was the primary duty of the king or pharaoh.

Maccabees: A second-century BCE Jewish liberation movement that won independence from the Seleucids of Persia.

Mahayana: One of the two major branches of Buddhism and the principal form practiced in most of East Asia.

megachurch: A Protestant Christian church, generally independent, that attracts large crowds—generally more than 2,000. Megachurches are usually headed by charismatic pastors who are noted for their preaching.

messiah: In Judaic tradition, a leader who would deliver the Israelites from bondage; more broadly, a savior figure. Christianity adopted the term in this latter sense and applied it to Jesus Christ. The word literally means "anointed one" or "chosen one."

missionary: A traveling member of a religion who proselytizes, or attempts to convert others to his or her faith.

moksha: Release from worldly existence as manifested in repeated reincarnations; the primary spiritual goal of Hinduism and Jainism.

monastery: A dwelling that houses monks or nuns, people who have taken vows and are dedicated to a religious life that is secluded from the secular world. Monastic traditions are found in both Christianity and Buddhism.

monotheism: The doctrine or belief that there is only one god.

mystery religions: Various cults of the Greco-Roman world that required secret initiation rites for their members.

mysticism: The doctrine or belief that direct knowledge of the divine, or spiritual truth, is attainable through intuition or insight beyond ordinary sensory perception or rationalization.

myth: A sacred narrative about deities or cultural heroes, usually set in a distant past (sometimes called a heroic or golden age) and generally believed to be true within its culture or religious group of origin.

nirvana: The primary spiritual goal of Buddhism; literally the "blowing out" or extinction of existence, manifested as liberation from rebirth and its attendant suffering. The enlightened state that the Buddha is said to have attained.

oracle: The medium through which divine messages or purposes are revealed, such as the preaching of an inspired prophet.

pagan: From Latin *paganus*, "peasant"; applied in the early centuries CE to people living in the countryside at a time when Christian worship was primarily urban. Today, one whose form of worship is outside an established religion; one who worships nature deities or idols, or who is irreligious.

patriarch: Title of the highest-ranking leader in an Eastern Christian church.

Pentecostal: Christians who strive to share the experience of Jesus's first followers on the Jewish feast of Pentecost, when they experienced a profound spiritual transformation and acquired the ability to speak in mysterious languages ("tongues"). A Pentecostal movement emerged in the early twentieth century and remains strong today.

Pietism: A Christian movement originating in the seventeenth-century Lutheran Church that stressed individual faith over reliance on church doctrine. The movement was later influential in many branches of Protestantism.

polytheism: The doctrine or belief in many deities.

pope: Spiritual and administrative leader of the Roman Catholic Church and the bishop of Rome. Popes wielded great political power in the past, and they are still influential in world affairs today. Catholic doctrine maintains that the pope is the direct successor to Saint Peter, Christ's apostle and traditionally the first head of the church.

predestination: The philosophy that all actions and events have been predetermined by a divine power. It has appeared in various forms in several religions, notably that of ancient Greece and, more recently, in Calvinist Christian theology.

Protestant: A member of a Christian church that is neither Roman Catholic nor Eastern Orthodox. Many Protestant churches originated during the Reformation.

purgatory: A place where, according to some Christians, sinners are sent after death to be purified of the effects of their sins. Once purified, they can enter heaven. Purgatory is to be distinguished from hell, which is a place of punishment from which there is no release.

purusharthas: The four goals of human life in Hindu philosophy. The greatest of these is moksha.

qi: Originally a Daoist concept of a vital life force, qi (chi) is now a major element of a more general Chinese philosophy; many Western new religions, inspired by East Asian traditions, profess a belief in qi as well.

qigong: Any of a number of methods designed to regulate and increase the flow of positive qi (chi) energy in Chinese religions.

Reformation, the: Movement against perceived un-Christian excesses and practices of the Roman Catholic Church in sixteenth-century Europe. Led by Martin Luther, John Calvin, and others, the movement resulted in numerous Protestant denominations that no longer recognized the pope as their spiritual leader.

relic: The body, part of the body, or an object associated with (usually one that came into physical contact with) a saint. Significant traditions of relic veneration occur in several major religions, notably Christianity and Buddhism.

satya: A Sanskrit word meaning "truth," and one of five core ethical virtues in Jainism, as well as a major element in Hinduism and Buddhism; the word refers largely to practice of truthfulness and correctness of action.

Sephardic: Jews who settled in Spain or northern Africa, traced their origins to Mesopotamia, lived according to the Babylonian Talmud, and were influenced by Islamic culture. They are distinguished from the Ashkenazi, who settled in other parts of Europe.

shamanism: A religion in which the noncorporeal world of nature spirits, gods, demons, and ancestors is responsive only to shamans—priests or medicine men.

Shiite: Islamic denomination that believes in the infallibility of the political and religious leadership of imams who are descended from 'Ali ibn Abi Talib, cousin and son-in-law of Muhammad and the fourth caliph to succeed the prophet.

Sunni: The largest Islamic denomination; believes in the doctrine of following the Sunnah, or example, of Muhammad's life; Sunnis believe the first four caliphs were the rightful successors to Muhammad. Sunni Muslims constitute as much as 90 percent of the world's Muslim population.

syncretism: The reconciliation or union of differing religious beliefs; a process of religious growth through amalgamating different forms of faith or worship by joining rites, doctrines, and tenets.

Tao: See *Dao*.

taboo: An action prohibited by its associations with either the divine or the accursed.

Theravada: The oldest branch of Buddhism and the principal form practiced in most Southeast Asian countries.

Vodou (voodoo): A form of West African religion, brought to the Caribbean and Louisiana by slaves and perpetuated by their descendants in many western lands; a syncretistic faith that combines African traditional faith with Christianity.

Wicca: A modern version of the pagan, nature-oriented traditions Wiccans believe were practiced in western Europe before the arrival of Christianity.

wu wei: A central tenet of Daoism that roughly translates as "the action of no action." In contemporary terms, the term translates as "going with the flow."

yin yang: An ancient Chinese symbol that denotes the principles of duality, balance, and change in the universe. Opposing forces in nature are represented by black (yin) and white (yang).

yoga: A Sanskrit word meaning "union," which in Hinduism, Buddhism, and Jainism refers to spiritual practices that unite body, mind, and spirit with the divine. In the West the term is understood as a set of physical practices.

Zionism: A movement with roots in ancient times that was founded in its modern form in the nineteenth century to establish a homeland for Jews in West Asia where Judaism originated.

RESOURCES FOR FURTHER REFERENCE

BOOKS AND ARTICLES

al Faruqi, Isma'il Ragi, ed., and David E. Sopher, map ed. *Historical Atlas of the Religions of the World*. New York: Macmillan, 1974.

Armstrong, Karen. *A History of God: The 4,000-Year Quest of Judaism, Christianity and Islam*. New York: Ballantine Books, 1994.

Barnavi, Eli, ed. *A Historical Atlas of the Jewish People*. New York: Schocken Books, 1992.

Bellitto, Christopher M. *The General Councils: A History of the Twenty-One Church Councils from Nicaea to Vatican II*. New York: Paulist Press, 2002.

Bettenson, Henry, ed. *Documents of the Christian Church,* 2nd ed. New York: Oxford University Press, 1967.

Black, Jeremy, ed. *DK Atlas of World History*. New York: DK Publishing, 2000.

Blumberg, Jess. "Rasta Revealed." *Smithsonian*, January 2008.

Bowker, John. *The Complete Bible Handbook*. New York: DK Publishing, 1998.

———, ed. *Religions*. Cambridge, UK: Cambridge University Press, 2002.

———. *World Religions*. New York: DK Publishing, 2006.

Chadwick, Henry. *The Early Church*. New York: Dorset Press, 1967.

Chadwick, Owen. *A History of Christianity*. New York: St. Martin's Press, 1995.

Crim, Keith, ed. *The Perennial Dictionary of World Religions*. New York: Harper Collins, 1990.

Cross, F. L., and E. A. Livingstone, eds. *The Oxford Dictionary of the Christian Church,* 3rd ed. Oxford: Oxford University Press, 1997.

Davidson, Hilda Roderick Ellis. *Gods and Myths of Northern Europe*. New York, London: Penguin Books, 1990.

Dawson, Lorne L., ed. *Cults and New Religious Movements: A Reader*. Malden, MA: Blackwell, 2003.

Eliade, Mircea. *From Primitives to Zen*. San Francisco: Harper Collins College Division, 1978.

———, and Ioan P. Couliano. *The Eliade Guide to World Religions*. New York: Harper Collins, 1991.

Encyclopaedia Britannica 2003, deluxe ed., on CD. Chicago: Encyclopaedia Britannica, 1994–2003.

Encyclopedia of Islam and the Muslim World. Eds. Richard C. Martin, et al. Macmillan Reference Books, 2003.

Feder, Lillian. *Crowell's Handbook of Classical Literature*. New York: Thomas Y. Crowell, 1964.

Gorenfeld, John. *Bad Moon Rising: How Reverend Moon Created the Washington Times, Seduced the Religious Right, and Built an American Kingdom*. California: Polipoint Press, 2008.

Hammond, N. G. L., and H. H. Scullard. *The Oxford Classical Dictionary,* 2nd ed. London: Oxford University Press, 1970.

Hammond Concise World Atlas. Hammond World Atlas Corp., 2007.

Hammond World Atlas 5th ed. Hammond World Atlas Corp., 2007.

Hathorn, Richard Y. *Crowell's Handbook of Classical Drama*. New York: Thomas Y. Crowell, 1967.

Hinnells, John R., ed. *A New Dictionary of Religions,* rev. ed. Oxford: Penguin Books, 1994.

Holifield, E. Brooks. *Theology in America*. New Haven, CT: Yale University Press, 2003.

Hornblower, Simon, and Anthony Spawforth, eds. *Oxford Classical Dictionary,* 3rd ed. New York: Oxford University Press, 1996.

Jordan, Michael. *Encyclopedia of Gods*. New York: Facts on File, 1993.

Leeming, David. *The Oxford Companion to World Mythology*. New York: Oxford University Press, 2005.

Lyden, Jackie. "Pearl of the Desert: Searching the Silk Road City of Yazd for the True Iranians and Their Ancient, Modern Faith." *Washington Post*, March 12, 2000.

McBrien, Richard P., ed. *The Harper Collins Encyclopedia of Catholicism*. San Francisco: Harper Collins, 1995.

Miles, Jack. *God: A Biography*. New York: Vintage Paperback, 1995.

Miller, Stephen M., and Robert V. Huber. *The Bible: A History*. Oxford: Lion Publishing, 2003.

Miller, Timothy, ed. *America's Alternative Religions: SUNY Series in Religious Studies*. New York: State University of New York Press, 1995.

Multifaith Information Manual. Toronto: Ontario Multifaith Council on Spiritual and Religious Care, 1995.

Nhat Hanh, Thich. *Living Buddha, Living Christ*. New York: Riverhead Trade, 1997.

———, Thich. *The Heart of the Buddha's Teaching*. New York: Broadway Books, 1999.

Piggott, Stuart. *The Druids*. New York: Thames and Hudson, 1985.

Richardson, Cyril C., ed. *Early Christian Fathers*. New York: Collier Books, 1970.

Robinson, George. *Essential Judaism*. New York: Simon & Schuster, 2000.

Roesdahl, Else. *The Vikings*. Trans. Susan M. Margeson and Kirsten Williams. New York, London: Penguin Books, 1998.

Ross, Anne. *Pagan Celtic Britain: Studies in Iconography and Tradition*. London: Constable, 1992.

Salamone, Frank, ed. *Encyclopedia of Religious Rites, Rituals, and Festivals*. New York: Routledge, 2004.

Sharma, Arvind, ed. *Our Religions*. New York: Harper Collins, 1995.

Smart, Ninian, and Frederick Denny, eds. *Atlas of the World's Religions,* 2nd ed. New York: Oxford University Press, 2007.

Smith, Jonathan Z. *The HarperCollins Dictionary of Religion*. San Francisco: Harper Collins, 1995.

Werblowski, R. J. Zwi, and Geoffrey Wigoder, eds., *The Oxford Dictionary of the Jewish Religion*. New York: Oxford University Press, 1997.

WEB SITES

Adherents
www.adherents.com

American Humanist Association
www.americanhumanist.org

Amish Life and People
www.amish.net

Anthroposophical Society in America
www.anthroposophy.org

Aryan Nations
www.aryan-nations.org

The Association of Religion Data Archives
www.thearda.com

"Baal," by Alan Hefner. *Encyclopedia Mythica*, 1997.
http://www.pantheon.org/articles/b/baal.html

BBC Religions
www.bbc.co.uk/religion

The Central Intelligence Department
www.cia.gov/library/publications/the-world-factbook

Christadelphians
www.christadelphians.org

Church of the Brethren
www.brethren.org

Church of Christian Science
www.churchofchristianscience.org

The Church of Jesus Christ of Latter-day Saints
www.lds.org

The Church of Satan
www.churchofsatan.com

"The Code of Hammurabi," by Richard Hooker. Washington State University, World Civilizations, 1996.
http://www.wsu.edu/~dee/MESO/CODE.HTM

Compendium of Muslim Texts, University of Southern California
http://www.usc.edu/dept/MSA/fundamentals/hadithsunnah/bukhari

The Dalai Lama
www.dalailama.com/

"The Deuterocanon," St. Takla Orthodox Coptic Church, Alexandria, Egypt
http://st-takla.org/pub_Deuterocanon/Deuterocanon-Apocrypha_El-Asfar_El-Kanoneya_El-Tanya__8-First-of-Maccabees.html#Chapter%201

Earth Mysteries
http://www.britannia.com/wonder/michell2.html

Eckankar: Religion of the Light and Sound of God
www.eckankar.org

Encyclopedia of Islam Online. P.J. Berman, Th. Bianquis, C. E. Bosworth, E. van Donzel, W. P. Heinrichs, eds. Brill Academic Publishers.
http://www.brill.nl/default.aspx?partid=210&pid=27684

Global Anabaptist Mennonite Encyclopedia Online
www.gameo.org

Gods and Mythology of Ancient Egypt
http://www.touregypt.net/godsofegypt/index.htm

The Holy Spirit Association for the Unification of World Christianity
www.unification.org

International Humanist and Ethical Union
www.iheu.org

Jews for Jesus
www.jews-for-jesus.org

Krishna
www.krishna.com

"Layamon's Brut," Bartleby.com
http://www.bartleby.com/211/1112.html

"Mani and Manichaeism," Bibliotheca Philosophica Hermetica, J. R. Ritman Library
http://www.ritmanlibrary.nl/c/p/pub/on_pub/mani/mani.html

Manichaean Texts from the Roman Empire, Cambridge University
http://www.cambridge.org/catalogue/catalogue.asp?isbn=9780511206917&ss=fro

The Masanavi of Rumi
http://www.sacred-texts.com/isl/masnavi/index.htm

Megalithic Poems, Anthology
http://megalithicpoems.blogspot.com/2007/01/standing-stones-of-stenness-by-godfrey.html

Meta Religion
http://meta-religion.com

The Moravian Church in North America
www.moravian.org

New York Times
www.nytimes.com

The Pluralism Project at Harvard University
www.pluralism.org/resources/statistics/index.php

The Qur'an (Koran)
http://quod.lib.umich.edu/k/koran/browse.html

Readings on Druidism
http://www.wildideas.net/cathbad/pagan/dr-text.html

The Religious Society of Friends
www.quaker.org

Religious Tolerance
www.religioustolerance.org

Scientology
www.scientology.org

Seventh-Day Adventist Church
www.adventist.org

"The Sultanate of Women," by Leslie Peirce, 2003, Channel 4 History
http://www.channel4.com/history/microsites/H/history/e-h/harem.html

The Theosophical Society–Adyar
www.ts-adyar.org

The Theosophical Society in America
www.theosophical.org

The Theosophical Society, Pasadena
www.theosociety.org

Tibetan Government in Exile
http://www.tibet.com/

"Ugarit and the Bible," Quartz Hill School of Theology
http://www.theology.edu/ugarbib.htm

Unitarian Universalist Association of Congregations
www.uua.org

United Lodge of Theosophists
www.ult.org

The Virtual Center for Phoenician Studies
http://phoenicia.org/index.shtml

"West Semitic Religions," LookLex Encyclopedia
http://lexicorient.com/e.o/semitic_west_rl.htm

World of Traditional Zoroastrianism
www.zoroastrianism.com

World Wide Religious News
www.wwrn.org/index.php

Xinhua
http://www.xinhuanet.com/english

SOURCES AND ACKNOWLEDGMENTS

ACKNOWLEDGMENTS

Langenscheidt Publishers and Hylas Publishing would like to thank the Reverend Robert G. Anderson, Chaplain Supervisor, New York Presbyterian Hospital, Weill Cornell campus; the Carroll and Mechem families; Phaeton Group; R. Matthew Bliss El-Hajj; Marilyn Moore; Jeremy Murray; and David Rumsey Cartography Associates (http://www.davidrumsey.com).

CONTRIBUTING AUTHORS

Thomas Cussans

Hinduism, 134–141; Hinduism, 226–231; Daoism, 242–245; Hinduism, 304–307.

Robert Huber

Canaan and Phoenicia, 24–25; Greece and Early Rome, 32–41; Amerindian, 62–65; Australasia and Oceania, 66–67; Greece, 72–73; Rome, 74–85; Africa, 122–123; The Americas, 124–129; Polynesia, 130–131; Abrahamic Religions, 166–167; Judaism, 168–173; Christianity, 174–191; Judaism, 250–255; Christianity, 256–275; Indigenous Religions, 296–301; Judaism, 326–327; Christianity, 328–335; Religion and Modern Societies, 374–375.

Elizabeth Mechem

India, 46–53; East Asia, 54–61; The Foundations of Organized Religion, 71; South Asia, 104–111; East Asia, 112–121; Buddhism, 142–149; Jainism, 150–151; Sikhism, 152–155; Daoism, 156–159; Confucianism, 160–163; Shinto, 164–165; The Colonial Era to the 20th Century, 225; Religions of the World Today, 303; East Asian Folk and Popular Religion, 322–323.

Stuart A.P. Murray

Introduction, v; The Religions of the Ancient World, 1; Early Humans, 2–5; Shamanism, 6–7; Mesopotamia, 8–9; Egypt, 14–17; Canaan and Phoenicia, 20–23; Western Europe, 26–31; Persia, 42–43; The Eastern Mediterranean and Persia, 94–103; The Rise of the Major Religions, 132–133; Islam, 192–203; Islam, 276–291; Islam, 340–345.

Sarah Novak

Christianity, 336–339; Zoroastrianism, 348–349; Faith Groups and Communities, 350–359; New Religious Movements, Sects, and Cults, 362–369.

David West Reynolds, PhD

Europe, 86–91; Buddhism, 232–237; Jainism, 238–239; Sikhism, 240–241; Confucianism, 246–247; Shinto, 248–249; Indigenous Religions, 292–295; Indigenous Religions, 296–297 (contributing author); Religion and Modern Societies, 372–373, 376–379.

Jo Rose

Europe, 92–93.

Tricia Wright

Buddhism, 308–313; Jainism, 314–315; Sikhism, 316–317; Daoism, 318–319; Confucianism, 320–321; Shinto, 324–325; Baha'ism, 346–347.

PICTURE CREDITS

t–top, b–bottom, r–right, l–left, c–center

Photography Sources

JI–Jupiterimages Corporation; IO–IndexOpen; ISP–iStockphoto; BSP–Big Stock Photo; SS–Shutterstock; WI–Wikimedia Commons; SXC–stock.xchng; LOC–Library of Congress; NASA–National Aeronautics and Space Administration; NOAA–National Oceanic and Atmospheric Administration; DOD–US Department of Defence

Half title LOC **Title page** LOC **iv** LOC **v** David Rumsey **vii** LOC

PART ONE: The Religions of the Ancient World

viii–1 NASA/WI **3r** JI **3tl** Peter Zaharov/SS **3bl** Robert Hardholt/SS **5b** National Park Service **5tr** Bill McKelvie/SS **5cl** Matej Krajcovic/SS **7** JI **9tl** JI **9tr** JI **9br** John Said/SS **11t** JI **11c** Marie-Lan Nguyen/WI **11b** Tla2006/WI **13cr** JI **13bl** JI **13br** Chief Photographer's Mate Edward G. Martens/U.S. Navy/WI **14** JI **15r** Vannucci Roberto/SS **15tl** Captmondo/WI **15bl** JI **16tr** Irina Kuznecova/SS **16l** JI **17** JI **18** JI **19br** George Long,Society for the Diffusion of Useful Knowledge/David Rumsey Map Collection **19tl** JI **21tr** Marie-Lan Nguyen /WI/Musée du Louvre **21br** Rama/WI **21tl** William Hughes, Society for the Diffusion of Useful Knowledge/David Rumsey Map Collection **22** Claus Mikosch/SS **23** JI **25tl** Caravaggio **25cr** FB78/WI **25** JI/Clipart **27tr** David Hughes/SS **27br** Donald Rose **27bl** JI **29br** WI **29tl** Berig/WI **29c** Jorunn/WI **31tr** JI **31br** Malene Thyssen/WI **31tl** Nicolaus Germanius (after Ptolemy)/National Digital Library of Poland/Peacay/WI **33tr** volk65/SS **33cr** JI **33bl** Andrey Kudinov/SS **33bl** janprchal/SS **35tr** JI **35tl** JI **35cl** Styve Reineck/SS **35br** Johann Georg Trautmann/Andreas Praefcke/WI **36** JI **36** Marie-Lan Nguyen /WI/Museo Chiaramonti **36** Jerry Zitterman **36** Bibi Saint-Pol/WI **36** JI **36** JFKennedy/WI **36** Marie-Lan Nguyen /WI/Museo Altemps **36** Cyril Hou/SS **36** Bibi Saint-Pol/WI **36** Aaron Wood/SS **36** Marie-Lan Nguyen /WI **36** Tomada por Zaqarbal/WI **36** Michael Onisiforou/SS **37bl** Michael Onisiforou/SS **37br** Tomasz Otap **37tr** Bibi Saint-Pol/WI **39cr** vlas2000/SS **39br** Netfalls/SS **39** Netfalls/SS **41bl** Gustave Moreau/Miniwark/WI **41tr** Maurizio Farnetti/SS **41br** Roberto Zanasi/WI **42bl** JI **42tr** Marie-Lan Nguyen/WI **43** Shaunti/WI **45br** Siamax/WI **45tl** JI **45bl** JI **47cr** Atif Gulzar/SXC **47bl** PHGCOM/WI/British Musuem **49tl** BernardM/WI **49bl** Redtigerxyz/WI **49br** Neoptoleumus/WI **51tr** WI **51br** Tonis Valing/SS **51tl** Karen Givens/SS **53t** JI **53c** WI **53b** Beta m common/WI **54l** Guss/WI **54r** Chee Choon Fat/SS **55l** Kevin Zim/WI **55r** Editor at Large/WI **57tr** Zhou Yi/WI **57br** Kowloosnese/José-Manuel Benito Álvarez/WI/**57l** W. B. Pettus/LOC Vault Map Collection **59bl** William Perry/BSP **59tr** tamir niv **59br** Snowyowl/WI **59tl** Bill Perry/SS **61tl** Amcaja/WI **61br** JI **61tr** Sam Downes/SS **61cr** Chris **73**/WI **63tr** Tim

Kiser/WI **63bl** F. Weiss, National Park Service/Werewombat/WI **63br** Maximilian Dörrbecker/WI **65cl** Elena Fernadez Zabelguelskaya/SS **65cb** Carlos E. Santa Maria/SS **65br** Madman/WI **67br** Sam DCruz/SS **67tl** Sam DCruz/SS **69cr** Courtesy of the Anthropology Photographic Archive, Department of Anthropology, The University of Auckland **69tl** Xavier Marchant/SS **69br** Hiroshi Sato

PART TWO: The Foundations of Organized Religion

70–71 Peacay/WINicolaus Germanius **72tr** Vangelis/SS **72bl** Society for the Diffusion of Useful Knowledge/David Rumsey Map Collection **73br** Dr. Le Thanh Hung/SS **73tl** Marie-Lan Nguyen/WI **75b** Bjsamelsonjones/WI **75c** JI **75t** David Rumsey **77tl** Ryan Freisling/WI **77br** Mike Young/WI **77tr** Vicente Barcelo Varona **78** Mac/WI **79tr** Marie-Lan Nguyen/WI **79tl** Gustave Doré/Dover Publications, Inc. **79br** Rigobert Bonne/David Rumsey Map Collection **81cr** Gunnar Bach Pedersen/WI **81tl** Gustave Doré/Dover Publications, Inc. **81bl** Michelangelo Merisi da Caravaggio/The Yorck Project/Eloquence/WI **81br** S.P. Tregelles/Leszek Janczuk/WI **83tr** Wassily Sazonov/Butko/WI **83br** JI **83tl** The Yorck Project/WI **85bl** Marinus Claesz van Raymerswale/The Yorck Project/WI **85br** Ilker Canikligil/SS **85tr** Salamanderman/SS **87tl** Stan Zurek/WI **87tr** BishkekRocks/WI **87br** Peter Paul Reubens/Eloquence/The YorckProject/WI **89tl** Putney9/WI **89cr** Getty Images Photo Disc/IO **89bl** Rama/WI **89br** Lalupa/WI **91bl** Natrajdr/WI **91tr** Karl Briullov/WI **93bl** Berig/WI **93tr** JI **93br** Stbalbach/WI **95bl** M. Disdero/WI **95br** JI **95tr** Georges Jansoone/WI **96** NASA **97tl** Jansson Jansonius/Ludo29/WI **97tr** JI **99bl** Edward Quin/Sidney Hall/David Rumsey Map Collection **99cr** QuartierLatin1968/WI **99tl** Kitkatcrazy/WI **100l** Itai/WI **100r** Carly Rose Hennigan/SS **101** JI **103tr** PHGCOM/WI **103tl** Ginolerhino/WI **103bl** JI **103br** Gregory Gerber/SS **105** JI **107tl** Sacca/WI **107br** PHG/WI **109tl** Rachelle Burnside **109br** Arteki/SS **109cb** PHGCOM/WI **111tl** Arteki/SS **111tr** Vishal Shah/SS **111br** The Yorck Project/WI **113tr** Maros Mraz/WI **113br** Isura Ranatunga/WI **115bl** JI **115tr** Louis le Grand/WI **115br** Jari Bilén/SS **117tl** PHGCOM/WI **117br** Kladno Snajdr/Tomás Páv **117bl** Gary L. Brewer/SS **117tr** Clouston/SS **118** IO **119bl** JI **119tr** Jarno Gonzalez Zarraonandia **119br** JI **120bl** Buddhadl/SS **120br** JI **121bl** Eric Connor/WI **121br** Martin Valent/SS **123bl** LassiHu/WI **123br** Julius Schnorr von Carolsfeld/Dover Publications, Inc. **123tr** Dainis Derics/SS **124br** Tom Grundy/SS **124bl** JI **125** Videowokart/WI **127bl** Celso Diniz/SS **127cr** Gordon Galbraith **127tr** Daniel Loncarevic/SS **122–123** Le Roy H. Appleton/Dover Publications, Inc. **128** Peter Isotalo/WI **129t** Jarno Gonzalez Zarraonandia/SS **129b** Herbert Eisengruber/SS **130l** Vladimir Korostyshevskiy/SS **130tr** iofoto/SS **130br** Rivi/WI

PART THREE: The Rise of the Major Religions

132–133 Jewish National University Library
and the Department of Geography, the Hebrew
University of Jerusalem 135ct Sarvagnya/WI
135cr Nicholas/WI 135br Chris Howey/SS 135bl
Kodda/SS 136cl JI 136cb JI 136cr JI 137tl Ranveig/
WI 137ct Kharidehal Abhirama Ashwin/SS 137tr
salamanderman/SS 137cl photolibrary.com pty.
ltd./IO 137cb Durga/WI 137c Mikhail Nekrasov/SS
137cr JI 137br PHG/WI 139tl Vinayaraj/WI 139
Dmitry Chernobrov/SS 139 Asit Jain/SS 141tl
0399778584/SS 141tr sarah davies/ISP 141br
Holger Mette/SS 143cr Eric Connor/WI 143tl
Ernst Stavro Blofeld/WI 143bl Earl Eliason/ISP 144
TAOLMOR/SS 145br sf2301420max/SS 145tr Hu
Xiao Fang/SS 147tl Harald Høiland Tjøstheim/SS
147cr Amy Nichole Harris/SS 147br Mountain at
the Shanghai Museum/WI 148 Martin Mette/SS
149 Applebee/WI 150 Kuntal Paul/ISP 151 Ajay
Shrivastava/SS 152 Jeev/WI 153t Sam Dcruz/SS
153br Hari singh/WI 154 WI 155br WI 155tr
Sukh/WI 155cb Holger Mette/SS 156 Hannah/WI
157tr Cutienemo04/Shizhao/WI 157br David
Fullmer/BSP 158tl Guthrie/WI 158bl Guthrie/
WI 158cl Guthrie/WI 158ct Guthrie/WI 158cb
Guthrie/WI 158cr Guthrie/WI 158tr Guthrie/WI
158br Guthrie/WI 159tl Pericles of Athens/WI
159tr Myths and Legends of China, by E.T.C.
Werner 159br Myths and Legends of China, by
E.T.C. Werner 160l Edescas2/WI 160WI 161cr
From "Madrolle's Guide Books: Northern China,
The Valley of the Blue River, Korea." Hachette &
Company, 1912. Image from the Perry-Castañeda
Library Map Collection, Courtesy of the University
of Texas Libraries, The University of Texas at
Austin. 161b CYLU/SS 162 Hannah/WI 163tr
PericlesofAthens/WI 163bl Mountain at Shanghai
Museum/WI 164 JI 165tl Fg2/WI 165cr JI 165b
Craig Hansen/SS 166 Pieter Pietersz Lastman /WI
166 JI 166 The Deceiver/WI 166 BJU Museum
and Gallery/Benjamin West/Captain Phoebus/
WI166 Kyd/WI 167br Isidorus/Guntherus Ziner/
Ecemaml/WI 167bl Dsmdgold/WI 169bl Heretiq/
WI 169tr LLC, Vstock/IO 169cr Chadi Samaan
Brejnev/WI 171bl Francisco Ricci/Marcos Felipe/
WI 171br Markinal/WI 171tl Lucas Janszoon
Waghenaer/Joopr/WI 173tl The Yorck Project/WI
173cb Ladislav Faigl/WI 173tr Athanasius Kircher/
Ben/WI 174tr PKM/WI 174bl Villy/WI 175tr
JI 177br Birute Vijeikiene/SS 177tl Laurom/WI
177tr Laurascudder/WI 179br Dan Breckwoldt/SS
179bl David Rumsey 179cb Marjan Smerke/WI
179tl Srnec/WI 181tl Vassia Atanassova/WI 181br
Shakko/WI 183cr JI 183tr Disdero/WI 185bl JI
185br JI 185tr JI 187bl Pinpin/WI 187tr JI 187br
JI 189tl JI 189tr Muriel Gottrop/WI 189br JI
189bl JI 190l Hispalois/WI 190br Tomasz Otap/
SS 191bl László Szalai/WI 191tl Jarno Gonzalez
Zarraonandia/SS 191cr JI 193tl Humus sapiens/WI
193c JI 193br Ronen/SS 194 Senemmar/WI 195
Igiveup/WI 197tl Factoria singular fotografia/SS;
Holger Mette/SS 197br Factoria singular fotografia/
SS; Holger Mette/SS 197cr Grenavitar/WI 198
PHGCOM/WI 199tr Arlo K. Abrahamson/WI
199tl JI 201bl DrFO.Jr.Tn/WI 201br PHGCOM/WI
203br Avner Richard/SS 203tr JI

Chronology of World Religions

204 Vassil/SS 205 JI/Clipart 206 Jon Sullivan/WI
207 QuartierLatin1968/WI 208 Jean-Christophe
BENOIST/WI 209 Deror avi/WI 210 iofoto/SS 211
JI 212 Oosoom/WI 213tl Ben/WI 213br JI 214tl
Gizmo II/WI 214bl Jon Harald Søby/WI 215 Melba
Photo Agency/IO 216tl LOC 216bl peter schmelzle/
WI 217 Hugo Lopes/WI 218ct Fred J/WI 218bl
Piotrus/WI 219bl Victorian Traditions/SS 219ct
LOC 220 Sascha Burkard/SS 221 LOC 222 Tuvic/
WI 223tl Daniel Case/WI 223br Bradley Allen/WI

**PART FOUR: The Colonial Era to the
20th Century**

224–225 London: The Times/Cassell & Company/
Richard Andree 226t Fowler&Fowler/WI 226b
Fowler&Fowler/WI 227br Fowler&Fowler/Perry
Castaneda Library MapsCollection/WI 227tr
Dziewa/WI 227ct Airunp/WI 229ct Yann/WI 229bl
JI 229br salamanderman/SS 231ct PlaneMad/WI
231cr Immanuel Giel/WI 232bl Ralf-André Lettau/
WI 232br TAOLMOR/SS 233 Hailin Chen/SS
235tl Mario Bruno/SS 235br Kheng Guan Toh/SS
236 Mariusz S. Jurgielewicz/SS 237tr Keith Levit
Photography/IO 237br Vladimir Korostyshevskiy/
SS 239tl Ranveig/WI/the British Museum 239tr
Flicka/WI 239br Psychofarm/WI 241tl Sukh/WI
241br Holger Mette/SS 242 Carl Christian Franz
Radefeld 243 LOC 244 zhu difeng/SS 245tr 245cr
OhanaUnited/WI 247 Johny Keny/SS 248 LOC
249tl LOC 249tr Barakishidan/WI 249bl David
Monniaux/WI 251tl Deror avi/WI 251tr Alexey
Sergeev/WI 251bl LOC 253tl JI/Clipart 253tr
jpatava/SS 253bl Jarekt/WI 254 Gridge/WI/
May 16, 1948 edition of Jewish newspaper The
Palestine Post 255tl JI 255cr Anke van Wyk/SS
257cl Bruce C. Murray/SS 257bl JI 257br Lim
Yong Hian/SS 259c A-giâu/WI/1933 edition of
the Bible in the Southern Min language 259br
faberfoto/SS 261tl JI/Clipart 261tr Andrew
Balet/WI 261bl Kippy Lanker/SS 262 Sandulov
Anton/SS 263cr JI/Clipart 263br JI 265bl Denise
Kappa/SS 265cr Garion96/Evert Odekerken/WI
265tc JI/Clipart 267tl Anthony Correia/SS 267cl
spe/SS 267tr Omegatron/WI/Nicolaus Copernicus'
De revolutionibus orbium coelestium 267br Jon
Harald Søby/WI 269t JonHarder/WI 269cb LOC
271tl JI 271tr JI 271br LOC 273tr LOC 273br
Vladimir Korostyshevskiy/SS 275t Photos.com
Select/IO 275br Ng Yin Chern/SS 277tl JoJan/WI
277cr Giovanni Antonio Guardi/The Yorck Project/
Eloquence/WI 277br Robert Raderschatt/WI
279tl Piri Reis/FunkMonk/WI 279br Collection of
Albert Sorlin-Dorigny/Jastrow/WI 281tl Haiduc/
WI 281c Department of Islamic Art, Richelieu/
Jastrow/WI 281br Irakischer Maler/The Yorck
Project/Eloquence/WI 282 Meister der Jahângîr-
MemoirenThe Yorck Project/Eloquence/WI
283tl JI 283br Former collections of Salomon de
Rothschild/Department of Islamic Art, Richelieu/
Jastrow/WI 285cr Jam.si/SS 285br Marja-Kristina
Akinsha/SS 287tr Bontenbal/WI 287cr Daniel
DeSlover/SS 287 Yorkshirian/WI 289tl JI 289cr
Styve Reineck/SS 289br JI/Clipart 290tl Madden/
WI/LOC 290tr Movieevery/WI 290bl Don
Koralewski/US Departmemt of Defense/Jake73/
WI 293tl LOC 293cb JI 293br George Burba/SS
295cr JI 295br Vinicius Tupinamba/SS 297tr Tim
Ross/WI 297bl 297br Jose Gil/SS 298 Antilived/WI
299cl Laurens Groenendijk/SS 299tr Sandivas/WI
299br Natalia Bratslavsky/SS 301tl Guérin Nicolas/

WI 301tr urosr/SS 301br Jastrow/WI/Former
collections of Charles Ratton and Hubert Goldet

PART FIVE: Religions of the World Today

302–303 Data courtesy Marc Imhoff of NASA
GSFC and Christopher Elvidge of NOAA NGDC.
Image by Craig Mayhew and Robert Simmon,
NASA GSFC 305tl JeremyRichards/SS 305tr
TAOLMOR/SS 305br Colin Gregory Palmer/WI
306 Wikimedia Commons 307 Vishal Shah/SS 308
Bartosz Hadyniak/SS 309tl Bobak Ha'Eri/Bobak/
WI 309cr Louise Cukrov/SS 309c Kathy Konkle/
ISP 310 Zaporozhchenko Yury/SS 311t iCEO/SS
311tr oksana.perkins/SS 312 Tiffany Muff/BSP
313tl Golden Pixels/IO 313br Dhoxax/SS 314
TAOLMOR/SS 315b PRANAV VORA/SS 315cr
Joan Loitz/SS 316 salamanderman/SS 316–317
tigerbarb/SS 318 Tze Ming/SS 319cr Phil Date/
SS 319br Lvector/SS 321tr Uriah923/WI 321br
TAOLMOR/SS 322 Amber Rose and Neil Dvorak
323 LOC 325tl Rekishi-JAPAN/WI 325cr JI 325br
lullabi/SS 327tr Manfred Steinbach/SS 327bl JI
327br Lvector/SS 328 Michael Fritzen/SS 329
SS 330 Sophie Bengtsson/SS 331 Mark William
Penny/SS 332 urosr/SS 333 JI 334 Ron Zmiri/SS
335 Peter Elvidge/SS 337tl LOC 337tr photolibrary.
com pty. ltd./IO 338 Chee-Onn Leong/SS 339tl
LOC 339bl Bigbadswede/WI 339br JI/Clipat 341tl
Mikhail Levit/SS 341tr Axel Mauruszat/WI 341b
EML/SS 343tl Alica Q/SS 343tr JI 343br Winertai/
WI 345tl Aron Brand/SS 345cr Quasipalm/WI/
US Navy 346 Jill Battaglia/SS 347tl Joan Loitz/SS
347b salamanderman/SS 349tl Joel Blit/SS 349tr
Polimerek/Maziart/WI 349br Raffaello Sanzio/
Jacobolus/WI 350l JI 350r Edward Hicks/Cobalty/
WI 351l LOC 351r JI 352l Daniel Schwen/WI 352r
philip balisciano/ISP 353l Ralph R. Echtinaw/SS
353r Christina Richards/SS 354tl Fb78/WI/Spiezer
Chronik 354bl Jeff Whyte/SS 354br JI/Clipart 355bl
Tyler Olson/SS 355br Logawi /WI 356l JI 356tr
LOC 357cr Wladyslaw Sojka/WI 357bl JI 357bt
Maksim/WI 358cl JI/Clipart 358bl LOC 359tr
Vinicius Tupinamba/SS 359br JedSundwall/WI
362cr David Shankbone/SS 362cb JI 363tl Svetlana
Larina/SS 363b Svetlana Larina/SS 364tl United
Nations World Food Programme 364bl NadinaS/SS
365cr Evil saltine/WI 365c Modemac/WI 365br
lomarti/SS 366cl Bjarne Henning Kvaale/SS 366bl
JI/Clipart 367cb JI/Clipart 367br kamphi/SS 368c
JI/Clipart 368bl Monika Lewandowska/ISP 369cr
Zaphod/WI 369bl Linda/SS 373tr Crucifixion/WI
373b MSGT Michael E. Best/DOD/WI 375tl JG
Howes/WI 375tr Gertjan Hooijer/SS 376 Keith
Levit Photography/IO 377t Yanfei Sun/SS 377br
Bibi Saint-Pol/WI/ 379tl salamanderman/SS 379br
Galyna Andrushko/SS

Front cover: Jupiterimages Corporation (center);
AbleStock/IO (background); QT Luong/www.
terragalleria.com (tl); Michael Fuery (cl); Carly
Rose Hennigan/SS (bl); Holger Mette/SS (tr);
Richard Paul Kane/SS (cr); Can Balcioglu/SS (br)

Back cover: Jewish National University Library
and the Department of Geography, the Hebrew
University of Jerusalem (background); Liudmila
Gridina/SS (right); Holger Mette/SS (left)

Cartography by Neil Dvorak

Base maps by Mountain High Maps® Copyright ©
1993 Digital Wisdom®, Inc.

INDEX